LAURIE J. MULLINS
ORGANISATIONAL BEHAVIOUR IN THE WORKPLACE

WITH JACQUELINE McLEAN

TWELFTH EDITION

 Pearson

Harlow, England • London • New York • Boston • San Francisco • Toronto • Sydney • Dubai • Singapore • Hong Kong
Tokyo • Seoul • Taipei • New Delhi • Cape Town • São Paulo • Mexico City • Madrid • Amsterdam • Munich • Paris • Milan

PEARSON EDUCATION LIMITED
KAO Two
KAO Park
Harlow CM17 9SR
United Kingdom
Tel: +44 (0)1279 623623
Web: www.pearson.com/uk

First published in 1985 in Great Britain under the Pitman imprint (print)
Fifth edition published in 1999 by Financial Times Pitman Publishing (print)
Seventh edition published 2005 (print)
Eighth edition published 2007 (print)
Ninth edition published 2010 (print)
Tenth edition published 2013 (print and electronic)
Eleventh edition published 2016 (print and electronic)
Twelfth edition published 2019 (print and electronic)

© Laurie J. Mullins 1985, 2010 (print)
© Laurie J. Mullins 2012, 2016, 2019 (print and electronic)
Chapters 4, 6 © Linda Carter and Laurie J. Mullins 1993, 2007
Chapter 5 © Linda Carter 1993, 2007
Chapter 12 © Peter Scott 2016
Chapter 13 © Peter Scott 2019
Chapter 15 © Peter Scott 2010, 2013
Chapter 16 © David Preece 1999, 2007
CTZ © Pearson 2019 (print and electronic)

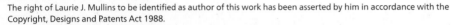

The Financial Times. With a worldwide network of highly respected journalists, *The Financial Times* provides global business news, insightful opinion and expert analysis of business, finance and politics. With over 500 journalists reporting from 50 countries worldwide, our in-depth coverage of international news is objectively reported and analysed from an independent, global perspective. To find out more, **visit www.ft.com/pearsonoffer.**

ISBN: 978-1-292-24548-5 (print)
         978-1-292-24550-8 (PDF)
         978-1-292-24553-9 (ePub)

British Library Cataloguing-in-Publication Data
A catalogue record for the print edition is available from the British Library

Library of Congress Cataloging-in-Publication Data
Names: Mullins, Laurie J., author. | McLean, Jacqueline E., contributor.
Title: Organisational behaviour in the workplace / Laurie J. Mullins with
  Jacqueline McLean.
Other titles: Management and organisational behaviour
Description: Twelfth edition. | Harlow, England ; New York : Pearson, [2019]
Identifiers: LCCN 2019019678| ISBN 9781292245485 (print) | ISBN 9781292245508
  (pdf) | ISBN 9781292245539 (epub)
Subjects: LCSH: Organizational behavior.
Classification: LCC HD58.7 .M85 2019 | DDC 658--dc23 LC record available at https://urldefense.proofpoint.
com/v2/url?u=https-3A__lccn.loc.gov_2019019678&d=DwIFAg&c=0YLnzTkWOdJlub_y7qAx8Q&r=zKTI3XC-TUJ
M0AsOJA2Iy8zK9anF7moqCccCkWx1Ygs&m=w2k6OVabVqUhXgB2VMmmiPYRSCz3zOk5obQcqtqoxLU&s
=7J-LWe9MBs2-b3bSdpIOj4pxB8FB6TrS2kI7ngy9geM&e=

10 9 8 7 6 5 4 3 2 1
23 22 21 20 19

Front cover image: © sturti/E+/Getty Images; Paul Bradbury/Caiaimage/Getty Images; Mint Images/
Mint Images RF/Getty Images; Maskot/Getty Images; Maskot/Getty Images; Inti St Clair/Getty Images
Print edition typeset in 9.5/12.5pt Frutiger Neue LT W1G by SPi Global
Print edition printed and bound in Slovakia by Neografia

To Pamela and for our families

Contents in brief

Contents in detail

Part 1
Organisational behaviour and work   21

Part 2
Focus on the individual   127

Part 3
Focus on groups and leadership 291

Part 4
Focus on the workplace   411

11 Organisational theory and structure   412

Part 5
Focus on organisational environment   559

15 Organisational culture and change   560

16 Strategy, corporate responsibility and ethics   600

17 Organisational performance and effectiveness 637

In acknowledgement and appreciation

A special tribute to my wife Pamela and families for their constant warmth, support and encouragement with this latest edition.

Special thanks and gratitude also to — including:

Colleagues Jacqueline McLean and Peter Scott for their valued contribution to this twelfth edition.

Gill and Richard Christy

Mike Crabbe and Mike Timmins

Hugo Misselhorn

Anne Riches

Jane Southall

And the fond memory of Karen Meudell

Francesca Mullins, Rebekah Darvill, Abigail Voller

Di and Mike Blyth, Jenny and Tony Hart, Lynn and Wayne Miller, Christine Paterson

Those managers who kindly gave permission to reproduce material from their own organisations and work environments.

The team at Pearson Education including: Victoria Tubb, Andrew Müller, Kelly Miller and Rachel Gear. Also to Simon Lake (hoping you are enjoying your retirement: happy memories).

From Jacqueline: Heartfelt gratitude for your invaluable support, advice and encouragement: Dr Kevin Gallimore, Dr Jie Liu, Prof Gary Akehurst, Alison Rowlands, Paul Walsh; my Mother, Isolyn McLean, Janet Foster, Minerva Streete-Boafoo, Eseata Steele, Elizabeth McLean and family.

From Peter: Thanks to Debbie and also the various students over the years who have had ideas about technology and organisations bounced off them.

External reviewers

The following reviewers approached by the publishers for their constructive comments that have helped shape this revised new edition.

Dr Sophie Bennett-Gillison, University of Aberystwyth

Dr Pattanee Susomrith, Senior Lecturer, School of Business and Law, Edith Cowan University, Australia

John Bateman, The University of Sussex Business School

Dr Sarah Warnes, UCL School of Management

Hugh M. Davenport, Senior Lecturer in Organisational Behaviour, University of Northampton

Dr Dieu Hack-Polay, University of Lincoln

Dr Emmanuelle Rey-Marmonier, Aberdeen Business School, Robert Gordon University

About the authors

Laurie Mullins has experience of business, local government, university administration and human resource management; an instructor in the Territorial Army; worked with the United Nations Association International Service, Voluntary Service Overseas; and professional and educational bodies including UNISON. Formerly a principal lecturer at Portsmouth Business School Laurie led the behavioural and human resource management group and was senior examiner for a range of university courses and professional organisations. Laurie has undertaken a visiting professorship at University of Wisconsin, USA; visiting fellowship at Royal Melbourne Institute of Technology University, Australia; guest speaker in South Africa; and frequent visiting lecturer in the Netherlands. Laurie is also author of *Essentials of Organisational Behaviour* and *Hospitality Management and Organisational Behaviour* both published by Pearson Education. His books have been translated into Russian, Chinese, Portuguese, Dutch and Greek with a Macedonian edition in progress. There has also been an edition in Braille. Laurie has the rare distinction for an academic author with an edition of *Management and Organisational Behaviour* featuring in both *The Guardian* and *The Times* bestseller lists of all paperbacks, both fiction and non-fiction.

About the contributors

Dr Jacqueline McLean is a Senior Lecturer in HRM and Organisational Behaviour in the Department of Business and Management at Manchester Metropolitan University. She is also Research Lead, Ethics and Governance Lead and Research Degrees Coordinator. Jacqueline is an experienced Educational Author, Consultant and Company Director and has been a Member of the Chartered Institute of Personnel and Development for over thirty-five years. Before joining academia, she held a number of personnel/ HRM/training roles in the commercial sector. Jacqueline's PhD research focused on knowledge management and new product development and explored how organisations, through their infrastructure, can utilise specialist knowledge to enhance innovation propensity.

Peter Scott is a Senior Lecturer at the University of Portsmouth Business School, specialising in organisational behaviour and employee relations. He has previously taught at the University of Bath and Manchester Metropolitan University. Peter's doctoral research was on craft skills and advanced manufacturing technology.

Publisher's acknowledgements

We are grateful for permission to reproduce the following copyright material:

Text

4 Pitman Publishing: *Introduction to Module 6, Organisational Behaviour,* Financial Times Mastering Management, FT Pitman Publishing (1997), p. 216. **4 Dryden Press:** Vecchio, R. P. *Organizational Behavior: Core Concepts,* sixth edition, The Dryden Press (2005). **8 John Wiley & Sons:** Wright, T. A. and Quick, J. C. 'The Role of Positive-Based Research in Building the Science of Organizational Behaviour', *Journal of Organizational Behavior,* vol. 30, 2009, pp. 329–36. **8 Southwestern Publishing Group:** Hellriegel, D., Slocum, J. W. and Woodman, R. W. *Organizational Behavior,* eighth edition, South-Western Publishing (1998), p. 5. **9 Southwestern Publishing Group:** From Hellriegel, D., Slocum, J. W., Jr. and Woodman, R. W. *Management,* eighth edition, South-Western Publishing (1998), p. 6. Reproduced by permission. **10 Pearson Education:** Robbins, S. P. and Judge, T. A. *Organizational Behavior,* thirteenth edition, Pearson Prentice Hall (2009), p. 50. **10 Confederation of British Industry:** 'Boosting Employability Skills' CBI http://cbi.org.uk (accessed 17 December 2014). **11 Pearson Education:** Maureen G., *Interactive Behaviour at Work,* third edition, Financial Times, Prentice Hall (2002) p. 8. Reprinted and electronically reproduced by permission of Pearson Education, Inc. **12 Crown copyright:** 'Forging Futures: Building Higher Level Skills through University and Employer Collaboration', UKCES, September 2014. **12 HarperCollins:** Your Brain at Work: Strategies for Overcoming Distraction, Regaining Focus, and Working Smarter All Day Long , October 6th 2009 by Harper Business. **12 HarperCollins:** Rock, D. Your Brain at Work, Harper Business, 2009. **25 Cambridge University Press:** Thomas, H., Smith, R. R. and Diez, F. (2013) *Human Capital and Global Business Strategy.* New York: Cambridge University Press, p. 3. **25 Elsevier:** Bontis, N., Dragonetti, N.C., Jacobsen, K. and Roos, G. 'The Knowledge Toolbox: A Review of Tools Available to Measure and Manage Intangible Resources', *European Management Journal,* vol. 17, no. 4, 1999, pp. 391–402. **25 Pearson Education:** Gratton L. *The Democratic Enterprise,* Financial Times Prentice Hall (2004). **27 Pearson Education:** Rollinson, D. *Organisational Behaviour and Analysis,* fourth edition, Pearson Education (2008), pp. 3–4. **27 Penguin Random House:** McGregor, D. *The Human Side of Enterprise,* Penguin (1987), p. 55. **33 Carol Publishing Group:** Shafritz, J. M. *Shakespeare on Management,* Carol Publishing Group (1992), p. xi. **34 Penguin Random House:** Handy, C. *Understanding Organizations,* fourth edition, Penguin Books (1993), p. 16. **34 Pearson Education:** Jones, G.R. *Organizational Theory, Design, and Change,* seventh edition, Pearson Education (2013), p. 30. **40 Pearson Education:** Gratton, L. *The Democratic Enterprise,* Financial Times Prentice Hall (2004), p. 208. **42 Institute of Administrative Management:** Stalker, K. 'The Individual, the Organisation and the Psychological Contract', *British Journal of Administrative Management,* July/August 2000, pp. 28–34. **45 Haymarket Media Group Ltd:** Hare, C. 'We Need to Embrace the Opportunities International Management Brings' *Management Today,* May 2012, p. 62. **47 Pearson Education:** Schneider, S. C. and Barsoux, J, *Managing Across*

Cultures, second edition, Financial Times Prentice Hall (2003) p. 167. **47 Ernest Hemingway Foundation:** John F. Kennedy, 10 June 1963. **48 Pearson Education:** From Brooks, I. *Organisational Behaviour: Individuals, Groups and Organisation,* fourth edition, Financial Times Prentice Hall (2009), p. 272. Reproduced with permission from Pearson Education Ltd. **49 Pearson Education:** Holden, N. J. *Cross-Cultural Management: A Knowledge Management Perspective,* Financial Times Prentice Hall (2002), p. 51. **53 Fred. Olsen Cruise Lines:** Thanks to Rachael Jackson. Fred. Olsen Cruise Lines. www.fredolsencruises.com. **62 Pearson Education:** Bouchikhi, H. and Kimberly, J. R., 'The Customized Workplace', in Chowdhury, S. (ed.) *Management 21C,* Financial Times Prentice Hall (2000), p. 215. Reproduced with permission from Pearson Education Ltd. **63 Haymarket Media Group Ltd:** Reeves, R. 'Reality Bites', *Management Today,* March 2003, p. 35. **65 Element Publisher:** Mann, S. Hiding the way we feel, faking what we don't: understanding the role of emotions at work, Element (1999). **66 Elsevier:** Gursoy, D., Boylu, Y. and Avci, U. 'Identifying the Complex Relationships Among Emotional Labour and Its Correlates', *International Journal of Hospitality Management,* vol. 30, (2011), pp. 783–94. **69 Kwansei Gakuin University Press:** From Smart, P. and Inazawa, K. Human resource management in the public sector, Kwansei Gakuin University Press (2011), p. 21. Reproduced with permission. **69 Spring Publications:** CIPD, 'Employee Outlook Survey: Employee views on working life', Spring 2017. **73 Institute of Administrative Management:** Lysons, K. 'Organisational Analysis', supplement to Manager, *The British Journal of Administrative Management,* no. 18, March/April 1997. Reproduced with permission of the Institute of Administrative Management. **74 Pearson Education:** Adapted from Gray, J. L. and Starke, F. A. *Organizational Behavior: Concepts and Applications,* fourth edition, Merrill Publishing Company (1988), p. 432. Reproduced with permission from Pearson Education Inc. **75 Professional Manager:** Law, S. 'Beyond the Water Cooler', *Professional Manager,* January 2005, p. 26. **75 Huffpost:** 'Love Your Work Colleagues: 10 Ways to Find Common Ground', *HuffPost Conversations,* http://www.huffingtonpost.co.uk/entry/love-your-work-colleagues-10-ways-to-find-common-ground_uk_58e61926e4b0917d3477545d (accessed 28 April 2017). **78 Crown copyright:** Department for Business Innovation & Skills (BIS). **78 ICSA: The Governance Institute:** Black, B. 'Family Friendly', Governance + Compliance, January 2014, pp. 52–3. **80 The Virtual Learning Materials Workshop:** Copyright © 2011 The Virtual Learning Materials Workshop. Reproduced with permission. **82 Haymarket Media Group Ltd:** Stern, S. 'My Generation', *Management Today,* March 2008, pp. 40–6. **84 Unum Limited:** 'The Future Workplace' Unum Limited 2014 www.unum.co.uk. **84 Associated Newspapers:** 'The World's Wackiest Workplace', Daily Mail July 5, 2017, pp. 30–1. **85 Crown copyright:** 'The Future of Work: Jobs and Skills in 2030', UKCES, 03.14. p. 8. **86 Haymarket Media Group Ltd:** 'Working Smarter– Anytime, Anywhere', *Management Today,* June 2016, p. 31. **90 The Clink Charity:** Thanks to Vanessa Frances, The Clink Charity www.theclinkcharity.org. **99 DMG Media:** Daily Mail, May, 5, 2017. **101 Acas National:** Podro, S. 'Riding out the storm: managing conflict in a recession and beyond', ACAS Policy Discussion Paper, ACAS, March 2010. **104 Coronet Books:** Townsend, R. Further Up the Organisation, Coronet Books (1985), p. 39. **104 Professional Manager:** Hart, J. 'Mind the Gap', *Professional Manager,* November 2002, pp. 22–3. **106 Crown Copyright:** The Advisory, Conciliation and Arbitration Service (ACAS). **107 Acas National:** 'Managing conflict at work'. ACAS, June 2014. Used with permission from Acas National. **109 Haymarket Media Group Ltd:** Randall, J. 'Home Truths', *Management Today,* June 2001, p. 31. **111 European Commission:** Stress at work – mind the gap',

Social Agenda, European Commission, no. 36 February 2014. **112 Acas National:** Advisory booklet – Stress at Work, HSE/ACAS September 2014. **112 Acas National:** ACAS News, issue 11, Spring 2008. **114 The Virtual Learning Materials Workshop:** Copyright © 2011 The Virtual Learning Materials Workshop. Reproduced with permission. **113 Haymarket Media Group Ltd:** Reeves, R. 'Reality Bites', *Management Today,* March 2003, p. 35. **115 Chartered Management Institute:** Scotchmer, A. 'A Place for Everything and Everything in Its Place', *Professional Manager,* vol. 16, no. 1, January 2007, pp. 30–1. **115 Haymarket Media Group Ltd:** Rigby, R. 'Under Pressure', *Management Today,* March 2010, pp. 50–2. **117 Crown copyright:** Health and Safety Executive, 'How to tackle work-related stress', publication INDG430, October 2009. **120 World Health Organization:** WHO, 2017. **120 Department of Health and Social Care:** Department of Health (2014). **122 Crown copyright:** 'Work related Stress, Anxiety and Depression Statistics in Great Britain 2016', Health and Safety Executive, www.hse.gov.uk. **123 M.O.D. Consulting:** Kindly provided by Hugo Misselhorn, M.O.D. Consulting, South Africa. **132 Travel Weekly Group:** 'Education: hotel schools' Caterer and Hotelkeeper, August 10, 2006. **132 British Psychological Society:** Briner, R. 'Feeling and Smiling', *The Psychologist,* vol. 12, no. 1, January 1999, pp. 16–9. **136 Penguin Random House:** Freud, S. *New Introductory Lectures on Psychoanalysis,* Penguin (1973). **140 Pearson Education:** Derek Rollinson, *Organisational Behaviour and Analysis: An integrated approach,* 4th ed. Pearson Education (2008). **141 Elsevier:** Adapted from Cattell, R. B. and Kline, P. *The Scientific Analysis of Personality and Motivation,* Academic Press (1977) Table 4.1, pp. 44–5. **142 W. W. Norton & Company:** Erikson, E. H. *Identity and the Life Cycle,* Norton (1980). **146 Pearson Education:** Adapted from Stephen Robbins and Timothy Judge, *Organizational Behaviour,* thirteenth edition, Pearson Prentice Hall (2009), p. 144. Reprinted and electronically reproduced by permission of Pearson Education, Inc. **147 Sage Publications:** Luthans, F. and Youssef, C. M. 'Emerging Positive Organizational Behavior', *Journal of Management,* vol. 33, no. 3, June 2007, pp. 321–49. **149 Bloomsbury Publishing:** Goleman, D. Emotional Intelligence, Bloomsbury (1996), p. 34. **150 Korn Ferry:** Boyatzis, R., Goleman, D. and Hay/McBer, Emotional Competence Inventory Feedback Report, Hay Group (1999). **150 Hay Group Limited:** Hay Group. Copyright © 1999 Hay Group Limited. All rights reserved. Reproduced with permission. **152 Sage Publications:** Higgins, J. 'The Six Habits Of Truly Inclusive Organisations', *Professional Management,* Summer 2016, pp. 29–35. **153 ICSA: The Governance Institute:** Cooper, P. 'Culture not cult' in interview with Nicholls, J. Governance + Compliance, October 2017, p. 21. **153 The Virtual Learning Materials Workshop:** Copyright © 2011 The Virtual Learning Materials Workshop. Reproduced with permission. **155 Crown Copyright:** United Kingdom Statistics Authority. Crown Copyright material is reproduced under terms of the Click-Use License. **156 Penguin Random House:** Saira Khan – star of The Apprentice television series. Khan, S. P.U.S.H. for Success, Vermilion (2006), p. 230. **156 Chartered Management Institute:** Francke, A, 'A Blueprint for Balance', *Professional Manager,* Summer 2016, p. 5. **157 Professional Manager:** Wilton, P. 'Diversity is a Blueprint for Business' *Professional Manager,* Spring 2014, p. 19. **158 ICSA: The Governance Institute:** Swabey, P. 'Red, Amber & Green', Governance + Compliance, May 2017, p. 24. **161 Penguin Books:** Susan Cain, Quiet: The Power of Introverts in a World That Can't Stop Talking, Viking an imprint of Penguin Books (2012) pp. 13–4. **162 Portsmouth Hospitals NHS Trust:** Extracts from Portsmouth Hospitals NHS Trust, Equality and Diversity Policy, 07 December 2015. Thanks to Ruth Dolby, Organisational Development Practitioner. **171 Kogan Page:** Clements, P. and Jones, J. *The Diversity 'Training Handbook': A Practical Guide to*

Understanding and Changing Attitudes, Kogan Page (2002), p. 9. **173 Chartered Institute of Personnel and Development:** Burgoyne, J., et al. 'The Debate Starts Here', in *People Management in Perspective: A Collection of Key Articles,* Published in the Last Year on Training and Development, IPD (April 1999), pp. 16–7. Reproduced with permission from the Chartered Institute of Personnel and Development (CIPD). **177 Lifespace Publishing:** Stewart, S. and Joines, V. *TA Today: A New Introduction to Transactional Analysis,* Lifespace Publishing (1987). **179 Pearson Education:** Maureen Guirdham, *Interpersonal Behaviour at Work,* third edition, Financial Times Prentice Hall (2002), p. 140. Reprinted and electronically reproduced by permission of Pearson Education, Inc. **181 Taylor & Francis:** Honey, P. 'Styles of Learning', in Mumford, A. (ed.) *Handbook of Management Development,* fourth edition, Gower (1994). **183 Professional Manager:** Gitsham, M. in conversation with Lucas, E. 'Learning With a Helping Hand', *Professional Manager,* vol. 18, no. 5, September 2009, pp. 22–25. **183 Action Learning Associates:** Action Learning Associates http://www .actionlearningassociates.co.uk/action-learning/ (accessed 10 June 2017). Used by Permission of Action Learning Associates. **184 Dods Group:** Cosgrove, E, 'Training Journal' 1 February 2015 http://www.trainingjournal.com/articles/feature/action-learning-unplugged. **185 Chartered Institute of Personnel & Development:** Mayo, A. and Lank, E. *The Power of Learning: A Guide to Gaining Competitive Advantage,* IPD (1994) pp. 135–6. **185 Crown Copyright:** From Atkins, M. J., Beattie, J. and Dockrell, W. B. *Assessment Issues in Higher Education,* Department of Employment (October 1993) p. 51. © Crown Copyright 1993. Crown copyright material is reproduced under terms of the Click-Use Licence. **187 Pearson Education:** Kerr, M. 'Knowledge Management', *The Occupational Psychologist,* no. 48, May 2003, pp. 24–6. **188 Institute of Administrative Management:** McLean, J. 'Does your organisation know what it knows'?, Manager, *The British Journal of Administrative Management,* Spring 2009, pp. 32–3. **189 SAGE Publications:** Hurst, D. K., Rush, C. and White, R. E. 'Top Management Teams and Organisational Renewal', in Henry, J. (ed.) *Creative Management,* Sage Publications (1991), pp. 232–53. **191 Chartered Management Institute:** Peck, T. 'The magic of enchantment', *Professional Manager,* May/June 2011, pp. 26–9. **191 Taylor & Francis Group:** Rickards, T., Runco, M. A. and Moger, S. (eds) *The Routledge Companion to Creativity,* Routledge (2009). **192 LinkedIn:** Alison Bagley, 'The Value of Mentoring in Improving Retention', *Manager,* Q4, 2016, p. 22. **194 The Virtual Learning Materials Workshop:** Copyright © 2011 The Virtual Learning Materials Workshop. Reproduced with permission. **195 Haymarket Media Group Ltd:** Garrett, A. (2012) Friends in high places, *Management Today,* October 2012, p. 50. www.managementtoday.com Reproduced with permission. **196 Chartered Institute of Personnel & Development:** 'Learning and Development Survey', 01 May 2015, Used with the permission of the publisher, the Chartered Institute of Personnel and Development, London (CIPD www.cipd.co.uk). **201 Virtual College:** Virtual College with thanks to Simon Falconer, Chief Marketing Officer. www.virtual-college.co.uk. **210 Pearson Education:** From Guirdham, M. *Interactive Behaviour at Work,* third edition, Financial Times Prentice Hall (2002), p. 162. Reproduced with permission from Pearson Education Ltd. **214 Penguin Random House:** McCrum, M. Going Dutch in Beijing, Profile Books (2007), p. vii. **216 Robson Books:** Block, J. R. and Yuker, H. E. *Can You Believe Your Eyes?,* Robson Books (2002), p. 163. Reproduced with permission. **218 Professor Richard King:** King, R. A. *Introduction to Psychology,* sixth edition, McGraw-Hill (1966). Figure 10.22, p. 339. Reproduced with permission from the author, Professor Richard King. **220 Methuen Publishing:** Adapted from Gregory, R. L. Odd Perceptions, Methuen

(1986), p. 71. **221 Taylor & Francis Group:** Wilson, P. R. 'Perceptual Distortion of Height as a Function of Ascribed Academic Status', *Journal of Social Psychology,* no.74, 1968, pp. 97–102. **221 Times Newspapers:** See, for example, Leitch, L. 'The Big Problem that Short Men Face', *The Times,* 24 June 2009. **223 Pearson Education:** From Guirdham, M. *Interactive Behaviour at Work,* third edition, Financial Times Prentice Hall (2002) p. 169. Reprinted and electronically reproduced by permission of Pearson Education, Inc. **229 McGraw-Hill Education:** Adapted from Mitchell, T. R. *People in Organisations,* second edition, McGraw-Hill (1982), p. 104. **230 George Bernard Shaw:** George Bernard Shaw. **231 Penguin Random House:** McCrum, M. *Going Dutch in Beijing,* Profile Books (2007) pp. 44–5. **232 Haymarket Media Group Ltd:** Pivcevic, P. 'Taming the Boss', *Management Today,* March 1999, p. 70. **232 Chartered Secretary:** McGuire, T. 'Don't Just Listen', Chartered Secretary, September 1998, p. 24. **234 The Virtual Learning Materials Workshop:** Copyright © 2009 The Virtual Learning Materials Workshop. Reproduced with permission. **237 Chartered Management Institute:** Nick Fitzherbert Applies the Rules of Magic to Coaching People in Communication Skills', www.fitzherbert.co.uk. **237 Nick Fitzherbert:** Nick Fitzherbert, www.fitzherbert.co.uk. Reproduced with permission. **238 Chartered Management Institute:** Baguley, P. 'Putting Your Message Across', *Professional Manager,* September 2009, pp. 33–5. **242 Royal College of Nursing:** Extracted with kind permission of Royal College of Nursing from 'Managing unacceptable behaviour guidelines' 03 October 2017. www.rcn.org.uk. **250 Academy of Management:** Mitchell, T. R. 'Motivation: New Directions for Theory, Research, and Practice', *Academy of Management Review,* vol. 7, no. 1, January 1982, pp. 80–8. **251 Pearson Education:** Farren, C. 'Mastery: The Critical Advantage', in Chowdhury, S. (ed.) *Management 21C,* Financial Times Prentice Hall (2000), p. 95. **252 The Irish Times:** August 2017 Brazilian international footballer Neymar. **252 Emerald Group Publishing Limited:** See, for example, Rudolph, P. A. and Kleiner, B. H. 'The Art of Motivating Employees', *Journal of Managerial Psychology,* vol. 4, no. 5, 1989, pp. i–iv. **253 Pearson Education:** Kets de Vries, M. 'Beyond Sloan: trust is at the core of corporate values' in Pickford, J. (ed.) *Financial Times Mastering Management 2.0,* Financial Times Prentice Hall (2001), pp. 267–70. **253 Institute of Administrative Management:** Blanchard, K. 'Do you get passionate at work'? *British Journal of Administrative Management,* Autumn 2011, p. 26. **254 Canongate Books Ltd:** Pink, D. H. Drive: The surprising truth about what motives us, *Canongate Books* (2011). **260 McGraw-Hill:** Steers, R. M. and Porter, L. W. *Motivation and Work Behaviour,* fifth edition, McGraw-Hill (1991), p. 35. **260 Haymarket Media Group Ltd.:** Saunders, A. 'Keep Staff Sweet', *Management Today,* June 2003, p. 75. **264 Cambridge University Press:** McClelland, D. C. *Human Motivation,* Cambridge University Press (1988). **269 Chartered Institute of Personnel & Development:** CIPD 'Strategic reward and total reward' CIPD Factsheet, Chartered Institute of Personnel and Development, March 2014. **272 Pearson Education:** Hannagan, T. *Management,* fourth edition, Financial Times Prentice Hall (2005), p. 363. **273 The Virtual Learning Materials Workshop:** Copyright © 2011 The Virtual Learning Materials Workshop. Reproduced with permission. **274 Chartered Management Institute:** 'Motivating your team', Checklist 068, Chartered Management Institute, November 2015. **275 Pearson Education:** Luthans, F. and Kreitner, R. *Organisational Behavior Modification and Beyond,* second edition, Scott Foresman (1985), p. 36. **277 Chartered Management Institute:** Tampoe, M. 'Knowledge Workers: The New Management Challenge', *Professional Manager,* Institute of Management, November 1994, p. 13. Reproduced with permission from Chartered Management Institute. **277 Institute of Management**

Publisher's acknowledgements xxv

Services: Matson, E and Prusak, L. 'Boosting the Productivity of Knowledge Workers' *Management Services,* vol. 57, no. 2, Summer 2013, pp. 14–5. **278 Hachette UK:** World famous Pike Place Fish Market, Seattle. Lundin, S., Paul, H. and Christensen, J. Fish: A Remarkable Way to Boost Morale and Improve Results, Hyperion Press (2001), p. 37. **279 Associated Newspapers:** For the full list see: www.dailymail.co.uk/ happiest jobs (accessed 22 March 2014). **279 Chartered Institute of Personnel & Development:** CIPD Employee Outlook, Spring 2017, p. 12. **281 Pearson Education:** Hackman, J. R. and Oldham, G. R. *Work Redesign,* first edition, © 1980, Addison-Wesley Publishing Company, Inc. (1980), Figure 4.6, p. 90. Reprinted and electronically reproduced by permission of Pearson Education, Inc., New York. **294 Taylor & Francis Group:** Adair, J. Effective Teambuilding, Gower (1986). **295 Pearson Education:** Schein, E. H. *Organizational Psychology,* third edition, Prentice Hall (1988), p. 145. **295 Belbin:** Belbin, R. M. *Beyond the Team,* Butterworth–Heinemann (2000). Copyright © 2000. Reproduced with permission from Belbin, www.belbin.com. **297 Institute of Administrative Management:** Lysons, K. 'Organisational Analysis', Supplement to *The British Journal of Administrative Management,* no. 18, March/ April 1997. **299 Virtual Learning Materials Workshop.:** Copyright © 2008 The Virtual Learning Materials Workshop. Reproduced with permission. **304 Green, J:** Cited in Green, J. 'Are Your Teams and Groups at Work Successful'?, *Administrator,* December 1993, p. 12. **305 Uppsala University:** Rickards, T. and Moger, S. T. 'Creative Leadership and Team Effectiveness: Empirical Evidence for a Two Barrier Model of Team Development', working paper presented at the Advanced Seminar Series, University of Uppsala, Sweden, 3 March 2009. **306 Sage Publications:** Haslam, S. A. *Psychology in Organizations: The Social Identity Approach,* second edition, Sage Publications (2004), p. 17. **306 Pearson Education:** Guirdham, M. *Interactive Behaviour at Work,* third edition, Financial Times Prentice Hall (2002), p. 118. **306 Pearson Education:** Guirdham, M. *Interactive Behaviour at Work,* third edition, Financial Times Prentice Hall (2002), p. 119. Reproduced with permission of Pearson Education Ltd. **309 McGraw-Hill:** Likert, R. *New Patterns of Management,* McGraw-Hill (1961). **310 Professional Manager:** Symons, J. 'Taking Virtual Team Control', *Professional Manager,* vol. 12, no. 2, March 2003, p. 37. **310 Pearson Education:** Francesco, A. M. and Gold, B. A. *International Organizational Behavior,* second edition, Pearson Prentice Hall (2005), p. 118. **312 Butterworth-Heinemann:** Belbin, R. M. *Team Roles at Work,* Butterworth-Heinemann (a division of Reed Elsevier UK Ltd) and Belbin Associates (1993), p. 23. Reproduced with permission. **316 Chartered Management Institute:** Newman, R. 'Love Games', *Professional Manager,* September/October 2011, pp. 19–23. **318 Houghton Mifflin:** For a comprehensive review of the 'risky-shift' phenomenon, see, for example, Clarke, R. D. 'Group Induced Shift Towards Risk: A Critical Appraisal', *Psychological Bulletin,* vol. 76, 1971, pp. 251–70. See also Vecchio, R. P. *Organizational Behavior,* third edition, Harcourt Brace and Company (1995). **318 Houghton Mifflin:** Janis, J. L. *Groupthink,* second edition, Houghton Mifflin (1982). **321 Thomson:** Charles J Margerison, *Team Leadership: A guide to success with Team Management Systems,* Thomson (2002), p. 8. **322 BBC:** 'The Joy of 9 to 5: Do We Need Managers?' BBC Radio 4 13 April 2016. **324 Professional Manager:** Powell, N. 'Teams Are a Mirror Image of Their Leaders', *Professional Manager,* vol. 16, no. 5, September 2007, p. 41. **324 Acas National:** ACAS Teamwork: Success Through People advisory booklet, ACAS (2007). **325 Academy of Management:** Townsend, A. M., DeMarie, S. M. and Hendrickson, A. R. 'Virtual Teams: Technology and the Workplace of the Future', *The Academy of Management Executive,* vol. 12, no. 3, 1998, pp. 17–29. **325 Virgin.com Limited:** Thiefels, J. 'Remote collaboration: It's not as hard as you think', Virgin, 2017, https://www.virgin.com/entrepreneur/remote-collaboration-its-not-as-hard-asyou-think (accessed 24 August 2018). **326 Rebecca Ranninger:** Rebecca Ranninger (2012), former Executive Vice President and Chief HR Officer of Symantec. **326 Gregory R. Berry:** Gregory R. Berry **328 Haymarket Media Group Ltd:** 'Take-home lessons: Tips from remote workers and their bosses', *Management Today,* March 2011, p. 49. www.managementtoday.com Reproduced with permission. **334 Caspian Publishing Limited:** CBI *The Path to Leadership: Developing a Sustainable Model within Organisations,* Caspian Publishing (2005), p. 4. **335 Emerald Group Publishing Limited:** Kent, T. W. 'Leading and Managing: It Takes Two to Tango', *Management Decision,* vol. 43, no. 7/8, 2005, pp. 1010–17. **336 Heinemann:** Drucker, P. F. *The Practice of Management,* Heinemann Professional (1989), p. 156. **339 Gower Press:** Adair, J. *Action-Centred Leadership,* Gower Press (1979), p. 10. Reproduced with permission from John Adair. **340 Haymarket Media Group Ltd:** Leena Nair, 'The Changing Face of the Leader', *Management Today,* June 2013, p. 53. **345 McGraw-Hill:** Adapted from Fiedler, F. E. *A Theory of Leadership Effectiveness,* McGraw-Hill (1967), p. 146. Reproduced with permission from Fred E. Fiedler. **345 Pearson Education:** Vroom, V. H. and Jago, A. G. *The New Leadership: Managing Participation in Organizations,* Prentice Hall (1988). **350 Simon & Schuster:** Bass, B. M. *Leadership and Performance Beyond Expectations,* Free Press (1985). **350 Pearson Education:** Yukl, G. *Leadership in Organizations,* seventh edition, Prentice Hall (2010). 15. Vroom, V. H. and Yetton, P. W. Leadership. **351 Haymarket Media Group Ltd:** Conger, J. 'Charisma and How to Grow It', *Management Today,* December 1999, pp. 78–81. **352 Kogan Page:** Adair, J. *The Inspirational Leader: How to Motivate, Encourage and Achieve Success,* Kogan Page (2003). **353 ICSA: The Governance Institute:** Lord Owen, 'The danger of runaway leadership', Governance + Compliance, May 2017, pp. 32–4. **355 The Virtual Learning Materials Workshop:** Copyright © 2008 The Virtual Learning Materials Workshop. Reproduced with permission. **356 The Financial Times Limited:** 'Responsible leadership', Financial Times. http://lexicon.ft.com/term=responsible-leadership. (Accessed 04 October 2014) **357 Penguin Books:** McGregor, D. *The Human Side of Enterprise,* Penguin (1987), p. 182. **357 Pearson Education:** Kouzes, J. M. and Posner, B. Z. 'The Janusian Leader', in Chowdhury, S. (ed.) *Management 21C,* Financial Times Prentice Hall (2000), p. 18. **359 Haymarket Media Group Ltd:** Reeves, R. and Knell, J. 'Your Mini MBA', *Management Today,* March 2009, pp. 60–4. **360 Acas National:** Acas Strategy Unit, 'The Acas framework for effective leadership', *Employment Relations Comment,* ACAS, September 2016. Used with permission from Acas National. **362 Professional Manager:** Cutler, A. 'A Good Fit Is Essential', *Professional Manager,* vol. 14, no. 3, May 2005, p. 38. Reproduced with permission from the Chartered Management Institute and Alan Cutler. **362 Oxford Leadership:** Bacon, B. 'Intuitive intelligence in leadership', Governance + Compliance, September 2013, pp. 24–5. **363 Institute of Administrative Management:** Blanchard, K 'Developing Your Leadership Point of View', Manager, *The British Journal of Administrative Management,* Spring 2010, p. 15. **363 Haymarket Media Group Ltd:** Benjamin, D. 'In my opinion', *Management Today,* May 2011, p. 58. **363 The Clemmer Group:** Clemmer, J. (2018). 'Management vs Leadership', https://www.clemmergroup.com/articles/management-vs-leadership/ (accessed 28 August 2018). **363 Harvard Business School Publishing:** Kotter, J. 'What Leaders Really Do', *Harvard Business Review,* December, 2001, pp. 3–12. **364 Pearson Education:** Yukl, G. *Leadership in Organisations,* eighth edition, Pearson Education (2013). **364 Sage Publications:** Northouse, P. G. *Leadership Theory and Practice,* sixth edition, Sage Publications

(2013). **364 Tim Hannagan:** Hannagan, T. *Management: Concepts & Practices,* fifth edition, Pearson Education, 2008. **364 Emerald Publishing Limited:** Armandi, B., Oppedisano, J. and Sherman, H. 'Leadership Theory and Practice: A "Case" in Point', *Management Decision,* 41/10, 2003, pp. 1076–88. **365 Warren Bennis:** Bennis, W. 'Leading Change: The Leader as the Chief Information Officer', in Renesch, J. (ed.), *Leadership in a New Era: Visionary Approaches to the Biggest Crises of Our Time,* Paraview Special Editions (2002), pp. 103–10. **365 Harvard Business School Publishing:** Kotter, J. 'What Leaders Really Do', *Harvard Business Review,* December, 2001, pp. 3–12. **365 The Clemmer Group:** Clemmer, J. (2018). 'Management vs Leadership', https://www.clemmergroup.com/articles/management-vs-leadership/ (accessed 28 August 2018). **367 Portsmouth Hospitals NHS Trust:** Extract from Portsmouth Hospitals NHS Trust 'Leading Together: Leadership Development Programme 2018' with kind permission from Abigail Wilson, Organisational Development Manager. **378 Taylor & Francis Ltd:** From Watson, T. J. *Management, Organisation and Employment Strategy,* Routledge & Kegan Paul (1986), p. 29. Reproduced by permission of the publishers, Routledge, a division of Taylor & Francis, Ltd. **377 Professional Manager:** Dib, F. 'Is Management a Science?', *Professional Manager,* Autumn 2014, pp. 38–9. **377 Pearson Education:** Foppen, J. W. 'Knowledge Leadership' in Chowdbury, S (ed) *Management 21C,* Financial Times Prentice Hall (2000) pp. 160–61. **378 Harvard Business School Publishing:** Hamel, G. with Breen, B. *The Future of Management,* Harvard Business School Press (2007), p. 20. **380 Chartered Institute of Personnel and Development:** 'Building Productive Public Sector Workplaces: Part One, Improving People Management', CIPD January 2010. **381 Elsevier:** Stewart, R. *The Reality of Management,* third edition, Butterworth Heinemann (1999), p. 6. **384 Pearson Education:** Robbins, S. P. *The Truth About Managing People,* second edition, Pearson Education, 2008, p. 202. **385 Haymarket Media Group Ltd.:** Bolchover, D. 'Why Mood Matters', *Management Today,* November 2008, pp. 46–50. **389 Gulf Publishing Company:** Blake, R. R. and McCanse, A. A. *Leadership Dilemmas – Grid Solutions,* Gulf Publishing Company (1991), p. 29. **389 Institute of Administrative Management:** Institute of Administrative Management. **389 Pearson Education:** Crainer, S. and Dearlove, D. (eds) *Financial Times Handbook of Management,* second edition, Financial Times Prentice Hall (2001), p. 364. **390 Pearson Education:** Gratton, L. *Living Strategy: Putting people at the Heart of Corporate Purpose,* Financial Times Prentice Hall (2002). Reprinted and electronically reproduced by permission of Pearson Education, Inc. **395 Springer:** Forte, R. 'How I See the Personnel Function', *Personnel Management,* vol. 14, no. 8, August 1982, p. 32. **395 Pearson Education:** Lynch, R. *Corporate Strategy,* fourth edition, Financial Times Prentice Hall, (2006), Chapter 7. **395 Investors in people:** www.investorsinpeople.com. **396 Investors in people:** www.investorsinpeople.com (accessed 15 November 2017) reprinted with permission. **398 Haymarket Media Group Ltd:** Berriman, J. 'The Most Effective Managers Focus on How Best to Get Their People to Collaborate', *Management Today,* December 2011, p. 86. **399 Chartered Management Institute:** Scott, M. in conversation with Goddard, J 'Performance management after the annual appraisal' *Professional Manager,* Summer 2016, pp. 37–9. Copyright © 2016 Chartered Management Institute. **400 Crown copyright:** 'Guidance to Good management' GOV.UK, 27 October 2014. **402 Berrett-Koehler Publishers:** Mintzberg, H. *Managing,* Financial Times Prentice Hall (2009), pp. 196–7. **402 Pearson Education:** Henry Mintzberg, *Managing,* Financial Times Prentice Hall (2009), p. 197. Compiled from various sources; my own favourites in italics. Reproduced with permission from

Pearson Education Ltd. **404 Society for Industrial and Organizational Psychology:** Pulakos, E. D. and O'Leary, R. S. 'Why Is Performance Management Broken?', *Industrial and Organizational Psychology,* 2011, pp. 146–64. **404 Pearson Education:** Aguinis, H. (2009). *Performance Management,* second edition. Upper Saddle River, NJ, US: Prentice Hall/Pearson Education. **404 Pearson Education:** Aguinis, H. (2009). Performance Management, second edition, Upper Saddle River, NJ, US: Prentice Hall/Pearson Education. **404 Harvard Business School Publishing:** The Performance Management Revolution Peter Cappelli Anna Tavis from the October 2016 Issue. **405 Dow Jones & Company, Inc:** Culbert, S. 'Get Rid of the Performance Review', *The Wall Street Journal,* 20 October 2008, http://online.wsj.com/article/SB1224263187484933.html (accessed 2 September 2018). **405 Emerald Group Publishing Limited:** Jones, D. 'The Future of Performance Management Beyond Appraisals', *Strategic HR Review,* vol. 15, no. 2, 2016, pp. 100–2. **407 Kogan Page:** Stewart, H. The Happy Manifesto: Make Your Organisation a Great Workplace – Now! Happy (2012), p. 121. Reproduced with permission. **418 Simon & Schuster:** Simon, H. A. *Administrative Behaviour,* third edition, Free Press (1976). **420 Haymarket Media Group Ltd.:** Stern, S. 'Guru Guide', *Management Today,* October 2001, pp. 83–4. **421 Macmillan Publishers:** Weber, M. The Theory of Social and Economic Organization, Collier Macmillan (1964). **422 Routledge and Kegan Paul:** Blau, P. M. and Scott, W. R. Formal Organizations, Routledge and Kegan Paul (1966). Reproduced with permission. **423 Haymarket Media Group Ltd:** Caulkin, S. 'Faceless Corridors of Power', *Management Today,* January 1988, p. 65. **424 Hachette UK:** Tibballs, G. *Business Blunders,* Robinson Publishing (1999). **428 Pearson Education:** Stead, B. A. *Women in Management,* Prentice Hall (1978), p. 190. **433 Houghton Mifflin Harcourt:** Silverman, D. *The Theory of Organisations,* Heinemann (1970), p. 147. **435 Hodder & Stoughton:** Bowey, A. M. *The Sociology of Organisations,* Hodder & Stoughton (1976). **435 Sage Publications:** Cooper, R. and Burrell, G. 'Modernism, Postmodernism and Organizational Analysis: An Introduction', *Organization Studies,* vol. 9, no. 1, January 1988, pp. 91–112. **436 Pearson Education:** Watson, T. J. *Organising and Managing Work,* second edition, Financial Times Prentice Hall (2006), p. 271. **438 Institute of Administrative Management:** McLean, J. 'Management Techniques and Theories', Manager, *The British Journal of Administrative Management,* August/September 2005, p. 17. Reproduced with permission. **438 MCB University Press:** Cheng, T., Sculli, D. and Chan, F. 'Relationship Dominance – Rethinking Management Theories from the Perspective of Methodological Relationalism', *Journal of Managerial Psychology,* vol. 16, no. 2, 2001, pp. 97–105. **438 Chartered Management Institute:** Robinson, L and Francis-Smythe, J. 'Managing to abstraction', *Professional Manager,* vol. 19, no.5, September 2010, pp. 36–8. **439 British Institute of Management:** Urwick, L. *A Short Survey of Industrial Management,* British Institute of Management, London (1950). **440 Emerald Group Publishing Limited:** Smith, I. and Boyns, T. 'British Management Theory and Practice: The Impact of Fayol', *Management Decision,* vol. 43, no. 10, 2005, pp 1317–34. **440 Penguin Books:** Pugh, D. S. and Hickson, D. J. *Writers on Organisations,* sixth edition, Penguin Books (2007), p. 96. **440 Henri Fayol:** Henri Fayol. **441 Penguin Books:** Pugh, D. S. and Hickson, D. J. *Writers on Organisations,* sixth edition, Penguin Books (2007), p. 100. **441 Emerald Group Publishing Limited:** Fells, M. J. 'Fayol Stands the Test of Time', *Journal of Management History,* vol. 6, no. 8, 2000, pp. 345–60. **441 EURAM:** Hatchuel, A. and Segrestin, B. 'A Century Old and Still Visionary: Fayol's Innovative Theory of Management', *European Academy of Management',* June 2018, pp. 1–14. **441 Emerald Group Publishing Limited:** Parker, L. D. and Ritson, P. 'Fads,

Stereotypes and Management Gurus: Fayol and Follett today', *Management Decision,* vol. 43, no. 10, 2005, pp. 1335–57. **441 Emerald Group Publishing Limited:** Fells, M. J. 'Fayol Stands the Test of Time', *Journal of Management History,* vol. 6, no. 8, 2000, pp. 345–60. **441 Emerald Group Publishing Limited:** Smith, I. and Boyns, T. 'British Management Theory and Practice: The Impact of Fayol', *Management Decision,* vol. 43, no. 10, 2005, pp. 1317–34. **441 Harvard Business School Publishing:** Mintzberg, H. 'The Manager's Job: Folklore and Fact', *Harvard Business Review,* vol. 53, no. 4, 1975, pp. 49–61. **441 Taylor & Francis Group:** Hales, C. (1993). *Managing Through Organization: The Management Process, Forms of Organization and the Work of Managers,* Routledge (1993) p. 3. **443 David Puttick:** Thanks to David Puttick, Vanguard. Reproduced with permission. **443 Random House:** Seddon, J. Freedom from Command & Control: A better way to make the work work, Vanguard Consulting Ltd. (2005). **445 Pearson Education:** Adapted from DuBrin, A. J. *Human Relations: A Job-Oriented Approach,* Reston Publishing/Prentice Hall (1978), pp. 296–7. Copyright © 1978. Reproduced with permission from Pearson Education Inc. **415 Pearson Education:** Jones, G. R. Organizational Theory, Design and Change, seventh edition, Pearson (2013). Reprinted and electronically reproduced by permission of Pearson Education, Inc. **422 Routledge and Kegan Paul:** Based on Blau, P. M. and Scott, W.R. *Formal Organizations,* Routledge & Kegan Paul (1966). **431 The Virtual Learning Materials Workshop:** Copyright © 2008 The Virtual Learning Materials Workshop. Reproduced with permission. **452 John Wiley & Sons:** Child, J. *Organization: Contemporary Principles and Practice,* second edition, Wiley (2015), p. 17. **452 Macmillan:** Forte, C. (Lord Forte) *Forte: The Autobiography of Charles Forte,* Sidgwick and Jackson (1986), p. 122. **452 John Wiley & Sons:** Parsons, T. 'Some Ingredients of a General Theory of Formal Organization', in Litterer, J. A. *Organizations: Structure and Behaviour,* third edition, Wiley (1980). **455 Oxford University Press:** Woodward, J. *Industrial Organization: Theory and Practice,* second edition, Oxford University Press (1980), p. 113. **460 Elsevier:** Drucker, P. F. *Management Challenges for the 21st Century,* Butterworth-Heinemann (1999), p. 11. **461 Macmillan Publishers:** Peter L. J. and Hull, R. *The Peter Principle,* Pan Books (1970), p. 22. **466 Pearson Education:** Senior, B. and Swailes, S. *Organizational Change,* fourth edition, Financial Times Prentice Hall (2010), p. 84. **471 Pearson Education:** Francesco, A. M. and Gold, B. A. *International Organizational Behavior,* second edition, Pearson Prentice Hall (2005), p. 246. **472 McGraw-Hill Education:** Rosenfeld, R. H. and Wilson, D. C. *Managing Organizations: Text, Readings and Cases,* second edition, McGraw-Hill (1999), p. 255. **472 Pearson Education:** Lynch, R. *Corporate Strategy,* fourth edition, Financial Times Prentice Hall (2006), p. 582. **475 Oxford University Press:** Dawson, S. and Wedderburn, D. 'Introduction' to Woodward, J. *Industrial Organization: Theory and Practice,* second edition, Oxford University Press (1980), p. xiii. **479 John Wiley & Sons:** Litterer, J. A. *The Analysis of Organizations,* second edition, John Wiley & Sons (1973), p. 339. Reproduced with permission from the estate of Joseph A. Litterer. **480 McGraw-Hill Education:** Robey, D. *Designing Organizations,* Irwin (1982), p. 59. See, for example, Fincham, R. and Rhodes, P. S. *The Individual, Work and Organization,* second edition, Weidenfeld and Nicolson (1992). **481 Pearson Education:** Schneider, S. C. and Barsoux, J. *Managing Across Cultures,* second edition, Financial Times Prentice Hall (2003), p. 101. **481 Pearson Education:** Watson, T. *Organising and Managing Work,* second edition, Financial Times Prentice Hall (2006), pp. 254–62. **481 John Wiley & Sons:** Cloke, K. and Goldsmith, J. *The End of Management and the Rise of Organizational Democracy,* Jossey-Bass (2002), p. 41. **483 Chartered Management Institute:** 'Deciding Whether

To Outsource', Checklist 079, Chartered Management Institute, September 2014. **485 HarperCollins:** Heller, R. *In Search of European Excellence,* HarperCollins Business (1997), p. 4. **485 Kaitlin Madden:** Madden (2010). **486 Raymond Hull:** Peter and Hull (1996:27). **486 Penguin Random House:** 'The Real Peter Principle: Promotion to Pain,' Hess, an occupational psychologist, p. 12. **486 Forbes Media LLC:** Benson, Li and Shue (2018) p. 30, p. 49. **487 William O. Beeman:** Beeman and Hess p. 48, p. 10. **488 Gaius Petronius:** Gaius Petronius, AD 66. **489 Investors in people:** for case study: Investors in People content provided by the UK Commission for Employment and Skills. www.investorsinpeople.co.uk. reprinted with permission. **470 Macmillan:** Based on Miner, J. B. Management Theory, Macmillan (1971), p. 47. **473 The Virtual Learning Materials Workshop:** Copyright ©2012 The Virtual Learning Materials Workshop. Reproduced with permission. **474 Pearson Education:** Lynch, R. Strategic Management, sixth edition, Pearson Education (2012), p. 464. Reprinted by permission of Pearson Education Ltd. **476 Oxford University Press:** Woodward, J. *Industrial Organization: Theory and Practice,* second edition, Oxford University Press (1980), p. 128. **477 Tavistock Publications Ltd:** Adapted from Perrow, C. *Organizational Analysis: A Sociological View,* Tavistock Publications (1970), p. 78. **482 Reed Business Information:** Copyright © Reed Business Information, reprinted with permission. **485 Pearson Education:** Gray, J. L. and Starke, F. A. *Organizational Behavior: Concepts and Applications,* fourth edition, © 1988. Reprinted and electronically reproduced by permission of Pearson Education, Inc., New York. **506 Penguin Random House:** Shirky, C. *Here Comes Everybody: The Power of Organizing without Organizations,* Penguin (2009). **508 European Foundation:** European Foundation for the Improvement of Living and Working Conditions, Global Competition and European Companies' Location Decisions. Background Paper, European Foundation (2008), p. 2. **509 Taylor & Francis Group:** Cited in Jackson, P. (ed.) *Virtual Working: Social and Organisational Dynamics,* Routledge (1999), p. 53. **510 Sage Publications:** Golden, T. 'Co-workers Who Telework and the Impact on Those in the Office: Understanding the Implications of Virtual Work for Co-worker Satisfaction and Turnover Intentions', *Human Relations,* vol. 60, no. 11, 2007, pp. 1641–67. **512 The Virtual Learning Materials Workshop:** Copyright © 2011 The Virtual Learning Materials Workshop. **514 Emerald Publishing Limited:** McDowall and Kinman (2017) p. 264. **516 Labour Research Department:** The main source for this case study is Labour Research Department 'The Enemy Within: Negotiating on Monitoring and Surveillance', Workplace Report, no. 97, December, 2011, pp. 15–6. **523 John Wiley & Sons:** Child, J. *Organization: Contemporary Principles and Practice,* second edition, Wiley (2015), p. 144. **524 John Wiley & Sons:** Cloke, K. and Goldsmith, J. *The End of Management and the Rise of Organizational Democracy,* Jossey-Bass (2002), p. 5. **524 Oxford University Press:** Wilson, F. M. *Organizational Behaviour and Work: A Critical Introduction,* third edition, Oxford University Press (2010), p. 222. **524 Pearson Education:** Watson, T. J. *Organising and Managing Work,* second edition, Financial Times Prentice Hall (2006), pp. 55–6. **527 McGraw-Hill Education:** McKenna, R. New Management, Irwin/McGraw-Hill (1999), pp. 430–1. **527 Oxford University Press:** Wilson, F. M. *Organizational Behaviour and Work: A Critical Introduction,* third edition, Oxford University Press (2010), p. 313. **528 Sage Publications:** Barker, J. R. 'Tightening the Iron Cage: Concertive Control in Self-Managing Teams', *Administrative Science Quarterly,* vol. 38, 1993, pp. 408–37. **528 John Wiley & Sons:** Child, J. *Organization: Contemporary Principles and Practice,* second edition, Wiley (2015), p. 144. **529 John Wiley & Sons:** Child, J. Organization: Contemporary Principles and Practice, second edition, Blackwell Publishing (2015),

p. 154. Reproduced with permission from Wiley-Blackwell. **532 Emerald Group Publishing Limited:** Caulkin, S. 'The Real Invisible Hand', *Management Today,* November 2011, pp. 40–4. **537 Penguin Random House:** Handy, C. B. *Understanding Organizations,* fourth edition, Penguin (1993), p. 131. **537 MOD Associates:** Misselhorn, H. *Values, Power and Problem Solving,* MOD Associates, South Africa, 10 March 2014. Reproduced with permission. **538 Professional Manager:** Mann, S. 'Oh I Heard It On the Grapevine', *Professional Manager,* July 1997, p. 33. **538 Haymarket Media Group Ltd:** Hazelhurst, J. 'The Way We Work Now', *Management Today,* June 2013, pp. 47–9. **540 John Wiley & Sons:** Owen, J. *The Death of Modern Management,* Wiley (2009), p. 230. **540 Pearson Education:** Yukl, G. *Leadership in Organizations,* seventh edition, Pearson (2010), p. 219. **542 Pearson Education:** Mills, D. Q. and Friesen, G. B. 'Empowerment', in Crainer, S. and Dearlove, D. (eds) *Financial Times Handbook of Management,* second edition, Financial Times Prentice Hall (2001), p. 323. **545 Institute of Administrative Management:** Bushe, G. R. 'The Skills of Clear Leadership', Manager, *The British Journal of Administrative Management,* Summer 2009, p. 26. **545 Haymarket Media Group Ltd.:** Gracie, S. 'Delegate Don't Abdicate', *Management Today,* March 1999, p. 94. **546 Elsevier:** Stewart, R. *The Reality of Management,* third edition, Butterworth Heinemann (1999), p. 180. **547 The Virtual Learning Materials Workshop:** Copyright © 2012 The Virtual Learning Materials Workshop. Reproduced with permission. **549 Ajit Ghosh:** Ghosh (2013:95). **549 Academy of Management:** *The Empowerment Process: Integrating Theory and Practice Academy of Management Review* Vol. 13, No. 3 Articles, Jay A. Conger and Rabindra N. Kanungo 1988. **559 Emerald Publishing Limited:** Honold (1997:210). **559 Emerald Publishing Limited:** Honold (1997:210). **559 Mayer Zald:** Zald, 1970:225. **551 Gerardo R. Ungson:** Mills and Ungson (2000:148). **537 Sergeant Keith Poultney:** With thanks to Sergeant Keith Poultney, Hampshire Constabulary for providing this information. **553 Crown copyright:** Section 39 of Evidence Act 1984 (PACE) that was enacted in January 1986 and any code of practice issued under the Act. **562 Amazon:** Attributed to Jeff Bezos founder and CEO, Amazon **562 Elsevier:** Stewart, R. *The Reality of Management,* third edition, Butterworth Heinemann (1999), p. 123. **563 Pearson Education:** Naylor, J. *Management,* second edition, Financial Times Prentice Hall (2004), p. 79. **564 Emerald Group Publishing Limited:** Atkinson, P. E. 'Creating Cultural Change', *Management Services,* vol. 34, no. 7, 1990, pp. 6–10. **564 ICSA: The Governance Institute:** Johnson, R. 'Changing corporate culture', *Governance & Compliance,* June 2013, p. 3. **569 The Financial Times Limited:** Thomas Cook waves an ungrateful goodbye to Harriet Green Alison Smith November 27, 2014. **570 Pearson Education:** Johnson, G., et al. *Exploring Strategy,* tenth edition, Pearson Education (2014). Reprinted and electronically reproduced by permission of Pearson Education, Inc. **571 Pearson Education:** Cartwright, J. *Cultural Transformation,* Financial Times Prentice Hall (1999), p. 34. **572 Acas National:** 'Effective Organisations: The People Factor', *Advisory Booklet,* ACAS, November 2001. **574 Institute of Administrative Management:** Clifton, K. 'Values Added', *Manager,* Autumn 2012, p 14. **574 ICSA: The Governance Institute:** Klugerman, M. 'Aspire higher: Changing organisational culture is never easy, but the rewards can be substantial', *Governance Compliance,* November 2017, pp. 30–2. **575 Chartered Secretary magazine:** This case was published originally in ICSA Global Outlook, a supplement to the May 2011 issue of Chartered Secretary magazine. **576 Emerald Group Publishing Limited:** Lewis, R. D. *The Cultural Imperative: Global Trends in the 21st Century,* Nicholas Brealey (2007). **578 Harvard Business School Publishing:** Tagiuri, R. and Litwin, G. H. (eds) *Organizational Climate,* Graduate School of Business

Administration, Harvard University (1968), p. 27. **582 University of Chicago Press:** Lewin, K. *Field Theory in Social Science,* Harper and Row (1951). **583 Macmillan Publishers:** Toffler, A. *Future Shock,* Pan Books (1970), p. 27. **587 Haymarket Media Group Ltd.:** In conversation with Saunders, A. 'How to cope with a changing world', *Management Today,* October 2012, pp. 52–5. **587 Haymarket Media Group Ltd.:** Lockhead, Sir M. 'In My Opinion', *Management Today,* September 2008, p. 12. **588 Haymarket Media Group Ltd.:** Reeves, R. and Knell, J. 'Your Mini MBA', *Management Today,* March 2009, pp. 60–4. **589 Chartered Management Institute:** Tranfield, D. and Braganza, A. *Business Leadership of Technological Change: Five Key Challenges Facing CEOs,* Chartered Management Institute (2007). **590 The Riches Group Pty Ltd:** Material in this section reproduced with kind permission of Anne Riches, creator of The Almond Effect® and author of CLUES: tips, strategies and examples for change leaders. For further information see www.AnneRiches.com. **591 SAGE Publications:** Dent, E. B., & Goldberg, S. G. Challenging "Resistance to Change". *The Journal of Applied Behavioral Science,* vol. 35, no. 1, 1999, 25–41. https://doi.org/10.1177/0021886399351003. **591 Elsevier:** Ford, J. D. and Ford, L. W. 'Stop Blaming Resistance to Change and Start Using It', *Organization Dynamics,* vol. 39, no. 1, 2010, pp. 24–36. **592 Sage Publications:** Dent, E. B., & Goldberg, S. G. (1999). Challenging "Resistance to Change." *The Journal of Applied Behavioral Science,* vol. 35, no. 1, 25–41. https://doi.org/10.1177/0021886399351003. **592 Elsevier:** Ford, J. D. and Ford, L. W. 'Stop Blaming Resistance to Change and Start Using It', *Organization Dynamics,* vol. 39, no. 1, 2010, pp. 24–36. **594 Echelon Learning Ltd:** Adapted with permission from David Hill, Director, Echelon Learning Ltd. **595 Chartered Management Institute:** 'Management 2020', *Commission on The Future of Management and Leadership,* Chartered Management Institute, July 2014, p. 33. www.managers.org.uk/management2020. Reproduced with permission. **563 Pearson Education:** Senior, B. and Swailes, S. *Organizational Change,* fourth edition, Financial Times Prentice Hall (2010), p. 161, Reprinted and Electronically reproduced by permission from Pearson Education, Inc., New York. **568 Pearson Education:** Rollinson, D. *Organisational Behaviour and Analysis: An Integrated Approach,* fourth edition, Financial Times Prentice Hall (2008), p. 592, Reprinted and Electronically reproduced by permission from Pearson Education, Inc., New York. **570 Pearson Education:** Johnson, G., Whittington, R., Scholes, K., Angwin, D. and Regnér, P. *Exploring Strategy,* tenth edition, p. 156. Reprinted and Electronically reproduced by permission from Pearson Education, Inc., New York. **577 Nicholas Brealey Publishing:** *The Cultural Imperative: Global Trends in the 21st Century,* Nicholas Brealey (Lewis, R.D. 2007) © 2003 Richard Lewis. Reproduced by permission of Nicholas Brealey Publishing. **582 Harper & Row:** Based on French, W. L., Kast, F. E. and Rosenzweig, J. E. *Understanding Human Behavior in Organizations,* Harper and Row (1985), p. 9. **584 The Virtual Learning Materials Workshop:** Copyright © 2011 The Virtual Learning Materials Workshop. Reproduced with permission. **603 Pearson Education:** Richard Lynch, *Strategic Management,* sixth edition – 2012 Pearson Education. Reprinted and electronically reproduced by permission of Pearson Education, Inc. **604 Haymarket Media Group Ltd.:** Stern, S. 'The Next Big Thing', *Management Today,* April 2007, p. 50. **604 Pearson Education:** Gratton, L. *Living Strategy: Putting People at the Heart of Corporate Purpose,* Financial Times Prentice Hall (2000), p. 18. **607 John Lewis Partnership:** http://www.johnlewispartnership.co.uk/about/our-principles.html. Used with Permission from John Lewis partnership. **608 Heinemann:** Drucker, P. *Managing for Results,* Heinemann Professional (1989). **612 Alistair Dryburgh:** Alistair Dryburgh, www.dontyoubelieveitblog.com (accessed 8 June 2012). **613 Institute of**

Administrative Management: Taylor, L. 'Why SMART goals need to get SMARTER', Institute of Administrative Management Newsletter, April 2017. **614 Red Carnation Hotels:** https://www.redcarnationhotels.com/about/core-values. Used by permission from Red Carnation Hotels. **617 United Nations:** https://www.unglobalcompact.org/what-is-gc/mission/principles. Reprinted with permission. **620 ICSA: The Governance Institute:** Handy, C. 'The glass towers', Governance + Compliance, March 2016, pp. 22–5. **621 ICSA: The Governance Institute:** Hilton, A. 'Ethical irony', Governance + Compliance, August 2016, pp. 12–3. **625 University of Portsmouth:** University of Portsmouth, Ethics Policy April 2017 www.port.ac.uk. **626 ICSA: The Governance Institute:** Bennett, M. 'Shaping the future', *Governance & Compliance,* June 2014, pp. 32–3. **625 Chartered Management Institute:** Chartered Management Institute, for full details, see www.managers.org.uk/code. Reproduced with permission. **625 University of Portsmouth:** University of Portsmouth, Ethics Policy April 2017 www.port.ac.uk. **632 Haymarket Media Group Ltd:** *Management Today* May 2011. p. 69. www.managementtoday.co.uk. Reproduced with permission. **633 Reach Publishers:** Misselhorn, A. *Head and Heart of Leadership,* (Reach Publishers, SA), (2012). p. 86. Reproduced with permission. **616 Pearson Education:** Rollinson, D. *Organisational Behaviour and Analysis: An Integrated Approach,* fourth edition, Financial Times Prentice Hall (2008), p. 592, Reprinted and Electronically reproduced by permission from Pearson Education, Inc., New York. **623 The Virtual Learning Materials Workshop:** Copyright © 2018 The Virtual Learning Materials Workshop. Reproduced with permission. **627 Equality and Human Rights Commission:** A Guide to Business and Human Rights: How Human Rights Can Add Value to Your Business. Equality and Human Rights Commission, June 2014. The copyright in the document this publication has been adapted from and all other intellectual property rights in that material are owned by, or licensed to, the Commission for Equality and Human Rights, known as the Equality and Human Rights Commission ("the EHRC"). **628 Elsevier Inc.:** Bart, C. K. 'Sex, Lies and Mission Statements', *Business Horizons,* Nov–Dec 1997, pp. 9–18. **629 Emerald Publishing Limited:** Khalifa, A. S. 'Three Fs for the Mission Statement: What's Next?', *Journal of Strategy and Management,* vol. 4, no. 1, 2011, pp. 25–43. **629 Harvard Business School Publishing:** Nash, L. 'Missions Statements: Mirrors and Windows', *Harvard Business Review,* March–April, 1988, pp. 155–56. **629 Emerald Publishing Limited:** Khalifa, A. S. 'Mission, purpose, and ambition: redefining the mission statement', *Journal of Strategy and Management,* vol. 5, no. 3, 2012, pp. 236–51. **629 Elsevier Inc.:** Bart, C. K. 'Sex, Lies and Mission Statements', Business Horizons, Nov–Dec 1997, pp. 9–18. **639 Management Consultancies Association:** Czerniawska, F. 'From Bottlenecks to BlackBerries: How the Relationship between Organisations and Individuals Is Changing,' Management Consultancies Association (September 2005). **640 Chartered Management Institute:** Lucas, E. 'Switched On to Innovation', *Professional Manager,* vol. 16, no. 3, May 2007, pp. 32–5. **640 Pearson Education:** Gratton, L. *The Democratic Enterprise,* Financial Times Prentice Hall (2004), pp. xiii–xiv. **641 Chartered Management Institute:** Scott, M. in conversation with Jimmy Wales, 'The end of control', *Professional Manager,* Winter 2016, p. 39. **642 McGraw-Hill Education:** O'Reilly, C. 'Corporations, Culture and Commitment: Motivation and Social Control in Organizations', in Steers, R. M., Porter, L. W. and Bigley, G. A. (eds) *Motivation and Leadership at Work,* sixth edition, McGraw-Hill (1996), p. 374. **643 Crown copyright:** Extracts from Macleod, D and Clarke, N. Engaging for Success: Enhancing performance through employee engagement, A report to Government, Department for Business, Innovation and Skills (2009). **647 The Virtual Learning Materials Workshop:** Copyright © 2011

The Virtual Learning Materials Workshop. Reproduced with permission. **644 Chartered Institute of Personnel & Development:** Employee engagement and motivation' Factsheet CIPD, 14 September 2017. **645 Professional Manager:** Rock, S. '12 Ways to Foster Amazing Employee Engagement' *Professional Manager,* Autumn 2016, pp. 50–3. **646 Penguin Random House:** Senge, P. M. *The Fifth Discipline: The Art of Practice of the Learning Organization,* Doubleday (1990). **649 HarperCollins:** Garratt, B. *The Fish Rots from the Head,* HarperCollins (1996). **649 Orpington:** Lane, T., Snow, D. and Labrow, P. 'Learning to Succeed with ICT', *The British Journal of Administrative Management,* May/June 2000, pp. 14–5. **651 Pitman Publishing:** Cane, S. *Kaizen Strategies for Winning through People,* Pitman Publishing (1996), p. 8. **651 Kaizen Institute:** https://uk.kaizen.com/home (accessed 14 February 2018). **651 Chartered Management Institute:** Van de Vliet, A. 'The New Balancing Act', *Management Today,* July 1997, pp. 78–80. **653 EFQM:** EFQM. Copyright © 2012 EFQM. The EFQM Excellence Model is a registered trademark of the EFQM. Reproduced with permission. **652 EFQM:** Material on EFQM Excellence Model reproduced with permission of EFQM www.efqm.org. **655 Professional Manager:** Mann, S. 'Cultivating influence', *Professional Manager,* January 2010, pp. 32–4. **656 Chartered Management Institute:** Saunders, A. 'Rebuilding management's good name', *Management Today,* May 2011, pp. 44–6. **657 Chartered Management Institute:** Birkinshaw, J. 'How to be a Better Boss', *Management Today,* September 2013, pp. 46–9. **658 Cengage Learning:** Rees, W. D. and Porter, C. *Skills of Management,* fifth edition, Thomson Learning (2001), p. 22. **661 Acas National:** Building Productivity in the UK' Acas Strategy Unit, June 2015. Used with permission from Acas National. **663 Boston Consulting Group:** Roghē, F., Toma, A., Kilmann, J., Dicke, R. and Strack, R. 'Organizational Capabilities Matter' The Boston Consulting Group, January 2012. **663 Elsevier:** Stewart, R. *The Reality of Management,* third edition, Butterworth-Heinemann (1999), p. 125. **663 The Boston Consulting Group:** Organizational Capabilities Matter © 2012, The Boston Consulting Group (BCG). **665 JPS Associates:** Hugo Misselhorn 'Do we fix the people or the organization?', 02 April 2016. www.jpsa.co.za. Reproduced with permission. **665 JPS Associates:** Adapted with permission from Hugo Misselhorn, JPS Associates www.jbsa.co.za. Reproduced with permission. **670 Haymarket Media Group Ltd.:** Stewart, H 'How to have a happy and productive office', *Management Today,* February 2012, pp. 38–42. **671 Crown copyright:** This case study is based on interviews conducted by the University of Plymouth with a human resources manager, a trade union representative and an organisation development Manager at Wiltshire Fire Service, along with discussions with Acas staff. TUPE refers to the "Transfer of Undertakings (Protection of Employment) Regulations 2006". The TUPE rules protect employees' rights when the organisation or service they work for transfers to a new employer. For more info see: www.acas.org.uk/tupe Reproduced with permission of Acas. Crown Copyright. Open Government Licence, details of which can be found here: http://www.nationalarchives.gov.uk/doc/open-government-licence/version/3/. **667 Gower Pub Co:** Marsick, V. J. and Watkins, K. E. *Facilitating Learning Organizations: Making Learning Count,* Gower (1999). **667 McGraw-Hill:** Pedler, M., Burgoyne, J. G. and Boydell, T. *The Learning Company: A Strategy for Sustainable Development,* McGraw-Hill (1991). **668 Sage Publications:** Thomsen, H. K. and Hoest, V. 'Employees' Perception of the Learning Organization', *Management Learning,* vol. 32, no. 4, 2001, pp. 469–91. **668 Harvard Business School Publishing:** Garvin, D. A., Edmondson, A. C. and Gino, F. 'Is Yours a Learning Organization?', Harvard Business Review, March, vol. 86, no. 3, 2008, pp. 109–16, 134. **668 Emerald Group Publishing Limited:** Grieves, J. 'Why We Should Abandon the Idea of the Learning Organization',

The Learning Organization, vol. 15, no. 6, 2008, pp. 463–73. **668 Emerald Group Publishing Limited:** Pedler, M. and Burgoyne, J. G. 'Is the Learning Organization Still Alive?', *The Learning Organization,* vol. 24, no. 2, 2017, pp. 119–26. **668 Emerald Group Publishing Limited:** Karkoulian, S., Messarra, L. C., and McCarthy, R. 'The Intriguing Art of Knowledge Management and its Relation to Learning Organizations', *The Journal of Knowledge Management,* 17, 2013, pp. 511–26. **403 The Virtual Learning Materials Workshop:** Copyright © 2011 The Virtual Learning Materials Workshop. Reproduced with permission. **45 The Virtual Learning Materials Workshop:** Copyright © 2011 The Virtual Learning Materials Workshop. Reproduced with permission. **15 The Virtual Learning Materials Workshop:** Copyright © 2011 The Virtual Learning Materials Workshop. Reproduced with permission. **364 Merriam Webster Online Dictionary:** Merriam Webster Online Dictionary https://www.merriam-webster.com/dictionary/leadership. Used with permission **364 Merriam Webster Online Dictionary:** Merriam Webster Online Dictionary https://www.merriam-webster.com/dictionary/management. Used with permission. **551 Merriam Webster Online Dictionary:** Merriam Webster Online Dictionary https://www.merriam-webster.com/dictionary/trust. Used with permission.

Photographs

003, 024, 032, 060, 064, 067, 169, 182, 189, 208, 215, 232, 249, 255, 294, 338, 352, 374, 379, 385, 392, 414, 421, 451, 464, 496, 498, 510, 523, 530, 535, 542, 580, 602, 610, 615, 622, 653, 662, Laurie Mullins: Laurie J. Mullins **063 Getty images:** Bloomberg/Contributor/Getty Images **090 BL Guardian News and Media Limited:** The Clink Charity **090 BR The Clink Charity:** The Clink Charity. **097 Laurie Mullins:** Laurie J. Mullins **103 Alamy:** imageBROKER/Alamy Stock Photo. **109, 109 Laurie Mullins:** Laurie J. Mullins **130 PEXELS:** Christina Morillo/PEXELS **145 Laurie Mullins:** Laurie J. Mullins **154 123RF:** Dmitriy Shironosov/123RF. **261, 261, 274, 274, 280, 280, 300, 300, 300 Laurie Mullins:** Laurie J. Mullins **313 Alamy:** Denise Kluivers/Alamy Stock Photo **343, 343, 430, 439, 439, 458, 458, 494, 494, 562, 562, 567, 567, 567, 583, 583 R Laurie Mullins:** Laurie J. Mullins **639, 639, 641, 641, 645 Laurie Mullins:** Laurie J. Mullins **007 B Getty ssimages:** sturti/E+/Getty images **008 M Alamy stock photo:** Tony Tallec/Alamy Stock Photo **007 M Alamy stock photo:** Mint Images Limited/Alamy Stock Photo **007 T Getty images:** Maskot/Getty images **008 T Alamy Stock Photo:** Inti St Clair/Blend Images/Alamy Stock Photo **039 Alamy:** Federico Caputo/Alamy Stock Photo **045 123RF:** Ilfede/123RF **045 Shutterstock:** Saipullah Srg/Shutterstock **077 Shutterstock:** Vitaly Titov/Shutterstock **116 Shutterstock:** Pixel-Shot/Shutterstock **149 Shutterstock:** 9'63 Creation/Shutterstock **212 Shutterstock:** Dean Drobot/Shutterstock **224 Shutterstock:** Photographee.eu/Shutterstock **308 Alamy:** Clive Chilvers/Alamy Stock Photo **430 R Shutterstock:** Zapp2Photo/Shutterstock **475 Shutterstock:** 3000ad/Shutterstock **505 Shutterstock:** Jkstock/Shutterstock **505 Shutterstock:** Shutterstock **583 Shutterstock:** ArtisticPhoto/Shutterstock **645 L Shutterstock:** Vgstockstudio/Shutterstock

Chapter 0
Your study of organisational behaviour

If you do not know where you are going how will you know if you have arrived?

Learning outcomes

After reading this chapter you should be more aware of:

- the meaning, nature and scope of organisational behaviour;
- the importance of social skills and employability;

- the structure, main features and contents of the book.

Outline chapter contents

Overview topic map: Chapter 0 – Your study of organisational behaviour

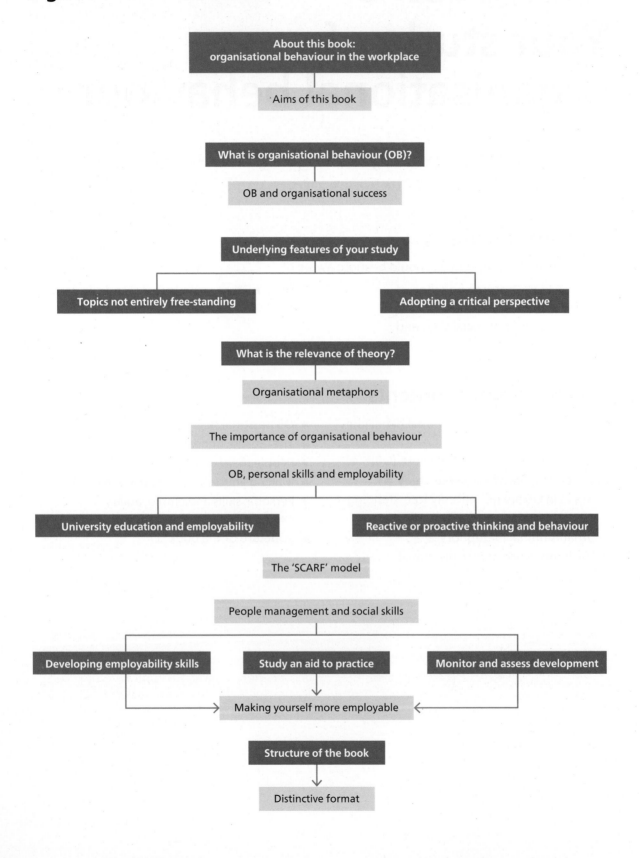

The hidden depth of an iceberg with up to 90 per cent of total mass below the surface

About this book: organisational behaviour in the workplace

This is an introductory text for those readers of organisational behaviour or related subjects interested in improving organisational performance through the behaviour and actions of people at work.

The activities of an organisation are directed towards the attainment of certain goals and also have social implications. Organisational behaviour is a wide and essentially multidisciplinary field of inquiry and should not be considered in a vacuum but related to the broader organisational context and external environment.

The concepts and ideas presented in this book provide a basis for contrasting perspectives on the structure, operation and management of organisations, and interactions among people who work in them. A central theme of the book is the nature of the people–organisation relationship.

Aims of this book

The aims of this book are to:

- indicate ways in which organisational performance may be improved through better understanding of the behaviour and actions of people at work;
- increase awareness of, and sensitivity to, personal skills and employability.

What is organisational behaviour (OB)?

At its basic, **organisational behaviour (OB)** is concerned with the study of human behaviour. It involves the understanding, prediction and control of behaviour of people within an organisational setting. The meaning of the term is not always clear and there are a number of closely related study areas with often similar descriptions such as organisational analysis, work psychology or organisation development but common definitions of organisational behaviour are generally along the lines of:

> **the study and understanding of individual and group behaviour and patterns of structure and management in order to help improve organisational performance and effectiveness.**

Study of organisational behaviour is usually interpreted more about the people within the work situation but it is difficul to divorce completely from broader social situations.

Clearly there is a multiplicity of interrelated factors that influence the decisions and actions of people as members of a work organisation. The scope for the examination of organisational behaviour is therefore very wide. There is also debate over the relationship between organisational behaviour, the human resource function, and management theory and practice.

Organisational Behaviour is one of the most complex and perhaps least understood academic elements of modern general management, but since it concerns the behaviour of people within organisations it is also one of the most central . . . its concern with individual and group patterns of behaviour makes it an essential element in dealing with the complex behavioural issues thrown up in the modern business world.

Source: Introduction to Module 6, Organisational Behaviour, Financial Times Mastering Management, FT Pitman Publishing (1997), p. 216.

However much of a cliché, it is still an inescapable fact that people are the main resource of any organisation. Without its members, an organisation is nothing; an organisation is only as good as the people who work within it. In today's increasingly dynamic, global and competitive environment understanding human behaviour at work and effective management of the people resource is even more important for organisational survival and success.

Vecchio suggests three reasons for studying organisational behaviour.

- **Important practical applications** that follow from an understanding and knowledge of OB and the ability to deal effectively with others in an organisational setting.
- **Personal growth** and the fulfilment gained from understanding our fellow humans. Understanding others may also lead to greater self-knowledge and self-insight.
- **Increased knowledge** about people in work settings, for example identification of major dimensions of leadership leading to the design leadership training programmes in organisations.[1]

Watson reminds us that the biggest challenge and most fascinating aspect that we face when trying to analyse organisations is its essential ambiguity. Organisations do not actually exist. The organisation in which you work or study is not something you can see, hear, touch, smell, kick, kiss or throw up in the air.[2]

OB and organisational success

Sooner or later every organisation has to perform successfully if it is to survive. An understanding of organisational behaviour is essential for organisational performance and effectiveness. In order to study the behaviour of people at work it is necessary to understand interrelationships with other variables that together comprise the total organisation.

The study of organisational behaviour embraces therefore an understanding of the interactions among:

- the nature and purpose of the organisation;
- formal structure and role relationships;
- the tasks to be undertaken and technology employed;
- organisational processes and the execution of work;
- the human element, informal organisation and behaviour of people;
- the process of management as an integrating and co-ordinating activity;
- social responsibilities and business ethics;
- the external environment of which the organisation is part; and
- the need for organisation success and survival.

How would YOU attempt to explain the meaning, significance and scope of organisational behaviour to a fellow student studying engineering?

Underlying features of your study

It is important always to remember that it is people who are being managed and people should be considered in human terms. Unlike physical resources, the people resource is not owned by the organisation. People bring their own perceptions, feelings and attitudes towards the organisation, systems and styles of management, their duties and responsibilities, and the conditions under which they are working. Human behaviour is capricious and scientific methods or principles of behaviour cannot be applied with reliability. It is also widely observed that you cannot study the behaviour of people without changing it.

A noticeable feature of organisational behaviour is the invariable difficulty in identifying a definitive solution to a particular situation. The absence of one single, 'right' answer can make study of the subject complex and frustrating and even may bring into question the value in studying the subject at all. Consider however the attraction of study for your personal development and confidence; the opportunity to test your thoughts and ideas with fellow students in a non-threatening environment; and to help prepare yourself for the realities of the work situation and progression in your future career.

Topics in OB are not entirely free-standing

The use of separate topic areas is a recognised academic means of aiding study and explanation of the subject. In practice, however, the activities of an organisation cannot be isolated neatly into discrete areas of study. Topics studied in OB should not be regarded, therefore, as entirely free-standing. Any study inevitably covers several aspects and used to a greater or lesser extent to confirm generalisations made about particular topic areas. Reference to the same studies to illustrate different aspects of management and organisational behaviour serves as useful revision and reinforcement and provides a more integrated approach to your study.

The majority of actions are likely to involve a number of simultaneous functions that relate to the total processes within an organisation. In order to study the behaviour of people at work it is necessary to understand interrelationships with other variables that together comprise the total organisation.

Consider, for example

A manager briefing departmental staff on a major unexpected, important and urgent task. Such a briefing is likely to include consideration of organisational culture, organisation and role structures, management of change, levels of hierarchy and authority, forms of communications, previous experience, delegation and empowerment, teamwork, leadership style, motivation and control systems. The behaviour of the staff will be influenced by a combination of individual, group, organisational and environmental factors.

Explain fully what other possible considerations YOU see as important? What do you see as the priorities for decision or action?

Adopting a critical perspective

You are encouraged to adopt a critical perspective towards your studies. Be prepared to analyse, question and challenge what you read in the text. What do YOU think and believe? Be prepared to change any preconceived beliefs. Consider also whose interests are best served by the preferred 'best' answer: for example senior managers, the general workforce, shareholders, trade unions, community.

At the end of each chapter you will find group discussion activities to help provoke personal responses to what you have just read. You are of course entitled to your own views but be conscious of your own bias or prejudices. The extent to which your point of view persuades other people will be influenced by clear, logical reasoning and supported by academic evidence.

Draw upon the views of your colleagues to share experiences and test not only your assumptions and ideas but also your skills of group interaction and influencing other people. References to the importance of skills throughout the text, together with the exhibits, case studies and assignments should serve to stimulate your awareness of the importance of underlying personal and employability skills necessary for effective performance.

You are encouraged to complement your reading by drawing upon your own observations and practical experiences. This can, of course, be from your university. You may also have work experience, even part-time or casual employment, in other organisations to draw upon. In addition, you will have contact with a range of other organisations such as supermarkets, local pubs and shops, bank or building society, fast-food restaurants, service station, doctor or dentist surgery. An analytical approach to contemporary examples from your own observations should help further both a critical perspective and your interest in the subject area.

Bear in mind that opportunities to develop personal skills are not always immediately apparent but embedded into your course of study. Adopt an inquisitive and enquiring mind. Search for both good and bad examples of organisational behaviour and people management, and the **manner** in which concepts and ideas presented in this book are applied in practice. Make a point of continually observing and thinking about the interpersonal and work-based skills exhibited. Use this awareness and knowledge to enhance development of your own employability skills and aid career progression.

W1A – A British comedy television series aired on BBC 2 in September 2017

This entertaining programme follows the life of Ian Fletcher, who works at the BBC as the 'head of values' – a role that requires him to redefine the entire BBC brand and tasked with clarifying and defining the core purpose of the BBC across all its activities. The series of half-hour programmes makes fun of ludicrous jargon and political correctness; and is a spoof about such subjects as structure, open-plan, hot-desking, communications, meetings, social interactions, stereotypical behaviour, inclusivity and other aspects of organisational behaviour.

The programme provides an amusing and stimulating way of thinking about the subject area. Despite the implausibility of the programme, it is easy to relate to what can actually happen in work organisations.

There are a number of references to the programme on the internet and it is available to buy on DVD.

What is the relevance of theory?

You should not be put off by the use of the word 'theory' in your studies. Most rational decisions are based on some form of theory. Theory provides a sound basis for action and contains a message on how people might behave. This may influence attitudes towards actual practice and lead to changes in patterns of behaviour. Theory further provides a conceptual framework and gives a perspective for the practical study of the subject. Together they lead to a better understanding of factors influencing patterns of behaviour in work organisations and applications of the process of management.[3] *McGregor* maintains that theory and practice are inseparable. Every managerial act rests on assumptions, generalizations, and hypotheses – that is to say, on theory. Although our assumptions are frequently implicit, sometimes quite unconscious, often conflicting; nevertheless, they determine our predictions that if we do a, b will occur.[4]

Patching suggests that all managers who think about what they do are practical students of organisational theory.

> **Theory is not something unique to academics, but something we all work with in arriving at our attitudes, beliefs and decisions as managers. It seems obvious to most of us that some theories are better than others. Many managerial discussions which we undertake in meetings focus upon trying to agree upon which theory will be best for a particular decision.[5]**

Organisational metaphors

Organisations are complex social systems that can be defined and studied in a number of ways. However one looks at the nature or disciplines of OB it is important to remember as *Morgan* points out:

> **the reality of organisational life usually comprises numerous different realities.**

Through the use of metaphors, Morgan provides a broad perspective on the nature of organisations and organisational behaviour and identifies eight different ways of viewing organisations – as machines, organisms, brains, cultures, political systems, psychic prisons, flux and transformation, and instruments of domination. These contrasting metaphors aid the understanding of the complex nature of organisational life and the critical evaluation of organisational phenomena.[6]

Metaphors offer an interesting perspective on how to view organisations. They provide a broader view of the dynamics of organisational behaviour and how to manage and design organisations. However, Morgan points out that these metaphors are not fixed categories and are not mutually exclusive. An organisation can be a mix of each and predominantly a combination of two or three metaphors. Furthermore, these combinations may change over a period of time.

A number of writers use metaphors to help describe organisations. For example, in discussing the role and logic of viewing the organisation in terms of metaphors, *Drummond* raises questions such as what an organisation is like and the power of metaphors in shaping our thinking, but also points out that all metaphors are partial and no metaphor can explain fully a particular phenomenon.[7]

The metaphor of an iceberg

A convenient way to perceive the organisation is an iceberg. For example, *Hellriegel, Slocum and Woodman* suggest: 'One way to recognise why people behave as they do at work is to view an organisation as an iceberg. What sinks ships isn't always what sailors can see, but what they can't see'.[8]

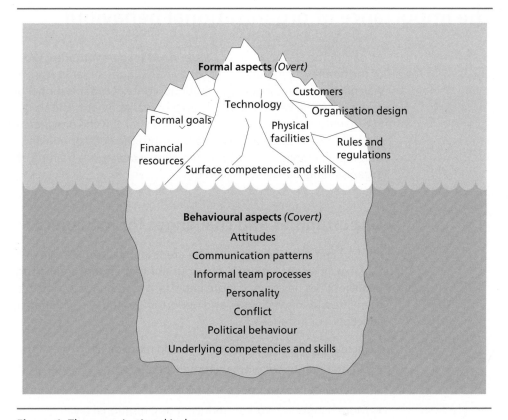

Figure 1 The organisational iceberg
Source: From Hellriegel, D., Slocum, J. W., Jr. and Woodman, R. W. *Management,* eighth edition, South-Western Publishing (1998), p. 6. Reproduced by permission.

The overt, formal aspects focus only on the tip of the iceberg (organisation). It is just as important to focus on what you can't see – the covert, behavioural aspects (*see* **Figure 1**).

The shadow side of organisations

Egan refers to the importance of the shadow side of the organisation: that is, those things not found on organisation charts or in company manuals – the covert, and often undiscussed, activities of people which affect both the productivity and quality of the working life of an organisation.[9] As *Howes* points out, the fiercest battles of the workplace may seem trivial yet they are nothing of the sort. 'Forget disagreements over strategies or policy – many of the bitterest workplace battles are fought over the prosaic matters of air conditioning and in-office music.' Underlying and unresolved disputes can brew animosity and resentment, and halt production.[10]

What metaphor would YOU use to help describe your university and/or any other organisation with which you are familiar?

The importance of organisational behaviour

As part of the *Financial Times Mastering Management* series, *Wood,* in his discussion of the nature of organisational behaviour, suggests that in its concern for the way people behave in an organisational context, organisational behaviour can be regarded as the key to the whole area of management. The study of behaviour in organizations is not just important, it is vital. It is the one area that can bring the collective wisdom of human history into the decision-making calculus of developing managers. The more technical a manager's training, the more important organisational behaviour becomes.[11]

Opportunities and challenges for managers

Robbins and Judge remind us there are few, if any, simple and universal principles that explain organisational behaviour but that understanding organisational behaviour has never been more important for managers than it is today. In short, there are a lot of challenges and opportunities today for managers to use OB concepts. For instance:

- Increasing age of typical employees in more developed countries;
- Greater number of women in the workplace;
- Broader ethnicity of people at work;
- More temporary workers reducing organisational loyalty;
- Demands for increased flexibility and coping with rapid change; and
- Working with and managing people in uncertain times.[12]

OB, personal skills and employability

An increasingly important feature of OB is the relationship with enhancing personal skills and employability within the workplace. The Confederation of British Industry (CBI) point out that in an increasingly competitive employment market, employers are looking beyond simple academic achievement when considering applicants for a job or internship. Many now expect to see evidence of other skills and achievements that boost someone's attractiveness as a potential employee.

> **Businesses want graduates who not only add value but who have the skills to help transform their organization in the face of continuous and rapid economic and technological change. All graduates – whatever their degree disciple – need to be equipped with employability skills.[13]**

A summary of factors bearing on the increased importance of interpersonal skills at work is given in **Figure 2**.

Recent years have seen attention given by the government and other employment and professional bodies to the importance of the supply and application of skills attainment for the prosperity of the UK economy. *The Chartered Institute of Personnel and Development (CIPD)* point out that in today's competitive and

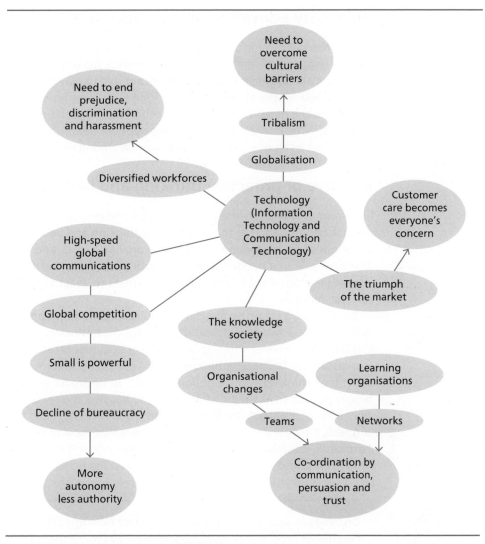

Figure 2 Factors bearing on the increased importance being placed on interpersonal skills at work
Source: Maureen Guirdham, *Interactive Behavior at Work,* 3rd edition, Financial Times Prentice Hall (2002), p. 8. Reprinted and electronically reproduced by permission of Pearson Education, Inc.

fast-changing world, the skills and capabilities of the workforce are vital to economic sustainability and growth. Workplace skills include the ability to:

- communicate with others;
- write and understand reports;
- perform numerical and analytical tasks;
- use computers to help solve problems.

Skills are important for both economic growth and prosperity, and for individuals and organisations. For the individual, skills determine their employment and earning potential. For organisations, skills are vital to meeting both current and future business demands. To be successful and competitive, businesses must ensure their talent and succession planning takes into consideration what skills need to be sourced, nurtured, developed and retained now, in order to create successful and productive workforces of the future.[14]

University education and employability

(The former) UKCES reports that higher education is well placed to play its part in helping to overcome the well-documented skills challenge. 'Collaborations between employers and universities have a significant role to play in providing the supply of highly skilled people to meet demand from businesses now and in the future.'[15] GOV. UK refer to the need for a better connection to bridge the gap between education and work.[16] The Prince's Trust also point out the human cost of skills shortages that could affect levels of productivity and morale among existing workforces.[17]

Reactive or proactive thinking and behaviour

Increasing competition, the pace of change and greater demands upon people at work has arguably led to more reactive thinking and behaviour. Many work situations of course require the ability to provide a quick and spontaneous response. There is however a danger of being caught too much by surprise and moving towards management by crisis. When you need to 'react' then this suggests you have lost the initiative.

By contrast, a proactive approach requires planned thought and anticipation of future events. *Edward de Bono* refers to proactive thinking as 'deliberate thinking' – this is not when we are driving or looking at documents sat at a desk or taking part in a discussion. Deliberate thinking means setting aside some time to do nothing other than thinking about a defined focus.[18] To be proactive you need to see the bigger picture, think about what is likely to happen and react in advance. Developing the ability of proactive thinking takes time and is energy consuming. *Misselhorn* suggests the difficulty with being proactive is that most of our behaviour from habit, familiarity, established routines and procedures do not require us to be proactive. The quickest and easiest routine works most of the time.[19]

Do YOU see yourself as a proactive thinker? How important is it if colleagues are reactive or proactive thinkers so long as they contribute fully to the activities of the team?

The 'SCARF' model

David Rock suggests that 'more people than ever are being paid to think, instead of just doing routine tasks'. Based on neuroscience studies, Rock has proposed a model of five domains of human social experience. In the same way as the brain reacts to primary threats and rewards the same happens also to social situations.

The five social concerns that drive human behaviour are, our:

Status –relative importance to others

Certainty – ability to predict the future

Autonomy – sense of control over events

Relatedness – sense of safety with others

Fairness – perception of fair exchanges between people.[20]

The aim of the model is interaction with other people in a way that minimises threats and maximises rewards. The five domains have clear relevance to the work situation discussed in later chapters, for example:

- position within the hierarchical structure and role relationships;
- clarity with expectations about your work and avoidance of stress;
- opportunities for autonomy and flexibility;
- interpersonal relationships and group working;
- the psychological contract.

You may find the SCARF model a useful framework of analysis and discussion as you proceed through your studies.

People management and social skills

Unlike technical or practical skills, social skills are more intangible. They are difficult to get a firm hold of, or to define and measure clearly. Social skills are often associated as 'soft skills' and regarded as a natural part of human behaviour. As a result, a common concern with attention to the skills shortage is lack of focus on people management, social skills and interpersonal behaviour. For example an important aspect of working with other people and leadership skills is an awareness and acceptance of individual differences and diversity.

Developing your employability skills

Increasingly, graduate recruiters are placing greater emphasis on key interpersonal and social skills, and attitudes. A first step in working harmoniously and effectively with other people is to know and understand yourself and the skill of self-management. Reflecting honestly on your personal strengths and weaknesses should help develop your level of competence. You cannot expect to influence the behaviour or actions of other people until you can effectively manage yourself. The continual development of employability skills as part of your university education and lifelong learning is important for:

- progressing your personal confidence and self-awareness;
- developing harmonious interpersonal relationships with colleagues and external contacts;
- initial attractiveness for appointment with a potential employer;
- maintaining a competent level of work performance;
- enhancing work motivation and job satisfaction; and
- helping to safeguard your career progression.

Many employers have structured programmes for the continued development of their staff. Your longer-term employment prospects will be enhanced when you are able to demonstrate a genuine and enthusiastic commitment to your own personal development.

Study as an aid to practice

Study is an aid to practice. A theme of this book is to provide an integrated view embracing both theory and practice. The ideas and concepts discussed provide you with opportunities to explore the underlying skills associated with the study of organisational behaviour.

As you progress through your studies, reflect upon what you have read and about the importance of social skills including:

- personal awareness and how you project yourself;
- openness to diversity, equality and inclusion;
- perceiving and understanding other people;
- written, verbal and non-verbal communications;
- social interactions with others and teamworking;
- personal organisation and time management;
- coping with change;
- coaching and mentoring; and
- working in a multicultural society.

Monitor and assess your development

It is recommended strongly that you maintain a portfolio of what you have learned, your personal development and the employability skills that you have attained or enhanced during your course of study. This can provide a useful basis of discussion with a potential employer. You may find it useful to assess progression of your personal skills and employability by reviewing your learning and development under the following broad headings, *see* **Figure 3**.

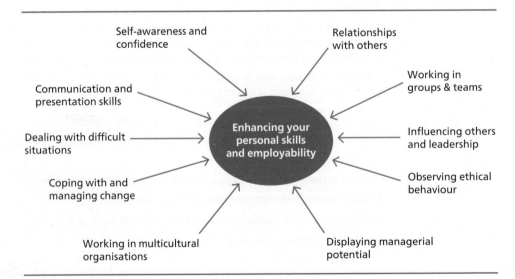

Figure 3 Broad headings for personal skills and employability

Making yourself more employable

Furnham points out educational qualifications are only one aspect of a person's assets they bring to the work situation and there are a number of other important fundamental issues considering a young person's employability. Furnham suggests five virtues employers want in all employees.

- Hardworking and productive, a conscientious work ethic, and to pitch up and pitch in. Honest, reliable and dependable.
- Smart, bright, curious, fast learners and not plodders. Inquisitive, widely read, interesting in understanding.
- Concept of rewardingness, warm and trustworthy, sensitive and well-adjusted, sociable and sufficiently altruistic.
- Signs of being leader-like, able to make decisions for which they are accountable and with good judgement. Taking initiative and the strain when it counts.
- Have the big picture and globally minded and who look ahead. Anticipate and adapt to the future without being a victim.

Some jobs require more than others and the desirable characteristics are not weighted equally but all five characteristics are important.[21]

Personal skills and employability exercise

Critical self-reflection is a positive activity that can challenge narrow preconceived thought processes, encourage creativity and provide a valuable personal learning and development experience.

At the end of each chapter is a 'Personal Skills and Employability Exercise'. This is designed to encourage you to think about further development of your social and work-based skills.

The appendix at the end of the book provides a review of features within the text that relate to employability skills. You are encouraged to ask yourself the extent to which you have enhanced your personal awareness and knowledge, and are better prepared to demonstrate your employability skills and aid your career progression.

How comfortable do YOU feel about the level of your future employability skills? How specifically do you hope to enhance your level of skills through the study of OB?

A summary of personal skills and employability is set out in the concept map, Figure 4.

Personal skills and employability   ASK

Skills for........
Organisations - vital to meet current and future business demands

Individuals - determine their employment and earning potential.

Working with others
People management, Social (soft) skills and Hard skills
Soft skills - a natural part of human behaviour.
Hard skills - those skills relating to a specific task or situation. Competence may be certificated

Examples of soft skills
- personal awareness & how you project yourself
- openness to diversity, equality and inclusion
- perceiving and understanding other people
- written, verbal and non-verbal communications
- social interactions with others and team working
- personal organisation and time management
- coping with change
- showing patience
- showing flexibility
- motivating others
- able to persuade
- coaching and mentoring;
- working in a multicultural society

Improving work performance
Applying the right .... **Attitude** - e.g. commitment, enthusiasm

Developing and using new... **Skills** - both soft and hard

Acquiring and using new... **Knowledge**

Developing employability skills
- Graduate recruiters are placing greater emphasis on key interpersonal and social skills, and attitudes.
- Know and understand yourself and the skill of self-management.
- Reflecting, honestly on your personal strengths and weaknesses should help develop your level of competence.
- To influence the behaviour or actions of other people you need to effectively manage yourself.

Examples of hard skills
- Writing and understanding reports
- Performing numerical and analytical tasks
- Using computers to help solve problems
- Understanding accounting & finance
- Knowledge and application of the law in the work place
- Foreign language skills
- Project management
- Customer knowledge

Many tasks require soft and Hard skills e.g.
Communicating - content of the message and how it is presented
Problem solving - selecting the technique(s) - involving colleagues

Monitor and assess your development
Maintain a portfolio of what you have learned - your personal development
- The employability skills you have attained or enhanced during your course of study.
- A useful basis for discussion with a potential employer
- Regularly assessing progression of your personal skills and employability by reviewing your learning and development under the following broad headings.

UK skills shortages
* Lack focus on people management, social skills and interpersonal behaviour.
* Need for awareness and acceptance of Individual differences and diversity.

Reactive or proactive thinking and behaviour
When you need to 'react' you may have lost the initiative.

To be proactive you need to see the bigger picture, what may happen? & react in advance

The continual development of employability skills as part of a university education and lifelong learning is important for:
- progressing your personal confidence and self-awareness
- developing harmonious interpersonal relationships with colleagues and external contacts
- initial attractiveness for appointment with a potential employer
- maintaining a competent level of work performance
- enhancing work motivation and job satisfaction and helping to safeguard your career progression.

Lifelong learning
through employers structured programmes and /or personal motivation
e.g. **Continuing Professional Development (CPD)**
MBA, MA, Msc, PhD

Enhancing your personal skills and employability
- Self-awareness and confidence
- Relationships with others
- Communication and presentation skills
- Working in groups and teams
- Dealing with difficult situations
- Influencing others and leadership
- Coping with and managing change
- Observing ethical behaviour
- Working in multicultural organisations
- Display managerial potential

Figure 4 Personal skills and employability
Source: Copyright © 2011 The Virtual Learning Materials Workshop. Reproduced with permission.

Structure of the book

For those familiar with previous editions of '*Management and Organisational Behaviour*' the revised structure of this edition entails attention to re-ordering throughout the text. Focus is on the overall plan of the book and sequence of contents between and within chapters.

In response to reviewer feedback this edition provides a clearer focus on undergraduate students of organisational behaviour. Efforts have been made to provide a text of manageable size and enhanced readability.

There is a logical flow to the sequencing of topic areas which follow the accepted broad pattern of individual, group, organisation and environment. In addition to this chapter the book is structured in five sections with seventeen chapters all within a broadly similar word count.

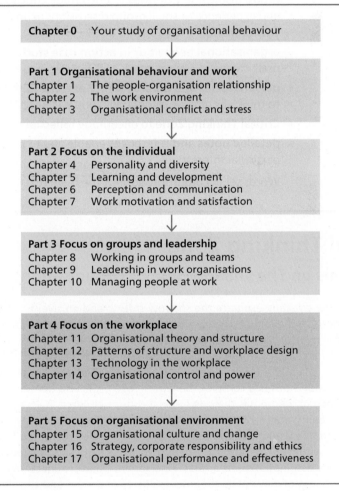

Distinctive format

Each chapter of the book is self-contained **with appropriate cross-referencing to other chapters.** This provides a flexible approach. Selection and ordering of chapters can be varied to suit the demands of particular courses of study or individual interests.

The book is written with a minimum of technical terminology and the format is clearly structured. Each chapter is supported with illustrations and practical examples and contains:

- **learning outcomes and outline chapter contents** at the start of the chapter to help you see what you will be reading and monitor progress through the book;

- **overview topic map** provides a visual representation of flow of main contents and links with other chapters. The collection of maps may be helpful for study and revision purposes;

- **'You' critical review questions** throughout the text to encourage your own critical thinking and reflection of what you have just read;

- **pictorial concept map** provides a 'mind map' of an important topic featured in the chapter (you may find a similar idea helpful for your studies and revision);

- **summary of key points** as a reminder of the chapter contents and an aid to revision;

- **group discussion activities** to encourage critical review and feedback, and experience of small group discussions in an open and non-threatening environment;

- **organisational behaviour in action case study** gives valuable insights into a practical real world situation and with tasks to encourage further thoughts.

- **personal skills and employability exercise** with clear objectives to encourage you to think about the personal skills you will need in your future career;

- **Critical Thinking Zone** to encourage reflections on a particular topic in the chapter;

- **detailed notes and references** enable you to pursue further any issues of particular interest.

Words set in **colour** throughout the main text indicate inclusion in the **Glossary.**

Critical Thinking Zone

Reflections on The Shadow Side of Organisations

In this zone, we critically evaluate the shadow side of organisations and examine whether the covert, informal aspects of organisational behaviour enable or hinder the completion of day-to-day business activities.

An organisation houses a complex menagerie of individuals, each of whom has their own social constructions of reality, their own perceptions of, and commitment to, the workplace and the idiosyncratic roles they play within it. They also have their own set of norms, values, assumptions and, arguably, personal agendas, which may or may not be congruent with, or aligned to, the espoused culture and deeply ingrained way of doing things that have evolved over time.[22] According to Linstead *et al.*,[23] these covert, hidden elements of the organisational iceberg metaphor[24] are often ignored, suppressed or overlooked by managers and the organisation at large because they are invisible, and therefore undiscussable, unmentionable

and elusive.[25,26] These elements conflate to form the shadow side of the organisation.[22,23,25]

Exploring the Shadow Side

The metaphor of the organisation possessing a shadow side was developed by Bowles[27] from the work of the eminent Swiss psychologist, Carl Jung. Jung's original thesis posited that everyone's personality has a shadow side (one of the four archetypes[28]), which is a composite of subconscious positive and negative characteristics that are unacknowledged, repressed, buried deep in our psyche and thus hidden from ourselves and others.[22] Arguably, recognising that we all have a Jungian shadow side enables us to understand how the metaphor can be applied in an organisational setting. Deeply entrenched social constructions and perceptions of reality, along with covert individual and collective assumptions, norms and values create and perpetuate shadow behaviours (such as the interplay of power and politics and enforcement

of personal ideologies and agendas[25]) that are hidden within the organisation's metaphorical psyche.[27] Stacey[29] professes that the shadow coexists with the organisation's formal/legitimate system in a dynamic, covert, social, political and psychological melee. Both are in a constant state of flux and tension with each other and are maintained through a series of socially constructed negotiations and transactions that enable business activities to be undertaken[22] and political deals to be brokered.[25]

Life in the Shadows

Shadow behaviours are a fact of organisational life. They can be categorised as 'light' behaviours, which include corridor conversations, personality clashes and power struggles[30] and 'dark' behaviours, such as inappropriate absenteeism, suboptimal performance and bullying, which are injurious to both the organisation and individuals and may result in financial consequences.[23,31] In studying these behaviours, it may be rather tempting for us to view the shadow as exclusively possessing negative traits that are potentially damaging to the organisation and its members. However, Egan[25] and Pheiffer *et al.*[22] concur that the shadow can be a positive force and achieve things that the organisation's legitimate system cannot. *How* is this possible? Egan and Nicholls[30] suggest that the shadow can enable managers to perform their jobs more proficiently by engaging in 'accepted', though unconventional, behaviours (e.g. political game playing and wheeling and dealing) that are not an espoused part of the culture and therefore not sanctioned or endorsed by management. Furthermore, Egan and Nicholls proffer that the shadow initiates and effects change by enabling the status quo to be challenged and in doing so, unearths deep-rooted assumptions, values and beliefs that may be restricting the organisation from moving forward.

Can the Shadow be Managed?

Bowles and Linstead *et al.* concur that the shadow *cannot* be managed, due to its unmentionable, undiscussable and invisible nature. Further, Bowles caveats that any attempt to control it would not only be futile but also strengthen its fervour and drive it deeper into the organisation's metaphorical psyche. Ostensibly, the organisation is a social network, through which shadow behaviours such as gossip, rumours and the grapevine thrive and survive. According to Egan and Nicholls, the network is an informal, unofficial information-sharing medium that enables knowledge and other intel, which may otherwise be bound in red tape, to be disseminated throughout the organisation much faster than through official, legitimate channels. From a managerial perspective, one can appreciate the desire to control shadow social network behaviours, particularly as they can be a double-edged sword, cutting through the bureaucracy on the one hand and sabotaging and opposing change programmes and strategic goals and objectives on the other. Rather than trying to manage or control the shadow, Nicholls advocates that managers should embrace it as an omnipresent cultural facet and part of established organisational behaviour in the workplace. Similarly, Pheiffer *et al.* suggest that appreciating the shadow's presence can help managers understand the nature of, in this instance, politically-motivated behaviours, and the ways in which they can be leveraged to help the organisation experience growth through change, especially if it is in a state of apathy or decline.[32]

The Shadow: An Organisational Reality

To conclude, the shadow is an organisational reality that has the capacity to both enable and hinder the completion of day-to-day business activities. The shadow side of organisations is unlike any other system, procedure or process that can be measured, deconstructed and reconstructed, but its omnipresence can be felt at every level and in every aspect of organisational behaviour in the workplace. Arguably, the shadow is not wholly light or dark, but has shades of grey. In accommodating the grey areas, McCabe[33] advocates that it may provide organisations with a lens through which they can create new states of consciousness and, in turn, identify and utilise alternative ways to behave, organise and govern themselves in the dynamic, global business environment.

Questions

Having read the above, answer the following questions.

1. *Critically discuss* the most *significant* features of the organisational shadow. *What* implications do they have for organisational behaviour in the twenty-first century workplace?

2. Bowles suggests that any managerial attempts to control the shadow are futile. *To what extent* do you agree with his view?

3. *How* can a knowledge and appreciation of our personal shadow help us to understand the complexities and interplay of shadow behaviours in the workplace?

Notes and references

1. Vecchio, R. P. *Organizational Behavior: Core Concepts,* sixth edition, The Dryden Press (2005).

2. Watson, T. J. *Organising and Managing Work,* second edition, Financial Times Prentice Hall (2006), p. 55.

3. See, for example, Billsberry, J. 'There's Nothing So Practical as a Good Theory: How Can Theory Help Managers Become More Effective?', in Billsberry, J. (ed.) *The Effective Manager: Perspectives and Illustrations,* Sage Publications (1996), pp. 1–27; and Naylor, J. *Management,* second edition, Financial Times Prentice Hall (2004), pp. 13–15.

4. McGregor, D. *The Human Side of Enterprise,* Penguin (1987), p. 6.

5. Patching, K. *Management and Organisation Development,* Macmillan Business (1999), p. 11.

6. Morgan, G. *Creative Organisation Theory,* Sage Publications (1989), p. 26

7. Drummond, H. *Introduction to Organisational Behaviour,* Oxford University Press (2000).

8. Hellriegel, D., Slocum, J. W. and Woodman, R. W. *Organizational Behavior,* eighth edition, South-Western Publishing (1998), p. 5.

9. Egan, G. 'The Shadow Side', *Management Today,* September 1993, pp. 33–8.

10. Howes, L. 'The Real Workplace Battle', *Professional Manager,* Winter 2014, pp. 60–3.

11. Wood, J. 'Deep Roots and Far From a "Soft" Option', *Financial Times Mastering Management,* Financial Times Pitman Publishing (1997), p. 217.

12. Robbins, S. P. and Judge, T. A. *Organizational Behavior,* thirteenth edition, Pearson PrenticeHall (2009) p. 50.

13. 'Boosting Employability Skills' CBI http://cbi.org.uk (accessed 17 December 2014).

14. 'Skills Development in the UK Workplace: Factsheet', CIPD, 15 May 2017.

15. 'Forging Futures: Building Higher Level Skills through University and Employer Collaboration', UKCES, September 2014.

16. 'Growth Through People', UKCES, 25 November 2014.

17. 'The Skills Crunch,' Prince's Trust, 2014.

18. De Bono, E. 'The Power of Proactive Thinking'. http://management-issues.cm/opinion/5883/the power of proactive thinking (accessed 14 April 2017).

19. Misselhorn, H. 'Proactive Versus Reactive Thinking', JPS Associates, www.jpsa.co.za, March 2017.

20. Rock, D. *Your Brain at Work,* Harper Business (2009).

21. Furnham, A. 'How to Make Yourself More Employable: The New Employability Skills of the 2016 Worker' Insights, *Chartered Management Institute,* 6 May 2016.

22. Pheiffer, G., Griffiths, D. and Andrew, D. 'Understanding the Dynamics of Corporate Social Responsibility using the Concept of the Shadow Side', *Social Responsibility Journal,* vol. 2, issue 2, 2006, pp 136–141.

23. Linstead, S., Maréchal, G. and Griffin, R.W. 'Theorizing and Researching the Dark Side of Organization', *Organization Studies,* vol. 35, issue 2, 2014, pp 165–188.

24. Hellriegel, D., Slocum, J.W., Jr. and Woodman, R.W. *Management,* sixth edition, South-Western Publishing (1998).

25. Egan, G. 'The Shadow Side', *Management Today,* September, 1993, pp. 33–8.

26. Lennox, M. 'Model Strategy for Change Management', *Management Development Review,* vol. 7, no. 6, 1994, pp 16–19.

27. Bowles, M. L. 'The Shadow Side', *Organization Studies,* vol. 12, issue 3, 1991, pp. 387–404.

28. Jung, C.G. 'The Archetypes and the Collective Unconscious'. Read, H., Fordham, M., Adler, G. and McGuire, W. (eds), *The Collected Works of C.G. Jung,* Vol. 9, Part 1, Princeton, NJ: Princeton University (1959).

29. Stacey, R. *Complexity and Creativity in Organizations,* Berrett-Koehler, San Francisco, CA (1996).

30. Nicholls, T. 'Embracing the Shadow Side of Organisational Life', HR Zon (2016), https://www.hrzone.com/lead/culture/embracing-the-shadow-side-of-organisational-life, accessed 5 June 2018.

31. Griffin, R.W. and O'Leary-Kelly, A. (eds) *The Dark Side of Organizational Behaviour,* San Francisco: Jossey-Bass (2004).

32. Handy, C. *Understanding Organizations,* fourth edition, Penguin (2007).

33. McCabe, D. 'Light in the Darkness? Managers in the Back Office of a Kafkaesque Bank', *Organization Studies,* vol. 35, issue 2, 2014, pp. 255–78.

Part 1
Organisational behaviour and work

Chapter 1
The people–organisation relationship

In an increasingly competitive business environment it is important to understand the nature of the people–organisation relationship and main influences on behaviour in the workplace.

Learning outcomes

After completing your study of this chapter you should have enhanced your ability to:

- explain the significance of the people–organisation relationship;
- detail a multidisciplinary perspective and interrelated influences on behaviour;
- explain analysis of the organisation as an open system;
- outline the contribution of Human Resource Management;
- evaluate the nature and importance of the psychological contract;
- detail systems of organisation and management;
- assess the impact of globalisation, and the international and cultural context.

Outline chapter contents

Overview topic map: Chapter 1 – The people–organisation relationship

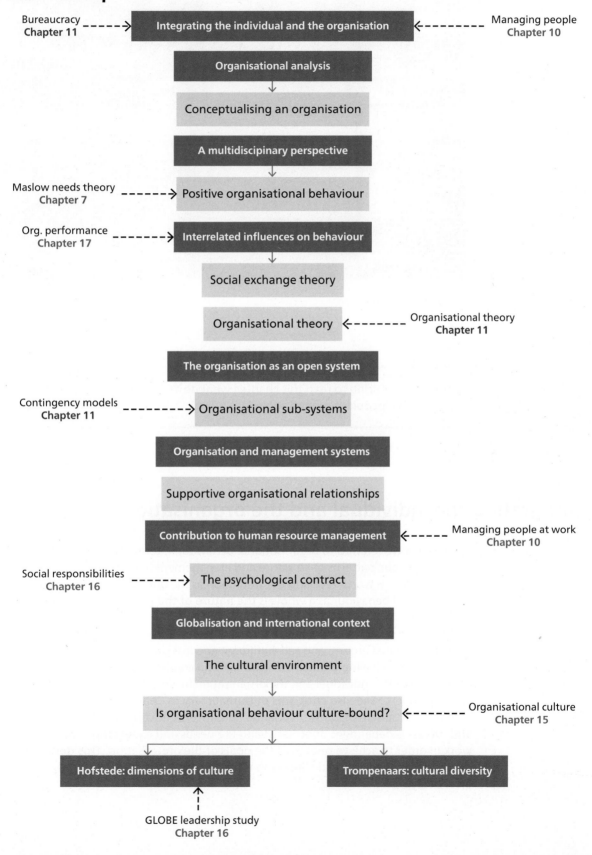

Bureaucracy
Chapter 11 - - - - →

Integrating the individual and the organisation

← - - - - - - - Managing people
Chapter 10

Organisational analysis

Conceptualising an organisation

A multidiscipinary perspective

Maslow needs theory
Chapter 7 - - - - - →

Positive organisational behaviour

Org. performance
Chapter 17 - - - - - →

Interrelated influences on behaviour

Social exchange theory

Organisational theory

← - - - - - - Organisational theory
Chapter 11

The organisation as an open system

Contingency models
Chapter 11 - - - - - - →

Organisational sub-systems

Organisation and management systems

Supportive organisational relationships

Contribution to human resource management

← - - - - Managing people at work
Chapter 10

Social responsibilities
Chapter 16 - - - - →

The psychological contract

Globalisation and international context

The cultural environment

Is organisational behaviour culture-bound?

← - - - - - Organisational culture
Chapter 15

Hofstede: dimensions of culture

Trompenaars: cultural diversity

GLOBE leadership study
Chapter 16

People and organisation!

Before commencing to read this chapter, what do YOU understand by the nature of the people–organisation relationship?

Integrating the individual and the organisation

In Chapter 0 we referred to organisational behaviour in terms of individual and group behaviour, patterns of structure and management and organisational performance. It is worth recalling this definition as the underlying basis for organisational behaviour as a whole is **the nature of the people–organisational relationship.**

One of the strongest critics of the formal organisation is *Argyris* who claims this restricts individual growth and self-fulfilment and in a psychologically healthy person, causes a feeling of failure, frustration and conflict. Argyris calls for closer integration of the individual and the organisation in a more 'authentic' relationship for its members.[1] **See also criticisms of bureaucracy in Chapter 11.**

In an atmosphere of constant change and uncertainty organisational survival and success is dependent upon satisfying the needs and expectations of people at work in order to achieve or exceed the goals of the organisation. **This demands creating an organisational climate in which people work both willingly and effectively.**

Perception of treatment by the organisation

People generally respond in the manner in which they are treated. It could be argued that the majority of people come to work with the original attitude of being eager to do a good job and desirous of performing well to the best of their abilities. Where actual performance fails to match the ideal this is largely a result of how people perceive they are treated by the organisation. Many problems in the people–organisation relationship arise from the manner in which decisions and actions of the organisation are actually carried out. Often, it is not so much the intent but the manner of implementation that is the root cause of staff unrest and dissatisfaction. For example, staff may agree (even if reluctantly) on the need for the organisation to introduce new technology to retain its competitive efficiency but feel resentment about the lack of prior consultation, effective retraining programmes, participation in agreeing new working practices and wage rates.

A heavy responsibility therefore is placed on managers – on the processes, activities and styles of management. Attention must be given to the work environment and appropriate systems of motivation, job satisfaction and rewards. It is important to remember that improvement in organisational performance will come about only through people. **See the discussion on managing with and through people in Chapter 10.**

Management of human capital

Over the years a number of writers have suggested organisations do not fully recognise people as a vital asset or how best to invest in them.[2] Attention to a more strategic approach to the management of people at work has given rise to the concept of **human capital** (HC) and acceptance of the belief that the way organisations manage people affects their performance. Although there is no generally agreed definition the term is widely used to denote a strategic approach to people management that focuses on issues critical to the success of an organisation. A popular definition is that by *Thomas* who defines HC as 'the people, their performance and their potential in the organisation'.[3] A fuller definition is given by *Bontis* as:

> the human factor in the organisation; the combined intelligence, skills and expertise that gives the organisation its distinctive character. The human elements of the organisation are those that are capable of learning, changing, innovating and providing the creative thrust which if properly motivated can ensure the long-term survival of the organisation.[4]

Gratton refers to three interrelated elements of human capital – intellectual, emotional and social – which have implications for both individuals and organisations.

- **Intellectual capital** is at the heart of individual development and creation of knowledge and personal value. This enables the exercise of choice.
- **Emotional capital** enables continual growth and fulfilment of ambition. It is maintained through self-awareness and insight.
- **Social capital** arises from forging of relationships. Traditional hierarchical roles and responsibilities are being replaced by integrated structures and relationships of trust and reciprocity.[5]

According to the *CIPD* many modern-day organisations have come to realise the organisation's intangible assets such as knowledge and skills of employees is fundamental to creating value and attaining competitive advantage. A growing body of evidence demonstrates a positive link between the development of HC and performance and underlines the vital role social capital plays at both the individual and organisational level in terms of creating value and stimulating new knowledge and innovation. At the individual level HC theory suggests investment in education and training increases skill level and productivity so justifying higher earnings. At the organisational level HC can help in the creation of competitive advantage and facilitate strategic outcomes.[6]

> How would YOU describe the essential characteristics that make for a meaningful and successful people–organisation relationship?

Organisational analysis

In order to study the behaviour of people within organisations it is necessary to have some understanding of the operations and functioning of organisations as a whole. Accordingly, although the main focus of this book is on the more micro level of organisational behaviour (OB) there is inevitably a close interrelationship with a broader approach that might be termed organisational analysis (OA). In terms of study of the subject area there is little clear distinction between the two approaches both of which are concerned with the people–organisation relationship. This is a recurring theme and integral feature of the contents of this book.

For example, the examination of people as individuals, their motivations, behaviour in group situations, relationships with colleagues and responses to styles of leadership styles cannot be divorced from a wider study of different ideas and approaches to the structure and management of organisations as a whole and to applications of organisational theory, **discussed in Chapter 11.** *See* **Figure 1.1**.

Conceptualising an organisation

Rollinson identifies a number of ways in which to conceptualise an organisation.

- **As artefacts** – organisations do not exist in nature but brought into existence by humans.
- **Goal directed** – created to serve some purpose although not everyone necessarily has the same common goal or is aware of the goals pursued by the organisation.
- **Social entities** – although a one-person business can be conceived, organisations usually exist of more than one person and normally this is how the term is meant.
- **Structured activity** – human activity is deliberately structured and coordinated into identifiable parts or service in order to achieve a purpose or goals of the organisation.
- **Nominal boundaries** – it is usually possible to identify nominal boundaries that provide some consensus about who or what is part of the organisation or belong elsewhere.

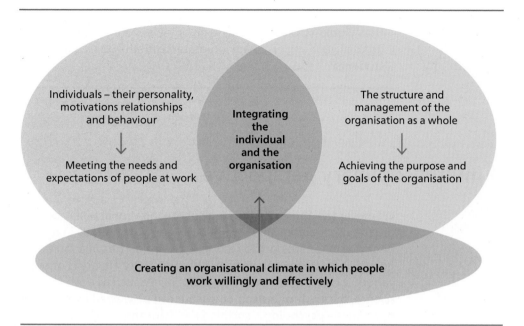

Figure 1.1 Integrating the individual and the organisation

On this basis, Rollinson provides a basic definition of an organisation as:

Social entities brought into existence and sustained in an ongoing way by humans to serve some purpose, from which it follows that human activities in the entity are normally structured and coordinated towards achieving some purpose or goals.[7]

Strictly, organisations have no goals, only people do. Success of the organisation is measured by the progress of people satisfying goals set by people. This gives rise to the questions of to what extent:

- Does an organisation have one common set of goals or is there diversity among the various goals of different departments or sections of the organisation?
- Individual members obtain satisfaction of their own goals (needs and expectations) through the attainment of organisational goals?

If organisational goals and personal goals are pulling in different directions, disharmony and conflict will arise and performance is likely to suffer. Ideally people may realise their own personal goals by helping the organisation to satisfy its goals. Only when organisational goals are shared by members of the organisation will complete integration be achieved. In practice this is unlikely and as *McGregor* for example points out:

Perfect integration of organizational requirements and individual goals and needs is, of course, not a realistic objective. In adopting this principle, we seek that degree of integration in which individuals can achieve their goals by directing efforts towards the success of the organization.[8]

Organisational goals, objectives and policy are discussed in Chapter 16.

How would YOU conceptualise an organisation? How well do you believe the goals of your university are integrated with the goals of members of staff and students?

A multidisciplinary perspective

Whatever the approach, the study of organisational behaviour and the people–organisation relationship cannot be undertaken entirely in terms of a single discipline. It is necessary to recognise the influences of a multidisciplinary, behavioural science perspective. Although there are areas of overlap among the various social sciences and related disciplines such as economics and political science, the study of human behaviour can be viewed in terms of three main disciplines – **psychology**, **sociology** and **anthropology**. All three disciplines have made an important contribution to the field of organisational behaviour **(see Figure 1.2).**

A **psychological** approach with the main emphasis on the individuals of which the organisation is comprised. The main focus of attention is on the individual as a whole person, or what can be termed the 'personality system', including, for example, perception, attitudes and motives. Psychological aspects are important but by themselves provide too narrow an approach for the understanding of organisational behaviour. Our main concern is not with the complex detail of individual differences and attributes *per se* but with the behaviour and management of people within an organisational setting.

A **sociological** approach concerned with a broader emphasis on human behaviour in society. Sociological aspects can be important. The main focus of attention is on the analysis of social structures and positions in those structures – for example, the relationship between the behaviour of leaders and followers. A number of sociology writers seem set on the purpose of criticising traditional views of organisation and management. Many of the criticisms and limitations are justified and help promote healthy academic debate. However, much of the argument tends to be presented in the abstract and is lacking in constructive ideas on how, in practical terms, action can be taken to improve organisational performance.

Anthropologists are more concerned with the science of humankind and the study of human behaviour as a whole. As far as organisational behaviour is concerned the main focus of attention is on the cultural system, the beliefs, customs, ideas and values within a group or society, and the comparison of behaviour among different cultures – for example, the importance to Muslim women of wearing trousers to work. People learn to depend on their culture to give them security and stability and they can suffer adverse reactions to unfamiliar environments.

The contribution of relevant aspects of psychology, sociology and anthropology underpins the field of organisational behaviour. We need also to consider the relevance and applications of philosophy, ethics and the law.

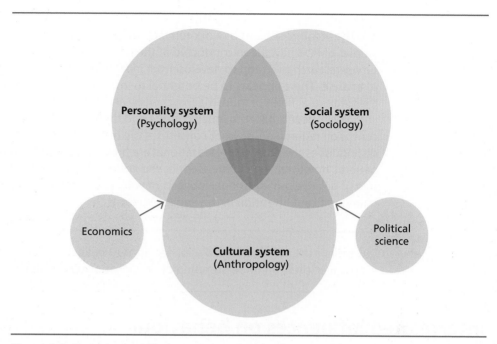

Figure 1.2 Organisational behaviour: a multidisciplinary approach

Positive organisational behaviour (POB)

A different approach to OB is that of positive organisational behaviour (POB) which takes a functionalist or positivist approach. In recent years increasing attention has been given to **positive psychology** which is defined broadly as: 'the scientific study of what makes life most worth living'. Although arguably originated by Maslow in his hierarchy of needs theory in 1954 **(see Chapter 7),** positive psychology is associated with the work of *Martin Seligman* in 1998.[9] Rather than focus on finding out what was wrong with people – the 'disease' model – positive psychology complements traditional psychology by focusing on determining how things go right and how to enhance people's satisfaction and well-being.

Peterson suggests that the topic of morale can also be placed under the positive psychology umbrella. Morale is used as a cognitive, emotional and motivational stance toward the goals and tasks of a group. In the same way that life satisfaction is an indicator of individual well-being, morale is an indicator of group well-being.[10]

Applications to the work situation

To what extent can positive psychology be applied to the work organisation? *Wong and Davey* maintain that each day in every organisation huge amounts of valuable resources are wasted because of human problems, wrong policies or poor training. The focus of leadership needs to be shifted from process and outcome to people and the development of social/emotional/spiritual capital. However, although positive psychology can be introduced into the workplace they question the ability of managers to apply this to employees in a meaningful way.[11]

Donaldson and Ko maintain that the primary emphasis of POB is in the workplace and the accomplishment of work-related outcomes and performance improvement. Studies of POB have been conducted at the micro- and meso-levels of analysis using survey research and tend to develop from individual to group to organisational levels of analysis. There appears to be potential to invigorate research and applications in the traditional fields of industrial psychology and organisational behaviour.[12]

POB has been subject to much critique and there still exists some measure of confusion regarding just what constitutes the realm of 'positive' behaviour, and what distinguishes the positive organisational agenda from organisational behaviour in general. However, despite the sceptics and critics, *Wright and Quick* believe that the role of positive organisational movement will continue to grow and prosper, and gain significant attention in the applied sciences.[13]

Which of the social science disciplines do YOU believe makes the greatest contribution to an understanding of organisational behaviour, and why?

Interrelated influences on behaviour

A multidisciplinary perspective provides contrasting but related approaches to the understanding of human behaviour in work organisations and presents a number of alternative pathways and levels of analysis. For our purposes a number of broad interrelated dimensions can be identified – the individual, the group, the organisation and the environment – which collectively influence behaviour in the workplace.

- **The individual.** Organisations are made up of their individual members. The individual is a central feature of organisational behaviour, whether acting in isolation or as part of a group, in response to expectations of the organisation, or as a result of the influences of the external environment. Where the needs of the individual and the demands of the organisation are incompatible, this can result in frustration and conflict.

- **The group.** Groups exist in all organisations and are essential to their working and performance. The organisation comprises groups of people and almost everyone in an organisation will be a member of one or more groups. Informal groups arise from the social needs of people within the organisation. People in groups influence each other in many ways and groups may develop their own hierarchies and leaders. Group pressures can have a major influence over the behaviour and performance of individual members. An understanding of group structure and behaviour complements knowledge of individual behaviour and adds a further dimension to the study of organisational behaviour.

- **The organisation.** Individuals and groups interact within the structure of the formal organisation. Structure is created to establish role relationships between individuals and groups, to provide order and systems and to direct the efforts of the organisation into goal-seeking activities. It is through the formal structure that people carry out their organisational activities to achieve aims and objectives. Behaviour is influenced by patterns of structure, technology, styles of leadership and systems of management through which organisational processes are planned, directed and monitored.

- **The environment.** Applications of organisational behaviour and effective human resource management take place in the context of the wider environmental setting, including the changing patterns of organisations and work. The broader external environment affects the organisation through, for example, internationalisation, technological and scientific development, economic activity, social and cultural influences, governmental actions, and corporate responsibility and ethical behaviour. The increasing rate of change in environmental factors has highlighted the need to study the total organisation and the processes by which the organisation attempts to adapt to the external demands placed upon it.

A framework of study

Chapter 0 pointed out that the study of organisational behaviour embraces an understanding of a wide range of interactions. In order to study the behaviour of people at work it is necessary to understand interrelationships with other variables that together comprise the total organisation. The bottom line is that sooner or later every organisation has to perform successfully if it is to survive. **Organisational performance and effectiveness is discussed in Chapter 17.**

This provides a convenient framework of study, *see* **Figure 1.3**.

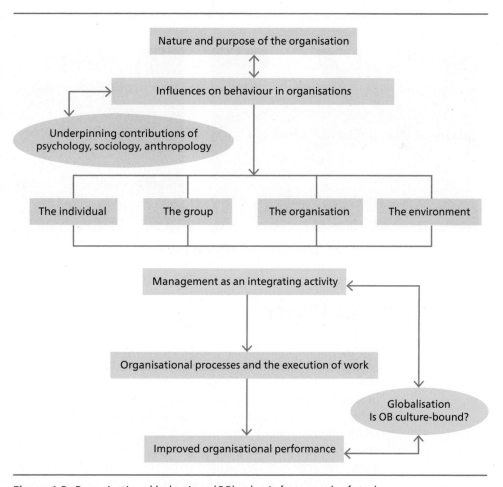

Figure 1.3 Organisational behaviour (OB): a basic framework of study

A spirituality perspective on organisational behaviour

Another interesting approach to organisational behaviour is that of spirituality. *Daniel Pink,* bestseller in business books, advocates we take spirituality seriously and maintains that human beings have a natural desire to find meaning in their lives beyond the material.[14] For example, clinical research for evidence of a spontaneous miracle in the life of Mother Teresa of Calcutta before she could be made a saint in the Catholic Church is an instance of avoiding the risk of assumption and wishful thinking.

Hugo Misselhorn, a renowned South African registered industrial psychologist, draws attention to a growing interest in the spiritual dimension in the workplace and exploration of passages in the Christian Bible that point to meaning or purpose in our lives beyond what we can see, touch, smell, hear and taste – or work out rationally. Misselhorn offers for consideration a spiritual perspective on organisational behaviour. There is more to human behaviour in the workplace than a clinical and 'scientific' application of the behavioural sciences devoid of a reference to God or a spiritual dimension in our lives.[15]

> What do YOU think about the meaning of spirituality in the workplace? Is it just 'pie in the sky' or a means of avoiding reality?

Left: House of The Virgin Mary, Ephesus, Turkey. Right: Prayer ribbons

Social exchange theory

An important feature that underlies the behaviour and interrelationships of people in organisations is that of **social exchange theory**. Rooted in cultural anthropology and economics, the central premise of social exchange theory is that a fundamental feature of human interaction is the exchange of social and material resources.[16] Social behaviour is determined by an exchange process. When people enter into a relationship with some other person there is the expectation of obtaining some kind of reward or benefit in exchange for giving something to the other person in return. Individuals seek to achieve a positive balance for themselves by maximising benefits and minimising costs of such exchanges. Social exchanges are influenced by a complex web of power relationships and as a result are not always equal but have an uneven balance of outcomes.[17]

Different relations and different expectations

The viability of social exchange theory relies on the assumption that individuals will engage in reciprocity and recognise the needs and wishes of other people. This draws attention to the importance of organisational climate. In different organisational relationships there will be different expectations of the content and balance of the exchange, for example between a senior manager and subordinate or between fellow team members. The level of satisfaction from the exchange will depend not just upon the actual outcomes but the individual's expectation of likely outcomes.

The perceived outcomes of a present relationship may also be viewed in consideration of both past relationships and potential future relationships. The nature of social exchanges impacts upon many other features of the people–organisation relationship discussed later including the psychological contract, patterns of communications, equity theory of motivation, group behaviour, leadership and management, control and power, and organisational culture.

Quoting the work of *Koster*,[18] a *CIPD* report comments that social exchange theory suggests employees may perceive investment in general skills as an investment in their development and thus may reciprocate by staying with the incumbent firm.[19]

Organisational theory

No single approach to organisational behaviour can provide all the answers. A central part of the study is the development of different thinking on and approaches to the structure, management and functioning of organisations, and their relationship with the external environment. This might be termed organisation theory. Managers reading the work of leading writers on the subject might see in their thoughts, ideas and conclusions a message about how they should behave. This will influence their attitudes towards actual practice and bring about change in behaviour.

Writing on organisational behaviour and management in some form or another can be traced back thousands of years. *Shafritz* makes an interesting observation about the contribution of William Shakespeare (1564–1616):

> **While William Shakespeare's contribution to literature and the development of the English language have long been acknowledged and thoroughly documented, his contribution to the theory of management and administration have been all but ignored. This is a surprising oversight when you consider that many of his plays deal with issues of personnel management and organizational behavior.** [20]

Importance of organisational theory

The study of organisation theory is important for the following reasons:

- It helps to view the interrelationships between the development of theory, behaviour in organisations and management practice.
- Theories are interpretive and evolve in line with changes in the organisational environment.

- Many of the earlier ideas are of continuing importance and later ideas tend to incorporate at least part of earlier ideas and conclusions.

However, if action is to be effective, the theory must be adequate and appropriate to the task and to improved organisational performance. It must be a 'good' theory. To be of any help to the practising manager, theory has to be appropriate. For example, *Lee* refers to the danger of adopting theories because they are teachable, rather than because they are effective.[21]

Charles Handy refers to analysis as an important prerequisite of action and the usefulness of conceptual frameworks to the interpretation of organisational phenomena. Concepts of organisation theory, properly used and understood, should: help one to *explain* the Past, which in turn

- Helps one to *understand* the Present and thus;
- To *predict* the Future which leads to;
- More influence over future events; and
- Less disturbance from the Unexpected.[22]

Gareth Jones suggests that knowledge about organisational design and change enables people to analyse the structure and culture of the organisation, diagnose problems and make adjustments that help the organisation achieve its goals.[23] **Figure 1.4** provides an outline of the relationship among organisation theory, structure, culture, design and change. **Organisational theory is discussed in more detail in Chapter 11.**

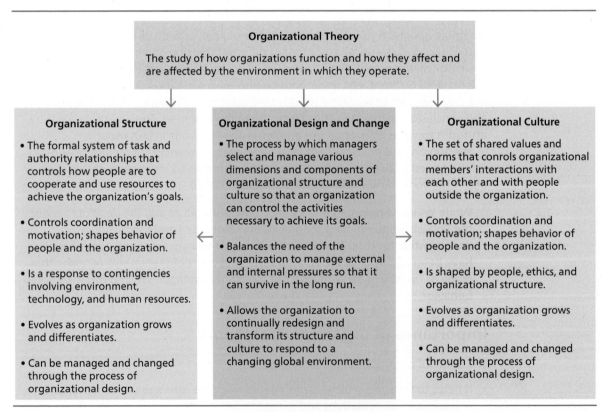

Figure 1.4 Relationship among Organisation Theory and Organisational Structure, Culture and Design and Change
Source: Jones G R *Organizational Theory, Design, and Change,* seventh edition, Pearson Education (2013), p. 30.

To what extent do YOU believe knowledge of organisational theory can help predict the future and results in less organisational disturbance from the unexpected?

The organisation as an open system

Organisations differ in many important respects, but also share common features, and can be viewed as open systems which take inputs from the environment (outputs from other systems) and through a series of activities transform or convert these inputs into outputs (inputs to other systems) to achieve some objective. By adopting the systems view of organisations, we can identify principles and prescriptions of structure and management that apply to business organisations in general. Differences in the application and operation of these principles and prescriptions as between one organisation and another are largely a matter only of degree and emphasis.

In terms of the **open systems model** the business organisation, for example, takes in resources such as people, finance, raw materials and information from its environment, transforms or converts these and returns them to the environment in various forms of outputs such as goods produced, services provided, completed processes or procedures in order to achieve certain goals such as profit, market standing, level of sales or consumer satisfaction. ***See Figure 1.5.***

All organisations need clear aims and objectives that will determine the nature of inputs, the series of activities to achieve outputs and the realisation of organisational goals. Feedback about the performance of the system, and the effects of its operation on the environment, is measured in terms of achieving aims and objectives. These common features make possible the application of general principles of organisational behaviour and the meaningful study of organisation theory. While general principles and prescriptions apply to all organisations,

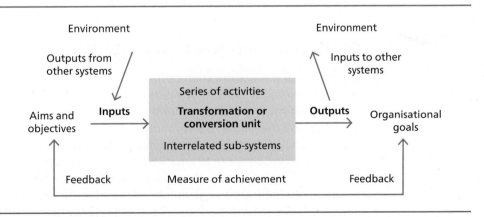

Figure 1.5 The open-systems model of organisations

differences in their type and purpose, goals and objectives and environmental influences highlight the nature of the people–organisation relationship. This aids the analysis of alternative forms of structure and management, methods of operation, styles of leadership and the motivations and behaviour of people employed by or working in different organisations.

Organisational sub-systems

Within the organisation (system) as a whole, each of the different transformation or conversion activities may themselves be viewed as separate **organisational sub-systems**. A framework of five main interrelated sub-systems as a basis for the analysis of work organisations can be identified as:

- **Task** – the goals and objectives of the organisation: the nature of inputs and outputs, and the work activities to be carried out in the transformation or conversion process;
- **Technology** – the manner in which the tasks of the organisation are carried out and the nature of work performance: the materials, systems and procedures, and equipment used in the transformation or conversion process;
- **Structure** – patterns of organisation, lines of authority, formal relationships and channels of communication among members: the division of work and co-ordination of tasks by which the series of activities is carried out;
- **People** – the nature of the members undertaking the series of activities: for example, their attitudes, skills and attributes; needs and expectations; interpersonal relations and patterns of behaviour; group functioning and behaviour; informal organisation and styles of leadership;
- **Management** – co-ordination of task, technology, structure and people, and policies and procedures for the execution of work: corporate strategy, direction of the activities of the organisation as a whole and its interactions with the external environment. *See* **Figure 1.6**.

Attention should be focused on the total work organisation and on interrelationships between the five main sub-systems – task, technology, structure, people and management. This provides a useful basis for the review of organisational performance and effectiveness.

Contingency models of organisation

Irrespective of the identification of sub-systems, the nature and scale of the series of activities involved in converting inputs to outputs will differ from one organisation to another in terms of the interrelationships between technology, structure, methods of operation and the nature of environmental influences. 'Contingency' models of organisation highlight these interrelationships and provide a further possible means of differentiation between alternative forms of organisation and management. The contingency approach takes the view that there is no one best, universal form of organisation. There are a large number of variables, or situational factors, that influence organisational performance. **(Contingency models are examined in Chapter 9.)**

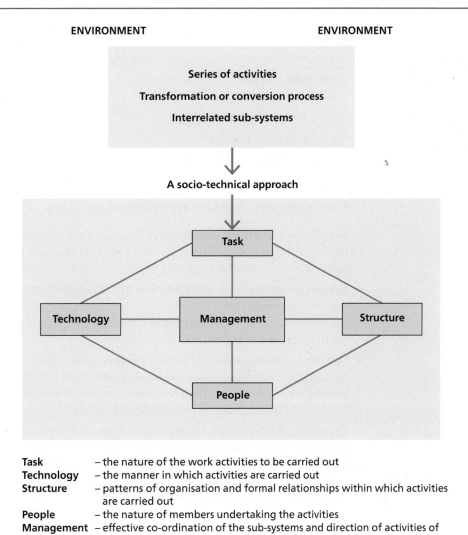

Figure 1.6 Organisational sub-systems

To what extent are YOU able to analyse the effectiveness of your university in terms of the five interrelated organisational sub-systems?

Organisation and management systems

The significance of the people–organisation relationship and management as an integrating factor was highlighted by *Likert* writing in the 1960s and 1970s.[24] On the basis of a questionnaire to managers in over 200 organisations and research into the performance characteristics of different types of organisations Likert established a profile of characteristics describing the nature of four different management systems in terms of a table of organisational variables under the headings of:

1. leadership processes;
2. motivational forces;
3. communication process;
4. interaction–influence process;
5. decision-making process;
6. goal-setting or ordering; and
7. control processes.

These management systems are designated by number:

- **System 1 – Exploitive authoritative.** Decisions are imposed on subordinates, motivation is based on threats, there is very little teamwork or communication; responsibility is centred at the top of the organisational hierarchy.
- **System 2 – Benevolent authoritative.** There is a condescending form of leadership, motivation is based on a system of rewards, there is only limited teamwork or communication; there is responsibility at managerial levels but not at lower levels of the organisational hierarchy.
- **System 3 – Consultative.** Leadership involves some trust in subordinates, motivation is based on rewards but also some involvement, there is a fair degree of teamwork, and communication takes place vertically and horizontally; responsibility for achieving the goals of the organisation is spread more widely throughout the hierarchy.
- **System 4 – Participative.** Leadership involves trust and confidence in subordinates, motivation is based on rewards for achievement of agreed goals, there is participation and a high degree of teamwork and communication; responsibility for achieving the goals of the organisation is widespread throughout all levels of the hierarchy.

Supportive organisational relationships

The nearer the behavioural characteristics of an organisation approach System 4, the more likely this will lead to long-term improvement in staff turnover and high productivity, low scrap, low costs and high earnings. Likert sets out three fundamental concepts of System 4 management. These are the use of:

- the principle of supportive relationships among members of the organisation and in particular between superior and subordinate;
- group decision-making and group methods of organisation and supervision; and
- high performance aspirations for all members of the organisation.

Supportive relationships are intended to enhance self-esteem and ego-building, contribute to subordinates' sense of personal worth and importance, and maintain their sense of significance and dignity. The superior's behaviour is regarded as supportive when this entails:

- mutual confidence and trust;
- helping to maintain a good income;

- understanding of work problems and help in doing the job;
- genuine interest in personal problems;
- help with training to assist promotion;
- sharing of information;
- seeking opinions about work problems;
- being friendly and approachable; and
- giving credit and recognition where due.

Likert refers to studies that suggest that employees generally want stable employment and job security, opportunities for promotion and satisfactory compensation. They want, also, to feel proud of their organisation and its performance and accomplishments. In System 4 management, superiors should therefore have high performance aspirations, but so also should every member of the organisation. To be effective, these high performance goals should not be imposed but set by a participative mechanism involving group decision-making and a multiple overlapping group structure. The mechanism should enable employees to be involved in setting high performance goals that help to satisfy their needs.

The ultimate people–organisation relationship?

Contribution of Human Resource Management (HRM)

At the heart of successful management is integrating the individual and the organisation, and this requires an understanding of both human personality and work organisations. People and organisations need each other and Human Resource Management (HRM) is an important part of this relationship. Although often studied as a separate subject area there is a substantial interrelationship between organisational behaviour and HRM as can be seen by the content of **Chapter 10.**

It is important always to remember that it is people who are being managed and people should be considered in human terms. Unlike physical resources, the people resource is not owned by the organisation. People bring their own perceptions, feelings and attitudes towards the organisation, systems and styles of management, their duties and responsibilities, and the conditions under which they are working.

Support for the process of management

Whatever the individual's orientations to work, the nature of the work organisation or cultural influences, efforts of members of the organisation need to be co-ordinated, directed and guided towards the achievement of its goals. HRM should serve to support the broader process of management and delivering organisational practices and the execution of work. It should help reconcile the needs of people at work with the requirements of the organisation and creation of an organisational climate in which people work willingly and effectively. (*See* **Figure 1.7.**)

The style of HRM adopted can be seen as a function of the organisation's attitudes towards people and assumptions about human nature and behaviour.

According to *Gratton,* for example:

When people are engaged and committed they are more likely to behave in the interests of the company and they have less need to be controlled and measured. In essence, engaged people can be trusted to behave in the interests of the company, in part because they perceived their interests to be the same as, or aligned with, the interests of the company.[25]

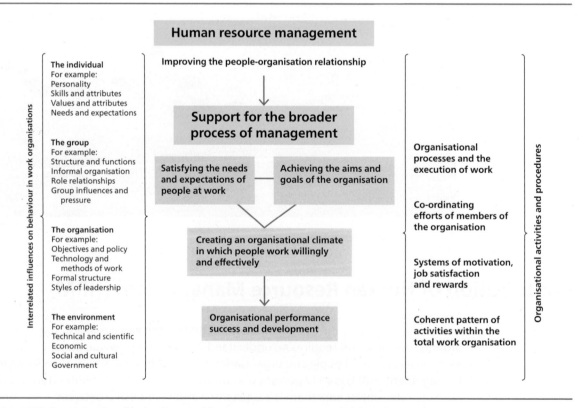

Figure 1.7 Organisational behaviour and human resource management

In what *specific* ways to YOU see human resource management activities contributing to the people–organisation relationship?

The psychological contract

One significant aspect of organisational behaviour and the people–organisation relationship is the concept of the **psychological contract**. This has its roots in social exchange theory and the relationship between the individual and the organisation. This is not a written document or part of a formal agreement but implies a series of mutual expectations and satisfaction of needs arising from the people–organisation relationship. The psychological contract covers a range of expectations of rights and privileges, duties and obligations that have an important influence on people's behaviour.

The psychology contract is also an important factor in the socialisation of new members of staff to the organisation. Early experiences of the people–organisation relationship have a major effect on an individual's perception of the organisation as a place to work and the quality of management, and can have a major influence on job satisfaction, attitude and levels of performance.

Nature and extent of expectations

The nature and extent of individuals' expectations vary widely, as do the ability and willingness of the organisation to meet them. It is difficult to list the range of implicit expectations that individuals have and these expectations also change over time. They are separate from any statutory requirements placed upon the organisation; they relate more to the idea of social responsibility of management **(discussed in Chapter 16).** The organisation will also have implicit expectations of its members. The organisational side of the psychological contract places emphasis on expectations, requirements and constraints that may differ from, and may conflict with, an individual's expectations. Some possible examples of the individual's and the organisation's expectations are given in **Figure 1.8**.

Process of balancing

It is unlikely that all expectations of the individual or of the organisation will be met fully. There is a continual process of balancing and explicit bargaining. The nature of these expectations is not defined formally and although the individual member and the organisation may not be consciously aware of them, they still affect relationships between them and have an influence on behaviour. *Stalker* suggests that successful companies are those that have the ability to balance the unwritten needs of their employees with the needs of the company. Such companies use a simple formula of Caring, Communicating, Listening, Knowing and Rewarding.

Individuals' expectations of the organisation
- Provide safe and hygienic working conditions.
- Make every reasonable effort to provide job security.
- Attempt to provide challenging and satisfying jobs, and reduce alienating aspects of work.
- Adopt equitable human resource management policies and procedures.
- Respect the role of trade union officials and staff representatives.
- Consult fully with staff and allow genuine participation in decisions that affect them.
- Implement best practice in equal opportunity policies and procedures.
- Reward all staff fairly according to their contribution and performance.
- Provide reasonable opportunities for personal development and career progression.
- Treat members of staff with respect.
- Demonstrate an understanding and considerate attitude towards personal problems of staff.

Organisational expectations of the individual
- Uphold the ideology of the organisation and the corporate image.
- Work diligently in pursuit of organisational objectives.
- Adhere to the rules, policies and procedures of the organisation.
- Respect the reasonable authority of senior members of staff.
- Do not take advantage of goodwill shown by management.
- Be responsive to leadership influence.
- Demonstrate loyalty, respect confidentiality and not betray positions of trust.
- Maintain harmonious relationships with work colleagues.
- Do not abuse organisational facilities such as email or internet access.
- Observe reasonable and acceptable standards of dress and appearance.
- Show respect and consolidation to customers and suppliers.

Figure 1.8 The psychological contract: possible examples of individual and organisational expectations

- **Caring** – demonstrating genuine concern for individuals working in the organisation;
- **Communicating** – really talking about what the company is hoping to achieve;
- **Listening** – hearing not only the words but also what lies behind the words;
- **Knowing** – the individuals who work for you, their families, personal wishes, desires and ambitions;
- **Rewarding** – money is not always necessary; a genuine thank-you or public recognition can raise morale.[26]

Moral contract with people

The changing nature of organisations and individuals at work has placed increasing pressures on the awareness and importance of new psychological contracts. *Ghoshal et al.* suggest the new management philosophy needs to be grounded in a very different moral contract with people. Rather than being seen as a corporate asset from which value can be appropriated, people are seen as a responsibility and a resource to be added to. The new moral contract also demands much from employees, who need to abandon the stability of lifetime employment and embrace the concept of continuous learning and personal development.[27]

> What examples can YOU give of the psychological contract between yourself and fellow students; and your university (or faculty/department)?

Globalisation and the international context

Many commentators have identified the increasingly international or global arena in which business organisations operate. This international environment and resultant cultural implications have a challenging impact upon the nature of the people–organisation relationship.

Globalisation may be viewed in different ways but in broad terms, refers to organisations integrating, operating and competing in a worldwide economy. The organisations' activities and methods of production are linked in locations across the world rather than confined nationally. The following factors are frequently cited as potential explanatory factors underlying this trend:

- improvements in international information and communication facilities leading to an increased consciousness of differences in workplace attitudes and behaviour in other societies;
- international competitive pressure – for example, the emergence of newly industrialised and/or free-market nations including for example the Far East region and former communist bloc countries;
- increased mobility of labour;
- international business activity, for example: overseas franchising or licensing agreements; outsourcing of business units to other countries (call centres provide a topical example); direct foreign investment and the activities of multinational corporations which, by definition, operate outside national boundaries;
- greater cross-cultural awareness and acceptance of the advantages of diversity.

A significant feature of globalisation for Western economies is the economic growth and development of countries known as BRIC: Brazil, Russia, India and China, and for some commentators BRICK to include Korea. Other commentators however question the extent to which the trend towards globalisation will continue. It is not spreading evenly and not all societies are in a position to trade on a global scale. Some chose to reject, or to even demonstrate against, the increasing movement towards globalisation.

The future of globalisation

Globalisation has been subjected to much criticism, in part at least due to lack of clarity as to its exact meaning and to the confusion about organisations that are very large-scale (such as Walmart in the USA) but have only a small proportion of their operations on a global basis. Globalisation has also become the subject of demonstrations and has been blamed for escalating inequalities in the developing world and endangering regional cultures. There appears to be a return to strong nationalistic tendencies in countries such as America and France.

By contrast, *McLean* maintains that globalisation is here to stay – it won't go away and if anything will get worse. 'We must face the realism that the world, and indeed organisations and the way they are managed, will never be the same. We must encompass these changes and harness the opportunities they present.'[28] *French*, however, reminds us that social trends are by their very nature, fluctuating. For example it is quite possible that the trend for global flows of workers may decrease in importance or even be reversed in the future.[29]

The cultural environment

Whatever the extent of globalisation, there are clear implications for organisational behaviour in accommodating international dimensions of management and cultural differences. There are also concerns about the loss of national or regional cultural identities. As organisations, and especially large business organisations, adopt a more global perspective this will have a significant effect on the broader context of organisational behaviour including diversity and inclusion, styles of leadership, systems of communication and human resource management. Globalisation will also impact on the nature of social responsibilities and business ethics with fears of increased inequalities at work.

The importance of people in business understanding cultural differences is illustrated by IBM, which publishes for members of staff a comprehensive guide to the main dimensions of culture and business, and an introduction to concepts, tips, resources and tools for building cross-cultural competencies across national, organisational, team and interpersonal barriers.

Variations in workplace attitudes and behaviour

Another advantage of adopting a cross-cultural approach to the study of organisational behaviour, and to the management of people more generally, lies in the recognition of variations in workplace attitudes and behaviour between individuals and groups in different cultural contexts. As an example Japanese corporate culture is permeated by unquestioning obedience and loyalty. This at least in part was said to be a reason for the Toshiba accounting scandal in 2015. In India people often have to work against an environment of chaos, corruption and lacking water or power in their homes.

In America, there is a strong commitment to the organisation (the corporation) and work and career are taken very seriously (as the author has experienced for himself). Hard work is accepted as part of the American way of life and good timekeeping is important. It is a long-hours culture and generally there is little concern for the work/life balance. There is a strong emphasis on political correctness and little banter or humour at work (again as the author found out to his cost), especially not in formal meetings. Americans do not like self-deprecation and find it strange that the British are prepared to laugh at themselves.

In China there is an enormous bureaucracy and hierarchy is an important indication of authority. In the business world you may need to deal with several ascending levels of management before reaching the senior manager. There can be an apparent lack of courtesy – and rather than being taken as given, respect and trust have to be earned. There is a strong superior–subordinate relationship, with staff often undertaking menial tasks for their boss.[30] In Japan and Korea, where society tends to be male-dominated, in the business world men are more likely to be taking the main role in setting agendas, communications and decision-making.

According to *Hare* we need to embrace the opportunities international management brings. All countries have their issues but whatever the customs, differences and similarities most cultures recognise the need to get something done. Successful international management boils down to five simple principles:

1. Listen well so you understand the rationale, motivations and outcomes desired by the other party.
2. Take time to do your research and homework.
3. Be courteous and polite, and mindful of local manners and customs.
4. Develop good working relationships through trust and respect.
5. Embrace the opportunities from international management.[31]

A summary of organisational culture is set out in the concept map Figure 1.9.

What do YOU see as the most significant impact of globalisation? What experiences do you have of different workplace attitudes and behaviours?

Examples of cultural environment

Organisational culture

* **Shared values and norms**
* **Development & change**
* **Culture and management**
* **Dimensions of culture**
* **Definitions**

Two definitions
(from very many)

"The collection of traditions, policies, beliefs and attitudes that constitute a pervasive context for everything we do and think in an organisation." (MCLEAN AND MARSHAL 1993)

'How things are done round here'
(DRENNAN 1992)

Organisation culture
Determines the way people in the organisation
* Regard and treat:
  - each other
  - their job
  - the organisation
* Approach their challenges
* Solve their problems
* Represent their organisation to:
  - customers /clients

* Shared values and norms
* Controls organisational members interactions with people inside and out side of the organisation
* Controls coordination and motivation shapes behaviours
* Is shaped by people ethics & structure
* Evolves as organisation grows and differentiates
* Can be managed & changed through organisational design

Top management set the formal culture of the organisation, but sub-cultures are very common:
- shift workers
- creative departments
- maintenance sections
- IT specialists in generalist organisations
In extreme cases, these subcultures can undermine the main organisation culture

Development & change
An organisation's culture is not necessarily constant, & may be subject to change over short or long timescales and/or the organisation type or size
Organisation size
Reasons for changing

Culture may change because of:
* Mergers & acquisitions
* Influential culture-determining staff leaving (or joining) the organisation
* Existing culture seen to be inappropriate to the business
* Existing culture contrary to new legislation
* Influential external stakeholder pressures

Setting the culture
Some tendencies in culture setting in smaller & larger organisations:

Smaller organisations	Larger organisations
• Highly dependent on owner / manager attitudes • Not always the subject of conscious thought • Subject to arbitrary change	• Formally related to business processes • Subject to more careful scrutiny & control • Not changed without debate

NB these are tendencies & not absolutes

Company policy implications
* If differences in environmental cultures are obvious, Western management theories are constrained
* If culture matters policies are less effective in different cultural environments
* Identical personnel policies may have differing effects in different countries
* Also perceptions of absenteeism; financial incentives; performance; quality costs; grievance procedures; labour turnover etc

Implications for training managers (INTL)
If destined to work abroad, they need a thorough familiarisation with the new culture using:
* Specialised cross-cultural training institutes, or
* Host country personnel to advise them

Hofstede
Working on national & regional cultural groupings, identified five dimensions of culture affecting organisations

Masculinity v Femininity
- Identified in the dominant value of the society

Masculinity concerned with:
- Assertiveness
- Acquisition of wealth & things
- Live to work
- Clear sex roles, leading to male dominance

Femininity concerned with:
- Quality of life
- Working to live
- Fluid sex roles, leading to equality

Power distance
Dimension relates to people as subordinates & their attitude to superiors. Large power distance mean superiors are held in awe as inaccessible (probably autocratic) persons /leaders

- Having a powerful superior whom one can blame (& praise) satisfies the need to avoid uncertainty
- Cultures with strong uncertainty avoidance trends don't take risks & don't conform to Maslow's perception of a hierarchy of human needs (Western)

Long-term/short-term orientation
(originally labelled 'Confucian work dynamism').
Countries scoring highly on Confucian work dynamism or long-term orientation exhibited a strong concern with time along a continuum, Therefore both past – & future oriented, preoccupation with tradition & concern with the effect of actions and policies on future generations.

Collectivist environment
Local employees need ties with the organisation for mutual loyalty & emotional dependence. Emphasises 'belonging' (Prefers non-capitalist order)

Uncertainty avoidance
- Low U.A suggests a culture of risk takers; a concern with performance & doing something to satisfy needs

2018 The virtual materials learning workshop

Figure 1.9   Personal skills and employability
Source: Copyright © 2011 The Virtual Learning Materials Workshop. Reproduced with permission.

Is organisational behaviour culture-bound?

While it can be valuable to apply organisational behaviour concepts to diverse cultural settings, it should also be borne in mind that some **universal** theories and models may, in reality, contain important culturally derived assumptions. When examining classical frameworks for understanding organisation structure *Schneider and Barsoux* point out: 'Theories about how best to organise – Max Weber's (German) bureaucracy, Henri Fayol's (French) administrative model, and Frederick Taylor's (American) scientific management – all reflect societal concerns of the times as well as the cultural background of the individuals.'[32]

It is unsurprising that writers on work organisations may themselves be influenced by their own cultural backgrounds when compiling their work: however, equally it should not be ignored. More significant still is the possibility that whole topics within organisational behaviour, *per se,* may be underpinned by a particular culturally derived frame of reference. *French* examines the extent to which universally applicable pressures or logics effectively rule out significant cultural variations in formal organisational arrangements, such as bureaucracy, as opposed to culture itself viewed as a variable within a range of factors influencing structure.[33]

Culture as understanding

'For our most basic common link is that we all inhabit this small planet, we all breathe the same air, we all cherish our children's future, and we are all mortal' (John F. Kennedy, 10 June 1963). There are a number of very good reasons why we could usefully understand cultural difference (and similarity) at work, based on new awareness contributing to our own effectiveness and moreover to the accomplishment of organisational goals. It could also be true to say that an appreciation of culture and its effects may be of intrinsic value. There could therefore be advantages to cross-cultural awareness which include:

- increased self-awareness;
- sensitivity to difference and diversity;
- questioning our own assumptions and knowledge;
- lessening ignorance, prejudice and hatred.

However, it would be wrong to think that increased cross-cultural awareness or activity will automatically bring about any of these outcomes.

Brooks is one of several commentators who draw our attention to the interlinked nature of culture and commonly held values. **Figure 1.10** illustrates the interplay between relevant factors affecting any one national culture.[34] You may wish to consider how these factors have combined to shape your own 'home' culture and that of one other country with which you are familiar.

Above all, those aspects of organisational behaviour that focus on individual differences and diversity, groups and managing people are the most clearly affected by culture and it is essential to take a cross-cultural approach to the subject. **(Organisation culture is discussed in Chapter 15.)**

Five dimensions of culture: the contribution of Hofstede

Geert Hofstede is one of the most significant contributors to the body of knowledge on culture and workplace difference. His work has largely resulted from a large-scale

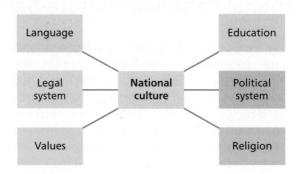

Figure 1.10 Factors affecting national culture
Source: From Brooks, I. *Organisational Behaviour: Individuals, Groups and Organisation,* fourth edition, Financial Times Prentice Hall (2009), p. 272. Reproduced with permission from Pearson Education Ltd.

research programme in the late 60s and early 70s involving employees from the IBM Corporation, initially in forty countries. In focusing on one organisation Hofstede felt that the results could be more clearly linked to national cultural difference. Arguing that culture is, in a memorable phrase, **collective programming** or **software of the mind,** Hofstede initially identified four dimensions of culture: power distance, uncertainty avoidance, individualism and masculinity.[35]

- **Power distance** relates to the *social distance among people* depending upon management style, hierarchical structure, willingness of subordinates to disagree with superiors, and the educational level and status accruing to particular roles.

- **Uncertainty avoidance** refers to the extent to which members of a society feel threatened by *ambiguity or unusual situations* or accepting of risks and uncertainty.

- **Individualism** describes the relatively *individualistic or collectivist ethic* evident in that particular society, for example the degree of respect for individual freedom or commitment to group membership.

- **Masculinity** refers to a continuum between *'masculine' characteristics,* such as assertiveness and competitiveness, *and 'feminine' traits,* such as caring, a stress upon the quality of life and concern with the environment.

A fifth dimension of culture, **long-term/short-term orientation,** was originally labelled 'Confucian work dynamism'. This dimension developed from the work of *Hofstede and Bond* in an attempt to locate Chinese cultural values as they impacted on the workplace.[36] Countries which scored highly on Confucian work dynamism or long-term orientation exhibited a strong concern with time along a continuum and were therefore both past- and future-oriented, with a preoccupation with tradition but also a concern with the effect of actions and policies on future generations.

Evaluation of Hofstede's work

Extremely influential, the seminal work of Hofstede has been criticised from certain quarters, for example for its simplicity and limited practical application. In common with other writers in this area there is a focus on the national rather than the regional level. The variations within certain countries, for example Spain, can be more or less significant. Again in common with other contributors Hofstede's classifications include medium categories which may be difficult to operationalise, accurate though they may be. Some may also find the masculinity/femininity dimension unconvincing and itself stereotypical. Other writers have questioned whether Hofstede's findings remain current. *Holden* summarises this view: 'How many people have ever thought that many of Hofstede's informants of three decades ago are now dead? Do their children and grandchildren really have the same values?'[37]

See also discussion on global leadership and organisational behaviour effectiveness (GLOBE) in Chapter 9.

Cultural diversity: the contribution of Trompenaars

Another significant contributor to this area of study is *Fons Trompenaars* whose later work is co-authored with *Charles Hampden-Turner.*[38] Trompenaars' original research spanned fifteen years, resulting in a database of 50,000 participants from fifty countries. It was supported by cases and anecdotes from 900 cross-cultural training programmes. A questionnaire method comprised a significant part of the study which involved requiring participants to consider their underlying norms, values and attitudes. The resultant framework identifies seven areas in which cultural differences may affect aspects of organisational behaviour:

- Relationships and rules. Here societies may be more or less **universal,** in which case there is relative rigidity in respect of rule-based behaviour, or **particular,** in which case the importance of relationships may lead to flexibility in the interpretation of situations.

- Societies may be more oriented to the **individual** or **collective.** The collective may take different forms: the corporation in Japan, the family in Italy or the Catholic Church in the Republic of Ireland. There may be implications here for such matters as individual responsibility or payment systems.

- It may also be true that societies differ in the extent to which it is thought appropriate for members to show emotion in public. **Neutral** societies favour the 'stiff upper lip', while overt displays of feeling are more likely in **emotional** societies.

- In **diffuse** cultures, the whole person would be involved in a business relationship and it would take time to build such relationships. In a **specific** culture, such as the USA, the basic relationship would be limited to the contractual. This distinction clearly has implications for those seeking to develop new international links.

- **Achievement**-based societies value recent success or an overall record of accomplishment. In contrast, in societies relying more on **ascription,** status could be bestowed on you through such factors as age, gender or educational record.

- Trompenaars suggests that societies view **time** in different ways which may in turn influence business activities. The American dream is the French nightmare. Americans generally start from zero and what matters is their present performance and their plan to 'make it' in the future. This is '*nouveau riche*' for the French, who prefer the '*ancien pauvre*'; they have an enormous sense of the past.

- Finally it is suggested that there are differences with regard to attitudes to the **environment.** In Western societies, individuals are typically masters of their fate. In other parts of the world, however, the world is more powerful than individuals.

Trompenaars' work is based on lengthy academic and field research. It is potentially useful in linking the dimensions of culture to aspects of organisational behaviour which are of direct relevance, particularly to people approaching a new culture for the first time.

How would YOU evaluate the contribution of Hofstede and Trompenaars to a greater understanding of organisational behaviour and cultural diversity?

Critical Thinking Zone

Reflections on the Psychological Contract

In this zone, we critically discuss the concept of the psychological contract and evaluate the extent to which it is key to understanding the dynamics of the people–organisation relationship.

The psychological contract is one of the most contested concepts in the HR arena. It has generated widespread interest, discourse and debate from both academics and practitioners, in a bid to develop a clearer understanding of the factors that may influence greater levels of individual engagement, commitment and motivation in the workplace.[39–41] The antecedents of the psychological contract can be traced back to the work of Argyris,[42] whose 'psychological work contract' theory defined the employment relationship as being rooted in the perceptions and values that are held by the individual and organisation.[39] As highlighted earlier in the chapter, the concept is also premised on the social exchange theory. Blau[43] posited that the people–organisation relationship is predicated on subjective interchange and social relationships and the extent to which these are reliant on unspecified or subconscious, socially constructed obligations or mutual expectations. Like the organisational shadow, these obligations and expectations are invisible, intangible and implicit, but if breached, can have a major impact on organisational behaviour in the workplace.[44]

Is the Psychological Contract a Theory, Measure or Construct?

According to Guest,[40] the psychological contract nestles (albeit rather awkwardly) between organisational psychology and employment relations. He suggests that it is neither a theory, nor measure, but a 'hypothetical construct' (p. 650), derived from a 'legal metaphor'. Cullinane and Dundon[39] concur and proffer that it is an 'ideological construct' (p. 123). Guest strongly questions whether the comparison to a 'legal contract' is appropriate, given that the construct implies the presence of a mutual agreement between parties. However, as the bedrock of the psychological contract is implicit, embedded, subjective perception, 'agreement exists in the eye of the beholder',[45] thus rendering any idea of an agreement between both parties in the people–organisation relationship intrinsically problematic.[39] Guest adds that the inherent implicitness and subjectivity of the psychological contract undermines the notion of an agreement, as its terms are stored in the mind rather than a filing cabinet or a safe. Therefore, neither party can be sure whether their expectations and obligations are the same, or indeed, have been met. Noting the multiple paradoxes surrounding the psychological contract, Cullinane and Dundon advocate that it should be recognised as a 'social exchange interaction' (p. 119), rather than a contract in its metaphorical sense.

When is the Psychological Contract Formed?

Arguably, the psychological contract is formed from the point at which a newcomer enters the organisation. The induction and socialisation processes orient the individual to the organisation and its norms and values, in preparation for their transition from an 'outsider' to 'insider'.[46] This process may invariably lead to individual assumptions and perceptions about what the organisation deems as appropriate behaviour and the consequences of conforming to, or deviating from, the implied and explicit terms of the formal contract of employment.[40,41,47] However, Herriot[48] claims that the individual's expectations of, and obligations to, their employer may be socially constructed over many years and shaped by their experiences in previous organisations. Individuals with little or no experience, including those on short-term or temporary contracts may, through the socialisation process, form what Sherman and Morley[49] refer to as an 'anticipatory psychological contract'. Although the contract is ambiguous and basic, it will be a vehicle to guide how the newcomer interacts with their new organisation.

Is the Psychological Contract Transactional or Relational?

According to Dabos and Rousseau[50] and Hui et al.,[51] there are three types of psychological contract. First, the transactional contract characterises obligations that are primarily based on short-term economic transactions with little or no loyalty. Individuals are paid to perform a fixed set of duties and responsibilities and the employer is not obligated to provide opportunities for training and development. Second, the relational contract is based on mutual loyalty, stability and trust and the individual's high emotional and attitudinal commitment to the organisation. Finally, a balanced, or hybrid, contract incorporates aspects of both the transactional and relational contracts, but the focus here is on the employer's obligation to develop the individual and provide career support. Arguably, the type of psychological contract that is formed by the individual may be linked to prior subjective perceptions and positive or negative experiences from previous employments.

Implications for Organisational Behaviour in the Workplace

McDonald and Makin,[52] Guest and Cullinane and Dundon all concur that a major implication for organisational behaviour in the workforce is the perceived breach or violation of the psychological contract. A breach occurs when an individual perceives that the organisation has not honoured or lived up to one or more of its obligations. *How* can the breach be identified? Cullinane and Dundon profess that the extent to which the psychological contract has been breached is difficult to quantify, due to its inherently unspecified and implicit nature. However, Jensen et al.[44] suggest that breaches are visible and manifested in counterproductive work behaviours that are, in themselves, violations of organisational norms and contrary to its legitimate interests. The authors link such behaviours to the type of perceived psychological contract the individual has with the organisation. For example, they posit that a relational contract breach results in the engagement of abusive behaviour, revenge and other means of retaliation, such as withdrawal. Breach of the transactional contract may provoke aggression and making threats and inappropriate comments. One can draw parallels with 'light' and 'dark' organisational shadow behaviours that could also be counterproductive.[53-55] Along with psychological contract breaches, these collective behaviours have a huge impact on the organisation and its members and can result in substantial costs, if not addressed by managers.

Understanding the Dynamics of the People–Organisation Relationship

To conclude, studying the psychological contract is key to understanding the dynamics of the people–organisation relationship. It is a complex, paradoxical construct that is embedded in the social exchange theory and subjective perception of both parties. It is an important lens through which individual perceptions, behaviours and experiences are filtered,[56] making it key to developing a knowledge and appreciation of how they impact on collective organisational behaviour in the workplace.

Questions

In view of the above, answer the following questions:

1. Guest and Cullinane and Dundon argue that the psychological contract is a hypothetical, ideological construct. *To what extent* do you agree with their view?

2. In exploring the nature of the psychological contract, Guest[40] (p. 652) stated that 'where the implicit encounters the implicit, the result may be two strangers passing blindfold and in the dark, disappointed at their failure to meet.' *Critically discuss* his statement and its implications for managing organisational behaviour in the workplace.

3. The counterproductive work behaviours that emanate from a breach of the psychological contract share parallels with light and dark organisational shadow behaviours. *What,* in practice, can the organisation do to 'manage' the psychological contract and avoid potential breaches or violations?

Summary – Chapter 1 'The people–organisation relationship'

The underlying basis for organisational behaviour is the nature of the people–organisation relationship. A more strategic approach to the management of people at work has given rise to the concept of human capital. It is necessary to recognise a multidisciplinary perspective to the study of organisational behaviour viewed in terms of interrelated aspects of the individual, the group, the organisation and the environment. There is a close relationship between organisational behaviour and organisational analysis. Organisational theory can influence actual practice and bring about change in behaviour. Viewing the organisation as an open system with interrelated sub-systems makes possible the analysis of principles and prescriptions that apply to organisations in general. A management system of supportive relationships is likely to lead to higher productivity. People and organisations need each other and there is a clear relationship between OB and the human resource function. The psychological contract implies a series of informal mutual expectations and satisfaction of needs arising from the people–organisation relationship. A major challenge facing managers today arises from an increasingly international or global business context. Applications of organisational behaviour are subject to the wider cultural environment and it is important to recognise major dimensions of culture.

Group discussion activities

Undertake each of these exercises and the critical review and reflections in small groups as indicated by your tutor. First, form your own views and then share and compare in open discussion with colleagues.

Reflect honestly on the extent to which: (i) you influenced the thinking and ideas of your colleagues; and (ii) you were influenced by your colleagues.

To what extent was your group able to reach consensus?

On behalf of the group, agree one of your members to produce a brief written summary of the discussion and prepared to present the conclusions in a plenary session.

Activity 1

It is often said that people are every organisation's most important asset. This is perfectly true but people are not like other assets. As well as being valuable in their own right – in terms of performance, skills and creativity – it is individual employees who bind every other aspect of working life together.

'The People Factor – engage your employees for business success', ACAS, March 2014, p. 4

(a) What does this statement actually mean to you and fellow members of your group?

(b) What exactly is meant by 'individual employees binding every other aspect of working life together'?

(c) To what extent do departmental members of staff in your own university appear to be valued as an important asset?

(d) Why is it that although the importance of people as the most important asset is often preached by organisations, this rarely seems to be the reality?

(e) How does this activity relate to your study of organisational behaviour?

Activity 2

(a) Differences in status and power mean the psychological contract is always balanced in favour of the organisation. Managers will *expect* individuals to display loyalty and commitment, put in extra hours and effort. Individuals can only *hope* for some commensurate fair reward now or later.

(b) To what extent do you believe:

    (i) the majority of people come to work with the *original* attitude of being eager to do a good job and desirous of performing well to the best of their abilities; and

    (ii) the suggestion of human capital theory that investment in education and training of individuals increases skill level and productivity so justifying higher earnings.

(c) Performance of people at work is determined predominantly by the work ethic and idiosyncratic behaviour of individuals, and a complex combination of social factors and unofficial working methods. In reality, management has only limited influence.

Activity 3

(a) National culture is not only an explanation of human beliefs, values, behaviours and actions, it is arguably one of the most significant features underlying your study of organisational behaviour.

(b) Using the studies of Hofstede and Trompenaars consider how dimensions of cultural differences influence the behaviour of people at work. Where possible draw upon the experiences of international colleagues or those colleagues whom have spent some time in other countries.

Organisational behaviour in action case study

Fred. Olsen Cruise Lines

An increasingly significant sector of the hospitality and leisure industry is that of the cruise sector. In an ever-growing and continually-evolving cruise industry, the delivery of a memorable personal service experience is particularly significant as an integral part of organisational effectiveness. A record 1.9 million holidaymakers from the UK and Ireland took an ocean cruise in 2016, proving that the wide choice of cruise holiday experiences, worldwide destinations and high levels of service offered on a cruise holiday cannot be beaten. *

Successful cruise management is a combination of travel agency, hotel and leisure activities, onboard entertainment and organised tours. It entails a complex and involved series of processes, both at sea and in different ports of call, quite unlike those experienced in most other business organisations.

Some particular factors to consider include, for example:

* continual heavy guest occupancy and usage, with rapid turnover, mass entry and exit

* 'people logistics' – attending to the complex transportation needs of guests pre- and post-cruise, and the logistics of a broad variety of shore excursions in different locations

* a wide range of onboard activities and events throughout the day and evening
* the highest standards of safety and security, maintenance, logistics and tender operations
* relationships with Head Office, Technical Department, Port Authorities, Pilots etc.
* expectations of high-quality cuisine, design and mix of menus, special dietary requirements
* health and hygiene, with large numbers of guests and crew in continual close contact
* crew resource deployment and rotation-planning, with the unavailability of additional agency or temporary staff, unlike land-based organisations. Need for flexible working practices in response to the demands of the business
* accommodating annual leave requirements, complex international flight arrangements for some crew members, and managing opportunities for time on shore
* change-over of crew at the end of contracts – maintaining business continuity

Cruising is associated with a high level of service delivery; based on preconceived expectations, guests can be very demanding. Guest satisfaction is dependent to a very large extent on the people: in particular, the day-to-day contact with – and care and attention from – members of the crew; and also travel with fellow like-minded guests.

Different cruise ships tend to focus on a particular range of guests, for example younger people, families with children, more mature and perhaps less able people. Although not exclusively, Fred. Olsen's target clientele is guests over 55, and some itineraries stipulate adult travellers only.

Fred. Olsen Cruise Lines has a Norwegian heritage, but is a British-based company, and dates back to 1848. It is one of the only family-run cruise lines in the world. The company has stylish, smaller-sized ships, departing from five regional UK ports. The ships have capacities between 800 and 1350 guests: large enough to provide the facilities desired by guests, but small enough to enable a 'closer' exploration of a wide range of exciting destinations. Emphasis is on a comfortable, friendly atmosphere – delivered 'with a smile' – by caring and attentive crew. Guests are welcomed as individuals in a relaxed, familiar 'home-from-home' ambience. Among a number of accolades in recent years, Fred. Olsen Cruise Lines has been voted 'Best Ocean Cruise Line' in the 'Silver Travel Awards' in 2016 and 2017, recognised for its excellent customer service, attention to detail and strong brand standards by cruisers over 50.

Members of crew come from a wide and diverse range of cultures and backgrounds, with a majority from the Philippines, Thailand, Indonesia and India: especially among room stewards and restaurant staff. There is also a noticeable cultural mix among top managers; from different religions, age groups and often different ways of working. The crew work long hours in often difficult and demanding conditions, and are away from their homes and, in many cases, young families, for up to nine months. Mixing socially is important.

Despite these different backgrounds, a noticeable feature is the strong, mutually-supportive teamwork across the Fred. Olsen fleet. Crew members are ready to help each other whenever needed, usually without direction from management. Supervisors are often seen helping out with routine duties to support their colleagues. A high number of Fred. Olsen crew members return to complete further contracts and have been engaged over many years with the company. In fact, Fred. Olsen has one of the highest staff retention rates of any cruise line, with some staff serving several decades with the company, and even generations of the same family working across the fleet.

Gratuities to crew members are an accepted custom throughout the cruise industry. Tips are a recognised feature of the reward system for good performance. It is up to guests to opt out of payment or vary the amount, at their discretion.

Management's concern and support for the welfare of its crew is of prime importance. At the same time, the nature of cruising demands attention to a safe and secure environment, for both guests and crew. This demands a management structure with clear lines of authority, directed leadership and good order. Strong discipline must be maintained at all times.

Fred. Olsen prides itself on providing exceptional service by anticipating, meeting and exceeding its guests' expectations when they are on board its ships. Despite the continually evolving and highly competitive nature of the industry, Fred. Olsen attracts a high level of 'repeat guests' – that is, loyal customers who have cruised with the company at least once before. On a typical Fred. Olsen cruise, more than half of the guests are repeat customers, which is one of the highest return rates of any major cruise line. A particularly noticeable feature of guest feedback is the extremely favourable and complimentary comments regarding the level of attention from courteous and ever-smiling crew members.

* CLIA UK & Ireland Cruise Review 2016, published March 2017. https://www.cruiseexperts.org/media/5863/clia-uk-ireland-cruise-review-2017-final-sml.pdf

Source: Thanks to Rachael Jackson. Fred. Olsen Cruise Lines. www.fredolsencruises.com

Tasks

1. Explain particular features of organisational behaviour raised by this case study.

2. The company has a particular attraction for discerning, traditional guests, predominately in the 55-plus age bracket. What additional considerations do you think this creates for both crew and management?

3. What do you think are the most important factors that explain the high level of repeat guests on Fred. Olsen cruise ships?

4. Discuss specific ways in which this case study draws attention to the importance of the people–organisation relationship.

Chapter 1 – Personal skills and employability exercise

Objectives

Completing this exercise should help you to enhance the following skills:

* Obtain a clearer picture of your own and other people's attitudes to studying.
* Explore the likely importance of work to you and your orientation to work.
* Relate responses to your personal learning and development.

Exercise

Form into small groups, preferably including any colleagues whom you have not yet got to know very well and/or from a different ethnicity. Discuss openly and honestly how you each feel regarding your attitude, enthusiasm and motivation towards studying.

For example:

1. What do you find most satisfying about studying?
2. What do you find least satisfying about studying?
3. How well are you able to concentrate on your studies?
4. To what extent do you enjoy studying for its own sake or only as a means to an end?
5. What do you find most distracting or difficult about your studies?
6. Is it possible to learn how to improve the skill of studying?
7. What rewards most encourage you in your studying?
8. At what time of the day and for how long at a time do you usually study best?
9. Do you prefer to fit studies around leisure time or enjoy leisure more if you have studied first?
10. What is the single most important feature of effective studying?

> **Discussion**
>
> ✳ How do your responses compare with those of your colleagues? Do any of the responses surprise you?
>
> ✳ To what extent do you believe the responses are a true indication of a work ethic? What do you see as the characteristic traits of a person with a healthy work ethic?
>
> ✳ How far do you agree with the contention that 'we are employed for our skills but valued for our attitudes'?

Notes and references

1. Argyris, C. *Integrating the Individual and the Organization,* Wiley (1964).
2. See, for example: Reeves, R. 'People in the Equation', *Management Today,* November 2004; and Coppin, A. 'Getting the Measure of Your People Assets', *Professional Manager,* vol. 14, no. 5, September 2005.
3. Thomas, H., Smith, R. R. and Diez, F. (2013) *Human Capital and Global Business Strategy.* New York: Cambridge University Press, p. 3.
4. Bontis, N., Dragonetti, N.C., Jacobsen, K. and Roos, G. 'The Knowledge Toolbox: A Review of Tools Available to Measure and Manage Intangible Resources', *European Management Journal.* Vol. 17, no. 4, 1999, pp. 391–402.
5. Gratton, L. *The Democratic Enterprise,* Financial Times Prentice Hall (2004).
6. 'Human Capital Theory: Assessing the Evidence for the Value and Importance of People to Organisational Success', Technical report, CIPD, May 2017.
7. Rollinson, D. *Organisational Behaviour and Analysis,* fourth edition, Pearson Education (2008), pp. 3–4.
8. McGregor, D. *The Human Side of Enterprise,* Penguin (1987), p. 55.
9. Seligman, M. E. P. and Csikszentmihalyi, M. 'Positive Psychology: An Introduction', *American Psychologist,* vol. 55, no. 1, Jan 2000, pp. 5–14.
10. Peterson, C., Park, N. and Sweeney, P. J. 'Group Well-being: Morale from a Positive Psychology Perspective', *Applied Psychology: An International Review,* vol. 57, 2008, p. 20.
11. Wong, T. P. and Davey, M. A, 'Best Practices in Servant Leadership', *School of Global Leadership & Entrepreneurship,* Regent University, July 2007.
12. Donaldson, S. I. and Ko, L. 'Positive Organizational Psychology, Behaviour and Scholarship: A Review of Emerging Literature and Evidence Base', *The Journal of Positive Psychology,* vol. 5, no. 3, May 2010, pp. 177–91.
13. Wright, T. A. and Quick, J. C. 'The Role of Positive-based Research in Building the Science of Organizational Behaviour', *Journal of Organizational Behavior,* vol. 30, 2009, pp. 329–36.
14. Pink, D. *A Whole New Mind,* Penguin (2006).
15. Misselhorn, H. 'Spirituality in the Workplace' JPS Associates, October 2016.
16. Homans, G. C. 'Social Behaviour as Exchange', *American Journal of Sociology,* vol. 63, no. 6, 1958, pp. 597–606. See also, Thibaut, J. W. and Kelley, H. H. *The Social Psychology of Groups,* Wiley (1959).
17. Blau, P. *Exchange and Power in Social Life,* Wiley (1964). See also: Bacharach, S. B. and Lawler, E. J. *Power and Politics in Organizations,* Jossey-Bass (1980).
18. Koster, F., De Grip, A. and Fourage, D. 'Does Perceived Support in Employee Development Affect Personnel Turnover?' *International Journal of Human Resource Management,* vol. 22, no. 11, 2011.
19. 'Human Capital Theory: Assessing the Evidence for the Value and Importance of People to Organisational Success', Technical report, CIPD, May 2017.
20. Shafritz, J. M. *Shakespeare on Management,* Carol Publishing Group (1992), p. xi.
21. Lee, R. A. 'There is Nothing so Useful as an Appropriate Theory' in Wilson, D. C. and Rosenfeld, R. H. *Managing Organisations: Text, Reading and Cases,* McGraw Hill (1990), p. 31.
22. Handy, C. *Understanding Organizations,* fourth edition, Penguin Books (1993), p.16.
23. Jones, G. R. *Organizational Theory, Design, and Change,* seventh edition, Pearson Education (2013).
24. Likert, R. *New Patterns of Management,* McGraw-Hill (1961).
25. Gratton, L. *The Democratic Enterprise,* Financial Times Prentice Hall (2004), p. 208.
26. Stalker, K. 'The Individual, The Organisation and The Psychological Contract', *British Journal of Administrative Management,* July/August 2000, pp. 28–34.
27. Ghoshal, S., Bartlett, C. A. and Moran, P. 'Value Creation: The New Millennium Management Manifesto',

in Chowdhury, S. (ed.) *Management 21C,* Financial Times Prentice Hall (2000), pp. 121.

28. McLean, J. 'Globalisation Is Here to Stay', *Manager, The British Journal of Administrative Management,* June/July 2006, p. 16.

29. French, R. *Cross-Cultural Management in Work Organisations,* second edition, Chartered Institute of Personnel and Development (2010), p. 4.

30. See, for example, Slater, D. 'When in China . . .', *Management Today,* May 2006, pp. 46–50 and also,. Goldthorpe, J. H., Lockwood, D., Bechofer, F. and Platt, J. *The Affluent Worker,* Cambridge University Press (1968).

31. Hare, C. 'We Need to Embrace the Opportunities International Management Brings' *Management Today,* May 2012, p. 62.

32. Schneider, S. C. and Barsoux, J, *Managing Across Cultures,* second edition, Financial Times Prentice Hall (2003) p. 167.

33. French, R. *Cross-Cultural Management in Work Organisations,* second edition, Chartered Institute of Personnel and Development (2010).

34. Brooks, I. *Organisational Behaviour: Individuals, Groups and Organisation,* fourth edition, Financial Times Prentice Hall (2009), p. 286.

35. Hofstede, G. *Culture's Consequences: International Differences in Work-Related Values,* Sage Publications (1980).

36. Hofstede, G. and Bond, M. H. 'The Confucius Connection: From Cultural Roots to Economic Growth', *Organisational Dynamics,* Spring 1988, pp. 4–21.

37. Holden, N. J. *Cross-Cultural Management: A Knowledge Management Perspective,* Financial Times Prentice Hall (2002), p. 51.

38. Trompenaars, F. and Hampden-Turner, C. *Riding the Waves of Culture,* second edition, Nicholas Brealey (1999).

39. Cullinane, N. and Dundon, T. 'The psychological contract: a critical review', *International Journal of Management Reviews,* vol. 8, issue 2, 2006, pp. 113–129.

40. Guest, D. 'Is the psychological contract worth taking seriously?', *Journal of Organizational Behaviour,* vol. 19, Special Issue: The Psychological Contract at Work, 1998, pp. 649–64.

41. Guest, D. 'The psychology of the employment relationship: an analysis based on the psychological contract', *Applied Psychology,* 53, 2004, pp. 541–55.

42. Argyris, C. *Understanding Organizational Behaviour,* Homewood, IL: Doresy (1960).

43. Blau, P. *Exchange and Power in Social Life.* New York: Wiley (1964).

44. Jensen, J.M., Opland, R.A. and Ryan, A.M. 'Psychological Contracts and Counterproductive Work Behaviours: Employee Responses to Transactional and Relational Breach', *Journal of Business Psychology,* vol. 25, 2010, 555–68.

45. Rousseau, D. *Psychological Contracts in Organizations: Understanding Written and Unwritten Agreements,* Thousand Oaks, CA: Sage (1995).

46. Antonacopoulou, E. P. and Güttel, W. 'Staff induction practices and organizational socialization', *Society and Business Review,* vol. 5, no. 1, 2010, pp. 22–47.

47. ACAS Contracts of Employment http://www.acas. org.uk/index.aspx?articleid=1577 (accessed 7 June 2018).

48. Herriot, P. H. 'Selection as a Process', in Smith, M. and Robertson, I. T. (eds), *Advances in Staff Selection,* Chichester, UK: Wiley (1989), pp. 171–87.

49. Sherman, U. P. and Morley, M. J. 'On the Formation of the Psychological Contract: A Schema Theory Perspective', *Group and Organization Management,* vol. 40, issue 2, 2015, pp. 160–92.

50. Dabos, G. E. and Rousseau, D. M. 'Mutuality and reciprocity in the psychological contracts of employees and employers', *Journal of Applied Psychology,* 89, 2004, pp. 52–72.

51. Hui, C., Lee, C. and Rousseau, D. (2004). 'Psychological Contract and Organizational Citizenship Behaviour in China', Investigating Generalizability and Instrumentality, *Journal of Applied Psychology,* 89, pp. 311–21.

52. McDonald, D. J. and Makin, P. J. 'The psychological contract, organisational commitment and job satisfaction of temporary staff', *Leadership and Organization Development Journal,* vol. 21, issue 2, 1999, pp. 84–91.

53. Griffin, R. W. and O'Leary-Kelly, A. (eds) *The Dark Side of Organizational Behaviour,* San Francisco: Jossey-Bass (2004).

54. Linstead, S., Maréchal, G. and Griffin, R. W. 'Theorizing and Researching the Dark Side of Organization', *Organization Studies,* vol. 35 (2), 2014, pp. 165–88.

55. Nicholls, T. 'Embracing the Shadow Side of Organisational Life', HR Zone (2016), www.hrzone.com/ lead/culture/embracing-the-shadow-side-of-organisational-life (accessed 5 June 2018).

56. O'Leary-Kelly, A. M., Henderson, K. E. and Ashforth, B. E. 'Psychological Contracts in a Nontraditional Industry: Exploring the Implications for Psychological Contract Development', *Group and Organization Management,* vol. 39, issue 3, 2014, pp. 326–60.

Chapter 2
The work environment

Recognition of the nature of the work and the environment in which it takes place is a central feature of the study of organisational behaviour.

Learning outcomes

After completing your study of this chapter you should have enhanced your ability to:

- assess work as a central life issue;
- explain orientations to work and the work ethic;
- review the nature and significance of emotional labour;
- debate the nature of work and the organisational setting;
- detail characteristics of the formal and informal organisation;
- evaluate the importance of work/life balance;
- debate the workplace of the future.

Outline chapter contents

Overview topic map: Chapter 2 – The work environment

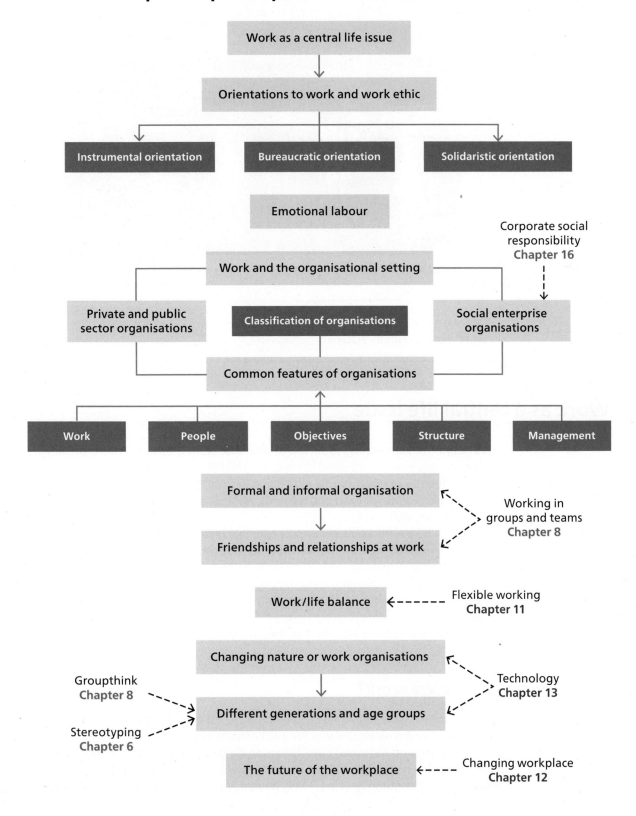

Not all working environments are as familiar as an office

 Before commencing to read this chapter – think carefully about what does 'work' really mean to YOU?

Work as a central life issue

It is evident from almost any social interaction that work is central to life generally and to how a person is perceived more specifically. Work in the form of occupation is a major feature of how our role or position in society is viewed by others. And according to *Hughes,* for example, the work we do is also a significant indication of our value in society.[1]

Work can help fulfil a number of purposes including providing the individual with a sense of perceived identity. Many people see themselves primarily in terms of their career and what they do at work. It defines who they are. *Waller* suggests that work inevitably plays a key role in challenging yourself, developing and learning, especially in the knowledge economy. With increasing flexible working it is harder to tell when we are off duty and work is rarely 'finished'.[2] As boundaries between work and free time blur people become absorbed by their work/life balance, **discussed later in this chapter.**

Why do we work?

To what extent is work ingrained as something we are expected to do and to be productive? Donkin maintains that for most citizens everywhere work remains about earning a living and not much else.[3] However, for most people today work in one form or another is clearly a major part of their lives, and many people spend a large proportion of their time working. Many people appear to have a passion for work into which they prioritise their effort, interest and time and from which they gain a high degree of personal satisfaction. For some people who do not necessarily have any financial motivation, work appears to provide a sense of purpose and a structure to their day. It is often even explained as 'a reason to get up in the morning'. Even after retirement from their occupation people with a high work passion often continue to feel uncomfortable unless they are actively involved in work rather than purely leisure pursuits.

In praise of idleness?

In a classic provocative 1932 essay 'In Praise of Idleness', *Bertrand Russell* puts forward an interesting view that the road to happiness and prosperity lies in an organised diminution of work. Russell suggests work of two kinds. The first kind is unpleasant and ill paid. The second is telling other people what to do and is pleasant and highly paid. The second kind is capable of indefinite extension: there are not only those who give orders, but those who give advice as to what orders should be given. Usually two opposite kinds of advice are given simultaneously by two organised bodies of men, this is called politics. The skill required for this kind of work is not knowledge of the subjects as to which advice is given, but knowledge of the art of persuasive speaking and writing.

Russell also refers throughout Europe to a third group of people, more respected than either of the classes of workers who, through ownership of land, are able to make others pay for the privilege of being allowed to exist and to work. Unfortunately their idleness is only rendered possible by the industry of others; indeed their desire for comfortable idleness is historically the source of the whole gospel of work. The last thing they have ever wished is that others should follow their example.[4]

> To what extent is work part of YOUR identity? Is your first reaction on meeting someone influenced by the work they do?

The changing nature of work

Whatever your view of this essay, what is clear is how the nature of work itself has changed over the past ninety years. From work primarily as a wage and means of survival; the growth and power of trade unions; an emphasis on manufacturing and apprenticeship with repetitive mundane work; few professionally qualified managers and development of business schools; labour disputes, discord and mass industrial relations; broadening work horizons but times of uncertainty, rapid pace of change, working longer and harder, more flexible working, and the impact of information technology.[5]

In their discussion of the twenty-first-century organisation, *Bouchikhi and Kimberly* refer to the customised workplace that represents a radical departure from commonly accepted principles and techniques.[6] They summarise the main differences between nineteenth, twentieth, and twenty-first century paradigms – *see* **Table 2.1**.

An overview of the work environment is given in Figure 2.1.

Table 2.1 Contrasting the paradigms

	19th century	20th century	21st century
Theory of personhood	Interchangeable muscle and energy	A subordinate with a hierarchy of needs	Autonomous and reflexive individual
Information and knowledge	The province of management alone	Management-dominated and shared on a limited basis	Widely diffused
The purpose of work	Survival	Accumulation of wealth and social status	Part of a strategic life plan
Identification	With the firm and/or with the working class	With a social group and/or the firm	The disenfranchised self
Conflict	Disruptive and to be avoided	Disruptive but tolerated and can be settled through collective bargaining	A normal part of life
Division of labour	Managers decide, employees execute	Managers decide, employees execute thoughtfully	Employees and managers decide and execute
Power	Concentrated at the top	Limited, functional sharing/ empowerment	Diffused and shared

Source: Bouchikhi, H. and Kimberly, J. R., 'The Customized Workplace', in Chowdhury, S. (ed.) *Management 21C,* Financial Times Prentice Hall (2000), p. 215. Reproduced with permission from Pearson Education Ltd.

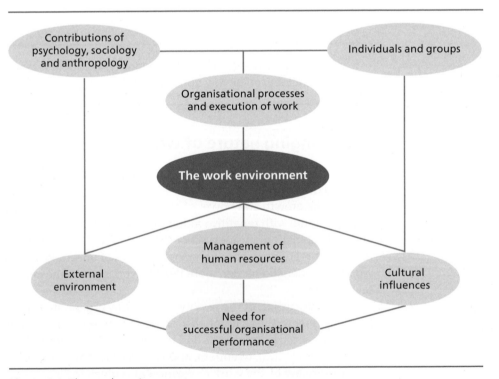

Figure 2.1 The work environment

Orientations to work and work ethic

People differ in the manner and extent of their involvement with, and concern for, work. From information collected about the work situation, organisational participation and involvement with work colleagues, and life outside the organisation, *Goldthorpe et al.* identified three main types of orientation to work: instrumental, bureaucratic and solidaristic.[7]

- Individuals with an **instrumental orientation** define work not as a central life issue but in terms of a means to an end. There is a calculative or economic involvement with work and a clear distinction between work-related and non-work-related activities.

- Individuals with a **bureaucratic orientation** define work as a central life issue. There is a sense of obligation to the work of the organisation and a positive involvement in terms of a career structure. There is a close link between work-related and non-work-related activities.

- Individuals with a **solidaristic orientation** define the work situation in terms of group activities. There is an ego involvement with work groups rather than with the organisation itself. Work is more than just a means to an end. Non-work activities are linked to work relationships.

Opportunities and choices

Some people may well have a set motivation to work, whatever the nature of the work environment. However, different work situations may also influence the individual's orientation to work. For example, the lack of opportunities for teamwork and the satisfaction of social expectations may result in an instrumental orientation to work and a primary concern for economic interests such as pay and security. In other situations where there are greater opportunities to satisfy social needs, membership of work groups may be very important and individuals may have a more solidaristic orientation to work. This often appears to be the case, for example, with people working in the hospitality industry.

According to *Bunting,* although some people in poorly paid jobs requiring long hours do not have other options, for the majority there is a degree of choice in how hard they work. People make their own choices. If they want to work hard, or if they wish to opt out and live the good life, it is up to them.[8] As the number of baby-boomers (born between 1946 and 1963 and typified by a search for security) decline and the proportion of Generation Y (born between 1980 and 1995 and typified by travel first, then a career) increases this will have a further impact on the future world of work.[9] **(See a fuller discussion later in this chapter.)**

Cultural influences

National culture is also a significant influence on orientations to work. For example, *Reeves* comments on the importance of conversation for effective organisational relationships but how this is resisted in the British work culture.

> The Protestant version of the work ethic prevails, implying heads-down work, focused agendas, punctuality, efficiency. In French and Spanish offices, it takes

the first hour to kiss everyone, the second to discuss local gossip and the third to pop out for a coffee and croissant. In Britain, these activities would count as sexual harassment, time-wasting and absenteeism. Many firms have built cafés or break out areas and then discovered people are too scared to use them for fear of looking work-shy.[10]

Internationally there are clear differences between those who work to live and those live to work. For example, Americans and Japanese have an acknowledged very serious attitude to work with apparent acceptance of the demands for regular long hours and forsaking weekends. Work often appears to come first ahead of family time together or holidays. A work ethic of this extent is generally unwelcomed in Europe where regular free time is viewed as an essential part of the work environment.

Is a relaxed work ethic too relaxed?

How would YOU describe your orientation to work? What influences do YOU think determine your work ethic and to what extent do you expect your perspective of, and attitude to work, to change over time?

Emotional labour

Traditionally workplaces were seen as rational, logical places where emotions were excluded or seen in a negative light. The term **emotional labour** arose from *Hochschild's* study into how employees are expected to manage their emotions to exhibit publicly observable specified personal attitudes, facial expressions and bodily displays. Emotional labour is sold for a wage and therefore has exchange value.[11] The original research was of flight attendants in US Delta airlines but many jobs require a display of certain emotions where customer care is linked inextricably with making people feel good. This could include those involved in service-based activities such as care centres, nursing, hospitals, airports, stores, call centres, teaching, social work, dental offices.

There are many forms of emotional labour that require a person to manage a wide range of feelings. For example, the 'toxin handlers' such as divorce lawyers who job is to deliver bad news; and those such as firefighters who face a real chance of actually experiencing pain or loss of their own. Hochschild refers to the polar extremes of emotional labour represented by flight attendants and bill (debt) collectors but who in some ways have similar jobs. Both jobs are subject to changing economic conditions but while the flight attendant is required to *enhance* customer status, the bill collector typically *deflates* customer status. Emotional behaviour distinguishes between **surface acting** – deceiving others and disguising what we feel; faking or pretending by displaying emotion without feeling or experiencing it; and **deep acting** – deceiving oneself this is not a negative reaction; thinking, visualising to induce the emotion in the situation. Deep acting as the edge over surface acting.

While acknowledging the possible cost of conflict or stress, hierarchical control or the worker become estranged or alienated from an aspect of self, Hochschild maintains that emotional labour is potentially good. No customer wants to experience lapses in courtesy or to deal with a surly waitress, crabby bank clerk or flight attendant deliberately avoiding eye contact.

Hochschild draws attention to gender and suggests emotion labour is important in different ways for men and women who tend to undertake different kinds of work. On the whole women tend to specialise more as flight attendants and men as bill collectors. *Wilson* also draws attention to emotional labour as not being 'gender neutral' and to the link between sexuality and emotions. Jobs requiring significant amounts of emotional labour are dominated by women. They are often required to display the sex stereotype in order to be effective in their work.[12]

Acting or hiding emotions

Jobs involving emotional labour are those that involve:

- face-to-face contact with the public;
- producing an emotional state in another person; or
- the exercise of control over the employees' emotional activities.

Emotional labour involves the acting or hiding of emotions. *Mann* identifies three potential situations involving the match between emotions felt and emotions displayed in work roles.

- **Emotional harmony** – where the individual actually feels the emotion required of the display rules and social expectations. This is not emotional labour because the individual is not hiding or facing emotions);
- **Emotional dissonance** – when the emotions displayed for the purposes of the job role are not the emotions actually felt;
- **Emotional deviance** – occurs when the person displays the emotions felt but these are not the ones that are expected to be displayed.[13]

Emotional labour in the hospitality and leisure industry

Many organisations place strategic importance on the customer's perception of service quality and particularly in the hospitality and leisure economy. Companies such as Disney, Marriott, TGI Fridays openly ask their employees to consider themselves on stage when front of house. Identifying the complex relations between emotional labour, *Gursoy et al.* analyse the need to display particular emotions at work and the impact this has on the workforce. 'Unless they are dealing with a task of a negative nature, tourism and hospitality employees are expected to display positive and pleasant emotions, more specifically they are expected to be happy, jolly and cheerful'.[14]

A study by *Chu et al.* 'When we are on stage we smile', points out that some degree of emotional labour is 'critical to the very nature of service and hospitality as the interaction between employees and customers is a significant component of the service encounter which can affect the service quality'. The study considers the emotional effect of 'surface acting' on the staff member and concludes that the emotional dissonance felt when an employee is required to display emotions which are not the real feelings (surface acting) leads to emotional exhaustion and a lack of job satisfaction. However, when an employee tries to feel the required emotion (deep acting) this tends to lead to increased job satisfaction.[15]

What examples of emotional labour have YOU witnessed? What appeared to be the reactions of the people involved?

Work and the organisational setting

For the purposes of our study we view work as taking place within the context of a formal organisational setting. The purpose, nature, objects and structure of an organisation and the environment in which it is operating has an overriding effect on the actual meaning and nature of work, and the manner in which work is actually carried out. All organisations have some function to perform. Through collaborative action, members of an organisation can achieve a synergistic effect and enable objectives to be achieved that could not be attained by the efforts of individuals on their own.

There are many different types of organisations that come in all forms, shapes and sizes, and set up to serve a number of purposes and to meet a variety of needs. Not only are there many different types of organisations, cultural differences in countries can reflect different conceptions of what actually is an organisation.[16] Although we may not always be conscious of it, organisations have a continual and significant influence on both society and our daily lives. Wikipedia list the largest companies by revenue starting with Walmart, State Grid, China National Petroleum; and the top 100 global franchise, starting with McDonald's, KFC, Burger King. One of the world's largest hubs Heathrow Airport handles a million and half passengers every week from 82 nationalities and one third of all UK exports pass through.

Organisations however range in size and influence from extremely large and internationally powerful to the small local one-person corner shop. Think of the multiplicity range of different organisations with diverse purpose, size, structure and staffing and how the operations of these organisations impact upon society and either directly or indirectly upon our daily lives. *See* **Figure 2.2** and consider the examples you could add. A prison and a university could be considered two types of organisations towards the ends of a possible continuum, *see* **Figure 2.5 later in this chapter.**

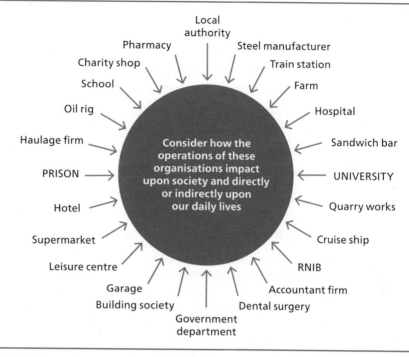

Figure 2.2 Organisations, society and daily lives

The setting influences the organisation

Think also about the different nature of the workplace and what is likely to influence the extent to which you would be happy working in one form of organisation as opposed to another.

Classification of organisations

In order to relate the study of organisational behaviour to one particular type of organisation as distinct from another, it is helpful to group similar types of organisations together. This enables generalisations to be made on the basis of certain characteristic features of organisations within a particular grouping. Organisations can be distinguished by, for example, their nature and type, goods or services provided, size, aims and objectives, and the people who are employed by or who work in them. Organisations can, therefore, be classified in a number of ways and different writers have emphasised particular features of organisations.

A common classification of organisations is by major purpose. This leads to a distinction between, for example,

- **economic**– such as business firms, private equity, partnerships;
- **mutual** – employee-owned such as co-operatives or building societies;
- **public service** – such as government departments, local authorities and hospitals;
- **social enterprise** – social or environmental concerns such as fair trading;
- **protective** – such as the military, trade unions and police forces;
- **social or associative** – such as clubs and societies;
- **religious** – such as churches, monasteries and mosques;
- **political** – such as political parties, pressure groups;
- **educational** – such as universities, colleges and training centres; and
- **voluntary and community** – such as Citizens Advice Bureaux, RNLI, hospital radio.

Such distinction, however, tends to lack refinement, and not all organisations fit simply into one classification. Social enterprise organisations have both social and financial objectives. Many universities combine business consultancy with teaching. Some hospitals are concerned as much with training and/or research as with treatment of patients. One could debate the main purpose of a prison: is it, for example, corrective, protective, penal or educational?

The main purpose of a trade union is seen, presumably, as protection of the interests of its members through their wages and working conditions, but many trade unions also have strong social, educational and political interests. Many organisations serve more than one goal, but although they are multi-purpose organisations it is usually possible to identify one predominant goal (or purpose) by which the organisation can be classified, however crude this classification may be.

What have YOU noticed about the most significant features of organisational behaviour in the different types of organisations?

Private and public sector organisations

Organisations can traditionally be distinguished in terms of two generic groups: private enterprise organisations and public sector organisations. The distinction can be made broadly on the basis of ownership and finance, and the profit motive. **Private-enterprise organisations** are owned and financed by individuals, partners, or shareholders in a joint stock company, and are accountable to their owners or members. They vary widely in nature and size, and the type and scope of work that is carried out. **The nature of work is directed towards a commercial nature such as profit, return on capital employed, market standing or sales level.**

Public-sector organisations are created by government and include, for example, municipal undertakings and central government departments, which do not have profit as their goal. Municipal undertakings such as local authorities are 'owned' by the council tax payers and business ratepayers and financed by

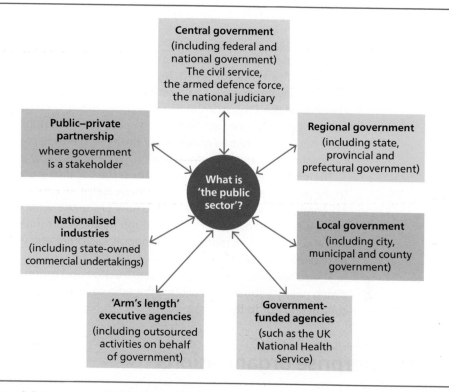

Figure 2.3 Seven aspects of the public sector
Source: From Smart, P. and Inazawa, K. *Human Resource Management in The Public Sector,* Kwansei Gakuin University Press (2011), p. 21. Reproduced with permission.

council taxes, business rates, government grants, loans and charges for certain services. Central government departments are 'state owned' and financed by funds granted by parliament. Public sector organisations have political purposes and do not distribute profits. Any surplus of revenue over expenditure may be reallocated through improved services or reduced charges. **Within public sector organisations work is directed to the provision of a service to, and the well-being of, the community.**

Smart and *Inazawa* suggests that although the size, scope and structure of the public sector differ extensively between different countries there are seven common features which define the public sector in terms of seven main aspects of activity[17] **(see Figure 2.3).**

The CIPD employee outlook survey reports an increase in several scores for employees in the public sector: job satisfaction, opportunities for employee voice, aspects of engagement, trust and confidence in senior leaders. Provision for opportunities to grow is also more likely for public sector workers than employees from the private and voluntary sectors.

Source: CIPD, 'Employee Outlook Survey: Employee views on working life', Spring 2017.

What do you think are the reasons for these findings?

Not-for-profit organisations

The increasing scale of privatisation and the blurring of commercial interests and social interests have led to an alternative classification of organisations: those run for **profit**; and those clearly **not-for-profit.** Not-for-profit organisations include on the one hand charities, private societies and most religious organisations, and on the other hand National Health Service hospitals, universities, prisons and most government and local authority departments. However, even in not-for-profit public sector organisations there has been increased government pressure to ensure cost-effectiveness, investment by private sector involvement, and efficiency and economy in their operations.

There has been much controversy over the contracting out of state-run institutions to the private sector. *Gwyther* for example questions whether this is a 'failed experiment' and suggests few would now praise the services of the railways or the utilities. Gwyther also refers to the tough business of running Britain's private jails; and queries with low margins, a monopoly customer and volatile users has the system reached breaking point?[18]

The collapse in January 2018 of construction and group service giant Carillion owing nearly £3bn lead to extensive media coverage over the controversy of contracting out to the private sector.

Social enterprise organisations

In recent years increasing attention has been given to a particular form of organisation that brings together aspects of both the private and public sectors – the **social-enterprise organisation**. Although they function as companies, work is directed to their main concern with the community in general rather than shareholder value or specific public interest. Social enterprise organisations promote the well-being of society but are not charities and they suggest elements of both capitalism and socialism.

Unlike not-for-profit organisations, social enterprise organisations have a triple bottom line trading in goods and/or services with social, environmental and financial objectives. However, as the name suggests they have a primary concern with a social purpose and the creation of social value. An underlying question for social enterprise organisations is the extent to which they can be both successful and responsible? **See the discussion on corporate social responsibility in Chapter 16.** Social enterprises are very diverse and may take a number of different forms including community enterprises, farmers' markets, leisure trusts, recycling, transport and energy, provision of local services, and job creation and training. In the public sector there are many examples of social enterprises in primary and community health, care and welfare services.[19]

Another example is Jamie Oliver's project 'Fifteen', which offered disadvantaged young people opportunities for a career in the restaurant industry. Other well-known examples include the Eden Project, The Big Issue, Café Direct and Divine Chocolate. **See also the work of the Clink Charity in the Organisational Behaviour in Action Case Study at the end of this chapter.**

International examples

Social enterprise organisations are also developing internationally. A common theme is empowering people and harnessing their skills and abilities. A particular example of a social enterprise organisation is Grameen Bank, which provides microcredit loans without collateral to rural villages in Bangladesh. In Singapore there is a non-profit 'Social Innovation Park' that acts as a form of incubator for start-up social enterprises including a dance centre which channels profits to bursaries for low-income students, cooking and deportment lessons for plus-sized people, and opportunities for individuals with untapped talents to showcase their original creations or to perform a dance or song.

An example of social enterprise in the Arabian Gulf is Sidab women in Oman who have mastered the formation of their own small business to market their sewing and photography, Omani home cooking and henna applications. The European Commission also recognises the increasing potential of social enterprises as pioneers in developing new markets and creating sustainable jobs. However, entrepreneurs may lack business skills and there is a lack of measurement of the social value generated.[20]

How do YOU see the main differences in the nature of work in private enterprise, public sector and social enterprise organisations? In which type of organisation would you most prefer to work?

Common features of organisations

Whatever their classification all organisations have their own individual character, culture and sense of identity and differ in their attributes, processes and methods of working. Despite the differences it must be remembered that all organisations are structures of people. Through collaborate action members can achieve a synergistic effect. They exist in order to achieve objectives and to provide satisfaction for their members. There are at least three common features of any organisation: people, objectives and structure.

It is the interaction of **people** in order to achieve **objectives** that form the basis of an organisation. Some form of **structure** is needed by which people's interactions and efforts are channelled and co-ordinated. We can add to these a fourth factor: management. The interrelationship of people, objectives and structure, together with the efficient **management of non-human and human resources,** will determine the success or failure of the organisation and the extent of its effectiveness **(see Figure 2.4).**

Differences in applications

Despite these common features the structure, management and functioning of individual organisations will vary because of differences in their nature and type, respective goals and objectives, and the behaviour of the people who work in them. Consider for example just two types of organisations towards the opposite ends of a possible continuum – say a maximum-security prison and a university largely concerned with academic research – as a framework on which to focus attention. We can appreciate readily that although both types of organisation will be concerned with the basic activities of organisation and management, their actual procedures and methods of operation, orientation and behaviour of members and actual nature of work will differ considerably **(see Figure 2.5).**

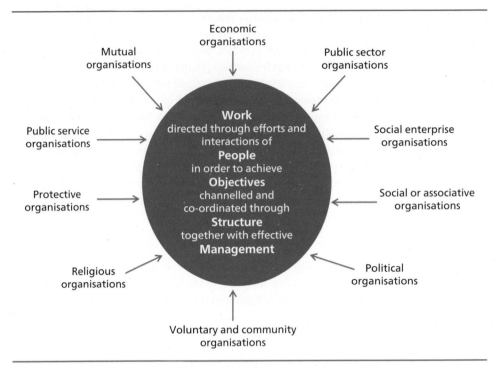

Figure 2.4 Common features of organisations

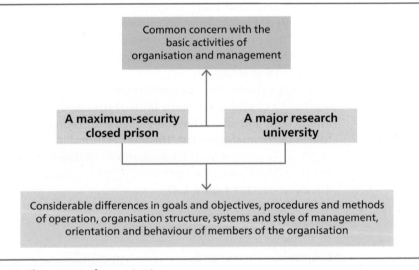

Figure 2.5 The nature of organisations

 What do YOU see as the major difficulties and long-term future of social enterprise organisations?

Formal and informal organisations

So far we have been looking at the nature of formal organisations – that is, organisations deliberately planned and structured to meet stated objectives. However, a major feature of the work environment is that whatever the type or nature of an organisation or its formal structure, an informal organisation will always be present **(*see* Figure 2.6)**.

A **formal organisation** is deliberately planned and created with stated objectives. It is a pattern of roles, hierarchy of authority and responsibility. The object of co-ordination is activities, not people. An organisation chart may give a representation of the formal structure. Other examples of the formal organisation are rules and regulations, policy manuals, standing orders and job descriptions. The formal organisation can exist independently of the membership of particular individuals.

By contrast the **informal organisation** arises from the interaction of people working in the organisation, their psychological and social needs, and the development of groups with their own relationships and norms of behaviour, irrespective of those defined within the formal structure. The informal organisation is flexible and loosely structured, relationships may be left undefined, and membership is spontaneous with varying degrees of involvement.

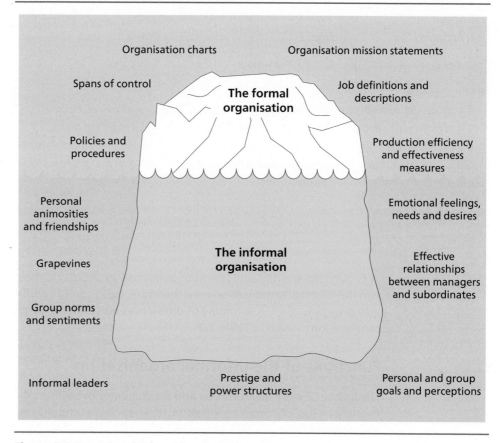

Figure 2.6 Formal and informal organisations
Source: Lysons, K. 'Organisational Analysis', supplement to Manager, *The British Journal of Administrative Management,* No. 18, March/April 1997. Reproduced with permission of The Institute of Administrative Management.

Table 2.2 Comparison of the formal and the informal organisation

Characteristic	Formal organisation	Informal organisation
1 Structure		
A Origin	Planned	Spontaneous
B Rationale	Rational	Emotional
C Characteristics	Stable	Dynamic
2 Position terminology	Job	Role
3 Goals	Profitability or service to society	Member satisfaction
4 Influence		
A Base	Position	Personality
B Type	Authority	Power
C Flow	Top-down	Bottom-up
5 Control mechanisms	Threat of firing, demotion	Physical or social sanctions (norms)
6 Communication		
A Channels	Formal channels	Grapevine
B Networks	Well-defined, follow formal lines	Poorly defined, cut across regular channels
C Speed	Slow	Fast
D Accuracy	High	Low
7 Charting the organisation	Organisation chart	Sociogram
8 Miscellaneous		
A Individuals included	All individuals in work group	Only those 'acceptable'
B Interpersonal relations	Prescribed by job description	Arise spontaneously
C Leadership role	Assigned by organisation	Result of membership agreement
D Basis for interaction	Functional duties or position	Personal characteristics, ethnic background, status
E Basis for attachment	Loyalty	Cohesiveness

Source: Adapted from Gray, J. L. and Starke, F. A. *Organizational Behavior: Concepts and Applications,* fourth edition, Merrill Publishing Company (1988), p. 432. Reproduced with permission from Pearson Education Inc.

Group relationships and norms of behaviour exist outside the official structure and the informal organisation may, therefore, be in conflict with the aims of the formal organisation. A summary of differences between the formal and the informal organisation is given in **Table 2.2.**

Functions of the informal organisation

The nature of work environment and activities and behaviour of people is influenced strongly by this informal organisation. It can serve a number of important functions and provides for:

- **satisfaction of members' social needs** and a sense of personal identity and belonging.

- **additional channels of communication** – for example, through the 'grapevine', information of importance to particular members is communicated quickly.
- **means of motivation** – for example, through status, social interaction, peer rating, variety in routine or tedious jobs, and informal methods of work.
- **feeling of stability and security,** and through informal 'norms' of behaviour can exercise a form of control over members.

The informal organisation, therefore, has an important influence on the morale, motivation, job satisfaction and performance of staff. It can provide members with greater opportunity to use their initiative and creativity in both personal and organisational development. Covert and informal activities may also have economic consequences for the organisation in terms of added values and/or costs that escape ordinary accounting procedures.[21]

> Buying a coffee machine and water cooler could be the most important investments a company ever makes in its future. For it's at these social hubs of office life that the real business often gets done, as part of a casual chat or chance meeting.[22]

(The importance and nature of groups, and reasons why people form into groups, both formal and informal, are discussed in Chapter 8.)

Friendships and relationships at work

One particular aspect of the informal organisation that has received increasing attention is the possible effects of personal friendships and relationships at work, and potential conflict between the informal and formal organisation. For example, according to *Vernon,* whilst work is one of the best sources of friends as well as the most desirable place to have them, the trouble is that friendships at work are full of ambiguities. For friendships the trouble with work is that you are there to be useful: to do something for a client, team or boss. Professional friendships will always be influenced and possibly determined by the utility factor.[23] Potential conflict between personal freedom and team performance is discussed in **Chapter 8**.

The Code of Conduct for the *Royal Bank of Scotland* refers to the responsibility to speak up if something is wrong. No one has the authority to tell any colleague to do or ignore something against the Bank's values or policies or is illegal. Avoid financial conflicts of interest by never making transactions for personal gain, or on behalf of friends or family and take action and tell a manager if there is a potential or suspected conflict of interest.[24]

Workplace relationships: ten ways to love your work colleagues

A feature in *HuffPost Conversations* suggests that workplace relationships can have a positive impact on your lives. Work colleagues can feel like a second family, provide social and emotional support, make your job more enjoyable, and encourage employee engagement in the workplace. Drawing on the work of Max Blumberg there are ten ways to find common ground with your co-workers.

- **Look for similarities** – we tend to be attracted to people socially similar to ourselves so look for common ground to use in a social situation.

- **Keep it positive** – and be consistent and predictable, and try not to let your neuroses hang out.
- **Start a conversation** – show interest in another person and ask open questions.
- **Do something nice for them** – remember the principle of reciprocity is a key to befriending a co-worker.
- **Turn up to work more often** – many friends now meet through social media so to improve person-to-person real life friendships go to work more.
- **Take it slow** – don't rush, work scenario friendships take longer to develop than ordinary social ones.
- **Do your research** – the work environment is more structured and formal so you need to think more about perception.
- **Respect their privacy** – don't be a nosy snoop or dig too deep into everybody else's business.
- **Avoid confrontation** – if you don't get along with another colleague, don't confront the issue but try to avoid the situation.
- **Remember it's worth the investment** – even if you are shy or have a busy social or demanding family life remember it is worth getting to know your colleagues.[25]

To what extent do YOU see friendships and relationships at work as in potential conflict with the formal organisation? Are there examples that colleagues can share?

Work/life balance

We have looked at the importance, nature and some main features of the work environment as an integral feature of human civilisation. But what role do, or should, organisations play in the lives of their staff or with broader concerns for the work/life balance? What are the ethical considerations and how much also depends upon the individual's orientations to work?

It is not easy to determine the extent to which attention to the quality of working life and the work/life balance is based on the exercise of a genuine social responsibility and a moral or ethical motivation; or based primarily on the pursuit of economic efficiency and motivated through good business practice and enlightened self-interest. Opinions appear to be divided. For example, *Sternberg*, whilst recognising the importance of treating employees ethically, does not support the belief that a business should be run for the benefit of its employees or should, by action or by omission, encourage employees to have inappropriate expectations of the business.[26]

The European Commission, however, still stresses the importance of helping people to improve their work/life balance, and continues to unveil a series of packages to update existing EU legislation. The Commission also draws attention to the interactions between work/life balance and public policy. The way people balance competing demands may influence, for example, the number of children people choose to have, or if they decide to work or not. Public policy itself influences these choices: the existence of public provision of care for children and other dependants, for instance, or legal rights to family-related leave.[27]

Is work/life balance still important?

Popular press articles often suggest that work is still a large component of what gives meaning to people's lives and provide examples of big lottery or pools winners staying in work and often in their same, even apparently routine, jobs. Other surveys and reports continue to suggest that the workplace is no longer a central feature of social activity. For a majority of people the main reason for work remains the need for money to fulfil the necessities of life. However, much still appears to depend on the extent of an individual's social contacts and activities outside of the work situation.

Many staff still have specific places of work and agreed times in which to undertake their duties. However, technology and the internet allow for greater flexibility in work schedules. So-called knowledge workers, who work from home on computers, with greater control over their roles and work times, arguably have improved motivation and productivity.

In a thought-provoking article, *Reeves* questions the extent to which progress has been made in establishing a healthy equilibrium between our working day and personal time and if work/life balance is still an issue or already past its sell-by date. The phrase has been contested for the presumption that life is better than work and that the two are separable in a clear-cut way that allows a calculation of 'balance' between them. Continuing concern with the issue cannot be explained simply with reference to working hours. Work/life balance is moving towards a concern with flexibility and parenting. It taps into a desire for greater autonomy at work, a shift in gender roles within the family, the possibilities of technology and an intensification of working life.[28]

The *Advisory, Conciliation and Arbitration Service* (ACAS) point out that the pace of change is now more rapid than ever and with organisations under constant pressure

I am happy with my work/life balance: how about you?

to match the requirements of customer and business there is a need for work/life balance and flexible working.[29] **(Flexible patterns of working are discussed in Chapter 12.)**

Family structure and work satisfaction

The *Department for Business, Innovation & Skills (BIS)* draws attention to the continuing importance of family structure and work satisfaction.

> **The issue of how to promote the balance of work and family responsibilities is a major policy concern and has deserved increasing scholarly activity attention in recent years. As this report has shown the relationship between the labour market and the household is an important determinant in understanding people's living conditions in current society. Particularly, this is the case for women who traditionally have assumed most of the duties in the rearing of children while in the last few decades have increasingly been incorporated in the labour market to pursue a professional career.**

BIS point out that work/life balance (WLB) policies play an important role in worker satisfaction and this effect seem to be gender-neutral. Male workers in 'family-friendly' environments also experience higher levels of job satisfaction and involvement.[30]

Business Link also emphasise the business benefits of improved work/life balance. It can enable employees to feel more in control of their working life and lead to increased productivity, lower absenteeism and a happier, less stressed workforce. Flexible working and work/life balance policies will also foster a more positive perception of an employer. This can lead to better relations with employees and greater staff loyalty, commitment and motivation, reducing staff turnover and recruitment costs.[31]

A family-friendly model

According to *Black* employers that promote a healthy work/life balance maximise productivity and optimise their corporate performance. In order to attract the best staff there is a rise in the family-friendly employer offering best packages to staff including flexible working conditions and characteristics to promote a happy and healthy work/life balance. Black suggests five, not mutually exclusive, reasons: the commercial reality of flexible working; the contribution of female leadership; advantages of diversity; an aid to recruitment; demographic changes. Black also suggests three parts to a family-friendly model.

- **Culture** – This important aspect comes from management. You need someone very senior involved and the message must be clear.
- **Emotional and developmental** – Coaching and mentoring to help parents get clarity on choices they will need to make.
- **Practical** – Solutions to support the culture such as networks, childcare and elderly care support. The old networks of friends and families that once existed do not exist so clearly in modern, flexible working life.

To what extent do YOU believe concern for work/life balance should form part of the ethical concern or underlying values of an organisation?

Changing nature of work organisations

Increasing business competitiveness, globalisation, shifting labour markets, rapid technological progress, the move towards more customer-driven markets, a 24/7 society and demands of work/life balance have led to a period of constant change and the need for greater organisational flexibility. The rapid spread of new technology and the impact of various socio-economic and political factors have attracted increasing attention to the concept of corporate responsibilities and business ethics **(discussed in Chapter 16).**

The combination of these influences is transforming the way we live and work. And this clearly has significant implications for organisational behaviour. It is important to understand how organisations function and the pervasive influences which they exercise over the behaviour and actions of people in the workplace.

The impact of technology

As technology continues to advance and change, it has a major impact on the work environment including: location, structure and pace of work; nature and design of jobs; systems of management, supervision and control; customer relationships; patterns of communication; security; and the informal organisation and social interactions. **These topics are discussed more fully in Chapter 13.**

Humanisation of organisations

The evolving nature of work organisations and the social context has led to a climate of constant change and the need for greater organisational flexibility. Managers need to be aware of new psychological contracts and to adopt alternative styles of management. *Cloke and Goldsmith* refer to the rise of organisational democracy. There is a demand for alternative organisational practices, and a far-reaching transformation has already begun, based on the idea that management as a system fails to open the heart or free the spirit. The age of management is coming to an end and the real push for the future is for more authentic human relationships and the humanisation of organisations as crucibles for personal growth and development.[32]

A summary of the changing context of work including topics discussed in subsequent chapters is set out in the concept map Figure 2.7.

The changing context of work

- Traditional v. Emergent work contexts
- Employee skills in the new organisation
- Work/life balance
- Flexible working rights

Flexible working rights

Anyone can ask their employer to allow flexible working patterns, but in the UK the government has introduced a statutory right in order to encourage applications. This legal framework allows someone to request flexible working if the person:

- is an employee with 26 or more weeks' service and
- has a child under the age of six (or disabled child under 18) and
- is responsible for that child and is applying to care for that child

or

- is someone caring for an adult living at the same address as the employee

If these conditions are met, the employer must give the request "Serious consideration". Employers can refuse on certain "business Grounds" described in the legislation

> Remember – employees sometimes just need time away from work to pursue their own personal interests!

Work/life balance

Factors associated with increased emphasis on the Work situation

- Deep interest in the nature of the work itself
- Income a high priority
- Employee unempowered and not confident
- Organisation norms expect attendance
- Organisation pay dictated by time attendance
- Employee has home problems and would rather be at work.

Early trades unions demanded that on working days a worker should have: 'Eight hours work, eight hours leisure, and eight hours sleep'

Factors associated with increased emphasis on Life outside work

- Formal recognition by the organisation that employees have commitments other than work (including child/elderly people care)
- Employee outputs based on results, not time attended
- Excellent organisational ICT systems, enabling easy communication with employees
- Organisation climate resulting in confident employees

Traditional & emergent work Contexts compared

Some observed differences between traditional & emergent organisations include the following:

Note 1 These are Tendencies can exceptions can Often be Found!

Note 2 the nature Of the ion's Organisational demand work / many traditional A 'traditional' Approach

Characteristic	Traditional	Emergent
Organisation structure (1)	Many management layers	Few management layers
Organisation structure (2)	Hierarchical	Flexible
Career path for employees (1)	Heavily organisation influenced	Principally based on individual's own plans
Career path for employees (2)	Based in very few organisations	Based in many organisations
Employee development	Largely restricted to current job	Aimed at future as well as current job
Organisation output	Product/service based	Knowledge based
Management style (1)	More formal	More relaxed
Management style (2)	Inward-looking	More broadly based on outside society
Decisionmaking	Often hierarchical	Frequently collective
Workplace	Office location based	Field or home based

Employee skills in the new organisation

Emergent organisations tend to have fewer management positions. One implication for employees is that in addition to their own technical or professional expertise a working competency is needed in such topics as:

- **Clerical and administrative work** – because support staff are increasingly seen as an unwarranted overhead expense
- **Information & Communications Technology (ICT)** – because emerging organisations are highly dependent on new technologies
- **Advanced personal communication systems** – especially for field or embossed workers
- **'Customer-facing' skills** – because employees increasingly deal with customers/clients
- **Financial skills** – to help in understanding the business as a whole
- **Change-coping and change management capabilities** – because rapid changes in the business are a common feature

Figure 2.7 The changing context of work
Source: Copyright © 2011 The Virtual Learning Materials Workshop. Reproduced with permission.

Silly workplace rules

All workplaces need rules. But it is clear that some rules are simply ridiculous. Some companies seem to make rules designed to alienate and disengage their staff.

Amongst some of silly workplace rules that have been reported are:

Time Keeping – At one business if you were two minutes you were docked 15 minutes worth of pay – at another staff weren't allowed to travel more than 20 metres from the building at lunch time in case they were late in returning.

Silent Treatment – Employees reported not being able to speak out loud except in 'designated areas'. Others were told not to say 'hello' to a customer – it could only be 'good morning' or 'good afternoon'.

Beverage Blunders – Some workplaces banned their staff from drinking water; another refused to let staff walk up and down stairs carrying liquids; worse still at least one company would not let staff have drinks on their desks in case they spilled anything.

Toilet Trouble – One of the most common ridiculous rules is a strict time frame on toilet breaks – as little as three minutes. Some firms require their staff to ask for permission to head to the toilet and some even searched their employees before they could go to the loo.

Dress Code Dummies – A number of reports have come to light of having to wear specifically coloured clothes to match the businesses colours, often women have been banned from wearing trousers. Perhaps, mostly insanely of all, one worker was sent home for refusing the dress down on 'dress down Friday'.

Different generations and age groups

Much attention is being given to the consequences from demographic changes and in particular the political, social and economic outcomes of an ageing population. *Management Today* commissioned a survey from FreshMinds looking at the future world of work and the contrasting attitudes and perspectives of three different generations and age groups:

- the confident, footloose, wire-free **Generation Y** (born between 1980 and 1995 and typified by travel first, then a career);
- the mellow **baby-boomers** (born between 1946 and 1963 and typified by a search for security); and
- the pig-in-the-middle **Generation X** (born between 1964 and 1980 and typified by after the slog, the rewards).

From the on-line survey of 1000 people, supplemented by three extensive focus-group sessions, emerges 'a complex picture of a workforce in a state of flux, struggling to come to terms with the changed realities of today'. This new world of work is termed 'Work 2.0'. As the number of baby-boomers declines and the proportion of Generation Y increases this will have an impact on the work environment.

Generation X have another three decades at work but this is a different world of work from the one they entered fifteen or so years ago and there is less confidence and few guarantees about their financial future.

By contrast, **Generation Y** will have fewer problems in adapting to the changed realities of the twenty-first century. For example, they are likely to be more technologically sophisticated.

Encouraging the three different age groups to work happily as a team will require imagination on all sides and competent management. For example, the influence of the war on the baby-boomers and the search for security is not something understood readily by Generations X or Y. The message from Alistair Leathwood, managing director of FreshMinds Talent, is that the rules of engagement at work have changed. 'Work 2.0 signals a new social contract between employers and employees – one premised upon short-term commitment, flexibility and, most importantly, one where the employee's loyalty to their employer is not expected to be any greater than what little the employer provides to its staff.'[33]

Although these generational characteristics are broad stereotypes and differences will clearly exist between individuals, they may help provide an understanding of contrasting work orientations and attitudes, job security, and work/life balance; and with implications for social interactions, motivation, and styles of leadership and management.[34] **(See also stereotyping in Chapter 6.)**

Aside from Generations X and Y and the baby-boomers, as people live and work longer there will be a wider spread of age groups in the workforce.

Technology and social media

In a discussion concerning the impact of technology and social media, *Gazzaley and Rosen* identify three additional generations of Americans. Added to the baby-boomers, Generation X and Generation Y are:

- Net Generation (1980–1989);
- iGeneration (1990–1999);
- Generation C (born in the new millennium).

Although younger generations believe they can multitask better than older generations, their real-life behaviours and performance suffer when concurrently engaged in activities using multiple forms of media.[35]

Different motivations

The different generations are motivated by different things. With increasingly more Generation Y stepping into managerial roles *Anne Riches* questions the antagonism from Generation X and the baby-boomers towards Generation Y. For many baby-boomers and Generation X job security is a big concern. They have to respond to different values, drivers and fears. They are fearful of not having enough money to fund their retirement or become concerned with increases in rates on hefty mortgages. Generation Y are not frightened by the future. Most do not own property yet or cannot afford it. They are not inspired or motivated by the threat of being fired, not promoted or no salary increase. Generation Y will not stay in a job they don't enjoy with people they don't like. In an era of flat wages growth why shouldn't Generation Y decide to move on if they get fed up with their manager, the organisational culture or just want to explore other things?[36]

Ageism the last taboo?

A number of commentators suggest that age is the most common form of discrimination, and possible more in high-tech companies. *Gale* maintains that in a society worshipping youth, older workers are often unfairly overlooked. Well-managed diversity results in less risk of groupthink **(discussed in Chapter 8)** yet age is far behind gender or race on the diversity agenda. Older workers struggle to get equal treatment and employers tend to invest less in their training and development, and unfortunately ageist views are unlikely to go anywhere fast. Gale reports an example of a senior manager on the receiving end of age discrimination but who would still hire younger candidates. There is a long way to go when even victims of prejudice believe it is justified. There is however progress with companies such as B&Q, McDonald's, BMW and Barclays making a conscious decision to employ older workers.[37]

What examples can YOU provide of significant difference in perspectives and attitudes to work of different generations? How important is an ageing population to the study of organisational behaviour?

B&Q is one company that has encouraged older workers to apply for jobs in stores, valuing their DIY knowledge and experience
Source: Management Today, Issue 3, 2017, p. 43.

The future of the workplace

As part of a round-table debate hosted by the Royal College of Art, *Gwyther* questions what effect the workplace becoming more fragmented will have on the culture of an organisation? Is it a weakness that people aren't communicating face to face on a regular basis?[38]

A survey report commissioned by financial protection company Unum highlights that the approach to the workplace will need to be significantly different in the future (2030). With an increasingly turbulent social, political and economic environment human resource departments must take care to enable people to work better for longer. The needs of employees change constantly and rapidly and organisations will need to be responsive to these changes. *'The workplace of the future is going to be increasingly people-centric, and organisations competing for talent will need to respond by being more supportive of their staff than ever before'.*

The report reviews key trends of a changing workplace:

- **The Ageless Workforce** – the rise of an ageless workplace promotes the idea of working forever and enables 'returnment' instead of retirement.
- **The Mindful Workplace** – workplace care will need to deliver a new set of values nurturing health and performance of the mind.
- **The Intuitive Workplace** – delivering a lean and agile work culture to create an all-encompassing, intelligent and intuitive working environment.
- **The Collaborative Workplace** – promoting open social exchange and a flat organisation to create a collaborative, co-operative and convivial workplace.[39]

Workers at Google take catnaps in £5,000 sleep pods and hold meetings in a caravan. You can get a staff pass for your dog, the canteen serves free lobster – but don't you dare get fat!

Source: 'The World's Wackiest Workplace', *Daily Mail* 5 July, 2017, pp. 30–31.

How do YOU view the workplace of the future and working for organisations such as B&Q or Google? Do you feel encouraged or fearful?

Hot-desking

An increasing number of organisations are introducing clear desks or hot-desking. LEGO's London office removed the idea of employees having their own dedicated desk and managers working in offices in favour of 'activity-based working'. Instead of the traditional department the concept aims to encourage cross-organisation collaboration. If a member of staff vacates a desk for longer than 90 minutes they have to clear the desk for use by someone. Employees are free to manage their own space but must keep papers to a minimum and not leave out confidential paperwork. They can use a meeting room, a quiet zone or general office area.[40]

Some people express concern about added stress, and health and safety concerns from working in a hot-desking environment and the greater use of shared space and equipment.

Homeworking

Another feature of the flexible changing nature of the workplace is the growth in homeworking. Most commentators suggest the benefits outweigh drawbacks.[41]

However it appears that few homeworkers carry out all or the majority of their work at home. Benefits to the organisation include reduced overheads, increased productivity, wider choice when hiring, and more ideas from a wider diverse workforce.[42] The greatest barrier to homeworking success is that of trust and managerial attitude about employees needing to be seen to be considered productive.[43]

Working from home does not appeal to everyone and needs to be managed well especially for full-time homeworkers. Many report a feeling of detachment from work and miss interaction with colleagues. Without a clocking-off time or commute homeworkers may find it difficult to unwind after work.

Future jobs and skills

A report from UKCES points out that it is not possible to predict the future but aims to influence and challenge thinking in a constructive, creative way. If current trends continue, the UK workforce will be multi-generational, older, more international with women playing a stronger role. The highly skilled will push for better work–life balance but others will experience greater insecurity of employment and income. With shrinking workforces fewer employees will be able to enjoy long-term contracts. The report details trends shaping the future of UK jobs and skills up to 2030.[44] **(See Figure 2.8.)**

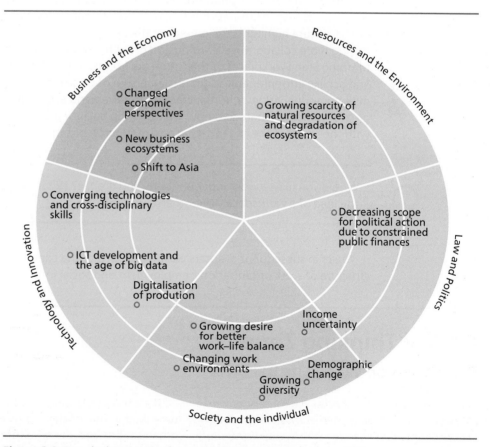

Figure 2.8 Trends shaping the future of UK jobs and skills up to 2030
Source: 'The Future of Work: Jobs and Skills in 2030', UKCES, 03.14, p. 8.

Workspace hosting

An increasingly popular movement is the use of shared short-term workspaces. Online companies such as Spacehop or OfficeRiders use online platforms through which people rent space in their home to professionals and businesses in which to work or hold meetings.

> For 20 euro, I'm spending the day in Tarek's Parisian flat, in the new world of work. While companies like WeWork are popularising the concept of co-working in shared spaces, companies like OfficeRiders are going a step further into the sharing economy – it's an Airbnb for workspaces, where homeowners like Tarek rent out their underutilised rooms to entrepreneurs, freelancers, start-ups, or people on business trips, like me, who'd prefer not to work in a Starbucks.
>
> *Source:* 'Working smarter – anytime, anywhere', *Management Today,* June 2016, p. 31.

A feature in *Management Today* notes the word 'workspace' rather than workplace in recognition that work can happen anywhere. The nature of the work we do, when and how we do it is becoming more individual. More than half of young people expect eventually to work independently or in small enterprises. In response some large corporations are moving away from traditional hierarchies and creating more agile business models, cross-functional teams and matrixed working.

The feature highlights the emergent theme of 'democratisation' of the workplace driving more collaborative learning and growth. Examples are Zappos.com, WL Gore, Morning Star. Workplaces of the future are likely to encourage employees to think and act like entrepreneurs with full ownership of particular domains or projects and minimum supervision or bureaucracy. The on-demand economy is about creating greater choice in where and how we work: the balancing of individualisation of work with the needs of the organisation and productive output.[45]

Would you like to work independently and mobile? What are your thoughts on the idea of a workspace rather than a workplace?

Topics in subsequent chapters will discuss further the changing nature and structure of work organisations, employment and social interactions.[46]

Critical Thinking Zone
Reflections on Work–Life Balance

In this zone, we critically discuss the concept of work–life balance and evaluate whether it is still an important feature of organisational life in the twenty-first century workplace.

The concept of work–life balance (WLB) has been described as one of the top three challenges facing organisations and the HR profession.[47] Theory and practice suggests that a major challenge has been the implementation, take up and monitoring of programmes that were intended to give the workforce a greater level of harmony between their work and personal lives and provide more flexibility in how, where and then they complete work tasks.[48] A further challenge has been working with multiple, subjective perceptions of the concept and the value that end users may or may not attach to organisational initiatives that are in place.[49]

In general, work–life balance has also become a rather contested phrase. Gregory and Milner[50] assert that the word 'balance' is inappropriate in this context, as it infers that work is not an integral part of life and it is somehow possible to trade one against the other. Beatson[48] and Lutz[51] concur and argue that a more contemporary parlance should be 'work–life blend' as there are times in life when, despite the best intentions, people struggle to find a clear dichotomy between the two. The dissonance caused by this metaphorical tug of war can lead to inter-role conflict, tension and psychological distress.[52] In consideration of this, Lutz concludes that the notion of balance is an idealistic, unachievable standard, the naive pursuit of which can result in a continuous sense of failure.

Is Work–Life Balance Still an Important Feature of Organisational Life?

Arguably, the answer to this question is 'yes.' However, the importance that is ascribed to WLB may, as we established above, be a matter of subjective opinion between employers who offer the benefits and individuals who may or may not use them. Regardless of the complexities and challenges surrounding the concept, work is busier now than ever. The globalised, boundaryless, 24/7, hyperconnected, always on society has promulgated a culture where the business world never sleeps and individuals have constant access to work.[53] MacCormick et al.[54] describe this phenomenon as 'job creep.' To stem this tide, legislative changes, along with a raft of WLB campaigns, have reinforced the efforts of employers and HR managers to provide working arrangements that are more flexible, diverse and mutually beneficial to all parties concerned. Yet, despite employers' positive attitudes towards, and commitment to, WLB and the mutual benefits that can be derived from its implementation, including increased production, a reduction in absenteeism and enhanced job satisfaction,[55] evidence suggests that some individuals are not utilising the statutory or organisational-based initiatives that their employers

provide. This is highlighted in the CIPD UK Working Lives Survey.[56] The study found that only 9% of employees sampled ($n = 5215$) use flexitime arrangements that are in place (33% don't use) and only 6% work from home (34% don't). These findings infer that *something* is clearly preventing these individuals from making use of WLB initiatives. But *what* is it?

According to McCarthy et al.[57] and Daverth et al.,[58] one reason could be the relationship between line managers and their staff. Their research suggests that managers who have a proximal or close relationship with their staff, and are supportive of their work context, make a major difference between engagement and non-engagement in WLB initiatives. Beatson[59] argues that managers can also be a *barrier,* either due to staff perceptions that they are unsupportive or because the organisation, through its culture and practices, has not effectively communicated the availability of, and support for, opportunities to achieve more flexibility in their work.

The Impact of WLB on Organisational Behaviour in the Workplace

While the benefits of WLB to both individuals and the organisation are well documented in the literature and research data and cannot be discounted, the CIPD[60] has raised concerns that WLB initiatives are excessively focused on meeting the needs of carers and parents. Beauregard[49] concurs and caveats that organisations should be mindful of the potential 'backlash' from childfree staff, who believe that such initiatives are unfair and skewed towards parents, resulting in increased workloads if they do not use them. This clearly has implications for organisational behaviour in the workplace. Beauregard advises that those affected might overtly display their dissatisfaction by arriving at work late without permission to do so, create their own flexibility to redress the perceived inequity or take longer breaks than are normal or acceptable.

Different Strokes for Different Folks

To conclude, WLB is still an important feature of organisational life in the twenty-first-century workplace. However, people's wants, needs and expectations of work and life differ. What might be overwork to one person may be equilibrium to another. Whether it is a matter of subjective perception or people's reality, the search for balance or harmony and the decision to engage in WLB initiatives, should, arguably, be a personal choice and what feels right for them and their context. As Sara Just, Executive Producer of PBS News Hour in the US, stated 'the truth is my work–life balance tilts pretty hard toward work. I know we are supposed to fight that, but . . . if you love what you do, why apologise for the imbalance?'.[61]

Questions

As we have seen, WLB is a controversial concept. With the above in mind, and based on your experiences, answer the following questions.

1. *What other* reasons can you identify that may be discouraging individuals from engaging with WLB initiatives, particularly as they are geared towards providing a more flexible approach to work?

2. Evidence suggests that WLB initiatives are not working in the way in which they were intended. *What alternative* benefits could an organisation introduce to encourage more widespread engagement with, and participation in, flexible work practices?

3. *What other challenges* does WLB present to managers and HR practitioners in managing organisational behaviour in the twenty-first-century workplace?

Summary – Chapter 2 'The work environment'

For most people work is a central life issue and to a person's perceived identity. Work is ingrained as something we are expected to do and to be productive. People differ in the manner and extent of their involvement with and concern for work. Work takes place within the context of an organisational setting and has an overriding effect on the meaning, nature and direction of work. Organisations can be classified in a number of ways. A traditional distinction is between private enterprise and public sector. Emotional labour is when employees are required to manage their emotions or feelings at work. A major feature of the work environment is the informal organisation which arises from the interaction of people and their psychological and social needs, and group relationships. Increasing attention is focused on the work/life balance and the role organisations should play in concerns for the quality of working life. Work organisations today are facing greater uncertainty, constant change, the need for greater flexibility and the impact of information technology. Attention is also being given to demographic change and an ageing population. Approach to the workplace needs to be significantly different in the future. One increasing popular movement is the use of shared short-term workspaces rather than workplaces.

Group discussion activities

Undertake each of these activities in small groups as indicated by your tutor. Before you start your discussion establish a non-threatening environment within the group and confirm confidentiality will be honoured.

First, form your own views and then share and compare in open critical discussion with colleagues. Reflect honestly on the extent to which: (i) you influenced the thinking and ideas of your colleagues; and (ii) you were influenced by your colleagues.

To what extent was your group able to reach consensus?

Agree one of your members to produce a brief written summary of the discussion and prepared to present in a plenary session.

Activity 1

Refer to the classification of organisations in pages 67–68. From each of *any five* of the ten classifications, select one particular organisation of your choice.

Now, for *each* of your chosen five organisations, identify what you believe are:

(a) significance features that are characteristic of the organisation

(b) the essential nature of the purpose and direction of work

(c) specific details of the actual workplace.

In which of your chosen organisation do you think you would most prefer to work, and why?

Activity 2

(a) An individual's orientation to work and underlying work ethic is the strongest influence on their motivation and organisational performance. The actions of management have only a minimal effect. How far do you agree with this contention?

(b) What is your view of emotional labour? What personal experiences have you been involved in? How comfortable are you in managing your feelings and displaying certain expected emotions? To what extent do you believe there is a moral issue in expecting employees to demonstrate emotional labour?

Activity 3

Young people's career expectations are increasingly mobile and the concept of workspaces – co-working in shared spaces – suggests that work can be undertaken anywhere.

(a) To what extent does this concept appeal to you? What do you see as the potential advantages and disadvantages of workspaces?

(b) Set out in detail how you see the nature of the workplace in (say) five to ten years' time. What do you think is the *single* most significant change and how well are you prepared to embrace this change?

Organisational behaviour in action case study

The Clink Restaurants

It might be any training restaurant, smart, modern with a four-course menu. The meals are well cooked and served, typical of any College or University training restaurant. However, the security search, entry through locked gates, barbed wire and high walls suggest something different. Guests are not permitted to enter with sharp items, mobile phones, lipstick or cameras. They are security checked in advance when making reservations and must produce photo ID before they enter.

The Clink Charity operates four training restaurants of which two are inside the prison wall.

There are 84,405 adults in prison in England and Wales, of those released sadly 46%* of them go back to prison within the first year of release and for those serving sentences of less than 12 months this increases to 60%. The sole aim of The Clink Charity is to reduce reoffending rates by training and placing our graduates upon their release from prison into employment in the hospitality industry. Since launching the first Clink Restaurant at HMP High Down in 2009 we now have seven projects which achieve outstanding results by offering our 5-step integrated programme.

Prisoners at The Clink work a 40-hour week simulating a professional working environment. Our dedicated full-time trainers and assessors work closely with the prisoners to help them gain their City & Guilds NVQs qualifications. Upon release our support workers help the graduates find employment, housing and then mentor them weekly, helping them reintegrate back into society. During the last 12 months, The Clink has been able to train up to 160 prisoners a day and in total trained 384 prisoners. Of the 92 Clink graduates released 89 went into full-time employment and 3 into rehab. Between them they had gained 138 full NVQ level 2 qualifications.

We currently operate four Clink Restaurants, at HMP High Down, HMP Cardiff, HMP Brixton and HMP Styal. By dining at one of our restaurants you are supporting our training and giving the prisoners the experience they require. The menus are created around the changing seasons, fresh local produce and the City and Guilds syllabus. Each restaurant also offers facilities for corporate events and private dining. In addition to the restaurants, we operate Clink Gardens at HMP Send and HMP High Down to achieve City & Guilds NVQs in horticulture. Fruit, vegetables and herbs from the gardens are used by the restaurants along with eggs from our chickens.

Clink Events provides catering beyond the prison walls for corporate and charity events. It gives prisoners and homeless clients from the Centrepoint charity the opportunity to train to gain qualifications in event catering and prepare for full-time employment. We now have over 250 employers willing to

take on Clink graduates subject to a satisfactory interview. Such as Hilton Hotels, The Royal Lancaster Hotel, Roast Restaurant and Harbour and Jones. To date we have won more than 57 awards, including The Centre for Social Justice – Social Enterprise Award in March 2017.

Our catering industry ambassadors who include Albert Roux, Prue Leith, Cyrus Todiwala, Antonio Carluccio, Giorgio Locatelli, Daniel Galmiche, Lisa Allen, Thomasina Miers and many others work with us to deliver masterclasses in our kitchens and restaurants and introduce Clink graduates to prospective employers. The Justice Datalab published in November 2016 a report that highlights prisoners going through The Clink Charity training programmes are 41% less likely to reoffend. The report states that the charity has achieved a 'statistically significant result'. In order to show a fair assessment, Clink Graduates that qualified for analysis were measured comparatively to individuals that have not received The Clink's intervention but were similar in circumstance.

We are currently building our central production kitchen for Clink Events and also looking for future sites in UK prisons. The Clink Charity's aim is to see more than 1,000 highly trained and qualified Clink graduates enter employment each year by 2020. We are proud that with our partner HMPPS we continue to achieve extraordinary outcomes while fulfilling our key objective of reducing re-offending. We have done this in an affordable and value for money way while fulfilling our core values of compassion, professionalism and integrity in an environment that sometimes seems bleak with so many daily challenges. We hope that The Clink has demonstrated what can be achieved when society engages collectively to help those who want and deserve a second chance.

* Ministry of Justice (2016) Population and capacity briefing for Friday 17 June 2016, London: Ministry of Justice

Source: Thanks to Vanessa Frances at, The Clink Charity www.theclinkcharity.org

Tasks

1. Give a detailed account of your view of this example of organisational behaviour in the workplace. Is there anything that was a particular surprise?

2. Consider the issues that would need to be addressed when employing these staff within the hospitality industry.

3. Identify and consider potential benefits to the individuals, the organisation and to society generally.

Chapter 2 – Personal skills and employability exercise

Objectives

Completing this exercise should help you to enhance the following skills:

* Appreciate the changing nature of work organisations.
* Come to terms with an ageless workforce.
* Develop harmonious working relationships among different age groups.

Exercise

Demographic changes and an ageing population mean an individual's perceived underlying work ethic is likely to be influenced at least in part by their generation and age group. The rise of the ageless workforce gives rise to increasingly complex patterns of the working environment.

Referring to each of the different generations mentioned in the text:

1. Identity what you see as the most likely causes of potential disharmony or conflict including the following:

Orientation to work
Career structure
Technology and social media
Motivations
Ageism

2. Explain fully what actions you would take to help overcome disagreements or discrimination and encourage harmonious team working.

Discussion

* To what extent can you accept differences in attitude among different generations?

* How do you feel about potentially working with colleagues from a range of age groups?

* What examples of different orientations to work have you observed with mature students or those on part-time or post-graduate courses?

Notes and references

1. Hughes, E. C. 'Work and the Self' in Rohrer, J. H. and Sherif, M. (eds) *Social Psychology at the Crossroads,* Harper (1951), pp. 313–23.
2. Waller, D. 'Are You What You Do?', *Management Today,* October 2008, pp. 42–6.
3. Donkin, R. *The Future of Work,* Palgrave Macmillan (2010).
4. Betrand Russell, 'In Praise of Idleness', by Richard Nordquist, http://grammar.about.com/od/classicessays/a/praiseidleness.htm (accessed 27 June 2012).
5. 'Modern World of Work', BBC 2 Television, March 2011.
6. Bouchikhi, H and Kimberly, J. R. 'The Customised Workplace', in Chowdhury, S. (ed.) *Management 21C,* Financial Times Prentice Hall (2000), pp. 207–19.
7. Goldthorpe, J. H., Lockwood, D., Bechofer, F. and Platt, J. *The Affluent Worker,* Cambridge University Press (1968).
8. Bunting, M. *Willing Slaves,* HarperCollins (2004).
9. Stern, S. 'My Generation', *Management Today,* March 2008, pp. 40–6.
10. Reeves, R. 'Reality Bites', *Management Today,* March 2003, p. 35.
11. Hochschild, A. R. *The Managed Heart: Commercialization of Human Feeling,* University of California Press (1983) and updated edition (2012).
12. Wilson, F. M. *Organizational Behaviour and Work,* fourth edition, Oxford University Press (2014).
13. Mann, S. *Hiding the Way we Feel, Faking What we Don't: Understanding the Role of Emotions at Work,* Element (1999).
14. Gursoy, D., Boylu, Y. and Avci, U. 'Identifying the Complex Relationships Among Emotional Labour and its Correlates', *International Journal of Hospitality Management,* vol. 30, 2011, pp. 783–94.
15. Chu, K., Baker, M. and Murrmann, S. 'When We are on Stage We Smile; The Effects of Emotional Labour on Employee Work Outcomes', *International Journal of Hospitality Management,* vol. 31, 2012, pp. 906–15.
16. Schneider, S. C. and Barsoux, J. *Managing Across Cultures,* second edition, Financial Times Prentice Hall (2003).
17. Smart, P. and Inazawa, K. *Human Resource Management in the Public Sector,* Kwansei Gakuin University Press (2011).
18. Gwyther, M. 'A Failed Experiment?', *Management Today,* issue 2, 2017, pp. 11, 47–9.
19. See, for example, 'Social Enterprises as a New Type of Employer', *Employment Relations Matters,* ACAS, issue 11, June 2008, pp. 3–5.
20. 'The Lessons from the Ground', *Social Agenda,* European Commission, No. 32, February 2013.

21. Egan, G. 'The Shadow Side', *Management Today,* September 1993, pp. 33–8.
22. Law, S. 'Beyond the Water Cooler', *Professional Manager,* January 2005, p. 26.
23. Vernon, M. 'Office Friends: Who Needs Them?', *Management Today,* September 2005, pp. 59–61.
24. 'This is Our Code', Royal Bank of Scotland Group, 8 July 2013.
25. 'Love Your Work Colleagues: 10 Ways To Find Common Ground', HuffPost Conversations, http://www.huffingtonpost.co.uk/entry/love-your-work-colleagues-10-ways-to-find-common-ground_uk_58e61926e4b0917d3477545d (accessed 28 April 2017).
26. Sternberg, E. *Just Business: Business Ethics in Action,* second edition, Oxford University Press (2000), pp. 124–5.
27. 'Juggling Act: How the EU is Helping People Improve Their Work–Life Balance', *Social Agenda,* European Commission, issue 19, December 2008, pp. 15–20.
28. 'Reeves, R. 'Still Juggling After All These Years', *Management Today,* June 2007, pp. 36–43.
29. Flexible Working and Work–Life Balance', ACAS, September 2010.
30. Perez, A. M. 'Family Structure and Work Satisfaction: Can Work–Life Balance Policies Foster Happiness in the Workplace?' Department for Business, Innovation & Skills, November 2009.
31. 'Meet the Need for Work/Life Balance' Business Link www.businesslink.gov.uk/bdotg (accessed 26 October 2011). See also Armitage, K. 'Can We Really Achieve a Life/Work Balance?', *The British Journal of Administrative Management,* July/August 2001, pp. 14–15.
32. Cloke, K. and Goldsmith, J. *The End of Management and the Rise of Organizational Democracy,* Jossey-Bass (2002).
33. Stern, S. 'My Generation', *Management Today,* March 2008, pp. 40–6.
34. See, for example, Searle, I. 'Out With the Old, In With the New', *Governance + Compliance,* October 2013, pp. 20–2.
35. Gazzaley, A. and Rosen L. D. *The Distracted Mind: Ancient Brains in a High-Tech World,* MIT Press (2016), p. 144.
36. Riches, A. 'Are Gen Y Creating Havoc with Your Life?' www.info@anneriches.com, 3 May 2017.
37. Gale, A. 'Is Ageism the Last Taboo?', *Management Today,* issue 3, 2017, pp. 40–3.
38. Gwyther, M. 'The Future of the Workplace', *Management Today,* June 2011, pp. 57–9.
39. 'The Future Workplace' Unum Limited 2014 www.unum.co.uk.
40. 'Should We All Have Clear Desks?', Insights, *Professional Manager,* Autumn 2015, pp. 12–13.
41. See, for example: Willis, B. 'Out of Office', *Professional Manager,* Summer 2014, pp. 66–8.
42. 'Homeworking – A Guide for Employers and Employees', ACAS, May 2014.
43. Sutherland, A. 'Agile but Fragile: The Changing Face of UK Homeworking – What Work Best for Whom?' ACAS, July 2014.
44. 'The Future of Work: Jobs and Skills in 2030', UKCES, 03.14.
45. 'Welcome to the Future of Work', *Management Today,* June 2016, pp. 30–2.
46. See, for example, Hazelhurst, J. 'The Way We Work Now', *Management Today,* June 2013, pp. 46–9.
47. McCarthy, A., Darcy, C. and Grady, G. 'Work–Life Balance Policy and Practice: Understanding Line Manager Attitudes and Behaviours,' *Human Resource Management Review,* 20, 2010, pp. 158–67.
48. Beatson, M. 'How Does Work–Life Balance Change how "Good" Your Job Is?' CIPD Blog https://www.cipd.co.uk/Community/blogs/b/mark_beatson/posts/how-does-work-life-balance-change-how-good-your-job-is (accessed on 3 May 2018).
49. Beauregard, T. A. 'Fairness Perceptions of Work–Life Balance Initiatives: Effects on Counterproductive Work Behaviour', *British Journal of Management,* vol. 25, 2014, pp. 792–89.
50. Gregory, A. and Milner, S. 'Editorial: Work–life Balance: A Matter of Choice?' *Gender, Work and Organization,* vol. 16, no. 1, 2009, January, pp. 1–13.
51. Lutz, J. *It's Time To Kill The Fantasy That Is Work–Life Balance,* Forbes, https://www.forbes.com/sites/jessicalutz/2018/01/11/its-time-to-kill-the-fantasy-that-is-work-life-balance/#45e5bac470a1 (accessed 5 May 2018).
52. Moen, P., Kelly, E. and Huang, R. 'Fit Inside the Work-Family Black Box: An Ecology of the Life Course, Cycles of Control Reframing', *Journal of Occupational and Organizational Psychology,* 81, 2008, pp. 411–33.
53. Ross, J. P., Intindola, M. L. and Boje, D. M. 'It Was the Best of Times; It Was the Worst of Times: The Expiration of Work–Life Balance', *Journal of Management Enquiry,* vol. 26, (2), 2017, 202–15.
54. MacCormick, J. S., Dery, K. and Kolb, D. G. 'Engaged or Just Connected? Smartphones and Employee Engagement, *Organizational Dynamics',* vol. 41, (3), 2012, pp. 194–201.
55. Department for Innovation and Skills, Fourth Work-Life Balance Employer Survey (2013), BIS Research Paper, December (2014).
56. CIPD, UK Working Lives Survey Report: The CIPD Job Quality Index, Chartered Institute of Personnel and Development, London (2018a).
57. McCarthy, A., Cleveland, J. N., Hunter, S., Darcy, C. and Grady, G. 'Employee Work–Life Balance Outcomes

in Ireland: A Multilevel Investigation of Supervisory Support and Perceived Organizational Support', *The International Journal of Human Resource Management,* vol. 24, no. 6, 2013, pp. 1257–76.

58. Daverth, G., Hyde, P. and Cassell, C. 'Uptake of Organisational Work–Life Balance Opportunities: The Context of Support', *The International Journal of Human Resource Management,* vol. 27, no. 15, 2016, pp. 1710–29.

59. Beatson, M. Working–Life-Balance, Blend or Bedlam? CIPD Blog (2014), https://www2.cipd.co.uk/community/blogs/b/mark_beatson/archive/2014/04/03/working-life (accessed 3 May 2018).

60. CIPD, Flexible Working Practices, Factsheet, Chartered Institute of Personnel and Development, 20 September (2018b) https://www.cipd.co.uk/knowledge/fundamentals/relations/flexible-working/factsheet (accessed 27 November 2018).

61. Just, S. 'There may not be perfect work–life balance. . . and that's OK by me', PBS NewsHour, 3 July, https://www.pbs.org/newshour/nation/may-perfect-work-life-balance-that's-ok (2015).

Chapter 3
Organisational conflict and stress

Conflict and stress are two underlying realities of work organisations and have a significant influence for the study of organisational behaviour.

Learning outcomes

After completing your study of this chapter you should have enhanced your ability to:

- Explain relationships between work, health and well-being;
- Review the nature, scope and effects of conflict at work;
- Identify contrasting perspectives of conflict;
- Assess the management of conflict in the workplace;
- Explore the nature, sources and impact of work related stress;
- Debate whether stress is necessarily to be avoided;
- Evaluate measures for coping with harmful effects of stress.

Outline chapter contents

Overview topic map: Chapter 3 – Organisational conflict and stress

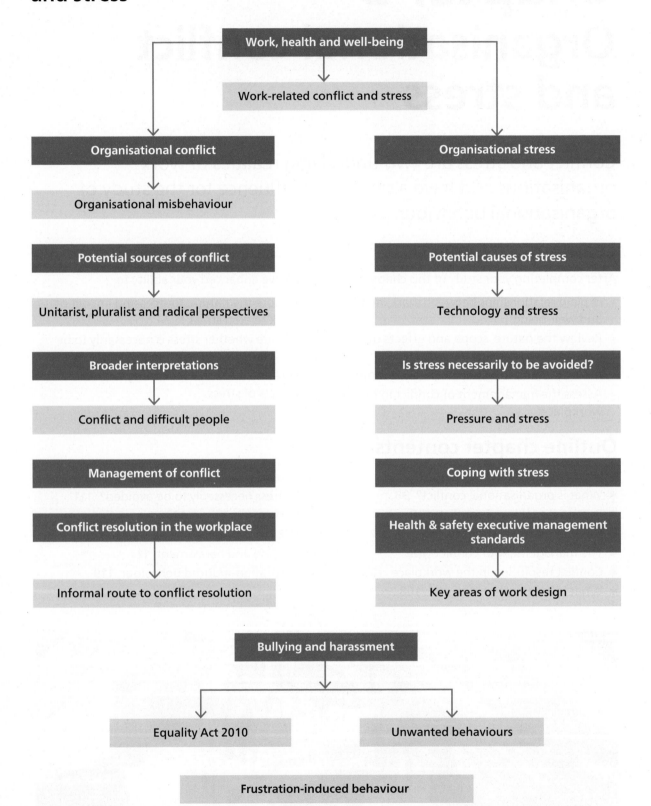

Related influences discussed in other chapters

Conflict and stress can come from many angles

Before commencing to read this chapter – what exactly do YOU understand by the words 'conflict' and 'stress'? What do you think is the significance of their study for organisational behaviour?

Work, health and well-being

There is growing recognition of the relationships among work, health and well-being including for example government initiatives such as 'Fit for Work'. Work-related ill health results in both high personal and organisational costs. The nature of work and the way in which it is undertaken are clearly potential major influences on our general health and well-being.

Work is generally good for your health. Higher rates of absence and illness are associated with *lower* levels of work demands, control and support.[1] The CIPD maintains well-being creates workplaces which support health and happiness so that people can flourish and reach their potential. It involves creating an environment that actively promotes a state of contentment, benefiting both employees and the organisation.[2] Harmonious relationships have the potential to make workplaces healthy and productive with motivated people, but good employment relationship practices are also necessary.

Work-related conflict and stress

Two major realities of organisational behaviour that have a significant influence on work and well-being are conflict and stress, and can be aggravated by bullying and harassment **(see Figure 3.1).** Incidents of conflict and stress are influenced in many ways by the general nature of the working environment including group behaviour, leadership and HRM, structure, and technology, discussed in later chapters. Emotional labour **discussed in Chapter 2** is another potential source of conflict or stress. The two forces of conflict and stress are often interrelated. Conflict in many of its forms can have a contributory influence on stress, and people under stress may be more inclined to experience situations of conflict. The European Commission states that work-related stress is one of the biggest health and safety factors that we face

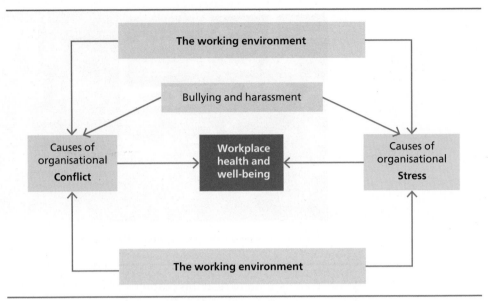

Figure 3.1 Workplace health and well-being

in Europe today. The Commission also draws attention to the gap between the legal obligations of EU employers to manage stress and psychosocial risk at the workplace and practices actually observed. Numerous examples confirm work-related stress can be approached in the same manner as other health and safety issues.[3]

Health and well-being the hospitality industry

Maintaining a high level of workplace health and well-being is challenging in any environment but is particularly pronounced for example in the hospitality industry. Problems arise from a number of factors including: people-intensive and pressurised working environment; both production and on-demand service operations; long hours, often in excess of 65 a week; relatively low pay often the legal minimum and due in part to many part time or casual staff; many units operate 24 hours and every day; a transient workforce often with social issues.[4] *Berger and Brownell* identify major behavioural consequences of organisational conflict and stress in the hospitality industry as leading to eating disorders, increased smoking, alcohol and drug abuse, violent tendencies and accident proneness.[5]

What is organisational conflict?

Most of us will understand what is commonly meant by organisational conflict and be aware of its existence and effects. Conflict involves the perception of the state of mind of another person or persons. We all see things in different ways and have our own set of values, beliefs and opinions. Individual perception results in different people attaching different meanings to the same stimuli.

Conflict is a term that can be defined and interpreted in a number of ways. For our purpose we see **conflict** as behaviour intended to obstruct the achievement of some other person's goals. Conflict is based on the incompatibility of goals and arises from opposing behaviours. It can be viewed at the individual, group or organisation level. Conflict can be related to power and politics, hierarchical structure, or styles of management or leadership. But conflict can also arise at any level of an organisation and from many different situations or actions, for example clashes of personality, grievances against a senior member of staff, or team friction or rivalry.

Organisational misbehaviour

Ackroyd and Thompson use the term 'organizational misbehaviour' to refer to 'anything you do at work which you are not supposed to' and usually interpreted as anything unacceptable to management. Management establish boundaries that distinguish acceptable and non-acceptable behaviour from employees. The actions of employees are then judged as falling one side or the other of these boundaries.[6]

There are however many forms of organisational misbehaviour that can give rise to potential conflict at work and can range from:

- deliberate time wasting and/or to enhance overtime;
- misuses of the telephone or internet;
- cheating, fiddles, petty theft; to
- fraud, vandalism or sabotage.

In educational establishments cheating such as plagiarism is an increasing concern about organisational misbehaviour.

Student cheats with invisible ink

Students are smuggling notes written with invisible ink into university exams, according to an official report. It is said one law student last year wrote 24 pages of invisible ink notes in a statute book which was allowed to be taken to the exam. She then used a tiny ultra-violet torch to read them. The report from the Office of Independent Adjudicator said: She was seen using the notes by other students and the invigilator who retained the statute book as evidence'. The student was failed in all her modules as punishment. Universities UK, which represents vice chancellors, said cheating was taken extremely seriously.

Source: Daily Mail, 5 May 2017.

Yew and Gregory look at organisational misbehaviour in terms of management–employee relations and the nature of control and power in the workplace. Examples range from harassment to workplace romance with negative behaviour such as favouritism towards the partner. Rumour and gossip are often viewed as misbehaviour but can be an important means of communication about what is actually happening. More often than not, individuals engage in organisational misbehaviour either to benefit the individual, to benefit the organisation, or with the intention to damage and hurt a particular individual, organisation asset or social unit.[7] An overview of organisational conflict is set out in **Figure 3.2.**

What is your view of organisational misbehaviour? To what extent do YOU see it as a normal pattern of human behaviour in the workplace or more particularly an issue of management control and power?

There are many potential sources of organisational conflict, including those arising from: **individual factors** such as, personality characteristics, illness or stress, personal

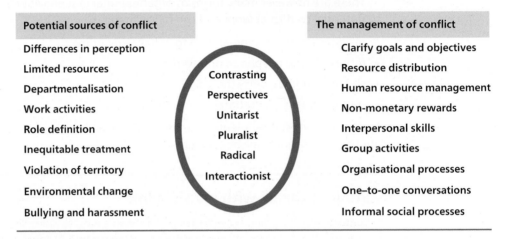

Figure 3.2 An overview of organisational conflict

friendships, relationships and romance in the workplace; **group factors** such as team roles, patterns of interaction and group norms, friction between the informal and formal organisation; **organisational factors** such as authority structures, systems of communication.

Potential sources of conflict

- **Differences in perception.** We all see things in different ways and have our own set of values, beliefs and opinions. Differences in perception result in individuals attaching different meanings to the same stimuli. As perceptions become a person's reality, value judgements can be a potential major source of conflict. **(The importance of perception is discussed in Chapter 6.)**

- **Limited resources.** Most organisational resources are limited and individuals and groups have to fight for their share; for example, at the time of the allocation of the next year's budget or when cutbacks have to be made. The greater the limitation of resources such as in an organisation with reducing profits or revenues, the potential for conflict is likely to be intensified.

- **Departmentalisation and specialisation.** Most work organisations are divided into departments with specialised functions. Because of familiarity with the manner in which they undertake their activities, managers tend to turn inwards and to concentrate on the achievement of their own particular goals. When departments need to co-operate, this is a frequent source of conflict. Differing goals and internal environments of departments are also a potential source of conflict, for example between task and element function **(discussed in Chapter 11).** In *Woodward*'s study of management organisation of firms in this country she comments on the bad relationships between accountants and other managers. People concerned with works accounting tended to see their role as one of controlling and sanctioning one rather than servicing and supportive. Line managers resented this attitude and retaliated by becoming aggressive and obstructive.[8]

- **Nature of work activities.** Where the activities of one person are dependent upon the work of others there is potential for conflict. For example a worker expected to complete the assembly of a given number of components each day but must reply on another worker forwarding the part-assembled components in good time. If reward and punishment systems are perceived to be based on performance levels, then the potential for conflict is even greater. If the work of a department is dependent upon the output of another department, a similar situation could arise, especially if this situation is coupled with limited resources.

- **Role definition.** A role is the expected pattern of behaviours associated with members occupying a particular position within the structure of the organisation. In practice, the manner in which people actually behave may not be consistent with their expected pattern of behaviour. Problems of role incompatibility and role ambiguity arise from inadequate or inappropriate role definition and can be a significant source of conflict. **(Role structure is discussed in Chapter 8.)**

- **Inequitable treatment.** A person's feeling of unjust treatment, say in the operation of HR policies and practices or in reward and punishment systems, can lead to tension and conflict. For example, according to the equity theory of motivation **(discussed in Chapter 7),** the perception of inequity will motivate a person to take action to restore equity, including changes to inputs or outputs, or through acting on others.

- **Violation of territory.** People tend to become attached to their own 'territory', for example, area of work, clients, room, chair or parking space; or through access to information or membership of groups. Ownership of territory may be conferred formally, for example by organisation charts, job descriptions or management decisions; it may be established through procedures, for example circulation lists or membership of committees; or it may arise informally, for example through group norms, tradition or perceived status symbols. If a person's territory is violated this can lead to the possibility of retaliation and conflict. Where people choose to meet can have a symbolic value. If a subordinate is summoned to meet in a manager's office this might be perceived as signalling higher status. If the manager chooses to meet at the subordinate's place of work, or on neutral territory, this may be a signal that the manager wishes to meet more as an equal.

- **Environmental change.** Changes in an organisation's external environment, such as increased competition, government intervention, new technology or changing social values, can cause major areas of conflict. For example, a fall in demand for, or government financial restrictions on, enrolments for a certain discipline in higher education can result in conflict over the allocation of resources. If the department concerned is a large and important one and led by a powerful head, there could be even greater potential for conflict.

- **Bullying and harassment** is discussed later in this chapter.

According to *Podro,* conflict in the workplace can be divided into three categories:

- **Organised conflict,** which manifests itself as strike action or action short of strike, wildcat strikes, and occupations etc.;

- **Overt individual conflict** such as formal grievances raised over working conditions; and
- **Latent conflict** where the signs of unrest, discontent and disengagement are expressed through increased absence levels and higher turnover, a drop in performance, more fractious interpersonal relationships between managers and the managed which can lead to an increase in bullying and harassment.[9]

What do YOU believe are the possible main causes of conflict in the workplace? What type of conflict would be likely to give you the most concern, and why?

It might be expected that a healthy organisational climate would be reflected by complete harmony in working relationships, loyalty and common commitment to the goals and objectives of the organisation. This view of work organisations as 'happy families' is perhaps a worthwhile and creditable ideal and as such appears to be implied by a number of management writers. For example *Drucker* makes the point that each member of the organisation should contribute towards a common goal and their efforts must all pull in the same direction without gaps or duplication of effort. If not, instead of teamwork, there is friction, frustration and conflict.[10]

Clearly, conflict can have adverse effects on attitudes and behaviour, morale and motivation, sickness absence or organisational performance. Extreme cases of conflict can give rise to excessive emotional or physical stress with very upsetting, or even tragic, consequences for some people. Common definitions of conflict tend to be associated with negative features and situations which give rise to inefficiency, ineffectiveness or dysfunctional consequences. The traditional view of conflict is that it is bad for organisations. Conflict is perceived as disruptive and unnatural and represents a form of deviant behaviour that should be controlled and changed.

Unitarist and pluralist perspectives

Such traditional views appear to imply a **unitarist perspective** of the organisation **(discussed in Chapter 11).** The natural state of the organisation is viewed as an integrated, co-operative and harmonious whole. There is an image of the organisation as a team with a common source of loyalty and one focus of effort. But if one accepts the idea of a **pluralist perspective** to work organisations, conflict is not necessarily a bad thing but can be an agent for evolution and internal and external change. The pluralist manager is more likely to accept that conflict in organisations requires careful handling and attempt to reconcile rival interests.

The radical perspective

The **radical perspective** is associated with the ideas of writers such as Karl Marx and the structuralist approach to organisations and management.[11] It challenges the traditional view of conflict in society and sees organisations in terms of disparity in power and control between owners and workers. Conflict is an inherent feature of the unequal nature of organisational life and a means of bringing about change.[12] Collective bargaining is not seen as particularly helpful in a system stacked against the workers. Conflict is a natural part of the class struggle. The design of organisation structure, management systems and the choice of technology all form part of the struggle for power and control within the work organisation.

According to the radical approach, the design of organisation structure, management systems and the choice and use of technology all form part of the struggle for power and control within the work organisation. Greater attention should be given to relationships between the formal and informal aspects of the organisation and the study of conflict between the needs of the individual and those of the organisation, and between workers and management.

Deprivation of freedom and the radical perspective?

To what extent do YOU believe work organisations can ever be truly like 'happy families' or that it is a worthwhile and creditable view but just too idealistic and simplistic?

Broader interpretations of conflict

A more recent view of conflict is the **interactionist perspective**, which believes that conflict is a positive force and necessary for effective performance. This approach encourages a minimum level of conflict within the group in order to encourage self-criticism, change and innovation, and to help prevent apathy or too great a tolerance for harmony and the status quo.[13] Conflict *per se* is not necessarily good or bad but an inevitable feature of organisational life and should be judged in terms of its effects on performance. Even if organisations have taken great care to try to avoid conflict, it will still occur. Conflict will continue to emerge despite management attempts to suppress it.

The current view appears to recognise conflict can be interpreted more broadly than in the traditional view. *Townsend* sees conflict as a sign of a healthy organisation – up to a point.

A good manager doesn't try to eliminate conflict; he tries to keep it from wasting the energies of his people . . . If you're the boss and your people fight you openly when they think you're wrong – that's healthy. If your people fight each other openly in your presence for what they believe in – that's healthy. But keep all the conflict eyeball to eyeball.[14]

Constructive conflict

Conflict, then, is not necessarily a bad thing. It can be seen as a 'constructive' force and in certain circumstances it can be welcomed or even encouraged. Healthy conflict can help generate innovation and seen as an aid to incremental improvement in organisation design and functioning, and to the decision-making process. Conflict can be an agent for evolution, and for internal and external change. Properly identified and handled, it can help to minimise the destructive influences of the win–lose situation.

In a discussion of conflict at board level, *Dunne* refers to the destructive force of failure to manage conflict. However, if the board focuses on a combination of the right strategy, right resources and right governance; and executives on strategic options, delivering the business plan and operational and financial integrity, then there is a much better chance of achieving a healthy degree of constructive conflict and sustained high performance.[15]

Conflict and 'difficult people'

The idea of conflict as inevitable is discussed by *Irvine,* who suggests that if you ask a group of managers about the nature and level of conflict they experience, the majority will tell you honestly that apart from the odd minor tiff, there is not much conflict about. There are, however, 'difficult people'. Irvine suggests a shift away from blaming individuals and their personalities, recognising instead that it is through normal human interaction that outward expressions of difference are produced.[16]

It should be considered how relationships between older employees and younger managers, where experience is on one side and power on the other, can lead to conflict. It is very easy for an experienced manager in a conflict with an older employee to consider them 'difficult' where in fact they should be exploring the reasons behind behavioural patterns. If appropriate steps are not taken, the relationship can quickly end up with both parties feeling undermined and threatened.

According to *Mannering,* conflicts, misunderstandings and personality clashes are usually at the root of the problem when employees become unhappy at work. There is an erosion of our social framework, and the work environment has become more competitive with pressure to have the best jobs and gadgets. People are placed into teams with people they would possibly never choose to associate with. Mannering suggests that people can be 'difficult' for a number of reasons but it is important not to concentrate on the negative points. Negativity is the most difficult behaviour to overcome or change as it constantly undermines what the team is trying to achieve.

In order to help defuse conflict, it is important to draw a fine line between firm management and aggressive behaviour. Humour may help defuse a situation but it is more important to stay calm and professional. Improved communications and relationships may help but if someone is determined not to co-operate, then there will be conflict. Mannering makes the point that although you cannot please everyone all the time, avoidance is not an option for dealing with difficult people. Managers must develop solid coping mechanisms and do their best in the particular situation.[17]

> To what extent do YOU believe that most conflict at work is due to a combination of negativity and 'difficult people'? How much do you think humour helps to resolve conflict?

The management of conflict

Much has been written about the nature and implications of conflict as a social process. Whatever the relevance and importance of this debate it is not so much the extent to which it is possible, or desirable, to create a totally harmonious working environment but how conflict when found to exist is handled and managed. Although a certain amount of organisational conflict may be seen as inevitable, there are a number of ways in which management can attempt to avoid harmful effects of conflict in order to achieve a positive rather than negative influence in the workplace. Many of these ideas will be discussed in later chapters. The strategies adopted will vary according to the nature and sources of conflict outlined above. Bear in mind that managing conflict takes time and effort but attempting to establish a climate of mutual trust, consideration and respect is worthwhile.

- **Clarification of goals and objectives.** Continual refinement and communication of goals and objectives, role definitions and performance standards will help to avoid misunderstandings and conflict. Focusing attention on superordinate goals that are shared by the parties in conflict may help to defuse hostility and lead to more co-operative behaviour.

- **Resource distribution.** Although it may not always be possible for managers to increase their allocated share of resources, they may be able to use imagination and initiative to help overcome conflict situations – for example, making a special case to higher management; greater flexibility to transfer funds between budget headings; delaying staff appointments in one area to provide more money for another area.

- **Human resource management.** A participative and supportive style of leadership and managerial behaviour together with careful attention to just and equitable HR policies and procedures may help reduce areas of conflict. For example, an attitude of respect and trust; encouraging personal self-development; creating a work environment in which staff can work co-operatively; recognition of trade unions and their officials. An open-door policy and identifying potential causes of disputes may help avoid conflict.

- **Non-monetary rewards.** Where financial resources are limited, it may be possible to pay greater attention to non-monetary rewards. Examples are job design; more interesting, challenging or responsible work; increased delegation or empowerment; improved equipment; flexible working hours; attendance at courses or conferences; unofficial perks, or more relaxed working conditions.

- **Development of interpersonal skills.** This may help engender a better understanding of one's own behaviour, the other person's point of view, communication processes and problem-solving. Attention to body language may also assist people to work through conflict situations in a constructive manner. Where possible encourage addressing disputes early on a one-to-one basis.

- **Group activities.** Attention to the composition of groups and to factors that affect group cohesiveness may reduce dysfunctional conflict. Overlapping group membership with a 'linking-pin' process, and the careful selection of project teams or task forces for problems affecting more than one group, may also be beneficial. **(See also Chapter 8.)**

- **Organisational processes.** Conflict situations may be reduced by attention to such features as the nature of the authority structure; work organisation; patterns of communication and sharing of information; democratic functioning of the organisation; unnecessary adherence to bureaucratic procedures and official rules and regulations.

 How successful are YOU in using interpersonal process skills to help avoid conflict in group activity situations with your fellow students? What do you notice about the body language within the group?

Conflict resolution in the workplace

Having one-to-one conversations about issues requires a great deal of sensitivity and empathy. *The Advisory, Conciliation and Arbitration Service* (ACAS) suggest you must try to:

- listen to what individuals are saying and try to recognise any underlying causes of unhappiness or stress;
- ask questions in a calm and measured way to put the other person at ease and let them speak freely;
- rephrase or reinterpret what's been said so that problems can be seen in a different light;
- make connections between interests of the individual and that of the team or organisation;
- lead by example and set the right tone for people;
- respect diversity and equality.

There are three common responses to conflict; Fight, Flight or Freeze, to which Acas suggest a fourth – Face it. This means responding to a problem in a calm and rational way with a planned approach[18] **(see Figure 3.3).**

An informal route to conflict resolution

From an analysis of five case studies, *Saundry and Wibberley* found that in larger organisations, effective conflict management revolves around informal social processes underpinned by high-trust relationships between key organizational

Individual conflict in the workplace

Definition: *"Conflict may be expressed formally as disciplinary action or employee grievances but also by disagreements and clashes between colleagues and between managers and their staff."*

How do you respond to conflict?

There are three common responses to conflict – which way do you respond?

Fight	You react in a challenging way. At work this might mean shouting or losing your temper.
Flight	You turn your back on what's going on. This is a common reaction – by ignoring a problem you hope it will go away.
Freeze	You are not sure how to react and become very passive. You might begin to deal with the issue but things drift or become drawn out through indecision.

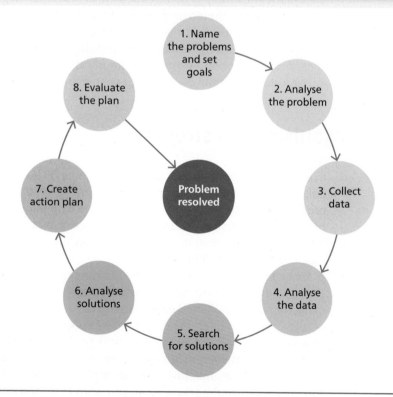

Figure 3.3 Conflict problem-solving cycle

Source: 'Managing conflict at work', ACAS, June 2014. Used with permission from ACAS National.

stakeholders. However these relationships are threatened by more centralised models of HR, and the lack of confidence and capability of line managers to deal with difficult issues. Evidence suggests conflict management was seen as a lower order skill and the support of senior managers was crucial. There is a need for developing structures of employee representation and increased investment in developing the skills and confidence of line managers. The analysis highlights the importance of communications between managers and staff and the positive role of performance management systems and employee engagement in conflict situations.[19]

Hirshman and Wakeling claim that latest research indicates many managers have little choice in managing individual conflict. They can go either for the 'informal chat' approach or the potentially safer procedural route. Particularly in larger organisations the default position for conflict management is too often rather formal. Hirshman and Wakeling refer to renewed interest in emotional intelligence and refining people skills. They question if between intuition and procedure there is a middle ground for managers to feel more certain of defusing potential conflict. However with a more psychological approach, managers may be concerned about trusting their emotions and feel perplexed or alienated by the fear of internal criticism. But there is scope to learn more about emotions and behaviours. Increasing psychological awareness of the workplace can benefit employee, manager and organisation.[20]

The importance of early informal resolution to conflict is emphasised by *CIPD* who refer to US research that suggests employees spend an average of 2.7 hours a week in conflict at work. Most organisations manage conflict through formal procedures as prime HR responsibilities but in some cases HR has become more distant from operations and arguably do not see conflict resolution as sufficiently strategic. Greater attention should be given to the value of conflict resolution skills and early informal action including mediation and similar approaches that aim to genuinely resolve conflict such as facilitated conversations with line managers. Much conflict arises from poor or non-existent communication and conflict resolution skills are only an extension of normal dialogue between managers and their teams.[21]

What is organisational stress?

In addition to organisational conflict, a major and related influence on the work/life balance, **discussed in Chapter 2,** is the extent to which employees suffer from organisational stress. **Stress** is a complex and dynamic concept. It is a possible source of tension and frustration, and can arise through a number of interrelated influences on behaviour, including the individual, group, organisational and environmental factors **discussed in Chapter 1.**

York contends that despite all the business-speak, people get seriously vague when it comes to definitions and raises the question: what is stress? Is it a new name for an old-fashioned condition such as unhappiness or overwork, or is it peculiar to our uniquely pressured times? York suggests there is something in the idea that stress isn't just about hard work or unhappiness, but about conflict, confusion and frustration. It's about the anxiety generated by multi-tasking and balancing priorities, meeting contradictory demands, about knowing where to start and papering over the cracks when you want to do too much.[22]

Level of scepticism

Understandably perhaps there is a level of scepticism about the amount of attention given to stress, and a number of press and other articles feature the 'myth' of work stress. For example, an interesting report from the Institute for Social and Economic Research suggests that claims of workplace pressure may be misplaced. Levels of job satisfaction and mental distress vary systematically according to the day of the week on which respondents are interviewed. Stress appears to disappear on Friday and Saturday. When genuine dissatisfaction was found, it tended to be because employees were working too few or too many hours. However, the main cause of stress was money difficulties, caused by unemployment or debt. The research casts a question mark over the generous compensation regularly handed out by the courts to employees claiming they suffer from stress.[23]

Randall comments that 'Whichever lawyer first hit on the idea of promoting stress as either a reason for not going to work or a way to make others cough up could hardly have done more damage to Britain's work ethic than if he or she had arranged a quintupling of dole payments.'[24]

Stress is a very personal experience, as is the response of each individual to it and their beliefs about how best to cope with the causes and effects. *Gwyther* points out that although stress appears to have become public health enemy number one and is viewed as the culprit of myriad complaints, the term is bandied about far too readily and there is a need to stand back and attempt to get things into some sort of perspective. A measure of stress is natural. A degree of stress at work is no unhealthy thing and without it nothing would ever get done.[25]

Despite the scepticism however, an increasing number of surveys report perceived or actual increases in levels of stress and contend that stress at work is one of the biggest problems in European companies and one of the major adverse influences on the quality of working life and work performance. There have also been a number of highly publicised reports of successful legal claims based on the effects of stress.[26] The *CIPD* annual absence survey indicates that stress is still one of the main causes of short- and long-term absence.[26] The Health and Safety Executive report that in 2015/16 stress accounted for 37 per cent of all work-related ill-health cases and 45 per cent of all working days lost due to ill health.[27]

Work stress takes many possible forms and means different things to different people

To what extent do YOU believe stress is a serious and worsening reality of the work situation or too much of a fashionable trend with little real substance?

Potential causes of work stress

Whatever the effects, it is generally acknowledged that stress is potentially part of everyday working life. It occurs for a variety of reasons, including individual differences and types of personality; occupation and actual stressful nature of the job; whether working in the private or public sector; and organisational conflict **(discussed earlier in this chapter).** External economic pressures such as a result of recession also accounts for an increase in stress.

Other sources of stress at work include the following:

- **Restructuring of organisations** and reductions in staffing levels resulting from demands for improved business competitiveness and lower operating costs has placed greater pressures on remaining staff.
- **The long-hours culture,** increased workloads and work intensification, together with unreasonable deadlines.
- **Excessive rules and regulations,** and greater bureaucratic burdens especially among professional groups.
- **Organisational changes** such as redundancies and the loss of key members of staff that place extra demands on managers.
- **Authoritarian styles of leadership and management,** for example *Donaldson-Fielder* points out: line managers' competences for tackling stress are in need of greater empathy, listening skills and integrity.[28]
- **Interpersonal relationships at work,** especially with team colleagues; poor communications; office politics.
- **Lack of empowerment and autonomy over control of work.** Stress is often caused by the hierarchical structure of the organisation or lack of delegation and empowerment.
- **Organisation structure and role relationships.** Lack of clarity about expected patterns of behaviour, or role conflict, is a potential source of stress **(discussed in Chapter 8).**

Technology and stress

Technology can be an underlying influence on work-related conflict and levels of stress. Whatever the type of organisation, with the advent of ICT (information, communication and technology) operations can be conducted 24/7 and from a wide range of locations. Staff are far more constantly and easily contactable and expected to deliver everything faster. This can lead to greater pressure on individuals, a reluctance to switch off and a blurring between work and home life. There are possible concerns over the use of technology for workplace surveillance and control. Many people find the high levels of emails and expectations to provide a prompt response an added source of stress. *Rosen* comments on iDisorder, changes to your brain's ability to process information and relate to the daily use of media and technology. This can result in signs and symptoms of psychological disorders such as stress sleeplessness and a compulsive need to check in with all your technology.[29] ***See* also Chapter 13.**

According to the European Commission the most common causes of work-related stress are: job reorganisation or job insecurity (72 per cent), hours worked or workload (66 per cent), unacceptable behaviour such as bullying or harassment (59 per cent), lack of support to fulfil your role (57 per cent), lack of clarity on roles or responsibilities (52 per cent) and limited possibilities to manage own work patterns (46 per cent). Moreover, employees affected by stress are not in a position to deploy full potential and contribute as much as they could to the development of the company for which they work. Not to mention the human costs and lifelong repercussions of psychosocial diseases for the employees concerned and their families.[30]

Cultural differences

To what extent do causes of stress vary according to different cultures? There is some evidence to suggest that the incidence of stress does not vary noticeably among different cultures. For example Type A personalities, who are competitive and thrive on hard work and long hours **(discussed in Chapter 4)** exhibit similar levels of stress across the United Kingdom, Hungary, Italy, Israel and the United States.[31] From a study of European Canadians, East Asian Canadians and Japanese exchange students *Tweed et al.* identified variations between culture and ways of coping with stressful events.[32] Another study of a diverse set of countries across the Anglo world, China and Latin America suggests that stress caused by long working hours can be mitigated by a strong social support network such as families or friends.[33]

What apparent similarities or differences have YOU observed about reactions to stress among your colleagues with different personalities or from different cultures?

Is stress necessarily to be avoided?

A certain amount of stress may not necessarily be seen as a bad thing and perhaps even help promote a higher level of intensity and motivation to get work done. It is arguable that stress is a normal motivating factor, and in moderation and in short spells, stress may be good for you. It is important to bear in mind, however, that stress is potentially very harmful. But what is the distinction between pressure and stress? 'Pressure' can be seen as a positive factor that may be harnessed to help people respond to a challenge and function more effectively. 'Stress' may be regarded as a continuous negative response arising from extreme pressure or other demands and the individual's inability to cope.

Difference between pressure and stress

According to the Health and Safety Executive (HSE), people get confused about the difference between pressure and stress. Pressure can be positive and a motivating factor, and is often essential in a job. It can help us to achieve our goals and perform better. Stress occurs when this pressure becomes excessive. Stress is a natural reaction to too much pressure. HSE defines work stress as: 'The adverse reaction people have to excessive pressures or other types of demand placed on them at work.' Stress is not an illness – it is a state.

If stress becomes too excessive and prolonged, mental and physical illness may develop. Stress can hit anyone at any level of the business and recent research shows that work-related stress is widespread and is not confined to particular sectors, jobs or industries. A person experiences stress when they perceive the demands of their work are greater than their ability to cope. However, stress can also result from having too few demands, as people will become bored, feel undervalued and lack recognition.[34] Work-related stress can be approached on different levels – individual worker, work organisation, national and EU level. Aside from the legal obligations, stress is a problem for the individual, their work organisation and society, and work-related stress problems are increasing.

Attention to job design

Two employees work doing the same job as part of a small team. When a new manager arrives one of the employees is given the more difficult work, while the other is given the more routine repetitive tasks. The employee with the challenging work begins to work longer hours in order to get his work completed on time. After a few weeks he is frequently off sick due to the pressure of work. The other employee does the routine work easily and has time left with nothing to do. She soon feels bored and starts to make mistakes and not complete tasks due to lack of motivation. The manager holds a meeting with the employees to discuss the problems. The manager agrees to look at the job design and reorganise work duties. Training is arranged so that both employees can undertake some of the more challenging work and the routine work is distributed more fairly.

Source: Advisory booklet – Stress at Work, HSE/ACAS September 2014.

According to *Kate Cobb* the issue of pressure is a complex one though some small changes can make all the difference in assisting you. Cobb refers to two separate aspects of stress:

- pressure that comes from outside, for example working to imposed deadlines when you have many other tasks to perform as well. This places emphasis on your planning skills;
- pressure from within and self-imposed, for example if you are a perfectionist and everything has to be 'just so' in your work. This suggests you should look at why you have developed this attitude and learn to be a little easier on yourself.[35]

It is important to bear in mind that although management may believe that a moderate level of stress can be a spur to increased work performance, employees are unlikely to perceive this in the same way and dispute what is regarded as an acceptable level of stress or excessive pressure. While some amount of stress can be useful as a spur to motivation it is important to avoid the adverse reaction. This can include physical symptoms such as headaches, stomach problems and muscle tension, and mental symptoms such as anxiety and depression. These reactions can be extremely debilitating and result in reduced productivity, absenteeism and poor morale in the workplace.[36]

To what extent does pressure help motivate YOU to improve your performance? Is this pressure more from outside or self-imposed from within?

A summary of the nature and causes of stress is set out in the concept map, Figure 3.4.

Coping with stress

There are a number of measures by which individuals and organisations can attempt to reduce the causes and harmful effects of stress. There are also many suggested techniques to help individuals bring stress under control – for example, changing one's viewpoint, identifying causes of distress, effective time management **(discussed in Chapter 16),** expanding one's social network, laughing and telling jokes, relaxation training, working on stress reduction and appreciating that some stress can be useful. However, there are not always easy remedies for stress and much depends upon the personality of the individual.

Techniques such as relaxation therapy may help some people, although not others, but still tend to address the symptoms rather than the cause. Organisations also need to give greater attention to training, support and counselling and to the work organisation and job design. However, *Briner* suggests that talking therapies certainly can be useful in some circumstances but if problems of high-level stress-related issues are caused by a poor working environment or poor management, then counselling is unlikely to help or, if it does, the effects are likely to be only short-lived.[37]

Effective communications and conversation

Effective two-way communications at all levels of the organisation are clearly important in helping to reduce or overcome the level of stress. Staff should feel able to express their true feelings openly and know they will be listened to. However, in addition to good communications, *Reeves* refers to the importance of conversation for maintaining relationships and suggests a case for a conversation culture. The ability to hold good-quality conversations is becoming a core organisational and individual skill. Unlike communication, conversations are intrinsically creative and roam freely across personal issues, corporate gossip and work projects. 'Conversations are a defence against stress and other mental health problems. People with good social relationships at work are much less likely to be stressed or anxious.'[38]

Stress

- what is stress?
- how can stress be caused?
- how can you identify stress?
- what can you do to avoid stress?

Stress
- The result of a person being pushed beyond the limit of his or her natural capacity
- After the cause is removed the person does not return to his or her previous state

All managers work under pressure. When pressure becomes too high the manager experiences unacceptable stress. Organisations need to reduce stress in managers to the level of challenge.

The cause of stress
- work load
- personality
- physical factors

Confused working
- conflicting priorities
- disordered environment
  – continual interruptions
- too little feedback/feedback too late
- distorted feedback/too much information
- ambiguity – unclear objectives
- too little control

Physical fitness
- low physical fitness increases vulnerability to stress
- large frequent meals reduce fitness
- smoking
- drinking
- little sleep
- little exercise

Old age
- problems from paced work
- problems from poor feedback
- fear of underemployment, redundancy, and depreciation

Underemployment
- Too little depending on actions
  - job ignored
  - job deprecated
- Stress generated by fear
  - loss of job
  - loss of face (to others or self)
- Underemployment from
  - recruiting to too high a standard
  - recruiting to keep up establishment
  - transfer to avoid redundancy
  - overpayment preventing leaving
  - cancellation of expectations

Overworking
- Too great a responsibility
- Too close supervision
  - too little room for manoeuvre
  - negative feedback only
- Too much control
  - too fast an assembly line
  - poorly paced work

Driving
- always trying to get things done
  generally
  - poor team member
  - doesn't suffer fools
  - prefers short term problems
  stress from UNDEREMPLOYMENT

performance / drive (motivation & movement)

Internal response to stress
- If things go wrong he or she takes it out on themselves
  - generally introvert
  - withdrawing
  - careful
  - stress from OVERWORKING

Organisational strategies for reducing stress

Training
- Induction
- Specific training
- Time planning
- Assertiveness
- Stress awareness

Examine reward Systems
- Pay
- Other benefits
- Intangible rewards

Review organisational Aims, objectives & systems
- Needs & objectives change with time
- Systems need to reflect these changes

Employing change Consultants
- When major change is contemplated

Relaxation techniques
Consider new techniques, diet analysis, counselling & advice systems. Organisations can support through: relaxation, Alexander technique, yoga, Tai Chi, sports and cultural activities

Employee appraisal
- Target setting
- Controlling expectations

Personal crises outside of work
- Promotion → Increase in discretionary part of the job
- Increase work load → No one with whom to discuss difficulties
- Working late → Work becomes an obsession
- Off work for a long spell with acute depression → Exhaustion & anxiety Stress-related absence – loses more days per year than industrial action

Identifying stress
- Unusual behavior
- Flying off the handle more than usual
- Tiredness
- Not getting the job done
- Nervousness
- Blaming others
- Acute stress from major strain
- Chronic stress – from long-term strain

Avoiding stress (chronic stress)
- Keep fit & sleep enough
- Plan relations & limit work time
- Don't get worked up at work
- Decide if you are doing the right job
  - What do you want from life
  - Death is nature's way of telling you to slow down!

External response to stress
- If things go wrong he or she takes it out on other people
- Generally – extrovert
  status conscious
  decisive decision taker
  stress from confused working

Types of stress
Acute • Short term can be caused by Sharp increase / decrease in orders
  - Key staff leaving / sickness in others
  - Industrial disputes / strikes
  • Long term caused by
  - Lack of clarity of organisational goals
  - Protracted takeover negotiations
  - Promotion above manager's level of competence
  - Non-supportive organisational systems

Avoiding stress (acute stress)
- Decide if you are doing the right job
- If under threat take deeper breaths
  - pace the interview
  - answer one question at a time
  - answer question with question
  - keep calm, watch how you appear to others

Figure 3.4 Stress
Source: Copyright © 2011 The Virtual Learning Materials Workshop. Reproduced with permission.

A growing number of organisations are introducing an email-free day to encourage staff to use the telephone or walk across the corridor to talk more with one another.

Informing members of staff in the first place about what is happening especially at times of major change, involving them proactively in the change process, and allowing people to feel in control and exercise their own discretion reduces uncertainty and can help minimise the potential for stress. Managers can do much to create a psychologically supportive and healthy work environment. Treating people with consideration, respect and trust, giving full recognition and credit, getting to know members of staff as individuals, and placing emphasis on end results can all help to reduce stress. Managers should attempt to be role models and through their language and body language indicate to others that they are dealing effectively with their own work pressures.

Use of kaizen principles

Another interesting approach to reducing stress is through the use of the Japanese kaizen principles **(see also Chapter 17).** According to *Scotchmer,* applying the kaizen 5S method (translated into English as sort, straighten, shine, standardise and sustain) can help increase efficiency and productivity, raise morale and lower an individual's stress levels. 'The busier you are the tidier your desk should be; that is if you wish to get ahead and deliver more with less stress.'[39]

Individual needs and expectations

Rigby points out that stress at work is getting worse and the problem for those who would seek an easier life is that big-money jobs generally come with a big chunk of hassle attached. People suffering from high stress at work should try switching to a job more in tune with their individual needs and expectations. Rigby suggests five prescriptions for those seeking a lower-stress job and a healthier, more satisfying work/life balance.

- **Stability and security** – consider professional jobs, those requiring specialised technical knowledge or jobs in obscure sectors such as industry and food technology.

- **Personal contact** – forging strong relationships with customers and colleagues can be great for stress relief but avoid frontline contact with overbearing customer-care departments or call centres.

- **Right kind of boss** – unless you have a good boss look for a job that gets you out on your own a lot or allows flexible working, or become self-employed.

- **Change, pressure and perception** – look for firms changing fast because they are leading the way, but avoid working for a firm where change is imposed because it is trying to catch up. Consider also the public perception of how far the job is important or socially useful.

- **Potential for fulfilment** – even if the work is hard and long, look for jobs that are creative or engaging or provide a sense of worth or satisfaction.[40]

How well do YOU cope with stress? What actions do you take to avoid or reduce your levels of stress? To what extent do you discuss any concerns with your colleagues?

HSE management standards

The Health and Safety Executive (HSE) has developed the Management Standards approach to tackling work-related stress. These Standards represent a set of conditions that, if present, reflect a high level of health, well-being and organisational performance. It is based on the familiar 'Five steps to risk assessment' model, requiring management and staff to work together. *See* **Figure 3.5.**

Key areas of work design

The six Management Standards cover the primary sources of stress at work and if not properly managed are associated with poor health and well-being, lower productivity and increased sickness absence.[41]

- **Demands** – includes workload, work patterns and the work environment.
- **Control** – how much say a person has in the way they do their work.
- **Support** – includes the encouragement, sponsorship and resources provided by the organisation, line management and colleagues.
- **Role** – whether people understand their role within the organisation and whether the organisation ensures that they do not have conflicting roles.
- **Change** – how organisational change (large or small) is managed and communicated in the organisation.
- **Relationships** – promoting positive working to avoid conflict and dealing with unacceptable behaviour.

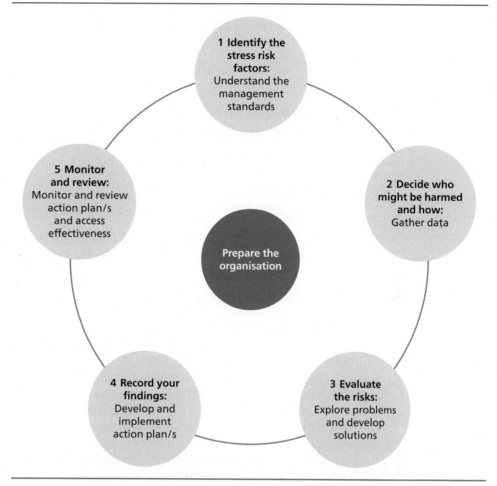

Figure 3.5 The Management Standards approach: five steps to risk assessment
Source: Health and Safety Executive, 'How to tackle work-related stress', publication INDG430, October 2009.

Bullying and harassment

Bullying and harassment can clearly have a serious adverse effect on workplace health and well-being. Despite increasing awareness of the problem, according to the CIPD bullying and harassment remain significant issues in the workplace. The conflict created can lead to high levels of stress resulting in increased sickness absence, higher labour turnover, less productive and effective teams. A workplace environment free from hostility enables people to achieve higher levels of job satisfaction and contribute more effectively to organisation success.[42]

The Equality Act 2010

Under the Equality Act 2010 harassment is defined widely as unwanted conduct that has the purpose or effect of violating a person's dignity or creating an intimidating, hostile, degrading, humiliating or offensive environment for that person. Harassment is when the unwanted behaviour is related to one of the following:

- age;
- sex;
- disability;
- gender (including gender reassignment);
- marriage and civil partnership;
- pregnancy and maternity;
- race;
- religion or belief;
- sexual orientation.

Harassment in the workplace can occur even if the effect is unintended but when a person has reasonably considered that such conduct has that effect.

Unwanted behaviours

Bullying is not defined in law but is characterised by Acas as 'offensive, intimidating, malicious or insulting behaviour, an abuse or misuse of power through means that undermine, humiliate, denigrate or injure the recipient'. Bullying and harassment are unwanted behaviour that may be between two individuals or involve groups of people; it might be obvious or insidious; it may be a persistent or isolated incident. For practical purposes people making a complaint define what has happened to them as unwelcome, unwarranted and causing a detrimental effect. Bullying and harassment can take many forms and is not necessarily face to face. It may incur through written communications, visual images, email, phone or automatic supervision methods. [43] Bullying and harassment is not only a lack of dignity and respect at work but such unwanted behaviour can lead to conflict and a high proportion of stress-related illnesses. According to *Luisa Cheshire* bullying is rife in the workplace and this trend is on the rise.[44]

Bullying and harassment is not only a human concern with possible physical and/ or psychological damage: it can lead to poor morale, high turnover, unrest and lack of respect for management, and lower performance. Organisations need to have a clearly stated formal policy, good behaviour and examples from senior staff, effective human resource management, and safe reporting procedures. *Evesson and Oxenbridge* report that workplace bullying is a serious problem in Britain. It is a source of considerable individual suffering, weakening organisational performance and negative outcomes for society and the economy. The complexity of workplace bullying poses a challenge to those seeking to prevent and manage such behaviours but in many workplaces bullying is not taken seriously enough.[45]

To what extent do YOU believe bullying and harassment is evident in (i) workplaces generally and (ii) your own university? What action would you propose to reduce incidents of unwanted behaviours?

Frustration-induced behaviour

Incidence of conflict or stress can lead to the individual experiencing a feeling of frustration at the inability to satisfy their own needs and expectations from the work situation. For example this may result from a person strongly at odds with a manager whom is perceived to be deliberately blocking promotion; or the personality of an individual who prefers a quiet life without confrontation and upset easily by any form of aggravation. In either event conflict or stress could result in frustration-induced behaviour. There are two possible sets of outcomes: constructive behaviour or frustration.

- **Constructive behaviour** is a positive reaction and can take two main forms: problem-solving for example removing the barrier and bypassing the non-co-operative superior; or restructuring through substitution such as taking an additional part-time job, asking to work in a different department, or reassessing work/life balance.

- **Frustration** is a negative response to the blockage of a desired goal and results in a defensive form of behaviour which can be summarised under four broad headings: aggression, regression, fixation and withdrawal.[46] However, these categories are not mutually exclusive. Many forms of frustration-induced behaviour at work are a combination of aggression, regression and fixation.

Aggression is a physical or verbal attack on some person or object, for example striking a supervisor, rage or abusive language, destruction of equipment or documents, or malicious gossip about a superior. Where a direct attack cannot be made against the actual barrier or blocking agent, because for example where the source is feared, as with a powerful superior, aggression may be displaced towards some other person or object. With **displaced aggression** the person may a scapegoat for the outlet of frustration – for example picking arguments or being short-tempered with colleagues or slamming the filing cabinet. A more constructive form of displaced aggression is working off frustrated feelings through demanding physical work or sport, or perhaps by shouting/cursing when alone or in the company of an understanding colleague.

- **Regression** is reverting to a childish or more primitive form of behaviour – for example sulking, crying, tantrums or kicking a broken machine or piece of equipment.

- **Fixation** is persisting in a form of behaviour which has no adaptive value and continuing to repeat actions which have no positive results – for example the inability to accept change or new ideas, repeatedly trying a machine which clearly will not work, or even insisting on applying for promotion even without the support of your manager.

- **Withdrawal** is apathy, giving up or resignation – for example arriving at work late and leaving early, sickness and absenteeism, refusal to accept responsibility, avoiding decision-making, passing work over to colleagues or leaving the job altogether.

It is important that managers attempt to reduce potential frustration-induced behaviour through, for example: equitable recognition and rewards; effective communications; participative style of management; attempting to understand the individual's perception of the situation.

Critical Thinking Zone
Reflections on Health and Well-Being

In this zone, we critically examine the concept of health and well-being and evaluate whether organisations are doing enough to promote the welfare of their most valuable assets.

Work is an innate and necessary part of our everyday lives. On average, we spend an estimated one-third of our lives at work.[47] Indeed, the ever-increasing, blurred lines between our home and work lives caused, in part, by the twenty-first century, hyperconnected workplace, has meant that many of us find it difficult, if not impossible at times, to leave our work at the door when we finish for the day and leave our personal lives at the door when we arrive at work.[48] This inability to achieve equilibrium between our work and home lives (see Chapter 2: Critical Thinking Zone: Reflections on Work–Life Balance), has created a culture whereby individuals may succumb to organisational pressures and behavioural norms to put their jobs before their families and personal lives by working longer hours, resulting in excessive strain and burnout.[49] Moreover, Caicedo et al.[50] profess that other workplace stressors, such as incessant organisational change, staff shortages and poor relationships with managers and colleagues, may have a negative effect on overall health and well-being and, as a consequence, reduce productivity and organisational effectiveness. Hence, the promulgation of debate and research in health and well-being in the past two decades.[48,51]

Deconstructing Health and Well-Being

Employee well-being is an inclusive and complex concept, with its roots embedded in a multiplicity of fields, including HRM, healthcare, psychology, sociology and organisational behaviour.[51,52] It is a major concern for organisations as it can have both a positive and negative influence on individual and organisational performance. Well-being can be defined as the overall *quality of work* experienced by the individual in the workplace.[53] This feeds into the quality of work life construct, which Sirgy et al. (p. 242)[54] define as 'employee satisfaction with a variety of needs through resources, activities and outcomes stemming from participation in the workplace.' Yeo and Li[55] proffer that individuals perceive they have attained a quality of work life, and thus satisfaction, when their primary expectations are appropriately met. One could argue that these are the same expectations and obligations that are subjectively perceived via the transactional, relational and balanced psychological contracts individuals may have formed with the organisation[56,57] (See Chapter 1: Critical Thinking Zone: Reflections on the Psychological Contract). Furthermore, Sirgy et al. and Yeo and Li contend that the expectations that are shrouded within the quality of work life construct are associated with the satisfaction of various needs on Maslow's Hierarchy. For example, satisfaction with: workplace facilities (physical needs); compensation and benefits (security needs); opportunities to engage in social networking and collaboration (affiliation needs); autonomy and decision making (esteem needs) and strategic planning and involvement (self-actualisation needs).

On a slightly different note, Fisher[58] likens well-being to 'happiness', which is manifest in positive attitudes, good moods and emotions. She suggests that experiencing feelings of happiness are also linked to high levels of job satisfaction, employee engagement and affective organisational commitment; again, symptomatic of a relational psychological contract.

According to Grant et al.,[52] employee well-being is premised on three main dimensions. First, the psychological dimension relates to happiness and the subjective, positive experiences individuals have in the workplace. Second, physical health and well-being encapsulate aspects of stress, injuries and diseases and the provision of healthcare services as part of, for example, employee assistance programmes.[59] Third, the social well-being dimension characterises the quality of peer and hierarchical relationships in the workplace. The three dimensions are mirrored in the World Health Organization's depiction of the concept of health. They define it as 'a state of complete physical, mental and social well-being and not merely the absence of disease and infirmity.'[60] As we can see, there are clear definitional overlaps between health and well-being. This is also recognised by the Department of Health.[61] who argue that 'there is a two-way relationship between well-being and health: health influences well-being and well-being itself influences health.' The evidential interrelationship between the two concepts have a significant influence on organisational behaviour in the workplace. This recognition can enable managers to develop strategies to promote a quality of work life that is conducive to commitment, engagement, productivity and, arguably, a positive relational psychological contract.

Reality not Rhetoric!

The CIPD's research reported that many organisations are proactively adopting a range of initiatives to support and manage individuals with disabilities, mental health issues and long-term health conditions, such as flexible working and access to employee assistance programmes that offer counselling and occupational health services.[59] However, Cooper and Suff[62] caveat that organisations need to become *more* conscious of the micro and macroenvironmental complexities surrounding people's lives, which may negatively impact on their overall welfare. Organisations can thus provide individuals with key emotional support from managers, which has been evidenced to decrease burnout and the negative effects of other health-related issues,[63] along with tailored support, such as the initiatives mentioned above. This may ensure that individuals remain a valued part of the workforce and retain their knowledge, skills and experience within the business.

Protecting Valuable Assets

To conclude, although evidence suggests that organisations are generally promoting health and well-being in the workplace, The CIPD[48] caveat that too many are not taking employee well-being seriously enough and

therefore not doing enough to facilitate a healthy, happy and harmonious workplace. If, as espoused, people are an organisation's greatest asset, managers need to supplement their rhetoric with proactivity, place the health and well-being of their workforce high on the strategic agenda and thus foster a good quality of work life that generates tangible benefits for all parties concerned in the people-organisation relationship.

Questions

Based on the above, answer the following questions.

1. Evidence suggests that health and well-being are inextricably linked, bonded by a two-way relationship. With reference to theory, *critically analyse* the key similarities and differences between the concepts.

2. Quality of work life is an importance construct within the health and well-being debate. *Critically evaluate* the link between the construct and transactional, relational and balanced psychological contracts. *What* are the implications for organisational behaviour in the workplace?

3. The CIPD advocates that organisations should be more conscious of the micro and macroenvironmental complexities surrounding people's lives and how they impact on their health and well-being. *How* can organisations do this in practice?

Summary – Chapter 3 'Organisational conflict and stress'

Conflict and stress at work are realities of organisational behaviour with significant influence on work and well-being. Conflict can be defined and interpreted in a number of ways but is based on incompatibility of goals and arises from opposing behaviours. There are contrasting perspectives of conflict and the extent to which it is necessarily a bad thing or an agent for evolution and change. A certain amount of conflict may be inevitable but there are a number of ways in which to avoid the harmful and negative outcomes in the workplace. A related influence on work/life balance is the extent of work stress. There is scepticism about the attention given to stress but it is a personal experience as is the response of each individual. Stress at work is a potential source of mental and physical ill-health. There is debate on the difference between pressure and stress and the extent to which pressure can be seen as a positive factor. There are a number of measures by which individuals and organisations can attempt to reduce harmful effects of stress. Bullying and harassment are unwanted behaviours that display lack of dignity and respect at work, and can lead to conflict and stress-related illnesses. Conflict and stress can result in frustration-induced behaviour.

Group discussion activities

Undertake each of these activities in small groups as indicated by your tutor. Before you start your discussion establish a non-threatening environment within the group and confirm confidentiality will be honoured.

First, form your own views and then share and compare in open critical discussion with colleagues. Reflect honestly on the extent to which: (i) you influenced the thinking and ideas of your colleagues; and (ii) you were influenced by your colleagues.

To what extent was your group able to reach consensus?

Agree one of your members to produce a brief written summary of the discussion and be prepared to present in a plenary session.

Activity 1

(a) Drawing on the ideas of unitarist, pluralist, radical and interactionist perspectives consider the extent to which you see conflict as a constructive positive force likely to inspire improved work performance.

(b) Now describe specific situations in which you see conflict more of a constructive force rather than a negative or disruptive influence.

(c) How much agreement is there on conflict as an inherent feature of organisational life and that structure, management systems and choice of technology all form part of the struggle for power and control?

(d) To what extent should your lecturers be encouraged deliberately to arouse constructive conflict? What are the possible dangers and how might the idea be perceived by students from different cultural backgrounds?

Activity 2

Work-related stress, depression or anxiety is defined as a harmful reaction people have to undue pressures and demands placed on them at work. Stress is more prevalent in public service industries, such as education; health and social care; and public administration and defence. By occupation, jobs that are common across public service industries (such as healthcare workers; teaching professionals; business, media and public service professionals) show higher levels of stress as compared with other jobs.

(a) What do you think are the main reasons for higher levels of stress in public service industries?

(b) To what extent is the potential level of stress likely to affect your choice of career?

Source: 'Work related Stress, Anxiety and Depression Statistics in Great Britain 2016', Health and Safety Executive, www.hse.gov.uk

Activity 3

(a) People may be busy and under pressure, but stress is far too much an over-used word and has become something of a fashion trend. Many people appear to compete for who is most stressed. The biggest danger is that the more people talk about stress, the more likely they will really become stressed.

(b) Suggestions for coping with a high level of stress, for example adjusting your viewpoint, changing your job or relaxation therapy, may be well intended but are difficult to implement and have little adaptive value. Stress is predominately a feature of a person's personality and must be accepted as such.

(c) To what extent are situations outside of the work organisation (for example domestic, economic, accommodation) likely to have an adverse effect on work-related stress?

(d) How well does your personality allow you to cope with stress?

What conclusions did you draw and to what extent was the discussion helpful to group members?

Organisational behaviour in action case study – based on real events

The production manager (Jack), quality control manager (Josh) and planning manager (Jill) work for a company producing PVC raw materials for customers making a variety of PVC products such as clothing, tarpaulins, seat covers, plastic containers etc. Here is a conversation on the shop floor between them concerning a customer complaint about the PVC raw materials.

Josh: I wish your department would give more attention to quality, Jack. We can only do a 10 per cent check on quality from our random sampling. Now we have this complaint from a customer about quality on a batch we produced last week. And the boss is real mad... was real mad when I told him.

Jack: Why the heck didn't you come to me first?... this puts me in a bad light before I have a chance to investigate and do something. You have assumed that the factory is to blame... it could have been...

Josh: You always have some excuse and start blaming others... like blaming me for poor quality control checks. You've even put pressure on our department to be retrained, or even fired, for poor quality control, when you know we are under pressure with increased sales. Have you forgotten....?

Jack: (Interrupts) Why don't you let me finish my sentence before you cut in and attack me?

Josh: Well you're always finding fault with me. So now you know what it's like. Anyway, what did you want to say?

Jack: I wanted to suggest that our complicated delivery schedule can cause confusion.

Josh: It's you chaps that make it complicated. I've already checked with Jill on planning and also checked despatch. There was nothing wrong with the order. This is clearly a production mess up...

Jack: Well I'm going to check with Jill's schedule anyway to make sure we have got the right production schedule...

Josh: Go ahead... perhaps you will be able to blame Jill.

Jack: What the hell are you talking about?... who said anything about blame? I'm just trying to get to the facts before taking the rap for something we didn't do.

Josh: Well I don't know about that Jack. As I walk through the plant, I'm not convinced that some of your supervisors and operators really pay enough attention to quality and the correct operating procedures.

Jack: You're a real pain in the arse Josh! (shouting)

Josh: So are you... (shouting)

Jill walks in and notices the tension.

Jill: What's the problem chaps?

Jack: Josh is blaming production for a quality problem from a customer complaint and...

Josh: Not blaming, simply stating a fact that...

Josh: That's absolute bull!

Jill: It seems that you chaps have two problems. A problem with the job – the complaint – and a problem with your conflict. I can't see you solving the complaint until you manage your conflict better.

Source: Kindly provided by Hugo Misselhorn, M.O.D. Consulting, South Africa.

Case study tasks

1. What do you see as the underlying cause of the conflict between Jack and Josh?

2. If you were Jill, how would you encourage Jack and Josh to investigate the complaint?

3. How would you attempt to avoid further conflict?

Chapter 3 – Personal skills and employability exercise

Objectives

Completing this exercise should help you to enhance the following skills:

* Understanding factors that impact upon work conflict and stress
* Assess benefits from your course of study
* Participate in preparing a plenary report

Exercise

PART 1 – Look back at the Organisational Behaviour in Action case study in this chapter. To what extent can you relate the situation in this case to potential sources of conflict discussed in the text of the chapter:

* Differences in perception
* Limited resources
* Departmentalisation and specialisation
* Nature of work activities
* Role definition
* Inequitable treatment
* Violation of territory?

PART 2 – Think of any stressful situation(s) you have experienced either during your university studies and/or any type of work experience you have had. Explain fully the nature of the situation and the causes, symptoms and consequences, and how you attempted to deal with the situation. How successful were you?

NOW, explore fully the extent to which you can relate the contents and discussion in this chapter to the situation(s) you experienced.

PART 3 – Share and discuss your findings in a small group situation and elect a spokesperson to report back in plenary session.

Discussion

∗ How far have been able to relate your course of study to actual situations of conflict and stress?

∗ To what extent do you perceive any relationship between conflict, stress and gender or ethnicity?

∗ How would you best prepare your university colleagues to deal with potential conflict and stress in the work environment?

Notes and references

1. 'Health, Work and Wellbeing', ACAS, March 2012.
2. 'Well-Being at Work', CIPD, 5 April 2017.
3. 'Stress at Work – Mind the Gap', *Social Agenda,* European Commission, no. 36 February 2014.
4. For further information, see: Mullins, L. J. and Dosser, P. *Hospitality Management and Organisational Behaviour,* fifth edition, Pearson Education (2013).
5. Berger, F. and Brownell, J. *Organisational Behaviour for the Hospitality Industry,* Pearson Prentice Hall (2009).
6. Ackroyd, S. and Thompson, P. *Organizational Misbehaviour,* Sage Publications (1999).
7. Yew, L. T. and Gregory, G. 'Organisational Misbehaviour: Should Management Intervene?' 26 July 2011. http://thebornepost.com/2011/07/26/organisational-misbehaviour-should-management-intervene (accessed 30 April 2017).
8. Woodward, J. *Industrial Organization: Theory and Practice,* second edition, Oxford University Press (1980), p. 113.
9. Podro, S. 'Riding out the Storm: Managing Conflict in a Recession and Beyond', ACAS Policy Discussion Paper, ACAS, March 2010.
10. Drucker, P. F. *The Practice of Management,* Heinemann Professional (1989), p. 119.
11. For an account of the Marxist critique, see, for example, Johnston, R. 'Hidden Capital', in Barry, J., Chandler, J., Clark, H., Johnston, R. and Needle, D. (eds) *Organization and Management: A Critical Text,* International Thomson Business Press (2000), pp. 16–35.
12. Salaman, G. *Class and Corporation,* Fontana (1981).
13. See, for example, Robbins, S. P. and Judge, T. A. *Organizational Behavior,* thirteenth edition, Pearson Education (2009).
14. Townsend, R. *Further Up the Organisation,* Coronet Books (1985), p. 39.
15. Dunne, P. 'Balance on the Board', *Governance + Compliance*, April 2014, pp. 24–7.
16. Irvine, L. 'Conflicts of Interest', *Manager, The British Journal of Administrative Management,* March/April 1998, pp. 8–10.
17. Mannering, K. 'Working with "Prickly" People', *Professional Manager,* vol. 19, no. 1, January 2009, pp. 32–4.
18. 'Managing Conflict at Work', ACAS, June 2014.
19. Saundry R. and Wibberley, G, 'Workplace Dispute Resolution and the Management of Individual Conflict – A Thematic Analysis of Five Case Studies', ACAS Research Paper, June 2014.
20. Hirshman, A. and Wakeling, A. 'The Road Less Travelled? Taking the Informal Route to Conflict Resolution', *Employee Relations Comment,* ACAS, July 2016.
21. Simms, J' There's More than One Way to Solve a Dispute', CIPD, 25 July 2017. www.cipd.co.uk.
22. York, P. 'Getting a Grip on Stress', *Management Today,* October 2001, p. 105.
23. Taylor, M. 'Tell me Why I Don't Like Mondays', Working Paper of the Institute for Social and Economic Research, October 2002.
24. Randall, J. 'Home Truths', *Management Today,* June 2001, p. 31.
25. Gwyther, M. 'stressed for Success', *Management Today,* January 1999, pp. 22–6.
26. 'Absence Management' Annual survey report, CIPD, November 2016.

27. 'Work Related Stress, Anxiety and Depression Statistics in Great Britain 2016', Health and Safety Executive http://www.hse.gov.uk (accessed 16 August 2017).

28. Donaldson-Fielder, A. in Hirshman, A. and Wakeling, A. 'The Road Less Travelled? Taking the Informal Route to Conflict Resolution', *Employment Relations Comment,* ACAS July 2016.

29. Rosen, L. *iDisorder: Understanding Our Obsession with Technology and Overcoming Its Hold on Us,* St Martin's Press (2012).

30. 'Stress at work – mind the gap', *Social Agenda,* European Commission, no. 36, February 2014.

31. Liu, C., Spector P. E. and Shi, L. 'Cross-National Job Stress: A Quantitative and Qualitative Study', *Journal of Organisational Behavior,* February 2007, pp. 209–39.

32. Tweed, R. G., White, K. and Lehman, D. R. 'Culture, Stress and Coping: Internally and Externally Targeted Control Strategies of European Canadians, East Asian Canadians and Japanese', *Journal of Cross-Cultural Psychology,* vol. 35, no. 6, 2004, pp. 652–8.

33. Spector, P. E. 'A Cross-National Comparative Study of Work-Family Stressors, Working Hours and Well-Being: China and Latin America versus the Anglo World', *Personnel Psychology,* Spring 2004, pp. 119–42.

34. 'What is stress?' Health and Safety Executive http://www.hse.gov.uk/stress (accessed 18 August 2017).

35. Cobb, K. 'Handling Pressure: Developing Skills for Mangers to Stay Resilient', *Manager: The British Journal of Administrative Management,* Winter 2011, pp. 24–5.

36. *ACAS News,* issue 11, Spring 2008.

37. Briner, R. 'Ask the Experts', *Professional Manager,* July/August 2011, p. 38.

38. Reeves, R. 'Reality Bites', *Management Today,* March 2003, p. 35.

39. Scotchmer, A. 'A Place for Everything and Everything in its Place', *Professional Manager,* vol. 16, no. 1, January 2007, pp. 30–1.

40. Rigby, R. 'Under Pressure', *Management Today,* March 2010, pp. 50–2.

41. 'What are the Management Standards for work related stress?', Health and Safety Executive http://www.hse gov.uk/stress (accessed 1 May 2017).

42. 'Harassment and Bullying at Work', CIPD, 1 August 2016.

43. 'Bullying and Harassment at Work' ACAS, June 2014 and 'Conference: ACAS Directions' 11 January 2016.

44. Cheshire, L. 'Silent Assassins', *Professional Manager,* Summer 2015, pp. 51–5.

45. Evesson, J and Oxenbridge, S. 'Seeking Better Solutions: Tackling Bullying and Ill-Treatment in Britain's Workplaces' *ACAS Policy Discussion Paper,* November 2015.

46. See, for example, Brown, J. A. C. *The Social Psychology of Industry,* Penguin (1986).

47. Ahmad, S. 'Paradigms of Quality of Work Life', *Journal of Human Values,* 19 (1), 2013, pp. 73–82.

48. CIPD, 'Health and Well-Being at Work', Survey Report, Chartered Institute of Personnel and Development, May, 2018.

49. Beauregard, T. A. 'Direct and Indirect Links Between Organizational Work–Home Culture and Employee Well-Being', *British Journal of Management,* vol. 22, 2011, pp. 218–37.

50. Caicedo, M. H., Mårtensson, M. and Roslender, R. 'Managing and Measuring Employee Wellbeing: A Review and Critique', *Journal of Accounting and Organizational Change,* vol. 16, no. 4, 2010, pp 436–59.

51. Vakkayil, J., Torre, E. D. and Giangrew, A. '"It's not how it looks!" Exploring Managerial Perspectives on Employee Wellbeing', *European Management Journal,* 35, 2017, pp. 548–62.

52. Grant, A. M., Christianson, M. K. and Price, R. H. 'Happiness, Health or Relationships? Managerial Practices and Employee Well-Being Tradeoffs', *Academy of Management Perspectives,* vol. 21, no. 3. 2007, pp. 51–63.

53. Warr, P. *Work, Unemployment and Mental Health,* Oxford: Clarendon Press (1987).

54. Sirgy, M. J., Efraty, D., Siegel, P. and Lee, D. J. 'A New Measure of Quality of Work Life (QWL) Based on Need Satisfaction and Spillover Theories', *Social Indicators Research,* 55, 2001, pp. 241–302.

55. Yeo, R. K. and Li, J. 'Working out the Quality of Work Life', *Human Resource Management International Digest,* vol. 19, no. 3, 2011, pp. 39–45.

56. Dabos, G. E. and Rousseau, D. M. 'Mutuality and Reciprocity in the Psychological Contracts of Employees and Employers', *Journal of Applied Psychology,* 89, 2004, pp. 52–72.

57. Hui, C., Lee, C. and Rousseau, D. 'Psychological Contract and Organizational Citizenship Behaviour in China, Investigating Generalizability and Instrumentality', *Journal of Applied Psychology,* 89, 2004, pp. 311–21.

58. Fisher, C. D. 'Happiness at Work', *International Journal of Management Reviews,* vol. 12, 2010, pp. 384–12.

59. Joseph, B. and Walker, A. 'Employee Assistance Programmes in Australia: The Perspectives of Organizational Leaders Across Sectors', *Asia Pacific Journal of Human Resources,* 55, 2017, pp. 177–91.

60. World Health Organization 'Constitution of WHO: Principles', 2017, http://www.who.int/about/mission/en (accessed 6 June 2018).

61. Department of Health 'The Relationship Between Wellbeing and Health', A Compendium of Factsheets: Wellbeing Across the Lifecourse, Health Improvement Analytical Team, January, 2014, pp. 1–3.

62. Cooper, C. and Suff, R. In Health and Well-Being at Work Survey Report, Chartered Institute of Personnel and Development, May, 2018.

63. Thompson, C. A. and Prottas, D. J. 'Relationships Among Organizational Family Support, Job Autonomy, Perceived Control and Employee Well-being', *Journal of Occupational Health Psychology,* 11, 2006, pp. 100–118.

Part 2
Focus on the individual

Chapter 4
Personality and diversity

Personality is a defining feature of individual differences and qualities, and an essential part of the study of organisational behaviour in the workplace.

Learning outcomes

After completing this chapter you should have enhanced your ability to:

- explain the nature of personality as a feature of individuality;
- outline theoretical approaches and the work of leading writers;
- assess the application of personality studies to the workplace;
- evaluate the value of personality 'tests' and assessments;

- explain the nature of significance of emotional intelligence;
- explore the nature and importance of diversity in the workplace;
- focus on relationships between personality and work performance.

Outline chapter contents

Overview topic map: Chapter 4 – Personality and diversity

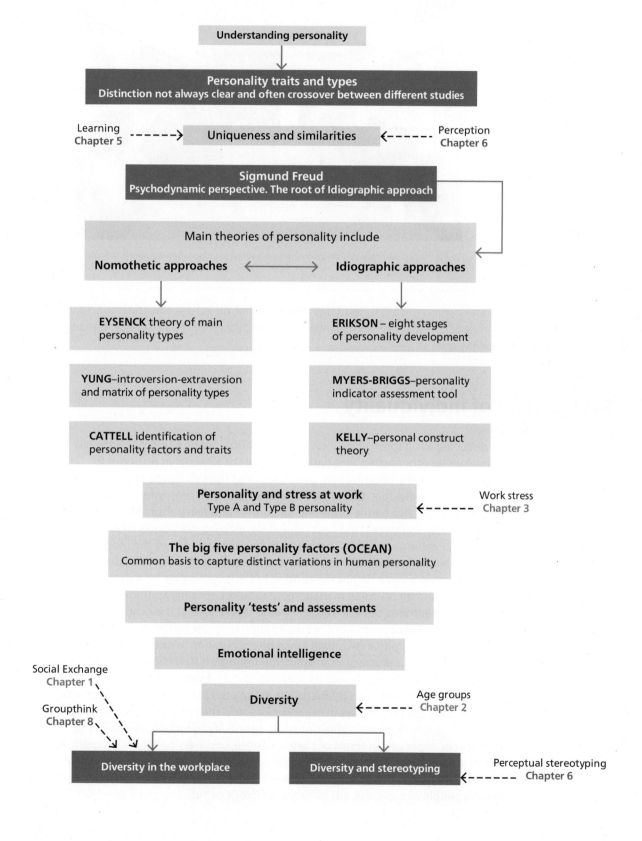

Source: https://www.pexels.com/photo/people-gathering-inside-white-building-1181408/

Before commencing to read this chapter, what do YOU see as the importance of an understanding of personality and diversity to your study of organisational behaviour?

Recognition of individuality

As discussed in Chapter 1, the individual is a central feature of organisational behaviour whether acting in isolation or as part of a group, in response to expectations of the organisation, or as a result of the influences of the external environment. Individual differences can foster creativity, enjoyment and satisfaction at work but can also be the potential for conflict and frustration. Managers are required to be competent at selecting and developing individuals who will be valuable to the organisation. They need to be observant about the individuals who are capable of effective performance, have the potential for development, and work well with other people within the context of the organisation as a whole.

Effective human resource management requires not only an understanding of individual employees but also recognition of the culture of the organisation. What is expected and accepted in one work situation may not be the same in another. For instance, creativity and individuality may be encouraged in one organisation but undermined by bureaucracy in another. It is important to recognise, respect and value individual differences and be sensitive to contrasting needs.

Maintaining harmonious relationships in the workplace has always been a key skill, but the speed of change in organisations and the external environment places increasing pressure on individuals at work. Sensitivity to individual needs and differences, especially in terms of their resilience, becomes particularly significant when organisations embark on change initiatives. When change appears to be externally imposed this may demand new mindsets, attitudes and perceptions that enable people to cope and adjust to the different world.

How do individuals differ?

Our sense of self is shaped by inherited characteristics and by influences in our social environment. Differences among individuals include: ethnic origin, physique, gender, early family experiences, social and cultural factors, national culture, motivation, perception. The impact of early family life and the country in which we live – has a significant part to play in our identity. Most social scientists agree that both inherited and environmental factors are important in our development, and the way these factors interact is the key to our adult personality. However, scientists differ with regard to the weight they place on these factors, some believing personality is influenced most heavily by inherited characteristics, others that environmental factors are most important. Developmental influences such as ageing and health also arguably affect personality characteristics.

Some of these characteristics are shared with others such as individuals from the same ethnic group or who have the same ability levels or who share similar physical attributes. But our uniqueness stems from the dynamic ways in which these inherited and environmental factors combine and interact. Central to the way in which it is possible to differentiate between individuals including their behaviour, actions and performance at work is an understanding of personality: the heart of individual differences. Every member of the organisation need to know themselves, understand their uniqueness and the impact of their own personality on others.

The workplace brings together a diverse mix of individual personalities. An integral and essential feature of individuality is diversity, **discussed later in this chapter.** An understanding of the way people learn is fundamental to an appreciation of individual differences and **is considered in Chapter 5.** The process of perception and communications **is examined in Chapter 6.** All contribute to a greater understanding of self and others.

Understanding personality

Personality may be viewed as consisting of stable characteristics that explain why a person behaves in a particular way. So, for instance, independence, conscientiousness, agreeableness and self-control are examples of personality characteristics. However, it is only when we see/hear/observe a person that we can gain an understanding of their personality. For example, a person who is independent may show that characteristic by displaying a strong sense of self-sufficiency. We would expect the person to take the initiative and not depend on other people. Furthermore, if the characteristic is 'stable' we can rely on this being a consistent part of the person's behaviour. We would be surprised if the person one day demonstrated autonomy and initiative and the next withdrew and delayed any decisions.

There are times when we might be surprised by somebody's behaviour and feel they are 'acting out of character'. Of course this would be known only if we had an understanding of their 'typical behaviour' in the first place. Individuals may exaggerate or suppress certain personality traits, for example if they are under stress or influenced by drink/drugs. Managers need to learn the art of 'reading' and understanding people's behaviour in order to manage relationships effectively.

Personality is clearly of importance in any work situation, and stress and dissatisfaction often results from personality clashes. Personality is arguably even more important in certain types of organisation such as in the service economy. For example a key element of reviews in the highly competitive cruise industry is the personality of members of the crew. A number of writers suggest that for hotel managers, personality is more important than other factors. *Ineson,* points out that 'Research has confirmed that personality is a key contributor to effective management especially in the service sector where well developed personal and interpersonal competencies are key to managerial success.'[1] The general manager of the Four Seasons Hotel, Qatar indicates what he looks for in hotel managers: 'if graduates are too academic they tend not to last'.[2]

Emotions in work behaviour

Traditionally, workplaces were seen as rational, logical places where emotions were excluded or seen in a negative light, and in **Chapter 2** we discussed the nature of emotional labour and how workers can become estranged from their own feelings. *Briner* challenges psychologists to broaden research to throw light on the complexities of emotions in the workplace. He notes that organisations specify the emotions they would like their employees to feel in the mission statements and in more subtle ways in terms of the rewards and career enhancements people receive when they display appropriate emotions. However, he suggests that little is known about the incidence of emotion at work and the part it plays in work behaviours.[3] The illustration shown in **Table 4.1,** although simplistic, plots a possible sequence of events and the effects of power of rewards and on psychological well-being. **Note also the discussion on emotional intelligence later in this chapter.**

Table 4.1 A sequence of work emotions, thought and behaviour

- Jane is asked to carry out a difficult project, usually given only to more experienced colleagues. She feels valued, flattered and trusted – also a little worried.
- While working hard on the project her emotions range from excitement and elation to fear and frustration.
- She completes the task well and feels proud and relieved.
- Jane tells her boss and shows her completed work.
- Boss gives no thanks or praise and picks out a trivial error.
- Jane then feels resentful and angry and thinks that she will never again 'put herself out' for her boss. Also feels exploited.
- Thinks about looking for another job.
- Doesn't volunteer to do additional tasks any more.
- Starts to feel sad and disappointed.
- Updates her CV and regularly starts looking at job advertisements.

Source: Briner, R. 'Feeling and Smiling', *The Psychologist,* vol. 12, no. 1, January 1999, pp. 16–19.

To what extent can you identify with Jane? Do YOU believe enough attention is given to psychological well-being and the role of emotions in your university?

Personality traits and types

Studies of personality can be divided into two main approaches, those looking at different aspects of personality, such as specific traits or competencies labelled nomothetic; and those taking a broader view of the type of individual personality as a whole, labelled as idiographic. Neither approach can be regarded as right or wrong; each views personality from different underlying assumptions. Some writers see traits concerned more with quantitative differences and types with qualitative differences. It is not always easy to see a clear difference between trait and type theories. There is often some crossover between the different studies and doubt about under which heading to classify a particular theory of personality.

The nomothetic approach

This is a measurable and specific perspective that looks at *the identification of traits and personality as a collection of characteristics.* These characteristics are ones that can be described, identified and measured and therefore can be subjected to observation and tests. This perspective is especially helpful for managers when they are involved in the selection, training and development of individuals. Nomothetic approaches tend to view environmental and social influences as minimal and view personality as consistent, largely inherited and resistant to change. Although they would not diminish the difficulties that measuring personality brings, nomothetic approaches would claim that it is possible to measure and predict the ways in which personality types would behave given certain circumstances.

Nomothetic researchers closely align themselves to studies that are 'scientific' in a positivistic sense. (The term positivism refers to the branch of science that is exclusively based on the objective collection of observable data – data that are beyond question.) Such an approach transfers methods used in natural sciences to the social world. Some psychologists are interested in describing and measuring characteristics and comparing individuals' scores. Does this person exhibit more or less than 'average' of this particular trait? Being able to predict behaviour is a major aim and outcome of this approach.

The idiographic approach

This is a more holistic and dynamic perspective which insists that managers take into account a 'whole' understanding of the individual at work. The individual's personality is more complex to be seen just as a collection of traits. This may also require going beyond the study of pure psychology to an understanding of the societal context in which the person lives. These are called idiographic approaches and are particularly pertinent in understanding motivation, career development and team relationships.

Idiographic approaches are concerned with understanding the uniqueness of individuals and the development of the self-concept. They regard personality development as a process that is open to change. They regard individuals as responding to the environment and people around them and see the dynamics of the interactions as playing a critical part in shaping personality.

Criticisms of the two approaches

The measurement of traits is seen as largely inappropriate in that one person's responses may not be comparable to another's. They suggest that personality assessment is not a valid method of understanding the unique ways in which a person understands and responds to the world. The depth and richness of a person's personality cannot be revealed in superficial paper-and-pencil questionnaires. Furthermore, the categories defined by psychologists are too narrow in scope and depth. However, the term *type* has been used in different ways and is the source of some confusion. There is criticism that the complex nature of personality cannot be explained with a small number of specific types. Individuals do not fall simply into broad type theories such as extrovert and introvert **discussed later in this chapter,** but lie somewhere within a wider continuous dimension.

Theory and the world of work

The application of theory to the world of work is not always easy and some find the process confusing when theory does not match with their experiences. Psychological investigations emphasise the complexity and variety of individual behaviour, and insist that simple answers and explanations are generally inadequate. The study of personality provides an excellent example of some of the complexities involved in applying psychological theory in practice.

Consider two individuals who share similar characteristics. They are both twenty-four years old and have lived in the same area; both have a first-class honours degree in pharmacy and they have identical personality assessment profiles. However, we would still predict individual differences with regard to, for example, their attitude and performance in the workplace. The complexities of the process pose a number of questions that interest psychologists and evoke different responses. **Figure 4.1** identifies the links between the dynamics of personality and life's experiences.

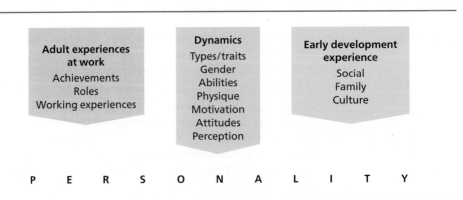

Figure 4.1 To what extent does our personality remain constant?

What do YOU believe is the *single* most distinguishing feature of an individual's personality? What *one* word would you use to describe your personality?

Uniqueness and similarities

Tables 4.2 and 4.3 focus on two major issues of prime importance in the study of personality. First, is personality a constant throughout our lifetime, which remains resistant to change and circumstances? Second, to what extent can we measure and compare individuals on the basis of their personality? This second question assumes that it is possible to distinguish personality characteristics in the first place. Trying to make sense of the nature of personality has resulted in a prolific number of theories,

Table 4.2 The role of early experiences – what is their impact?

Environment is significant Approach taken by idiographic theorists	Inherited characteristics are significant Approach taken by nomothetic theorists
The personalities of the two pharmacists described above are the culmination of experiences. Their personalities have been shaped by the people around them from their very earliest years. Early family life – the relationship between family members, the size of the family, the rewards and punishments exercised by parents – would have had an influence on the type of person each is now. In other words, the environment and early learning experiences have significantly contributed to their personality development.	The pharmacists inherited a genetic make-up which would remain core and would be resistant to change. Early experiences, while they may shape the person to a certain extent, do not alter the inherited make-up. Intelligence, physical appearances, physiological reactions are 'wired' in from birth – the 'core' of the individual is a 'given'.

Table 4.3 Is it possible to 'measure' an individual's personality?

No, personality is unique Approach taken by idiographic theorists	Yes, there are identifiable traits Approach taken by nomothetic theorists
Idiographic approaches do not believe it is possible to put personal characteristics to the test. Our very uniqueness makes comparisons difficult, if not impossible. Is it appropriate to consider the 'strength' of a trait? Our pharmacists may not always reveal their true 'self' – at times circumstances may force them to 'mask' their preferred ways of behaving. Our pharmacists may not reliably report on their own behaviour or there may be a real difference between what they say and what others see. Critics of questionnaires believe answering 'set' questions is 'forcing' responses to questions that may not be relevant. Instead it may be more appropriate to use open-ended techniques. This ensures that individuals use their own definitions and allows for greater understanding about their motivations and causes of behaviour.	Identifying an individual's personality typically refers to distinguishing traits or types. Personality traits are usually identified by what people do the behaviour they exhibit, e.g. sociability. Psychologists have designed questionnaires asking people to report on the way they feel or behave. They claim that this is a legitimate way of assessing personality. These self-reporting questionnaires would then be subject to quantitative methods. It is therefore possible to quantify the strength of a person's trait and to enable comparisons to be made with others. Such information then becomes a basis for prediction. For example, if a person has a high score on extraversion, it would be possible to predict the way in which the individual might behave in a given situation.

with some psychologists focusing solely on the unique make-up of individuals, others drawing comparisons between individuals or looking for broad similarities in aspirations and goals.

In a work context we tend to be more interested in understanding 'what' an individual's personality is rather than why it is as it is. Furthermore, it is important to understand how various personality characteristics relate to performance at work. The idiographic approach enriches our understanding of 'why' and the nomothetic approach explores the 'what' of personality.

The same but different

 How would YOU distinguish between Nomothetic and Idiographic approaches? To what extent does discussion of the two approaches help your study and understanding of personality?

Sigmund Freud – a psychodynamic perspective

A discussion on personality would not be complete without a mention of *Sigmund Freud* (1856–1939) who was at the root of the ideographic approach. His psychological approach is based on the role of the inner self and unconscious, and emphasised the importance of:

- early childhood experiences, particularly parental relationships and dealing with trauma;
- different levels of consciousness and the influence of the unconscious mind on behaviour;
- understanding the 'whole' person in relation to their past.[4]

Early childhood experiences were seen by Freud as paramount in understanding the adult personality. He described the development of all individuals as one

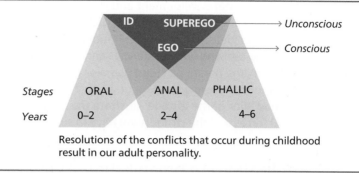

Resolutions of the conflicts that occur during childhood result in our adult personality.

Figure 4.2 Representative of Freud's personality theory, development and structure

which progressed through a number of stages: (i) oral; (ii) anal; and (iii) phallic **(see Figure 4.2)**. These changes are, for Freud, significant in that if the child finds the stage too difficult and the conflicts too hard and traumatic, an arrested development or 'fixation' could result. This means that the problems associated with the stage may be relived at a later time in adult life.

The personality structure of the individual develops as the child comes to terms with the new changes at each stage of life. Each stage was characterised by an internal struggle of domination by three personality structures – the **id, ego** and **superego** – as well as external conflict with outside relationships.

- **Id** is present at birth and consists of the instinctive, biological and hedonistic part of self. The id contains our inherited drives, desires and needs, which demand immediate gratification.

- **Ego** which develops out of the id has to make sense of the internal conflict in our mind between the id and superego and the external world. The ego is the decision-making part of our personality and is engaged in rational and logical thinking. It is governed by the reality principle.

- **Superego** is the last component to develop and consists of learned values and moral standards, and our sense of right and wrong. It is the part of personality that is influenced by significant others in our life.

The id and superego are in conflict with each other, with the id desiring certain behaviours and the superego attempting to discipline and control behaviour. These conflicts and tensions, rooted in the past and repressed within the unconscious, were seen by Freud as the key to an understanding of adult personality. In summary, Freud saw adult personality as being largely determined by the strength of inner drives and impulses and the resolutions of these tensions within early childhood experiences. Freud's overwhelming interest lay in understanding the conflicts that exist for the person and how people come to terms with their anxieties and tensions. His interest therefore lay in understanding the whole person and not in identifying traits or types.

Criticism of Freud

Freud's theory is controversial and subject to heavy criticism on the grounds that: it is subjective and unscientific; no attention was given to the impact of cultural or environment; a heavy emphasis on early childhood makes it highly deterministic; and it disregards later development and changes. His theory should, however, be seen in its historical context and in terms of its impact upon the development of later theories and ideas. In a review of Freudian theory *Andrews and Brewin* cite research supporting oral and anal tendencies and offer support for some of his ideas on depression and paranoia. Freud was also given positive review concerning 'slips of the tongue'. These incidents occur when what was actually said was not intended. For Freud 'slips of the tongue' illustrate the conflict that can exist between our mental forces and the struggle we have in suppressing our desires.[5]

Applications to organisational behaviour

With regard to organisational behaviour, Freud's theory still has much to offer with respect to understanding stress at work. When the going gets tough it is easy to slip into habitual ways of responding that have been learned as children. Within the working context, such behaviour may be seen as inappropriate and yet bring immediate relief or comfort to the individual. Instances include regressing into temper tantrums or gaining relief by excessive eating or drinking and can be seen to protect the ego from a painful memory or unwanted impulse. Freud labelled these **defence mechanisms.** The most readily observable ones in the workplace include:

- **Regression** – adopting childhood patterns of behaviour;
- **Fixation** – inflexible and rigid behaviour or attitudes;
- **Rationalisation** – elaborate 'covering-up' of ideas/motives;
- **Projection** – attributing feelings and motives to others.

(See also the discussion on frustrated behaviour in Chapter 3.)

Interest in the power of the unconscious has led some writers to consider the impact of repressed desires and wishes on organisational behaviour. These have been succinctly reviewed by *Gareth Morgan* who uses the metaphor of a 'Psychic Prison' to visualise and emphasise its power. Such an image suggests that people are trapped by their unconscious. As prisoners of their personal history, they are constantly struggling to control their unwanted impulses which lead to repression and dysfunctional activities at work.[6]

How comfortable would YOU feel in attempting to justify the relevance of Freud's work for the study of OB to a sceptical colleague studying a different subject area?

Nomothetic approaches

Main writers under this heading include:

- Eysenck's theory of main personality types;
- Yung's introversion–extraversion and matrix of personality types; and
- Cattell's identification of personality factors and traits.

Hans Eysenck

Hans Eysenck (1916–97) believed that personality was largely inherited and that we are born with differing physiological tendencies. He identified two major individual differences extroversion and introversion; to which he added two further dimensions of neuroticism and stability to define four distinct personality types.

- stable extraverts (sanguine) with traits such as being talkative, responsive, easygoing, lively, carefree;
- unstable extraverts (choleric) with traits such as being impulsive, changeable, excitable, restless;
- stable introverts (phlegmatic) with traits such as being calm, even-tempered, peaceful, thoughtful;
- unstable introverts (melancholic) with traits such as being anxious, moody, reserved, pessimistic.

Individuals in Eysenck's theory could, therefore, be one of four main personality types. His aim was to produce objective evidence of personality differences using large samples of the population.[7] However, it unlikely that anyone will be a complete example of one particular type. So each type would lead to a predisposition of traits that would, itself, lead to the likelihood of certain behaviours. For instance, a person typed as an extravert would predictably talk over things with someone to help them think it through, while an introvert would prefer to mull it over before talking about the issue. Although Eysenck still divides personality into four types his work is moving more towards trait theories.

Although Eysenck's theory appears simplistic, it has an impressive amount of supporting research evidence. His approach has immediate appeal to managers in organisations who are concerned with predicting the future behaviour of their employees, either for selection or promotion. Given the evidence that personality is a useful predictor of behaviour, it is not surprising that the use of psychometric tests has grown substantially over the past decade and that the majority of large companies use occupational tests.[8] **(Further information about testing is given later in this chapter.)**

Carl Jung

Carl Jung's (1875–1961) theory is of particular significance in that it bridges the psychoanalytic approach (of writers such as Sigmund Freud) with modern approaches of personality test design. His theory identifies life energy as concerned with hopes and goals of the future and not just of the past. Jung describes three levels of personality:

- a conscious level (daily reality);
- an unconscious level (contains our unique complexes);
- a collective unconscious level (store of universal and evolutionary experiences).

According to Jung people have a psychological preference for introversion or extraversion and the balance between their inner self or the external world. Introverts are directed more towards their own internal feelings and actions, and tend to avoid social situations. Extraverts are outgoing, active and enjoy interactions

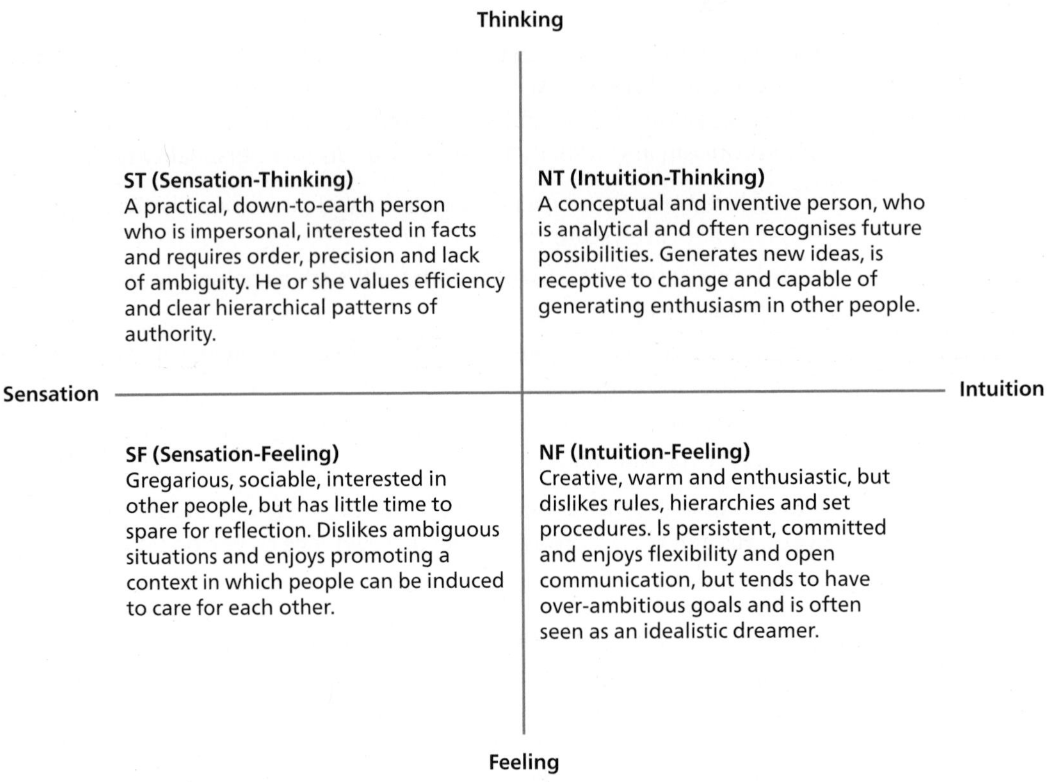

Thinking

ST (Sensation-Thinking)
A practical, down-to-earth person who is impersonal, interested in facts and requires order, precision and lack of ambiguity. He or she values efficiency and clear hierarchical patterns of authority.

NT (Intuition-Thinking)
A conceptual and inventive person, who is analytical and often recognises future possibilities. Generates new ideas, is receptive to change and capable of generating enthusiasm in other people.

Sensation ——————————————————————————————— Intuition

SF (Sensation-Feeling)
Gregarious, sociable, interested in other people, but has little time to spare for reflection. Dislikes ambiguous situations and enjoys promoting a context in which people can be induced to care for each other.

NF (Intuition-Feeling)
Creative, warm and enthusiastic, but dislikes rules, hierarchies and set procedures. Is persistent, committed and enjoys flexibility and open communication, but tends to have over-ambitious goals and is often seen as an idealistic dreamer.

Feeling

Figure 4.3 Jung's personality types
Source: Derek Rollinson, *Organisational Behaviour and Analysis: An integrated approach,* fourth edition, Pearson Education (2008).

with other people. This basic dichotomy is expanded into four additional factors: thinking, sensing, feeling, feeling and intuition which provide a matrix of four personality types **(*See* Figure 4.3).**

Sensation-Thinking (ST)	Sensation-Feeling (SF)
Intuition-Thinking (NT)	Intuition-Feeling (NF)[8]

Raymond Cattell

Cattell's (1905–98) work resembles Eysenck's in the methods used to study personality. He used quantitative, objective techniques in order to analyse his data and followed traditional scientific procedures in order to understand the basic dimensions of personality. He identified two main types of personality traits:

- **surface traits** – that seem to cluster together consistently and are observable in behaviour such as assertiveness;
- **source traits** – such as self-discipline, that can only be inferred and seem to underlie and determine the traits which are likely to 'surface' into behaviour.

Table 4.4 Cattell's personality factors

Factor	High score	Low score
A	Outgoing	Reserved
B	More intelligent (abstract thinker)	Less intelligent (concrete thinker)
C	Higher ego strength (emotionally stable)	Lower ego strength (emotionally unstable)
E	Dominant	Submissive
F	Surgency (optimistic)	Desurgency (pessimistic)
G	Stronger superego strength (conscientious)	Weaker superego strength (expedient)
H	Parmia (adventurous)	Threctia (timid)
I	Presmia (tender-minded)	Harria (tough-minded)
L	Protension (suspicious)	Alaxia (trusting)
M	Autia (imaginative)	Praxernia (practical)
N	Shrewdness	Artlessness (unpretentious)
O	Insecure – guilt-proneness	Self-assured
Q1	Radicalism	Conservatism
Q2	Self-sufficiency	Group dependence
Q3	High self-concept control (controlled)	Low self-concept control (casual)
Q4	High ergic tension (tense, frustrated)	Low ergic tension (relaxed, tranquil)

Adapted from Cattell, R. B. and Kline, P. *The Scientific Analysis of Personality and Motivation,* Academic Press (1977) Table 4.1 pp. 44–5.

Unlike Eysenck, Cattell did not 'type' individuals but used 'traits' as his main personality descriptor. They also differed with regard to the determinants of personality: Eysenck viewed the inherited physiological basis as the main determinant, whereas Cattell was more interested in taking social factors into account when understanding an individual's personality. The original work identified twelve source traits, or primary factors, but was revised to sixteen which form the basis of the Cattell Sixteen Personality Factor (16 PF) Questionnaire. **See Table 4.4.** Both theorists have contributed to a lively debate about personality structure and its measurement and in doing so have advanced the selection techniques available to managers.[9]

Which of the above Nomothetic approaches do YOU think has the greatest value in helping your understanding of personality – and why? What do your colleagues think?

Idiographic approaches

Idiographic approaches emphasise the development of the individual and of individuals' views of themselves – their self-concept. Supporters of idiographic approaches are critical of the nomothetic approach that attempts to categorise individuals on the basis of group data. They argue that the techniques used to collate the group data are questionable and the outcome inappropriate to an understanding of personality. For the idiographic researchers, personality is expressed through the experiences and development of the individual. It cannot be understood outside a social context and has to be studied in the light of individuals' own perceptions of their world. Idiographic researchers would always take into account the social circumstances of the person and in particular the relationships with others, family life and social conditions. In early childhood strong personal relationships and unconditional love are essential for later fulfilment and psychological growth.

Main writers under this heading include:

- Erikson's eight stages of personality development;
- Myers–Briggs' personality indicator assessment tool; and
- Kelly's personal construct theory.

Erik Erikson

Erik Erikson's (1902–94) theory is a good example of the idiographic approach. He viewed personality development as continuing throughout life, and was interested in the effect of experiences on the development of the self-concept and how different individuals resolved personal conflicts. Erikson recognised the importance of early childhood in establishing certain basic concepts of trust, autonomy and initiative, but also claimed that all stages of life produce different tensions and conflicts.

For Erikson, there are eight distinct stages of life, each of which produces different tensions and conflicts that have to be resolved.

- Stage 1 – Trust (year 1)
- Stage 2 – Autonomy (years 2–3)
- Stage 3 – Initiative (years 4–5)
- Stage 4 – Industry (years 6–11)
- Stage 5 – Identity (years 12–18)
- Stage 6 – Intimacy (young adult)
- Stage 7 – Generativity (middle age)
- Stage 8 – Integrity (old age).[10]

Successful resolution of these conflicts produces a healthy personality, whereas difficulties in earlier stages may produce problems later on. Erikson's theory not only makes considerable sense in terms of face validity (i.e. the 'it feels right' factor), it also links with other research indicating that managers' motivations and goals change with age (see also *Hunt,* who identified nine different career/life stages[11]).

The Myers–Briggs Type Indicator® (MBTI®)

Jung is probably best known for his constructs that form the foundation for the MBTI personality indicator. The **Myers–Briggs Type Indicator (MBTI)** assessment tool was designed by *Isabel Briggs Myers* and *Katherine Briggs* who applied the rigours of systematic testing to Jung's personality functions and attitudes.[12] Jung identified differences between individuals in terms of their libidinal energy that could flow outwards to the external world (extravert) or inwards to their inner world (introvert).

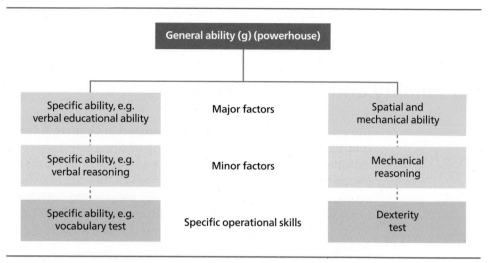

Figure 4.4 Leadership styles and the Myers–Briggs types

Personality differences would also be manifest through differing cognitive functions of thinking, feeling, sensation and intuition. The Myers–Briggs assessment added a further dimension of style of living. The MBTI tool has promoted considerable research interest, particularly with regard to the correlation between personality types, occupations and management style **(*see* Figure 4.4).**

The MBTI assessment tool has been in and out of fashion over the years and there is constant debate about its continuing relevance or usefulness. For example, *Vernon* maintains that Jung's ideas have become an integral part of business and that many don't even realise they were his in the first place. Advocates of Jung's analytical psychology believe his legacy is still underexploited and despite its risks MBTI is still the most popular non-clinical measure of personality type.[13]

Kelly's personal construct theory

Although it can fall broadly under the heading of idiographic, *Kelly's* (1905–1967) theory of personal constructs does not just consider personality development; it considers the whole person in terms of their perceptions, attitudes and goals. Personality is the individual's way of construing and experimenting with their world, and Kelly was critical of separating the study of personality apart from the 'whole' person.

The underlying theme of Personal Construct Theory is that people organize their experiences with the world into conceptual classifications called *constructs*. Observation of the behaviour of other people leads to our hypotheses – personal constructs – about the social world. Based on perceptions of, and personal experiences with, their environment each individual shapes their own unique set of constructs that are important to them. Kelly maintains that these constructs manifest themselves as polar opposites. We develop a wide range of constructs that we can challenge and change over time. How a person organises and prioritises their constructs influences their judgements, actions and decisions.

Inherent differences in people's personal constructs can lead to bias in research. For Kelly it was important to take data from one individual (idiography) and to employ a technique to cope with the collection of qualitative data. He developed the Repertory Grid in order to measure an individual's construct of the world. Kelly was thus able to employ a clear and valid measure within an idiographic approach and the repertory technique has become increasingly important as a research tool. It enables the person to use their own constructions of the world but in such a way that they are comparable and measurable.[14]

Personality and stress at work

The significance of stress at work is **discussed in Chapter 3.** Personality is a contributing factor in the understanding of stress. Stress is a complex topic: it is individually defined and is intrinsically tied into an individual's perceptual system. Everyone has a range of comfort within which they can feel steady and safe. Stress occurs when the individual feels that they are working outside of that comfort zone. Individuals will differ when they feel discomfort. The effects of stress will differ too; for some, the incidence of stress may energise and activate but for others it may immobilise.

Type A and Type B personality

Two polar sets of behaviour that link with personality and health have been identified by medical students *Friedman and Rosenman,* who identified recurring patterns of personality in patients suffering from premature heart disease.[15] Individuals with a **Type A personality** are excessively competitive, thrive on hard work and long hours, and have little interests outside work. They work under moderate to high levels of stress and exhibit characteristics such as:

- a high need for achievement;
- extreme competitiveness;
- impatience with obstacles to the completion of tasks;
- aggressiveness;
- a tendency to move and speak rapidly;
- an aversion to idleness;
- restlessness and urgency about time.

Individuals with a **Type B personality** are considered to exhibit the opposite characteristics from Type A. They are not preoccupied with achievement, are easy-going, rarely impatient, not easily frustrated, enjoy leisure time, and move and speak slowly. Type B personalities may still have high levels of drive and ambition but are more relaxed, work at a steady pace and do not exhibit a sense of time urgency.

According to Friedman and Rosenman, Type A personalities are far more vulnerable to heart attacks than Type B personalities. Individuals who have a personality classified as Type A are more likely to suffer from heart disease under severe stress than individuals with a Type B personality. With training, Type A personalities can change to a Type B provided they are sufficiently aware and find time to implement change strategies.[16]

Type a people and team performance

Gratton reports on what happens when Type A people, for whom time urgency is crucial; get to work together with less time-urgent people. Type A people are likely to pay a great deal of attention to the passage of time, constantly check the time remaining and see time as their enemy. Typically they will be very efficient in their use of time, and will use deadlines to prioritise tasks and increase their work pace. Type A people have the potential to keep things moving and active but can have a detrimental impact.[17] A study by *Waller et al.* found that where teams were responsible for completing creative tasks, Type A time-urgent people tended to impose strict, linear schedules on members and this reduced the innovative performance of the team.[18]

Diversity but the same smile

How clearly do YOU see yourself as a Type A or Type B? Do your colleagues tend to agree? To what extent do you think your 'Type' will help or hinder your future career?

The big five personality factors

For many years identification of personality traits has been a dominant subject of research in the UK and the USA. A more prominent development is general acceptance of a broad body of evidence which suggests that five basic dimensions provide a common basis by which to capture distinct variations in human personality. These common factors are more clusters of super traits, not personality types, and are known as the Big Five[19] often expressed in the acronym OCEAN (or sometimes CANEO):

- **O**penness/closed-mindedness
- **C**onscientiousness/heedlessness
- **E**xtroversion/introversion
- **A**greeableness/hostility
- **N**euroticism/stability **(*see* Figure 4.5.)**

The big five and work performance

The big five form the basis of standard personality questionnaires that determine positive or negative scores for each dimension. Results from a wide number of studies have shown that these factors can be identified as being significant in measuring the variation between people.[20] Of these, conscientiousness has the highest positive link with high levels of job knowledge and performance across a range of occupations.[21] However, some researchers are critical of the descriptors used.[22]

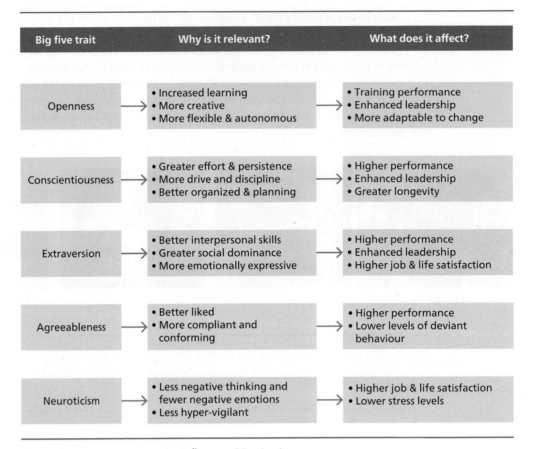

Big five trait	Why is it relevant?	What does it affect?
Openness	• Increased learning • More creative • More flexible & autonomous	• Training performance • Enhanced leadership • More adaptable to change
Conscientiousness	• Greater effort & persistence • More drive and discipline • Better organized & planning	• Higher performance • Enhanced leadership • Greater longevity
Extraversion	• Better interpersonal skills • Greater social dominance • More emotionally expressive	• Higher performance • Enhanced leadership • Higher job & life satisfaction
Agreeableness	• Better liked • More compliant and conforming	• Higher performance • Lower levels of deviant behaviour
Neuroticism	• Less negative thinking and fewer negative emotions • Less hyper-vigilant	• Higher job & life satisfaction • Lower stress levels

Figure 4.5 How Big Five traits influence OB criteria

Source: Adapted from Stephen Robbins and Timothy Judge, *Organizational Behaviour,* 13th edition, Pearson Prentice Hall (2009), p. 144. Reprinted and electronically reproduced by permission of Pearson Education, Inc.

Bentall suggests they are 'tainted by the investigators' values' and continues: 'I suspect that most people will have a pretty clear idea of where they would like to find themselves on the dimensions of neuroticism, extraversion, openness, agreeableness and conscientiousness.' He questions the ethical and political nature of the scales.[23] The relationship between personality and work performance is also questioned by *Robertson* who suggests that the only two of the five dimensions linked consistently with high levels of performance are conscientiousness and emotional stability.[24]

Despite these reservations, the strength and value of the Big Five model has been extolled in a review by *Lord and Rust,* who conclude that the five-factor model has become the linchpin that holds personality assessment together, at least within the work context. The model links the study of assessment instruments within the HR field to research in personality and related areas carried out within clinical and mainstream psychology fields.[25] Support for the big five is also provided by *Luthans and Youssef* who report that the personality traits have been found to be related strongly to performance and also to:

- **individual-level outcomes** such as happiness and physical and psychological health, spirituality and identity;
- **interpersonal-level outcomes** such as quality of relationships with peers, family and romantic others; and

- **organisational or social-level outcomes** such as occupational choice, satisfaction, performance, community involvement, criminal activity and political ideology.[26]

> What value do YOU place on 'The Big Five' model of personality for an understanding of work performance and the practice of human resource management?

Personality 'tests' and assessments

Much has been written about the value and validity of personality tests and questionnaires particular as a method of selection. Do they actually measure what they claim to measure? It should be noted that the word 'test' is often taken to refer to measures of intelligence, achievement and developed abilities, and aptitude for particular tasks. Measures of interests, social attitudes, emotional stability or traits of personality are usually referred to as questionnaires or profiles, or similar. **Answers are regarded as common or uncommon, typical or untypical, rather than right or wrong, good or bad.**

The word 'test' is therefore usually avoided in such measures, as, for example, the Cattell 16PF Questionnaire. Also, the terms 'personality tests' and 'psychometric tests' are often used interchangeably. Strictly however, personality tests measure only enduring characteristics of an individual whereas a psychometric test measures a broader range of all psychological characteristics. Most people will have taken a 'test' of one kind or another by the time they are an adult in employment. Such measures are perceived to be useful as an objective discriminating tool, but they are not without controversies and sensitivities. To be considered as a psychological instrument it must be **objective, standardised, reliable, valid** and **discriminating** (but not discriminatory). The choice of any assessment measure should be based on a number of other key features such as its acceptability, practicality, time, costs and perceived and actual added value.

Applications in the workplace

It would be rare for organisations not to consider the personality of a candidate at a selection interview. For some organisations, personality is a major criterion for selection or rejection. The hospitality industry, for example, is well known for the emphasis placed on the potency of personality. Although the interview remains the most usual method of selection there is an increasing use of psychometric measures. Personality questionnaires can be particularly valuable for personal development or used within team-building and development programmes. They can initiate discussion about individual differences, the importance of diversity in teamworking and the strengths that each personality type can bring to the working situation. Personality questionnaires can be a helpful diagnostic tool at the start of a coaching session or as a preliminary to a team-building process – an audit of strengths and weaknesses.

Use and limitations of tests and assessments

Despite increasing popularity, there are still widespread doubts and criticisms about the use and value of personality questionnaires in predicting performance at work. All methods of assessment have limitations. They can sample behaviour only at one particular moment in time. Some individuals are very nervous and may not perform at their best and indeed some may feel indignant that they are obliged to take a test at all. Great skill is required, therefore, in the administering of tests or questionnaires and in the interpretation of results. A suitable physical environment is also important. The possible reaction of candidates must be considered. Some might find any form of 'test' something of an ordeal or regard it as an unpleasantness.

Goss suggests that the use of personality assessments not only is an infringement of the individual's privacy but also leads to unfortunate organisational consequences, with 'cloning' as an outcome. Such techniques can be perceived as a form of social engineering and an insidious form of organisational control.[27] Aware of these problems, the British Psychological Society has produced guidelines and codes of practice for users of psychometric tests. Furthermore, evidence is emerging to show that where personality questionnaires have been specifically designed and related to work characteristics, prediction and validity scores are much higher.[28]

Administered properly psychological measures may provide an additional source of information only, but they can:

- make more systematic and precise decisions about people;
- predict future performance and reduce uncertainty;
- provide more accurate descriptions of people and their behaviour.

However, it must be remembered that:

- they may be expensive and time-consuming;
- without proper professional practice, they can be misused and results abused;
- they may be seen as an intrusion;
- they may be regarded as inappropriate;
- practice may have an effect on test results.

A major consideration is how to avoid any risk of cultural bias.

Personality and social expectations

Although personality may be a powerful determinant of potential effectiveness, account must also be taken of the social rules and expectations within the workplace. People learn the behaviour expected of them and may mask their true preferences. We can respond in ways that are not 'true to type' and required to take on roles at work that may run counter to our preferences. For instance, an introverted academic lecturer may prefer to be reflective and have time to think but will be required to 'perform' in front of 200 undergraduate students and expected to respond immediately to questions. We have to learn coping strategies and adaptive skills, but for some people stress may result. Furthermore, different temperaments may be rewarded at different times depending on whether an organisation is going through a period of growth or retrenchment. In one situation recognition may be given for exciting promotional activity and product development, but other personality characteristics may be needed if there is a period of slow-down and attention to detail and costs.

How much do we worry about social expectations?

Have YOU ever undertaken a personality 'test' or assessment? What was your reaction? If not, would you be happy to undergo such a 'test'? What about your colleagues?

Emotional intelligence (EI)

An important related concept of personality is that of emotional intelligence EI (or EQ, for Emotional Quotient). Developed originally by *Salovey and Mayer*,[29] EI is generally attributed to *Goleman* who in 1955 published his ground-breaking work. Goleman agreed that the classical view of intelligence was too narrow. He felt that the emotional qualities of individuals should be considered. Goleman identified the key characteristics of EI as: *abilities such as being able to motivate oneself and persist in the face of frustrations; to control impulse and delay gratification; to regulate one's moods and keep distress from swamping the ability to think; to empathise and to hope.*[30]

Emotional intelligence is the sum of a range of interpersonal skills that form the public persona including the emotional qualities of individuals. Goleman's model outlines five main EI constructs.

- Self-awareness
- Self-regulation
- Social skill
- Empathy
- Motivation

Emotional competencies are not innate talents, but rather learned capabilities that must be worked on and can be developed to achieve outstanding performance.

The Hay Group, working with Goleman, have identified eighteen specific competencies that make up the four components of emotional intelligence and have

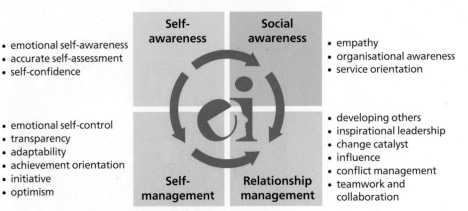

Figure 4.6 Emotional Intelligence Competence Model
Source: Hay Group. Copyright © 1999 Hay Group Limited. All rights reserved. Reproduced with permission.

produced an inventory designed to measure emotional competence (*see* **Figure 4.6**). The Emotional Competence Inventory defines EI as 'The capacity for recognising our own feelings and those of others, for motivating ourselves and for managing emotions within ourselves and with others.'[31]

Significance of emotional intelligence at work

EI has received considerable attention as a key aspect of both personal success and managing other people effectively. People capable of controlling their own emotions, who can relate meaningfully to the emotions of others and are comfortable in social situations are likely to be successful in the work situation. *Landale* refers to *EI* as the glue that holds people and teams together. With flatter work structures there is increasing proximity for us to build the relationships we need – fast, so it should really be no surprise to find it very much in demand. Empathy is important in EI as this involves how a person self-manages and addresses how to engage with the emotions of others. There seems little doubt that managers and leaders who have trained up in EQ have far more initiative in dealing with organisational life. Stress will always exist at work, but EQ gives people the tools and ways of thinking to manage it to their advantage.[32]

According to *Dann,* becoming highly self-aware allows an individual to recognise inner and outer conflict and develop more proactive self-management. Developing greater social awareness allows the fostering of productive relations and a greater degree of engagement between employees and management. A manager with a high EI benefits both the organisation and the individual.[33] The *Chartered Management Institute* points to the importance of emotional responses at work. Individuals with substantial EI recognise their emotions and physical reactions and are better able to deal with resulting potential outcomes. EI is identified as one of the key softer skills emphasised frequently as important for success in leadership and management.[34]

However, *Alexander* reports on research concerning the negative uses and dark side of emotional intelligence, and questions what happens when people start using it to manipulate others in order to further their own careers. Those on the dark side of EI will scrutinise the emotions of others but are adept at controlling their own emotional displays. For example, bosses with negative EI in mind may focus on employees' emotions for cynical purposes. Employees looking to profit by dark EI may constantly scrutinise a superior's emotions for ways to enhance how they are estimated by attuning to the superior's state of mind.[35]

Recognition of diversity

The workplace brings together a diverse mix of individual personalities. An integral and essential feature of individuality is diversity. We have seen from the discussion above that people are not homogeneous. **Diversity** focuses on the multiplicity of differences among people – on the variety of people as heterogeneous groupings. Individual differences are the basis of diversity. Diversity is relevant to anything which may affect workplace relationships and achievements. However, valuing differences is easier said than done. It means relating and working with people with different personalities who hold different perspectives and views, bringing different qualities to the workplace, having different aspirations and different customs and traditions. Differences are challenging; they question people's views, perceptions and attitudes and require individuals to see things from an alternative frame of reference.

From equal opportunities to managing diversity

Equal opportunities relate to legislation intended to outlaw discrimination and extends to nine areas of protected characteristics: age, disability, gender, gender reassignment, marriage and civil partnership, pregnancy and maternity, race, religion or belief, sexual orientation. Although diversity in the workplace relates to treating everyone equally, it complements and further develops initiatives on equal opportunities and preventing discrimination. The *Chartered Management Institute* point out that diversity management goes beyond what is required by legislation. The focus is on individuals rather than minority groups and comprises an approach which recognises and values differences and aims to make positive use of the unique talents and perspectives within the workforce.[36]

Six habits of truly inclusive organisations

Joanna Higgins suggests that acceptance of diversity programmes is patchy and progress slow but refers to six habits of truly inclusive organisations. They:

1. **Have a story** – and articulate in clear and simple terms the purpose and values of their diversity and inclusion measures.
2. **Lead by example** – behaviour from top management sends the strongest measure about the strength of the company's commitment.
3. **Develop empathy** – inclusive workplaces thrive on tolerance and respect for 'the other'.
4. **Give people a voice** – giving everyone a 'safe space' to talk freely whether in meetings or networks.
5. **Use evidence** – using data both to expose weak spots and monitor progress of talent-development groups.
6. **Recruit for difference** – in order to enrich your organisation with more varied viewpoints you have to recruit them.[37]

What *exactly* do YOU understand by 'diversity'? How well does your university attempt to provide a fully inclusive organisation? Give specific examples of how you have benefited by studying in a diverse working environment.

Diversity in the workplace

A joint report from the CBI and TUC, supported by the Equality and Human Rights Commission, suggests that promoting diversity in the workplace and employing people solely on the basis of their ability can bring many real business benefits. These include:

- increasing employee satisfaction, which helps attract new staff and retain those already there, reduces recruitment costs, and can increase productivity;
- understanding better how the company's diverse customers think and what drives their spending habits, or how they access markets they have not previously been able to tap into so effectively;
- finding enough workers to fill skills gaps in areas with tight labour markets, where there are not enough 'obvious candidates' for the vacancies they have.

The report also makes clear that diversity can be improved through positive action – such as encouraging applications from types of people who have not in the past applied for jobs, additional training, providing support networks or adapting work practices – but not positive discrimination.[39]

Diversity and social class

Although many firms pat themselves on the back for their diversity policies, *Reeves* suggests that in fact social mobility in Britain is in steady decline and class inequality is not dead. If businesses continue to run a 'people like us' strategy when it comes to talent, they risk blunting their own competitive edge. Whilst it is possible to look diverse by hiring and promoting a diverse range of 'posh' people rather than a monopoly of posh straight white men, the standard diversity agenda misses the more subtle inequalities of class.[39]

Global business diversity

The chair of CMI Race, Pavita Cooper questions whether the business case for diversity is solely about cognitive diversity and thinking differently. Although cognitive diversity is important it is necessary also to reflect an increasingly global market.

> You have to make decisions around products, around services, around communications, about what your website looks like, about how you talk to your future talent pool – surely you need some reflection of the customer base you are serving? For many organisations that is what is driving this push for better diversity.[40]

A summary of equality at work is set out in the concept map in Figure 4.7.

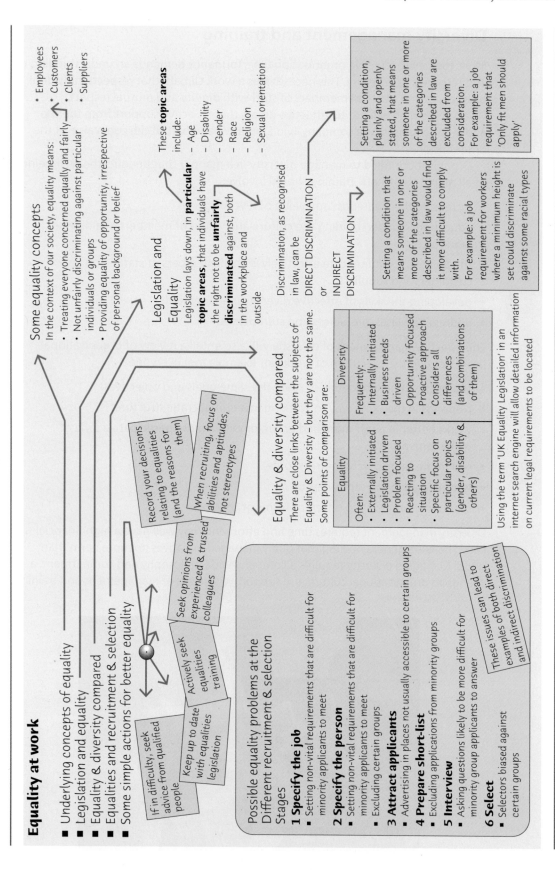

Figure 4.7 Equality at work

Diversity management and training

More than ever, effective organisational performance demands an understanding of, and response to, diversity. This necessitates a work climate that respects individual differences and treats all members of staff with dignity and mutual respect. Diversity training will not be effective unless there is active support from the top and it is recognised as a company-wide initiative and part of the core value of the organisation.

Organisations need to manage diversity in a manner that benefits the well-being of all members of staff. Training should involve:

- increasing the awareness and value of diversity;
- education in understanding the culture and values of members of a diverse workforce;
- the ability to communicate effectively with all members of staff – and also customers and suppliers;
- developing the skills of effective diversity management;
- addressing biases, prejudices and stereotypes.

The effective management of diversity will also entail a review of organisational processes and the execution of work. For example, not everyone

- shares the same work ethic or seeks the same goals and objectives;
- responds in the same way to working in a bureaucratic structure;
- works better in a self-managed group or with a more participative style of management;
- will fit the same psychometric profile;
- is motivated in the same way; or
- reacts the same way to different forms of control.

Diversity management requires time and effort and may well have a high financial cost. There is a general feeling that badly managed initiatives do more harm than good. Managing diversity requires a company-wide philosophy and commitment, a change to organisational culture and supportive systems of management and training.

UKSA – equality and diversity policy

'UKSA is committed to being an equal opportunities employer and to achieving equality of opportunity for all employees. ONS values and welcomes diversity and all employees are entitled to work in an environment free from discrimination and harassment.

Our equality and diversity policy aims to ensure that existing employees and applicants for jobs are treated fairly and within the law. No UKSA employees or applicants for jobs in UKSA should receive less favourable treatment on unjustifiable grounds because of their: sex, marital or civil partnership status, age, race, disability, responsibility for dependants, religion or belief (actual or perceived), sexual orientation (actual or perceived), transgender status, pregnancy, political beliefs, trade union activities, working patterns or contract status.

UKSA supports a range of flexible working patterns to enable employees to balance home and work responsibilities and treats people fairly, irrespective of their working arrangements.'

Key points of Equality and Diversity work at UKSA:

- The Director General of UKSA chairs the Equality and Diversity Steering Group which sets the strategic direction for all equality work in the organisation, as well as scrutinising, and monitoring staff data.

- UKSA has senior sponsors for each of its 15 diversity network groups.

- UKSA meets its statutory equality duties as a public authority and is committed to achieving best practice in promoting equality and eliminating discrimination and harassment. To aid this UKSA participates in a number of equality benchmarking exercises and recently became the first organisation to receive the 'Gold Standard' in the Business Disability Forum's Disability Standard.

- Promoting equality is core to the expectations UKSA staff should have of the organisation as an employer, and in the expectations UKSA has of its workforce. All staff are required to have an objective that covers equality and diversity which forms part of their performance review.

UKSA has a detailed Diversity & Inclusion Strategy (2017–2020) and detailed action plans which cover:

- Gender Action Plan
- Disability Action Plan
- Work Life Balance working Action Plan
- Ethnicity Action Plan

Source: United Kingdom Statistics Authority. Crown Copyright material is reproduced under terms of the Click-Use Licence.

Can YOU provide examples of people within your university who may be guilty (even innocently) of stereotyping? What specific action would you recommend to help overcome stereotyping?

Diversity and stereotyping

Diversity also challenges many traditional stereotypes **(discussed in Chapter 6).** Stereotyping infers that people within a particular perceived category are assumed to share the same personality traits or characteristics. Stereotypes are a means of making simplified judgements of other people instead of coping with a range of individual stimuli. Stereotyping attributes to all individuals the characteristics or tendencies of the categorisation as a whole.

A greater understanding of cultural differences in non-verbal communications and body language will help improve interpersonal relationships.

> There have been instances in my life, both at home and at work, when people have felt I'm a little crazy because I am pushy, outspoken, energetic, competitive, enthusiastic, driven and strong. Crazy, because that's not what's expected of an Asian woman. Crazy, because it's not what the majority of people are like. And crazy, because they think they know me better than I know myself.
>
> Saira Khan – star of *The Apprentice* television series[41]

Gender diversity

One of the most significant and important aspects of managing diversity is that of gender equality, and the participation of men and women in the workforce. One of our initial perceptions and classifications of another individual and their likely personality is usually the identification of their gender. How does this perception affect our behaviour?

- What difference does it make if our work group is predominantly male or female?
- Do women and men have different experiences at work?
- If organisations are rational and neutral institutions – why should gender make a difference?
- Does it matter that many classic theories have been based on research carried out on men, by male researchers?
- What has been the influence of diversity policies on work behaviour and on the position of women in organisations?

Laura Spira and Helen Pitcher maintain that it is unfortunate that diversity has become synonymous with gender in media discussions. They raise the debatable issue of voluntary or mandatory quotas. Material diversity in the boardroom is not always synonymous with a well-performing board. Although there is some argument to correlate gender diversity with effective performance this should not ignore other bases for argument.[42]

Ann Francke, Chief Executive CMI maintains there is evidence that gender balance bolsters business results in three important ways.

- **Improved financials** – better returns on sales and equity, and growth at micro and macro level;
- **Better culture** – inclusivity boosts employee and customer satisfaction and generates more innovative ideas;
- **Less risky decision-making** – diversity helps eliminate groupthink, at the core of every major business breakdown over the past 20 years.[43] **(Groupthink is discussed in Chapter 8).**

Managing an ageing workforce

The focus on diversity has drawn attention to managing the generation gap and the increasing numbers of older people in the workforce. The EU refers to the ageing population, to the future shrinking of the working-age population and to the whole world ageing fast. Working longer is not enough. We need to empower older people to participate and contribute to their communities so that they can remain autonomous as long as possible. This requires a more age-friendly and inclusive society.[44]

Now that the UK default retirement age of sixty-five has been removed there will be an increasing challenge to manage an intergenerational workforce. *Barnes* suggests that at worst, young workers can see their older colleagues as dinosaurs, set in their ways and blocking creativity, as well as their own path to promotion. Older workers too can feel threatened by the energy and technological ease of their younger colleagues or impatient with their brashness and lack of experience. Managers need to recognise and harness differences in skills, motivations and work routines to deliver high-quality output and mutual learning.[45]

- In **Chapter 2** attention was drawn to three different generations and age groups in the workplace. As people live and work longer there will be a wider spread of age groups in the workforce. Wilton, for example, suggests a fourth generation that of 'Homelanders' born after 9/11 changed the world for ever.

- It is now clear that late Baby Boomers and early Gen X are not retiring early has implication for pensions, retirement and health policies. This may help to highlight that age issues should have as high a profile as gender equality and racial diversity in the workplace; something that does not always happen.

Criticisms and limitations

Despite potential benefits from diversity, there are a number of criticisms and perceived limitations. While acknowledging that the positive management of diversity aims to promote an inclusive culture in which individuals are valued and respected, the Chartered Management Institute points out that diversity management should not be mistaken for equal opportunities or be merely a question of legal compliance. Managers should avoid handling diversity issues insensitively; invading employees' privacy; failing to consult and gain commitment throughout the organisation; or falling into an 'us' and 'them' mentality.[46]

Individuality and groups

Social interaction is a natural feature of human behaviour and group working is a major feature of organisational life. Strong and cohesive groups can have beneficial effects for the organisation but there are potential disadvantages. There is arguably a potential conflict with workforce diversity because of the need to consider staff both as individuals and also as members of a group. The greater the compatibility of its members and the more homogeneous the group, the greater the danger of the group developing its own subculture. Members may display a critical attitude towards people outside the group or members of other groups. Encouraging individuality and at the same time expecting group co-operation and teamwork are potential triggers for tension. **Group cohesiveness is discussed in Chapter 8.**

Diversity can also be threatened by power relationships. The concept of social exchange theory **(discussed in Chapter 1)** suggests that social exchanges are influenced by a complex web of power relationships and as a result are not always equal but have an uneven balance of outcomes. Those individuals at the lower end of power relationships, perhaps for example part-time or casual workers or ethnic minorities may arguably be disadvantaged.

Concern for moral and social issues

A major concern with the increasing attention to diversity is that too much attention is given to the advantages for the organisation rather than to broader moral or social issues and the ethical arguments for equality of treatment. In arguing the case for combining heterogeneity and homogeneity, *Nordström and Ridderstråle* suggest that although quite often people talk favourably about diversity since it supposedly promotes a better atmosphere and equality, the typical manager is persuaded to change the mix of people at the company for economic reasons.[47] *Kirton and Greene* believe that the 'business case' should be broadened to include wider issues of social justice and social responsibility.[48]

According to *Lucas,* one of the key messages the experts want to get across is that paying attention to diversity isn't just a moral obligation, it's an organisational imperative. Workers in organisations where diversity is valued generally feel more engaged with their employer and are more likely to stay on board. If the organisation builds a reputation as an 'enlightened' employer, it will be able to attract the best people at a time when talent is at a premium. Drawing on the expertise of its diverse workforce will help create new and improved products and services to help get ahead in competitive, global markets.[49]

The simple message from *Swabey* (Policy and Research Director at ICSA: the Governance Institute) is clear: **'Diversity is important but the aim should surely be that it ceases to be an issue in our society.'**[50]

Do YOU believe there should be a specific programme of diversity training for students? What is your opinion of the quality of diversity management in your university?

Critical Thinking Zone

Reflections on the Dark Side of Emotional Intelligence

In this zone, we critically evaluate the dark side of emotional intelligence and explore its impact on organisational behaviour in the workplace.

Over the past two decades, emotional intelligence (EI) has become a widely contested, debated and emotive topic in the fields of management and psychology.[51] Its original espousal by Salovey and Mayer[52] and subsequent development by Goleman[53] and Goleman and Boyatzis,[54] has catalysed a growing industry for practitioners and academics with, it could be argued, two key aims in mind. First, to popularise EI as a management tool and technique to develop, among other things, the pursuit of more effective leadership, the optimisation of performance and catalyse changes in individual and organisational behaviour.[55] Second, to empiricise and address the conceptual, theoretical and measurement paradoxes surrounding EI and its perceived and espoused relationship with established personality factors.[55,56,57]

Exploring the Dark Side of EI

While EI has received glowing references from both practitioners and academics, in terms of how the construct can enable us to become more in tune with, and aware of, our own and others' emotions,[51,57] Bariso[58] argues that the concept can no longer be viewed as 'inherently virtuous'. In the past, proponents of EI (e.g. leaders, educators and policy makers), have, rather enthusiastically, touted it as a panacea for all ills, to solve a raft of issues ranging from personal problems (e.g. bullying) and organisational difficulties such as poor employee engagement, in the hope that it will foster a more caring and nurturing workplace.[57] However, Bariso and Grant[57] caveat that EI has both a 'light' and 'dark' side and individuals can therefore use it in ethical and unethical ways to promote their own ends.

Metaphorically, Bariso describes EI as power, inferring its potential capacity to corrupt. On this note, Bariso and Grant suggest that history is riddled with a litany of examples of high profile leaders who have demonstrated elevated levels of EI and achieved national and international notoriety for their unique ability to manipulate others through, for example, using a knowledge of people's emotions to influence their behaviour. Bariso argues that consciously or subconsciously, we are all culpable of exercising this behaviour, a classic of example of which is being nice to someone who has something that we want or can do something for us, such as helping to advance our careers. Grant and Kilduff, Chiaburu and Menges[59] concur and highlight new evidence, which suggests that when individuals sharpen their emotional skills,

they become more adept at manipulating and motivating others to act in ways that may be contrary to their own beliefs, value systems and best interests. Bariso questions whether this behaviour is unethical and concludes 'in the end, it depends. . . EI can be an especially dangerous tool in the wrong hands.' Kilduff et al. adds 'the manipulation of others' emotions for strategic ends are behaviours evident not only on Shakespeare's stage but also in offices and corridors where power and influence are traded' (p. 147). One could argue that this is a demonstration of the Jungian shadow at play and symptomatic of the dark behaviours that can be injurious to both individuals and organisations.[60,61] (See Chapter 0: Critical Thinking Zone: Reflections on the Shadow Side of Organisations).

Gaming EI Tests

Arguably, a key tenet of EI is measurement of one's emotional quotient (EQ) using self-testing and self-perception tests. Tobak[62] caveats that engagement with these tests can lead to 'gaming' whereby respondents manipulate their answers to achieve high EQ scores. He argues that although the test questions are phrased in a number of different ways to try and improve their accuracy, the overall results can be distorted by individuals who display certain personality traits and are thus skilled at controlling and understanding their emotions. Tobak noted 'the more delusional, narcissistic and sociopathic you are, the easier it is to game the test.' Respondents are therefore more likely to appear they are 'as self-aware and empathetic as a Zen Master or Buddhist Monk.' Tobak and Antonakis[63] contend that testing for EQ is not scientific and, in many instances, may not have been subject to rigorous research. They therefore conclude that such tests are fundamentally flawed and their results are meaningless, leaving more opportunities for dark behaviours to be manifested and perpetuated by those who seek to wield power and influence over others.

Implications for Organisational Behaviour in the Workplace

To conclude, although EI can enable us to become more emotionally aware of our own and other's emotions, Grant and Tobak caveat that like the organisational shadow, the dark side of EI is pervasive and can be used as a weapon to manipulate people and exercise a modicum of control over their emotions. This clearly has implications for organisational behaviour in the workplace. One could argue that the heart of EI is behavioural change; changing how we think, feel, act and perceive ourselves and others around us, including the organisation at large. It could be further argued that the dark behaviours that emanate from the somewhat Machiavellian exploitation of EI, obscures the original, well-meaning tenets and objectives of the concept. However, given that our emotions and behaviours are, like the Jungian shadow, mainly subjective, subconscious and buried deep within us, it is no surprise that the dark side of EI is interplayed on the organisation's metaphorical stage.

Tobak contends that the change in individual and organisational behaviour espoused by EI is somewhat utopian and cannot be achieved by taking a test, attending a seminar or reading a book. He notes 'if that were the case – if it really were that simple – people would not need years of therapy, hard work and discipline to change their behaviour.' Tobak maintains his scepticism and concludes 'study emotional intelligence all you want, it won't change a thing.'

Questions

With the above in mind, answer the following questions.

1. Bariso argues that EI can no longer be viewed as 'inherently virtuous.' With reference to theory and practice, *critically discuss* his viewpoint.

2. The dark side of EI can be likened to the Jungian shadow. *Compare and contrast* the two concepts and identify the implications for organisational behaviour in the workplace.

3. Bariso argues that we are all culpable of consciously and subconsciously using a knowledge of people's emotions to influence their behaviour. *To what extent* do you agree with his views?

Summary – Chapter 4 'Personality and diversity'

Personality is a defining feature of individual differences and qualities. Individual differences can foster creativity, enjoyment and satisfaction at work but there can also be potential for frustration and conflict. Discussion of personality concerns uniqueness and similarities. Studies on personality can be divided into those looking at specific traits and those taking a broader view of type of individual personality. Two main approaches to theoretical studies of personality are labelled nomothetic and idiographic but the distinction is not always clear and there is often crossover between different studies. Personality is a contributory factor in the understanding of stress at work. Psychometric 'tests' and personality questionnaires may help identify individual characteristics but are subject to doubts and criticisms about their predictive value of performance at work. An important related concept of personality is emotional intelligence (EI) which focuses on the range of the individual's interpersonal skills and emotional qualities. The workplace brings together a diverse mix of personalities. Diversity focuses on the multiplicity of individual differences among people. Valuing differences is not easy; diversity challenges traditional stereotypes and demands effective management.
An increasing number of organisations appear to recognise the value of diversity but there potential criticisms including concern for moral and social issues.

Group discussion activities

Undertake each of these exercises in small groups as indicated by your tutor. Before you start your discussion establish a non-threatening environment within the group and confirm that confidential will be honoured.

First, form your own views and then share and compare in open discussion with colleagues. Reflect honestly on the extent to which: (i) you influenced the thinking and ideas of your colleagues; and (ii) you were influenced by your colleagues.

To what extent was your group able to reach consensus?

Agree one of your members to produce a brief written summary of the discussion and prepared to present in a plenary session.

Activity 1

If you're still not sure where you fall on the introvert–extrovert spectrum, you can assess yourself here. Answer each question 'true' or 'false', choosing the answer that applies to you more often that not.*

1. _____ I prefer one-on-one conversions to group activities.
2. _____ I often prefer to express myself in writing.
3. _____ I enjoy solitude.
4. _____ I seem to care less than my peers about wealth, fame and status.
5. _____ I dislike small talk, but I enjoy talking in depth about topics that matter to me.
6. _____ People tell me that I'm a good listener.
7. _____ I'm not a big risk-taker.
8. _____ I enjoy work that allows me to 'dive in' with few interruptions.
9. _____ I like to celebrate birthdays on a small scale, with only one or two close friends or family members.
10. _____ People describe me as 'soft-spoken' or 'mellow'.
11. _____ I prefer not to show or discuss my work with others until it's finished.
12. _____ I dislike conflict.
13. _____ I do my best work on my own.
14. _____ I tend to think before I speak.
15. _____ I feel drained after being out and about, even if I've enjoyed myself.
16. _____ I often let calls go through to voice mail.
17. _____ If I had to choose, I'd prefer a weekend with absolutely nothing to do to one with too many things scheduled.
18. _____ I don't enjoy multitasking.
19. _____ I can concentrate easily.
20. _____ In classroom situations, I prefer lectures to seminars.

Source: Susan Cain, *Quiet: The Power of Introverts in a World That Can't Stop Talking*, Viking an imprint of Penguin Books (2012) pp. 13–14.

*This is an informal quiz, not a scientifically validated personality test. The questions were formulated based on characteristics of introversion often accepted by contemporary researchers.

(a) Discuss your answers with colleagues. To what extent do they agree with you?

(b) What conclusions do you draw?

Further information may be provided by your tutor.

Activity 2

Think carefully and honestly about:

(a) How you are perceived by other people generally and in particular your colleagues.

(b) How confident are you in your own abilities?

(c) To what extent do you deliberately seek out new challenges?

(d) Whether you get upset easily if things do not go your way.

(e) Are you a good listener?

(f) The extent to which you can impose self-discipline.

(g) Do most people respect you and your opinions?

(h) How comfortable are you meeting with new people?

Activity 3

Asian members of staff can sometimes be considered 'over-subservient' towards guests and appear to accept frivolous requests or complaints too readily. Guests used to this approach then seem quick to complain strongly if they do not receive what they regard as the same level of response from, say, Eastern European members of staff.

(a) If you were head receptionist in a multi-cultural international hotel how would you handle this situation?

(b) What do you see as most challenging working with people in a multi-cultural environment?

Organisational behaviour in action case study
Portsmouth Hospitality NHS Trust, Equality and Diversity Policy

Portsmouth Hospitals NHS Trust promotes equality with due regard to the protected characteristics of age, disability, gender reassignment, marriage and civil partnership, pregnancy and maternity, race, religion or belief, sex and sexual orientation. The trust has a comprehensive Equality and Diversity policy, including:

Purpose

The management of equality and diversity is important as it will help to:

∗ ensure the services we provide are accessible to all people; actively promote equality; and are free from unlawful discrimination;

* develop services which best meets the needs of our diverse communities;

* eliminate from our services, policies and decision making, any adverse impact on the promotion of equality and inclusion for our patients and staff; and

* enhance the corporate reputation of the organisation.

Definitions

Equality is not about treating everyone the same. Equality recognises that:

* everyone has individual needs and the right to have those needs respected;

* inequality exists and that unlawful discrimination needs to be tackled;

* employment and Trust services should be accessible to all; and

* it is about treating people fairly where everyone can participate and have the opportunity to fulfil their potential.

Diversity is about respecting and valuing individual difference. Diversity recognises that:

* everybody is different;

* we need to understand, value, and respect those differences; and

* diversity can include individuals and groups with varying backgrounds, experiences, styles, perceptions, values and beliefs.

A diversity approach aims to recognise, value and manage differences to enable all patients, service users and staff to contribute and realise their full potential. Diversity challenges us to recognise and value all differences in order to make a better working environment and ensure an excellent service for all people.

The Equality Impact Group (EIG)

The EIG has responsibility for ensuring development and delivery of the Equality and Diversity strategy. The EIG is set up with delegated responsibility from the Trust Board to lead on the Equality and Diversity agenda and monitor progress to ensure it provides equality with regards to access, experience and outcome.

The EIG will:

* provide long-term and continuing support and leadership, for equality and diversity across the Trust

and in support of legal and regulatory obligations; and

* monitor Divisions on their progress in embedding equality and diversity through the performance management of the Trust Equality Standard.

Managers

All managers have a responsibility to adhere to this policy and bring it to the attention of staff in their work area in order to establish and maintain an inclusive environment free of unlawful discrimination. Managers have a responsibility to:

* set a positive example by treating others with respect and setting standards of acceptable behaviour;

* promote an inclusive working environment where unlawful discrimination is unacceptable and not tolerated;

* ensuring any allegations of discriminatory behaviour or practices are correctly investigated and appropriate action taken in accordance to the Trust Bullying and Harassment Policy and Management of Violence and Aggression Policy;

* ensure their teams work effectively together;

* ensure staff are given equal opportunity to access learning and development opportunities;

* consult with the Human Resources Team and Equality and Diversity Manager for advice and support regarding E&D issues;

* assisting with monitoring of compliance within their area of responsibility; and

* implement the Equality Standard.

Staff

All staff have personal responsibility for their own behaviour and ensuring they comply with the Equality Act 2010 and are expected to:

* understand the Trust Values and how this impacts on everything we do;

* have a personal responsibility to adhere to the Policy. Staff should not undertake any acts of discriminatory practice in the course of their employment for which they will be personally liable;

* help promote an inclusive environment by treating everyone with dignity and respect;

* respecting and responding to the diverse needs of staff, service users and others;

* appropriately challenge and/or report behaviour that may be considered to be offensive when directed against themselves or others in accordance to the Trust Bullying and Harassment Policy;

* have a responsibility to bring any potentially discriminatory actions or practice to the attention of their Line Manager or the Human Resources Department; and

* implement the Trust Equality Standard.

Source: Extracts from Portsmouth Hospitals NHS Trust, Equality and Diversity Policy, 07 December 2015. Thanks to Ruth Dolby, Organisational Development Practitioner.

Tasks

1. To what extent do you identify with the definitions of equality and diversity?

2. What do you think of the idea of an Equality Impact Group (EIG)?

3. Would you recommend a similar EIG for other organisations including your university?

Chapter 4 – Personal skills and employability exercise

Objectives

Completing this exercise should help you to enhance the following skills:

* Mindful of your own attitudes and behaviours towards individual differences
* Acceptance of the dimensions, benefits and impact of diversity
* Develop greater respect and empathy towards other people

Exercise

For each of the following ten statements you are required to make notes in order to indicate *honestly and fully* the extent to which you:

1. Believe in managing diversity for moral and social reasons.

2. Are happy mixing with people from different cultures.

3. Resist stereotyping or profiling individuals into general categories of people.

4. Show patience and understanding when dealing with people whose English language is limited.

5. Accept that positive discrimination can sometimes be fully justified.

6. View diversity as distinctly different from political correctness.

7. Enjoy learning about different cultures and values.

8. Believe that diversity enriches the working lives of all employees.

9. Feel comfortable working closely with a colleague who has a different sexual orientation.

10. Are willing to take orders from someone much younger or much older than yourself, or from the opposite gender.

Discussion

After completing the questionnaire, pair with a colleague – where possible with a different ethnicity, culture, gender or age group – and compare and discuss critically both sets of responses.

* To what extent were you each surprised by the responses or comments from your colleague?

* What do you and your colleague believe are the greatest obstacles to a harmonious truly diverse workforce? How much consensus between you is there?

* Detail fully in writing what have your learnt about your awareness of, and attitude and adaptability, to diversity.

Notes and references

1. Ineson, E. 'The Contribution of Personality to Graduate Managerial Training', *International Journal of Contemporary Hospitality Management,* vol.3, 2011, pp. 630–8.
2. 'Education: Hotel Schools' *Caterer and Hotelkeeper,* 10 August, 2006.
3. Briner, R. 'Feeling and Smiling', *The Psychologist,* vol. 12, no. 1, January 1999, pp. 16–19.
4. Freud, S. *New Introductory Lectures on Psychoanalysis,* Penguin (1973).
5. Andrews, B. and Brewin, C. R. 'What Did Freud Get Right', *The Psychologist,* vol. 13, no. 12, December 2000, pp. 605–7.
6. Morgan, G. *Images of Organization,* second edition, Sage Publications (1997).
7. Eysenck, H. J. *Eysenck on Extraversion,* Crosby Lockwood Staples (1973).
8. Jung, C. G. *Analytical Psychology: Its Theory and Practice,* Routledge and Kegan Paul (1968). See also Jacobi, J. *Psychology of C. G. Jung,* seventh edition, Routledge and Kegan Paul (1968).
9. Howarth, E. 'A Source of Independent Variation: Convergence and Divergence in the Work of Cattell and Eysenck', in Dreger, R. M. (ed.) *Multivariate Personality Research,* Claiton (1972).
10. Erikson, E. H. *Identity and the Life Cycle,* Norton (1980).
11. Hunt, J. W. *Managing People at Work: A Manager's Guide to Behaviour in Organisations,* third edition, McGraw-Hill (1992).
12. Myers, I. B. *Introduction to Type,* sixth edition, Consulting Psychologists Press (1998); and Myers, K. D. and Kirby, L. K. *Introduction to Type Dynamics and Development,* second edition, Consulting Psychologists Press (2000).
13. Vernon, M. 'Why Jung Still Matters', *Management Today,* June 2011, pp. 4–50.
14. Kelly, G. A. *The Psychology of Personal Constructs,* Norton (1955). See also Kelly's theory as described by Bannister, D. and Fansella, F., in *Inquiring Mind: The Theory of Personal Constructs,* Penguin (1971), pp. 50–1.
15. Friedman, M. and Rosenman, R. *Type A Behavior and Your Heart,* Knopf (1974).
16. Rosenmann, R., Friedman, F. and Straus, R. 'A Predictive Study of CHD', *Journal of the American Medical Association,* vol. 89, 1964, pp. 15–22; and Warr, P. and Wall, T. *Work and Well Being,* Penguin (1975).
17. Gratton, L., *Hot Spots,* Financial Times Prentice Hall (2007).
18. Ibid., p. 83.
19. McCrae, R. R. and Costa, P. T. 'More Reasons to Adopt the Five-Factor Model', *American Psychologist,* vol. 44, no. 2, 1989, pp. 451–2.
20. Bayne, R. 'The Big Five versus the Myers-Briggs', *The Psychologist,* January 1994, pp. 14–17.
21. Barrick, M. R. and Mount, M. K. 'The Big Five Personality Dimensions and Job Performance: A Meta-Analysis', *Personnel Psychology,* Spring 1991, pp. 1–26.
22. Mount, M. K., Barrick, M. R. and Strauss, J. P. 'Validity of Observer Ratings of the Big Five Personality Factors', *Journal of Applied Psychology,* April 1994, p. 272.
23. Bentall, R. P. 'Personality Traits May be Alive, They may Even be Well, but Are They Really Useful?', *The Psychologist,* July 1993, p. 307.
24. Robertson, I. 'Undue Diligence', *People Management,* no. 22, November 2001, pp. 42–3.
25. Lord, W. and Rust, J. 'The Big Five Revisited: Where Are We Now? A Brief Review of the Relevance of the Big Five for Occupational Assessment', *Selection and Development Review,* vol. 19, no. 4, August 2003, pp. 15–18.

26. Luthans, F. and Youssef, C. M. 'Emerging Positive Organizational Behavior', *Journal of Management,* vol. 33, no. 3, June 2007, pp. 321–49.

27. Goss, D. *Principles of Human Resource Management,* Routledge (1994).

28. Gibbons, P., Baron, H., Nyfield, G. and Robertson, I. 'The Managerial Performance and Competences', conference paper given at the British Psychological Society Occupational Psychology Conference, University of Warwick, January 1995.

29. Salovey, P and Mayer, J. D. 'Emotional Intelligence', *Imagination, Cognition and Personality,* vol. 9, 1990, pp. 185–211.

30. Goleman, D. *Emotional Intelligence,* Bloomsbury (1996), p. 34.

31. Boyatzis, R., Goleman, D. and Hay/McBer, *Emotional Competence Inventory Feedback Report,* Hay Group (1999).

32. Landale, A. 'Must Have EQ', *Manager: The British Journal of Administrative Management,* February/March 2007, pp. 24–5.

33. Dann, J. 'Managing Your Emotions', *Professional Manager,* January 2015.

34. 'Emotional Intelligence', Checklist 178, Chartered Management Institute, March 2008.

35. Alexander, R. 'The Dark Side of Emotional Intelligence', *Management Today,* April 2011, pp. 46–50.

36. 'Managing for Diversity' Checklist 152, Chartered Management Institute, February 2014.

37. Higgins, J. 'The Six Habits of Truly Inclusive Organisations', *Professional Management,* Summer 2016, pp. 29–35.

38. 'Talent not Tokenism: The Business Benefits of Workforce Diversity', CBI and TUC, June 2008.

39. Reeves, R. 'Worth not Birth', *Management Today,* September 2013, pp. 36–9.

40. Cooper, P. 'Culture not Cult' in interview with Nicholls, J. *Governance + Compliance,* October 2017, p. 21.

41. Khan, S. *P.U.S.H. for Success,* Vermilion (2006), p. 230.

42. Spira, L. F. and Pitcher, H. 'Questioning Quotas' *Governance + Compliance,* April 2014, p. 18.

43. Francke, A. 'A Blueprint for Balance', *Professional Manager,* Summer 2016, p. 5.

44. 'Older and More Diverse', *Social Agenda,* The European Commission Magazine, no 26, March 2011, pp. 11–14.

45. Barnes, H. 'Managing the Generation Gap', *Manager, The British Institute of Administrative Management,* Autumn 2010, p. 30.

46. Wilton, P. 'Diversity is a Blueprint for Business' *Professional Manager,* Spring 2014, p. 19.

47. Nordström, K. and Ridderstråle, J., 'Funky Inc.,' in Crainer, S. and Dearlove, D. (eds) *Financial Times Handbook of Management,* second edition, Financial Times Prentice Hall (2001), p. 63.

48. Kirton, G. and Greene, A. M. *The Dynamics of Managing Diversity,* Butterworth Heinemann (2000).

49. Lucas, E. 'Making Inclusivity a Reality', *Professional Manager,* vol. 16, no. 4, July 2007, pp. 32–5.

50. Swabey, P. 'Red, Amber & Green', *Governance + Compliance,* May 2017, p. 24.

51. Chen, A. S. Y., Bian, M. D. and Hou, Y. S. 'Impact of Transformational Leadership on Subordinate's EI and Work Performance, *Personnel Review,* vol. 44, no. 4, 2015, pp. 438–53.

52. Salovey, P. and Mayer, J. D. 'Emotional Intelligence', *Imagination, Cognition, and Personality,* vol. 9, no. 2, 1990, pp. 185–211.

53. Goleman, D. *Emotional Intelligence,* Bantam Books, New York, NY (1995).

54. Goleman, D. and Boyatzis, R. E. 'Emotional Intelligence has 12 Elements: Which Do You Need to Work On?' *Harvard Business Review,* 6 February 2017, https://hbr.org/2017/02/emotional-intelligence-has-12-elements-which-do-you-need-to-work-on (accessed 7 July 2018).

55. Lindebaum, D. 'Rhetoric or Remedy? A Critique on Developing Emotional Intelligence', *Academy of Management Learning and Education,* vol. 18, no. 2, 2009, pp. 225–37.

56. Conte, J. M. 'A Review and Critique of Emotional Intelligence Measures', *Journal of Organizational Behaviour,* 26, 2005, pp. 433–40.

57. Grant, A. The Dark Side of Emotional Intelligence, 2014, https://www.theatlantic.com/health/archive/2014/01/the-dark-side-of-emotional-intelligence/282720/ (accessed 7 July 2018).

58. Bariso, J. *EQ Applied: The Real-World Guide to Emotional Intelligence,* Borough Hall: Germany (2018).

59. Kilduff, M., Chiaburu, D. S. and Menges, J. I. 'Strategic use of Emotional Intelligence in Organisational Settings: Exploring the Dark Side', *Research in Organizational Behaviour,* 30, 2010, pp. 129–52.

60. Linstead, S., Maréchal, G. and Griffin, R. W. 'Theorizing and Researching the Dark Side of Organization', *Organization Studies,* vol. 35 (2), 2014, pp 165–88.

61. Griffin, R. W. and O'Leary-Kelly, A. (eds) *The Dark Side of Organizational Behaviour,* San Francisco: Jossey-Bass (2004).

62. Tobak, S. Don't Believe the Hype Around 'Emotional Intelligence', 2014, https://www.entrepreneur.com/article/237459 (accessed 15 July 2018).

63. Antonakis, J. 'On Why "Emotional Intelligence" Will Not Predict Leadership Effectiveness Beyond IQ or the "Big Five": An Extension and Rejoinder', *Organizational Analysis,* vol. 12, no. 2, 2004, pp. 171–82.

Chapter 5
Learning and development

An understanding of the ways in which people learn and develop is an implicit feature of the study of organisational behaviour.

Learning outcomes

After completing your study of this chapter you should have enhanced your ability to:

- explain the importance of learning and development ;
- distinguish between behaviourist theories and cognitive approach;
- debate the value of different theories and studies about learning;
- assess the nature and importance of learning styles;

- review the importance of knowledge management and its impact on learning;
- explain the nature and importance of creativity in organisations;
- evaluate the importance of mentoring and coaching for learning and development.

Outline chapter contents

Overview topic map: Chapter 5 – Learning and development

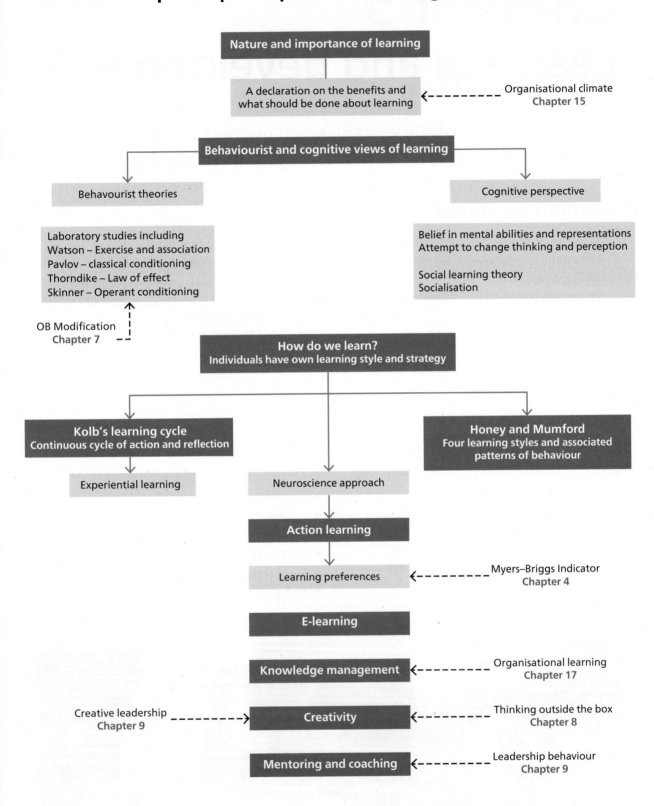

The monk has to learn to feed himself: the start of developing a way of life

Before commencing to read this chapter — reflect upon what YOU understand about what the nature of learning involves and how people learn.

The nature and importance of learning

The underlying purpose of learning and development is to improve both individual and organisational performance. Globalisation and technological advances have heightened the pace of change, including the relative importance of different occupations and skills, and transformed the way we live and work. Learning inevitably involves an examination of how change takes place. **Learning** is generally defined in terms of the acquisition of knowledge that leads to a relatively permanent change in behaviour which results from experience. Individuals may experience a temporary change in behaviour because of, for example, maturation or ageing, short-term factors such as tiredness or alcohol. These temporary changes are of a different nature to those associated with the process of learning which results in knowledge or a relatively permanent change in behaviour. Learning can be a deliberate and formal process or an unintentional outcome of natural activity or progression.

It is important to understand how people learn and develop their knowledge and skills in order to cope effectively with the complex and changing demands of the workplace. Attention must be given to the management of learning within organisations. Managers also need to develop their personal development aspirations with the goals of the organisation. An understanding of how people learn is a highly significant area of study and has been of continual interest in the development of psychology as a science. Learning is a function of the inner workings of our mind and has created a number of methodological difficulties. Every person learns in their own way and are good at learning some things, for example art or music; and less so with other things, for example IT skills. Some main forms of learning and development are set out in **Figure 5.1.**

Attitudes and social behaviour

Individuals differ in their learning capabilities, their style and their creative responses. Imagine for example these scenarios:

- a student attending an action learning set
- a person undertaking a fork-lift truck driving lesson
- a trainee observing a manager deal with an irate customer
- a nurse measuring blood pressure for the first time
- a manager completing a learning portfolio
- an older employee introduced to a new financial computer system.

These scenarios all share the common feature that learning has taken or is about to take place. They demonstrate that a discussion of learning involves not only knowledge and skills but also attitudes and social behaviour. Learning implies a different internal state which may result in **new behaviours and actions** (for example, a new skill such as taking blood pressure) or **new understanding and knowledge** (for example, a new subject area such as finance). Sometimes behaviour and knowledge coincide (for example, learning a language, becoming IT literate); at other times people will learn to act in certain ways without an underlying understanding of the reasons why (for example, operating machinery without an understanding of its mechanical features).

Individual learning is a lifelong process that is essential if people are able to cope with the changing nature of work organisations. *Payne and Whittaker,* for example, maintain that business can only be competitive with a highly skilled, highly educated workforce. They stress the importance of skills for the future and lifelong learning as the only way to keep abreast of the pace of change in a technological age, requiring flexible labour markets that operate in an increasingly global economy.[1]

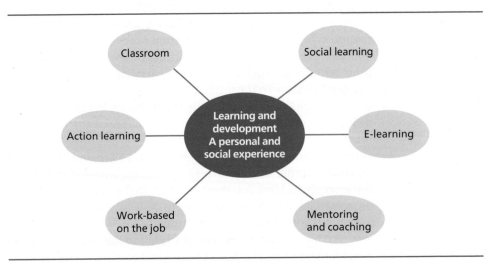

Figure 5.1 Main forms of learning and development

How prepared are YOU to readily accept new behaviours and actions, and new understanding and knowledge?

Much of what we learn takes place without any necessary deliberations or assessments. Learning can be seen to be a continuous and automatic process, often taking place in a social context. The spontaneous nature of learning can be observed in young children's play as they imitate and model their behaviour and attitudes on the people around them. Learning has an active and dynamic nature. As active participants, we engage and relate to the people around us. Our ability to learn will be affected by both our innate potential and our social experiences.

Learning, therefore, links the individual to the social world and is both a personal and a social experience. Often learning is an event that is shared with others. The process may be a deliberate sharing of information or guiding behaviour — as, for example, in the parent—child relationship when parents are attempting to socialise the child into acceptable ways of behaving or in organisations where new members are taught opening phrases when answering the telephone or how to greet a customer. At other times it is the actual sharing of the learning experience — going through the same learning process — which makes the process challenging and valuable. It is through the support of others that individuals can find both strength and rewards.

Learning occurs in many ways; information or skills may be imparted quite explicitly and at the same time the values and attitudes of the trainer will also be implicitly communicated. Learning is a rich experience. At times we may be learning 'incidentally' as we acquire, process and remember information automatically. *Crainer and Dearlove* maintain that if learning is work, such as brainstorming seminars with an atmosphere of deliberate playfulness, it is ineffective. The learning that sticks has a joy of discovery, playfulness and should extend to cover the entire working day.[2]

Learning and emotions

Learning implies that an individual has experienced 'something', has stored that experience and is able to refer to and/or use it at a later time. Learning and memory are inextricably linked. There are many factors that influence both the rate and enjoyment of learning **(see Figure 5.2).** The rewards and punishments levelled at us in the past will affect our motivation and attitudes towards learning in the present and the future. Expectations of others and the climate that surrounds us will determine our readiness to learn.

Feelings generated by the process of learning are very powerful and often tend to be pleasurable. A sense of achievement that often accompanies the completion of a learning process can lead to an enhancement of an individual's self-worth and esteem. However, learning can also be an uncomfortable experience; it can 'shake an individual's comfort zones'; it can provide new and alarming perceptions and can be disruptive and anxiety-provoking. An illustration of this has been noted by trainers in diversity who need to challenge individuals' attitudes and perceptions when there is evidence of prejudice.'[3]

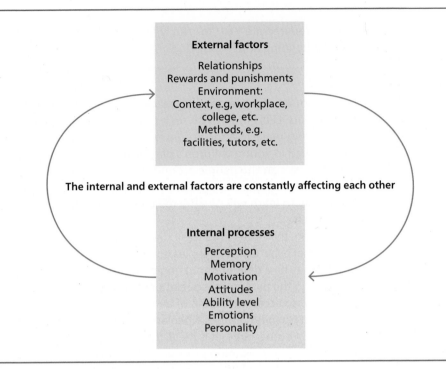

Figure 5.2 Factors influencing the learning process

A declaration on learning

Eight distinguished scholars on learning in organisations launched a declaration summarising their collective thoughts on the nature of learning, its benefits and what should be done about learning. They singled out learning as a key process for individuals, organisations and for society as a whole for the twenty-first century. They believe that it is too easy to take learning for granted and treat it as an automatic part of the human condition. They claim that individuals frequently do not organise or plan their learning and they leave the evaluation of learning to chance. Typically individuals fail to check what exactly they can do better or differently as a result of the learning experience.[4] Two parts of the declaration are shown in **Table 5.1.**

General climate of the organisation

If learning can result in the benefits outlined by Burgoyne *et al.* in Table 5.1, it is clearly in the organisation's best interest to ensure it utilises the knowledge and skills of all its employees. But how do organisations achieve these outcomes? In some organisations learning is still left to chance: the individual employee is expected to 'pick up' behaviour, attitudes and skills. Much learning appears to come about as a natural consequence of the demands of the job, overcoming problems and interactions with colleagues. That is, learning achieved through experience. It becomes difficult, therefore, to separate how learning occurs without taking some account of the relationship between employee and manager and the general climate of the organisation **(discussed in Chapter 15).**

Table 5.1 A declaration on learning: John Burgoyne, Ian Cunningham, Bob Garratt, Peter Honey, Andrew Mayo, Alan Mumford, Michael Pearn, Mike Pedler

Learning: the central issue for the 21st century	The benefits
Learning is the most powerful, engaging, rewarding and enjoyable aspect of our personal and collective experience. The ability to learn about learning and become masters of the learning process is the critical issue for the next century.	The following benefits assume that the learning in question has both morally acceptable intent and outcome:
Our understanding of learning has generally been restricted to formal teaching and training. It is often seen as unrelated to daily life and work. Systems of accreditation are sometimes used as a way of unfairly discriminating between individuals and are often felt to be irrelevant to real needs. The biggest missed opportunity for policy-makers and leaders is the failure to capitalise on the collective learning ability of people.	For individuals • Learning is the key to developing a person's potential • Learning to learn is the key to effective learning • Learning enables the individual to meet the demands of change • The capacity to learn is an asset that never becomes obsolete • Embracing learning helps the individual to acknowledge that learning is more than formal education and training
Organisational leaders need to harness relevant knowledge and experience so that the organisation as a whole and the people who comprise it can learn more effectively. The same principle applies at community, national and international levels. Every person, team and organisation both survives and progresses through the ability to internalise and act upon this fundamental truth.	For organisations • Learning increases everyone's capacity to contribute to the success of organisations • Learning enables the organisation to be more effective in meeting its goals • Learning emancipates the organisation through clarification of purpose, vision, values and behaviour • A focus on learning, planned and unplanned, formal and informal, produces a wider range of solutions to organisational issues • Learning helps to achieve a better balance between long-term organisational effectiveness and short-term organisational efficiency
This declaration does not contain all there is to say on the subject of learning. It does, however, reflect the thinking of the eight signatories. The declaration is designed to stimulate and encourage dialogue.	For society • Society survives and thrives through learning • A focus on capturing and sharing learning contributes to a more cohesive society • Individual and collective learning reinforces the informed, conscious and discriminating choices that underpin democracy • Learning helps to enhance the capacity of individuals to create a more fulfilled society

Source: Burgoyne, J., et al. 'The Debate Starts Here', in *People Management in Perspective: A Collection of Key Articles Published in the Last Year on Training and Development,* IPD (April 1999), pp. 16–17. Reproduced with permission from the Chartered Institute of Personnel and Development (CIPD).

How far can YOU identify with the individual benefits of learning set out in a 'declaration of learning' in Table 5.1? To what extent do YOU experience a feeling of pleasure from the learning process?

Behaviourist and cognitive views of learning

Early classic studies of learning offer explanations for simple learning situations. The principles arising from laboratory experiments remain applicable to an understanding of organisational behaviour. The effects of rewards and punishment (the ways in which behaviour can be shaped and modified) have considerable relevance in understanding the motivation of individuals and the culture of organisations. **These are called behaviourist theories** and underlined by a belief in specific actions. These theories are based on the assumption that our behaviour, and actions and reactions to stimuli in our environment are a result of the learning process. These behaviours can therefore be modified or unlearned.

Dissatisfaction with the earliest theories led researchers to consider more complex learning situations. '**Cognitive theories**' are underlined by a belief in our mental abilities and representations. Learning is based on our feelings and what takes place in our minds rather than our behaviour. These theories attempt to change our thinking and perception and have particular application to an understanding of individual differences in learning situations. They offer models that explain the process of learning and take into account different preferences and styles.

Behaviourist theorists of learning

Theories of learning have their roots in the history of psychology and some of the earliest experimental psychologists focused their attention on animal learning and were keen to develop laws of learning. They were interested only in behaviour that could be objectively measured and they designed experiments that maximised key scientific conditions: **control**, **reliability** and **validity**. A school of psychology called **behaviourism** developed out of these early research studies. As the name suggests, researchers were interested in the study of behaviour and those actions that could be observed, measured and controlled. Ideas and thoughts in people's minds were considered inaccessible to objective, scientific measurement and were therefore excluded from study.

Main theories under this heading include:

- law of exercise and association;
- classical conditioning;
- law of effect;
- operant conditioning.

Exercise and association

John B. Watson (1878–1958) developed the **law of exercise and association.** This refers to the process that occurs when two responses are connected and repeatedly exercised. Watson was particularly interested in the study of fixed habits and routines.[5] In organisational life we can see evidence of this in the habits and routines at work. These behaviours can become 'locked-in', believed to be 'the only way' of completing certain tasks — a part of cultural life; it is as if they are fixed into beds of concrete. Speech is a further illustration of our routine habits. The predictability of a greeting provides acknowledgement of our existence — when people say 'How are you?' they do not expect to be given a rundown of your medical history. The rhetorical question is really saying, 'Hello — I see, acknowledge and recognise you.'

Classical conditioning

Ivan Pavlov (1823–1899)[6] working in Russia, developed a theory called **classical conditioning**. His laboratory experiments demonstrated how instinctive reflexes, such as salivation, could be 'conditioned' to respond to a new situation and a new stimulus **(see Figure 5.3)**. Pavlov, through his repeated experimental studies, showed the power and strength of association. How can we relate these experiments on dogs to behaviour at work? There are times when our body responds more quickly than our mind. We may have an initial panic reaction to a situation without necessarily realising why. Physiological reactions may be appropriate in times of stressful situations — our body may be in a state of readiness to run (fight or flight reaction).

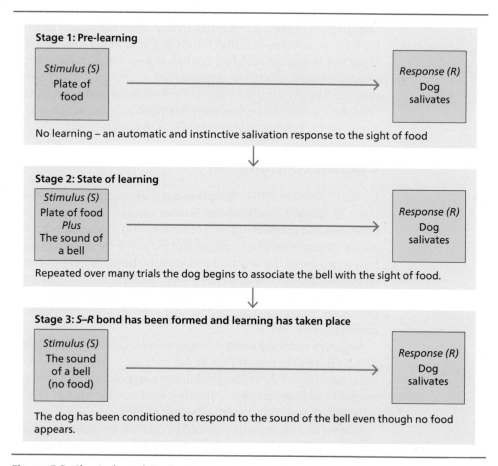

Figure 5.3 Classical conditioning

At other times our reactions may be 'conditioned' because of previous associations of pain, guilt or fear. Smells and sounds are particularly evocative and may release physiological reactions akin to the Pavlovian experiments. Thus sitting in a waiting room at the dentist's and hearing the sound of the drill may invoke an increase in our blood pressure or heart rate — nothing to do with any actual pain we may be experiencing. Returning to school for a parents' evening may invoke feelings of 'dread' or 'pleasure' depending on our own childhood experiences of school and its associations. Training for some occupations may depend upon learned associations and automatic reactions, an example being initial military training. If fire drills are to be successful, immediate reaction to the bell or siren is essential.

How would YOU attempt to argue against the view that Pavlov's work has little practical application to learning in the classroom situation?

Law of effect

Edward Thorndike's (1874–1949) work drew attention to the outcomes of learning — **the Law of Effect.** All learning is a process of stimulus-response (S-R). The strength of the S-R link is dependent upon the extent to which the experience is pleasurable. Behaviour that results in a favourable outcome is more likely to be repeated. Thorndike watched animals in new situations and noted how they learned to adapt successfully to the environment. He noted that in his experiments there were no flashes of insight shown but learning would occur by **trial and error.** Over time these correct responses were 'stamped in'. If an action was successful and led to a reward, the behaviour was more likely to be repeated.[7]

Operant conditioning

Burrhus F. Skinner (1904–90) advanced the ideas of Thorndike and produced a thesis of **operant conditioning**. Skinner's experiments on animals showed the effects of reward and punishment on animal learning. Unlike classical conditioning, learning was rewarded after the response had occurred. He proved that a response would be learned when the animal associated the behavioural response with a reward (or reinforcement) and could be broken with punishment. Partial reinforcement strengthened the stimulus—response bond and the behaviour was more resistant to extinction. The reward seemed to hold even greater importance when it was given intermittently.[8]

Negative reinforcement was also shown to be powerful. These experiments demonstrated the importance of the stimulus—response bond, but the reward was the prevention of something painful or nasty occurring. *Not* being shocked is the reward in such experiments. Negative reinforcement is not punishment. **Punishment** is trying to break the stimulus—reward bond.

Skinner and his researchers applied operant conditioning theory to many experimental situations. He demonstrated the power and control of simple learning principles: the identification of a stimulus and a reward following a successful response. He was able to train animals to perform complex acts by a process known as 'shaping'. Behaviour is shaped through a series of small but successive steps, with rewards given for those responses which approximate the desired end result.

Operant conditioning in work situations

The technique of shaping (modifying and controlling behaviour) and the identification of the stimulus—response bond can be applied to work situations. Illustrations of the power of rewards can be seen in almost any work organisation, for example: bonuses, commission, prizes for reaching sales targets, 'employee of the month' awards. Intermittent reinforcement is another useful outcome of Skinner's research. If an employee always receives a reward, does its value diminish? Skinner's research would say 'yes'. There is an interesting parallel with this concept in Transactional Analysis whereby too many positive verbal comments (called strokes) are described as 'marshmallow throwing'.[9]

A difficult problem with the application of operant conditioning is that Skinner was dealing with 'hungry' animals; they had a clear drive to eat and therefore a plate of food was, no doubt, a reward. It is far more complex when we consider **rewards for people.** We may all have our own definitions of a 'reward'. Although money might be a suitable reward for some employees, others may prefer to have 'time out' or a symbolic gesture of the work they have achieved. So having a photograph on public display may be a proud and rewarding moment for some but other employees may be acutely embarrassed. How organisations reward their employees makes a statement about what they value. How different pay practices affect organisational and individual performance is a critical aspect of reward management.

The same principle applies to people's perception of punishment. Inappropriate behaviour at work can be punished directly by, for example, withholding rewards or by initiating the company's disciplinary procedure. Some managerial actions may be perceived as punishment, for example being sent on a training course, not being sent on an international assignment. Whether the punishment is real or perceived, it is likely to cause feelings of resentment in the mind of the employee. Hence, punishment results in negative psychological outcomes. Although the employee may comply with requirements, it is likely that resentment will lead to anger and/or apathy and psychological revenge.

Some organisations endeavour to exercise tight control over their employees' language and behaviour. Training new employees is a form of 'shaping' behaviour in line with written training objectives. As employees demonstrate their responses, they may be rewarded with a tick in the training box or a 'badge' that they wear on their clothing. Learning occurs incrementally, with the task divided into sub-goals, each with its own reward. Sometimes shaping can occur in training centres where peer assessment can add further power to the modification process.

See also the discussion on organisational behaviour modification in Chapter 7.

How effective do YOU believe operant conditioning is as an effective method of learning in (i) the classroom and (ii) the workplace?

Cognitive perspective of learning

Focusing only on behaviour is useful but limited and cannot explain all forms of learning. The understanding and application of basic factual knowledge can arguably be learned through operant conditioning, for example computer-based training for call centre staff. However, more advanced levels of learning require more active brain processes. The inner mind has particular relevance to understanding how, what and why people learn. Personality, perceptions, motivations and attitudes will all play their part in helping or hindering the learning process.

Behaviourism cannot easily explain the natural curiosity that humans have, the great desire to learn, to make sense of their environment and to feel competent in activities. Neither can it explain the extent of incidental learning that takes place. Observing changes in behaviour is only part of the learning process. To understand how and why people learn, attention must be given to myriad individual factors including plans, ambitions and goals.

Research conducted in the last century highlighted the fact that the process of learning was more complex than simple stimulus—response associations. *Tolman* showed that rats allowed to wander freely through a maze to find food were capable of learning an image (a cognitive map) of the maze that they would use at a later time if their initial route was blocked.[10]

Social learning theory

Supporters of the behavioural school appear to have neglected the influence of broader social interactions. An influential writer *Albert Bandura* draws attention to the importance of environmental influences on observable behaviour. **Social learning theory** is based on the premise that people learn by observing and interacting with others and through imitation. Even aggressive behaviour can arguably be learned by imitation. The concept of 'self-efficacy' refers to a person's perception of themselves and a belief in their ability to act in a particular way and successfully achieve a task.[11] People with a high level of self-efficacy tend to exhibit high work performance without becoming stressed.

People learn by watching others. The term 'modelling' was coined by *Miller and Dollard* to explain learning by imitating others and 'role models' as a label for those individuals who are held up as examples of good practice.[12] So, the trainee observing how to prepare a soufflé will imitate the actions of their role model. Interpersonal skills can also be learned by observation and new recruits, by watching others, will 'pick up' the habits and techniques of those around them. Miller and Dollard's research brought attention to cognitive functions of thinking, perception, attention and memory in addition to behavioural responses. So, for instance, a trainee watching a supervisor deal with a customer complaint would need to attend to the customer's emotions, note the reaction of the supervisor and learn how the 'lessons' of this interaction could be applied to another situation.

Socialisation

Social learning also relates to the **socialisation** of new members of staff into the culture of the organisation and expected standards of behaviour and action. This occurs by learning through experience and observing and imitating other

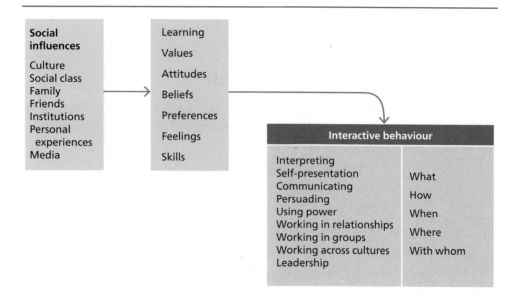

Figure 5.4 Learning: how we acquire our interpersonal skills
Source: Maureen Guirdham, *'Interpersonal Behaviour at Work'*, 3rd Edition, Financial Times Prentice Hall (2002), p. 140. Reprinted and electronically reproduced by permission of Pearson Education, Inc.

people as role models. For example working within the hierarchical structure, how to address other members of staff, physical appearance, recognising the informal organisation, acceptance of the psychological contract. Some organisations, for example IBM, attempt to reduce potential conflict by indoctrinating employees to share the same interest as management. The socialisation process may take place on a more formal basis for example through buddy systems, structured induction courses, probationary period of employment.

Guirdham points out that a key element of socialisation is how to interact with other people. Learning is the key to how interpersonal skills develop. **Figure 5.4** illustrates the relationships between skills and social influences developed through learning.[13]

 How would YOU evaluate the experience of socialisation into your university course? What suggestions do you have to enhance the process?

How do we learn?

Learning styles indicate various approaches to, or methods of, learning and the ways in which people learn. This approach recognises that individuals have their own learning style and strategy. This influences how people prefer to learn. Some cognitive theorists have emphasised the cyclical nature of learning and its active nature. *Professional Manager* magazine refers to the continuing controversy over learning styles or even if such styles really exist. But what is probably true is that students often have preferences for the way they are taught and more enthusiastic about learning if taught in this way.[14] Although there are a number of models of learning style, two of the best known and useful are that of David Kolb and that of Peter Honey and Alan Mumford.

The Kolb learning cycle

Kolb's learning cycle is typical of this approach and is one used frequently in the management literature.[15] Learning and development passes through a continuous cycle of action and reflection:

- Concrete experiences;
- Observational and reflective;
- Abstract conceptualisation;
- Active experimentation **(see Figure 5.5).**

The model provides useful insights into the nature of learning:

- It demonstrates that there is no end to learning but only another turn of the cycle.
- Learners are not passive recipients but need actively to explore and test the environment.
- It identifies the importance of reflection and internalisation.
- It is a useful way of identifying problems in the learning process.

Experiential learning

The approach emphasises the importance of the synthesis between an individual's behaviour and the evaluation of their actions. Reflection on what has been learned in order to experiment with new situations and to become aware of new possibilities is a vital part of the learning process. This **experiential learning** is the very essence of action learning; going through the cycle that learners are exposed to, applying, reflecting and testing out their learning. This encourages individuals in habits compatible with the notion of lifelong learning. It is therefore no surprise that Kolb

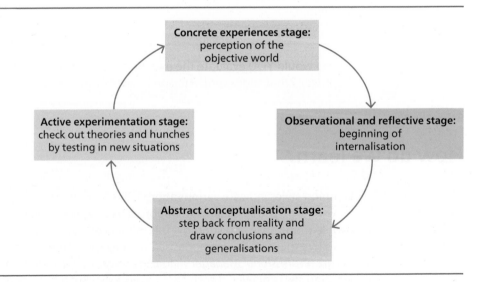

Figure 5.5 Kolb's learning cycle

addresses his ideas to managers and suggests that experiential learning will enable managers to cope with change and complexity.

Kolb and his colleagues suggest that partnerships between education and industry should create feedback loops which enable interactions between ideas and action — certainly ideas which fit well into a learning organisation framework and into the concept of the management of knowledge. **Action learning and knowledge management are considered later in this chapter.**

Can YOU give an example of anything you have learned from application of Kolb's learning cycle? What about your colleagues?

Honey and Mumford styles of learning

When applying the learning cycle to the study of individual differences, Kolb demonstrated that individuals may have a preference for one of the key stages and therein lies their learning style. His work, developed by Honey and Mumford, has been applied to managerial behaviour.[16] Kolb identified four different styles of learning:

- **accommodative** — strong preference for concrete experiences and active experimentation (hands-on);
- **divergent** — preference for concrete experiences, but to reflect on these from different perspectives;
- **assimilative** — prefers to swing between reflection and conceptualisation and will use inductive reasoning to develop new theory;
- **convergent** — prefers to apply ideas, will take an idea and test it out in practice.

Honey and Mumford simplified Kolb's learning cycle and refined his learning style questionnaire. They also identify four learning styles and associated pattern of behaviour.

- **Activists — What's new? I'm game for anything.** Activists are enthusiastic, flexible and open-minded. They like the challenge of new experiences, but can become bored with long-term routine procedures. Activists enjoy the here and now. They tend to think first and consider consequences later.
- **Reflectors — I'd like time to think about this.** Reflectors are cautious and slow to reach conclusions. They stand back and observe and like to think things through carefully. By collection and analysis they maintain a big picture perspective. At discussions and meetings, reflectors prefer to adopt a low profile and take a back seat.
- **Theorists — How does this relate to that?** Theorists are logical and disciplined, and value rationality and objectivity. They assimilate disparate facts in order to understand coherent theories. Theorists tend to be perfectionists and reject subjectivity, lateral thinking or flippancy.
- **Pragmatists — How can I apply this in practice?** Pragmatists like to experiment and seek and try new ideas or theories. They enjoy challenges and problem-solving. Pragmatists are practical, down-to-earth, quick to make decisions and quickly bored with long-term discussions.[17]

The researchers claim that an understanding of one's learning style will enhance learning effectiveness, whether as a trainee or as a tutor. Although all styles are necessary, individuals tend to be more comfortable with and focus on one particular style. An integrated and effective learner will be equipped to manage all four styles even though they may have a preference for one. Knowing your learning style may help avoid repeated mistakes by attempting activities to enhance alternative styles. For example, if you tend to 'jump in at the deep end', consider spending time reflecting on experiences before taking action.

Neuroscience approach to learning

The *CIPD* draw attention to a critique of the work of Kolb and Honey and Mumford, and the shift away from simplistic learning styles. Such models are oversimplified and there is advancing research into how psychology and neuroscience can support the design and delivery of effective learning. Cognitive insights and neuroscientific findings are less prescriptive than the learning styles approach. Attention is focused on more flexible learning strategies and the process of how people think and learn. The learner chooses the approach that is most appropriate to the task in hand. CIPD refer to models that highlight learning as a stress free and enjoyable experience for effective outcomes and that learning increases as threats are minimised and rewards maximised. However, the application of neuroscience to learning is still advancing and there is need to seek further evidence and assessment of the approach.[18]

To what extent are you a dreamer and explorer?

Action learning

Learning includes social learning and also has a reflective element as members are asked to reflect on their experience and learning. Typically, **action learning** involves a small group of learners (action learning set) meeting regularly to undertake a practical, organisational-based project. It is based on real work issues and designed to help develop both the manager and the organisation. Action learning was developed by *Reg Revans,* who argues that managerial learning is learner-driven and a combination of 'know-how' and 'know-that'. It involves participants working together to find solutions to actual problems and reflecting on their experiences. According to Revans, the learning process may be expressed by the equation: Learning (L) is based on a combination of programmed knowledge or instruction (P) and insightful questioning (Q), so that: $L = P + Q$.[19]

The emphasis is on learning and self-evaluation by doing, with advice and support from tutors and other course members. It is therefore essentially a learner-driven process. Action learning can be contentious compared with traditional programmed knowledge of development. There may be no formal structure and the process demands flexibility with attention focused on questioning and challenging. The process can be daunting for some people and a supportive atmosphere is essential. However, *Gitsham* maintains that experiential learning is one of the most effective ways to build leadership skills. 'Action learning and learning through projects where you are in the real world engaging with people is very valuable.'[20]

Yukl refers to action learning as an approach often used for combining formal training with learning from experience. An alternative approach is to link projects to a process of mutual coaching and mentoring. Project participants identify their own learning objects and the group meets periodically to devise solutions to problems, evaluate progress and discuss what was learned.[21]

The CIPD provide a link to 'action learning associates' who explain learning as a continuous process best achieved with an open, probing mind, an ability to listen, question and explore ideas. Action learning is the process of bringing thinking and action into harmony.[22] *See* **Figure 5.6.**

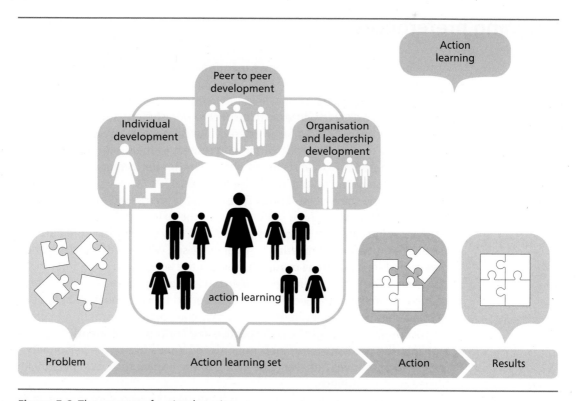

Figure 5.6 The process of action learning
Source: Action Learning Associates http://www.actionlearningassociates.co.uk.action-learning (accessed 10 June 2017). Used by Permission of Action Learning Associates.

Have YOU ever been involved in an action learning experience? If so, with what effect? If not, how far does the idea appeal to you as a potential learning situation?

An example of action learning is a programmed approach by Mencap a leading UK charity for people with learning disability. The approach was intended to provide support for area operational managers offering space and time to discuss and explore in an honest and open way ongoing issues with colleagues facing the same challenges. The programme consisted of eight action learning sets each with up to eight participants carefully selected for diversity. Each set met for a full day every six weeks, a total of nine times. Participation was impressively high often involving long hours of travel and/or overnight stay. Evaluation was conducted through a thematic feedback report after each round; mid-point and final online questionnaire evaluations; and final celebration event with focus groups feedback and recommendations for the future. The programme contributed to a real culture shift in Mencap and began a new way to work in a different way, providing more engagement with their role, their colleagues and the organisation.

Source: Cosgrove, E, 'Training Journal' 1 February 2015 http://www.trainingjournal.com/articles/feature/action-learning-unplugged

Learning preferences

At the beginning of this chapter we mentioned that every person learns in their own way and differ in their learning capabilities, their style and their creative responses. For example, *Eysenck has* shown links between personality and learning and that introverts and extraverts differ with respect to punishment and reward. Whereas introverts are more likely to be affected by punishment, extraverts' performance is enhanced by reward. They also differ with respect to their retention of short- and long-term material; extraverts tend to have a better performance at short-term intervals whereas the reverse is true for introverts.[23]

Studies using the Myers—Briggs Type Indicator **(discussed in Chapter 4)** also reveal differences in learning preferences for the sixteen personality types. Such differences indicate that introverts work best if they can think before participating or ask questions before completing tasks or exercises, whereas extraverts work best if they can interact in a small group and/or talk the lesson over with other individuals. However, some of the interesting research has been completed on the interaction between trainer and trainee. Thus, an extraverted trainer who is also high on 'sensing' may positively evaluate students who are active, energetic and practical, but may overlook the thoughtful introspective and conceptual students.[24] Such studies highlight the necessity for trainers not only to be sensitive to the personality needs of the group of trainees but also to be aware of the impact their own personality has on the learning experience.

Mayo and Lank suggests that organisations need to recognise the simple fact that different people learn in different ways and should take the following actions:

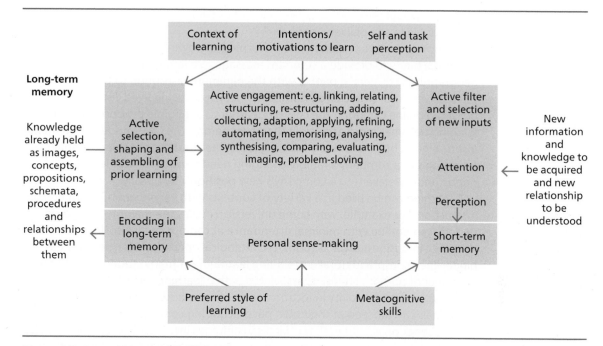

Figure 5.7 A cognitive model of learning

Source: From Atkins, M. J., Beattie, J. and Dockrell, W. B. *Assessment Issues in Higher Education,* Department of Employment (October 1993) p. 51. © Crown Copyright 1993. Crown copyright material is reproduced under terms of the Click-Use Licence.

- give people the opportunity to discover their most natural learning style;
- offer learning opportunities that suit people with different learning styles;
- recognise the need to complete the full learning cycle;
- help people to translate the learning cycle into an upwards continuous spiral of learning.[25]

A complex model of learning

Given the complexity of learning, how can managers make the best sense of the theories, concepts and frameworks? Models of learning such as that shown in **Figure 5.7** are inevitably complex. However, the model might stimulate questions and could help in the preparation and design of learning programmes. For example has sufficient consideration been given to the abilities of employees, preference for learning styles, and the best methods to be used?

E-learning

There is an increasing use of technology as a means of enhancing the learning situation. **E-learning** (short for electronic learning) *comprises self-contained learning and using the computer through the internet, or an intranet,* is now a global phenomenon and is central to many organisations. According to The Virtual College, although previously e-learning received a bad press with concerns that the use of a computer would remove the human element of learning, it has now been embraced as a valuable lesson delivery medium.[26]

It is not difficult to see why on-line learning is growing in popularity. It offers the opportunity to provide a standard message to a large number of widely geographically dispersed people with the minimum disruption to their working and private lives. And, where large numbers of learners are involved, learning materials delivered online can bring the cost per learner to negligible proportions. Thus, learning becomes more accessible than ever before. *The Chartered Management Institute* point out that since e-learning is internet-based it has the potential to respond to a company's rapidly changing needs, and offer new learning opportunities relevant to a company's new position very quickly.[27]

E-learning can be used in a variety of contexts with varying amounts of personal interaction. For example, with some university courses the majority of study is undertaken on-line with minimal attendance at campus or face-to-face tuition. However, in business organisations, technological and culture barriers appear to hinder the widespread uptake of on-line learning. For many students, there are a number of potential benefits associated with e-learning including: open access to education and flexibility in location and timing; quicker delivery of training; individuals can proceed at their own pace; acquiring computer skills; monitoring and feedback on activities. Potential disadvantages include: concerns over quality of content; maintaining motivation and danger of procrastination; lack of team working and social interaction.

The challenge involved in e-learning is not simply teaching in a different way. Rather, it means rethinking the whole nature of the teaching/learning process. It is clear that e-learning is more appropriate for the acquisition of knowledge and there are doubts about its application to the development of interpersonal social skills. Despite all of these reservations, as information communications technology develops and as people want to learn exactly what they need to know, with the minimum disruption to their lives, e-learning will become an increasingly significant part of training, either pre-course preparation or post-course evaluation and refreshment of knowledge.

How comfortable are YOU with the use of technology as a means of learning? Do you believe e-learning endangers personal interaction and the development of social skills?

Knowledge management

As mentioned previously, it is clearly in the best interests of the organisation to develop the knowledge and skills of its employees. Learning at the individual or group level impacts on the learning, development and performance of the organisation as a whole, and the process of learning is influenced by the general climate of the organisation. An increasingly important aspect of organisational performance is the idea of **knowledge management**. Although there is no generally recognised definition knowledge is defined in terms of a range of practices or processes to identify, capture, share, develop and apply knowledge to benefit organisational performance. Growth will continue as more collaborative IT applications become available. Knowledge management is related to business strategy, information technology, human resource management and people management, and can therefore be linked to **organisational learning discussed in Chapter 17.**

Explicit and tacit knowledge

Nonaka argues that competitive advantage is founded in the ability of companies to create new forms of knowledge and translate this knowledge into innovative action. He says that 'the one sure source of lasting competitive advantage is knowledge' and describes the different kinds of knowledge that exist in organisations and the ways in which knowledge can be translated into action.[28] Nonaka distinguishes explicit and tacit knowledge.

- **Explicit knowledge** is that held consciously in mental focus by an individual. It is easily communicated, quantified and available to others in various forms such as language, mathematical expression or printed matter.

- **Tacit knowledge,** however, is internalised and an individual may not be consciously aware of it. It is personal and specific to the individual and more akin to wisdom that is inarticulate, understood but rarely described. Although more problematic, because it is not so easily disseminated, tacit knowledge is arguably as important as explicit knowledge.

According to Nonaka, those companies able to use both kinds of knowledge will make the creative breakthroughs. He suggests that the knowledge-creating companies systematically ensure that the tacit and explicit feed into each other in a spiral of knowledge. Tacit knowledge is converted into explicit knowledge by articulation and that explicit knowledge is used within an individual's cognitive understanding by a process of internalisation. It perhaps is no surprise that 'knowledge management' has been the subject of hype in the management literature and has been extolled as the route to the Holy Grail of competitive advantage.

The importance of knowledge management

A substantial number of benefits have been identified by researchers of KM that no doubt have contributed to the surge of interest. *Kerr* identifies seven reasons why KM is an important area:

- business pressure on innovation;
- inter-organisational enterprises (e.g. mergers, takeovers, etc.);
- networked organisations and the need to co-ordinate geographically dispersed groups;
- increasingly complex products and services with a significant knowledge component;
- hyper-competitive marketplace (decreasing life cycles and time to market);
- digitisation of business environments and IT revolution;
- concerns about the loss of knowledge due to increasing staff mobility, staff attrition and retirements.[29]

McLean suggests that although many early management techniques have been relegated to the vaults of history, knowledge management shows no sign of disappearing from boardroom discussion. Knowledge management has become a major driver of organisational change and wealth creation.

> **Knowledge management aims to empower individuals and organisations to deal with real-life problems and issues which they face on a day-to-day basis. It also challenges them to identify ways in which they can 'know what they know' and use that conscious knowledge to assist their organisations to be a competitive force against rivals.**[30]

Embedded within the business

The success of knowledge management would depend on the culture of the organisation and its priority in sharing learning and knowledge, and has roots in the learning organisation. From an examination of the changing shape of knowledge sharing practices in organisations, *Burton* refers to criticisms of KM including that it can morph into a version of content management and rapidly become a specialist discipline with practitioners talking in abstract terms. Burton suggests the principles of knowledge management are not something where you bring in a specialist team to manage all your knowledge for you. It is something that has to be embedded within the business.[31]

The *Chartered Management Institute* points out that effective knowledge management can be a vital source of competitive advantage. It can enhance the ability to learn from past failures and be a driver for new ideas and more timely responses to change. However, this requires an integrated strategic approach with support from top management and a culture where knowledge is embedded in the skills, competencies and experience of the workforce over the long term.[32]

Organisational memory

In the past, organisations may have relied largely on the stability of the organisation's structure for knowledge transmission. Managers would tend to know who to go to for advice and would seek out the older and experienced employees who held the 'know-how'. This knowledge and wisdom, accumulated over years of work, was a precious store of information. However, such a store was rarely formalised or articulated and would be communicated only on an informal basis. Communication to the next generation of employees was an important part of the organisation's culture and socialisation process.

Older employees were useful as a source of knowledge and guidance for younger ones. Many held the role of an informal mentor and were much appreciated by their younger subordinates. (**Mentoring and coaching are discussed later in this chapter.**) More flexible forms of structure, increasing rates of staff turnover, widening generation and age groups, downsizing and outsourcing have a major effect on the extent of what may be termed 'organisational memory'. Not only are relationships disrupted by the restructuring of the business, but also there is the potential for the complete loss of this powerful and important reservoir of knowledge and understanding.

In what ways do YOU believe that knowledge management is likely to be affected by widening generations and age groups in the workforce?

Knowledge management takes many forms

Creativity

With a continuing turbulent and uncertain environment, organisations have an increasing need to foster a culture of creativity. For organisations to be innovative and maintain competitive advantage, creative solutions are required. Organisations need employees with the potential for both development and creativity. There are numerous definitions of **creativity** but it is defined generally, for example by *Goodman* in terms such as 'the process of generating new ideas or concepts' or more specifically such as 'the application of imaginative thought which results in innovative solutions to many problems'. Creativity is often linked with 'innovation' but this term is generally associated with the development of a new products or services.

According to *Goodman:* 'Actively creative people have a talent for getting to the heart of a problem. They are not confused by detail and by the need to invoke standard approaches.' There tends to be consensus in the literature that suggests such individuals have a desire for originality, non-conformity and the opportunity to experiment and express new ideas. A difference can also be drawn between those people who are productive in terms of the number of ideas they can create and those individuals who have entrepreneurial capabilities and are able to bring the ideas to the marketplace.[33]

Promoting a culture of creativity

The importance of the skill of creativity has received increasing attention in recent years, lending a so-called soft edge of organisational behaviour to the business literature. Strategic management writers suggest that managers will be required to go beyond rational/logical thinking and use their senses of feeling, creativity and intuition to create businesses for the future. *Hurst et al. for example* refer to The Creative Model of management, which is 'built on the philosophical assumption that the real world which surrounds the organisation is a dynamic construct enacted by the members of the organisation over time.'[34]

Such a view suggests that personality, sensitivity, creativity and communication skills are going to be the requirements of the future. It also requires managers to be proactive in their search for root causes to problems and be imaginative in solving them. In order to promote creativity employees must feel motivated and there must be a supporting environmental climate and organisation structures. Managers and supervisors need to adopt a style of behaviour and leadership based on openness, respect and trust that encourages the generation and implementation of new ideas. **See transformational or creative leadership in Chapter 9.**

Imaginative thought may lead to new ways of seeing things that may be novel for the person or completely novel in time. According to *Lois Burton* 'creativity is often viewed as a talent which resides only in a few and many will not see it necessarily as part of their role. In the twenty-first-century workplace, as well as building on existing knowledge, we need to develop new cultures which focus on developing creativity in everyone.' Burton refers to two parts to our imagination: **synthetic imagination** which enables us to analyse previous and imagine scenarios based on that experience and knowledge; and **creative imagination** which enables us to develop completely new and different ideas and concepts to solve problems and achieve goals. Organisations moving from good to great, however are learning to trust ideas from the creative imagination as well.[35]

Lucas comments that: 'Organisations are toying with improvisation to help managers work together better in teams, release creativity and improve their presentation skills. However the key to gaining acceptance is getting past people's scepticism about its value in the workplace. Rigid structures are all very well but they can and do inhibit free thinking, which is vital for creativity, improving business performance and engaging with your audience.'[36]

Blocks to creativity

People often lack confidence in their ability to be creative and organisations may set up a number of blocks. It is therefore understandable that creativity is suppressed and devalued. Amongst the common blocks to personal creativity are:

- **Emotion** — fear and anxiety about making errors or looking foolish to your peers
- **Communication** — suitability or otherwise of the style, method or skill in dealing with issues
- **Perception** — habit and stereotyping; and an over-reliance on the tropes of the past
- **Culture** — culture and attitudes not being constructive
- **Environment** — what surrounds us – available facilities, the mindset of others and other external stress factors
- **Process** — the lack of skill or technique in process matters; finding a quick solution.

A distinction can be made in Goodman's list between the first four features, which are aspects of the individual's psyche and repertoire of skills and the last two, which are functions of the culture of the organisation. Unless there is a culture of creativity and interest in re-construction, it is more likely that individuals will use their creativity and resourcefulness outside the organisation or against the organisation rather than for the organisation. Despite the doubts and blocks, learning to be creative is encouraged by many writers through exercises and activities to stretch and develop imagination in wild and novel ways — often referred to as 'thinking outside the box'. **These include procedures such as lateral thinking and brainstorming, discussed in Chapter 8.**

The magic of enchantment

In an age of austerity and tight finances, *Peck* refers to employees being beguiled by the magic of enchantment. Employees need to embrace the goals and values of the organisation needing less direction or supervision. Enchantment is a three-stage process by providing a MAP:

Mastery — the ability to master new skills and improve themselves at work

Autonomy — the ability to work independently and not have someone breathing down your neck

Purpose — working for a higher calling than simply making money.

If people are enabled to master new skills while working autonomously on meaningful goals you will enchant them into wanting to do things rather than being made to. They are empowered and know what to do because they know what the organisation stands for.[37]

Creativity and context

Rickards, Runco and Moger see creativity as a complex and compelling area of study that is as difficult to define as it is to achieve. In a thought-provoking series of contemporary articles, they explore how creativity can be better understood and used in a range of contexts including innovation and entrepreneurship; environmental influences, knowledge management, personal creativity and structured interventions. Rickards *et al.* refer to creativity occurring within particular contexts, two of the most important being cultural and organisational. These do not act merely as influences and determinants, however, but instead are also influenced by creativity. 'It is simplistic to think that contexts are always the influence and creative thinking the result. Instead, interplay implies that environments act on and are influenced by creative people and their efforts.'[38]

To what extent do YOU have a creative imagination? In what ways have you been encouraged to, or dissuaded from, a more creative approach to your studies?

Mentoring and coaching

Organisations need to offer learning and development opportunities which simultaneously challenge and support together with effective procedures that enable people to harness their potential. This requires creativity to engage and motivate people emotionally to operate at their limits. So, how are employees to learn and acquire the skills that are necessary to further their career progression?

An integral part of this process is the role of mentoring and coaching. Both mentoring and coaching are concerned with helping individuals to take responsibility for their learning and development. Although there is confusion about the two terms, that are often used interchangeably, practitioners usually perceive a clear difference.

- **Mentoring** aims to facilitate the individual's capability and potential, to enhance their performance and to achieve their ambitions and career progression. Mentors are there to offer advice, guidance, support and feedback. Mentoring tends to focus on long-term development and the mentor is typically not the line manager but an expert in an area or a leader within the organisation. Rapport and confidentiality is essential for either relationship to work effectively. Mentoring can also serve as a means of socialisation and encouraging a sense of membership.

- **Coaching** is a supportive relationship aimed at developing the individual's self-awareness. Coaching is usually a line management function with focus on knowledge and skills relating to specific tasks or activities that can be monitored and measured. There is an emphasis on performance. However, a coach does not 'fix' someone or solve their problems or assume an 'expert's' position; rather they try to draw out the wisdom from within.

Mentoring is widely regarded today as a two-way process with benefit to both parties. One of the joys of mentoring others can be to know that you have helped others develop and grow. *Bagley* distinguishes a mentor from a coach or teacher **(Figure 5.8)** but points out the likely downfall if someone takes on a mentoring role more for the perceived benefit to their own career. The mentor must be sure to focus on the person they are mentoring; not trying to manipulate the person but sharing experiences and knowledge in a supportive manner.[39]

Mentor	Coach
Usually a senior member of staff with experience of the business	Usually a member of staff with expertise in a specific skill or discipline
Works with the person being mentored to identify their ambitions for personal and professional development	Teaches the person to improve and develop their skills in a specific business area
Builds a trusting relationship with the person to enable a 'safe space' to discuss and learn	Relationship based on a pupil/teacher dynamic
Works with a person to create a programme of development and learning and supports them through challenges and opportunities	Imposes a programme of learning onto an individual or team to meet business needs
Always delivers mentoring on a one to one basis, providing the mentored person with individual focus	May coach individuals and teams, not necessarily focused on one person but on the development needs of the business
Someone who doesn't work with the person they mentor on a daily basis	Usually someone who works closely with that person or team

Figure 5.8 Mentoring and coaching
Source: Alison Bagley, 'The Value of Mentoring in Improving Retention', *Manager*, Q4, 2016, p. 22.

Managers as mentors

There is some debate on the extent to which managers can be both effective in in their own role and also as effective mentors. Managers have always been informal mentors and coaches — some relishing this role with the required portfolio of skills, some being more hesitant and others having a negative influence and acting as a 'block' rather than a steer to their subordinates. The extent to which managers can also be effective mentors is dependent upon the type of leadership behaviour exhibited, for example directive, supportive or participative; the confidence of subordinates; and the extent to which their tasks are highly structured with clearly defined goals.[40] **Leadership behaviour is discussed in Chapter 9.**

Benefits of mentoring and coaching

Potential benefits of an organisation developing a mentoring and coaching culture seem to be well recognised. According to *Whitaker,* mentoring is becoming increasingly popular as a powerful personal development and empowerment tool as an effective way of helping people to progress in their careers. Mentoring is to support and encourage people to manage their own learning in order to maximise their potential, develop their skills, improve their performance and become the person they want to be.[41]

The *Advisory, Conciliation and Arbitration Service* (ACAS) refers to the many forms of coaching including life coaching, skills coaching and business coaching. Most coaching is motivated by a desire to change, and improve, the way things are currently done. This might mean changing the way someone interacts with their colleagues, improving levels of skill or performance or acting as a positive role model. Coaching can be used in a many ways including:

- support for employees undergoing a change of role or career;
- personal development;
- improving individual performance;
- focusing on productivity;
- motivating individuals to change aspects of their behaviour at work.

Coaching and mentoring help to develop bonds between colleagues at work by emphasising the importance of personnel development. One-to-one interactions will also help to nurture working relationships based on openness and understanding. Some organisations use coaching to help employees manage specific work or life situations. For example, maternity coaching can help mothers manage the transition from work to maternity leave and back to work again.[42]

Sabin maintains there are many stages within your career life cycle when coaching provides a practical solution to help individuals determine control, over what is best for their career and families. By contrast *Brinkman* argues the danger of coaching is never being allowed to resist the craze for never-ending improvement. Constant self-development and improvement may be the cause of exhaustion and emptiness.[43]

Despite criticisms about the unethical process, the potential benefits of an organisation developing a coaching culture seem to be well recognised. According to *Dean* coaching allows the individual to examine their own thoughts, priorities and challenges. It is a tool used by successful organisations to drive and retain their best people. Coaching increases motivation, helps generate new ideas and can have significant and quantifiable effects on performance.[44]

A summary of formal mentoring is set out in the concept map, Figure 5.9.

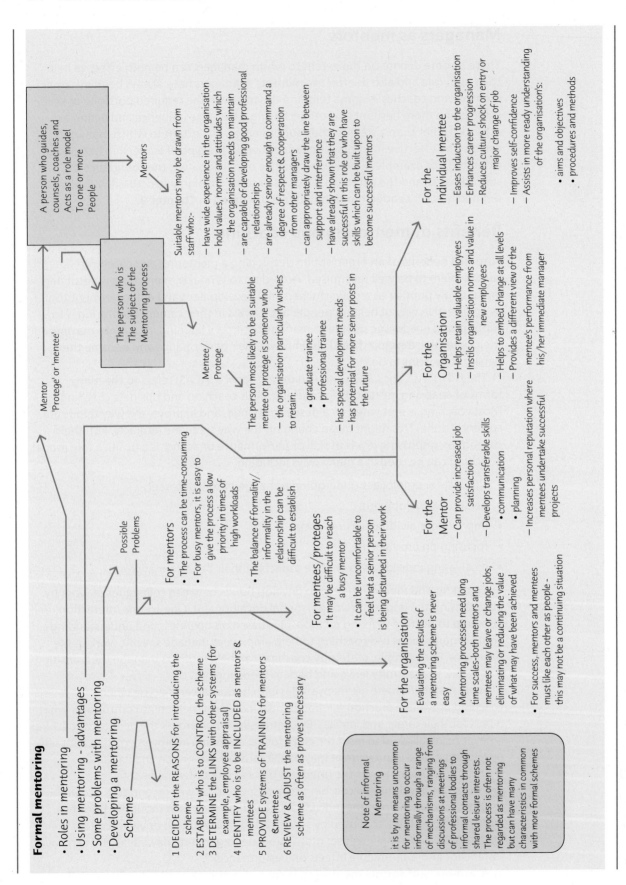

Figure 5.9 Formal mentoring

Source: Copyright © 2011 The Virtual Learning Materials Workshop. Reproduced with permission.

Unilever's global mentoring programme

Unilever's global mentoring programme started in 2009 to fulfil the specific business objective of accelerating more women into senior leadership positions. 'Before, mentoring was quite informal,' says global talent manager Katherine Ray. 'This was designed to speed up the transition between certain high-level roles.'

Patricia Corsi, Unilever's brand development director for laundry products in Europe, joined the programme two years ago, and when her first mentor left the company she was paired with Pier Luigi Sigismondi, Unilever's chief supply chain officer and a member of the worldwide executive board.

Corsi, who came to the UK from Brazil four years ago, says: 'I wanted to have an opportunity to learn from a much more experienced professional and to get a different point of view on my career next steps.' She was also eager to learn from someone who had made a similar geographic move – Sigismondi is originally from Italy and has worked in Venezuela – and had some specific management issues to discuss. She explains: 'Sometimes you have a situation where you have to influence stakeholders. I wanted to find out how to convey one message, how do I make this message really strong and convincing?'

Sigismondi says the first meeting was not about formal objectives, however, but about getting to know each other. 'It's important that you treat your mentee as a person, not as an employee,' he says. 'So we started talking about ourselves, and this was the biggest surprise for her, because she was never expecting me to be myself and to actually tell her about what my challenges are where I sit,'

The pair have met every couple of months during the year for two hours at a time, and Corsi makes a point of preparing carefully for each meeting. She says: It's important he feels I am committed to this programme and I really value his time, which I know is precious.'

For his part, Sigismondi says it is essential in any mentoring relationship to have 'rules of engagement': there must be a mutual interest, a clear commitment to invest the time, and respect. But he also believes that to be most effective, mentoring crosses the boundary of the merely professional, and explores deeper personal questions. 'That unleashes many of the self-confidence issues that you need to face in order to grow professionally.'

His approach, he says, is to come to each meeting with a fresh perspective that Corsi will not have considered: 'It keeps her thinking after the meeting on how to improve, how to see things differently and how to grow as a person.' And Corsi says: 'The value is immense, not just because he's on the Unilever board, but because Pier Luigi is a very inspiring person.'

She concludes: 'Knowing people believe in you drives you to do more and better. I'm very reassured about my role in Unilever, how the company sees me, and I have clarity on where I'm going. I really, really treasure this relationship with my mentor.'

Source: Garrett, A. (2012) Friends in high places, *Management Today*, October 2012, p. 50. www.management-today.com Reproduced with permission

What value do YOU place on the mentoring and coaching process as an aid to learning and development? How well does the process work in your university?

Applications of learning theory

Some of the major areas where it is possible to apply theories of learning to organisations include the following.

Self-development

- Learning what to 'do' (for example, skills and knowledge).
- Learning how to 'be' (role behaviour).
- Learning the ropes (socialisation process and culture) and the social rules (norms and attitudes).

Development of others

- Personal development — training others and developing their potential (including skills of mentoring and coaching).
- Development of planned learning events.

Development of learning culture

- Policy development — developing policies for 'learning organisations'; coping with changes and development; enabling 'loose', creative and lateral thinking.

Learning and development practices

The CIPD 2015 survey of learning and development (L&D) reports in-house methods of delivery remain more popular than external methods and expected to grow further in use. L&D professionals expect to see a continuing shift towards integration with business strategy and more emphasis on monitoring and evaluation.[45] The most commonly used and most effective learning and development practices are set out in **Figure 5.10.**

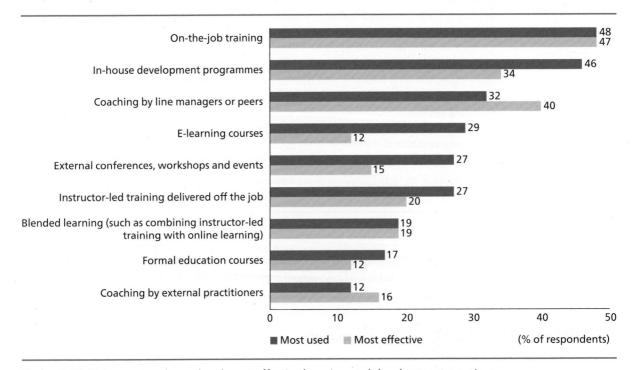

Figure 5.10 Most commonly used and most effective learning and development practices
Source: 'Learning and Development Survey', 1 May 2015, Used with the permission of the publisher, the Chartered Institute of Personnel and Development, London (CIPD www.cipd.co.uk).

Critical Thinking Zone
Reflections on Knowledge Management

In this zone, we critically discuss the concept of knowledge management and evaluate whether an organisation, in reality, can manage the knowledge of its workforce.

Over the past two decades, discourse and debate regarding the importance of knowledge and knowledge management within the post-industrial economy has gained momentum. The shift in paradigm from land, capital and labour to knowledge as the fourth factor of production[46] has transferred the focus from manufacture (production with the hands) to mentofacture (production with the mind[47]) and catalysed the realisation that knowledge is an intangible, commoditable asset that can yield sustainable competitive advantages for organisations.[48]

The Origins of Knowledge Management

Brinkley[49] and DiMattia and Oder[50] posit that the emergence and development of knowledge management has been influenced by three significant changes in the business environment. First, globalisation opened up markets and enabled the internationalisation of knowledge-based industries, such as education, research and development (R&D) and IT services. It created a global marketplace for knowledge workers and the utilisation of their specialist knowledge, skills and expertise to innovate new products, services and processes. Second, the drive for organisational 'leanness and meanness' in the 1980s and 90s led to a raft of downsizing activities, resulting in the exodus of specialist and operational knowledge, leading to major knowledge and skills gaps.[51] To mitigate against this, many organisations implemented knowledge management strategies such as codification,[52] in a bid to capture tacit knowledge and transform it into explicit, tangible formats (e.g. documents, blueprints and reports), to retain the knowledge for future use. Third, technological advancements in information and communication technologies (ICT), such as the internet, intranets and enterprise resource planning (ERP) systems,[53,54] have helped to service the proliferation of geographically dispersed and networked organisations and the necessity to disseminate explicit knowledge to those who need it, when they need it, regardless of time zones and location.[50]

The Roots of Knowledge Management

Theorists attest that the roots of knowledge management are firmly embedded in a multiplicity of diverse disciplines, ranging from organisational theory to anthropology and management strategy.[55] Over the years, a wide theoretical foundation has served to stimulate considerable debate within these fields and enabled a better understanding of how knowledge is created, stored, retrieved, shared and applied within organisations.[56] However, Jashapara[57] caveats that managerial uncertainty still pervades as to what knowledge management is all about and whether it can, in reality, be implemented as a strategy to manage intangible assets. In an attempt to address this uncertainty, it is necessary to first explore the nature of knowledge.

The Nature of Knowledge

The quest for knowledge and how it can be managed is an old one. It has been at the forefront of human thought since the beginning of time and debated by classic Greek philosophers, including Plato and Aristotle and twentieth century thinkers such as Polanyi[58] and Ryle.[59] Simply defined, knowledge is 'information that changes something or somebody, either by becoming grounds for actions or by making an individual (or institution) capable of different or more effective action' (Drucker: 24).[60] Both Drucker and Nonaka and Takeuchi[61] relate knowledge to human action and change through the medium and utilisation of information. Davenport and Prusak,[62] however, view knowledge as a fluid mixture of framed experiences that are, essentially, socially constructed and originated and applied in the minds of knowers. Expert insight, which is a key constituent of knowledge, is tacit in nature and, over time, is consciously and subconsciously embedded in documents, repositories (e.g. knowledge management systems or intranets) and the organisation's routines, practices, norms and processes.[63] In essence, knowledge forms a major part of the organisation's cultural fabric and helps to shape its identity to its members, the business community and society at large. Classic examples of this are knowledge-based organisations such as Google, Microsoft and Apple, who are recognised not only for the goods and services they offer to consumers and businesses but also for the vast knowledge base of their workforce, whose specialist knowledge is, without doubt, commoditised for competitive advantage.

Debates about Knowledge

The definitions proffered by Drucker and Davenport and Prusak raise arguments and debates about whether knowledge exists independently of individuals; whether, metaphorically, the individual is knowledge[64] and whether knowledge is something individuals have or something they do.[65] Delving deeper within this debate, two competing perspectives are unearthed: objectivist and practice-based,[66] both of which have implications for knowledge management and organisational behaviour in the workplace.

The Objectivist Perspective

In this debate, knowledge is perceived as an object or commodity that individuals possess. Knowledge exists independently in their minds and can thus be 'objectified' through externalisation[61] and transferred and commoditised intra and inter-organisationally.[67] As knowledge is seen as a collection of objective facts, both knowledge and understanding can be developed that are free from individual subjectivity and bias.

The Practice-Based Perspective

From this perspective, knowledge is embedded in practice and thus cannot be separated from human action, to which Drucker and Nonaka and Takeuchi allude. Instead of being regarded as something people have, as in the objectivist perspective, Blackler[65] attests that knowledge becomes *knowing,* as it is embodied in and carried, taught, passed on and used and misused by people.[60] As knowing is socially constructed, subjective and influenced by a multiplicity of personal and organisational experiences that have developed over time, it can never be bias free and cannot, wholly, be separated from the knower and objectified into explicit knowledge. This, then, poses further questions whether knowledge is capable of being managed.

Hard and Soft Knowledge Management

The concept of knowledge management can be defined from two approaches, hard and soft,[68] which reflect the objectivist and practice-based perspectives explored above. First, hard knowledge management refers to a process of knowledge creation, capture,

dissemination and utilisation, via ICT,[69] to enhance the organisation's performance. The focus here is on the adoption of a codification strategy,[52] which externalises tacit knowledge that has been disembodied from knowers, and objectified into explicit formats. Second, soft knowledge management is, one could argue, more humanist than the hard approach because it focuses on developing and motivating knowledge workers and keeping their tacit knowledge and expertise in a 'state of fluid gestation' (Schulz and Jobe: 144)[70] through the deployment of a personalisation strategy.[52] This enables knowledge workers to socialise[61] and interact with other experts face to face, in, for example, a community of practice.[71]

Can Knowledge and Knowing be Managed?

To conclude, based on the discussions presented, it could be argued that an organisation, in reality, *cannot,* wholly, manage the knowledge of its workforce, due, in part, to the highly tacit, subjective, socially constructed, personal and idiosyncratic nature of knowledge and knowing.[63,72] Bordum[73] proffers that the notion of 'managing knowledge' becomes problematic when we consider that managers experience a reversal of the 'knowledge—power' relationship in situations where they have to manage experts and specialists in their field, who may be more knowledgeable and thus be perceived to have a greater level of power. Bordum argues that organisations may turn this potential negative into a positive by codifying specialist knowledge into explicit formats and embedding it into procedures, processes and activities, which may serve to not only reduce an organisation's reliance on knowledge workers but also redress the perceived power imbalance. He caveats that managers must not forget that 'there is always a (tacit) basis of knowing the knowledge, which cannot be managed' (p. 53). As Cook and Brown[74] (p. 385) contend 'tacit knowledge cannot be turned into explicit knowledge, nor can explicit knowledge be turned into tacit'. This paradox has additional implications for managing knowledge and, indeed, organisational behaviour in the workplace, as organisations must consider implementing an infrastructure that underpins the deployment of codification and personalisation (hybrid) knowledge management strategies and developing a culture that supports the creation, sharing and utilisation of explicit and tacit knowledge for competitive advantage.

Questions

In light of the above, answer the following questions.

1. Theorists espouse that the advent of globalisation, downsizing and rapid technological advances catalysed the emergence and development of knowledge management. With reference to literature and practical examples, *what other* twentieth and twenty-first century changes have influenced the concept?

2. *Compare and contrast* the objectivist and practice-based perspectives of knowledge. *What* implications do they have for hard and soft knowledge management?

3. Theory and practice suggest that knowledge and knowing cannot, in reality, be wholly separated or managed. *Critically evaluate* the implications of this for organisational behaviour in the workplace.

Summary – Chapter 5 'Learning and development'

An understanding of ways in which people learn and develop is a dynamic concept and fundamental feature of organisational behaviour. Learning takes place in a variety of ways and a range of situations. Lifelong learning is essential to cope with the changing nature of work organisations. The behaviourist approach to learning was interested in laboratory studies of behaviour and actions that could be observed, measured and controlled. The cognitive perspective gives attention to how and why people learn. Social learning theory draws attention to the influence of social interactions and imitation, and the process of socialisation. Two major models of how we learn include the Kolb learning cycle and Honey and Mumford styles of learning. Action learning places emphasis on learning and self-evaluation by doing. Learning via technology (e-learning) is central to many organisations. It arises in a number of forms and can be used in a variety of different contexts. An important aspect of effective organisational performance is the idea of knowledge management which is linked to organisational learning. In order to maintain competitive advantage the importance of a creative organisational culture has received increasing attention in recent years. Mentoring and coaching may contribute to an organisational climate in which individuals take responsibility for their own learning, personal development and empowerment.

Group discussion activities

Undertake each of these activities in small groups as indicated by your tutor. Before you start your discussion establish a non-threatening environment within the group and confirm confidentiality will be honoured.

First, form your own views and then share and compare in open critical discussion with colleagues. Reflect honestly on the extent to which: (i) you influenced the thinking and ideas of your colleagues; and (ii) you were influenced by your colleagues.

To what extent was your group able to reach consensus?

Agree one of your members to produce a brief written summary of the discussion and prepared to present in a plenary session.

Activity 1

Prepare a paper setting out in bullet-point format the *contrasting* potential benefits, applications and shortcomings of:

(a) Traditional models of learning

(b) Social learning theory

(c) Action learning

(d) E-learning

(e) The use of computer games as part of the curriculum

Activity 2

A study by US psychologists suggested that you remember and recall more from writing notes by longhand rather than into a laptop or tablet computer.

Your tutor will arrange for members of your seminar group to watch a video recording of a lecture they have not seen previously.

Half the group have only pen and paper and half a laptop or tablet to make notes during the recording or immediately after.

Thirty minutes later your tutor will chair a joint discussion with both groups and ask a series of recall and comprehension questions based on the recording.

Meet again in your separate groups:

(a) What conclusions do you draw from the discussion and to what extent do they support the original study?

(b) What if any are the implications for the process of learning and development?

Activity 3

(a) University courses should be designed less around knowledge of academic disciplines and more to take account of the skills and abilities necessary in the workplace and for career advancement.

(b) Traditional methods of student assessment are too rigid and restrictive in responses expected from students. The underlying search for standard answers discourages approaching your studies with an open mind, leaves little allowance for originality and stifles creativity.

(c) Testing *what* has been learned is ingrained in our society and accounts largely for the ways individuals are compared and evaluated. This is too short-sighted. Far more attention should be given to *why* and *how* a person has learned and practical applications of learning.

Organisational behaviour in action case study

E-learning: Leicester Medical School

The background

The University of Leicester is ranked in the top one per cent of universities in the world by the Times Higher Education. Its Medical School celebrated its 40th anniversary in 2016 and has recently completed a £42 million build of state of the art facilities. The way in which Healthcare Practitioners work is changing and Leicester Medical School strives to make everything clinically-relevant whilst incorporating new technologies. For example, the Medical School is the first in the UK to equip each new pre-clinical-phase student with a free iPad.

The challenge

Medicine is obviously a sensitive issue with patient confidentiality of utmost importance. It is crucial that workers in the sector are aware of the ramifications of how and to whom they talk about their work. In practice, the lines between private and professional lives are becoming blurred by digital and social media. The General Medical Council publishes guidance which students must read and agree to adhere to, but they might not envision the different practical implications of this guidance. Terese Bird, Educational Designer at the University of Leicester, commented: 'As the pitfalls are easy to fall into, some students are on the side of caution by closing down from social media altogether or they just use it personally but not professionally'.

There are, however, huge potential benefits which can be realised by using digital communication appropriately within the medical profession. For example, it can be used as a way of tapping into the experience of a doctor who, in the past, has come across rare patient symptoms. 'The GMC stresses that its official guidelines recognise the potential professional benefits of using social media appropriately and we wanted our medical students to be aware of the positives as well,' explained Terese.

The solution

In April 2015, the Medical School first engaged with Virtual College about its interactive 'Managing your Professional Digital Profile' online resources. These have been created in conjunction with subject matter expert, Bernadette John, previously Digital Professionalism Lead for Kings College London. The course incorporates fictional case studies to illustrate how individuals can make the most of digital and social media without risk to themselves or their organisation. The online course provides an opportunity to question and encourages thinking, interaction and engagement. Leicester Medical School bought licences in June 2015 to enable it to provide the course to its students. 'Within medicine, it has always been important to track and provide proof. The university needs to know that it has done its duty in making students aware of digital professionalism and can provide reports, if necessary.'

The results

Within 4 months, virtually all of Leicester Medical School's year one, two and three students had taken the online 'Managing your Professional Digital Profile' course. Terese commented: 'It was easy to give students access to the resources via the learning management system.'

'I could see who had completed the course and nudge the few who hadn't.'

'As far as I am aware not many medical students in the UK are getting similar social media professionalism training.'

'All of our students have iPads, and their learning material is all formatted for study on iPads, including apps they use in class such as for quizzes and interactivity between lecturer and student.'

'The Virtual College course was perfect in that the material was written by a medical staff instructor, the software is interactive and engaging and runs nicely on iPads, and plus I have access to the data to check students' engagement.'

'It would be costly to offer this learning content on a face to face basis, and costly for me to try and build something similar, and it would be difficult to get the time on the curriculum to cover this by traditional methods.'

'For topics like this, in particular, e-learning can provide a rapid and cost effective solution for us, which is more likely to deliver engagement and retention. I like the fact that the course gives students an opportunity for feedback.'

'Use of e-learning within the Medical School is only going to grow in the future.'

Source: Virtual College with thanks to Simon Falconer, Chief Marketing Officer. www.virtual-college.co.uk.

Tasks

1. Discuss how best to overcome problems with the blurred lines between private and professional lives by digital and social media.

2. What potential benefits do you see by increased use of digital communication within the medical profession?

3. Apart from the medical profession to what extent do you see the general use of e-learning only going to grow in the future? What examples can you provide?

Chapter 5 — Personal skills and employability exercise

Objectives

Completing this exercise should enable you to enhance the following skills:

* Participate meaningfully in a role play activity.
* Demonstrate the skills required in mentoring and coaching.
* Sensitivity to your personal relationships with other people.

Exercise

Role play: manager/supervisor

You are a manager in a large Accounts Department. A junior member of staff, Chris, one of the most energetic people, has asked for some of your time and is coming to see you in a couple of minutes. You're not sure what it's about but you have had concerns about the amount of work Chris appears to take on. The supervisor has advised you that Chris takes on anything that needs doing and is always the first to volunteer for new projects. This has been particularly so over the past few months and the supervisor is beginning to worry about health issues as Chris looks very drained at the moment.

You obviously want Chris's enthusiasm to remain high but you don't want a stressed or burnt-out employee. You may be unsure how much to act as a mentor or a manager. Decide how you will approach the issue and how you might get Chris to moderate the workload.

Role play: employee/Chris

You have been in the Accounts Department for a little over a year now and really love your job. In fact, since you and your partner split up a few months ago you've really thrown yourself into your work. It's nothing for you to work late into the evening and quite often at weekends. There are so many exciting things to get involved with that there isn't enough time to do as much as you'd like. Besides, your social life isn't exactly buzzing at the moment and you've never got hooked into any particular hobbies or pastimes. Your supervisor is full of praise for your performance, giving you a high rating on your objectives. You've also making rapid progress during your time in the department. However, you have felt a bit drained recently and find it hard to switch off.

You have asked to see the manager about an exciting new piece of work you've heard about. You'd really like to get involved in it. You don't want to give up your other stuff though.

Discussion

* What do you believe is the best training method for developing coaching and mentoring skills?

* How would you attempt to ensure the transparency necessary for good coaching whilst maintaining confidentiality about personal circumstances?

* Debate critically what you have learned from undertaking this activity.

Notes and references

1. Payne, E. and Whittaker, L. *Developing Study Skills,* second edition, Financial Times Prentice Hall (2006), p. xxi.
2. Crainer, S. and Dearlove, D. *Financial Times Handbook of Management,* third edition, Pearson Education (2004), p. 750.
3. Clements, P. and Jones, J. *The Diversity 'Training Handbook': A Practical Guide to Understanding and Changing Attitudes,* Kogan Page (2002), p. 9.
4. Burgoyne, J., Cunningham, I., Garratt, B., Honey, P., Mayo, A., Mumford, A., Pearn, M. and Pedler, M. 'The Debate Starts Here', in *People Management in Perspective: A Collection of Key Articles Published in the Last Year on Training and Development,* IPD (1999), pp. 16–17.
5. Watson, J. B. *Behaviourism,* JB Lippincott (1924).
6. Pavlov, I. *Conditioned Reflexes,* Oxford University Press (1927).
7. Thorndike, E. L. *The Fundamentals of Learning,* Teachers College, New York (1932).
8. Skinner, B. F. *Science and Human Behaviour,* Macmillan (1953) and Skinner, B. F. *About Behaviourism,* Jonathan Cape (1974).
9. Stewart, S. and Joines, V. *TA Today: A New Introduction to Transactional Analysis,* Lifespace Publishing (1987).
10. Tolman, E. C. *Purposive Behavior in Animals and Men,* Appleton-Century-Crofts (1932).
11. Bandura, A. *Social Learning Theory,* Prentice Hall (1977).
12. Miller, N. E. and Dollard, J. C. *Personality and Psychotherapy,* McGraw-Hill (1950).
13. Guirdham, M. *Interactive Behaviour at Work,* third edition, Financial Times Prentice Hall (2002).
14. 'The Way We Learn', Insights, *Professional Manager,* Summer 2015, pp. 16–17.
15. Kolb, D. A. *Experiential Learning: Experience as the Source of Learning and Development,* Prentice Hall (1985).
16. Honey, P. and Mumford, A. *The Manual of Learning Styles,* third edition, Honey (1992).
17. Honey, P. 'Styles of Learning', in Mumford, A. (ed.) *Handbook of Management Development,* fourth edition, Gower (1994).
18. 'Psychology and Neuroscience in Learning', CIPD, 29 June 2017, www.cipd.co.uk.
19. Revans, R. *ABC of ACTION Learning,* Chartwell-Bratt (1983).
20. Gitsham, M. in conversation with Lucas, E. 'Learning with a Helping Hand', *Professional Manager,* vol. 18, no. 5, September 2009, pp. 22–5.
21. Yukl, G. *Leadership in Organizations,* seventh edition, Pearson Prentice Hall (2010).
22. 'What is Action Learning?', Action Learning Associates. http://www.actionlearningassociates.co.uk/action-learning/ (accessed 10 June 2017).
23. Eysenck, M. 'Learning, Memory and Personality', in Eysenck, H. J. (ed.) *A Model of Personality,* Springer (1981), pp. 169–209.
24. Hirsch, S. K. *Using the Myers–Briggs Type Indicator in Organisations,* second edition, Consulting Psychologists Press Inc. (1991).

25. Mayo, A. and Lank, E. *The Power of Learning: A Guide to Gaining Competitive Advantage,* IPD (1994) pp. 135–6.

26. 'What is E-learning?', *Virtual College* https://virtual-college.co.uk/help/what-is-e-learning (accessed 8 June 2017).

27. Chartered Management Institute, http://mde.managers.org.uk/members/Searchsummary.aspx?term=e-learning# (accessed 8 June 2017).

28. Nonaka, I. 'The Knowledge Creating Company', in Starkey, K. (ed.) *How Organizations Learn,* International Thomson Business Press (1996), pp. 18–32.

29. Kerr, M. 'Knowledge Management', *The Occupational Psychologist,* no. 48, May 2003, pp. 24–6.

30. McLean, J. 'Does Your Organisation Know What It Knows?', *Manager, The British Journal of Administrative Management,* Spring 2009, pp. 32–3.

31. Burton, G. 'Knowledge Empowered', *Manager,* Spring 2013, pp. 28–31.

32. 'Knowledge Management', Checklist 166, *Chartered Management Institute,* February 2016.

33. Goodman, M. *Creative Management,* Prentice Hall (1995), p. 86.

34. Hurst, D. K., Rush, C. and White, R. E. 'Top Management Teams and Organisational Renewal', in Henry, J. (ed.) *Creative Management,* Sage Publications (1991), pp. 232–53.

35. Burton, L. 'Creativity and Innovation: The power of imagination', *Manager, The British Journal of Administrative Management,* Autumn 2009, p. 25.

36. Goodman, M. *Creative Management,* Prentice Hall (1995).

37. Peck, T. 'The Magic of Enchantment', *Professional Manager,* May/June 2011, pp. 26–9.

38. Rickards, T., Runco, M. A. and Moger, S. (eds) *The Routledge Companion to Creativity,* Routledge (2009).

39. Bagley, A., 'The Value of Mentoring in Improving Retention', *Manager,* Q4, 2016, p. 22.

40. For further discussion, see: Misselhorn, H. 'To Mentor or to Manager' November 2016. www.jpsa.co.za.

41. Whitaker, H. 'Speak the Same Language', *Governance + Compliance,* April 2014, pp. 54–5.

42. 'Front Line Managers', ACAS, June 2014.

43. 'Do You Really Need a Life Coach?' *Professional Manager,* Autumn 2017, pp. 12–13.

44. Dean, J. 'What is the No. 1 Tool for Managers?' *Training Journal,* March 2017, pp. 30–3.

45. CIPD 'Learning and Development Survey', 1 May 2015, www.cipd.co.uk.

46. Drucker, P. F. *The Post Capitalist Society.* New York: Harper Business (1993).

47. Pedler, M., Burgoyne, J. and Boydell, T. *The Learning Company: A Strategy for Sustainable Development.* London: McGraw-Hill (1991).

48. Leal-Rodriguez, A. L., Roldan, J. L., Leal, A. G. and Ortega-Gutierrez, J. 'Knowledge Management, Relational Learning and The Effectiveness of Innovation Outcomes', *The Service Industries Journal,* vol. 33 (13–14), 2013, pp. 1294–311.

49. Brinkley, I. *The Knowledge Economy: How Knowledge is Reshaping The Economic Life of Nations,* London: The Work Foundation (2008).

50. DiMattia, S. and Oder, N. 'Knowledge Management: Hope, Hype or Harbinger?' *ERIC Library Journal,* vol. 122 (15), 1997, pp. 33–5.

51. Piggott, S. E. A. 'Internet Commerce and Knowledge Management: The Next Megatrends', *Business Information Review,* vol. 14 (4), 1997, pp. 169–72.

52. Hansen, M. T., Nohria, N. and Tierney, T. 'What's Your Strategy for Managing Knowledge?', *Harvard Business Review,* vol. 77 (2), March/April, 1999, pp. 106–16.

53. Farzaneh, M., Vanani, I. R. and Soharbi, B. 'A Survey Study of Influential Factors in the Implementation of Enterprise Resource Planning Systems', *International Journal of Enterprise Information Systems,* vol. 9 (1), 2013, pp. 76–96.

54. Gressgård, L. J., Amundsen, O., Aasen, T. M. and Hansen, K. 'Use of Information and Communication Technology to Support Employee-driven Innovation in Organisations: A Knowledge Management Perspective', *Journal of Knowledge Management,* vol. 18 (4), 2014, pp. 633–50.

55. Chae, B. and Bloodgood, J. M. 'The Paradoxes of Knowledge Management: An Eastern Philosophical Perspective, *Information and Organization',* vol. 16, 2006, pp. 1–26.

56. Janz, B. and Prasarnphanich, P. 'Understanding the Antecedents of Effective Knowledge Management: The Importance of Knowledge-centred Culture', *Decision Sciences,* vol. 34 (2), 2003, pp. 351–84.

57. Jashapara, A. *Knowledge Management: An Integrated Approach,* second edition. Harlow: Financial Times Prentice Hall (2011).

58. Polanyi, M. *The Tacit Dimension.* London: Routledge & Kegan Paul (1967).

59. Ryle, G. *The Concept of Mind.* London: Hutchinson (1949).

60. Drucker, P. F. *The New Realities.* Revised Edition. Oxford: Routledge (2007).

61. Nonaka, I. and Takeuchi, H. *The Knowledge Creating Company: How Japanese Companies Create the Dynamics of Innovation.* Oxford: Oxford University Press (1995).

62. Davenport, T. H. and Pruzak, L. *Working Knowledge: How Organizations Manage What They Know,* second edition, Boston: Harvard Business School Press (2000).

63. Gourlay, S. 'Tacit knowledge, tacit knowing, or behaving?' *Proceedings of the 3rd European Organizational Knowledge, Learning and Capabilities Conference,* 5–6 April 2002, Athens, Greece, pp. 1–24.

64. Nonaka, I. and Peltokorpi, V. 'Objectivity and Subjectivity in Knowledge Management: a review of 20 top articles', *Knowledge and Process Management,* vol. 13 (2), 2006, pp. 73–82.

65. Blackler, F. 'Knowledge, Knowledge Work and Organisation: An Overview and Interpretation', *Organization Studies,* vol. 16 (6), 1995, pp. 1021–46.

66. Hislop, D. *Knowledge Management in Organisations: A Critical Introduction,* third edition, Oxford: Oxford University Press (2013).

67. Sveiby, K. E. *The New Organizational Wealth: Managing and Measuring Knowledge-Based Assets.* San Francisco: Berrett-Koehler Publishers, Inc. (1997).

68. Mason, D. and Pauleen, D. 'Perceptions of Knowledge Management: A Qualitative Analysis', *Journal of Knowledge Management,* vol. 7 (4), 2003, pp. 38–48.

69. Hlupic, V., Pouloudi, A. and Rzevski, G. 'Towards an Integrated Approach to Knowledge Management: "Hard", "Soft" and "Abstract" Issues', *Knowledge and Process Management,* vol. 9 (2), 2002, pp. 90–102.

70. Schulz, M. and Jobe, L. A. 'Codification and Tacitness as Knowledge Management Strategies: An Empirical Exploration', *Journal of High Technology Management Research,* 12, 2001, pp. 139–65.

71. Cheng, E. C. K. and Lee, J. C. K. 'Developing Strategies for Communities of Practice', *International Journal of Educational Management,* vol. 28 (6), 2014, pp. 751–64.

72. Dixon, N. M. *Common Knowledge: How Companies Thrive By Sharing What They Know.* Boston: Harvard Business Press (2000).

73. Bordum, A. 'From Tacit Knowing to Tacit Knowledge – Emancipation or Ideology?', *The Critical Quarterly,* vol. 44, issue 3, 2002, pp 50–4.

74. Cook, S. and Brown, J. S. 'Bridging Epistemologies: The Generative Dance between the Organizational Knowledge and Organizational Knowing', *Organization Science,* vol. 10 (4), 1999, pp. 381–400.

Chapter 6
Perception and communication

An understanding of perception and interpersonal communication is at the root of organisational behaviour, and effective personal and work relationships.

Learning outcomes

After completing your study of this chapter you should have enhanced your ability to:

- explain the nature and importance of the perceptual process;
- detail internal and external factors that provide meaning to the individual;
- assess the importance of perceptual illusions, and distortions and errors;
- identify difficulties in judgements about and perceiving other people;
- outline the nature and significance of attribution theory;
- explain the importance of language and communications in perception;
- evaluate non-verbal communication, body language and impression management.

Outline chapter contents

Overview topic map: Chapter 6 – Perception and communication

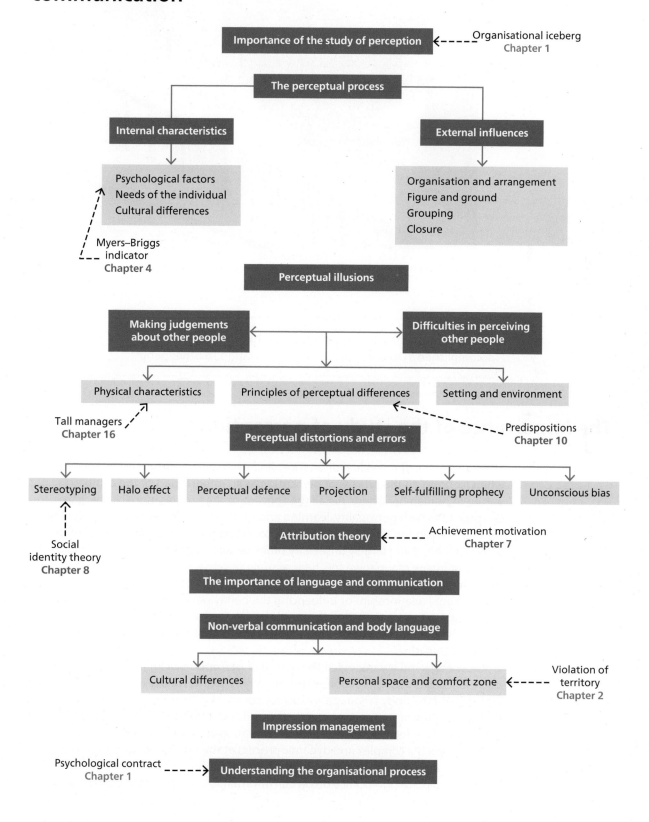

Cruise ship nearing Somalia. Perception: fear or security?

Before commencing to read this chapter think seriously about how accomplished YOU are in perceiving and relating to other people.

The importance of the study of perception

The significance of individual differences and diversity is particularly apparent when focusing on the process of perception as an integral part of the complex nature of human behaviour. Recall the concept of the organisational iceberg in **Chapter 1.** As with personality, learning and motivation (discussed in the following chapter) perception is part of the hidden, covert behavioural aspects taking place in someone's head and largely unseen by other people. We all have our own unique picture or image of what we see, hear, assume or sense. Without an understanding of our own perceptions and those of others we will not be effective with interpersonal relationships or influencing the behaviour of other people.

Perception can be viewed as the way in which we see the 'reality' of the world around us: our own way of looking at and relating to our environment and the people within it.

Knowledge and awareness of the nature of perception can help develop insights about ourselves and interactions with others. The words we use and speak, the way we look and the body language we display communicate our view of the world. Recognising the importance of perception and communications in guiding behaviour is essential for effective personal and work relationships with others.

Perception is a complex and dynamic process at the root of our understanding, behaviour and actions. We do not passively receive information; we analyse and judge it, and place significance on certain information and disregard others. We may also be influenced by our expectations so that we perceive what we expect to 'see' or 'hear'. Any situation can be analysed in terms of its perceptual connotations. A situation may be the same but the interpretation of that situation by two individuals may be vastly different. Consider, for instance, the following situation.

A member of senior management has sent an email to departmental managers directing them to provide statistics of overtime worked within their section during the past six months and projections for the next six months. Mixed reactions could result:

- One manager may see it as a reasonable and welcome request to provide information in the hopeful expectation that this will help lead to improved staffing levels.
- Another manager may extremely upset and suspect the information will be used by senior management to order cutbacks in future overtime in order to reduce staffing costs.
- A third manager may see it as an unreasonable demand, intended only to enable management to exercise closer supervision and control over the activities of the section.
- A fourth manager may have no objection to providing the information but is suspicious that it may lead to possible intrusion into the running of the section.
- Yet another manager may see it as a positive action by management to investigate ways of improving efficiency throughout the organisation.

Each of the departmental managers has their own different perception of the email which could be influenced, for example, by their working relationship with senior management or previous experiences. Their perceived reality and understanding of the situation provokes individual reactions. In addition, there are likely to be mixed reactions to the use of email as the means of communication in this instance.

How YOU would be likely to perceive such a directive and how would you react to senior management's use of email?

The perceptual process

It is not possible to have an understanding of perception without taking into account its sensory basis. Perception does not follow a neat step-by-step programme and *Misselhorn* for example suggests normally we do not manage our perceptions very well. Our attention, recognition, interpretations, responses and further responses to feedback happen very quickly. A number of perceptions happen simultaneously and help us form general interpretations and impressions of reality. It is not a conscious process but a spontaneous one we have difficulty in controlling. As a consequence, we perceive and respond with little conscious challenge to question what we think we have perceived.[1]

A model of general perception processes is given in **Figure 6.1**.

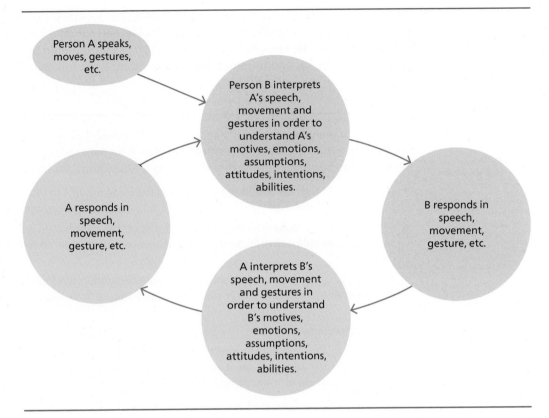

Figure 6.1 Cycle of perception and behaviour
Source: From Guirdham, M. *Interactive Behaviour at Work,* third edition, Financial Times Prentice Hall (2002), p. 162. Reproduced with permission from Pearson Education Ltd.

Selectivity in attention and perception

Our sensory systems have limits and we are not able to attend to everything in our environment. The physical limits therefore demand we are selective in our attention and perception. Early pioneer work by psychologists has resulted in an understanding of universal laws that underlie the perceptual process. It seems that we cannot help but search for meaning and understanding in our environment. The way we categorise and organise this sensory information is based on a range of factors including the present situation, our emotional state and any experiences of the same or a similar event.

Some information may be considered highly important and result in immediate response. In other instances, the information may be simply 'parked' or assimilated in other ideas and thoughts. Some of our 'parked' material may be forgotten or, indeed, changed and reconstructed over time.[2] We should be aware of the assumptions made throughout the perceptual process, below our conscious threshold. We have learned to take for granted certain constants in our environment do not need to spend time and energy seeing things afresh and anew. We make a number of inferences throughout the entire perceptual process. Although these inferences may save time and speed up the process, they may also lead to distortions and inaccuracies, **discussed later in this chapter.**

Perception as information processing

It is common to see stages of perception described as an information-processing system – **see Figure 6.2**: (top-down) information (stimuli) (Box A) is selected at one end of the process (Box B), then interpreted (Box C) and translated (Box D), resulting in action or thought patterns (Box E). However, it is important to note that such a model simplifies the process and although easy to understand, does not do justice to the complexity and dynamics of the process. In certain circumstances, we may select information out of the environment because of the way we categorise the world. The dotted line illustrates this 'bottom-up' process.

For instance, if a manager has been advised by colleagues that a particular trainee has managerial potential, the manager may be specifically looking for confirmation those views are correct. This process has been known as 'top-down' because the cognitive processes are influencing the perceptual readiness of the individual to select certain information. This emphasises the active nature of the perceptual process. We do not passively digest the information from our senses, but actively attend to and indeed, at times, seek out certain information.

Meaning to the individual

The process of perception explains the manner in which information (stimuli) from the environment around us is selected and organised to provide meaning for the individual. Perception is the mental function of giving significance to stimuli such as shapes, colours, movement, taste, sounds, touch, smells, pain, pressures and feelings. Perception gives rise to individual behavioural responses to particular situations.

Despite the fact that a group of people may 'physically see' the same thing, each have their own version of what is seen – their perceived view of reality. Consider, for example, the image (published by W. E. Hill in *Puck,* 6 November 1915) shown in **Figure 6.3.** What do you see? A young, attractive, well-dressed woman or an older,

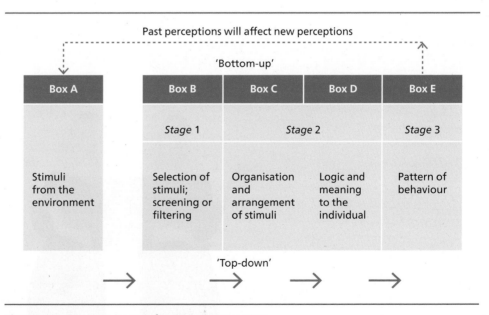

Figure 6.2 Perceptions as information processing

Figure 6.3

poor woman? Or can you now see both? *And who can say with certainty that there is just the one, 'correct' answer?*

Why do we attend to certain stimuli and not to others? There are two important factors to consider in this discussion. The process of perceptual selection is based on both **internal** characteristics relating to the state of the individual; and the environment and influences **external** to the individual.

Same situation, different selectivity

What did YOU see *first* in Figure 6.3 and how clear was it to identify? Do you think the figure you identified says anything about your personality? What do your colleagues think?

Internal characteristics

As individuals we may differ in terms of our sensory limits or thresholds and also the ability to discriminate between stimuli. For instance, it may not be possible for the untrained to distinguish between different types of wine but this would be an everyday event for the trained sommelier. We may also differ in terms of the amount of sensory information needed to reach our own comfortable equilibrium. Some individuals would find loud music at a party or gig uncomfortable and unpleasant, whereas for others the intensity of the music is part of the total enjoyment. Likewise, if we are deprived of sensory information for too long this can lead to feelings of discomfort and fatigue.

Psychological factors

Psychological factors will also affect what is perceived. These internal factors, such as personality, learning and motives, will give rise to an inclination to perceive certain stimuli with a readiness to respond in certain ways. This has been called an individual's perceptual set *(see* **Figure 6.4).** Differences in the ways individuals acquire information have been used as one of four scales in the Myers–Briggs Type Indicator **(discussed in Chapter 4).** They distinguish individuals who 'tend to accept and work with what is given in the here-and-now, and thus become realistic and practical' (sensing types) from others who go beyond the information from the senses and look at the possible patterns, meanings and relationships. These 'intuitive types' 'grow expert at seeing new possibilities and new ways of doing things'. *Myers and Briggs* stress the value of both types and emphasise the importance of complementary skills and variety in any successful enterprise or relationship.[3]

Needs of the individual

The most desirable and urgent needs will almost certainly affect an individual perceptual process. A manager deeply engrossed in preparing an urgent report

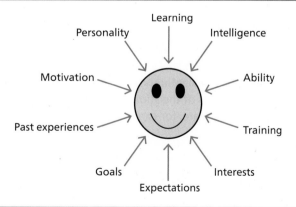

Figure 6.4 Factors affecting an individual's perceptual set

may screen out ringing telephones, the sound of computers, people talking and furniture being moved in the next office, but will respond readily to the smell of coffee brewing. Members of a church choir might well form a perception of the minister quite different from that of a parishioner seeking comfort after the recent death of a close relative. The 'Pollyanna Principle' claims that pleasant stimuli will be processed more quickly and remembered more precisely than unpleasant stimuli. However, it must be noted that intense internal drives may lead to perceptual distortions of situations (or people) and unwillingness to absorb certain painful information.

Cultural differences

Ways in which people interact are also subject to cultural differences and such differences may be misconstrued. Embarrassment and discomfort can occur when emotional lines are broken. This was demonstrated in a classic American study that researched the experience of Japanese students visiting the USA for the first time. The Japanese students faced considerable challenges in adapting to the new culture of social interaction including casual visits and phone calls at midnight to the host room-mate; opposite-sex partners holding hands or kissing in public places; and males cooking and shopping in the household or by themselves.[4]

In certain cultures, such as the USA, it is 'normal' to explain all details clearly, explicitly and directly. In other cultures the 'spelling out' of all the details is unnecessary and embarrassing. *McCrum* refers to a joke circulated on the Web by disaffected UN staff. A worldwide survey was conducted by the UN. The only question asked was: 'Would you please give your honest opinion about solutions to the food shortage in the rest of the world?'

> **The survey was a failure. In Africa they didn't know what 'food' meant; in India they didn't know what 'honest' meant; in Europe they didn't know what 'shortage' meant; in China they didn't know what 'opinion' meant; in the Middle East they didn't know what 'solution' meant; in South America they didn't know what 'please' meant; and in the USA they didn't know what 'the rest of the world' meant.[5]**

Ways in which words are used and the assumptions made about shared understanding are dependent upon an individual's culture and upbringing. Cultural differences often lead to stereotypical views. **See also cultural differences in non-verbal communication and body language later in this chapter.**

External influences

Knowledge, familiarity or expectations about a given situation or previous experiences will influence perception. External factors refer to the nature and characteristics of the stimuli. There is usually a tendency to give more attention to stimuli which are, for example:

- Large
- Moving
- Intense
- Loud

- Bright
- Novel
- Repeated
- In strong contrast to their background.

How many of the eight stimuli listed above do these sheep display?

Any number of these factors may be present at a given time or in a given situation. The use of these stimuli is a key feature in the design of advertising. (Think of your own examples.) It is the **total pattern** of the stimuli together with the **context** in which they occur that influence perception. For example, it is usually a novel or unfamiliar stimulus that is more noticeable, but a person is more likely to perceive the familiar face of a friend among a group of people all dressed in the same-style uniform (*see* **Figure 6.5**).[6]

We are familiar with the expression 'what on earth is that doing here?' The sight of a fork-lift truck on the factory floor in a manufacturing organisation is likely to be perceived quite differently from one in the corridor of a university. A jet ski (left temporarily by a neighbour moving house) in the garage of a person known to be scared of water is likely to elicit such a remark: yet the sight of numerous jet skis on the beach is likely to pass without comment. The word 'terminal' is likely to be perceived differently in the context of: (i) a hospital, (ii) an airport, or (iii) a computer firm. Consumer psychologists and marketing experts apply these perceptual principles with extraordinary success for some of their products. (Again, think of your own examples.)

Organisation and arrangement of stimuli

The Gestalt School of Psychology led by Max Wertheimer claimed the process of perception is innately organised and patterned. It described the process as one that has built-in field effects. In other words, the brain can act like a dynamic, physical field in which interaction among elements is an intrinsic part. The Gestalt School produced a series of principles, which are still readily applicable today. Some of the most significant include the following:

- figure and ground;
- grouping;
- closure.

Figure 6.5 Is everybody happy?
Source: Block, J. R. and Yuker, H. E. *Can You Believe Your Eyes?,* Robson Books (2002), p. 163. Reproduced with permission.

Figure 6.6

Figure and ground

The figure and ground principle states figures are seen against a background. The figure does not have to be an object; it could be merely a geometrical pattern. Figure and ground relationships are often reversible, as in the popular example shown in **Figure 6.6.** What do you see first? A white chalice (or small stand shape) in the centre of the frame or the dark profiles of twins facing each other on the edge of the frame? Now look again. Can you see the other shape?

The figure and ground principle has applications in work situations. It is important employees know and able to attend to the significant aspects (the figure) and treat other elements of the job as context (background). Early training sessions aim to identify and focus on the significant aspects of a task. Stress could occur for those employees who are uncertain about their priorities and are unable to distinguish between the significant and less significant tasks. They feel overwhelmed by the 'whole' picture.

Grouping

The grouping principle refers to the tendency to organise shapes and patterns instantly into meaningful groupings or patterns on the basis of their proximity or similarity. Parts close in time or space tend to be perceived together. For example, in **Figure 6.7a,** the workers are more likely to be perceived as nine independent people, but in **Figure 6.7b,** because of the proximity principle, the workers may be perceived as three distinct groups of people. Consider the importance of the layout of the room and tables for a large wedding reception and the perception of people in terms of both the table where they are sat, and with whom they are grouped!

Taxi firms often use the idea of grouping to display their telephone number. In the example below, which of the following numbers – (a), (b) or (c) – is most likely to be remembered easily?

(a) 0231667474   (b) 02316 67474   (c) 023 166 7474

Similar parts tend to be seen together as forming a familiar group. In the following example there is a tendency to see alternate lines of characters – crosses and noughts (or circles). This is because the horizontal similarity is usually greater than the vertical similarity. However, if the page is turned sideways the figure may be perceived as alternate noughts and crosses in each line.

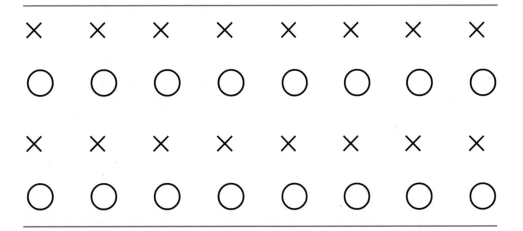

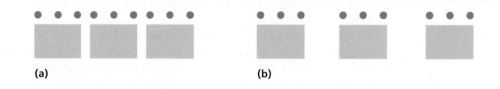

Figure 6.7

It is interesting to note when asked to describe this pattern many people refer to alternate lines of noughts and crosses – rather than crosses and noughts. There is also an example here of the impact of cultural differences, mentioned earlier. The author undertook a teaching exchange in the USA and gave this exercise to a class of students. Almost without exception the students described the horizontal pattern correctly as alternate rows of crosses and noughts (or zeros). The explanation appears to be that Americans do not know the game as 'noughts and crosses' but refer to it as 'tic-tac-toe'.

Closure

There is also a tendency to complete an incomplete figure – to fill in the gaps (mentally) and to perceive the figure as a whole. This creates an overall and meaningful image for the individual rather than an unconnected series of lines or blobs. In the example in **Figure 6.8**[7] most people are likely to see the blobs as either the letter B or the number 13, possibly depending on whether at the time they had been more concerned with written material or dealing in numbers.

However, for some people, the figure may be described in terms of just a series of eleven discrete blobs or perceived as some other (to them) meaningful pattern/object.

Figure 6.8
Source: King, R. A. *Introduction to Psychology,* 6th edition, McGraw-Hill (1966), Figure 10.22, p. 339. Reproduced with permission from the author, Professor Richard King.

How good are YOU at the organisation and arrangement of stimuli and in particular distinguishing the significant aspects (the figure) from the ground?

Perceptual illusions

Here are some examples to help you judge your perceptive skills. In **Figure 6.9** try reading aloud the four words. It is possible that you find yourself 'caught' in a perceptual set that means that you tend to pronounce 'machinery' as 'MacHinery' as if it too were a Scottish surname.

In **Figure 6.10,** which of the centre blue circles is the larger – A or B?

Although you may have guessed that the two centre circles are in fact the same size, the circle on the right (B) may well **appear** larger because it is framed by smaller circles. The centre circle on the left (A) may well **appear** smaller because it is framed by larger circles.

In **Figure 6.11** try saying the *colour* of the word, *not* the word itself.

The physiological nature of perception is of relevance here in the discussion of illusions. Why does the circle on the right in Figure 6.10 look bigger? Why is it difficult to say the colour, not the word? These examples demonstrate the way our brain can be fooled. Indeed, we make assumptions about our world that go beyond the pure sensations our brain receives.

M-A-C-D-O-N-A-L-D
M-A-C-P-H-E-R-S-O-N
M-A-C-D-O-U-G-A-L-L
M-A-C-H-I-N-E-R-Y

Figure 6.9

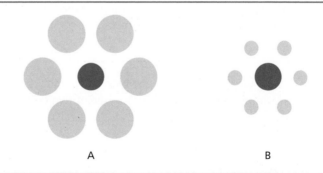

| A | B |

Figure 6.10

BLUE	GREY	YELLOW	MAUVE
BLACK	ORANGE	GREEN	RED
WHITE	PURPLE	BLUE	BROWN

Figure 6.11

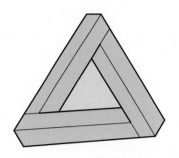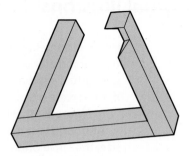

Figure 6.12
Source: Gregory, R. L. *Odd Perceptions,* Methuen (1986), p. 71. Reprinted by permission of the publishers, Routledge, a division of Taylor & Francis Ltd.

Beyond reality

Perception goes beyond the sensory information and converts patterns to a three-dimensional reality that we understand. This conversion process, as we can see, is easily tricked. We may not be aware of the inferences we are making as they are part of our conditioning and learning. The Stroop experiment in **Figure 6.11** illustrates this perfectly.[8]

An illustration of the way in which we react automatically to stimuli is the illusion of the impossible triangle **(see Figure 6.12).** Even when we know the triangle is impossible we cannot stop ourselves from completing the triangle and attempting to make it meaningful. We go beyond what is given and make assumptions about the world, which in certain instances are wildly incorrect. Psychologists and designers may make positive use of these assumptions to project positive images of a product or the environment. Colours may be used to induce certain atmospheres in buildings; designs of wallpaper or texture of curtains may be used to create feelings of spaciousness or cosiness. Packaging of products may tempt us to see something as bigger or perhaps more precious.

How well did YOU manage with the perceptual illusions? To what extent did the examples help you judge your perceptive skills? What about your colleagues?

Making judgements about other people

The way we organise and make judgements about what we have perceived is to a large extent based on experiences and learning. We may not always be aware of our pre-set assumptions but they will influence the way we interpret the behaviour of others. It is important to be aware of the inferences and assumptions we make which go beyond the information given. A manager might know more about person A, a member of staff who was or has become a good friend, is seen in a variety of social situations and with whom there is a close relationship; than about person B, a member of staff in the same section as A and undertaking similar duties, but with whom there is only a formal work relationship and limited social acquaintance.

These differences in relationship, information and interaction might well influence the manager's perception if asked, for example, to evaluate the comparative work performance of A and B.

Judgement of other people can also be influenced by perceptions of such stimuli as:

- role or status;
- occupation;
- ethnicity, gender and age;
- physical factors and appearance; and
- non-verbal communication and body language **(discussed later in this chapter).**

Physical characteristics and appearance

There are frequent popular articles referring to the suggestion that tall people both men and women, are more likely to be successful both socially and professionally.

Perceived height based on academic status

An unknown English visitor from Cambridge was introduced to a class of American students divided into five equal groups. The visitor was described to each group differently as a student, an instructor, a lecturer, a senior lecturer, a professor. After the visitor left each group was asked to estimate the height of the visitor. The mean estimated height varied higher with each group according to the ascribed academic status.

Source: Wilson, P. R. 'Perceptual distortion of height as a function of ascribed academic status', *Journal of Social Psychology*, no. 74, 1968, pp. 97–102.

Arianne Cohen comments on taller people who look down on shorter colleagues are perceived to have confidence and respect. In an interesting account celebrating the lives of tall people Cohen maintains that height is a pivotal piece of identity and the most defining force in our lives. Height determined her choice of sports (swimming), boyfriends (tall), social circle (tall), my college (tall), and my personality (big enough to fill the tall).[9] Another example is the appointment (June 2009) of the new speaker of the House of Commons, John Bercow, who is 5ft 6in in height. This appointment prompted newspaper articles about 'heightism' and perceptions about the 'shorter man'.[10]

In a discussion of physical attributes and good leadership, *Dib* suggests that 'we seem to associate the effectiveness of leaders with certain personality traits, which are in turn assumed as a consequence of their looks.' Examples are gender, hair colour, face, height, ethnicity and weight.

> **Of course there is no scientific evidence of correlation between height and intelligence, or height and the ability to lead people. Yet tall people are massively overrepresented in leadership roles. Similarly, other illogical preferences on hair colour, weight and facial features have nestled into our subconscious through societal, cultural and historical channels, and continue to affect the decisions we make and the leaders we turn to.**

Dib reports that there are convincing arguments for why we need to confront and overhaul ingrained preconceptions and stereotypes.[11]

Note also that *Mintzberg* includes 'tall' in a composite list of basic managerial qualities.[12] **(See Figure 10.8 in Chapter 10.)**

Difficulties in perceiving other people

There are a number of well-documented difficulties that arise when perceiving other people. Many of these problems occur because of our limitations in selecting and attending information. This selectivity may occur because:

- we already know what we are looking for and are therefore 'set' to receive only the information which confirms our initial thoughts;
- previous training and experience have led us to shortcut and see only a certain range of behaviours;
- we may group features together and make assumptions about their similarities.

The Gestalt principles apply equally well to the perception of people as to the perception of objects. Thus we can see, for example, that if people live in the same geographical area, assumptions may be made about not only their wealth and type of accommodation but also their attitudes, their political views and even their type of personality.

Principles of perceptual differences

The way we see others, the habits formed, the associations made and assumptions we make lead us to make errors and distortions when perceiving others. The principles of perceptual differences explained earlier apply to the way we perceive others. Some examples might be as follows:

- **Grouping** – the way in which a manager may think of a number of staff – for example, either working in close proximity; or with some common feature such as all IT staff, all graduate trainees or all older workers; as a homogeneous group rather than a collection of individuals, each with their own separate identity and characteristics.
- **Figure and ground** – a manager may notice a new recruit and set them apart from the group because of particular characteristics such as age, appearance or physical features.
- **Closure** – the degree to which unanimity is perceived and decisions made or action taken in the belief that there is full agreement with staff when, in fact, a number of staff may be opposed to the decision or action.

The way in which managers approach the performance of their jobs and the behaviour they display towards subordinate staff are likely to be conditioned by predispositions about people, human nature and work. An example of this is the style of management adopted on the basis of McGregor's Theory X and Theory Y suppositions, **discussed in Chapter 10.** In making judgements about other people it is important to try to perceive their underlying intent and motivation, not *just* the resultant behaviour or actions.

Perception of people's performance can be affected by the organisation of stimuli. In employment interviews, for example, interviewers are susceptible to contrast

What do YOU see as the greatest difficulty in perceiving other people? What errors have you made and what was the cause and result of those errors?

effects and the perception of a candidate may be influenced by the rating given to immediately preceding candidates. Average candidates may be rated highly if they follow people with low qualifications, but rated lower when following people with higher qualifications.[13]

Dynamics of interpersonal perception

Unlike perception of an object that just exists, when you perceive another individual they will react to you and be affected by your behaviour – the dynamics are all-important. The interaction of individuals provides an additional layer of interpretation and complexity. The cue we may attend to, the expectation we may have, the assumptions we may make, the response pattern that occurs, leave more scope for errors and distortions. We not only perceive the stimulus (that is, the other person), we also process their reactions to us at the same time they are processing our reactions to them. Thus interpersonal perception differs from the perception of objects because it is a continually dynamic and changing process. The perceiver is a part of this process who will influence and be influenced by the other people in the situation (*see* **Figure 6.13**).[14]

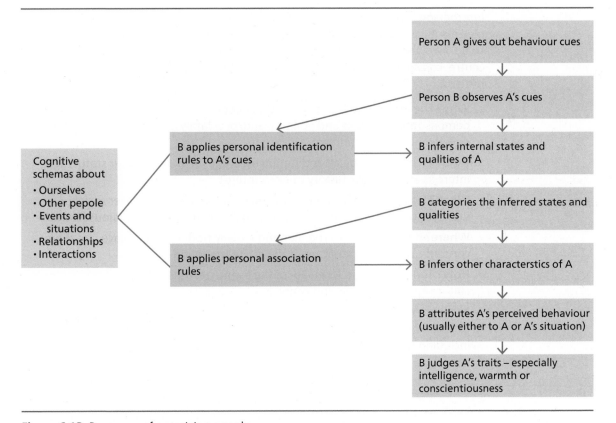

Figure 6.13 Processes of perceiving people
Source: From Guirdham, M. *Interactive Behaviour at Work,* third edition, Financial Times Prentice Hall (2002), p. 169. Reprinted and electronically reproduced by permission of Pearson Education, Inc.

Interpersonal perception is a two-way street

Setting and environment

Interpersonal perception is also affected by the setting and environment which may play a critical part in establishing rapport. For example, if you have been, or were to be, involved in a formal meeting such as attending an in-house development centre, consider the following situations that may all influence the perceptual process.

- **Why?** The extent to which you see the meeting as a chance to be visible and demonstrate your skills and abilities, and/or a catalyst for promotion or new development opportunities.
- **Who?** Who else will be attending the meeting, for example their status, age, interests and previous history or encounters?
- **When?** Does the date or time of the meeting cause concern over social or domestic commitments or is the meeting in the middle of a religious festival?
- **Where?** If the location of the meeting is away from the workplace, are there concerns over travel or nature of the accommodation?
- **How?** The staging and formality of the event, demonstration of organisational culture including power and control.
- **Past experience?** If you have attended previous development events your expectations and perception may be further influenced by that experience including the nature of feedback.

What other examples can YOU relate when the setting and environment has made a significant influence on establishing rapport with another person(s)?

Perceptual distortions and errors

We have seen our perception results in different people seeing different things and attaching different meanings to the same stimuli. Every person sees things in their own way and as perceptions become a person's reality this can lead to misunderstandings. The accuracy of interpersonal perception and the judgements made about other people are influenced by the:

- nature of the relationship between the perceiver and the other person;
- amount of information available to the perceiver and the order in which information is received;
- nature and extent of interaction between the two people.

Five main features that can create particular difficulties and give rise to perceptual problems, bias or distortions in our dealings with other people are:

- stereotyping;
- the halo effect;
- perceptual defence;
- projection;
- self-fulfilling prophecy.

To which could be added a sixth

- unconscious bias

See **Figure 6.14.**

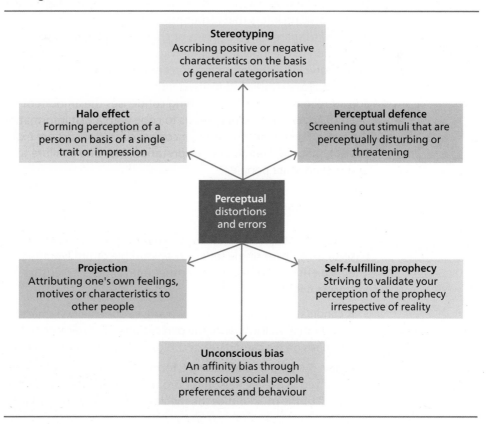

Figure 6.14 Causes of perceptual distortions and errors

Stereotyping

This is the tendency to ascribe positive or negative characteristics to a person on the basis of a general categorisation and perceived similarities. The perception may be based more on certain expected characteristics than on recognition of that person as an individual. It is a form of typecasting. **Stereotyping** is a means of simplifying the process of perception, making sense of the world and judgements of other people instead of dealing with a range of complex and alternative stimuli. When an individual is judged on the basis of the group to which it is perceived that person belongs and with the same characteristics, we are stereotyping. Pre-judgements are made without really knowing whether such judgements are accurate; they may be wildly wrong.

Common stereotyping may be based on, for example:

- **Nationality** – Germans are orderly and industrious; Australians like cricket.
- **Occupation** – accountants are boring; librarians are serious and undemonstrative.
- **Age** – young people are unreliable, old people do not want to learn new ideas.
- **Physical** – people with red hair have a fiery temperament; people with visible tattoos are exhibitionists.
- **Education** – graduates are intelligent; graduates from Oxford or Cambridge are especially bright.
- **Social** – unemployed people are lazy, immigrants do not want to learn English.
- **Politics** – Labour voters favour strong trade unions, Conservative voters support private enterprise.

(See also the discussion of Social Identity Theory in Chapter 8.)

Stereotyping infers that all people within a particular perceived category are assumed to share the same traits or characteristics and can block out accurate perception of the individual or individual situation. A significant social implication of stereotyping is therefore the perception held about particular groups of people based on, for example, ethnicity, gender, disability, appearance, sexual orientation, age, or religious belief. Stereotyping condenses the amount of information we need to know and thus enables us to cope with a vast information flow. However, the consequences of attributing incorrect characteristics are extremely negative. Stereotyping can lead to misinterpretation, bias and a failure to try and really understand other people.[15]

The halo effect

The **halo effect** is the process by which perception of a person is formulated on the basis of a single (or single series of) favourable or unfavourable trait or impression. The halo effect tends to shut out other relevant characteristics of that person. Some examples might be as follows:

- A candidate for employment, who arrives punctually, is smart in appearance and friendly may well influence the perception of the selectors, who then place less emphasis on the candidate's technical ability, qualifications or experience for the job.
- A new member of staff who performs well in a first major assignment may be perceived as a likely person for promotion, even though that assignment is not typical of the usual duties the member of staff is expected to undertake.

- A single trait, such as good attendance and timekeeping, may become the main emphasis for judgement of overall competence and performance rather than other considerations such as the quantity, quality and accuracy of work.

A particular danger with the halo effect is that where quick judgements are made on the basis of readily available stimuli, the perceiver may become 'perceptually blind' to subsequent stimuli at variance with the original perception and (often subconsciously) notice only those characteristics that support the original judgement. **(See also the self-fulfilling prophecy, discussed below.)**

The rusty halo effect

The process may also work in reverse: the **rusty halo effect**. This is where general judgements about a person are formulated from the perception of a negative characteristic. For example, a candidate is seen arriving late for an interview. There may be a very good reason for this and it may be completely out of character. But on the basis of that one particular event the person may be perceived as a poor timekeeper and unreliable. Another example may be a new member of staff who performs poorly in a first major assignment. This may have been due to an unusual set of circumstances and not typical behaviour, but the person may still be perceived as a bad appointment.

Perceptual defence

People may tend to select information supportive of their point of view and choose not to acknowledge contrary information. **Perceptual defence** is the tendency to avoid or screen out certain stimuli that conflict with strongly held values and are perceptually disturbing or threatening. For example, a manager who has refused steadfastly to support promotion for a member of staff against the advice of other colleagues may select only unfavourable information which supports that decision and ignore favourable information which questions that decision.

Projection

Attributing, or projecting, one's own feelings, motives or characteristics to other people is a further distortion which can occur in the perception of other people. Judgements of other people may be more favourable when they have characteristics largely in common with, and easily recognised by, the perceiver. **Projection** may also result in people exaggerating undesirable traits in others that they fail to recognise in themselves.

Perception is distorted by feelings and emotions. Projection may be used as a means of attempting to externalise difficult or uncomfortable feelings. For example, a manager concerned about possible redundancy may perceive other managers to be even more concerned. People have a tendency to perceive others less favourably by projecting certain of their own feelings or characteristics onto them. As another example, supervisors may complain that their manager did not work hard enough to secure additional resources for the department when in fact the supervisors failed to provide the manager with all the relevant information and statistics. However, projection may also be used to externalise positive feelings onto other members of staff by attempting to create an overstated and unrealistic level of expectations and performance.

Self-fulfilling prophecy

A common feature of social interaction is the concept of the **self-fulfilling prophecy** (sometimes known as the Pygmalion effect), a term that is usually attributed to *Merton.*[16] The essence of the prophecy is that simply because it has been made, this will cause it to happen. People strive to validate their perceptions irrespective of the actual reality. People's beliefs or expectations influence their actions and behaviour in such a way as to make the beliefs or expectations more likely to come true. If staff believe a rumour (prophecy) that there will be no promotions or bonuses for the foreseeable future, they are likely to behave in such a way that their performance would not justify promotion or bonuses (even if the rumour was not true).

The expectation of managers has a powerful influence on the behaviour and performance of staff. If a manager expects only minimal performance from staff, they are not likely to perform to the best of their abilities. Therefore, managers need to establish an organisational framework and supportive culture that reinforces positive performance expectations at all levels of the organisation. Staff should also be encouraged to have high self-expectations of performance through working towards common goals.

Unconscious bias

Dan Robertson, diversity and inclusion director of Employers Network for Equality and Inclusion, in conversation with *Davies,* draws attention to our 'preferred people preferences' that affect our unconscious social preferences. This type of bias may be demonstrated in 'micro-behaviours'.

> **For example, we may exhibit an affinity bias, where we respond positively to people who are similar to us or with whom we have something in common. We might give that person more airtime in a meeting, or agree more often with what they say. In contrast, we might cut short those with whom we do not have an affinity or disregard their viewpoints.**

These are subtle, unconscious behaviours and different from overt and discriminatory behaviour. Robertson maintains that such **unconscious biases** are hard wired into us. We cannot eliminate them altogether so it is important to be aware of them and to change the way we work.[17]

To what extent do YOU identify with perceptual distortions or errors? Think *honestly* of occasions when your reality has led to errors and/or misunderstandings.

Attribution theory

Part of the process of perceiving other people is to attribute characteristics to them. We judge their behaviour and intentions on past knowledge and in comparison with other people we know. It is our way of making sense of their behaviour. This is known as **attribution theory** which is related to interpersonal perception in organisations. Attribution is the process by which people interpret the perceived causes of behaviour. The initiator of attribution theory is generally recognised as *Heider,* who suggests behaviour is determined by a combination of **perceived** internal forces and external forces.[18]

Internal forces relate to personal attributes such as ability, skill, and amount of effort or fatigue. **External forces** relate to environmental factors such as organisational rules and policies, manner of superiors, or the weather. Behaviour at work may be explained by the locus of control, that is whether the individual perceives outcomes as controlled by themselves or by external factors. Judgements made about other people will also be influenced strongly by whether the cause is seen as internal or external.

Basic criteria in making attributions

In making attributions and determining whether an internal or external attribution is chosen, *Kelley* suggests three basic criteria: distinctiveness, consensus and consistency.

- **Distinctiveness.** How distinctive or different was the behaviour or action in this particular task or situation compared with behaviour or action in other tasks or situations?
- **Consensus.** Is the behaviour or action different from, or in keeping with, that displayed by most other people in the same situation?
- **Consistency.** Is the behaviour or action associated with an enduring personality or motivational characteristic over time, or an unusual one-off situation caused by external factors?

Kelley hypothesised that people attribute behaviour to internal forces or personal factors when they perceive **low distinctiveness, low consensus** and **high consistency.** Behaviour is attributed to external forces or environmental factors when people perceived **high distinctiveness, high consensus** and **low consistency.**[19] An example of these criteria related to a student who fails a mid-sessional examination in a particular subject is given in **Table 6.1.**

Implications of attribution theory

Employees with an internal control orientation are more likely to believe they can influence their level of performance through their own abilities, skills or efforts.

Table 6.1 Example of criteria in making attributions

	Distinctiveness	Consensus	Consistency
Internal attribution	Student fails all mid-sessional examinations	Student is the only one to fail	Student also fails final examination
External attribution	Student gains high marks in other mid-sessional examinations	All students in the class get low marks	Student obtains a good mark in final examination

Source: Adapted from Mitchell, T. R. *People in Organisations,* second edition, McGraw-Hill (1982), p. 104.

Employees with an external control orientation are more likely to believe that their level of performance is determined by external factors beyond their influence. People with a high achievement motivation may perceive successful performance is caused by their own internal forces, ability and effort rather than by the nature of the task or by luck.

If members of staff fail to perform well on their tasks they may believe external factors are the cause and as a result reduce the level of future effort. However, if staff perform well but the manager perceives this as due to an easy task or to luck, the appropriate recognition and reward may not be given. If staff perceive that good performance was due to ability and/or effort, the lack of recognition and reward may well have a demotivating effect. **(Achievement motivation is discussed in Chapter 7.)**

What is YOUR view of Attribution Theory? To what extent do YOU have an internal control orientation and belief that you can influence your own level of performance?

The importance of language and communication

Language plays an important role in the way we perceive and communicate with the world. It not only labels and distinguishes the environment for us but also structures and guides our thinking patterns. Our language is part of the culture we experience and learn to take for granted. Culture differences are relevant because they emphasise the impact of social learning on the perception of people and their surroundings. Language not only reflects our experience but also shapes whether and what we experience. It influences our relationships with others and with the environment.

Consider a situation where a student is using a library in a UK university for the first time. The student is from South Asia where the word 'please' is incorporated in the verb and intonation; a separate word is not used. When the student requests help, the assistant may consider the student rude because they did not use the word 'please'. By causing offence the student has quite innocently affected the library assistant's perceptions. Much is also communicated in how words are said and in the silences between words. In the UK speech is suggestive and idiomatic speech is common: 'Make no bones about it' (means get straight to the point), 'Sent to Coventry' (means to be socially isolated). And action is implied rather than always stated: 'I hope you won't mind if I' (means 'I am going to') 'I'm afraid I really can't see my way to . . . ' (means 'no').

Conversational pitfalls

A well-known quotation, attributed to George Bernard Shaw, is:

England and America are two countries divided by a common language.

From frequent visits to America, the author can give numerous personal testimonies to this, including these actual words: 'I am just going to the trunk (boot of the car) to get my purse (handbag), fanny bag (bum bag) and money wallet (purse).'

McCrum gives some examples of conversational pitfalls.[20] (Many of which the author can attest to from personal experience.)

Australia	talking disparagingly about Aboriginal people
China	human rights; Tibet, Taiwan; sex; religion; bureaucracy
Far East	confusing Japanese, Chinese or Korean
Greece, S. Cyprus	asking for Turkish coffee
India	poverty; sex; dowry deaths
Ireland	referring to Great Britain as the 'mainland'; talking about 'the British Isles' to include Ireland; asking why they use euros rather than pounds sterling
Latin America	talking about 'Americans' to mean just North America
Mexico	nepotism
The Netherlands	calling the country 'Holland' (inaccurate and offensive to people not from the Holland provinces)
New Zealand	using the term 'mainland' for either North or South islands; mispronouncing Maori place-names
Northern Ireland	asking people whether they're Catholic or Protestant
Russia	corruption, contract killings, etc.
South Africa	banging on about apartheid (it ended some time ago)
Spain	criticism of bullfighting
US South	the Confederate flag

Source: McCrum, M. *Going Dutch in Beijing,* Profile Books (2007) pp. 44–5.

Non-verbal communication and body language

We have referred previously to the significance of non-verbal communication and body language. This includes inferences drawn from posture, gestures, touch, the use of hand signals, extent of eye contact, tone of voice or facial expressions and personal space (proxemics). As an example, in the restricted space of aircraft cabin crew make frequent use of facial expressions and silent hand signals to communicate with each other and with passengers.

According to *Mehrabian,* in our face-to-face communication with other people as much as 93 per cent of the messages about our feelings and attitudes come from non-verbal channels. The overall liking communicated by simultaneous facial, vocal and verbal messages can be expressed as

Only 7 per cent verbal from the words we use; but

38 per cent from our voice and how the words are said; and

55 per cent from facial expressions.

Significantly, if there is any conflict between facial and vocal parts of the communication, the facial expression typically dominates.[21]

Although actual percentages may vary, there appears to be general support for this contention. According to *Pivcevic*: 'It is commonly agreed that 80 per cent of communication is non-verbal; it is carried in your posture and gestures, and in the tone, pace and energy behind what you say.'[22] *McGuire* suggests that when verbal and non-verbal messages are in conflict, 'Accepted wisdom from the experts is that the non-verbal signals should be the ones to rely on, and that what is not said is frequently louder than what is said, revealing attitudes and feelings in a way words can't express.'[23]

In our perceptions and judgement of others it is important therefore to observe and take careful note of their non-verbal communication. Consider the simple action of a handshake and extent to which this can provide a meaningful insight into personality. Does a firm handshake by itself necessarily indicate friendship and confidence? Is a limp handshake a sign of shyness or lack of engagement with the other person? The reality is that body language is not a precise science. One gesture can be interpreted in several ways. It may give a possible indication of a particular meaning but by itself cannot be interrupted with any certainty. Crossing your arms is often taken as a sign of defensiveness but could equally mean that the person is cold or finds this a comfortable position.[24] Despite these limitations, it is essential that managers have an understanding of non-verbal communication and body language and are fully cognisant of the possible messages they are giving out.

Communication without speaking

The Donald Trump Handshake

There is frequent comment that a significant way of expressing a sense of control in business and politics is through a firm handshake. Following Donald Trump's election as US President there was a great deal of media attention given to his unusual handshake when meeting with other world leaders. As an example it was quoted that the meeting with French President Emmanuel Macron and Donald Trump saw the pair grip each other's hand so firmly their knuckles turned white. A handshake encounter with Japanese Prime Minister Shinzō Abe lasted an awkward 19 seconds. The significance of Donald Trump's 'weird' styles of handshake has caught the interest of many commentators and body language experts.

Cultural differences

There are many cultural variations in non-verbal communications, extent of physical contact and differences in the way body language is perceived and interpreted. A few examples:

- Italians and South Americans tend to show their feelings through intense body language, while the Japanese tend to hide their feelings and have largely eliminated overt body language from interpersonal communication.
- When talking to another person, the British tend to look away spasmodically, but Norwegians typically look people steadily in the eyes without altering their gaze.
- In many European countries people are greeted with three or four kisses on the cheek and pulling the head away may be taken as a sign of impoliteness.
- When the Dutch point a forefinger at their temples this may be a sign of congratulations for a good idea, rather than a less complimentary implication.
- With many Asian cultures not only is pointing with the finger very rude, sitting with your feet pointing at a person is also insulting.

Personal space and comfort zone

Different cultures have specific values related to 'proxemics', that is the use of personal space and 'comfort zone'. Arabs tend to stand very close when speaking to another person but most Americans when introduced to a new person will, after shaking hands, move backwards a couple of steps to place a comfortable space between themselves and the person they have just met. One reason why Americans tend to speak loudly is that their sense of personal space is twice that of the British.[25] **(See also discussion on violation of territory in Chapter 3.)**

What specific examples can YOU give of cultural difficulties in non-verbal communication and body language?

A concept map of interacting and networking with other people is set out in Figure 6.15.

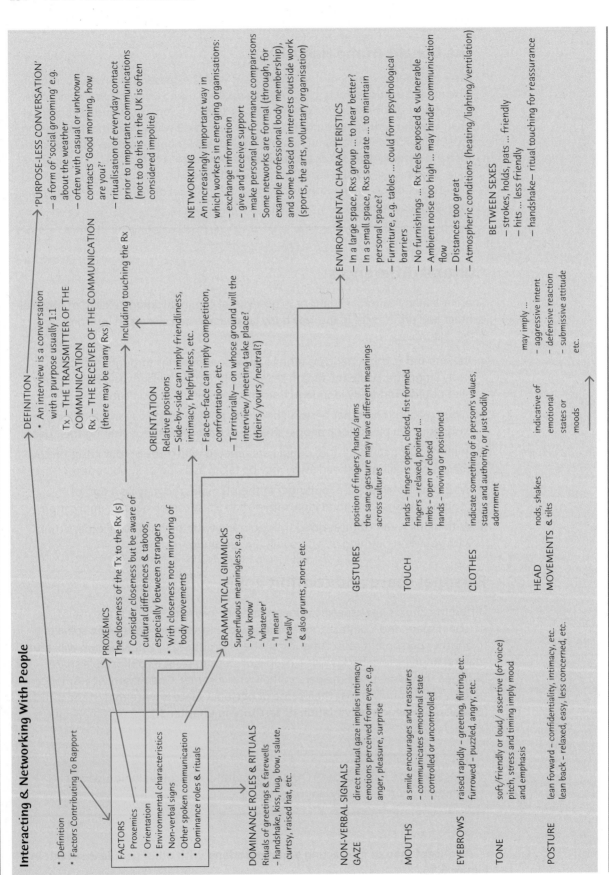

Figure 6.15 Interacting and networking with people

Source: Copyright © 2009 The Virtual Learning Materials Workshop. Reproduced with permission.

Don't stand so close to me! Why 3ft is perfect distance from a stranger

MIND the gap... because the closest a Briton can stand next to a stranger without feeling uncomfortable is three feet.

Coming any nearer makes us awkward – even if we don't show it.

Researchers found that Argentines were the most relaxed with strangers and set a limit of 76.5cm before they felt uneasy. Romanians liked to keep the biggest gap, at 1.39m.

Despite having a reputation for standoffishness, the study revealed that Britons were not the most pro-

Mail Foreign Service

tective about their personal space. At an average distance of 99.4cm, the UK was ranked 26th in a list of 42 countries whose citizens feel most ill at ease with strangers.

We were more comfortable at closer distances than those in China, Portugal or Brazil.

The study said cultural differences could be behind the differences – but other factors were at play. In general, those in warmer countries were more likely to want to stand closer,

but older generations and women prefer to be further apart. The research, led by academics at the University of Wroclaw in Poland, involved asking almost 9,000 participants from 42 countries to point out on a graphic how close they would stand to a stranger.

Both Americans and Germans are more at ease at closer distances than the British. It could explain why Theresa May had an awkward exchange with Angela Merkel last year – holding each other in a half-hug rather than a full embrace.

WHO NEEDS MOST PERSONAL SPACE?

	Country	Distance		Country	Distance
1	Romania	1.39m	30	USA	95.3cm
2	Hungary	1.30m	34	Greece	91.2cm
3	Saudi Arabia	1.26m	35	Spain	90.5cm
4	Turkey	1.23m	36	Russia	89.1cm
5	Uganda	1.21m	37	Slovakia	88.8cm
6	Pakistan	1.19m	38	Austria	88.1cm
7	Estonia	1.18m	39	Ukraine	85.5cm
8	Colombia	1.17m	40	Bulgaria	81.3cm
9	Hong Kong	1.16m	41	Peru	79.6cm
10	China	1.15m	42	Argentina	76.5cm
26	UK	99.4cm			

Daily Mail 31 March 2017

Impression management

In some situations we all attempt to project our attitudes, personality and competence by paying particular attention to our appearance and the impact this may have on others. This has been labelled **'impression management'** (or self-presentation)[26] and is noticeable particularly in the organisational context with attempts to enhance how one is perceived by other people. The selection interview is an obvious illustration. Some information is given more weight than other information when an impression is formed. It would seem that there are central traits that are more important than others in determining our perceptions.

What information do we select and why? The social situation consists of both verbal and non-verbal signals. Non-verbal signals include:

- bodily contact
- proximity
- orientation
- head movements
- facial expressions
- gestures
- posture
- direction of gaze
- dress and appearance
- non-verbal aspects of speech.

Verbal and non-verbal signals are co-ordinated into regular sequences, often without the awareness of the parties. Although you not be aware of it and probably haven't consciously developed it, *Lucas* refers to the importance of the 'personal brand' that we all have and about the messages we send with our dress, voice and body language.[27]

The timing of information also seems to be critical in the impressions we form. For example, information heard first tends to be resistant to later contradictory information. In other words, the saying 'first impression counts' is supported by research.[28] It has also been shown that a negative first impression is more resistant to change than a positive one.[29] However, if there is a break in time we are more likely to remember the most recent information.

What information do we select and why? The social situation consists of both verbal and non-verbal communication discussed above. These signals or cues are co-ordinated into regular sequences, often without the awareness of the parties. *Rigby* points out that although it would be good to think all managers view staff as equal and judged only on results, there are still plenty of ways in which people discriminate. Eleven factors that hold back your career are:

- dress sense
- appearance
- body modification
- accent
- education
- parentage
- height
- hair
- weight
- politics
- religion.[30]

Snap judgements

Despite becoming somewhat clichéd, *Everett* reminds us of the truth of the expression that 'you never get a second chance to make a first impression'. It takes five to seven seconds to make a first impression. Starting with non-verbal impact, body language, dress and appearance, quality and clarity of voice and then what we say.[31] Research by *Willis and Todorov* demonstrated people respond intuitively to facial appearance so rapidly that an exposure time of no more than a tenth of a second is sufficient to form an impression of whether or not you trust someone. Longer exposure time increases confidence in judgements but do not alter significantly the first impression.[32]

Dress code and culture

The meanings we ascribe to these non-verbal signals are rooted in our culture and early socialisation. Thus it is no surprise that there are significant differences in the way we perceive such signals. For instance, dress codes differ in degrees of formality. *Schneider and Barsoux* summarise some interesting cultural differences. For example: Northern European managers tend to dress more informally than their Latin counterparts. Personal style is important for Latin managers, while Anglo and Asian managers do not want to attract attention. French women think it strange that American businesswomen dress in 'man-like' business suits (sometimes with running shoes).[33]

Ziolo discusses how the collective set of each generation differs due to different life experiences, work ethic and culture. Even if we have to make large generalisations, an understanding of sartorial trends of each generation can lead to a better understanding of the culture that guides them. For *most* senior managers and executives hailing from the old school, clothing is not an expression of self, but a business uniform and, a suit is the norm. Younger employees are more likely to see work as part of what defines them and where expression of personality matters.[34]

Perception and interpersonal communications

It is difficult to consider the process of interpersonal perception without commenting on how people communicate. Communication and perception are inextricably bound. How we communicate with colleagues, boss, subordinates, friends will depend on our perception of them, our 'history' with them, and their emotional state. *Fitzherbert* draws an interesting comparison between magic, perception and communication.

> Magicians are acutely aware that the moment people see, hear, feel, taste or smell anything it automatically triggers a range of expectations and perceptions in their minds. In effect, it opens up a 'file' in their brain that tells them what they already know about the subject and rejects anything that doesn't fit. Magicians build their communication and effects around the expectations and perceptions they trigger.

Clarity and impact aside, communication will be effective only if you can convince the audience about what you are telling them or showing them. Fitzherbert sets out twenty rules of perception and communication, shown in **Figure 6.16**.[35]

Getting your message across

Baguley points out that workplace communications can have a variety of aims and objectives, and if it's going to be successful there must be a two way process. Channels of communication are proliferating but many people still struggle to get

Engagement	Attention	Impact	Conviction
1 The framework for any communication is determined by the **expectations and perceptions** that you **trigger**	**5** Concentrated attention requires a **single point of focus**	**12** The senses offer **five different ways** into the brain	**17** To be convincing you, yourself, must **be convinced**
2 Expectations and perceptions can be reinforced or diminished by **prestige, atmosphere and environment** and **desire**	**6** Attention **tracks from left to right**, then settles at the left	**13** Firsts and lasts are remembered	**18** Doubts are reduced by **openness**, but may be increased by **over-stressing**
3 Communication can only register effectively when it builds on **what the audience already knows**	**7** The audience will look where you **look**, where you **point**, where you **tell them** to look	**14** Negatively impede communication as they need unscrambing before the meaning can be interpreted	**19** People put more reliance on something they have **worked out for themselves**
4 The brain filters out most information it receives, leaving only what it considers important	**8** Curiosity, movement, sound, contrast and anything that is new or different are friends *and* foes. Each has the potential to seize attention	**15** Over-familiarity leads to 'invisibility'	**20** People's reactions are influenced by those of their **peers**
	9 The **wider environment** can often add to or detract from your message	**16** Sustained impact depends on transferring information **to long-term memory**	
	10 Every element of your **content** will either **add to or detract** from your message		
	11 Attention is sustained by variation, which **shortens mental time**		

Figure 6.16 Twenty rules of perception and communication
Source: Nick Fitzherbert, www.fitzherbert.co.uk. Reproduced with permission.

their message across effectively. It is important to use the right medium form your message: 'I'm appalled by incidents like, for example, sacking employees by text message'. To be a good communicator, Baguley suggests you need the following skills and understanding.

- Listen actively, rather than passively.
- 'Wear the other person's shoes' and understand the why and how of where that other person is coming from.
- Empathise with what's being said and felt by the other person.
- Be aware of and carefully observe body language.
- Plan your communication to take into account your objectives, the needs and abilities of the other person, the social and physical environment of the communication, and the nature of the message.[36]

Importance of feedback

Feedback is a vital ingredient of the communication process. We may misjudge the receiver and regard our communication as unsuccessful, but unless we have some feedback from the other party we may never know whether what we have said or done was received in the way it was intended. The feedback may reaffirm our perceptions of the person or it may force us to review our perceptions. In our dealings with more senior staff the process of communication can be of special significance, including non-verbal communication, posture and tone.[37]

What is YOUR view of the comparison between magic, perception and communication? How far do you identify with Fitzherbert's twenty rules?

Understanding the organisational process

The process of perception and interpersonal communication has been outlined as selective and subjective: we perceive the world in our own terms and expect the world to 'fit' into our constructs. Throughout our development we learn to distinguish what is important and significant (figure) from information that is additional and contextual (ground). This process is repeated when we join new organisations or take a new job within the same organisation. Fitting into the organisation involves selecting information that is necessary from that which is less significant. At times, the process can be distorted and we can also be 'tricked' into seeing the world in particular ways.

Although some organisations may discriminate, stereotyped perceptions are not always calculated: they are often made automatically and without conscious thought – in much the same way as we may be tricked by visual illusions. In fact, perceptual illusions are a very appropriate way of understanding the organisational setting. For any organisation to be effective it is imperative that the staff are competent to undertake their work and satisfy the 'psychological contract' **(discussed in Chapter 1).** Part of the role of managers is to select and train individuals whom they predict will perform successfully on the job, and then to monitor and assess their competence for promotion. Accordingly, it is clearly important for managers to be aware of their own prejudices and assumptions. By opening channels and encouraging and developing all staff, trust might be fed back into the system from which equality and inclusion could flourish.

Critical Thinking Zone
Reflections on Cultural Differences

In this zone, we critically discuss cultural differences and examine how organisations can manage and utilise cultural nuances and idiosyncrasies for competitive advantage.

The advent and subsequent march of globalisation, which former U.S. President, Bill Clinton[38] (p. 274), proclaimed as 'the central reality of our time,' has carved a dynamic, multicultural corporate landscape and drawn societies closer together than ever before in a diverse and culturally-rich global village.[39] The conflation of rapid and intense political, economic, socio-cultural and technological forces have created and transformed marketplaces, economies, industries and jobs across the globe, to the extent where citizens of the metaphorical village are working together and conducting business, communicating and interacting with each other in ways that were, in the past, deemed improbable.[40] With this in mind, organisations are faced with the challenge of managing a multicultural workforce in national and international contexts, along with cultural nuances, norms and values that are idiosyncratic to each country and society. Managers and individuals must therefore understand the essence of cultural differences and how they influence working relationships and overall business success.[41]

Understanding Cultural Differences

Over the past three decades, a plethora of anthropological studies have been proffered by theorists such as Hofstede[42,43] and Trompenaars and Hampden-Turner,[44] each of which has attempted to raise awareness and develop our understanding of different cultural dimensions that characterise global nations. From this perspective, Søderberg and Holden[45] view culture as an amalgam of assumptions, norms and values that are transmitted to the next generation by socialisation. Essentially, it is characterised as something members of a community have or belong to. These norms, values,

assumptions and indeed traditions differ from country to country and, arguably, a lack of understanding of these differences and how they originated give rise to stereotypes,[46] misperceptions, misjudgements and mistakes in managing relationships with the organisation's members, stakeholders and customers.[47]

Lewis[48] (p. 17) proffers that our positive and negative perceptions and general attitudes to cultural differences have emerged as a result of 'brainwashing'. He notes 'we think our minds are free, but like captured American pilots in Vietnam and North Korea, we have been thoroughly brainwashed.' He attributes these reactions to 'collective programming,' which, he claims began when we were born and have been reinforced and perpetuated throughout our lifetime and interplayed both in and outside the workplace. Lewis argues that our programming 'convinces us that we are normal, others eccentric.' Fitzpatrick[49] concurs and suggests that the meanings, interpretations, stereotypes and misperceptions that we ascribe to cultural norms and differences are influenced, regulated and negotiated as part of our social constructions of reality. These have developed over time and are, in part, shaped by our interactions with, and experiences of, working with diverse cultures. Lewis[48] and Fitzpatrick indicate that, rightly or wrongly, there is an element of predetermination and predictability in the way we behave.[46]

The Missing Link

While the models of Hofstede and Trompenaars and Hampden-Turner have provided us with a snapshot of cultural nuances, Lewis[50] argues that their preoccupation with dimensions such as time, religion and nationality has overlooked the missing link: *behaviour*. Based on his research, which began in the 1990s, he concluded that human beings can be clearly dichotomised into three categories. First, Linear-active, incorporating, for example, Britain, North America and Northern Europe. Second, Reactive, which includes all the main countries in Asia, apart from the Indian sub-continent (hybrid) and third, Multi-Active, such as Southern Europe, South America and the Middle East. Lewis[50] proffers that although these global cultures are geographically diverse and differ in terms of their values, beliefs and religions, *behaviourally,* they can be classified as a group, because they follow the same behavioural pattern and display similar traits and commonalities, such as emotion, expressive body language, variable work ethic, primacy of family bonds and relationship orientation.

What Does this Mean for Organisational Behaviour in the Workplace?

Lewis[51] suggests that placing a focus on national behaviours and the cultural roots that define them, both in terms of business and society, can assist organisations to predict and calculate, with a surprising amount of accuracy, how individuals will cooperate with, and respond to, each other in the workplace. Is it that *simple,* though? One could argue that it isn't. Lewis[51] and Fitzpatrick, and indeed Hofstede in his original definition of culture, suggest that our views, perceptions, misperceptions, misjudgements et al are a by-product of our social constructions and collective programming that began when we were born and have continued through child and adulthood. Like the Jungian shadow, these are deep-rooted, hidden and surfaced when we are confronted with situations that require us to interact, work and do business with people from other cultures. Hoecklin[52] (p. ix) caveated that if shadow behaviours, as they pertain to our views of other cultures, are not managed, cultural differences may lead to 'management frustration, costly misunderstandings and even business failures.' In this respect, cross-cultural management can be utilised by organisations as a strategy to mitigate against the rather negative portrait painted by Hoecklin and a tactic to deal with conflict, friction and miscommunication that arise as a result of cultural clashes.[45] Managing cultural differences can also ensure that a diverse workforce can be utilised as a strategic, organisational asset rather than a liability.[53] Additionally, engaging in cross-cultural awareness training can help to reduce the negativity associated with culture shock,[54] equip managers with the requisite knowledge and skills to effectively

bridge the gap between different cultures and help the organisation's members to minimise the risk of judging and indeed misjudging others based on their own deep-rooted subjective biases and stereotypes.[41]

The Effects of Collective Programming

To conclude, due to the effects of collective programming, organisations can, to some extent though not fully, manage cultural nuances and idiosyncrasies. Our own culture, and how we perceive other cultures, is deeply ingrained within us and is part of our cultural fabric and what defines us as human beings. Importantly, Schneider and Barsoux[55] and Lewis[48] point out that the task of understanding and managing cultural differences is not to contain or neutralise diversity but to build on and exploit it. Hoecklin concurs but caveats that before an organisation contemplates utilising cultural differences as competitive advantage, its assumptions, and those of its members, must change. Rather than being an obstacle to conducting business across diverse cultures, a multicultural workforce can yield a variety of tangible benefits to organisations, including diversity of knowledge, skills, expertise, world views, innovation and creativity. However, for these benefits to be leveraged and differentness celebrated, Holden[47] concludes 'culture and its consequences must be managed and this, by general consent, is no easy task.'

Questions

In view of the above, answer the following questions.

1. Globalisation has played a major role in creating a culturally-rich global village. *What* other factors have contributed to the rise in the multicultural workplace?

2. Lewis, Fitzpatrick and Hofstede proffer that our assumptions, misperceptions and misjudgements about cultural differences are socially constructed and, to a lesser or greater extent, pre-programmed. *What* implications does this have for organisational behaviour in the workplace?

3. *How* can organisations 'effectively' manage cultural differences for competitive advantage?

Summary – Chapter 6 'Perception and communication'

Perception is a complex and dynamic process at the root of our understanding, behaviour and action. We all have our unique image of how we interpret the 'reality' of the world around us. Perception gives rise to individual behavioural responses in given situations. The process of perception is based on both internal characteristics in terms of our sensory limits or thresholds and external influences related to the nature of the stimuli. It is important to be aware of potential perceptual illusions. Making judgements about other people is not easy and there are many potential difficulties. Perception results in different people attaching different meanings to the same stimulus. This gives rise to a number of potential perceptual distortions and errors. Attribution is the process by which people interpret the perceived causes of behaviour. Language plays an important part in the way we perceive and communicate with the world. This includes cultural differences, non-verbal communication and body language, and impression management. Part of the process of perception is to attribute characteristics to other people. Perception and interpersonal communication are inextricably bound and are selective and subjective. Managers should be aware of their own perceptual prejudices, assumptions and perceptions that influence style of behaviour and relationship with other staff.

Group discussion activities

Undertake each of these activities in small groups as indicated by your tutor. Before you start your discussion establish a non-threatening environment within the group and confirm confidentiality will be honoured.

First, form your own views and then share and compare in open critical discussion with colleagues. Reflect honestly on the extent to which: (i) you influenced the thinking and ideas of your colleagues; and (ii) you were influenced by your colleagues.

To what extent was your group able to reach consensus?

Agree one of your members to produce a brief written summary of the discussion and prepared to present in a plenary session.

Activity 1

(a) Have you every avoided telling anyone that you are a student for fear of being stereotyped?

(b) To what extent do you think judgements are made about other people on the basis of:
* height
* other physical characteristics
* speech and/or dress
* car they drive
* preferred reading books
* timekeeping
* leisure interests or activities

(c) In the television programme *Only Fools and Horse*, how far do you think people identify with Del's Reliant Robin car as being 'the right image' for him?

Activity 2

Impression management gives rise to the question of ethical issues. Many organisations undertake induction and training courses in an effort to 'coach' staff how to display an impression in the manner expected of them. John Lewis for example, sends recruits to theatre school to gain confidence in how to impress customers.

(a) To what extent do you see impression management as potentially undermining mutual acceptance and trust as a basis for effective interpersonal relationships?

(b) How far should people at work be free to be themselves rather than a 'false' persona demanded by the organisation?

(c) Can you see any possible connections between impression management and emotional labour discussed in **Chapter 2**?

Activity 3

Most people feel uncomfortable or even intimidated if the territory of their personal space is invaded. Not only are there differences in specific values of 'comfort zones' among cultures but there are also different limits within the same UK culture when people stand too close. These limits range from 3ft 8in for strangers, 2ft 6in for house-mates, 1ft 10in for friends, 1ft 7in for family members, to 1ft 5in for partners.

(*Daily Mail,* 3 July 2017)

(a) How strongly do you feel about your preferred comfort zone and to what extent can you relate to these limits?

(b) Explain how you likely to react to invasion of your personal space.

Organisational behaviour in action case study

Royal College of Nursing: Managing unacceptable behaviour

If someone is communicating with you in an unacceptable way, be it face to face, over the phone or in written form, there are steps you can take to try and de-escalate the situation. The following tips aim to help you do this and should always be employed as a first step in the process of managing unacceptable behaviour.

Face-to-face and/or verbal incidents

✱ Act as a role model for appropriate behaviour.

✱ Address the person directly and politely.

✱ Slow down the conversation and ask the person to repeat what they said.

✱ Give the person honest and constructive feedback, be specific.

✱ Ask them to stop behaving in an unacceptable manner and explain that if they don't you will remove yourself from the situation/end the phone call.

✱ When an individual appears to be distraught, employing the following skills may help you to calm them.

Non-verbal listening skills

* Maintain eye contact.
* Keep your facial expression neutral.
* Ensure your body language is professional but open.
* Keep a level tone of voice.
* Talk at a steady pace, avoid rushing.

Verbal listening skills

* Ask open, relevant questions.
* Paraphrase what they have said to show you are listening.

If the individual's unacceptable behaviour continues, repeat your request for them to stop and let them know you will take the matter further. If the situation is escalating face to face and you need assistance, find a colleague to support you as soon as possible. If you feel at all under threat, remove yourself from the situation immediately and put a distance between yourself and the individual involved. You must also consider calling the police if you believe the threat to you or others may be severe.

Written incidents

* Take your time reading through the email or letter.
* Pick out the points that need responding to and the evidence of unacceptable behaviour.
* Consider whether it would be more constructive to call the individual to discuss their email or letter, and employ the skills listed for verbal incidents.
* If you choose to write back, be clear and polite, acknowledge their concerns.
* Highlight where you believe their behaviour has breached our Respect Charter and include a copy if appropriate.

* Ask them to treat you respectfully and explain that if they don't, you may have to refuse to communicate with them.
* Talk to your RCN supervising officer/senior officer for further advice on handling the situation.

Recovering from incidents

* Incidents of unacceptable behaviour can have a substantial impact on our accredited representatives, their well-being, productivity, and their relationships with our members.
* If you are affected by an incident, you are encouraged to seek support to reflect on and recover from what took place. Talk to your relevant RCN supervising officer/senior officer. They will offer guidance on recording and reporting the incident, and explore what further support you may need.

Source for the case: Extracted with kind permission of Royal College of Nursing from 'Managing unacceptable behaviour guidelines' 3 October 2017, www.rcn.org.uk

Tasks

1. What do you think of the idea of a written set of guidelines on managing unacceptable behaviour? Would you recommend similar guidelines for universities?
2. In what ways can you relate this case study to your reading of perception and communication?
3. How well do you believe you could handle and de-escalate a challenging situation?

Chapter 6 – Personal skills and employability exercise

Objectives

Completing this exercise should help you to enhance the following skills:

* Reflect on your understanding of, and behaviour towards, other people.
* Review your personal experiences of the process of interpersonal perception.
* Learn and understand more about your inner self.

Part 1

Look back at the different reactions from five managers to the situation referred to at the start of this chapter. What do you think might be the underlying reasons for the individual responses and how might these responses relate to the perceptual process?

Part 2 – Exercise

You are required to work in small self-selecting groups *with colleagues you trust and feel comfortable with, and with whom confidences are assured.*

Relate honestly and fully:

1. **(a)** your bias and prejudices about other people; and

 (b) bias and prejudices you perceive in other people.

2. Examples when you have been guilty of:

 (a) Making a pre-judgement about an individual without really knowing the true circumstances. To what extent did you then filter stimuli to receive only that which supported your initial reactions? How did you eventually resolve or reconcile this pre-judgement?

 (b) Perceptual errors or misjudgements arising from:

 * halo and/or rusty halo effect

 * projection

 * self-fulfilling prophecy

 What action did you take subsequently and to what extent were the misjudgements or errors resolved?

Discussion

* What were your colleagues' reactions to your revelations? Did anything surprise you? Or them?

* To what extent has undertaking this exercise made you more aware of your own perceptions and how you perceive other people?

* What have you learnt from undertaking this exercise and how has it helped you to avoid similar situations in the future?

Notes and references

1. Misselhorn, H. J. *Understanding and Managing Your Organisation,* fifth edition, MOD Consulting (2004).
2. Kohler, I. 'The Formation and Transformation of the Visual World', *Psychological Issues,* vol. 3, 1964, pp. 28–46, 116–33.
3. Myers, I. B. *Introduction to Type,* Oxford Psychologists Press (1987).
4. Ling, C. and Masako, I. 'Intercultural Communication and Cultural Learning: The Experience of Visiting Japanese Students in the US', *The Howard Journal of Communications,* vol. 14, 2003, pp. 75–96.
5. McCrum, M. *Going Dutch in Beijing,* Profile Books (2007), p. vii.
6. Block, J. R. and Yuker, H. E. *Can You Believe Your Eyes?,* Robson Books (2002).

7. Morgan, C. T. and King, R. A. *Introduction to Psychology,* third edition, McGraw-Hill (1966), p. 343.

8. Stroop, J. R. 'Studies of Interference in Serial Verbal Reactions', *Journal of Experimental Psychology,* vol. 4, no. 18, 1935, pp. 643–62; and Penrose, L. S. and Penrose, R. 'Impossible Objects: A Special Type of Illusion', *British Journal of Psychology,* part 1, February 1958.

9. Cohen, A. *The Tall Book: A Celebration of Life from on High,* Bloomsbury (2009).

10. See, for example, Leitch, L. 'The Big Problem That Short Men Face', *The Times,* 24 June 2009.

11. Dib, F. 'The Anatomy of a Leader', *Professional Manager,* September/October 2012, pp. 34–8.

12. Mintzberg, H. *Managing,* Financial Times Prentice Hall (2009).

13. Wexley, K. N., Yukl, G. A., Kovacs, S. Z. and Sanders, R. E. 'Importance of Contrast Effects in Employment Interviews', *Journal of Applied Psychology,* vol. 56, 1972, pp. 45–8.

14. Guirdham, M. *Interactive Behaviour at Work,* third edition, Financial Times Prentice Hall (2002).

15. See, for example, Stewart-Allen, A. L. 'Changing the Mindset about Americans', *Professional Manager,* vol. 15, no. 5, September 2006, p. 37.

16. Merton, R. K. *Social Theory and Social Structure,* Free Press (1957).

17. Davies, C. M. 'You are Blind to Your Bias', *Professional Manager,* September/October 2012, p. 53.

18. Heider, F. *The Psychology of Interpersonal Relations,* John Wiley & Sons (1958).

19. Kelley, H. H. 'The Process of Causal Attribution', *American Psychologist,* February 1973, pp. 107–28; Goffman, E. *The Presentation of Self in Everyday Life,* Penguin (1971).

20. McCrum, M. *Going Dutch in Beijing,* Profile Books (2007), pp. 44–5.

21. Mehrabian, A. *Tactics of Social Influence,* Prentice Hall (1970).

22. Pivcevic, P. 'Taming the Boss', *Management Today,* March 1999, p. 70.

23. McGuire, T. 'Don't Just Listen', *Chartered Secretary,* September 1998, p. 24.

24. See, for example, James, J. *The Body Language Bible,* Vermilion (2008).

25. For other examples of cultural differences, see French, R. *Cross-Cultural Management in Work Organisations,* second edition, Chartered Institute of Personnel and Development (2010).

26. Goffman, E. *The Presentation of Self in Everyday Life,* Penguin (1971).

27. Lucas, E. 'Check the Label', *Professional Manager,* November 2009, pp. 22–5.

28. Miller, N. and Campbell, D. T. 'Recency and Primacy in Persuasion as a Function of the Timing of Speeches and Measurements', *Journal of Abnormal and Social Psychology,* 59, 1959, pp. 1–9.

29. Hodges, B. 'Effect of Volume on Relative Weighting in Impression Formation', *Journal of Personality and Social Psychology,* 30, 1974, pp. 378–81.

30. Rigby, R. 'What's Holding Him Back', *Management Today,* December 2009, pp. 54–6.

31. Everett, L. 'First Impressions', *Governance + Compliance,* November 2012, p. 54.

32. Willis, J and Todorov, A. 'First Impressions: Making up Your Mind after a 100-ms Exposure to a Face', *Psychological Science,* vol. 17, no. 7, 2006.

33. Schneider, S. C. and Barsoux, J. *Managing Across Cultures,* second edition, Financial Times Prentice Hall (2003), p. 29.

34. Ziolo, K. 'A Stitch in Time', *Professional Manager,* July/August 2011, pp. 31–3.

35. 'Nick Fitzherbert Applies the Rules of Magic to Coaching People in Communication Skills', www.fitzherbert.co.uk. See also Fitzherbert, N. 'Magic Tricks in Communication', *Professional Manager,* vol. 14, no. 5, September 2005, pp. 32–3.

36. Baguley, P. 'Putting your Message Across', *Professional Manager,* September 2009, pp. 33–5.

37. See, for example, Pivcevic, P. 'Taming the Boss', *Management Today,* March 1999, pp. 68–72.

38. Clinton, W. J. 'Remarks to the Opening of the National Summit on Africa, February 17, 2000,' *Public Papers of the Presidents of the United States,* William J. Clinton, January 1 to June 26, 2000.

39. McLean, J. and Lewis, R. D. 'Communicating Across Cultures,' *British Journal of Administrative Management,* Summer 2010, pp. 30–1.

40. Liu, C. H. and Lee, H. W. 'Cross-cultural Communication,' *Review of Business Research,* vol. 8, no. 6, 2008, pp 138–42.

41. CIPD. International Culture, Factsheet, Chartered Institute of Personnel and Development, 18 July 2016, https://www.cipd.co.uk/knowledge/culture/working-environment/international-culture-factsheet (accessed 25 July 2018).

42. Hofstede, G. *Culture's Consequences: International Differences in Work-Related Values,* Sage (1980).

43. Hofstede, G. 'Dimensionalizing Cultures: The Hofstede Model in Context,' *Online Readings in Psychology and Culture,* 2 (1), 2011, pp. 1–26.

44. Trompenaars, F. and Hampden-Turner, C. *Riding the Waves of Culture: Understanding Cultural Diversity in Global Business,* McGraw-Hill (1998).

45. Søderberg, A. M. and Holden, N. 'Rethinking Cross-cultural Management in a Globalising Business World,' *International Journal of Cross-Cultural Management,* vol. 2(1), 2002, pp. 103–21.

46. Clausen, L. 'Moving Beyond Stereotypes in Managing Cultural Difference: Communication in Danish-Japanese Corporate Relationships,' *Scandinavian Journal of Management,* 26, 2010, pp. 57–66.

47. Holden, N. *Cross-Cultural Management: A Knowledge Management Perspective,* Financial Times, Prentice Hall (2002).

48. Lewis, R. D. *When Cultures Collide: Leading Across Cultures,* third edition, Nicholas Brealey International (2006).

49. Fitzpatrick, F. 'Taking the "Culture" out of "Culture Shock" – A Critical Review of Literature on Cross-cultural Adjustment in International Relocation', *Cultural Perspectives on International Business,* vol. 13, no. 4, 2017, pp. 278–96.

50. Lewis, R. D. 'The Lewis Model-Dimensions of Behaviour,' 2015, https://www.crossculture.com/the-lewis-model-dimensions-of-behaviour/ (accessed 25 July 2018).

51. Lewis, R. D. *When Cultures Collide: Leading Across Cultures,* fourth edition, Nicholas Brealey Publishing (2018).

52. Hoecklin, L. *Managing Cultural Differences: Strategies for Competitive Advantage,* Addison Wesley (1995).

53. Stahl, G. K., Mäkelä, K., Zander, L. and Maznevski, M. L. 'A Look at the Bright Side of Multicultural Team Diversity,' *Scandinavian Journal of Management,* 26, 2010, pp. 439–47.

54. Dewald, B. and Self, J. T. (2008). 'Cross-cultural Training for Expatriate Hotel Managers: An Exploratory Study,' *International Journal of Hospitality Management and Tourism Administration,* vol. 19 (4), 2008, pp. 352–64.

55. Schneider, S. and Barsoux, J. L. (1997). *Managing Across Cultures,* Prentice Hall (1997).

Chapter 7
Work motivation and satisfaction

The relationship between the organisation and its members is influenced by what motivates them to work and the rewards and fulfilment they derive from it.

Learning outcomes

After completing this chapter you should have enhanced your ability to:

- explain the significance and underlying concept of motivation;
- detail various needs and expectations of people at work;
- examine content theories of motivations and work of leading writers;
- review process theories of motivation and relevance to particular work situations;

- assess broader approaches to work motivation and satisfaction;
- explore the nature and dimensions of job satisfaction;
- evaluate relationships between work motivation, satisfaction and performance.

Outline chapter contents

Overview topic map: Chapter 7 – Work motivation and satisfaction

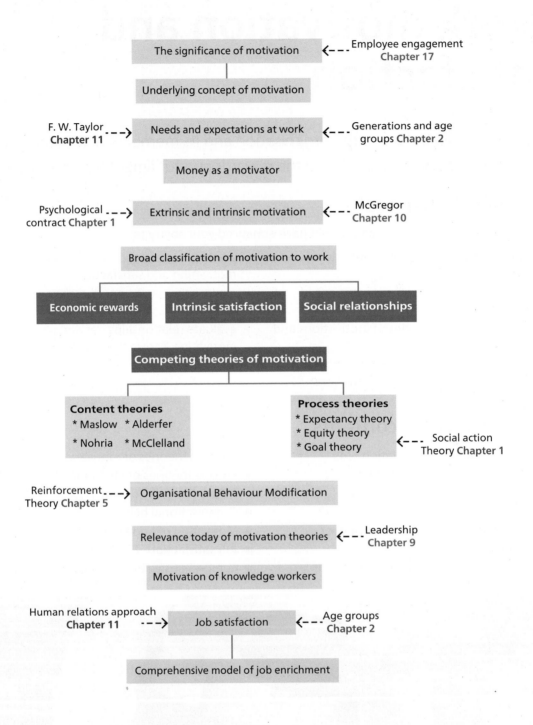

A satisfactory job

Before commencing to read this chapter think hard about what would really motivate YOU most to give of your best at work.

The significance of motivation

Effective organisational performance is dependent upon human activity and the efforts of members of staff. The more highly motivated the workforce the more likely success of the organisation in achieving its goals and objectives. Motivation is at the basis of all organisational activity. The manager needs to know how best to elicit the co-operation and motivation of staff, and direct their efforts to achieving the goals and objectives of the organisation.

The study of **motivation** is concerned with why people behave in a certain way and do what they do. In general terms, motivation can be described as the direction and persistence of action. It is concerned with why people choose a particular course of action in preference to others, and why they continue with a chosen action, often over a long period and in the face of difficulties and problems.[1] There is a fine line between employee motivation and engagement. **Employee engagement is discussed fully in Chapter 17.**

From a review of motivation theory, *Mitchell* identifies four common characteristics which underlie the definition of motivation:

- Motivation is typified as an individual phenomenon. Every person is unique and major theories of motivation allow for this uniqueness to be demonstrated in one way or another.

- Motivation is described, usually, as intentional. Motivation is assumed to be under the worker's control, and behaviours that are influenced by motivation, such as effort expended, are seen as choices of action.
- Motivation is multifaceted. The two factors of greatest importance are: (i) what gets people activated (arousal); and (ii) the force of an individual to engage in desired behaviour (direction or choice of behaviour).
- The purpose of motivational theories is to predict behaviour. Motivation is not the behaviour itself and it is not performance. Motivation concerns action and the internal and external forces which influence a person's choice of action.

On the basis of these characteristics, Mitchell defines motivation as 'the degree to which an individual wants and chooses to engage in certain specified behaviours'.[2] The *Chartered Management Institute* refers to motivation as the process of creating incentives and contexts that prompt individuals to action. In a workplace context this involves employee incentives to perform to the best of their ability.[3]

Needs and expectations at work

The underlying concept of motivation is some driving force within individuals by which they attempt to achieve some goal in order to fulfil some need or expectation. This concept gives rise to the basic motivational model, illustrated in **Figure 7.1.** People's behaviour is determined by what motivates them. Their performance is a product of both ability level and motivation.

$$\text{Performance} = \text{function (ability} \times \text{motivation)}$$

Kreitner et al. suggest that although motivation is a necessary contributor for job performance, it is not the only one. Along with ability, motivation is also a combination of level of skill, knowledge about how to complete the task, feelings and emotions, and facilitating and inhibiting conditions not under the individual's control.[4] However, what is clearly evident is that if the manager is to improve the work of the organisation, attention must be given to the level of motivation of its members. The manager must also encourage staff to direct their efforts (their

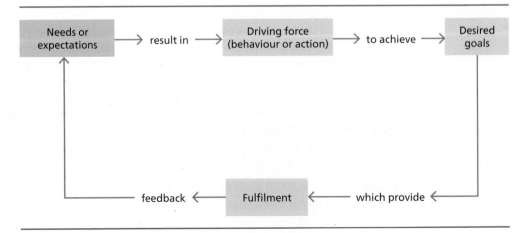

Figure 7.1 A simplified illustration of the basic motivational model

driving force) towards the successful attainment of the goals and objectives of the organisation.

But what is this driving force and what do people really want from work? What are people's needs and expectations and how do they influence behaviour and performance? Motivation is a complex subject, it is a very personal thing, and influenced by many variables. For example, *Farren* reminds us of the twelve human needs that have been around since the beginning of recorded history:

- family
- health and well-being
- work/career
- economic
- learning
- home/shelter
- social relationships
- spirituality
- community
- leisure
- mobility
- environment/safety.

'Work and private life in the new millennium will continue to revolve around the 12 human needs.'[5]

Early writers, such as F. W. Taylor, believed in economic needs motivation. Workers would be motivated by obtaining the highest possible wages through working in the most efficient and productive way. Performance was limited by physiological fatigue. For Taylor, motivation was a comparatively simple issue – what the workers wanted from their employers more than anything else was high wages. The ideas of F. W. Taylor and his 'rational–economic needs' concept of motivation **(discussed in Chapter 11)** and subsequent approaches to motivation at work have fuelled the continuing debate about financial rewards as a motivator and their influence on productivity.

Money as a motivator

Where there is little pleasure in work itself or the job offers little opportunity for career advancement, personal challenge or growth, many people may appear to be motivated primarily, if not exclusively, by money. Weaver suggests that for many hourly workers in the hospitality industry, such as dishwashing, waiting or housekeeping staff, the work does not change much among different companies and there is little attachment to a particular company. For such staff, *Weaver* proposes a 'Theory M' programme of motivation based on direct cash rewards for above-average performance. A percentage base is calculated from the average performance of workers on the staff.[6]

Different generations and age groups in the workforce **(discussed in Chapter 2)** are also likely to have contrasting sets of motivations. For example, the baby boomers may well be concerned primarily about job security, paying their large mortgages or funding their retirement with the demise of final salary pensions. Generation X may be concerned about the changing nature of the work organisation, their financial future and continuing job security for the rest of their working life. On the other hand, Generation Y may be more footloose, have less interest in or doubts about affording to buy their own home, and are less concerned about security or a long-term career.

For the vast majority of people, money is clearly important and a motivator at work **but** to what extent and **how** important depends upon personal circumstances and other satisfactions they derive from work. Although pay may still make people tick, there are a number of other important influences on motivation. For many people, the feeling of being recognised and valued appears more important than money in motivating them to stay in a particular job. Note also that money may seem important as symbolising successful task performance and goal achievement.

As *Chamorro-Premuzic and Fagan* point out few management topics have attracted as much discussion as the relationship between money and motivation. It seems that money is not a great motivator at work and under certain circumstances may even demotivate. Extrinsic incentives such as financial rewards may extinguish or crowd out intrinsic rewards such as engagement and job satisfaction. The authors also report on evidence which suggests that people are far more sensitive to the loss of money than the gaining of money. A pay rise may not necessarily make people happy but a pay cut will be sure to make them miserable.[7]

In August 2017 Brazilian international footballer Neymar moved from Barcelona to Paris Saint-Germain for a world record £200m transfer fee and reported to earn £540,000 per week after tax. Neymar was quoted widely as saying: 'I was never motivated by money. I thought all else about the happiness of my family regardless of money.'

 How important to YOU is job security and good pension provision in thinking about your future choice of career? What *single* factor would have most influence on your choice?

Extrinsic and intrinsic motivation

The various needs and expectations at work can be categorised in a number of ways – for example division into physiological and social motives or into extrinsic and intrinsic motivation.

- **Extrinsic motivation** is related to 'tangible' rewards such as salary and fringe benefits, security, promotion, contract of service, the work environment and conditions of work. Such tangible rewards are often determined at the organisational level and may be largely outside the control of individual managers.

- **Intrinsic motivation** is related to 'psychological' rewards such as the opportunity to use one's ability, a sense of challenge and achievement, receiving appreciation, positive recognition and being treated in a caring and considerate manner. Psychological rewards are those that can usually be determined by the actions and behaviour of individual managers.[8]

Broader intrinsic motivation

Popular press reports appear to indicate many people are increasingly motivated by broader concerns such as their work/life balance, opportunities for flexible working, career advancement and personal development and growth, and a feeling of identification with the values of the organisation. Motivation to work is also influenced by the changing nature of the work environment and the concept of the 'psychological contract' **(discussed in Chapter 1).**

According to *Kets de Vries,* the best-performing companies possess a set of values that creates the right conditions for high performance. In addition to the motivation needs system for physiological needs, sensual and enjoyment needs, and the need to respond to threatening situations, companies that get the best out of their people are characterised by a system based on a higher set of motivational needs:

- **attachment/affiliation** – concerning the need for engagement and sharing, a feeling of community and a sense of belonging to the company; and
- **exploration/assertion** – concerning the ability to play and work, a sense of fun and enjoyment, the need for self-assertion and the ability to choose.[9]

Developing a passion for work

Blanchard has identified eight critical employee needs that should be in place if organisations are to develop a passion for work and get the best out of their people and have them thrive.

- **Meaningful work** – people need to know that their work is worthwhile at both the individual and organisational levels and this is arguably the most important need.
- **Collaboration** – working in a culture and environment that is encouraging, collaborative and co-operative.
- **Fairness** – people expect to be treated with respect, ethically, fairly and justly.
- **Autonomy** – to have influence and input over how tasks are performed, and freedom to make personal decisions about their work.
- **Recognition** – the feeling they are making a positive contribution through praise and appreciation or other recognition for their achievements.
- **Growth** – opportunities to learn, grow and develop skills that lead to advancement in a chosen career.
- **Connectedness with leaders** – people need leaders they can trust and who share information and build rapport with them.
- **Connectedness with colleagues** – solid relationships with colleagues and co-workers in order to provide willingness to apply discretionary effort.[10]

Self-directed behaviour

Referring to the work of Douglas McGregor **(discussed in Chapter 10)**, *Pink* discusses extrinsic and intrinsic motivation in terms of Type X behaviour and Type I behaviour.

Type X behaviour is fuelled more by extrinsic desires with less satisfaction from an activity itself and more with the external rewards from activity. Type I behaviour is a way of thinking and approach to life centred around intrinsic motivators and with the internal satisfaction of an activity. No one exhibits either type of behaviour exclusively but we do have certain often clear dispositions. Pink maintains that in order to strengthen organisations we need to move from Type X to Type I behaviour.

Type I behaviour does not disdain money or recognition but once compensation is perceived as fair and equitable money is no longer as important as focusing on the work itself and recognition for accomplishments. According to Pink Type I behaviour is self-directed and promotes greater physical and mental well-being and dependent upon three nutrients of:

- Autonomy – over what you do, when how and who with;
- Mastery – the impulse for improvement and to get better at what matters;
- Purpose – the quest for excellence directed towards a larger purpose.[11]

In support of Pink, *Smallman* points out that pay was once the best way to woo potential employees with a mighty pay packet and to motivate current workers with a hefty bonus. But hard cash alone is no longer sufficient. It is necessary to change the record: people have always been motivated by aspiration, challenges and achievement. Smallman includes flexibility, gratitude and working environment as best non-monetary motivators.[12]

To what extent can YOU identify with Type I behaviour and motivation by aspiration, challenge and achievement?

Three-fold classification for review of motivation

Given the complex and variable nature of needs and expectations, the following is a simplistic but useful, broad three-fold classification as a starting point for reviewing the motivation to work (*see* **Figure 7.2**):

- **Economic rewards** – such as pay, fringe benefits, pension rights, material goods and security. This is an instrumental orientation to work and concerned with 'other things'.
- **Intrinsic satisfaction** – derived from the nature of the work itself, interest in the job, and personal growth and development. This is a personal orientation to work and concerned with 'oneself'.
- **Social relationships** – such as friendships, group working and the desire for affiliation, status and dependency. This is a relational orientation to work and concerned with 'other people'.

A person's motivation, job satisfaction and work performance will be determined by the comparative strength of these sets of needs and expectations and the extent to which they are fulfilled. For example, some people may make a deliberate choice to forgo intrinsic satisfaction and social relationships in return for high economic rewards and/or job security. For other people psychological well-being or social relationships would appear to be an important feature. For people working in caring organisations or the hospitality industry, where pay is often not very high, the interactions with other people and importance of supportive working relationships and good teamwork can be strong motivators at work.[13]

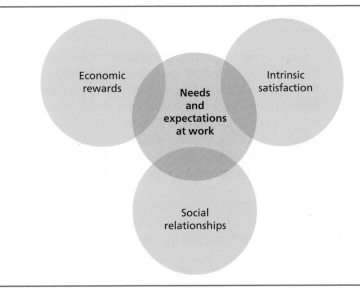

Figure 7.2 Needs and expectations of people at work

However the needs and expectations at work are categorised, a central motivational issue is the underlying importance of management as an integrating activity and employees have a feeling of connection with the organisation and their jobs. It is important to develop an organisational climate in which people work willingly and effectively. **(Employee engagement is discussed in Chapter 17.)**

The OB three-fold way: economic rewards, intrinsic satisfaction and social relationships

Competing theories of motivation

The complexity of motivation and lack of a ready-made solution or single answer for motivating people at work gives rise to many competing theories. These theories may all be at least partially true and help to explain the behaviour of certain people at certain times. They show there are many motives that influence people's behaviour and performance. Collectively, the different theories provide a framework within which to direct attention to the problem of how best to motivate staff to work willingly and effectively. These different theories of motivation are usually divided into two contrasting approaches: content theories and process theories.

It is important to emphasise these various theories are not conclusive and have their critics or subject to alternative findings. Many of these theories were not intended initially to have the significance that some writers have subsequently placed upon them. It is easy to quote an example that appears to contradict any generalised observation on what motivates people to work. Despite these reservations the different theories provide a basis for study and discussion, and for review of the most effective motivational style **(see Figure 7.3).** The manager must judge the relevance of these different theories, how best to draw upon them, and how they might effectively be applied in particular work situations.

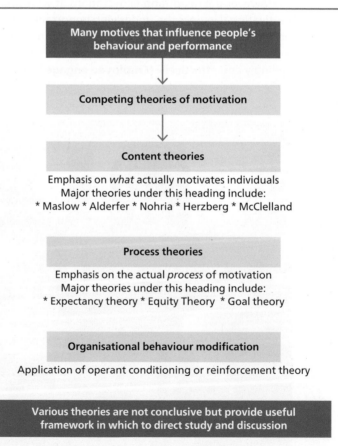

Figure 7.3 An overview of main theories of work motivation

How would YOU describe the comparative strength of economic rewards, intrinsic satisfaction or social relationships in determining your motivation to work?

Content theories of motivation

Content theories attempt to explain those specific things that actually motivate the individual at work. These theories are concerned with identifying people's needs and their relative strengths, and the goals they pursue in order to satisfy these needs. Content theories place emphasis on the nature of needs and what motivates. Major content theories of motivation include:

- Maslow's hierarchy of needs model;
- Alderfer's modified need hierarchy model;
- Nohria's four drives model of motivation;
- Herzberg's two-factor theory;
- McClelland's achievement motivation theory.

Maslow's hierarchy of needs theory

A useful starting point is the work of *Maslow* and his theory of individual development and motivation, published originally in 1943.[14] Maslow's basic proposition is that human needs are arranged in a series of levels, a hierarchy of importance. People are wanting beings, they always want more, and what they want depends on what they already have.

Maslow identified eight innate needs. However, the hierarchy is usually shown as ranging through five main levels, from, at the lowest level, physiological needs, through safety needs, love needs and esteem needs, to the need for self-actualisation at the highest level. The **hierarchy of needs** may be shown as a series of steps but is usually displayed in the form of a pyramid **(see Figure 7.4).** This is an appropriate form of illustration as it implies a thinning out of needs as people progress up the hierarchy.

- **Physiological needs.** Include homeostasis (the body's automatic efforts to retain normal functioning) such as satisfaction of hunger and thirst, the need for oxygen and to maintain temperature regulation. Also sleep, sensory pleasures, activity, maternal behaviour and, arguably, sexual desire.
- **Safety needs.** Include safety and security, freedom from pain or threat of physical attack, protection from danger or deprivation, the need for predictability and orderliness.
- **Love needs** (often referred to as social needs). Include affection, sense of belonging, social activities, friendships, and both the giving and receiving of love.
- **Esteem needs** (sometimes referred to as ego needs). Include both self-respect and the esteem of others. Self-respect involves the desire for confidence, strength,

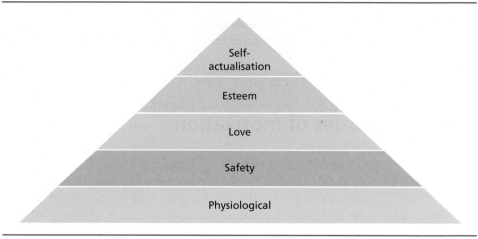

Figure 7.4 Maslow's hierarchy of needs model

independence and freedom, and achievement. Esteem of others involves reputation or prestige, status, recognition, attention and appreciation.

- **Self-actualisation needs.** Once a lower need has been satisfied, it no longer acts as a strong motivator. The needs of the next higher level in the hierarchy demand satisfaction and become the motivating influence. Only unsatisfied needs motivate a person. Thus Maslow asserts that '*a satisfied need is no longer a motivator*'. Maslow claims the hierarchy is relatively universal among different cultures, but recognises there are differences in an individual's motivational content in a particular culture.

Note however *John Adair* points out presenting Maslow's hierarchy as a pyramid gives the impression that greatest needs are in the lower levels. The pyramid should be inverted as physiological needs, for example, are limited but there are fewer limitations the further up you go.[15]

Do YOU agree that Maslow's hierarchy would be shown more meaningfully as an inverted pyramid? What alternative means of presentation can you suggest?

Degrees of satisfaction

Maslow points out a false impression may be given a need must be satisfied fully before a subsequent need arises. He suggests a more realistic description is in terms of decreasing percentages of satisfaction along levels of the hierarchy. The relative importance of these needs changes during the psychological development of the individual. Maslow subsequently modified his views by noting that satisfaction of self-actualisation needs by growth-motivated individuals can actually enhance these needs rather than reduce them. Furthermore, he accepted that some higher-level needs may still emerge after long deprivation of lower-level needs rather than only after their satisfaction.

Not necessarily a fixed order

Although Maslow suggests that most people have these basic needs in about the order indicated he makes clear for some people there will be a reversal, for example:

- Self-esteem may seem to be more important than love to some people. This is the most common reversal of the hierarchy. People who seek love may try to put on a show of aggressive, confident behaviour. They are not really seeking self-esteem as an end in itself but for the sake of love needs.

- For some innately creative people the drive for creativity and self-actualisation may arise despite lack of satisfaction of more basic needs.

- Higher-level needs may be lost in some people who will continue to be satisfied at lower levels only: for example, a person who has experienced chronic unemployment.

- Some people who have been deprived of love in early childhood may experience the permanent loss of love needs.

- A need satisfied over a long period of time may be undervalued. For example, people who have never suffered from chronic hunger may tend to underestimate its effects, and regard food as rather unimportant. A higher-level need may assume greater importance than more basic needs.

- People with high ideals or values may become martyrs and give up everything else for the sake of their beliefs.

Applications to the work situation

Based on Maslow's theory, once lower-level needs have been satisfied giving more of the same does not provide motivation. Individuals advance up the hierarchy as each lower-level need becomes satisfied. Therefore, to provide motivation for a change in behaviour, the manager must direct attention to the next higher level of needs that seek satisfaction. There are however a number of difficulties in relating Maslow's theory to the work situation. These include the following:

- People do not necessarily satisfy their needs, especially higher-level needs, just through the work situation but through other areas of their life as well. The manager would need a complete understanding of people's private and social lives, not just their behaviour at work.

- Individual differences mean that people place different values on the same need. For example, some people prefer what they see as the comparative safety of working in a bureaucratic organisation to a more highly paid and higher status position, but with less job security, in a different organisation.

- Some rewards or outcomes at work satisfy more than one need. Higher salary or promotion, for example, can be applied to all levels of the hierarchy. Even for people within the same level of the hierarchy, the motivating factors will not be the same. There are many different ways in which people may seek satisfaction of, for example, their esteem needs.

- Maslow viewed satisfaction as the main motivational outcome of behaviour. But job satisfaction does not necessarily lead to improved work performance.

Useful basis for evaluation

Although Maslow did not originally intend the need hierarchy should be applied to the work situation, it remains popular as a theory of motivation. Despite criticisms and doubts about its limitations, the theory has had a significant impact on management approaches to motivation and the design of organisations to meet individual needs. It is a convenient framework for viewing the different needs and expectations that people have, where they are in the hierarchy, and the different motivators that might be applied to people at different levels. The need hierarchy model provides a useful base for the evaluation of motivation at work. For example, *Steers and Porter* suggest a list of general rewards and organisational factors used to satisfy different needs **(see Table 7.1)**.[16]

Saunders contends that despite the time that has elapsed, Maslow's theory remains watertight.

> When prehistoric man first took shelter in a cave and lit a fire, he was satisfying his lowest – physiological and safety – needs. When a Buddhist achieves a state of nirvana, she is satisfying the fifth and highest – self-actualisation . . . The cave these days might be a three-bedroom semi with garden and off-street parking, but the fact remains that once we've got enough to feed, clothe and house our families money is a low-level motivator for most people. The dash for cash is soon replaced by the desire for recognition, status and ultimately (although Maslow reckoned that a lot of us never get this far) the need to express yourself through your work.[17]

Table 7.1 Applying Maslow's needs hierarchy

General rewards		Organisational factors
• Growth • Creativity • Advancement	Self actual-isation	• Challenging job • Opportunities for creativity • Achievement in work • Advancement in the company
• Status • Self-respect • Recognition	Esteem	• Job title • High-status job • Feedback from the manager
• Love • Affection • Sense of connection	Social	• Friendly supervision • Professional links • Connected work group
• Health • Employment • Security	Safety	• Safe working conditions • Job benefits • Job security/satisfaction
• Air • Water • Food	Physiological	• Pay • Friendly work environment • Perks

Source: Steers, R. M. and Porter, L. W. *Motivation and Work Behaviour*, fifth edition, McGraw-Hill (1991), p. 35.

How would YOU relate the twelve human needs identified by Farren earlier in this chapter with Maslow's need hierarchy?

Which of Maslow's Hierarchy of Needs model do we see here?

Alderfer's modified need hierarchy model

A modified need hierarchy model has been presented by *Alderfer*.[18] This model condenses Maslow's five levels of need into only three levels based on the core needs of existence, relatedness and growth (ERG theory):

- **Existence needs** concerned with sustaining human existence and survival and cover physiological and safety needs of a material nature.
- **Relatedness needs** concerned with relationships to the social environment and cover love or belonging, affiliation and meaningful interpersonal relationships of a safety or esteem nature.
- **Growth needs** concerned with the development of potential and cover self-esteem and self-actualisation.

A continuum of needs

Alderfer suggests individuals progress through existence needs to relatedness needs to growth needs as the lower-level needs become satisfied. However, these needs are more a continuum than hierarchical levels. More than one need may be activated at the same time. Individuals may also progress down the hierarchy. There is a frustration–regression process. For example, if an individual is continually frustrated in attempting to satisfy growth needs, relatedness needs may reassume most importance. The lower-level needs become the main focus of the individual's efforts.

Unlike Maslow's theory, the results of Alderfer's work suggest lower-level needs do not have to be satisfied before a higher-level need emerges as a motivating influence. The results, however, do support the idea that lower-level needs decrease in strength as they become satisfied. ERG theory states an individual is motivated to satisfy one or more basic sets of needs. Therefore if a person's needs at a particular level are blocked, attention should be focused on the satisfaction of needs at the other levels. For example, if a subordinate's growth needs are blocked because the job does not allow sufficient opportunity for personal development, the manager should attempt to provide greater opportunities for the subordinate to satisfy existence and relatedness needs.

Nohria's four drives model of motivation

Another theory similar to Maslow is that by *Nohria, Groysberg and Lee.* Based on a survey of a wide range of Fortune 500 and other companies they formulated a model to increase work motivation based on four basic innate drives:

* The drive to **acquire** – scarce goods and intangibles such as social status;
* The drive to **bond** – connections with individuals and groups;
* The drive to **comprehend** – satisfy curiosity and master the world around us;
* The drive to **defend** – against external threats and to promote justice.

For each of these drives there is primary organisational lever that frontline managers can use in order to best meet these deep needs and drives. Reward systems that value good performance fulfil the drive to acquire. A collaborative and open culture fulfils the drive to bond. Meaningful and challenging jobs fulfil the need to comprehend. Transparent performance management systems fulfil the drive to defend. All four levers are important and failure to adequately fulfil any one drive will impact on satisfaction of other drives. However, using all four levers simultaneously can lead to a noticeable increase in motivation and organisational performance.[19]

Herzberg's two-factor theory

The link between motivation, job design and satisfaction was established by *Herzberg* who a critical used critical incident method in interviews with 203 accountants and engineers from different industries in the Pittsburgh area of America. Subjects were asked to describe times when they felt exceptionally good or exceptionally bad about their present job or any previous job. Responses to the interviews were generally consistent and revealed that there were two different sets of factors affecting motivation and work. **This led to the two-factor theory of motivation and job satisfaction.**[20]

Hygiene and motivating factors

One set of factors are those which, if absent, cause dissatisfaction. These factors are related to job context, they are concerned with job environment and extrinsic to the job itself. These factors are the **'hygiene' or 'maintenance' factors** ('hygiene' being used as analogous to the medical term meaning preventive and environmental). The other set of factors are those that serve to motivate the individual to superior effort and performance. These factors are related to job content of the work itself. They are the **'motivators' or growth factors**. The strength of these factors will affect feelings of satisfaction or no satisfaction, but not dissatisfaction. **The opposite of dissatisfaction is not satisfaction but, simply, no dissatisfaction (*see* Figure 7.5).**

Figure 7.5 Representation of Herzberg's two-factor theory

Herzberg emphasises that hygiene factors are not a 'second-class citizen system'. They are as important as the motivators, but for different reasons. Hygiene factors are necessary to avoid unpleasantness at work and to deny unfair treatment. 'Management should never deny people proper treatment at work.' To motivate workers to give of their best, the manager must give proper attention to the motivators or growth factors. The motivators relate to what people are allowed to do and the quality of human experience at work. They are the variables which actually motivate people.

Evaluation of Herzberg's work

Herzberg's theory is a source of frequent debate. There are two common general criticisms of Herzberg's theory. One is the theory has only limited application to largely unskilled jobs or whose work is uninteresting, repetitive and monotonous, and limited in scope. Yet these are the people who often present management with the biggest problem of motivation. Some workers do not seem greatly interested in the job content of their work or with the motivators or growth factors. A second, general criticism concerns the critical incident methodology. People are more likely to attribute satisfying incidents at work, the motivators, as a favourable reflection on their own performance. The dissatisfying incidents, the hygiene factors, are more likely to be attributed to external influences and the efforts of other people.

Despite such criticisms, there is still evidence of support for the continuing relevance of the theory. For example, according to *Crainer and Dearlove,* Herzberg's work has a considerable effect on rewards and remuneration packages offered by organisations and the emphasis on self-development, career management and self-managed learning can be seen as having evolved from Herzberg's insights.[21]

Whatever the validity of the two-factor theory, much of the criticism is with the benefit of hindsight, and Herzberg did at least attempt an empirical approach to the study of motivation at work and job satisfaction. Furthermore, his work has drawn attention to the importance of job design in the 'quality of work life'. The work of Herzberg indicates it is more likely that good performance leads to job satisfaction rather than the reverse.

To what extent would YOU agree that Herzberg's two-factor theory still resonates strongly for an understanding of motivation and behaviour at work today?

McClelland's achievement motivation theory

McClelland's work originated from investigations into the relationship between hunger needs and the extent to which imagery of food dominated thought processes. From subsequent research McClelland identified four main arousal-based, and socially developed, motives:

- the **Achievement** motive;
- the **Power** motive;
- the **Affiliative** motive;
- the **Avoidance** motive.[22]

The relative intensity of these motives varies between individuals and also tends to vary between different occupations. Managers appear to be higher in achievement motivation than in affiliation motivation. McClelland saw the achievement need (n-Ach) as the most critical for the country's economic growth and success. The need to achieve is linked to entrepreneurial spirit and the development of available resources.

Research studies by McClelland use a series of projective 'tests' – Thematic Apperception Tests (TATs) – to gauge an individual's motivation. Individuals are shown a number of pictures in which some activity is depicted. They are asked to look briefly (10–15 seconds) at the pictures and then describe what they think is happening, what people in the picture are thinking and what events have led to the situation depicted.[23] The descriptions are used as a basis for analysing the strength of the individual's motives.

Characteristics of achievement motivation

Some individuals rate very highly in achievement motivation. They are challenged by opportunities and work hard to achieve a goal. Money is not an incentive but may serve as a means of giving feedback on performance. High achievers seem unlikely to remain long with an organisation that does not pay them well for good performance. Money may seem to be important to high achievers, but they value it more as symbolising successful task performance and goal achievement.

From empirical research McClelland identified four characteristics of people with a strong achievement need (n-Ach):

- **Moderate task difficulty and goals as an achievement incentive.** If the task is too difficult or too risky, it would reduce chances of success and gaining need satisfaction. If the course of action is too easy or too safe, there is little challenge in accomplishing the task and little satisfaction from success.

- **Personal responsibility for performance.** They like to attain success through the focus of their own abilities and efforts rather than by teamwork or chance factors outside their control. Personal satisfaction is derived from the accomplishment of the task and recognition need not come from other people.

- **Need for clear and unambiguous feedback on how well they are performing.** A knowledge of results within a reasonable time is necessary for self-evaluation. Feedback enables them to determine success or failure in the accomplishment of their goals and to derive satisfaction from their activities.

- **More innovative.** As they always seek moderately challenging tasks they tend always to be moving on to something a little more challenging. In seeking short cuts, they are more likely to cheat. There is a constant search for variety and for information to find new ways of doing things. They are more restless, avoid routine and also tend to travel more.

McClelland and Burnham have also suggested that as effective managers need to be successful leaders and to influence other people, they should possess a high need for power.[24] However, the effective manager also scores high on inhibition. Power is directed more towards the organisation and concern for group goals and is exercised on behalf of other people. This is 'socialised' power. It is distinguished from 'personalised' power that is characterised by satisfaction from exercising dominance over other people, and personal aggrandisement.

What do YOU believe is the most practical value of process theories for an understanding of work motivation in twenty-first century organisations?

Process theories of motivation

Process theories attempt to identify the relationships among dynamic variables that make up motivation and actions required to influence behaviour. These theories are concerned more with the actual process of motivation and how behaviour is initiated, directed and sustained. Many of the theories cannot be linked to a single writer, but major approaches and leading writers under this heading include:

- Expectancy theory – VictorVroom;
- Equity theory – Stacy Adams;
- Goal theory – Edwin Locke.

A more recent approach to the study of motivation is Attribution theory. Attribution is the process by which people interpret the perceived causes of behaviour. **Attribution theory was discussed in Chapter 6.**

Expectancy theory of motivation

The underlying basis of **expectancy theory** is that people are influenced by the expected results of their actions. Motivation is a function of the relationship between:

1. effort expended and perceived level of performance; and
2. expectation that rewards (desired outcomes) will be related to performance.

There must also be:

3. expectation that rewards (desired outcomes) will be expectation that rewards (desired outcomes) are available.

These relationships determine the strength of the 'motivational link' **(*see* Figure 7.6).** Performance depends upon the perceived expectation regarding effort expended and achieving the desired outcome. For example, desire for promotion will result in high performance only if the person believes there is a strong possibility this will lead to promotion. If, however, the person believes promotion to be based solely on age and length of service, there is no motivation to achieve high performance. A person's behaviour reflects a conscious choice between the comparative evaluation of alternative behaviours. **The choice of behaviour is based on the expectancy of the most favourable consequences.**

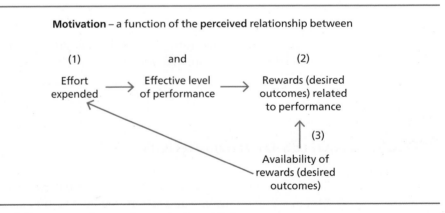

Figure 7.6 Expectancy theory: the motivational link

Vroom's expectancy theory

Vroom was the first person to propose an expectancy theory aimed specifically at work motivation.[25] His model is based on three key variables: **valence, instrumentality** and **expectancy** (VIE theory or expectancy/valence theory). The theory is founded on the idea that people prefer certain outcomes from their behaviour over others. They anticipate feelings of satisfaction should the preferred outcome be achieved.

- **Valence** – attractiveness of, or preference for, a particular outcome to the individual and its anticipated satisfaction. Valences of certain outcomes may be derived in their own right, but more usually derived from other outcomes to which they are expected to lead. An obvious example is money. Some people may see money as having an intrinsic worth and derive satisfaction from the actual accumulation of wealth. Most people, however, see money in terms of the many satisfying outcomes to which it can lead.

- **Instrumentality** – from which the valence of outcomes is derived. This leads to a distinction between first-level outcomes and second-level outcomes. First-level outcomes are performance-related. Some people may seek to perform well as part of their work ethic and without thinking about the expected consequences of their actions. Usually, however, performance outcomes acquire valence because of the expectation that they will lead to other outcomes as an anticipated source of satisfaction – second-level outcomes. Second-level outcomes are need-related. Many need-related outcomes are dependent upon actual performance rather than effort expended. People generally receive rewards for what they have achieved rather than for effort alone or through trying hard.

- **Expectancy** – when a person chooses between alternative behaviours which have uncertain outcomes, the choice is affected not only by the preference for a particular outcome but also the probability that the outcome will be achieved. This is expectancy. People develop a perception of the degree of probability that choice of a particular action will actually lead to the desired outcome. Expectancy relates effort expended to the achievement of first-level outcomes. Its value ranges between 0, indicating zero probability and 1, indicating certainty that an action will result in the outcome.

On the basis of Vroom's expectancy theory, it is possible to depict a general model of behaviour (*see* **Figure 7.7**).

Motivational force

The combination of valence and expectancy determines the person's motivation for a given form of behaviour. This is the **motivational force.** Expressed as an equation, motivation (*M*) is the sum of the products of the valences of all outcomes (*V*), times the strength of expectancies that action will result in achieving these outcomes (*E*). Therefore, if either, or both, valence or expectancy is zero, then motivation is zero. The choice between alternative behaviours is indicated by the highest attractiveness score.

$$M = \sum^{n} E \cdot V$$

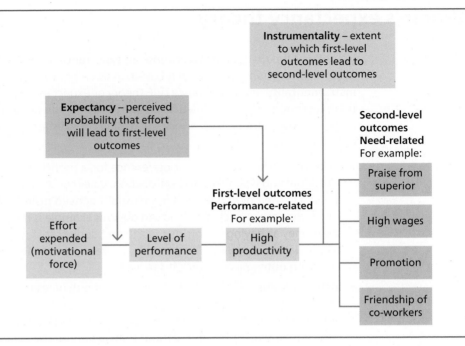

Figure 7.7 Basic model of expectancy theory

There are likely to be a number of outcomes expected for a given action. Therefore, the measure of $E \cdot V$ is summed across the total number of possible outcomes to arrive at a single figure indicating the attractiveness for the contemplated choice of behaviour.

Implications of expectancy theory

There are a number of versions of expectancy theory including work by Porter and Lawler.[26] The main elements tend to be similar and suggests development of a generally accepted approach. Expectancy models are not always easy to understand, or to apply. There are many variables which affect behaviour at work. A problem can arise in attempting to include a large number of variables or in identifying those variables which are most appropriate in particular situations.

Expectancy theory does, however, draw attention to the complexities of work motivation and provides further information in helping to explain the nature of behaviour. Expectancy theory indicates that managers should give attention to a number of factors, including the following:

- Establishing clear procedures for the evaluation of individual levels of performance and perceived relationships between effort–performance and rewards.
- Intervening variables such as abilities and traits, role perceptions, organisational procedures and support facilities, which, although not necessarily direct motivational factors, may still affect performance.
- Minimising undesirable outcomes which may result from a high level of performance, such as industrial accidents or sanctions from co-workers, or to result despite a high level of performance, such as short-time working or layoffs.

Strategic and total rewards

The value of rewards is an important aspect of expectancy theories of motivation. The CIPD distinguish between strategic rewards and total rewards.

Strategic reward is based on the design and implementation of long-term policies and practices to closely support and advance business or organisational objectives as well as employee aspirations. The concept of total reward encompasses all aspects of work that are valued by employees, including elements such as learning and development opportunities and/or an attractive working environment, in addition to the wider pay and benefits package.[27]

The need to maintain a strategic approach to motivation, development and performance of employees has resulted in many organisations giving greater attention to a more comprehensive approach of total rewards including attention to both extrinsic and intrinsic rewards **(discussed earlier in this chapter).** However, CIPD cautions some rewards are easier to provide than others.

How would YOU attempt to justify potential benefits of expectancy theory in modern work organisations to a sceptical manager or supervisor?

Equity theory of motivation

One of the major variables of satisfaction in expectancy theory is perceived available of rewards. This leads to consideration of another process theory of motivation – **equity theory**. Applied to the work situation, equity theory is usually associated with the work of *Adams*.[28] Equity theory focuses on people's feelings of how fairly they have been treated in comparison with the treatment received by others. It is based on social exchange theory **(discussed in Chapter 1).**

Social relationships involve an exchange process. For example, a person may expect promotion as an outcome of a high level of contribution (input) in helping to achieve an important organisational objective. People also compare their own position with that of others. They determine the perceived equity of their own position. Most exchanges involve a number of inputs and outcomes. According to equity theory, people place a weighting on these various inputs and outcomes according to how they perceive their importance. When there is an unequal comparison of ratios the person experiences a sense of inequity.

Behaviour as a consequence of inequity

A feeling of inequity causes tension, which is an unpleasant experience. It motivates the person to remove or to reduce the level of tension and perceived inequity. The magnitude of perceived inequity determines the level of tension and strength of motivation. Adams identifies six broad types of possible behaviour as consequences of inequity **(see Figure 7.8).**

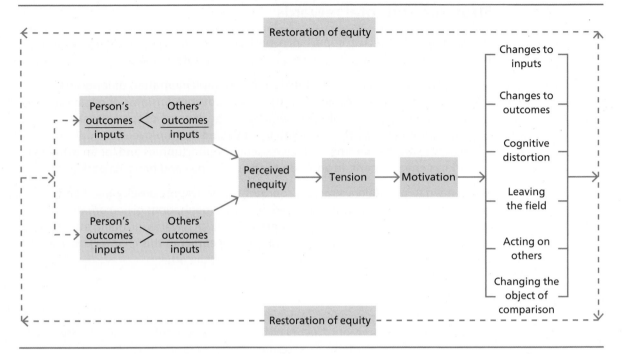

Figure 7.8 An illustration of Adams' equity theory of motivation

- **Changes to inputs** – increasing or decreasing level of inputs, for example through the amount or quality of work, absenteeism, or working additional hours without pay.
- **Changes to outcomes** – attempting to change outcomes such as pay, working conditions, status and recognition, without changes to inputs.
- **Cognitive distortion** – distorting, cognitively, inputs or outcomes to achieve the same results. Attempting to distort the utility of facts, for example the belief about how hard really working, the relevance of a particular qualification, or what they can or cannot obtain with a given level of pay.
- **Leaving the field** – trying to find a new situation with a more favourable balance, for example by absenteeism, request for a transfer, resigning from a job or from the organisation altogether.
- **Acting on others** – attempting to bring about changes in others, for example to lower their inputs or accept greater outcomes. The person may cognitively distort the inputs and outcomes of others, or alternatively try to force others to leave the field.
- **Changing the object of comparison** – changing the reference group with whom comparison is made. For example, where another person with a previously similar ratio of outcomes–inputs receives greater outcomes without any apparent increase in contribution, that other person may be perceived as now belonging to a different level in the organisation structure.

Managerial control

The manager may seek to remove or reduce tension and perceived inequity among staff by influencing these types of behaviour – for example attempting to change a person's inputs or encouraging a different object of comparison. People measure and compare their total inputs and outcomes so, for example, a working parent may prefer greater flexibility in working hours in return for lower monetary rewards. However, there are likely to be only two courses of action under the direct control of the manager. Outcomes can be changed by, for example, increased pay, additional perks or improved working conditions; or by instigating a person leaving the field through transfer, resignation or, as an extreme measure, dismissal. It is important to remember that equity theory is about the **perceived** ratio of inputs to outputs and these perceptions may not reflect the reality of the situation.

The ultimatum game

The **ultimatum game** is an economic behavioural game that can arguably be related to the concept of equity theory.[29] Two participants, A and B, are given the opportunity to split a given sum of money between them. The game is played anonymously and once only. One person (A) has to decide to make a one-time, take-it-or-leave-it, offer to B (ultimatum). If the other person (B) agrees to the division, both A and B keep their share of the money. However, if the offer is rejected neither person receives anything. Experiments indicate that if A offers around 50 per cent of the money then B will accept the offer. But if A offers a noticeably lesser amount than 50 per cent, B will typically refuse the offer in which case neither participant receives anything. One might expect B to accept because even a lesser amount, whatever the offer, is better than nothing.

The conclusion appears to be that people do not like to be taken advantage of, and in certain circumstances fairness in treatment is more important than money at work. Can you see how this might be related to perceptions of equity theory? Viewers of the ITV1 television quiz programme *Divided,* in which contestants have to agree how to divide a cash prize, may see a similarity with the ultimatum game.

Goal theory

Another theory usually considered under the heading of motivation to work is **goal theory**, or the theory of goal-setting **(see Figure 7.9).** This theory is based mainly on the work of *Locke*.[30] The basic premise is that people's goals or intentions play an important part in determining behaviour. Locke accepts the importance of perceived value, as indicated in expectancy theories of motivation, and suggests that these values give rise to the experience of emotions and desires. Goals direct work behaviour and performance and lead to certain consequences or feedback. People strive to achieve goals in order to satisfy their emotions and desires. Locke subsequently pointed out that 'goal-setting is more appropriately viewed as a motivational technique rather than as a formal theory of motivation'.[31]

Goal-setting and performance

The combination of **goal difficulty** –the extent to which it is challenging and demanding and the **extent of the person's commitment** regulates the level of effort expended. People with specific quantitative goals, such as a defined level of performance or a given deadline for completion of a task, will perform better than

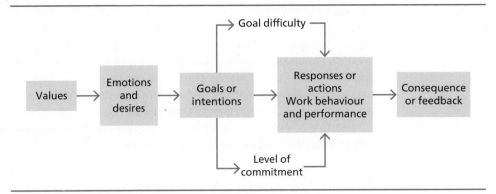

Figure 7.9 An illustration of Locke's theory of goal-setting

people with no set goal or only a vague goal such as 'do the best you can'. People who have difficult goals will perform better than people with easier goals.

Gratton refers to 'stretch goals' which are ambitious, highly targeted opportunities for breakthrough improvements in performance. These goals should stem from critical success indicators and come from deep discussions within the company, and from collaboration within and across task forces, and lead to the development of activities and tactics to achieve the goals.[32] People lacking positive motivation at work may also help gain improved results and a better sense of achievement by setting themselves specific goals and identifying tasks directly related to their work and measurable targets of time and performance.

Practical implications for the manager

Goal theory has a number of practical implications for the manager:

- Individuals lacking in motivation often do not have clear goals. Specific performance goals should systematically be identified and set in order to direct behaviour and maintain motivation.

- Goals should be set at a challenging but realistic level. Difficult goals lead to higher performance. However, if goals are set at too high a level or are regarded as impossible to achieve, this can lead to stress and performance will suffer, especially over a longer period.

- Complete, accurate and timely feedback and knowledge of results is usually associated with high performance. Feedback provides a means of checking progress on goal attainment and forms the basis for any revision of goals.

- Goals can be determined either by a superior or by individuals themselves. Goals set by other people are more likely to be accepted when there is participation. Employee participation in the setting of goals may lead to higher performance.

However it is viewed, the theory of goal-setting provides a useful approach to work motivation and performance. And *Hannagan* goes so far as to suggest: 'At present goal-setting is one of the most influential theories of work motivation applicable to all cultures.'[33]

A concept map of motivation and work is set out in Figure 7.10.

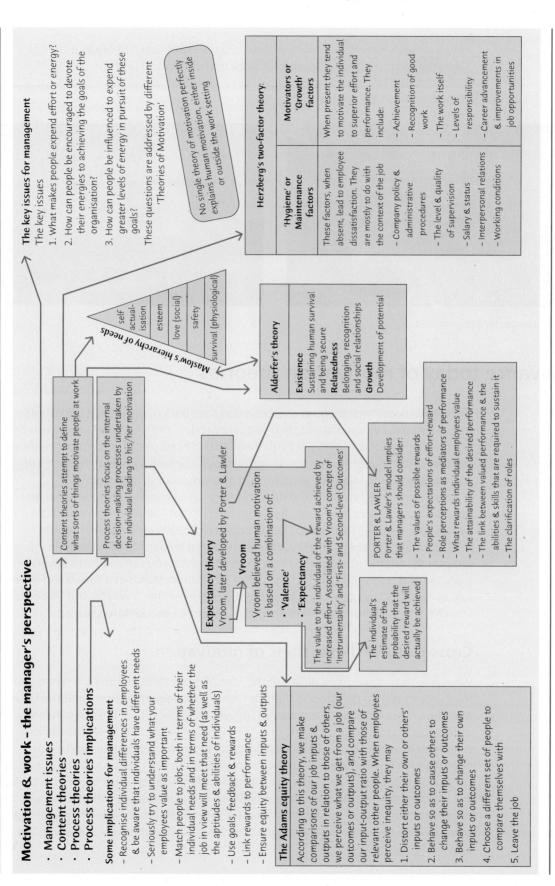

Figure 7.10 Motivation and work – the manager's perspective

Source: Copyright © 2011 The Virtual Learning Materials Workshop. Reproduced with permission.

How strongly can YOU identify with Equity theory or Goal theory as practical approaches to an understanding of work motivation and performance?

Goals are important to progress

Relevance today of motivation theories

Given that most major theories of motivation date back many years it is inevitable that questions are raised about their relevance today. The *Chartered Management Institute* suggest that looking at both theories and examples of good practice should stimulate your thoughts, give you insights into the behaviour and attitudes of those you work with, and initial ideas on how to motivate your own people.[34]

Whatever the relevance of the different theories of motivation, to what extent do individuals have control over their own level of motivation or how much is dependent upon the leadership they encounter? *Adair* reassesses the theories of Maslow and Herzberg in terms of action-centred leadership **(discussed in Chapter 9).** Adair also argues that the extent to which you can motivate anyone else is limited and refers to the fifty–fifty rule of motivation, that is as a rough and ready rule of thumb 50 per cent of motivation comes from within a person and 50 per cent from his or her environment, especially the leadership encountered there.[35]

Cross-cultural dimensions of motivation

Whatever the popularity of different theories of motivation, doubts are raised about their universality on the ground that they have not adequately addressed the factor of culture.[36] Are theories of motivation universally applicable or are there meaningful differences in motivation at work, or in life more generally, in different societies? A number of writers have questioned whether motivational theories and models originating in one culture are amenable to transference to other parts of the world. For example, *Francesco and Gold* stress systems of motivation must be flexible to take into account the meaning of work and relative value of rewards with the cultures the organisation operates. The authors devote a substantial proportion of a discussion of motivation to examining the extent to which American motivation theories are applicable outside the United States.[37]

One criticism of content theories of motivation centres on relative applicability in different circumstances, and the suggestion of variations across cultures falls within this line of reasoning. However, perhaps less obviously, process theories of motivation have also been criticised for being culture-bound. As they focus on process rather than content, such theories may appear to be more applicable in diverse cultural contexts. Nonetheless it has been suggested that process theories of motivation contain certain inbuilt assumptions that are themselves culturally derived.

Adler reminds us that expectancy models of motivation assume that individuals believe that they can, to some extent, control their environment and influence their fate. If, as in the cases of more fatalistic cultures such as China, people do not have the same sense of internal attribution, the expectancy model may have less force and therefore less applicability. When Adams's equity theory is applied across the world, differences in interpretation have been recorded.[38]

Organisational behaviour modification

Another possible approach to motivation is that of **organisational behaviour modification (OBMod)**. This is the application of learning principles to influence organisational behaviour. In particular it can be seen as a form of Skinner's operant conditioning, or reinforcement theory **(discussed in Chapter 5).** Reinforcement is a feature of the behaviourism approach and shaped by environmental influences. Reward for a particular form of behaviour is likely to result in the reinforcement of that behaviour. A negative outcome or lack of acknowledgement for the behaviour is likely to mean the behaviour will stop. *Luthans and Kreitner* suggest that OBMod 'represents a merging of behavioural learning theory on the one hand and organizational behaviour theory on the other'.[39]

According to Luthans and Kreitner, a major premise of OBMod is that positive consequence management is much more effective than negative consequence management. Organisations that encourage the members to learn and undertake desired behaviours and not to undertake undesired behaviours follow five main steps:

1 **Identify** the observable, objective and measurable behaviours relevant to the desired organisational performance.

2 **Measure** the frequency with which those behaviours actually occur under normal conditions. Provide baseline performance data as a point of reference to compare with changes in step 5.

3 **Determine** the antecedents of the behaviours, the reinforcements to encourage patterns of behaviour and the consequences that follow from those behaviours.

4 **Develop** an intervention strategy for change in order to strengthen desirable behaviours and weaken undesirable behaviours, through the use of operant conditioning and reinforcement theory including punishment if necessary.

5 **Measure and evaluate** systematically (using the same measure as in step 2) the extent to which the frequency of desired behaviours and undesired behaviours have changed, and improvements in organisational performance.

Applications of OBMod

To what extent can OBMod be applied effectively to improve motivation and performance in work organisations? OBMod works best for behaviours that are specific, objective and countable. There have been a number of studies in the United States that indicate positive results in behaviours that improved performance in reducing errors, attendance and punctuality, health and safety and customer service.[40]

In a study of a Russian textile factory, following the OBMod approach, workers were subjected to two forms of intervention – extrinsic rewards and social rewards. The extrinsic rewards provided valued American products, such as clothing, music tapes and hard-to-get foods, for improved performance. Social rewards such as attention, recognition and praise from supervisors were for performing specified actions such as checking looms, undertaking repairs and helping others. Both extrinsic and social interventions led to highly significant increases in performance. This contrasted with a previous participative job design approach that involved asking workers for ideas for improving performance and enriching their jobs that did not work. Researchers suggest cultural issues and the workers' past experiences may explain the failure of the participative intervention strategy, and that the OBMod approach has wider application.[41]

Although there appear to be a number of supporters in America, in the UK it is a controversial concept. Critics claim that OBMod is not an accepted theory of motivation and that there are too many individual differences for people to be treated as subjects of operant conditioning. OBMod is concerned only with shaping. There is the added criticism of a 'Big Brother' approach with excessive management manipulation and control over employees, more in line with scientific management. This in turn could also have the added disadvantage of discouraging individual initiative and adaptability to change circumstances. Workers subject to OBMod programmes may tend to ignore those aspects of voluntary behaviours, such as social support or assistance to colleagues that are not subject to direct reward and reinforcement.

Motivation of knowledge workers

Recent advantages in telecommunications and in scientific and technological knowledge have led to greater emphasis on the knowledge and expertise of staff, and importance of creativity. *Tampoe* suggests that at the core of the new industrial trend are the 'knowledge workers' – those employees who apply their theoretical and practical understanding of a specific area of knowledge to produce outcomes of a commercial, social or personal value. Performance of knowledge workers should be judged on both the cleverness of ideas and the utility and commercial value of their applied knowledge. Creativity is necessary and needs to be encouraged but should be bounded by commercial realism. This presents management with a new challenge of how to motivate the knowledge workers.[42]

Tampoe suggests that the personal motivation of knowledge workers is based on the value they place on the rewards they expect to earn at work. In addition to the individual's own motivation, the performance of knowledge workers is dependent upon four key characteristics (*see* **Figure 7.11**):

- task competence;
- peer and management support;

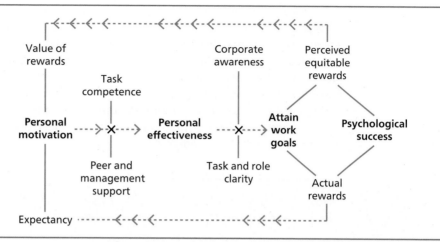

Figure 7.11 Motivating knowledge workers
Source: Tampoe, M. 'Knowledge Workers: The New Management Challenge', *Professional Manager*, Institute of Management, November 1994, p. 13. Reproduced with permission from Chartered Management Institute.

- task and role clarity; and
- corporate awareness.

The challenge to management is to ensure the effectiveness of the four key variables and to recognise the need for staff to supervise and manage themselves and the wider rewards expected by knowledge workers.

Climate of creativity

Whitmore suggests of course pay and conditions are important but in order to create a climate for creativity among employees, recognition must be given to the importance of two human needs that rise above all others and exist independent of race, creed and culture. Need for self-belief and the development of emotional intelligence; and the ever-present need that every human being has for a sense of meaning and purpose in their lives.[43]

Matson and Prusak of management consultants McKinsey & Company report that despite the high stakes in knowledge workers there is lack of understanding of what it takes to bolster their productivity. This lack of clarity is partly because knowledge work involves more diverse and amorphous tasks than do production or clerical positions, and partly because performance metrics are hard to come by in knowledge work. Knowledge workers spend half their time on interactions and in order to improve their productivity, companies should explore the barriers that impede these interactions:

- **Physical and technical** – including geographical distance, different time zones, lack of effective tools;
- **Social or cultural** – including rigid hierarchies or ineffective incentives;
- **Contextual** – the sharing and translating knowledge from colleagues in different fields;
- **Time** – or rather the perceived lack of time.[44]

Goffee and Jones suggest future prosperity rests with organisations that make their living from the knowledge they themselves are able to develop. Clever people are highly talented individuals with the potential to create disproportionate amounts of value from the resources that the organisation makes available to them. Keeping and leading the clever people who inhabit these organisations becomes a critical challenge.

Clever people do not like to be led or told what to do and are at their most productive when faced with really hard questions. Tell them something is not possible and they will be highly motivated to prove you wrong. They must be given enough space to try out new things and given recognition for their work. Goffee and Jones suggest that clever people can be difficult to lead and have developed new rules to help guide their leaders.[45]

How do YOU react to the word 'clever'? To what extent would you argue that knowledge workers are not necessarily clever?

Job satisfaction

Job satisfaction is complex and multifaceted, and can mean different things to different people. It is more of an attitude, an internal state and could for example be associated with a personal feeling of achievement, either quantitative or qualitative. There is undoubtedly an integral relationship between motivation, satisfaction and performance but the exact nature of this relationship is an issue of continuing debate. It is difficult to isolate job satisfaction as a single concept. For example Herzberg's two-factor theory discussed earlier is arguably more a theory of job satisfaction. Although the level of job satisfaction may well affect strength of motivation, this is not always the case. One view, associated with the early human relations approach, **discussed in Chapter 11**, is that satisfaction leads to performance. An alternative view is that performance leads to satisfaction.

> There is always a choice about the way you do your work, even if there is not a choice about the work itself. You always have a choice about the attitude you bring to the job.
>
> World famous Pike Place Fish Market, Seattle[46]

Dimensions of job satisfaction

There is doubt whether job satisfaction consists of a single dimension or a number of separate dimensions. Some workers may be satisfied with certain aspects of their work and dissatisfied with other aspects. The level of job satisfaction is affected by a wide range of variables relating to individual, social, cultural, organisational and environmental factors.

- **Individual factors** include personality, education and qualifications, intelligence and abilities, age, marital status, orientation to work.
- **Social factors** include relationships with co-workers, group working and norms, opportunities for interaction, informal organisation.
- **Cultural factors** include ethnicity, underlying attitudes, beliefs and values.

- **Organisational factors** include nature and size, formal structure, HR policies and procedures, nature of the work, technology and work organisation, styles of leadership, management systems, working conditions.
- **Environmental factors** include economic, social, technical and governmental influences.

These different factors all affect the job satisfaction of certain individuals in a given set of circumstances but not necessarily in others. For example in times of economic depression and fears of high unemployment, job security is likely to be a prominent concern. The FreshMinds survey **discussed in Chapter 2,** suggests that when it comes to job satisfaction it pays to be older. Apparently 100 per cent of older baby boomers (born between 1946 and 1963) are satisfied with their job, but only 66 per cent of Generation Y (typified by travel first, then a career) feel the same way. And Generation Y want more at work such as gym membership and sabbaticals.[47]

An increasingly important issue affecting job satisfaction and efficiency is the nature of the work environment. For example, *Reeves* draws attention to the importance of good interpersonal relations.

> **Over the years, a number of different surveys suggest good interpersonal relationships with colleagues is more important to enjoying your work than a high salary. In 2014, a Cabinet Office survey of life satisfaction of 274 different occupations found members of the clergy, farmers, fitness instructors, school secretaries, dental nurses and farm workers among those with modest salaries but high personal job satisfaction.[48]**

Meaningful work

Despite the uncertain economic environment, the CIPD reports a continuing increase in net job satisfaction up to 64% satisfied and 16% dissatisfied. Employees in the public sector are significantly more likely to be satisfied with their jobs (73%) than employees in the private sector (61%). Job satisfaction in the public sector has risen to levels not seen in the past eight years.[49] Employee job satisfaction by sector is shown in **Table 7.2**.

Table 7.2 Employee job satisfaction, percentage breakdown by sector (%)

	Overall	Private	Public	Voluntary
Very satisfied	21	21	20	22
Satisfied	43	41	52	45
Neither satisfied nor dissatisfied	20	22	14	14
Dissatisfied	12	12	12	15
Very dissatisfied	4	5	1	4
Don't know	0	0	–	–
Base: 2,224				

Source: CIPD Employee Outlook, Spring 2017, p. 12.

The idea that every employee is able to find meaningful work is challenged by *Chamorro-Premuzic* who suggests the notion is as unrealistic as everybody having an interesting or well-paid job. In recent years organisations have made efforts to make their jobs appear more appealing as compensation for the inability to satisfy other psychological needs. Unfortunately after a few months employee enthusiasm levels tend to decline. When it comes to meaning, Chamorro-Premuzic suggests it might be better for organisations to under-promise but over-deliver.[50]

What do YOU think are the main reasons for higher levels of job satisfaction in the public sector compared with the private sector? How far does this influence your likely career choice?

Comprehensive model of job enrichment

Attempts to improve intrinsic motivation must not only include considerations of job characteristics but also take account of individual differences and attributes, and people's orientation to work. A popular and comprehensive model of job enrichment has been developed by *Hackman and Oldham* (*see* **Figure 7.12**).[51] The model views job enrichment in terms of increasing five core job dimensions: skill variety, task identity, task significance, autonomy and feedback.

Five core dimensions

The five core job dimensions can be summarised as follows:

- **skill variety** – extent to which a job entails different activities and involves a range of skills and talents;
- **task identity** – extent to which a job involves completion of a whole piece of work with a visible outcome;
- **task significance** – extent to which a job has a meaningful impact on other people, either inside or outside the organisation;

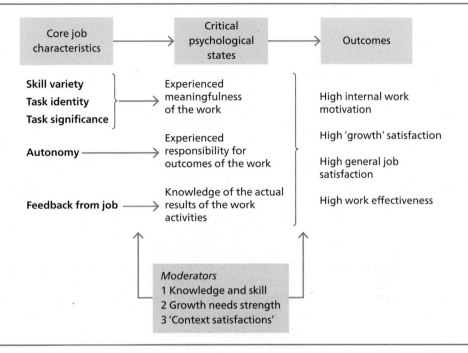

Figure 7.12 A job characteristics model of work motivation
Source: J. Richard Hackman and Greg R. Oldham, Work Redesign, 1st Ed. © 1980. Reprinted and Electronically reproduced by permission of Pearson Education, Inc. New York

- **autonomy** – extent to which a job provides freedom, independence and discretion in planning the work and determining how to undertake it;
- **feedback** – extent to which work activities result in direct and clear information on the effectiveness of job performance.

The extent of these core job dimensions creates three critical psychological states based on the individual's perception of:

- experienced value and meaningfulness of the work;
- experienced personal responsibility for the outcomes of the work; and
- clear knowledge of actual results of work activities and level of performance.

An example of a job with little enrichment could be that of a production assembly line worker or a kitchen porter, where all five core characteristics are likely to score low. An example of an enriched job could be that of a parish priest who draws upon a wide range of social skills and talents, who can usually identify with the whole task and whose job has clear and important meaning and significance. There is a very high level of autonomy and likely to be direct and clear feedback.

Job Diagnostic Survey: motivating potential score

From these five core job dimensions, Hackman and Oldham have developed an equation which gives a single index of a person's job profile. By answering a questionnaire – the Job Diagnostic Survey (JDS) – and by giving a score (between 1 and 7) to each job dimension, the person can calculate an overall measure of job enrichment, called the motivating potential score (MPS).

Examples of questions from the JDS are:

- How much variety is there in your job?
- To what extent does your job involve doing a whole and identifiable piece of work?
- In general, how significant or important is your job?
- How much autonomy is there in your job?
- To what extent does doing the job itself provide you with information about your work performance?

$$MPS = \frac{\{Skill\ variety\ +\ Task\ identity\ +\ Task\ significance\}}{3} \times Autonomy \times Feedback$$

The first three job dimensions of skill variety, task identity and task significance are averaged, since it is the combination of these dimensions which contributes to experienced meaningfulness of work. The remaining two job dimensions, autonomy and feedback, stand on their own. Since scores for skill variety, task identity and task significance are additive, this means that the absence of one dimension can be partially offset by the presence of the other dimensions. However, if either autonomy or feedback is absent then, because of the multiplicative relationship, the MPS would be zero. The job would offer no potential to motivate the person.

Critical Thinking Zone

Reflections on Motivating Knowledge Workers

In this zone, we critically evaluate the concept of the 'knowledge worker' and examine the ways in which they can be motivated to create, share and apply their specialist knowledge and expertise, both in and outside the organisation.

In 1999, Peter Drucker[52] predicted that 'the most valuable asset of a 21st-century institution (whether business or non-business) will be its knowledge workers and their productivity' (p. 79). Twenty years later, his prediction has become a reality. With the advent of the knowledge economy, not only has the volume of knowledge work in organisations intensified, the number of knowledge workers has increased, leading to an emphasis and reliance on the utilisation of theoretical, specialised knowledge that is hard to imitate by competitors.[53,54]

The Nature of Knowledge Work

Unlike manual 'blue collar' workers, knowledge 'gold collar' workers 'own the means of production'[52] (p. 87). Their work can be classed as primarily creative, intellectual and non-routine in nature. Importantly, the work also involves the creation and utilisation of theoretical/abstract knowledge,[53] which Dewhurst et al.[54] suggest is strategically significant to the organisation. Knowledge work encompasses a wide sphere of occupations, including engineering, medicine, teaching, consulting and law. Drucker[55] and Davenport[56] advocate that a major distinguishing feature of this work is the level of complexity or 'complicatedness' involved in doing the job. On this note, Reich[57] related knowledge workers to 'symbolic analysts', who identify, solve and negotiate/broker problems through the manipulation of symbols and utilisation of codified bodies of knowledge, such as reports, blueprints and other explicit documents. One could argue that such depictions of knowledge work and knowledge workers exclude a significant part of the workforce, who, in varying degrees, use tacit knowledge and knowing to do their jobs. Polanyi[58] posited that all knowledge has tacit/personal components, so in this respect, we could contend that all work is knowledge work, as we all use some type of knowledge to perform work tasks, whether it is highly intellectual, theoretical/abstract or contextual/practical.[53]

Motivating Knowledge Workers

Due to the nature of knowledge work and the intangible, tacitness of knowledge (see Chapter 5: Critical Thinking Zone: Reflections on Knowledge Management[59,60]), managing and motivating knowledge workers can be inherently problematic.[61] According to Bigliardi et al.[62] and Cetindamar et al.[63] they prefer to work in an environment that enables them to freely collaborate, both functionally and cross-functionally, with other experts, inside and outside the organisation. Part of this collaboration involves creating, sharing and applying specialist knowledge, which requires an element of co-location, trust, openness and collegiality.[64] Knowledge workers are perceived to be experts in their field and possess a stock of knowledge that is a rare, valuable, inimitable and non-substitutable strategic asset.[65,66] As such, they possess a degree of 'expert power' and thus prefer to work autonomously, without close supervision or direct control.[64]

Newell et al.[67] profess that this is a vitally important aspect of knowledge work. They suggest that problem-solving and creativity demand autonomy and knowledge workers should be motivated and encouraged to make the decisions on how they establish, plan, organise, coordinate and control their work. Importantly, Newell et al. caveat that the organisation is not in a position to deny knowledge workers their autonomy because, in line with Drucker's advocacy, they own the means of production and, ostensibly, have the power to share or hoard their specialist knowledge.[68] Newell et al. and Bigliardi et al. argue that management's primary role therefore is to provide an enabling context and culture that is conducive to knowledge work in all its forms.

Motivating Knowledge Workers through the Psychological Contract

Thite[69] (p. 29) contends that organisations can attract and retain top knowledge worker talent by forming a psychological contract with them that 'motivate them to generate and share knowledge in return for nurturing and nourishing their professional skills.' Given that managers cannot, as espoused, control how they work, entering into a relational psychological contract[70] may generate mutual loyalty, trust and stability and encourage reciprocity in terms of both parties' commitment to each other and the knowledge worker's emotional and attitudinal commitment to the organisation (see Chapter 1: Critical Thinking Zone: Reflections on the Psychological Contract). Carleton[71] notes that the knowledge worker–managerial relationship is crucial, insofar as it is the organisation's responsibility to provide a supportive culture and environment that encourages knowledge workers to thrive and flourish, given the strategic significance of their stock of specialist knowledge to the organisation. Carleton counsels that a breach or violation of the psychological contract is viewed as 'injustice' and may harbour negative knowledge worker behaviours and attitudes, leading to withdrawal, knowledge hoarding and a reduction in motivation and productivity.

Implications for Organisational Behaviour in the Workplace

To conclude, knowledge workers are a strategic asset to organisations, by virtue of their rare, valuable, inimitable and non-substitutable stock of specialist knowledge and know-how. Although literature espouses that they cannot be managed and controlled in a traditional sense, the onus appears to be on the organisation to foster an environment and, arguably, a reciprocal, relational psychological contract that motivates knowledge workers to create, share (rather than hoard) and apply their specialist knowledge and expertise with internal and external stakeholders. In its quest to motivate knowledge workers, Drucker[52] (p. 88) posits that 'management's job is to preserve the assets of the institution in its care.' He asserts that they must satisfy the needs of knowledge workers, who are 'owners of the human capital that gives the organisation its wealth-producing power.'

Questions

In view of the above, answer the following questions.

1. It could be argued that 'all work is knowledge work', which classifies everyone in the organisation as a 'knowledge worker.' *Justify* this argument, with reference to appropriate literature.

2. Motivating knowledge workers appears to be the remit of the organisation. *To what extent* is it the knowledge worker's responsibility to motivate themselves?

3. Knowledge workers are perceived to have expert power. *Consider* the potential problems that this may yield to a) organisational behaviour in the workplace, and b) the organisation's members who are not classed as knowledge workers.

Summary – Chapter 7 'Work motivation and satisfaction'

The relationship between the organisation and its members is influenced by what motivates them to work, and rewards and fulfilment derived from it. Motivation is at the basis of organisational activity. Individuals have a variety of changing, and often competing, needs and expectations at work which they attempt to satisfy in a number of ways. A person's work motivation, satisfaction and performance is determined by the comparative strength of economic rewards, intrinsic satisfaction, and social relationships. There are many competing theories that attempt to explain motivation at work. Content theories place emphasis on what actually motivates the individual. Main theories include those of Maslow, Alderfer, Nohria, Herzberg and McClelland. Process theories are concerned with the dynamic variables that make up motivation. Major approaches include expectancy theory, equity theory and goal theory. Another possible approach is organisational behaviour modification and application of learning principles to behaviour at work. These theories are not conclusive but provide a basis for study and discussion. Understanding the nature of job satisfaction and links with work motivation and performance is not easy. Satisfaction is an internal state associated with a feeling of personal achievement. Attention has also been given to a comprehensive model of job enrichment based on skill variety, task identity, task significance, autonomy and feedback.

Group discussion activities

Undertake each of these activities in small groups as indicated by your tutor. Before you start your discussion establish a non-threatening environment within the group and confirm confidentiality will be honoured.

First, form your own views and then share and compare in open critical discussion with colleagues. Reflect honestly on the extent to which: (i) you influenced the thinking and ideas of your colleagues; and (ii) you were influenced by your colleagues.

To what extent was your group able to reach consensus?

Agree one of your members to produce a brief written summary of the discussion and prepared to present in a plenary session.

Activity 1

(a) Some writers argue that people do not lack inherent motivation, only the right triggers to evoke their efforts. Others claim motivation can only truly come from within and attempts from other people to motivate have little lasting influence.

(b) It's all very well talking about a contented workforce, praise and recognition but at times of economic recession and uncertainty a secure job and high income are the only real motivators.

Activity 2

As a *forced-choice* exercise rate in order the importance of the three-fold classification of economic rewards, intrinsic satisfaction and social relationships plus *one* (only) classification of your own choice. Give supporting reasons and where possible specific examples in support of your rating.

Activity 3

(a) Motivation at work is very subjective and influenced by a range of variables including personality, age, cultural influences and unknown circumstances outside of work. Generalised theories of motivation cannot meet all individual circumstances and therefore are largely a waste of your study time.

(b) Motivating employees to improved performance is easy. An emphasis on clear, stretching but attainable goals, constructive feedback, an equitable system of rewards and leave them alone to get on with the job.

(c) The motivation of so-called knowledge workers is no different from motivating any other members of staff that is fair and reasonable recognition of their individual value to achieving the objectives of the organisation.

Organisational behaviour in action case study

A friend has unexpectedly inherited ownership of a 50-room family seaside hotel with restaurant and is concerned about the generally poor level of work performance, low motivation and morale, and disturbingly high staff turnover. You have been asked for your advice.

Imagine you are in your friend's position and:

* Detail fully the likely actions you would take to help overcome the present situation.

* Indicate clearly the priorities you would have in mind.

* Make clear any necessary reasonable assumptions.

* Explain fully how you might draw upon particular theories of motivation.

* In particular how would attempt to maintain the motivation and performance of the permanent position of chef compared with ad-hoc or seasonal members of staff?

* Explain what longer-term actions you would recommend.

Tasks

Share your observations with colleagues and discuss the extent to which you:

1. Avoided generalisations about what motivates other people.

2. Made assumptions (even if unintentional) about the work ethic of hotel staff.

3. Are able to distance yourself from your own work motivations.

4. Learnt from undertaking this exercise.

Chapter 7 – Personal skills and employability exercise

Objectives

Completing this exercise should help you to enhance the following skills:

* Review individual needs and expectations at work.
* Reflect upon your perceptions about the motives of other people.
* Matching work motivation and satisfaction with future employment.

Exercise – work in conjunction with a partner with whom you feel comfortable

FIRST write down your most likely preferred career choice. If you are not sure about a specific job at this stage explain the type of organisation or general nature of the work that most interests you.

THEN list in *rank order* the importance of these needs and expectations **to you as an individual.**

Where possible provide supporting examples including from any short-term or part-time work experience.

	YOU	PARTNER
1. Contributory pension scheme		
2. Long-term job security		
3. Safe working environment		
4. Harmonious working relationships		
5. Personal development and career progression		
6. Attractive benefits package (and perks)		
7. Leisure and sports facilities		
8. Size of the organisation		
9. Location		
10. Average age of working colleagues		
11. Group or team working		
12. Flexible working hours		
13. High basic salary		
14. Perceived status of the organisation and/or its work		
15. Wide diversity of members of staff		
16. Extent to which work involves high level of ICT		
17. Voluntary paid overtime		
18. Challenging work with a sense of achievement		
19. Autonomy on manner of undertaking tasks		
20. Employee share ownership scheme		

Exchange accounts with a partner before proceeding further

NOW taking turns you each play the role of 'devil's advocate' and question the extent to which the list of critical employee needs matches effectively with the likely pattern of future employment ambitions.

Compare and discuss critically accounts with your partner, and be prepared to explain and justify your views.

Discussion

* How difficult was it to avoid generalisations about what motivates other people?

* To what extent were you able to distance your own needs and expectations from work?

* What have your learnt and what conclusions do you draw from undertaking this exercise?

Notes and references

1. Krech, D., Crutchfield, R. S. and Ballachey, E. L. *Individual in Society,* McGraw-Hill (1962).
2. Mitchell, T. R. 'Motivation: New Directions for Theory, Research, and Practice', *Academy of Management Review,* vol. 7, no. 1, January 1982, pp. 80–8.
3. 'Motivating your team', Checklist 068, Chartered Management Institute, November 2015.
4. Kreitner, R., Kinicki, A. and Buelens, M. *Organizational Behaviour,* first European edition, McGraw-Hill (1999).
5. Farren, C. 'Mastery: The Critical Advantage', in Chowdhury, S. (ed.) *Management 21C,* Financial Times Prentice Hall (2000), p. 95.
6. Weaver, T. 'Theory M: Motivating with Money', *Cornell HRA Quarterly,* vol. 29, no. 3, November 1988, pp. 40–5.
7. Chamorro-Premuzic, T and Fagan, P. 'Money Talks, but do People still Listen?, *Management Today,* November 2014, pp. 50–3.
8. See, for example, Rudolph, P. A. and Kleiner, B. H. 'The Art of Motivating Employees', *Journal of Managerial Psychology,* vol. 4, no. 5, 1989, pp. i–iv.
9. Kets de Vries, M. 'Beyond Sloan: Trust is at the Core of Corporate Values' in Pickford, J. (ed.) *Financial Times Mastering Management 2.0,* Financial Times Prentice Hall (2001), pp. 267–70.
10. Blanchard, K. 'Do You Get Passionate at Work?' *British Journal of Administrative Management,* Autumn 2011, p. 26.
11. Pink, D. H. *Drive: The Surprising Truth About What Motives Us,* Canongate Books (2011).
12. Smallman, E. 'Money for Nothing', *Professional Manager,* Winter 2015, pp. 46–51.
13. For a fuller discussion, see Mullins, L. J. and Dossor, P. *Hospitality Management and Organisational Behaviour,* fifth edition, Pearson Education (2013).
14. Maslow, A. H. 'A Theory of Human Motivation', *Psychological Review,* 50, July 1943, pp. 370–96 and Maslow, A. H. *Motivation and Personality,* third edition, Harper and Row (1987).
15. Adair, J. *Leadership and Motivation,* Kogan Page (2006), p. 29.
16. Steers, R. M. and Porter, L. W. *Motivation and Work Behaviour,* fifth edition, McGraw-Hill (1991).
17. Saunders, A. 'Keep Staff Sweet', *Management Today,* June 2003, p. 75.
18. Alderfer, C. P. *Existence, Relatedness and Growth,* Collier Macmillan (1972).
19. Nohria, N., Groysberg, B. and Lee, L.-E. 'Employee Motivation: A Powerful New Model', *Harvard Business Review,* vol. 86 , July 2008, pp. 78–84.
20. Herzberg, F., Mausner, B. and Snyderman, B. B. *The Motivation to Work,* second edition, Chapman and Hall (1959).
21. Crainer, S. and Dearlove, D. (eds) *Financial Times Handbook of Management,* second edition, Financial Times Prentice Hall (2001), p. 361.
22. McClelland, D. C. *Human Motivation,* Cambridge University Press (1988).
23. For examples of pictures, see Osland, J. S., Kolb, D. A. and Rubin, I. M. *Organizational Behaviour: An Experimental Approach,* seventh edition, Prentice Hall (2001).

24. McClelland, D. C. and Burnham, D. H. 'Power Is the Great Motivation', *Harvard Business Review,* vol. 54, March–April 1976, pp. 100–10.

25. Vroom, V. H. *Work and Motivation,* Wiley (1964); also published by Krieger (1982).

26. See Porter, L. W. and Lawler, E. E. *Managerial Attitudes and Performance,* Irwin (1968), and Lawler, E. E. *Motivation in Work Organizations,* Brooks/Cole (1973).

27. CIPD 'Strategic Reward and Total Reward', CIPD Factsheet, Chartered Institute of Personnel and Development, March 2014.

28. Adams, J. S. 'Injustice in Social Exchange', in Berkowitz, L. (ed.) *Advances in Experimental and Social Psychology,* Academic Press (1965). Abridged in Steers, R. M. and Porter, L. W. *Motivation and Work Behavior,* second edition, McGraw-Hill (1979), pp. 107–24.

29. Werner, G., Schmittberger, R. and Schwarze, B. 'An Experimental Analysis of Ultimatum Bargaining', *Journal of Economic Behavior and Organization,* vol. 3, no. 4, December 1982, pp. 367–88.

30. Locke, E. A. 'Towards a Theory of Task Motivation and Incentives', *Organizational Behavior and Human Performance,* vol. 3, 1968, pp. 157–89.

31. Locke, E. A. 'Personal Attitudes and Motivation', *Annual Review of Psychology,* vol. 26, 1975, pp. 457–80.

32. Gratton, L. *Living Strategy: Putting People at the Heart of Corporate Purpose,* Financial Times Prentice Hall (2000), p. 193.

33. Hannagan, T. *Management,* fourth edition, Financial Times Prentice Hall (2005), p. 363.

34. 'Motivating Your Team', Checklist 068, Chartered Management Institute, November 2015.

35. Adair, J. *Leadership and Motivation,* Kogan Page (2006), p. 38.

36. See, for example, Cheng, T., Sculli, D. and Chan, F. S. 'Relationship Dominance – Rethinking Management Theories from the Perspective of Methodological Relationalism', *Journal of Managerial Psychology,* vol. 16, no. 2, 2001, pp. 97–105.

37. Francesco, A. M. and Gold, B. A. *International Organizational Behavior,* second edition, Pearson Prentice Hall (2005), p. 126.

38. Adler, N. J. *International Aspects of Organizational Behaviour,* third edition, South Western College Publishing (1997).

39. Luthans, F. and Kreitner, R. *Organisational Behavior Modification and Beyond,* second edition, Scott Foresman (1985), p. 36.

40. Stajkovic, A. D. and Luthans, F. 'Differential Effects of Incentive Motivators on Work Performance', *Academy of Management Journal,* vol. 44, no. 3, 2001, pp. 580–90.

41. Luthans, F., Stajkovic, A., Luthans, B. C. and Luthans, K. W. 'Applying Behavioral Management in Eastern Europe', *European Management Journal,* vol. 16, no. 4, August 1998, pp. 466–74.

42. Tampoe, M. 'Knowledge Workers – The New Management Challenge', *Professional Manager,* November 1994, pp. 12–13.

43. Whitmore, Sir J. 'Breaking Down the Barriers to Management Creativity', *Manager, The British Journal of Administrative Management,* May/June 2002, pp. 24–6.

44. Matson, E. and Prusak, L. 'Boosting the Productivity of Knowledge Workers' Management Services', vol. 57, no.2, Summer 2013, pp. 14–15.

45. Goffee, R. and Jones, G. 'How to Harness the Special Talents of Clever People', *Management Today,* September 2009, pp. 56–60.

46. Lundin, S., Paul, H. and Christensen, J. *Fish: A Remarkable Way to Boost Morale and Improve Results,* Hyperion Press (2001) p. 37.

47. Stern, S. 'My Generation', *Management Today,* March 2008, pp. 40–6.

48. For the full list see: www.dailymail.co.uk/happiest_jobs (accessed 22 March 2014).

49. 'Employee Outlook', CIPD Spring 2017.

50. Chamorro-Premuzic, T. 'Why Most Jobs are Meaningless', *Management Today,* April 2016, p. 60.

51. Hackman, J. R. and Oldham, G. R. *Work Redesign,* Addison-Wesley (1980).

52. Drucker, P. 'Knowledge-Worker Productivity: The Biggest Challenge', *California Management Review,* Winter, vol. 41, no. 2, 1999a, pp. 79–94.

53. Hislop, D. *Knowledge Management in Organisations: A Critical Introduction,* third edition, Oxford University Press (2013).

54. Dewhurst, M., Hancock, B. and Ellsworth, D. 'Redesigning knowledge work', *Harvard Business Review,* January–February, 2013, pp. 59–64.

55. Drucker, P. *Management Challenges for the 21st Century,* HarperCollins (1999b).

56. Davenport, T. H. *Thinking for a Living: How to Get Better Performance and Results from Knowledge Workers,* Harvard Business School Press (2005).

57. Reich, R. *The Work of Nations: A Blueprint for the Future,* Simon & Schuster (1991).

58. Polanyi, M. *The Tacit Dimension,* Routledge & Kegan Paul (1967).

59. Gourlay, S. 'Tacit knowledge, tacit knowing, or behaving?' *Proceedings of the 3rd European Organizational Knowledge, Learning and Capabilities Conference,* 5–6 April 2002, Athens, Greece, 2002, pp. 1–24.

60. Dixon, N. M. *Common Knowledge: How Companies Thrive By Sharing What They Know. Boston:* Harvard Business Press (2000).

61. Mládková, L., Zouharova, J. and Nový, J. 'Motivation and knowledge workers', *Procedia-Social and Behavioural Sciences,* vol. 207, 2015, pp. 768–76.

62. Bigliardi, B., Dormio, A. I., Galati, F. and Schuima, G. 'The Impact of Organisational Culture on the Job Satisfaction of Knowledge Workers', *The Journal of Information and*

Knowledge Management Systems, vol. 42, no. 1, 2012, pp. 36–51.

63. Cetindamar, D., Phaal, R. and Probert, D. *Technology Management: Activities and Tools,* Palgrave Macmillan (2010).

64. Ahmed, P. and Shepherd, C. *Innovation Management: Contexts, Strategies, Systems and Processes,* Financial Times Press (2010).

65. Bollinger, A. and Smith, R. 'Managing Organisational Knowledge as a Strategic Asset', *Journal of Knowledge Management,* vol. 5, no. 1, 2001, 8–18.

66. Lengnick-Hall, C. A. and Griffith, R. J. 'Evidence-based versus tinkerable knowledge as strategic assets: A new perspective on the interplay between innovation and application', *Journal of Engineering and Technology Management,* vol. 28, 2011, pp. 147–67.

67. Newell, S., Robertson, M., Scarbrough, H. and Swan, J. *Managing Knowledge Work and Innovation,* second edition, Palgrave Macmillan (2009).

68. Bartlett, C. A. and Ghoshal, S. 'Beyond Strategic Planning to Organisational Learning: Life Blood of the Individualised Corporation', *Strategy and Leadership,* vol. 26, no. 1, 1998, pp. 34–9.

69. Thite, M. 'Strategic Positioning of HRM in Knowledge-based Organizations', *The Learning Organization,* vol. 11, no. 1, 2004, pp. 28–44.

70. Dabos, G. E. and Rousseau, D. M. 'Mutuality and Reciprocity in the Psychological Contracts of Employees and Employers', *Journal of Applied Psychology,* vol. 89, 2004, pp. 52–72.

71. Carelton, K. 'How to Motivate and Retain Knowledge Workers in Organizations: A Review of the Literature,' *International Journal of Management,* vol. 28, no. 2, 2010, pp. 459–68.

Part 3
Focus on groups and leadership

Chapter 8
Working in groups and teams

The nature, operation and impact of groups and teams are an underlying feature of organisational behaviour and a major influence on the performance of people in the work situation.

Learning outcomes

After completing this chapter you should have enhanced your ability to:

- explain the nature and significance of work groups and teams;
- relate the nature of informal groups and group values and norms;
- examine factors which influence group cohesiveness and performance;
- assess the significance of social identity theory;

- identify characteristics of effective work groups and virtual teams;
- analyse individual roles and behaviour in group situations;
- debate the nature and performance of autonomous working groups.

Outline chapter contents

Overview topic map: Chapter 8 – Working in groups and teams

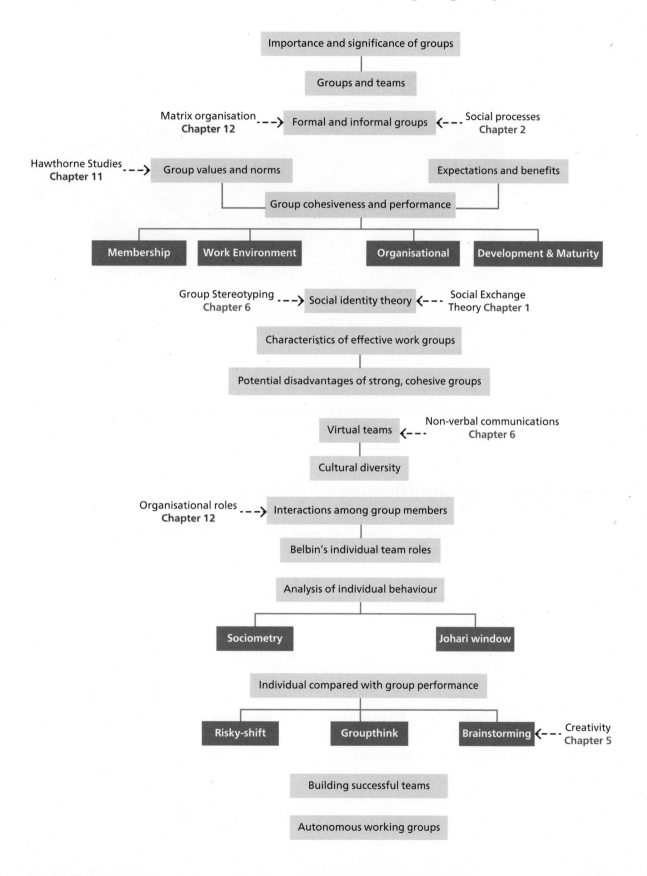

Group or team?

Before commencing to read this chapter reflect upon how YOU behave when working in a group and how this affects your job satisfaction and performance.

Importance and significance of groups

Groups are a characteristic of all social situations and an essential feature of any organisation. Work is a group-based activity and if the organisation is to function effectively it requires collaboration and co-operation among its members. The work organisation and its sub-units are made up of groups of people and almost every member of staff will belong to one or more group. Members of a group must co-operate in order for work to be carried out.

The working of groups and the influence they exert over their membership is an essential feature of organisational behaviour. People in groups influence each other in many ways and groups develop their own hierarchies and leaders. Group pressures can have a major influence over the behaviour of individual members and their work performance.

Adair suggests that a work group is a collection of people who share most, if not all, of the following characteristics:

- a definable membership;
- group consciousness;
- a sense of shared purpose;
- interdependence;

- interaction;
- ability to act in a unitary manner.[1]

Peterson and colleagues discuss the importance of morale as an indicator of group well-being. Attention of positive psychology to promote good life should include not only individuals but also groups within which individuals live, work, love and play. Groups should be a primary focus of research into health and well-being.[2]

Groups and teams

Although there is no single accepted definition, most people will readily understand what constitutes a group. The essential feature is that its members regard themselves as belonging to the group. A popular definition from *Schein* defines the group in psychological terms as:

> **any number of people who (1) interact with one another; (2) are psychologically aware of one another; and (3) perceive themselves to be a group.[3]**

It is not easy, however, to distinguish clearly between a group and a team. According to Acas, for example, the term 'team' is used loosely to describe many different groupings and a variety of labels are given to the types of teams. It is doubtful whether any definition of types of teams would be universally acceptable.[4]

Use of the word 'teams' has become increasingly fashionable in recent years. *Belbin* comments on the extent teamwork began to replace the more usual reference to groups and every activity was now being described as 'teamwork'. He maintains confusion in vocabulary should be addressed if the principles of good teamwork are to be retained. Belbin suggests there are several factors that characterise the difference between groups and teams (**see Figure 8.1**). The best differentiator is size: groups can comprise any number of people but teams are smaller with a membership between (ideally) four and six. The quintessential feature of a small,

	Team	Group
Size	Limited	Medium or large
Selection	Crucial	Immaterial
Leadership	Shared or rotating	Solo
Perception	Mutual knowledge understanding	Focus on leader
Style	Role-spread co-ordination	Convergence conformism
Spirit	Dynamic interaction	Togetherness persecution of opponents

Figure 8.1 Differences between a team and a group
Source: Belbin, R. M. *Beyond the Team,* Butterworth–Heinemann (2000). Copyright © 2000. Reproduced with permission from Belbin, www.belbin.com.

well-balanced team is that leadership is shared or rotates whereas large groups typically throw up solo leaders.[5]

Common usage of the two terms

While acknowledging the work of Belbin, it appears that the term 'group' is often used in a more general sense and 'team' in a more specific context. In common usage and literature, including in this book, there is a tendency for the terms 'groups' and 'teams' to be used interchangeably and based on personal preference. There is also the common usage of the two terms. For example, members of an orchestra or string quartet have to work closely together and co-ordinate in synchronisation but usually are referred to as a group rather than a team.

We continue to refer to 'group' or 'team' according to the particular focus of attention and the vocabulary of the quoted authors. Whereas all teams are, by definition, groups, it does not necessarily follow that all groups are teams. The *Chartered Management Institute* points out that a team is more than just a group of people who happen to work together. Increasingly, a team may be composed of people drawn from different functions, departments and disciplines whom have been brought together for a specific project.[6]

Whatever the debate on 'groups' or 'teams', what is clear is the increasing importance to organisations of effective group working or team working.

To what extent do YOU believe there is any benefit in attempting to distinguish in any meaningful way between a group and a team? What examples can you provide?

Formal and informal groups

Groups are formed as a consequence of the pattern of organisation structure and arrangements for the division of work, for example the grouping together of common activities into divisions or sections. **Formal groups** are created to achieve specific organisational objectives and are concerned with the **co-ordination of work activities.** People are brought together on the basis of defined roles within the structure of the organisation. The nature of the tasks to be undertaken is a predominant feature of the formal group. Goals are identified by management, and certain rules, relationships and norms of behaviour established.

Groups may result from the nature of technology employed and the way in which work is carried out, for example bringing together a number of people to carry out a sequence of operations on an assembly line. Groups may also develop when a number of people of the same level or status within the organisation see themselves as a group, for example departmental heads of an industrial organisation or chief officers of a local authority. Formal groups tend to be relatively permanent, although there may be changes in actual membership. However, temporary formal groups may also be created by management, as with for example the use of project teams in a matrix organisation. **(See also matrix structure in Chapter 12.)**

Social processes and informal organisation

The formal structure of the organisation, and system of role relationships, rules and procedures, will be augmented by interpretation and development at the informal level. Groups will also arise from social processes and the informal organisation, **discussed in Chapter 2. Informal groups** are based more on personal relationships and agreement of group members than on defined role relationships. They serve to satisfy psychological and social needs not related necessarily to the tasks to be undertaken. Informal groups may devise ways of attempting to satisfy members' affiliation and other social motivations lacking in the work situation.

Members of an informal group may appoint their own leader who exercises authority by consent of the members themselves. The informal leader may be chosen as the person who reflects the attitudes and values of the members, helps to resolve conflict, leads the group in satisfying its goals, or liaises with management or other people outside the group. The informal leader may change according to the particular situation facing the group. Although not usually the case, it is possible for the informal leader to be the same person as the formal leader appointed officially by management.

Membership of informal groups often cuts across the formal structure. They may comprise individuals from different parts of the organisation and/or from different levels of the organisation, vertically and diagonally, as well as from the same horizontal level. An informal group could also be the same as the formal group, or it might comprise a part only of the formal group **(see Figure 8.2).**

Major functions of informal groups

It is suggested that there are four major reasons for the existence of informal groups:

- **Habit of Informal groups.** In this context, there is a tendency for a set of values, norms and beliefs that guide group acceptance and group behaviour. Unless you subscribe to this same set of values and culture, you will be considered an 'outsider' and can be isolated.

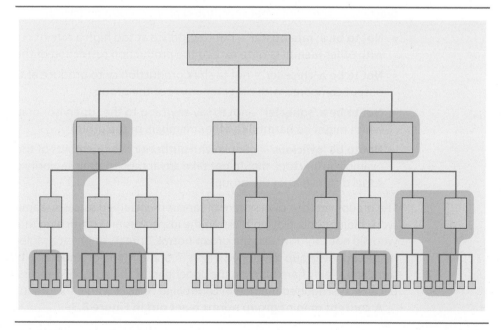

Figure 8.2 Examples of informal groups within the formal structure of an organisation

- **Communication.** Groups want all the information, either negative or positive, supplied to them that affects their welfare. If communication is not forthcoming they will seek to spread information in other ways amongst themselves.
- **Social Control.** Conformity is often enforced by ridicule, ostracism and even violence. An illustration of this can be found in the bank wiring room discussed in the previous section.
- **Interest and fun.** Jobs can be monotonous and fail to hold workers' attention, or perhaps hold few prospects. In these circumstances, works often compensate for lack of interest by time wasting activities; for instance talking, gambling, practical jokes and a culture of drinking.

Group values and norms

The classical approach to organisation and management tended to ignore the importance of groups and the social factors at work. As part of the human relations approach to organisations **(discussed in Chapter 11)**, the Hawthorne studies gave recognition to the work organisation as a social organisation and the importance of the group, and group values and norms, in influencing behaviour at work. One experiment involved the observation of a group of fourteen men working in the bank wiring room who formed their own sub-groups or cliques, with natural leaders emerging with the consent of the members. Despite a financial incentive scheme for the more work they did, the group decided on a level of output well below they were capable of achieving. Group pressures on individual workers were stronger than financial incentives offered by management.

Informal social relations

The group developed its own pattern of informal social relations and codes and practices ('norms') of what constituted proper group behaviour.

- **Not to be a 'rate buster'** – not to produce at too high a rate of output compared with other members or to exceed the production restriction of the group.
- **Not to be a 'chiseller'** – not to shirk production or to produce at too low a rate of output compared with other members of the group.
- **Not to be a 'squealer'** – not to say anything to the supervisor or management which might be harmful to other members of the group.
- **Not to be 'officious'** – people with authority over members of the group, for example inspectors, should not take advantage of their seniority or maintain a social distance from the group.

The group had their own system of sanctions including sarcasm, damaging completed work, hiding tools, playing tricks on the inspectors and ostracising those members who did not conform with the **group norms**. Threats of physical violence were also made and the group developed a system of punishing offenders by 'binging', striking someone a fairly hard blow on the upper part of the arm. This process of binging also became a recognised method of controlling conflict within the group.

A concept map of group norms is set out in Figure 8.3.

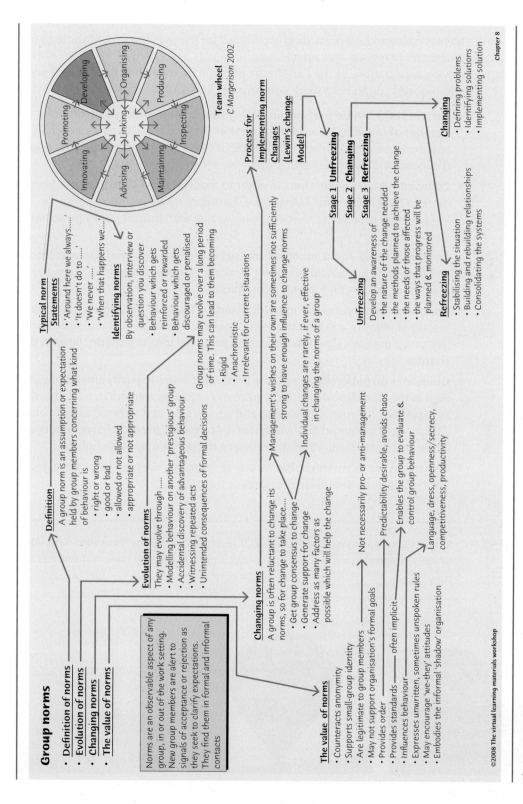

Group norms

- **Definition of norms**
- **Evolution of norms**
- **Changing norms**
- **The value of norms**

Norms are an observable aspect of any group, in or out of the work setting. New group members are alert to signals of acceptance or rejection as they seek to clarify expectations. They find them in formal and informal contacts

Definition

A group norm is an assumption or expectation held by group members concerning what kind of behaviour is
- right or wrong
- good or bad
- allowed or not allowed
- appropriate or not appropriate

Evolution of norms

They may evolve through .....
- Modelling behaviour on another 'prestigious' group
- Accidental discovery of advantageous behaviour
- Witnessing repeated acts
- Unintended consequences of formal decisions

Typical norm Statements
- 'Around here we always.....'
- 'It doesn't do to ......'
- 'We never ....'
- 'When that happens we.....'

Identifying norms

By observation, interview or question you discover
- Behaviour which gets reinforced or rewarded
- Behaviour which gets discouraged or penalised

Group norms may evolve over a long period of time. This can lead to them becoming
- Rigid
- Anachronistic
- Irrelevant for current situations

Changing norms

A group is often reluctant to change its norms, so for change to take place.....
- Get group consensus to change
- Generate support for change
- Address as many factors as possible which will help the change

Management's wishes on their own are sometimes not sufficiently strong to have enough influence to change norms

Individual changes are rarely, if ever, effective in changing the norms of a group

The value of norms
- Counteracts anonymity
- Supports small-group identity
- Are legitimate to group members
- May not support organisation's formal goals
- Provides order
- Provides standards ——— often implicit
- Influences behaviour
- Expresses unwritten, sometimes unspoken rules
- May encourage 'we-they' attitudes
- Embodies the informal 'shadow' organisation

Not necessarily pro- or anti-management

Predictability desirable, avoids chaos

Enables the group to evaluate & control group behaviour

Language, dress, openness/secrecy, competitiveness, productivity

Team wheel
C Margerison 2002

Process for Implementing norm Changes (Lewin's change Model)

Stage 1 **Unfreezing**
Stage 2 **Changing**
Stage 3 **Refreezing**

Unfreezing

Develop an awareness of
- the nature of the change needed
- the methods planned to achieve the change
- the needs of those affected
- the ways that progress will be planned & monitored

Refreezing
- Stabilising the situation
- Building and rebuilding relationships
- Consolidating the systems

Changing
- Defining problems
- Identifying solutions
- Implementing solution

©2008 The virtual learning materials workshop

Figure 8.3 Concept map of group norms

Source: Copyright © 2008 The Virtual Learning Materials Workshop. Reproduced with permission.

Expectations and benefits of group membership

Membership can be a rewarding experience for the individual, contribute to the promotion of morale and aid release of creativity and energy. Individuals have varying expectations of the benefits from group membership, both formal and informal, relating to both work performance and social processes.

- **Certain tasks can be performed only through the combined efforts of a number of individuals working together.** The variety of experience, knowledge and expertise among members provides a synergetic effect that can be applied to the increasingly complex problems of modern organisations.

- **Collusion between members** in order to modify formal working arrangements more to their liking – for example, by sharing or rotating unpopular tasks. Membership therefore provides the individual with opportunities for initiative and creativity.

- **Companionship and a source of mutual understanding and support from colleagues.** This can help in solving work problems and also to militate against stressful or demanding working conditions.

- **Membership provides the individual with a sense of belonging.** It provides a feeling of identity and the chance to acquire role recognition and status within the group or team. **(See the discussion on social identity theory later in this chapter.)**

- **Guidelines on generally acceptable behaviour.** Helps to clarify ambiguous situations such as the extent to which official rules and regulations are expected to be adhered to in practice, the rules of the game and what is seen as the correct actual behaviour. Allegiance to the group or team can serve as a means of control over individual behaviour and individuals who contravene the norms may be disciplined.

- **Protection for its membership.** Group or team members collaborate to protect their interests from outside pressures or threats.

In what specific ways have YOU benefited from group membership with your university colleagues? What expectations do you believe have not been satisfied fully?

It's all about working together

Group cohesiveness and performance

Social interaction is a natural feature of human behaviour and work organisation but ensuring harmonious relationships and effective teamwork is not an easy task. Co-operation is likely to be greater in a united, cohesive group. Members of a high-morale group are more likely to think of themselves as a group and work together effectively. Strong and cohesive work groups can, therefore, have beneficial effects for the organisation. There are many factors which affect group cohesiveness and performance that can be summarised under four broad headings: membership, work environment, organisational and **group development and maturity** as shown in **Figure 8.4.**

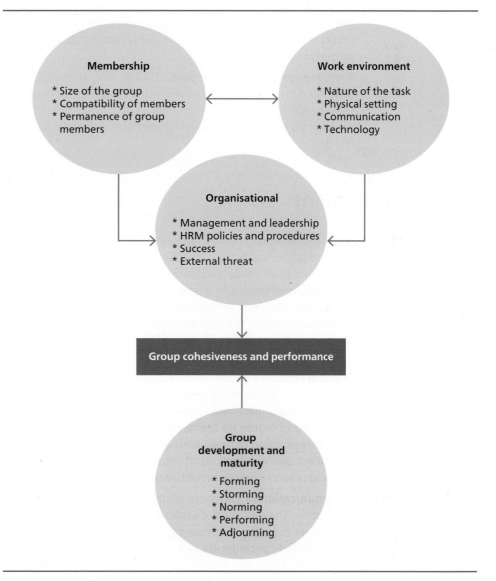

Figure 8.4 Factors contributing to group cohesiveness and performance

Membership

- **Size of the group –** As size increases problems arise with communications and co-ordination. When a group becomes too large it may split into smaller units and friction may develop between the sub-groups. It is difficult to put a figure on the ideal size of a work group. Much will depend upon other variables, but it seems to be generally accepted that cohesiveness becomes more difficult to achieve when a group exceeds ten to twelve members.[7] A figure of between five and seven is often quoted as an apparent optimum size for full participation within the group.

- **Compatibility of members –** The more homogeneous the group in terms of features as shared backgrounds, interests, attitudes and values of its members, the easier usually to promote cohesiveness. Other individual differences such as personality or skills of members, may serve to complement each other and help make for a cohesive group. However, conflict can arise in a homogeneous group where members are in competition with each other, for example with individual incentive payment schemes.

- **Permanence of group members –** Group spirit and relationships take time to develop. Cohesiveness is more likely when members of a group are together for a reasonable length of time and changes occur only slowly. A frequent turnover of members is likely to have an adverse effect on morale and on the cohesiveness of the group.

Work environment

- **Nature of the task –** Where workers share a common task or face the same problems, this may assist cohesiveness. The nature of the task may serve to bring people together when it is necessary to communicate and interact regularly – for example, members of a research and development team. If members of a group normally work at different locations they may still experience a feeling of cohesiveness when the task requires frequent communication and interaction – for example, security guards patrolling separate areas who need to check with each other on a regular basis.

- **Physical setting –** Where members of a group work in the same location or in close physical proximity to each other this may generally help cohesiveness. However, this is not always the case. For example, in large open-plan offices staff often tend to segregate themselves from colleagues and create barriers through the strategic siting of items such as filing cabinets, bookcases or indoor plants. Isolation from other groups of workers will also tend to build cohesiveness. This often applies to a smaller number of workers on a night shift.

- **Communications –** The more easily members can communicate freely with each other, the greater the likelihood of group cohesiveness. For example, difficulties in communication can arise with production systems where workers are stationed continuously at a particular point with limited freedom of movement. Physical conditions may limit effective communication, for example, the technological layout and high level of noise with some assembly line work. Changes in the nature of work including increasing demand for flexible working arrangements may restrict opportunities for social interaction and hamper internal group unity.[8]

- **Technology** – Technology is clearly a major influence on patterns of group operation and behaviour. The impact of information technology demands new patterns of work organisation and affects the formation and structure of groups. Improvements in telecommunications mean that support staff need no longer be located within the main production unit. Individuals may work more on their own, from their homes, shared offices or hotels, or work more with machines than with other people.

Organisational

- **Management and leadership** – The form of management and style of leadership adopted are major determinants of group cohesiveness. Teams tend to be a mirror image of their leaders. Cohesiveness will be affected by the manner in which the manager and senior staff give support, guidance and encouragement to the group; provide opportunities for participation; attempt to resolve conflicts; and give attention to employee relations.

- *Farrell* makes the point that managers are ultimately responsible for creating a balance in the workplace and should take the lead in setting standards of behaviour in teams.[9]

- **HRM policies and procedures** – Harmony and cohesiveness within the group are more likely to be achieved if HRM policies and procedures are well developed and perceived to be equitable, with fair treatment for all members. Attention should be given to the effects that appraisal systems, discipline, promotion and rewards, and opportunities for personal development have on members of the group.

- **Success** – Success is usually a strong motivational influence on cohesiveness and level of work performance. Success or reward as a positive motivator can be perceived by group members in a number of ways, for example the satisfactory completion of a task through co-operative action, praise from management, a feeling of high status, achievement in competition with other groups, or benefits gained, such as high wage payments from a group bonus incentive scheme.

- **External threat** – Cohesiveness may be enhanced by members co-operating with one another when faced with a common external threat, such as changes in their method of work or the appointment of a new manager. Conflict between groups will also tend to increase the cohesiveness of each group and the boundaries of the group become drawn more clearly. Even if the threat is subsequently removed, the group may continue to have a greater degree of cohesiveness.

Group development and maturity

The degree of cohesiveness is affected also by the manner in which groups progress through the various stages of development and maturity before getting down to the real tasks in hand. This process can take time and is often traumatic for the members. A popular model by *Tuckman* identifies five main successive stages of group progression and relationships: **forming**, **storming**, **norming**, **performing** and **adjourning**.[10]

- **Stage 1 – forming.** Initial formation of the group and bringing together individuals who identify tentatively the purpose, composition and terms of reference. Consideration is given to the hierarchical structure of the group, pattern of leadership, individual roles and responsibilities, and codes of conduct. There is likely to be considerable anxiety as members attempt to create an impression, to test each other and establish their personal identity within the group.

- **Stage 2 – storming.** As members of the group get to know each other better they will put forward their views more openly and forcefully. Disagreements will be expressed and challenges offered on the nature of the task and arrangements made in the earlier stage of development. This may lead to conflict and hostility. The storming stage is important because, if successful, there will be discussions on reforming arrangements for the working and operation of the group, and agreement on more meaningful structures and procedures.

- **Stage 3 – norming.** As conflict and hostility start to be controlled, members of the group will establish guidelines and standards and develop their own norms of acceptable behaviour. The norming stage is important in establishing the need for members to co-operate in order to plan, agree standards of performance and fulfil the purpose of the group.

- **Stage 4 – performing.** When the group has progressed successfully through the three earlier stages of development it will have created structure and cohesiveness to work effectively as a team. At this stage the group can concentrate on the attainment of its purpose and performance of the common task is likely to be at its most effective.

- **Stage 5 – adjourning.** This refers to the adjourning or disbanding of the group because of, for example, completion of the task, members leaving the organisation or moving on to other tasks. Some members may feel a compelling sense of loss at the end of a major or lengthy group project and their return to independence is characterised by sadness and anxiety. Managers may need to prepare for future group tasks and engendering team effort.

Another writer suggests that new groups go through the following five stages:

- the polite stage;
- the why are we here, what are we doing stage;
- the power stage, which dominant person will emerge;
- the constructive stage when sharing begins; and
- the unity stage – this often takes weeks, eating together, talking together.[11]

Creative leadership and group development

In an examination of creative leadership and team effectiveness, *Rickards and Moger* propose a modification to the Tuckman model and suggest a two-barrier model of group development. From their empirical studies of small groups and project teams,

Rickards and Moger put forward two challenges to the prevailing model of team development:

(i) Weak teams posed the question 'what is happening if a team fails to develop beyond the storm stage?'

(ii) The exceptional teams posed the question 'what happens if a team breaks out of the performance norms developed?'

The suggestion is that teams are differentiated by two barriers to performance. The weak barrier is behavioural and defeated a minority of teams; the strong barrier was a block to creativity or innovation, and defeated the majority of those teams who passed through the weak barrier. The two-barrier model provides a starting point for exploring the impact and influence of a team leader on the performance of teams. Rickards and Moger identified seven factors through which a leader might influence effective team development:

- building a platform of understanding;
- creating a shared vision;
- a creative climate;
- a commitment to idea ownership;
- resilience to setbacks;
- developing networking skills;
- learning from experience.[12]

Based on your own experience how far do YOU agree with Tuckman's five successive stages of group progression and relationships? How far do you support importance of the storming stage?

Social identity theory

Within work organisations there will be a number of different but overlapping groups representing a variety of functions, departments, occupations, technologies, project teams, locations or hierarchical levels. Organisational effectiveness will be dependent upon the extent to which these groups co-operate together, but often the different groupings are part of a network of complex relationships resulting in competitiveness and conflict. A feature of the importance and significance of group membership is the concept of social identity theory. *Tajfel and Turner* originally developed the idea of **social identity theory** as a means of understanding the psychological basis of inter-group discrimination.[13] Individuals are perceived as having not just one 'personal self' but a number of 'selves' derived from different social contexts and membership of groups. For a group to function effectively members must associate themselves as part of the group identity and values, and be prepared to forgo an individualistic stance.

Haslam refers to the relationship between individuals and groups in an understanding of organisational behaviour, and argues that in order to understand perception and interaction in organizational contexts we must:

do more than just study the psychology of individuals as individuals. Instead, we need to understand how social interaction is bound up with individuals' social identities – their definition of themselves in terms of group memberships.[14]

Social categorisation

Because of the need for a clear sense of personal identity, the groups or social categories with which we associate are an integral part of our self-concept (social identity). A natural process of human interaction is social categorisation by which we classify both ourselves and other people through reference to our own social identity. For example, membership of high-status groups can increase a person's perceived self-esteem. According to *Guirdham* 'self-categorisation is the process that transforms a number of individuals into a group'.[15] *See* **Figure 8.5.**

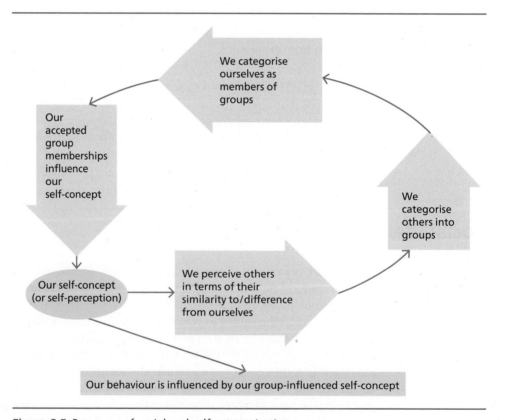

Figure 8.5 Processes of social and self-categorisation
Source: Guirdham, M. *Interactive Behaviour at Work,* third edition, Financial Times Prentice Hall (2002), p. 119. Reproduced with permission of Pearson Education Ltd.

We identify ourselves in terms of membership of certain social groupings and differentiate ourselves from other social groupings. This reinforces both social identity with our own category and negative perceptions and stereotypes towards out-groups. Stereotyping can lead to shared attitudes to other social groupings and to increased conflict amongst work groups. Examples of group stereotyping **(discussed in Chapter 6)** are associated with social identity theory. *Tajfel and Turner* suggest that the mere act of individuals categorising themselves as group members leads them to exhibit in-group favouritism. *Hewstone et al.* suggest that even without realising it, we tend usually to favour the groupings we belong to more than denigrate out-groups. Successful inter-group bias enhances self-esteem.[16] **(See also the discussion on social exchange theory in Chapter 1 and possible effects on group membership, norms and control.)**

How capable are YOU in forgoing an individualistic stance in order to view yourself as a member of a group and adopt group identity and values?

Characteristics of effective work groups

An underlying feature of an effective work group is a spirit of co-operation in which members work well together as a united team and with harmonious and supportive relationships. The characteristics are not always easy to isolate clearly but may be evidenced when members of a group exhibit:

- belief in shared aims and objectives;
- sense of commitment to the group;
- acceptance of group values and norms;
- feeling of mutual trust and dependency;
- full participation by all members and decision-making by consensus;
- free flow of information and communications;
- open expression of feelings and disagreements;
- resolution of conflict by the members themselves;
- lower level of staff turnover, absenteeism, accidents, errors and complaints.

Musical or dance ensembles make for an interesting study. Individual members may be brilliant soloists or dancers and often noted for their temperament but their performance is as much about the total blend and working noticeably well together as about musical or dance ability. By comparison, it is noticeable how managers of sporting teams often deliberately introduce new players, even to a successful team, in order to further increase competition, or rivalry, for places with the hope of achieving even greater success for the team as a whole.

An effective working group

Potential disadvantages of strong, cohesive groups

To develop effective work groups, attention should be given to those factors that influence the creation of group identity and cohesiveness. This may result in greater interaction between members, mutual help and social satisfaction, lower turnover and absenteeism, and often higher production.[17] However, strong and cohesive groups also present potential disadvantages. Working in groups may result in members spending too much time talking among themselves.

Cohesive groups do not necessarily produce a higher level of output. It may be remembered that in the bank wiring room experiment of the Hawthorne studies the level of output was restricted to a standard acceptable as a norm by the group. It is important that the manager attempts to influence the group during the norming stage when members are establishing their own guidelines and standards and their own norms of acceptable behaviour. Once a group has become fully developed, created cohesiveness and established its own culture it is more difficult for the manager successfully to change attitudes and behaviour of the group.

Strong, cohesive groups may develop a critical or even hostile attitude towards people outside the group or members of other groups. Groups may also compete against each other in a non-productive manner. This can be the case, for example, when group cohesiveness is based on common status, qualifications, technical expertise or professional standing. As a result, resentment and inter-group conflict may arise to the detriment of the organisation as a whole.

In order to help prevent, or overcome, unconstructive inter-group conflict, the manager should attempt to stimulate a high level of communication and interaction between groups. Yet, inter-group rivalry may deliberately be encouraged as a means of building stronger within-group cohesiveness. The

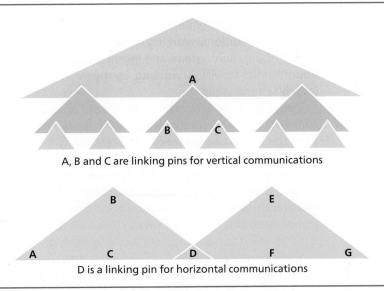

A, B and C are linking pins for vertical communications

D is a linking pin for horizontal communications

Figure 8.6 Representation of Likert's overlapping group structure and linking pins
Source: Likert, R. *New Patterns of Management*, McGraw-Hill (1961).

idea is that a competitive element may help to promote unity within a group. However, inter-group rivalry and competition need to be handled carefully and avoid development of 'win–lose' situations. Emphasis should be placed on overall objectives of the organisation and superordinate goals. These are goals over and above the issues at conflict and which, if they are to be achieved, require the co-operation of the competing groups.

Overlapping group membership

Part of the criteria for *Likert's* System 4 participative group management **(discussed in Chapter 1)** is the use of overlapping group structures.[18] The organisation functions best when members act, not as individuals, but as members of highly effective work groups. Likert proposes a structure based on overlapping group membership with a 'linking pin' process. The superior of one group is a subordinate member of, and the linking pin with, the next authority-level group. A structure of vertical overlapping groups helps to develop a committed team approach and improve the flow of communications, co-ordination and decision-making. Members of one group could also serve as linking pins between different groups on the same level such as functional, line or product-based work groups. This provides improved horizontal communications and coordination **(Figure 8.6)**.

Virtual teams

Combination of increasing globalisation, competition and widespread developments in information and communications technology has given greater emphasis to **virtual teams**. Instead of involving face-to-face proximity, virtual teams are a collection of people who are geographically separated but still need to work together closely. The primary interaction among members is by some electronic information and communication process. This enables organisations to function away from traditional working hours and the physical availability of staff. Computer-based information systems and increased wireless connectivity further the opportunities for virtual working. By their very nature, virtual teams are likely to be largely self-managed.

Virtual teams may lead to an increase in productivity through a reduction in commute time and greater personal flexibility. Organisations are able to establish a greater worldwide presence. Virtual teams can comprise people with different types of knowledge, help to reduce discrimination and provide wider employment opportunities. A potential difficulty is maintaining effective communications bearing in mind the lack of body language and non-verbal communication **(discussed in Chapter 6).** Virtual teams demand good leadership and management including competence in ICT. Virtual working is not always to the initial liking of all people and it is important to have a remote working strategy.

Some people seem clearly to welcome virtual working with the feeling of autonomy, freedom from distractions and interruptions, and less time and stress on commuting. However, despite the increase in remote working it does not appeal to everyone. Not everyone enjoys working on their own and miss group membership, social structure, contact and interaction. They may feel ignored by the organisation and experience an increasing feeling of isolation. For some people trust is difficult when you cannot see the other person. Without direct personal interaction some people find it difficult to motivate themselves. A sense of discipline and self-motivation is important for effective remote working.

Hall suggests the virtual team is a potential future compromise between fully fledged teams and well-managed groups but is sceptical it will actually create a 'third way'. Video conferences and Net communications are still poor substitutes for the crucible of personal interaction. Although once formed members may know each other but it is the importance of forming, norming and storming to make a team.[19]

Cultural diversity

Symons considers that one advantage of virtual team working is the clarity and richness of contributions when respondents are removed from the urgency of immediate interaction, and that this can be particularly relevant in cross-cultural groups. However, as the leader cannot influence by physical presence, and as hierarchies fade on-line, managing dispersed teams requires a range of subtly different leadership skills. It is important to develop mutual trust and a democratic approach of shared control and decision-making, and adopt the role and style of a coach. 'The leader has to establish and maintain ''credit'' with the group, as ''position power'' has little or no currency in virtual working.'[20]

One reason for the growth in virtual teams is increasing globalisation and team members working and living in different countries. This gives rise to potential difficulties of cultural diversity. As *Francesco and Gold* point out the more culturally diverse the members, the more difficult it is to manage a virtual team.

> **Cultural diversity, which will be increasingly common, adds to the complexity of managing virtual teams because different values, customs, and traditions require more leadership under conditions that reduce the ability to use direct leadership.[21]**

And according to *Murray,* although virtual working presents some unexpected benefits, if managing diversity in the workplace is a tough task for business leaders, the challenges of keeping executives from different backgrounds working together in various parts of the world is even more difficult. Virtual working does not eradicate the sort of cultural misunderstandings that can arise in a face-to-face situation.[22]

Hazelhurst points out that the rise of the virtual organisation is not a universal development and in emerging economies, the office is still a novelty and young people are clamouring to work in them. An office job is alive with exciting possibilities, as well as being a potent symbol of personal success.[23]

How comfortable do YOU feel about working in virtual teams? To what extent do you believe absence of group dynamics and social interactions reduce the effectiveness of virtual teams?

Interactions among group members

Whatever an individual's role within the structure of an organisation, if groups are to be successful and perform effectively, there must be a spirit of unity and co-operation. As *Crainer* reminds us, in most teams people will contribute individual skills, many of which will be different. However, referring to the work of *Obeng,*[24] Crainer points out that it is not enough to have a rag-bag collection of individual skills. For people to work successfully in teams, you need people to behave in certain ways and various behaviours of the team members must mesh together in order to achieve objectives. Some people are needed to concentrate on the task at hand, some to provide specialist knowledge and some to solve problems as they arise. You also need some people to make sure the whole team is contributing fully and some people to make sure that the team is operating as a cohesive social unit.[25]

Individual team roles

One of the most popular analysis of individual roles within a work group or team is that developed by *Meredith Belbin.* Belbin concludes that groups composed entirely of clever people, or of people with similar personalities, display a number of negative results and lack creativity. The most consistently successful groups comprise a range of roles undertaken by various members. The constitution of the group itself is an important variable in its success.[26]

A **team role** is a pattern of behaviour, characteristic of the way in which one team member interacts with another whose performance serves to facilitate the progress of the team as a whole.[27] Strength of contribution in any one role is commonly associated with particular weaknesses. These are called allowable weaknesses. Members are seldom strong in all nine team roles. A description of the evolved nine team roles is given in **Table 8.1.**

An extensive study by *Aritzeta, Swailes and Senior* point to a number of critical assessments of Belbin's work such as:

- concerns about the theoretical basis of the inventory;
- questions concerning the relationship between the role of personality and team roles;

Table 8.1 Belbin's evolved nine team roles

Roles and descriptions – team-role contribution		Allowable weaknesses
Plant	Creative, imaginative, unorthodox. Solves difficult problems.	Ignores details. Too preoccupied to communicate effectively.
Resource investigator	Extravert, enthusiastic, communicative. Explores opportunities. Develops contacts.	Over-optimistic. Loses interest once initial enthusiasm has passed.
Co-ordinator	Mature, confident, a good chairperson. Clarifies goals, promotes decision-making. Delegates well.	Can be seen as manipulative. Offloads personal work.
Shaper	Challenging, dynamic, thrives on pressure. Has the drive and courage to overcome obstacles.	Can provoke others. Hurts people's feelings.
Monitor-Evaluator	Sober, strategic and discerning. Sees all options. Judges accurately.	Lacks drive and ability to inspire others.
Teamworker	Co-operative, mild, perceptive and diplomatic. Listens, builds, averts friction.	Indecisive in crunch situations.
Implementer	Disciplined, reliable, conservative and efficient. Turns ideas into practical actions.	Somewhat inflexible. Slow to respond to new possibilities.
Completer	Painstaking, conscientious, anxious. Searches out errors and omissions. Delivers on time.	Inclined to worry unduly. Reluctant to delegate.
Specialist	Single-minded, self-sharing, dedicated. Provides knowledge and skills in rare supply.	Contributes on only a narrow front. Dwells on technicalities.

Source: Belbin, R. M. *Team Roles at Work,* Butterworth-Heinemann (a division of Reed Elsevier UK Ltd) and Belbin Associates (1993), p. 23. Reproduced with permission.

- lack of clear differentiation among the nine team roles;
- insufficient account of the type of task undertaken by the group;
- influence of organisational factors such as strategy, resources, structure, leadership and management style;
- a dominant psychological approach to understanding teamwork that needs to be complemented by socio-technical considerations.

However, despite negative criticisms the authors do not think it justifiable to suggest the team role theory is flawed. While evidence is mixed, they conclude, on balance, that the model and accompanying inventory have adequate convergent validity.[28]
See also discussion on organisational roles in Chapter 12.

Which team role do YOU believe you normally fit most comfortably? To what extent do you believe your colleagues would agree?

Analysis of individual behaviour

In order to understand and to influence the functioning and operation of a group or team, it is necessary to study patterns of interaction and the parts played by individual members. Not all skilled and capable individuals are necessarily good team players and for example it may sometimes be an advantage to have someone with a more sceptical attitude and open to change. The basic assumption behind the analysis of individual behaviour in groups is from the viewpoint of its function.

A popular classification of member roles in the study of group behaviour is that devised originally by *Benne and Sheats*.[29] The description of member roles performed in well-functioning groups is classified into three broad headings: group task roles, group building and maintenance roles, and individual roles.

- **Group task roles.** These assume that the task of the group is to select, define and solve common problems. For example, initiator-contributor, opinion seeker, co-ordinator, evaluator, recorder.
- **Group building and maintenance roles.** The analysis of member functions is oriented towards activities which build group-centred attitudes or maintain group-centred behaviour. For example, encourager, gatekeeper, standard setter, group commentator.
- **Individual roles.** These are directed towards the satisfaction of personal needs. Their purpose is not related either to group task or to the group functioning. For example, aggressor, blocker, dominator, help-seeker.

Sociometry

Originally developed by *Moreno* in 1953, **sociometry** is a method of indicating the feelings of acceptance or rejection among members of a group.[30] The basis of sociometry is usually 'buddy rating' or 'peer rating'. Each member is asked to nominate or to rate, privately, other members in terms of some given context or characteristic – for example, with whom they communicate, or how influential or how likeable they are. Questions may relate to either work or social activities. For example:

● Who would you most prefer or least prefer to work with closely?

● Who would make a good leader?

● With whom would you choose and not choose to have a drink in the pub or to go on holiday?

Positive and negative choices may be recorded for each person, although sometimes positive choices only are required. Sometimes individuals may be asked to rank their choices.

A sociogram is a diagrammatical illustration of the pattern of interpersonal relationships derived from sociometry and depicts choices, preferences, likes or dislikes and interactions between individual members. An advantage of a diagrammatical illustration is that it can also display a visual description of the structure of the group. It can indicate cliques and sub-groups, compatibility, and members who are popular, isolated or who act as links. **Figure 8.7** gives a simple illustration of an actual sociogram for a group of fifteen members with single, positive choices only.

1 G and M are popular (the stars) and most often chosen by members.

2 M is the link between two overlapping cliques, KML and MNO.

3 H and P are unpopular (isolated) and chosen least by members.

4 JKMO is a chain.

5 ABCD is a sub-group and separated from the rest of the members.

There are several methods of compiling and drawing sociograms, and a number of potential criticisms and limitations. Problems also arise over how to draw the sociogram and how to interpret the roles of individual members. However, if handled sensitively it can serve to encourage meaningful discussions on patterns of social interactions, group behaviour and the perceptions of individual members towards

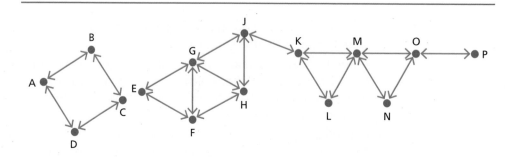

Figure 8.7 A simple illustration of a sociogram

each other. This can serve as a useful basis for the development of both employability and wider social skills.

Self-insight and the Johari window

A simple framework for looking at self-insight is the '**Johari window**'[31] (*see* **Figure 8.8**). This classifies behaviour in matrix form between what is known–unknown to self and what is known–unknown to others in order to encourage a reduction of the individual's 'hidden' behaviour through self-disclosure and of the 'blind' behaviour through feedback from others.

- **Hidden behaviour** is that which the individual wishes to conceal from, or not to communicate to, other group members. It is part of the private self. An important role of the group is to establish whether members conceal too much, or too little, about themselves from other members.

- **The blind area** (that is behaviour known to others but unknown to self) includes mannerisms, gestures and tone of voice and represents behaviour of the impact of which on others the individual is unaware. This is sometimes referred to as the 'bad breath' area. Members must establish an atmosphere of openness and trust in order that hidden and blind behaviours are reduced and the public behaviour enhanced.

Balance between team and individual

Group performance and the satisfaction derived by individuals are influenced by the interactions among members of the group. Individuals in groups interact extensively with each other and with other groups in the organisation. Working in a group is likely to be both psychologically rewarding, and potentially demanding experience for the individual. As an example **Figure 8.9** gives an unsolicited commentary from five final-year business studies degree students after completing a group-based assignment.

Friendships and relationships at work

Increasing attention has been given to the possible effects of friendships and relationships at work, and potential conflict between personal freedom and team performance. **(Recall the discussion in Chapter 2 on the informal organisation.)** While work may be one of the best sources of friends as well as the most desirable

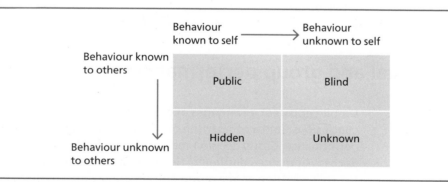

Figure 8.8 The Johari window

What we feel we have learned from working in a group

1 'We learned that we have to listen to everybody's points of view and take these into consideration.'

2 'We found that we had to be prepared to make certain sacrifices and adopted a democratic decision process. However, if an individual felt very strongly about a specific point and persisted with a valid argument then this had to be included.'

3 'We often felt frustrated.'

4 'It was time-consuming and difficult to schedule meetings due to differences in timetables and preferences in working hours.'

5 'We learned that it is good to pool resources because this increased the overall standard of the piece of work. We feel this was only because we all set high personal standards and expected these from our fellow group members. We learned that it is possible to work in other less productive groups where individual levels of achievement may decrease.'

6 'We learned that it is better to work in a smaller and not a larger group, as there is a tendency for individual ideas to be diluted.'

7 'Groups formed on the basis of friendship are not as effective as groups formed with work as the major influence. The former tend to be unproductive.'

8 'We found that it was good to get positive response, encouragement and feedback from team members. Likewise, it was demotivating to receive a negative response.'

9 'We learned a lot about our individual personalities.'

10 'We benefited from sharing personal experiences from our industrial placements.'

11 'It is important to separate work and personal relationships.'

Figure 8.9 unsolicited commentary from students after completing a group-based assignment

place to have them, the trouble is that friendships at work are full of ambiguities. For friendships the trouble with work is that you are there to be useful: to do something for a client, team or boss. Professional friendships will always be influenced and possibly determined by the utility factor.[32] Romance in the workplace presents managers with an interesting problem. 'On the one hand, you seek to shape a team with close bonds; a degree of flirtation may well accompany, even promote this. On the other; an ill-starred liaison that jeopardises, harmony and risks litigation is emphatically to be avoided'.[33]

What do YOU feel about participating in regular sociometry or other self-insight exercises in order to learn more about how you are perceived by your classmates?

Individual and group performance

Despite apparent advantages of group working it is difficult to draw firm conclusions from a comparison between individual and group or team performance. Group decision-making can be frustrating and stressful as well as costly and time-consuming. However, the general feeling appears to be that the collective power of a group outshines individual performance and working together as a team can produce better results and decisions. *Guirdham* for example

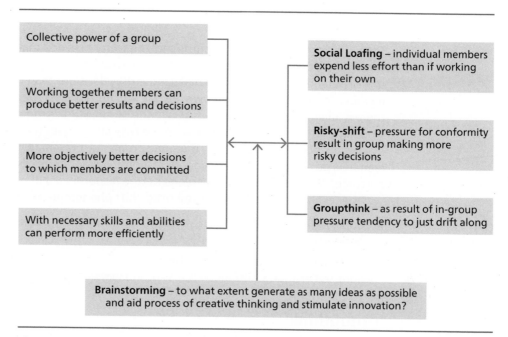

Figure 8.10 Individual compared with group performance

maintains that provided people have the special skills and abilities needed teams can perform functions and carry out projects better and more efficiently. Compared with individuals, groups can make objectively better decisions to which people feel more commitment.[34]

One might expect, therefore, a higher standard of decision-making to result from group discussion. There are, however, particular features of individual versus team performance, including:

* social loafing;
* risky-shift phenomenon;
* groupthink;
* brainstorming.

See **Figure 8.10.**

Social loafing

The concept of **social loafing (or the 'Ringelmann effect')** is the tendency for individual members of a group to expend less effort than if they were working on their own. A German psychologist, Ringelmann, compared results of individual and group performance on a rope-pulling task. Workers were asked to pull as hard as they could on a rope, performing the task first individually and then with others in groups of varying size. A meter measured the strength of each pull. Although the total amount of force did increase with the size of the work group, the effort expended by each individual member decreased with the result that the total group effort was less than the expected sum of the individual contributions.[35] Replications of the Ringelmann effect have generally been supportive of the original findings.[36]

The risky-shift phenomenon

This suggests that instead of the group taking fewer risks and making safer or more conservative decisions, the reverse is often the case. Pressures for conformity mean there is a tendency for groups to make more risky decisions than would individual members of the group on their own. People are arguably less averse to risk when there is an emotional bond with others in the group. Studies suggest that people working in groups generally advocate more risky alternatives than if they were making an individual decision on the same problem.[37] Presumably this is because members do not feel the same sense of responsibility for group decisions or their outcomes. 'A decision which is everyone's is the responsibility of no one.'

Other explanations offered for **the risky-shift phenomenon** include:

- People inclined to take risks are more influential in group discussions than more conservative people.
- Risk-taking is regarded as a desirable cultural characteristic that is more likely to be expressed in a social situation such as group working.[38]

'Groupthink'

The effectiveness of group behaviour and performance can be adversely affected by the idea of '**groupthink**'. This is when individual members of a group fail to speak out at what they believe is the wrong decision. From an examination of some well-known American policy-making including the 1961 Bay of Pigs fiasco *Janis* concluded that decisions can be characterised by groupthink which he defines as 'a deterioration of mental efficiency, reality testing, and moral judgment that results from in-group pressures'.[39] Groupthink results in the propensity for the group to just drift along. It is a generalised feature and can be apparent in any organisational situation where groups are relied upon to make important decisions.

Janis identifies a number of specific symptoms of groupthink:

- Illusion of invulnerability by excessive optimism and overestimating power of the group;
- Discrediting of negative feedback that contradicts group consensus;
- Unquestioned belief in the inherent morality of the group;
- Negative stereotyping of opponents or people outside the group, or to the acceptance of change;
- Pressure on individual members to conform and reach consensus so that minority or unpopular ideas may be suppressed;
- Self-censorship to avoid doubts or speaking against apparent consensus;
- Illusion of unanimity when to prevent disagreements silence is taken as agreement by the most vocal members;
- Mindguards' failure to pass on information or screening adverse information from outsiders.

Brainstorming

A **brainstorming approach** (sometimes referred to as 'thought showers' or 'cloud bursting' in order not to offend people with conditions such as epilepsy) involves a group of between six to ten members adopting a 'freewheeling' attitude and generating as many ideas as possible, the more wild or apparently far-fetched the better.[40] As an illustrative exercise a group may be asked to generate as many and varied possible uses as they can for, for example, a man or woman's leather belt. Brainstorming is based on encouraging members to suspend judgement, the assumption that creative thinking is achieved best by encouraging the natural inclinations of group members, and free association of ideas. The quantity of ideas will lead to quality of ideas.

There are a number of basic procedures for brainstorming.

- Maximum freedom of expression with a totally relaxed and informal approach. Members are encouraged to elaborate or build on ideas expressed by others and to bounce suggestions off one another.

- Initial emphasis is on the quantity of ideas generated, not the quality of ideas. No individual ideas are criticised or rejected at this stage, however wild or fanciful they may appear.

- Need for good reporting of all the ideas either in writing and/or by tape or video recording.

An interesting and popular exercise to help illustrate the suspension of initial perceived barriers and the encouragement of creative thinking is given in **Figure 8.11.** This exercise may also be used to compare individual and group/team-based performance.

One might reasonably expect that members of a brainstorming group would produce more creative problem-solving ideas than if the same members worked alone as individuals. Availability of time is an important factor. Over a longer period of time the group may produce more ideas through brainstorming than individuals could. Perhaps surprisingly there appears to be doubt about the effectiveness of brainstorming groups over nominal groups or individuals working under the same conditions.[41] However, any procedure which aids the process of creativity **(discussed in Chapter 5)** should be welcomed and there are a number of potential positive achievements in terms of related structural techniques for stimulating innovation.

In what particular situations do YOU believe there is value in a brainstorming approach? Explain the caveats you have concerning the potential effectiveness of brainstorming.

The task is to see if it is possible to touch each of the nine spots using only four straight, interconnected lines.

Figure 8.11 An example of creative thinking

Building successful teams

Whatever the debate about individual and group or team performance, effective team working is of increasing importance in modern organisations. *The Chartered Management Institute* point out that increasingly a team may be composed of people drawn from different functions, departments and disciplines who have been brought together for a specific project. Teams can play a key role in organisational success, but the development of good working relationships and practices is vital to team performance.[42]

Increasing attention to teamwork has placed greater attention on interpersonal skills. How people behave and perform as members of a group is as important as their behaviour or performance as individuals. Harmonious working relationships and good teamwork help make for a high level of staff morale and work performance. Teamwork is important in any organisation but may be especially significant in emergency and caring industries or service industries such as hospitality organisations where there is a direct effect on customer satisfaction.[43]

Yukl refers to the purpose of team building as being to increase cohesiveness, mutual co-operation and identification with the group. Based on research, theory and practice, Yukl identifies eight team building procedures:

- **Emphasise common interests and values** – collective identification is stronger when members agree about objectives, values, priorities, strategies and the need for co-operation.
- **Use ceremonies and rituals** – to increase identification with the group and make membership appear special. The use of rituals for initiation and retirement, and ceremonies for special occasions or events.
- **Use symbols to develop identification with the group** – such as team name, logo, insignia, emblem or particular colour to help create a special identity for the team.
- **Encourage and facilitate social interaction** – development of a cohesive group is more likely when members get to know each other on a personal basis and find social interactions satisfying.
- **Tell people about group activities and achievements** – keeping members informed about the plans, activities and achievements and how their work contributes to the success of the mission.
- **Conduct process analysis sessions** – frank and open discussions of interpersonal relationships and group processes including suggestions on how to improve effectiveness.
- **Conduct alignment sessions** – to increase mutual understanding among team members and to overcome negative stereotypes and attributions.
- **Increase incentives for mutual co-operation** – incentives based not individually but on group performance to encourage co-operation, such as bonus based on team performance.[44]

'Away days'

Another approach to team building is the use of activity-based exercises undertaken as part of corporate bonding, usually referred to as '**away days**'. The main objective is often the building of team spirit and working relationships involving formal team dynamics and assessment, although this may also be linked with a social purpose, for example to develop interactions with colleagues, improve motivation or to thank and reward staff. The idea of away days is subject to frequent criticism and even ridicule. Individuals may feel pressurised into participating for fear of not appearing to support management initiative or their group colleagues.

Margerison team wheel

From work with teams in major oil companies, *Margerison* concluded they lacked a common teamwork language to deal with team issues or for learning and development. After further work with *McCann* in a range of other organisations, Margerison identified nine key major skills necessary in every business and team that can improve your work contribution. The key to the system is the 'Team Wheel' – **Figure 8.12.**

The nine key factors cover all aspects of teamwork in every organisation. Linking is the all-encompassing area of co-ordination, and organisation success depends on how effectively members of the team link to achieve objectives.

- **Advising** – gathering and reporting information
- **Innovating** – creating and experimenting with ideas
- **Promoting** – exploring and presenting opportunities
- **Developing** – assessing and planning applications
- **Organising** – organising staff and resources
- **Producing** – concluding and delivering output
- **Inspecting** – controlling and auditing contracts and procedures

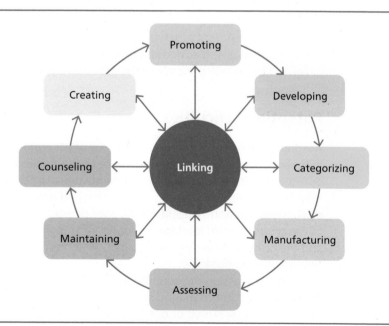

Figure 8.12 Margerison 'Team Wheel'
Source: Charles J. Margerison, *Team Leadership: A guide to success with Team Management Systems,* Thomson (2002), p. 8.

- **Maintaining** – upholding and safeguarding standards and values
- **Linking** – co-ordinating and integrating the work of others

The Team Wheel can also be used as a focus for reviewing both internal links between each member of the team and external linking with other teams and key stakeholders such as clients.[45]

Based on your own experience how far do YOU agree with Yukl's team-building procedures? Detail changes you would make to this list of procedures.

Autonomous working groups

An important development in work redesign and job enrichment is a form of work organisation based on autonomous work groups (or self-managed work groups) who are encouraged to manage their own work and working practices. The group operates without direct supervision and decides for itself how work should be distributed and carried out. Members of the group assume greater autonomy and responsibility for the effective performance of the work. With greater empowerment the belief is that members will feel more committed to the objectives and operations of the group.

Key features of the self-managed work group include the following:

- specific goals are set for the group but members decide the best means by which these goals are to be achieved and have greater freedom and wider discretion over the planning, execution and control of their work;
- collectively members of the group have the necessary variety of expertise and skills to undertake the tasks of the group successfully;
- the level of external supervision is reduced and the role of supervisor becomes more one of giving advice and support to the group. Feedback and evaluation are related to the performance of the group as a whole.

Potential difficulties

Autonomous working groups are not free of potential difficulties. With greater independence there may be a resistance to change and the acceptance of new ideas or responsibilities. With less management control internal battles other authority may develop within the group. A self-managed group is more likely to establish its own values and norms including the pace of work that may be at variance with those of the organisation. Developments with information communications technology and the growth of remote team working enable individuals to work collaboratively despite physical distance.

A radio discussion programme on the need for managers drew attention to the following: 'Self-managed structures are tribal and you are only in or out with the popular crowd or out on your own. In self-managed organisations, culture is compulsory and essential that everyone has to sign up to the prevailing ideology'.[46]

Skills to build self-managed teams

Cloke and Goldsmith refer to the special skills required for successful teamwork and list ten skills team members can develop in order to build innovative self-managing teams. All of these skills are interrelated, mutually reinforcing and dependent upon each of the others.[47]

- **Skill of self-management** – overcoming obstacles together; and building a sense of ownership, responsibility, commitment and efficiency within each team member.
- **Skill of communication** – collaboratively developing skills in becoming better listeners, communicating honestly about things that really matter.
- **Skill of leadership** – creating opportunities for each member to be skilled in order to serve as leader.
- **Skill of responsibility** – personal responsibility not only for their own work but for the work of every other member of the team in order to become self-managing.
- **Skill of supportive diversity** – allow team members to overcome prejudices and biases and not create winners and losers, reject outsiders or mistrust people who are different.
- **Skills of feedback and evaluation** – essential to improving learning, team communication and the quality of products, processes and relationships.
- **Skill of strategic planning** – identify challenges and opportunities collaboratively. Think long term, be proactive and focus on solutions rather than problems.
- **Skill of shaping successful meetings** – team meetings can be streamlined and made shorter, more satisfying and more productive, and result in expanded consensus.
- **Skill of resolving conflicts** – encourage members to improve skills in problem-solving, collaborative negotiation, responding to difficult behaviour and conflict resolution.
- **Skill of enjoyment** – most team members enjoy working together to accomplish difficult tasks, meeting high-performance challenges and producing results that benefit themselves and their teams, organisations and communities.

Role of team leader

Building successful teams requires effective leadership with an emphasis on trust, clear communications, full participation and self-management. In her discussion of the 'democratic enterprise' (organisations which can flourish economically and can also be places of excitement and stimulation, fulfilment and tranquillity), *Gratton* maintains that it is the leaders of the teams across the organisation who make the company vision a reality on a day-to-day basis. The team leaders are the creators of space in which choice and freedom can be exercised; they delineate the obligations and accountabilities contained within the business goals; they become role models for how members should behave; and they bring the philosophy of autonomy and personal development to realisation by the manner in which they act as mentors and coaches.[48]

A team rarely demonstrates more passion or behaves more positively than its leader. If you want to see the efficacy of a leader and his or her leadership style, then you need to look no further than the team he or she leads.

A cynical leader produces a cynical team; an innovative and creative leader will produce an innovative and creative team. A team that has energy, enthusiasm and innovation will be the product of leadership that shows the same qualities.

With the football business as an example, *Karen Brady* refers to the importance for any organisation, especially with a people business, of bringing staff with you, building a team around you, and how team ethic leads to success. 'It works because of respect for each other and knowing their strengths and weaknesses. We don't step into each other's territories but support them instead and leave each one to each role.'[49]

Continuous improvement and innovation

Acas strongly supports autonomous work groups. Reorganising the workforce into teams is not easy but when developed successfully team working has been shown to be a way of improving competitiveness and at the same time enhancing the quality of working life for employees. However, the concept of autonomous teams may be misleading as teams will always be answerable to management and rely on the provision of resources and other support. Acas suggest one of the best ways to ensure teams continue to develop is to move towards self-regulation and monitoring progress by assessing the level of dependence on management.

The Acas advisory booklet concludes that although self-regulation is necessary if the potential of team working is to be realised, teams will always need some degree of management direction. The task of management is to oversee the development of teams and provide the necessary support and training. Even when in place, teams will need constant monitoring and development. Team working is not a finite project but a process of continuous improvement and innovation.

> **The introduction of team working is a major step for an organisation to take. It is important that management, trade unions and employees ensure they know how team working will contribute to their business strategy and that it is likely to involve a long-term transformation.**[50]

To what extent do YOU agree support for autonomous working groups is much like the 'Emperor's new clothes' – good in theory but in reality rarely work well without supervision?

Critical Thinking Zone

Reflections on Managing Virtual Teams

In this zone, we critically discuss the phenomenon of virtual teams and explore the challenges of managing a team in the absence of co-location.

The utilisation of virtual teams as a medium to facilitate boundaryless, collaborative knowledge sharing, communication and task completion has risen dramatically in recent years and become the norm in many organisations[51,52] Defined as 'groups of geographically and/or organisationally dispersed co-workers that are assembled using a combination of telecommunications and information technologies to accomplish an organisational task'[53] (p. 18), virtual teams enable organisations to capitalise on increased resource utilisation, greater flexibility and wider access to knowledge, expertise and creativity outside the organisation's boundaries.[51,54] Significantly, Townsend *et al.*'s[53] definition posits that virtual teams are not exclusively found in geographically dispersed regions; they can be located within the same office or even country.

Dimensions of Virtuality

The extent of a team's virtuality is, according to Gibson and Cohen,[55] multidimensional and complex. Such complexity embodies three key dimensions, which Kirkman *et al.*[56] espouse transcend the technology used to support virtual working and the team's raison d'être. First, the proportion of time the team interact and work face-to-face compared to virtually. Second, the time they spend at any one location. In this dimension, the highest level of virtuality occurs when all team members work at geographically distant locations. Third, the proportion of time individuals devote to a virtual team project, which may only be a few hours a month, in comparison to time they spend on completing other duties. Berry[54] contends that a further defining feature is the amount of computer-mediated communication (CMC) technology the team uses. He proposes that the level of virtuality increases as the team's reliance on electronic communication intensifies.

Virtual Managerial Challenges

According to Dulebohn and Hoch,[57] despite widening research and theorisation on, and a growing practitioner interest in, virtual teams, little is known about how to successfully manage them and their dynamics. Managers are thus faced with a plethora of challenges, which Berry and Nydegger and Nydegger[58] advise must be addressed if virtual teams are to be effectively utilised within the organisation. First, communication can be hindered by the misinterpretation and miscommunication of messages, due to the absence of non-verbal cues, tone of voice and slow, delayed or missing information and feedback.[51] Second, engagement in teamwork and collaboration may be potentially lower, leading to reduced motivation and productivity. Third, team members may experience feelings of detachment and isolation from colleagues and the work itself, due to the absence of co-location, raised levels of social distance and lack of identity.[54,55] Fourth, managers may find it difficult, though, one could argue, not impossible, to manage and monitor performance, particularly in teams that operate in geographically dispersed and remote locations and in situations where levels of team cohesion, work satisfaction and co-operative behaviour have decreased.[55] Additionally, managers are challenged to address the major issue of a reduction in tacit knowledge creation, sharing and collaboration that are normally generated and enhanced through socialisation, co-location and face-to-face contact.[59, 60] This lack of interaction may lead to knowledge hoarding and protectionism,[61] a consequence of which is duplication of effort and increased costs.[62]

Working Differently, Not Onerously

The above scenario paints a rather negative and, arguably, onerous portrait of utilising virtual teams in the organisation. However, in support of virtual teams, Thiefels[63] insists that 'remote collaboration doesn't have to be hard.' She suggests, albeit simplistically, that all managers need to do to promote collaborative, virtual working is to assemble the organisation's basic communication tools, such as email and telephone, together with regular scheduled meetings. In this way, she espouses, 'you'll quickly realise that getting employees to collaborate virtually is similar to doing so in person . . . you have the tools and skills, you just have to use them differently.' Rebecca Ranninger,[64] former

Executive Vice President and Chief HR Officer of Symantec, argues that it is more complex than Thiefels infers. Although working flexibly and with more freedom has been a good and positive move for her organisation and has resulted in happier employees, she hints that the twenty first century, virtual, always on workplace has created a psychology whereby individuals find it more difficult to dichotomise between work and their home lives. Technology, she protests, has taken away 'the limitations of time and space.' Ranninger caveats that the communal-experience of sitting around a table, and the camaraderie it generates, is lost in a virtual world. She lamented 'how do we ensure that people have the same kind of experience they used to get sitting in a room when they are no longer in the same hemisphere?' She notes the importance of managers ensuring that virtual team members remain 'connected to work in a human way' and, crucially, do not become 'a voice on the phone and a line on a screen.'

Although virtual teams offer organisations greater flexibility, enhanced team member diversity and access to a wider global knowledge pool, Nydegger and Nydegger caveat that managers may resent their implementation because it might threaten their power base, due to the autonomous nature of virtual team working. To counter this, Ranninger suggests that organisations can initiate 'remote management' training, which develops specific skills and techniques to manage a local and international cadre of diverse individuals and the inevitable stresses and complexities that accompany managing virtual teams, regardless of their location and dimension of virtuality.

Implications for Organisational Behaviour in the Workplace

To conclude, virtual teams are a global phenomenon. As well as providing a raft of benefits to organisations,

in terms of increased flexibility and access to a wider pool of knowledge and expertise, Berry caveats that the adoption of virtual teams can only be successful if organisations create an environment that is conducive to effective virtual teamwork and importantly, invest in a technological infrastructure that supports the differing dimensions of virtuality and knowledge and informational needs of team members. To avert the negativities posed by the implementation of virtual teams, Nydegger and Nydegger posit that organisations must ensure their managers have bought into, and engaged with, virtualisation programmes and be appropriately supported and trained to manage the complexities of virtual working. If not, Berry advises that the failure or success of virtual teams, or indeed the organisation itself, 'may well be a consequence of inept leadership or management, more than a consequence of technology or other factors.'

Questions

In view of the above, answer the following questions.

1. Virtual teams can yield a raft of benefits to an organisation, but they also have their drawbacks. *Write* a balanced business case *for* the implementation of a virtual team. *Justify* your case with reference to theory and practice.

2. *How* can organisations mitigate against the feelings of detachment and isolation that Berry and Gibson and Cohen suggest virtual team members often experience?

3. Thiefels advocates that 'remote collaboration doesn't have to be hard.' *To what extent* do you agree with her view?

Summary – Chapter 8 'Working in groups and teams'

Groups are characteristic of all social situations and a major feature of the work organisation. The terms 'groups' and 'teams' are used interchangeably but it does not necessarily follow that all groups are teams. Formal groups are concerned with co-ordination of work activities. Within the formal structure informal groups develop to satisfy psychological and social needs. The manager's concern is members work together as a united, cohesive team with supportive relationships and prevent unconstructive inter-group conflict. Continuing globalisation and developments in ICT has given emphasis to the virtual teams. Members are geographically separated but still need to work together closely. To influence the working of groups it is necessary to understand and analyse patterns of interactions and roles played by individual members. It is difficult to draw any firm conclusion from comparison between group and individual performance. Growth of team work has led to increased interest in attention to social skills, competencies and leadership. Development in forms of work organisation has given rise to autonomous or self-managed working groups. How people behave and perform as members of a group is as important as their actions as individuals. Continual development and improvement is a necessary part of effective teamwork.

Group discussion activities

Undertake each of these activities in small groups as indicated by your tutor.

Before you start your discussion establish a non-threatening environment within the group and confirm confidentiality will be honoured.

First, form your own views and then share and compare in open discussion with colleagues.

Reflect honestly on the extent to which: (i) you influenced the thinking and ideas of your colleagues; and (ii) you were influenced by your colleagues.

To what extent was your group able to reach consensus?

Agree one of your members to produce a brief written summary of the discussion and prepared to present in a plenary session.

Activity 1

(a) Given the importance of social interactions and interpersonal relationships for morale, job satisfaction and work performance the main focus of your studies should be on the operations and management of the informal organisation.

(b) To gain a greater appreciation of teamwork attention should be given in the classroom to the management and functioning of accomplished musical ensembles and successful sports teams.

Activity 2

You are required to design and present an 'ice-breaker' exercise as a fun way to help groups of new students (or other new members or delegates) to get to know and interact with each other. The exercise should be **simple, easy to understand and undertake, entertaining, something to which all members of the team/group can contribute, and that can be completed within 30 minutes.**

Your tutor will be asked to decide which team has come up with the most novel, engaging and appropriate exercise.

If possible, attempt to employ the chosen exercise in a real-life situation. How successful was the exercise?

Activity 3

(a) Self-interest and opportunism are natural features of human behaviour and will always take precedence over demands and the best interest of teamwork.

(b) Discussion on building successful teams sounds fine in theory but ignores realities of the work environment. For example, managing groups of diverse people in a restaurant kitchen, production assembly line, gay pub, or professionals such as doctors or lecturers.

(c) Applying your knowledge and understanding of small group behaviour, evaluate the likely effectiveness of the jury trial system.

Organisational behaviour in action case study
Remote team working

Joanne Mooney, customer journey and online experience manager, British Gas, based in Stockport, and her boss, **Lucy Shadholt,** head of channel development for British Gas New Energy, based in Staines.

In the two years she's been working remotely for British Gas, Mooney has enjoyed the flexibility and greater access to her young family, and feels she mostly gets the balance right. 'You have to know when to switch off. At home, define your space, define your roles in the house, be disciplined in your working day, when it starts and stops. It's not always fair to the family – they know mummy's working, so they have to talk in hushed tones and that seems restrictive to them in their own home.' She had managed a call centre of 150 people and sometimes misses the banter. 'When I started, I was 100% working from home. I prefer the mix of the new role, where I'm getting out and meeting people. It's easier to build the relationship over the phone if you've met the person.'

Lucy Shadbolt, head of channel development for British Gas New Energy, is Mooney's boss. Since taking on the role in October she has built a team of 10, all of whom work at least part of the time remotely, including herself. 'It suits me; I get so much more done. The whole team love it,' she says. Shadbolt runs weekly meetings from the Staines office and is in regular contact with each team member. 'Some things are not suitable for conference calls. If I have to have a difficult conversation it needs to be face to face.' She's

confident she's getting good performance from each of them: 'You have to trust them. I make it clear with new team members that working from home is a privilege. If you give clear objectives it's easy to monitor output. People don't work 9 to 5, they work longer. It's not unusual to send an email at 10pm. Work is where your laptop is.'

Shadbolt acknowledges some aspects of her own career development are more difficult to achieve at arm's length – such as getting the ear of the boss. 'When I go into the office, where we hot-desk, I have to make an effort to position myself near my boss. You need to consciously build relationships when you don't have those water-cooler moments naturally occurring.'

Source: 'Take-home lessons: Tips from remote workers and their bosses', *Management Today,* March 2011, p. 49. www.managementtoday.com. Reproduced with permission.

Tasks

1. What particular problems do you envisage with remote team working?

2. Explain how would you attempt to establish mutual trust when you cannot see the other person?

3. Discuss fully the extent to which you would be happy as a remote team worker.

Chapter 8 – Personal skills and employability exercise

Objectives

Completing this exercise should help you to enhance the following skills:

* Evaluate the role(s) you play within the team and the contribution you make.
* Explore your relationships with other members of the team.
* Receive and give honest feedback about strengths and personal weaknesses.

In order to work well with other people, you need to know and understand yourself and be prepared to receive honest feedback from your colleagues. The effectiveness of a team can be enhanced by a genuine openness among its members.

Exercise

For this exercise, work in pairs with another team member – if possible from a different ethnicity, culture, gender or age group. You should both agree to honour confidentiality and to conduct the exercise as a means of providing constructive feedback.

Part 1 – refer to Belbin's nine team roles, Table 8.1 in the text of this chapter and ask the following question of each other.

1. For what role do you think I am most suited – and why?

Next refer to the Margerison Team Wheel Figure 8.12 in the text and ask the following question of each other:

2. In what ways can I contribute more to the work of the team?

Part 2

Now ask the follow-up questions below of each other:

3. Which member of the team do you believe I am most close to and which member most distant from?

4. What do you see as my major strengths and personal weaknesses as a member of the team?

5. What is it about me that you find most annoying?

6. In what ways could we help each other in our work?

7. How can I be a better all-round member of the team?

Discussion

After you have both completed these questions consider carefully and honestly:

* What have you learned about yourself from this activity?
* What response from your colleague surprised you the most?
* To what extent has this exercise helped you to understand how well you work as a team member? Put this in writing as an aid to discipline and for your personal reflection.

Notes and references

1. Adair, J. *Effective Teambuilding,* Gower (1986).
2. Peterson, C., Park, N and Sweeney, P. J. 'Group Well-being: Morale from a Positive Psychology Perspective', *Applied Psychology: An International Review,* vol. 57, 2008, pp. 19–36.
3. Schein, E. H. *Organizational Psychology,* third edition, Prentice Hall (1988), p. 145.
4. ACAS *Teamwork: Success Through People* advisory booklet, ACAS (2007), p. 24.
5. Belbin, R. M. *Beyond the Team,* Butterworth-Heinemann (2000).
6. 'Steps in Successful Team Building: Checklist 088', Chartered Management Institute, June 2011.
7. Lysons, K. 'Organisational Analysis', *Supplement to The British Journal of Administrative Management,* no. 18, March/April 1997.
8. Hazlehurst, J. 'The Way We Work Now', *Management Today,* June 2013, pp. 46–9.
9. Farrell, E. 'Take the Lead in Setting Standards of Behaviour in your Team', *Professional Manager,* vol. 19, no. 1, January 2009, p. 14.
10. Tuckman, B. W. 'Development Sequence in Small Groups', *Psychological Bulletin,* vol. 63, 1965, pp. 384–99; and Tuckman, B. W. and Jensen, M. C. 'Stages of Small Group Development Revised', *Group and Organizational Studies,* vol. 2, no. 3, 1977, pp. 419–27.
11. Cited in Green, J. 'Are Your Teams and Groups at Work Successful?', *Administrator,* December 1993, p. 12.
12. Rickards, T. and Moger, S. T. 'Creative Leadership and Team Effectiveness: Empirical Evidence for a Two Barrier Model of Team Development', working paper presented at the Advanced Seminar Series, University of Uppsala, Sweden, 3 March 2009. See also Rickards, T. and Moger, S. 'Creative Leadership Processes in Project Team Development: An Alternative to Tuckman's Stage Model?', *British Journal of Management,* Part 4, 2000, pp. 273–83.
13. Tajfel, H. and Turner, J. C. 'The Social Identity Theory of Intergroup Behavior', in Worchel, S. and Austin, L. W. (eds) *Psychology of Intergroup Relations,* Nelson-Hall (1986), pp. 7–24.
14. Haslam, S. A. *Psychology in Organizations: The Social Identity Approach,* second edition, Sage Publications (2004), p. 17.
15. Guirdham, M. *Interactive Behaviour at Work,* third edition, Financial Times Prentice Hall (2002), p. 118.
16. Hewstone, M., Ruibin, M. and Willis, H. 'Intergroup Bias', *Annual Review of Psychology,* vol. 53, 2002, pp. 575–604.
17. Argyle, M. *The Social Psychology of Work,* second edition, Penguin (1989).
18. Likert, R. *New Patterns of Management,* McGraw-Hill (1961).
19. Hall, P. 'Team Solutions Need Not Be the Organisational Norm', *Professional Manager,* July 2001, p. 45.
20. Symons, J. 'Taking Virtual Team Control', *Professional Manager,* vol. 12, no. 2, March 2003, p. 37.
21. Francesco, A. M. and Gold, B. A. *International Organizational Behavior,* second edition, Pearson Prentice Hall (2005), p. 118.
22. Murray, S. 'Virtual Teams: Global Harmony is their Dream', *Financial Times,* 11 May 2005.
23. Hazlehurst, J. 'The Way We Work Now', *Management Today,* June 2013, pp. 46–9.
24. Obeng, E. *All Change,* Pitman Publishing (1994).
25. Crainer, S. *Key Management Ideas: Thinkers That Changed the Management World,* third edition, Financial Times Prentice Hall (1998), p. 238.
26. Belbin, R. M. *Management Teams: Why They Succeed or Fail,* Butterworth-Heinemann (1981).
27. Belbin, R. M. *Team Roles at Work,* Butterworth-Heinemann (1993). See also: Belbin, M. *The Belbin Guide to Succeeding at Work,* A & C Black (2009).
28. Aritzeta, A., Swailes, S, and Senior, B. 'Belbin's Team Role model: Development, Validity and Applications for Team Building', *Journal of Management Studies,* vol. 44, no. 1, January 2007, pp. 96–118.
29. Benne, K. D. and Sheats, P. 'Functional Roles of Group Members', *Journal of Social Issues,* vol. 4, 1948, pp. 41–9.
30. Moreno, J. L. *Who Shall Survive?* Beacon House (1953). See also Moreno, J. L. and Jennings, H. H. *The Sociometry Reader,* Free Press of Glencoe (1960).
31. Luft, J. *Group Processes: An Introduction to Group Dynamics,* second edition, National Press (1970). (The term 'Johari window' was derived from a combination of the first names of the original authors, Joseph Luft and Harry Ingham.)
32. Vernon, M. 'Office Friends: Who Needs Them?', *Management Today,* September 2005, pp. 59–61.
33. Newman, R. 'Love Games', *Professional Manager,* September/October 2011, pp. 19–23.
34. Guirdham, M. *Interactive Behaviour at Work,* third edition, Financial Times Prentice Hall (2002), p. 498.
35. Kravitz, D. A. and Martin, B. 'Ringelmann Rediscovered: The Original Article', *Journal of Personality and Social Psychology,* May 1986, pp. 936–41.
36. See, for example, Karau, S. J. and Williams, K. D. 'Social Loafing: A Meta-analysis Review and Theoretical Integration', *Journal of Personality and Social Psychology,* October 1993, pp. 681–706: and Liden, R. C., Wayne, S. J., Jaworkski, R.A. and Bennett, N. 'Social Loafing: A Field Investigation', *Journal of Management,* vol. 30, no. 2 (2004), pp. 285–304.
37. Kogan, N. and Wallach, M. A. 'Risk-Taking as a Function of the Situation, the Person and the Group', in

Newcomb, T. M. (ed.) *New Directions in Psychology III,* Holt, Rinehart and Winston (1967).

38. For a comprehensive review of the 'risky-shift' phenomenon, see, for example, Clarke, R. D. 'Group Induced Shift Towards Risk: A Critical Appraisal', *Psychological Bulletin,* vol. 76, 1971, pp. 251–70. See also Vecchio, R. P. *Organizational Behavior,* third edition, Harcourt Brace and Company (1995).

39. Janis, J. L. *Victims of Groupthink,* Houghton Mifflin (1972) and Janis, J. L. *Groupthink,* second edition, Houghton Mifflin (1982).

40. Osborn, A. F. *Applied Imagination: Principles and Procedures of Creative Thinking,* Scribner's (1963).

41. See, for example: Jones, E. E. and Lambertus, D .D. 'Expecting Less from Groups: A New Perspective on Shortcomings in Idea Generation Groups', *Group Dynamics: Theory, research and practice,* vol. 18, No. 3 (2014) pp. 237–50.

42. 'Steps in Successful Team Building: Checklist 088', Chartered Management Institute, June 2011.

43. See, for example, Mullins, L. J. and Dossor, P. *Hospitality Management and Organisational Behaviour,* fifth edition, Pearson Education (2013).

44. Yukl, G. *Leadership in Organizations,* seventh edition, Pearson Prentice Hall (2010) pp. 374–7.

45. Margerison, C. J. *Team Leadership: A Guide to Success with Team Management Systems,* Thomson (2002).

46. 'The Joy of 9 to 5: Do We Need Managers?' BBC Radio 4 13 April 2016.

47. Cloke, K. and Goldsmith, J. *The End of Management and the Rise of Organizational Democracy,* Jossey-Bass (2002).

48. Gratton, L. *The Democratic Enterprise,* Financial Times Prentice Hall (2004).

49. Brady, K in conversation with Webber, M. 'Team Focus', *Manager,* Spring 2013, pp. 36–8.

50. ACAS *Teamwork: Success Through People* advisory booklet, ACAS (2007).

51. Klitmøller, A. and Lauring, J. 'When Global Virtual Teams Share Knowledge: Media Richness, Cultural Difference and Language Commonality', *Journal of World Business,* vol. 48, 2013, pp. 398–406.

52. Zander, L., Zettinig, P. and Mäkelä, K. 'Leading Global Virtual Teams to Success', *Organization Dynamics,* vol. 42, 2013, p. 237.

53. Townsend, A. M., DeMarie, S. M. and Hendrickson, A. R. 'Virtual Teams: Technology and The Workplace of The Future', *The Academy of Management Executive,* vol. 12, no. 3, 1998, pp. 17–29.

54. Berry, G. R. 'Enhancing Effectiveness on Virtual Teams: Understanding Why Traditional Team Skills Are Insufficient', *Journal of Business Communication,* vol. 48, no. 2, 2011, pp. 186–206.

55. Gibson, C. G. and Cohen, S. G. *Virtual Teams That Work: Creating Conditions for Virtual Teams Effectiveness* (2003), Jossey-Bass.

56. Kirkman, B. L., Rosen, B., Gibson, C. B., Tesluk, P. E. and McPherson, S. O. 'Five challenges to virtual team success: Lessons from Sabre Inc', *Academy of Management Review,* vol. 16, no. 3, 2002, pp. 67–79.

57. Dulebohn, J. H. and Hoch, J. E. 'Virtual Teams in Organizations', *Human Resource Management Review,* vol. 27, 2017, p. 574.

58. Nydegger, R. and Nydegger, L. 'Challenges in Managing Virtual Teams', *Journal of Business & Economics Research*', vol. 8, no. 3, 2010, pp. 69–81.

59. Nonaka, I. and Takeuchi, H. *The Knowledge Creating Company: How Japanese Companies Create the Dynamics of Innovation,* Oxford University Press (1995).

60. Ahmed, P. and Shepherd, C. *Innovation Management: Contexts, Strategies, Systems and Processes,* Financial Times Prentice Hall (2010).

61. Zhang, M. J. and Chen, H. 'Trust and Knowledge Sharing in Virtual Teams: The Case of China', *WHICEB Proceedings,* vol. 10, 2015, p. 192.

62. Patriotta, G., Castellano, A. and Wright, M. 'Coordinating knowledge transfer: Global managers as higher-level intermediaries', *Journal of World Business,* vol. 48, 2013, pp. 515–26.

63. Thiefels, J. 'Remote collaboration: It's not as hard as you think', Virgin, 2017, https://www.virgin.com/entrepreneur/remote-collaboration-its-not-as-hard-as-you-think (accessed 24 August 2018).

64. Ranninger, R. 'The evolution of work: One company's story', *The McKinsey Quarterly,* 2012, https://www.mckinsey.com/business-functions/organization/our-insights/the-evolution-of-work-one-companys-story (accessed 24 August 2018).

Chapter 9
Leadership in work organisations

The leader–follower relationship is reciprocal and effective leadership is a two-way process that influences both individual and organisational performance.

Learning outcomes

After completing this chapter you should have enhanced your ability to:

- explain the significance and nature of leadership in work organisations;
- contrast main approaches to, and studies of, leadership;
- explore different styles and forms of leadership;
- detail situational forces and variables in the leadership situation;

- explain the leadership relationship;
- examine the variables affecting effective leadership;
- review the nature and importance of leadership development.

Outline chapter contents

Overview topic map: Chapter 9 – Leadership in work organisations

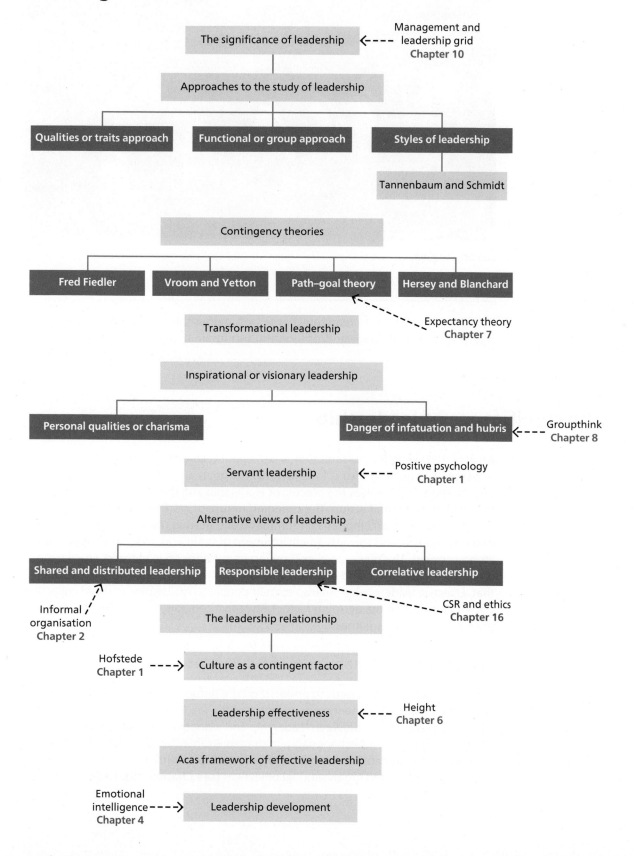

Leading the way

Before commencing to read this chapter, what does the term 'leadership' mean to YOU and what image and/or situation springs immediately to mind?

The significance of leadership

An essential element of organisational behaviour is co-ordinating the activities of people and guiding their efforts towards the goals and objectives of the organisation. This involves the process of leadership and the choice of an appropriate form of behaviour and action. The changing nature of work organisations involves moving away from an emphasis on command and getting results by the close control of the workforce; and towards an environment of teamwork coaching, support and empowerment. This places an ever-growing importance on leadership. Leadership is related to motivation and interpersonal behaviour.[1] A CBI report makes the point that 'Effective leaders, who can inspire their people to realise personal and collective potential, are often the deciding factor between a company being good at what it does and achieving greatness.'[2]

Leadership and management

The successful manager needs to understand the nature and influence of leadership and factors that determine the effectiveness of the leadership relationship. But what is the relationship between leadership and management? Although the two terms are often used interchangeably, management may be viewed as relating to people working within a structured organisation and with prescribed roles, in order to achieve stated organisational objectives **(see Chapter 10).** The emphasis of leadership is on interpersonal behaviour in a broader context. It is often associated with the willing and enthusiastic behaviour of followers.

Arguably there are differences between leadership and management. For example, *Zaleznik* explores difference in attitudes towards goals, conceptions of work, relations with others, self-perception and development.[3] Summarising the views of scholars who have attempted to differentiate between leading and managing, *Kent* draws attention to the following characteristics:

- managers do things right; leaders do the right things;
- managing is an authority relationship; leading is an influence relationship; and
- managing creates stability; leading creates change.

Kent suggests that although the ideas are provocative and stimulating, they provide a basis for a deeper understanding of the dynamics behind the two processes.[4]

Leadership role not clearly defined

The key point about leadership is that it does not necessarily take place within the hierarchical structure of the organisation. It occurs at different levels and manifested in different ways. Many people operate as leaders without their role ever being clearly established or defined. *Radcliffe* maintains that leadership is not mysterious, it's a completely natural human activity that is part of all of us. Leadership is plain and simple. The only qualification to be a leader is the desire to grow. It absolutely doesn't matter where you are in an organisation. There are only three aspects to leading: Future, Engage, Deliver.

- First, leading always starts in the Future;
- Second, if you want the help of others to create that Future, you need to Engage them;
- Third, in Deliver, you make things happen.[5]

Different perspectives

Despite continuing debate on management and leadership it is not easy to separate them as distinct activities. Many methods of management training can also be used as a means of measuring leadership style. For example, the Leadership Grid® **(discussed in Chapter 10)** was until recently known as the Managerial Grid®.

Mintzberg does not accept a distinction between the manager or the leader nor what any distinction means in the everyday life of organisations and poses the questions: how would you like to be managed by someone who doesn't lead; or why would you want to be led by someone who doesn't manage?[6] *Moorcroft* maintains there is little evidence to support one perspective over another but suggests overwhelming evidence that people like the idea of being a 'leader' and this may be the reason why the debate still rages, as it fulfils a need for differentiation.[7]

To what extent do YOU like the idea of being a leader? Could you be happy being managed by someone who doesn't lead?

Approaches to the study of leadership

There are many ways of looking at **leadership** and interpretations of its meaning. Leadership might be interpreted in simple terms, such as 'getting others to follow' or 'getting people to do things willingly', or interpreted more specifically, for example as 'the use of authority in decision-making'. It may be exercised as an attribute of position or because of personal knowledge or wisdom. Leadership might be based on a function of personality or it can be seen as a behavioural category. It may also be viewed in terms of the role of the leaders and their ability to achieve effective performance from others. Leadership can also be discussed in terms of a form of persuasion or power relationship.

It is difficult, therefore, to generalise about leadership, but essentially it is a **relationship through which one person influences the behaviour or actions of other people.** This means that the process of leadership cannot be separated from the activities of groups and effective teambuilding. Due to its complex and variable nature there are many different interpretations and alternative ways of analysing leadership. It is helpful, therefore, to have some framework in which to consider different approaches to study of the subject.

One way is to examine managerial leadership in terms of:

- qualities or traits approach;
- functional or group approach, including action-centred leadership;
- styles of leadership;
- contingency theories;
- transitional or transformational leadership;
- inspirational or visionary leadership;
- servant leadership; and
- alternative views **(see Figure 9.1).**

Qualities or traits approach

This approach assumes that leaders are born and not made. Leadership consists of certain inherited characteristics, or personality traits, which distinguish leaders from their followers. The **qualities approach** focuses attention on the man or woman in the job and not on the job itself. It suggests that attention is given to the selection of leaders rather than to training for leadership. *Drucker* (writing originally in 1955) makes the point that:

> **Leadership is of utmost importance. Indeed there is no substitute for it. But leadership cannot be created or promoted. It cannot be taught or learned.**[8]

However, attempts at identifying common personality, or physical and mental, characteristics of different 'good' or 'successful' leaders have met with little success.[9] Investigations have identified lists of traits that tend to be overlapping, contradictory or with little correlation for most features. It is noticeable that 'individuality' or 'originality' usually features in the list. This suggests little in common between specific personality traits of different leaders. It is perhaps possible therefore to identify general characteristics of leadership ability, such as self-confidence, initiative,

Qualities or traits approach

Assumes leaders are born and not made. Leadership consists of certain inherited characteristics or personality traits. Focuses attention on the person in the job and not on the job itself.

The functional or group approach

Attention is focused on the functions and responsibilities of leadership, what the leader actually does and the nature of the group. Assumes leadership skills can be learned and developed.

Styles of leadership

The way in which the functions of leadership are carried out and the behaviour adopted by managers towards subordinate staff. Concerned with the effects of leadership on those being led.

Situational approach and contingency models

The importance of the situation. Interactions between the variables involved in the leadership situation and patterns of behaviour. Belief that there is no single style of leadership appropriate to all situations.

Transformational leadership

A process of engendering motivation and commitment, creating a vision for transforming the performance of the organisation, and appealing to the higher ideals and values of followers.

Inspirational or visionary leadership

Based on the personal qualities or charisma of the leader and the manner in which the leadership influence is exercised.

Servant leadership

More a philosophy based on an ethical responsibility of leaders. A spiritual understanding of people; and empowering people through honesty, respect, nurturing and trust.

Alternative views of leadership

Broader approaches to the study of leadership, including shared and distributed leadership. Responsible leadership, and correlative leadership.

Figure 9.1 Framework for study of managerial leadership

intelligence and belief in one's actions, but research into this area has revealed little more than this.

Limitations of the traits approach

There are three further limitations with this approach.

- There is bound to be subjective judgement in determining who is regarded as a 'good' or 'successful' leader. (This can make for an interesting class discussion.)
- Lists of possible traits tend to be very long and often lack agreement on the most important.
- It ignores situational factors.

Even if it possible to identify an agreed list of more specific qualities, this would provide little explanation of the nature of leadership or development and training of future leaders. The qualities or traits approach gives rise to the questions of whether leaders are born or made and whether leadership is an art or a science. The important point, however, is that **these are not mutually exclusive alternatives.** Even if certain inborn qualities make for a good leader, these natural talents need encouragement and development. Even if leadership is something of an art, it still requires the application of special skills and techniques. Although there is still limited interest in the qualities, or traits, approach, attention has been directed more to other approaches to leadership. Discussions on 'great leaders' or examples of charismatic people who influence others is now more usually linked with transformational or inspirational leadership **discussed later in this chapter.**

What is it about people who YOU immediately think of as great leaders? How far do these people appear to share common personality characteristics?

Winston Churchill, Franklin D. Roosevelt and Joseph Stalin

Functional (or group) approach

This approach to leadership focuses attention not on personality nor the man or woman in the job, *per se,* but on the contents or **functions of leadership**. Leadership is always present in any group engaged in a task. The functional approach views leadership in terms of how the leader's behaviour affects, and is affected by, the group of followers. In contrast to the view of Drucker (referred to above) the functional approach believes the skills of leadership can be learned, developed and perfected. *Kotter* makes the point that successful companies do not wait for leaders to come along but actively seek out people with leadership potential and expose them to career experiences designed to develop that potential.[10]

Action-centred leadership

A general theory on the functional approach is associated with the work of *John Adair* and his ideas on **action-centred leadership** which focuses on what leaders actually *do*.[11] The effectiveness of the leader is dependent upon meeting three areas of need: to achieve the common **task;** for **team maintenance;** and **individual needs** of group members; symbolised by three overlapping circles **(*see* Figure 9.2).**

- **Task needs involve** achieving objectives and defining group tasks; organising the work, duties and responsibilities; controlling quality and performance.
- **Team maintenance needs** involve maintaining morale and team spirit; maintaining standards and discipline; training and communication within the group.
- **Individual needs** involve meeting needs of individual members and attending to personal problems; giving praise and status; reconciling conflicts between group needs and needs of the individual.

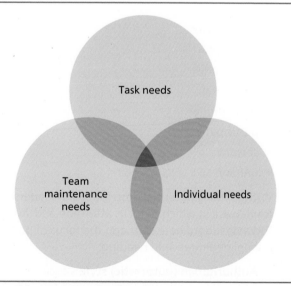

Figure 9.2 Interaction of needs within the group
Source: Adair, J. *Action-Centred Leadership*, Gower Press (1979), p. 10.
Reproduced with permission from John Adair.

Action by the leader in any one area of need will affect one or both of the other areas. The ideal position is where complete integration of the three areas of need is achieved. Adair's model of action-centred leadership is used as a basis for many leadership training courses.

Are leaders born or made?

There are times when leadership comes out of all of us. A few years ago, some of my team and I were caught up in the terrorist attack on the Taj Hotel in Mumbai. We were stuck inside, debris was falling and people were screaming. But a young member of staff rose to the situation and took care of us. This 22-year-old women guided is through the hotel and led us to safety. Nothing in her training had ever taught her how to respond in a situation like that, but she was calm, composed and unflappable. The way she exerted her authority was amazing. She showed me a lesson in leadership – you can lead in a moment, with your heart.

Leena Nair, 'The Changing Face of the Leader', *Management Today,* June 2013, p. 53.

Styles of leadership

In the work situation it has become increasingly clear that managers can no longer rely solely on the use of their position in the hierarchical structure. To get the best results the manager must also have regard for the need to encourage high morale, a spirit of involvement and co-operation, and a willingness to work. This gives rise to consideration of the style of leadership and provides another heading under which to analyse leadership behaviour. There are many possible ways of describing leadership style, such as for example:

- abdicatorial
- benevolent
- bureaucratic
- charismatic
- consultative
- dictatorial
- inspirational
- participative
- servant
- unitary.

With so many potential descriptions of leadership styles it is useful to have a broad framework in which to focus attention and study. The style of managerial leadership towards subordinate staff and the focus of power can therefore be considered within a simplified three-fold heading.

- **Authoritarian (autocratic) style** – focus of power is with the manager and interactions within the group move towards the manager. The manager alone exercises decision-making and authority for determining policy, procedures for achieving goals, work tasks and relationships, control of rewards or punishments.

- **Democratic style** – focus of power is more with the group as a whole and leadership functions are shared with greater interaction within the group with the manager more part of a team. Group members have a greater say in decision-making, determination of policy, implementation of systems and procedures.

- **Laissez-faire (genuine) style** – when members of the group are working well on their own the manager consciously makes a decision to pass the focus of power to members, allow them freedom of action to do as they think best but is readily available if help is needed. There is often confusion over this style of leadership behaviour. The word 'genuine' is emphasised because this is to be contrasted with the manager who could not care, who deliberately keeps away from the trouble spots and does not want to get involved. Members are left to face decisions that rightly belong with the manager. This is more a non-style of leadership or it could perhaps be labelled as abdication.

Continuum of leadership behaviour

One of the best-known works on leadership style is that by *Tannenbaum and Schmidt* (*see* **Figure 9.3**).[12] Originally written in 1958 and updated in 1973, their work

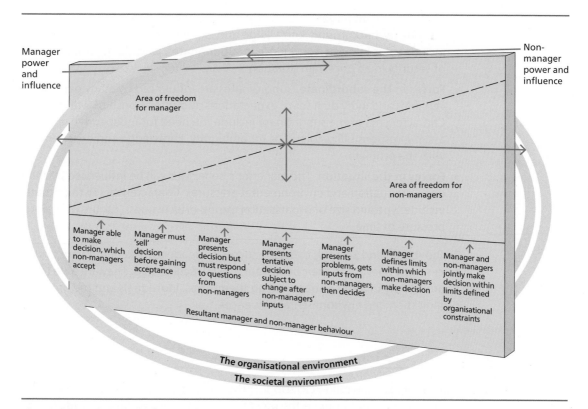

Figure 9.3 Continuum of manager/non-manager behaviour
Source: From Tannenbaum, R. and Schmidt, w. H. 'How to Choose a Leadership Pattern', *Harvard Business Review*, May/June 1973, p. 167. Copyright © 1973 by Harvard Business School Publishing Corporation; all rights reserved.

suggests a continuum of possible leadership behaviour available to a manager. The continuum presents a range of action related to the degree of authority used by the manager and to the area of freedom available to non-managers in arriving at decisions.

Neither extreme of the continuum is absolute as there is always some limitation on authority and on freedom. This approach can be seen as identifying four main styles of leadership by the manager: tells, sells, consults, joins.

- **Tells** – identifies a problem, makes decision and announces to subordinates, expecting them to implement without an opportunity for participation.
- **Sells** – makes decision but recognises possibility of some resistance and attempts to persuade subordinates to accept it.
- **Consults** – identifies problem, presents to the group and does not make a decision until having listened to advice and solutions suggested by subordinates.
- **Joins** – defines problem and limits within which the decision must be made, then passes to the group, with the manager as a member to make decisions.

Three main sets of forces

Tannenbaum and Schmidt suggest three factors, or forces, of particular importance in deciding what types of leadership are practicable and desirable. These are: forces in the manager, forces in the subordinate and forces in the situation.

- **Forces in the manager.** The manager's behaviour will be influenced by personality, background, knowledge and experiences. These internal forces include value-systems, confidence in subordinates, leadership inclinations, feelings of security in an uncertain situation.
- **Forces in the subordinate.** Subordinates are influenced by many personality variables and individual set of expectations about relationships with the manager. Characteristics of the subordinate include the need for independence, readiness to assume responsibility, tolerance for ambiguity, knowledge and experience to deal with the problem.
- **Forces in the situation.** The manager's behaviour will be influenced by the general situation and environmental pressures. Characteristics in the situation include type and size of organisation, group effectiveness, nature of the problem, pressure of time.

Tannenbaum and Schmidt conclude successful leaders are keenly aware of those forces most relevant to their behaviour at a particular time. They are able to behave appropriately in terms understanding themselves, individuals and the group, organisation and environmental influences.

To what extent would YOU support the contention that the Tannenbaum and Schmidt continuum is the most relevant framework for the study of leadership?

[Left] Directed leadership? [Right] Which style of leadership does this suggest?

Contingency theories of leadership

The continuum of leadership behaviour draws attention to forces in the situation as one of the main factors influencing the nature of managerial behaviour. The **contingency or situational approach** emphasises the situation as the dominant feature in considering characteristics of effective leadership. There are, however, limitations to this approach. There are people who possess the appropriate knowledge and skills and appear to be the most suitable leaders in a given situation, but who do not emerge as effective leaders. Also, in the work organisation, it is not usually practicable to allow the situation continually to determine who should act as the leader.

Despite limitations of the contingency approach, situational factors are clearly important. Contingency models focus on interactions between the variables involved in a leadership situation and patterns of leadership behaviour. Major contingency models of leadership include:

- Favourability of leadership situation – Fred Fiedler;
- Quality and acceptance of leader's decision – Vroom and Yetton;
- Path–goal theory – House, and House and Dessler;
- Readiness level of followers – Hersey and Blanchard.

Fiedler's contingency model

One of the first leader–situation models was developed by *Fred Fiedler* in his contingency theory of leadership effectiveness.[13] In order to measure attitudes of the leader, Fiedler developed a 'least preferred co-worker' (LPC) scale. This measures the rating given by leaders about the person with whom they could work least well. The questionnaire contains up to 20 items. Examples of items in the LPC scale are pleasant/ unpleasant, friendly/unfriendly, helpful/frustrating, distant/close, co-operative/ unco-operative, boring/interesting, self-assured/hesitant, open/guarded.

Each item is given a single ranking of between one and eight points, with eight points indicating the most favourable rating. For example:

Pleasant	:	:	:	:	:	:	:	:	Unpleasant
	8	7	6	5	4	3	2	1	

The LPC score is the sum of numerical ratings on all items for the 'least preferred co-worker'. The original interpretation of the LPC scale was that the leader with a high LPC score derived most satisfaction from **interpersonal relationships.** The leader with a low LPC score derived most satisfaction from performance of **the task and achieving objectives.** However, the interpretation of LPC has changed a number of times and there is still uncertainty about its actual meaning.

Favourability of the leadership situation

Fiedler suggests leadership behaviour is dependent upon favourability of the leadership situation. There are three major variables which determine the favourability of the situation and which affect the leader's role and influence:

- Leader–member relations – degree to which the leader is trusted and liked by group members, and their willingness to follow the leader's guidance.
- The task structure – degree to which the task is clearly defined for the group and the extent to which it can be carried out by detailed instructions or standard procedures.
- Position power – power of the leader by virtue of position in the organisation, and the degree to which the leader can exercise authority to influence (for example) rewards and punishments, or promotions and demotions.

From these three variables, Fiedler constructed eight combinations of group–task situations through which to relate leadership style **(see Figure 9.4).**

When the situation is **very favourable** (good leader–member relations, structured task, strong position power), or **very unfavourable** (poor leader–member relations, unstructured task, weak position power), then a **task-oriented leader** (low LPC score) with a directive, controlling style will be more effective.

When the situation is **moderately favourable** and the variables are mixed, then the leader with an **interpersonal relationship orientation** (high LPC score) and a participative approach will be more effective.

Position power, task structure and leader–member relations can be changed to make the situation more compatible with the characteristics of the leader. Fiedler's work has been subject to much debate and criticism but it does provide a further dimension to the study of leadership.[14] It brings into consideration the organisational variables that affect leadership effectiveness and suggests that in given situations a task-oriented, or structured, style of leadership is most appropriate. The 'best' styles of leadership will be dependent upon the variable factors in the leadership situation.

How far can YOU relate Fiedler's three sets of factors which influence favourability of the leadership situation to undertaking your course of study?

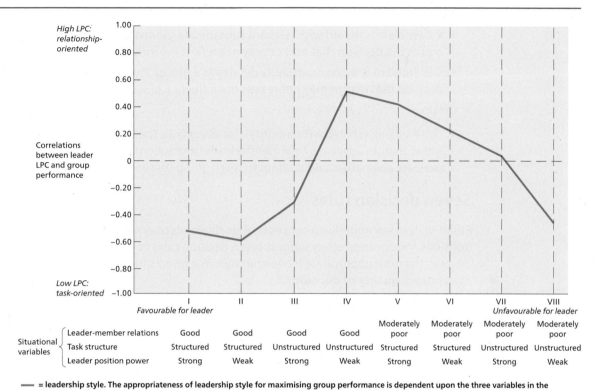

High LPC: relationship-oriented

Low LPC: task-oriented

Correlations between leader LPC and group performance

— = leadership style. The appropriateness of leadership style for maximising group performance is dependent upon the three variables in the leadership situation.

Figure 9.4 Correlations between leader's LPC scores and group effectiveness
Source: Adapted from Fiedler, F. E. A *Theory of Leadership Effectiveness*, McGraw-Hill (1967), p. 146. Reproduced with permission from Fred E. Fiedler.

Vroom and Yetton contingency model

Vroom and Yetton base their analysis on two main aspects of a leader's decision: its quality and its acceptance.[15]

- Decision quality, or rationality, is the effect that the decision has on group performance.
- Decision acceptance refers to the motivation and commitment of group members in implementing the decision.

A third consideration is

- the amount of time required to make the decision.

The Vroom and Yetton model suggests five main management decision styles and is sometimes viewed more as a model of decision-making and developed by *Vroom and Jago*.[16]

- Autocratic
  - A.I: Leader solves the problem or makes the decision alone using information available at the time.
  - A.II: Leader obtains information from subordinates but then decides on solution alone.

- Consultative
  - C.I: Problem is shared with relevant subordinates, individually. The leader then makes the decision that may or may not reflect the influence of subordinates.
  - C.II: Problem is shared with subordinates as a group. The leader then makes the decision that may or may not reflect the influence of subordinates.
- Group
  - G.II: Problem is shared with subordinates as a group. The leader acts as chairperson rather than an advocate. Together the leader and subordinates generate and evaluate alternatives and attempt to reach group consensus on a solution.

Seven decision rules

Based on two key underlying concepts of quality of decisions and acceptance of decisions, Vroom and Yetton suggest seven decision rules to help the manager discover the most appropriate leadership style in a given situation. The first three rules protect **quality of decisions.**

1 Is there a quality requirement such that one solution is likely to be more rational than another?
2 Is there sufficient information to make a high-quality decision?
3 Is the problem structured?

The last four rules protect **acceptance of decisions.**

1 Is acceptance of the decision by subordinates critical to effective implementation?
2 If you were to make the decision yourself, is it reasonably certain that it
3 Do subordinates share the organisational goals to be obtained in solving the problem?
4 Is conflict among subordinates likely in preferred solutions?

These rules indicate decision styles that the manager should **avoid** in a given situation and indicate the use of others. Decision-tree charts can be produced to help in the application of the rules and to relate the situation to the appropriate leadership style.

Path–goal theory

A third contingency model of leadership is the **path–goal theory**, the main work on which has been undertaken by *House,*[17] *House and Dessler*[18] and developed by *Nadler and Tushman.*[19] The model is based on the belief that the individual's motivation is dependent upon expectations that increased effort to achieve an improved level of performance will be successful, and expectations that improved performance will be instrumental in obtaining positive rewards and avoiding negative outcomes. This is the 'expectancy' theory of motivation, **discussed in Chapter 7.** Subordinates see leadership behaviour as a motivating influence to the extent that it means:

- satisfaction of their needs is dependent upon effective performance; and
- the necessary direction, guidance, training and support, which would otherwise be lacking, is provided.

Main types of leadership behaviour

House identifies four main types of leadership behaviour:

- Directive leadership – subordinates are expected to follow rules and regulations, know exactly what is expected of them and given specific directions.
- Supportive leadership – friendly and approachable manner displaying concern for the needs and welfare of subordinates.
- Participative leadership – consulting with subordinates and evaluation of their opinions and suggestions before making the decision.
- Achievement-oriented leadership – setting challenging goals, seeking improvement in performance and showing confidence in subordinates' ability to perform well.

Path–goal theory suggests different types of behaviour can be practised by the same person at different times in varying situations. By using one of the four styles of leadership behaviour the manager attempts to influence subordinates' perceptions and motivation, and smooth the path to their goals **(see Figure 9.5).**

Two main situational factors

Leadership behaviour is determined by two main situational factors: personal characteristics of subordinates and nature of the task.

- Personal characteristics of subordinates – how they react to the manager's behaviour and extent to which they see such behaviour as an immediate or potential source of need satisfaction.
- Nature of the task – relates to extent it is routine and structured or non-routine and unstructured.

Effective leadership behaviour is based, therefore, on both willingness to help subordinates and needs of subordinates for help. Leadership behaviour will be motivational to the extent it provides necessary direction, guidance and support, helps clarify path–goal relationships and removes any obstacles which hinder attainment of goals. For example, when a task is highly structured, the goals readily apparent and subordinates are confident attempts to further explain the job or to give directions are likely to be viewed as unacceptable behaviour. However, when a task is highly unstructured, the nature of the goals is not clear and subordinates lack experience a more directive style of leadership behaviour is likely to be welcomed by subordinates.

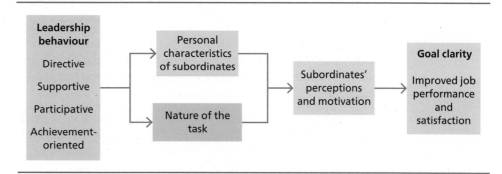

Figure 9.5 Representation of the path–goal theory of leadership

To what extent do YOU agree that although situational factors are a major determinant of leadership style, contingency models have little practical application?

Readiness of the followers or group

A major variable in the style of leadership adopted by the manager is the nature of subordinate staff. This view is developed by *Hersey and Blanchard* who present a form of situational leadership based on the 'readiness' level of the people the leader is attempting to influence. Readiness is the extent to which followers have the ability and willingness to accomplish a specific task. It is not a personal characteristic of the individual but how ready the individual is to perform a particular task.[20]

Readiness (R) is divided into a continuum of four levels: R1 (low), R2 and R3 (moderate) and R4 (high).

- R1 – low follower readiness – followers both *unable and unwilling* and who lack commitment and motivation; or who are *unable and insecure.*
- R2 – low to moderate follower readiness – followers *unable but willing* and who lack ability but motivated to make an effort; or are *unable but confident.*
- R3 – moderate to high follower readiness – followers *able but unwilling,* and who have ability to perform but are unwilling to apply their ability; or who are *able but insecure.*
- R4 – high follower readiness – followers both *able and willing* and who have ability and commitment to perform; or who are *able and confident.*

Task behaviour and relationship behaviour

For each of the four levels of maturity, the appropriate style of leadership is a combination of task behaviour and relationship behaviour.

- Task behaviour is the extent to which the leader provides directions for the actions of followers, sets goals for them and defines their roles and how to undertake them.
- Relationship behaviour is the extent to which the leader engages in two-way communication with followers, listens to them and provides support and encouragement.

From the combination of task behaviour and relationship behaviour derive four leadership styles (S): telling (S1), selling (S2), participating (S3) and delegating (S4). The appropriate leadership style corresponds with the readiness of the followers **(see Figure 9.6).**

- S1 – telling – emphasises high amounts of guidance (task behaviour) but limited supportive (relationship) behaviour. This style is most appropriate for *low follower readiness* (R1).
- S2 – selling – emphasises high amounts of both directive (task) and relationship behaviours. This style is most appropriate for *low to moderate follower readiness* (R2).

S1 – TELLING – emphasises high amounts of guidance (task behaviour) but limited supportive (relationship) behaviour. This style is most appropriate for *low follower readiness* **(R1).**
Leadership behaviour based on detailed instructions and close supervision

S2 – SELLING – emphasises high amounts of both directive (task) and relationship behaviours. This style is most appropriate for *low to moderate follower readiness* **(R2).**
Leadership behaviour based on explanation and discussion of decision

S3 – PARTICIPATING – emphasises high amounts of two-way communication and supportive (relationship) behaviour but low amounts of guidance (task behaviour). This style is most appropriate for *moderate to high follower readiness* **(R3).**
Leadership behaviour based on sharing ideas and facilitating decision-making

S4 – DELEGATING – emphasises little direction or support with low levels of both task and relationship behaviour. This style is most appropriate for *high follower readiness* **(R4).**
Leadership behaviour based on delegation of responsibility for decisions

---

Figure 9.6 Hersey and Blanchard's four leadership styles

- S3 – participating – emphasises a high amount of two-way communication and supportive (relationship) behaviour but low amounts of guidance (task behaviour). This style is most appropriate for *moderate to high follower readiness* (R3).
- S4 – delegating – emphasises little direction or support with low levels of both task and relationship behaviours. This style is most appropriate for *high follower readiness* (R4).

Development of subordinates

Hersey and Blanchard suggest the key to using situational leadership is any leader behaviour may be more or less effective according to the **readiness of the person** the leader is attempting to influence. The model draws attention to the importance of developing the ability, confidence and commitment of subordinates. Subordinates should be helped to develop in readiness to the extent they are able and willing to go. This development should take place by adjusting leadership behaviour through the four styles of telling, selling, participating and delegating.

Transformational leadership

Increasing business competitiveness and need for the most effective use of human resources has resulted in attention on how leaders revitalise or transform organisations. Based on the work of writers such as *Burns* this has given rise to a distinction between two fundamental forms of leadership: transactional leadership and transformational (or creative) leadership.[21]

- Transactional leadership is based on legitimate authority within the bureaucratic structure of the organisation. The emphasis is on the clarification of goals and objectives, work task and outcomes, and organisational rewards and punishments. Transactional leadership appeals to the self-interest of followers. It is based on a relationship of mutual dependence and an exchange process of 'I will give you this, if you do that.'

- Transformational (or creative) leadership, by contrast, is a process of engendering higher levels of motivation and commitment among followers. The emphasis is on generating a vision for the organisation and the leader's ability to appeal to higher ideals and values of followers, and creating a feeling of justice, loyalty and trust. In the organisational sense, transformational leadership is about transforming the performance or fortunes of a business.

Components of transformational leadership

Applying the ideas of Burns to organisational management, *Bass* proposed a theory of transformational leadership that argues that the leader transforms and motivates followers by:

1 generating greater awareness of the importance of the purpose of the organisation and task outcomes;

2 inducing them to transcend their own self-interests for the sake of the organisation or team; and

3 activating their higher-level needs.[22]

Transformational leadership is composed of four basic components:

- idealised influence – charisma of the leader, and respect and admiration of the followers;

- inspirational motivation – behaviour of the leader which provides meaning and challenge to the work of followers;

- intellectual stimulation – leaders who solicit new and novel approaches for the performance of work and creative problem solutions from followers; and

- individualised consideration – leaders who listen and give special concern to the growth and developmental needs of the followers.[23]

Set of guidelines

Based on a summary of theories and research findings, *Yukl* provides a set of guidelines for transformational leadership:

- Articulate a clear and appealing vision of what the organisation could accomplish or become to help people understand the purpose, objectives and priorities of the organisation, and help guide the actions and decisions of members.

- Explain how the vision can be attained and establish a clear link between the vision and a credible conventional yet straightforward strategy for attaining it.

- Act confident and optimistic about likely success, demonstrate self-confidence and conviction, and emphasise positive aspects of the vision rather than the obstacles and dangers.

- Express confidence in followers and their ability to accomplish the vision, especially when the task is difficult or dangerous, or when members lack confidence in themselves.

- Use dramatic, symbolic actions to emphasise key values and demonstrate leadership behaviour through highly visible actions including risking personal loss, self-sacrifice or acting unconventionally.

- Lead by example by recognising actions speak louder than words, exemplary behaviour in day-to-day interactions with subordinates and demonstrating consistency in daily behaviour.[24]

How would YOU distinguish between transactional and transformational leadership? Can you provide an example of each form of leadership and contrast the two styles?

Inspirational or visionary leadership

Successful transformational leaders are usually identified in terms of providing a strong vision and sense of mission, arousing strong emotions in followers and a sense of identification with the leader. Some writers see transformational leadership as the same thing as inspirational, visionary or charismatic leadership. Leadership today is increasingly associated with the concept of creating a vision with which others can identify, getting along with other people and the concept of inspiration. This might be considered as part of transformational leadership or arguably it has given rise to a new approach to leadership – that of **inspirational or visionary leadership**. Inspirational leadership is not concerned so much with the theory of leadership but more with the skills of motivating and inspiring people.

Goffee and Jones point out that the need for visionary leadership is becoming increasingly important. Traditional business hierarchies gave managers and workers a sense of their own position and what was expected of them. Now, as these hierarchies break down, it is leaders themselves who must fill the void, helping subordinates to understand their place and purpose. Personal leadership is beginning to replace organisational structure.[25]

Personal qualities or charisma

Leadership may be based on personal qualities, or charisma, of the leader and the manner in which influence is exercised. The concept of charismatic or inspirational leadership is not new and has been applied in the organisational context by writers such as Max Weber (1864–1920).[26] The importance of charisma for effective leadership today is emphasised by *Conger,* who also believes that many of the traits that make a successful leader can be taught, including charisma.

> **What you simply cannot learn is how to be passionate about what you do. You have to discover that for yourself, and passion is a big part of what drives a charismatic leader. It is also what motivates and inspires those who work for the charismatic leader.[27]**

However, the extent to which charismatic or inspirational leadership helps bring about improvement in organisational performance is open to debate. Conger also draws attention to the danger that the leader's vision, dynamism and inspirational nature are highly attractive to followers, which leads to a natural dependence. Staff see this extraordinary figure as a model to be emulated and the leader's abilities become the yardstick by which they measure their own performance. This is a potential source of leadership derailment. Dependence makes the followers more susceptible to deception.[28]

Adair argues that to be a truly inspirational leader one must understand the spirit within. All people have the potential for greatness. The inspirational leader connects with the led, appreciates the capabilities of others and through trust will unlock the powers in others. Adair refers to 'the inspired moment' – a recognition and seizure of a brief window of opportunity that can act as a powerful catalyst that inspires both the leader and the led.[29]

Important to trust this charismatic leader with dangerous conditions in Antarctica

Danger of infatuation and hubris

Kingsmill suggests that the belief that real change and transformation will come from a charismatic visionary may have an immediate appeal to some but all too often this can prove to be a shallow myth rather than a reality.

> **Grand strategies that never come to fruition, demoralised people whose voices are not heard and innovations that are stifled are all too often the real result of this preoccupation with the hero leader.[30]**

Tourish cautions infatuation with the myth of the great leader and suggests some scepticism is needed. Leadership clearly matters but it is only one ingredient of successful organisations. Whilst there are examples of charismatic individuals who exercise a profound positive effect on organisations and society there are also charismatic leaders who inflict enormous damage on people, organisations and society. There is a particular problem with people in positions of power in organisations who rarely receive sufficient criticism. Senior executives often shield themselves from interaction with others. Tourish points to the danger of hubris and need for greater humility and input from others.[31]

Lord Owen refers to the sense of invulnerability and hubris as an occupational hazard for leaders in all fields including business and questions whether hubris behaviour is a product of environment or a feature of personality. Lord Owen points out the need for boundaries against runaway leaders improving selection, education and evaluation by board members.

All too frequently, hubris – this dangerous mix of pride, ego, delusion, resistance to criticism and, in the case of a company or institution, groupthink – can create a culture capable of just about any mistake in the name of 'we know best'.[32]

(Groupthink was discussed in Chapter 8.)

How would YOU explain charisma? What examples can you give of charismatic people who have a profound positive and/or negative influence on your attitude and performance?

Servant leadership

In recent years renewed attention has been given to the idea of servant leadership originally proposed in 1970 by *Robert Greenleaf.*[33, 34] Rather than use of position power, servant leadership is more a philosophy based on ethical responsibility of leaders; a spiritual understanding of people; and empowering people through honesty, respect, nurturing and trust. A servant leader gives attention to the needs of people and the promotion of their personal development. The focus of leadership is on a supportive and participative style. A test of servant leadership is the extent to which the followers, that is those served, benefit. It might therefore be particularly appropriate in service organisations such as in the hospitality industry.[35] Servant leadership can be associated with the idea of positive psychology with an emphasis on human strengths, how things go right and how to enhance people's satisfaction and well-being, **discussed in Chapter 1.**

The focus of servant leadership

According to *Wong* the focus of leadership needs to shift from process and outcome to people and the future. **Servant leadership** represents a radical approach – it is humanistic and spiritual rather than rational and mechanistic. Command and control leadership no longer works because leaders must earn people's respect and trust. New types of leaders are needed to create new futures, and the challenge for leadership education is to:

- develop workers and unleash their creative potential;
- create a positive workplace that will attract and retain knowledge workers; and
- reinforce innovations and risk-taking to adapt to an uncertain future.

However, Wong acknowledges common criticism of servant leadership including it is: too restrictive, too unrealistic and impractical and would not work in situations such as military operations or prison systems. It is too idealistic and naïve, too closely related to Christian spirituality; and too foreign to a preferred alternative leadership style.[36]

Key values and examples

According to *Yukl* the values emphasised in servant leadership are primarily about helping people and fostering a relationship of trust and cooperation. Yukl lists seven key values and examples of how these might be expressed in a leader's behaviour.

- **Integrity** – open and honest communications, keeping promises and commitments, accepting responsibility for mistakes.
- **Altruism** – helping others and putting their need before your own, willing to takes risks and make sacrifices to benefit others.
- **Humility** – treats others with respect, avoids status symbols and privileges, modest about achievements, emphasises contributions of others.
- **Empathy and healing** – helps others cope with emotional distress, acts as mediator, encourages reconciliation.
- **Personal growth** – encourages development of individual confidence and ability, provides learning opportunities and mentoring and coaching.
- **Fairness and justice** – encourages and supports fair treatment, speaks out against unfair and unjust practices or policies.
- **Empowerment** – consults with others about decisions that affect them, provides autonomy and discretion, encourages expression of dissenting views.[37]

A summary of leadership is set out in the concept map in Figure 9.7.

Alternative views of leadership

In recent years the changing nature of the work organisation has drawn attention to different, broader approaches to the study of leadership including, shared and distributed leadership, responsible leadership and correlative leadership.

Shared and distributed leadership

As with servant leadership, the original idea of distributed leadership can be traced back many years. For example, *Mary Parker Follet* writing in 1941 envisioned management responsibility not just concentrated at the top of the hierarchy but diffused throughout the organisation from the depersonalising of orders and obeying the law of the situation.[38, 39]

Rather than a traditional view of a single, all powerful and visionary appointed leader; the underlying concept of **shared and distributed leadership** is of multiple leaders throughout the organisation. As opposed to hierarchical leadership, distributed leadership gives recognition to the sharing of the leadership function, power and decision-making among staff at all levels and positions including the role of the informal organisation **(discussed in Chapter 2)**. *Day, Groon and Salas* suggest that collective leadership from many different members of the organisation is of more importance than the actions of any individual leader.[40] With continuing pace of change, developments in ICT and uncertain economic environment, leadership functions will evolve and leadership roles change according to the situation. With increasing emphasis on teamwork attention has been focused on the significance of the leadership function for team performance. Greater awareness of the benefits from a more diverse workforce has also encouraged distributed leadership. *Hewlett* draws attention to the wider community leadership roles of ethnic minority staff who may hold only junior positions in the organisation.[41]

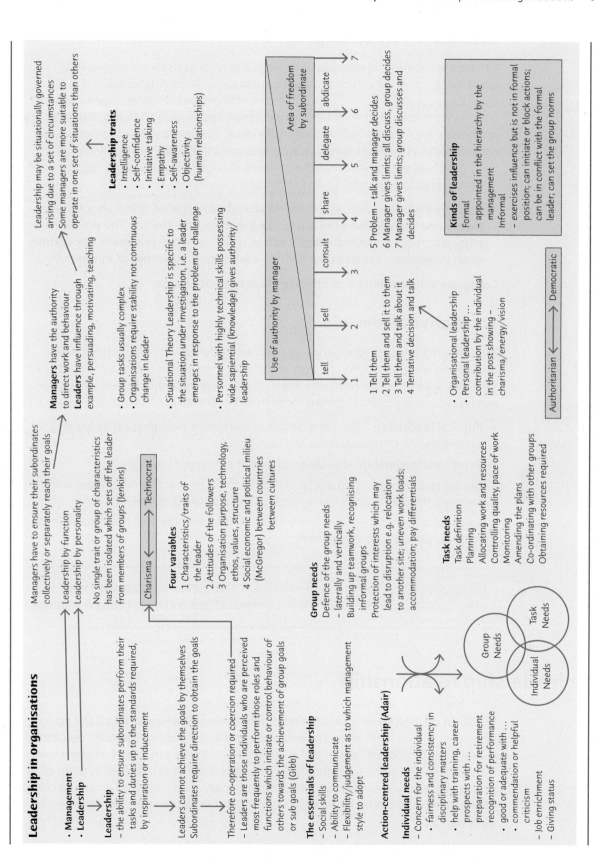

Figure 9.7 Leadership in organisations

Source: Copyright © 2008 The Virtual Learning Materials Workshop. Reproduced with permission.

Responsible leadership

The term **responsible leadership** has emerged as an organisation's approach to governance, social responsibilities and business ethics. According to *Business in The Community* the challenge for business leaders is to ensure the wider responsibilities of business are understood within their organisation and in society to demonstrate how a responsible approach to business will create value. Business leaders must demonstrate commitment to creating a fairer society and more sustainable future by fostering a culture that will encourage innovation, reward the right behaviours and regain trust.[42]

However, as the *Financial Times* points out:

> Responsible Leadership, as a business school subject area, is less about ethical theory and more about ethical practice based on case studies. The practice has a particular focus on an individual's values system and the pragmatic application of an individual's values in the real-life challenging dilemmas of business.[43]

Corporate responsibility and ethics is the subject of Chapter 16.

Correlative leadership

With the shift towards younger people becoming the power base within the work culture and wanting a different work experience from earlier generations, *Jones* calls for a new style of leadership for business. To add new attributes to leadership style involves four components labelled correlative leadership.

- **Physical leadership** – including design of workplace, own physical well-being, understanding of neuroscience and groupthink.
- **Emotional leadership** – the development of emotional intelligence.
- **Digital leadership** – using digital platforms to connect and communicate with people inside and outside the workplace and also to attract talent.
- **Spiritual leadership** – seeing every element of human life, and having deep and more purposeful conversations.[44]

Which *one* style or form of leadership are YOU most comfortable with from other people and which *one* style or form would you feel most happy practising?

The leadership relationship

Whatever the perceived approach an underlying feature of leadership is *the manner* in which the leader influences the behaviour and actions of other people. Leadership is a dynamic form of behaviour and there are a number of variables that affect the leadership relationship. For example, *Bass* reviews leadership influence in terms of persuasion, a power relation, an instrument of goal achievement, an emerging effect of interaction and the initiation of structure.[45] Four major variables are identified by *McGregor* as:

- the characteristics of the leader;
- the attitude, needs and other personal characteristics of the followers;

- the nature of the organisation, such as its purpose, its structure, and the tasks to be performed; and
- the social, economic and political environment.

McGregor concludes that 'leadership is not a property of the individual, but a complex relationship among these variables'.[46]

According to *Kouzes and Posner,* 'credibility is the foundation of leadership'. From extensive research in over 30 countries and response to the question of what people 'look for and admire in a leader, in a person whose direction they would willingly follow', people have consistently replied they want

> **leaders who exemplify four qualities: they want them to be honest, forward-looking, inspiring and competent. In our research our respondents strongly agree that they want leaders with integrity and trustworthiness, with vision and sense of direction, with enthusiasm and passion, and with expertise and a track record for getting things done.**[47]

Culture: A contingent factor?

Contribution of contingency approaches to leadership suggest contrasting types and styles of may be more or less appropriate in different situations. A consistent view expressed within the literature is that a major variable influencing choice of leadership style may be national culture. We should be wary of stereotyping the behaviour of leaders or subordinates, and many myths appear to have grown around notions of 'orderly' German, 'undisciplined' Italian and even 'obstructive' British workers. However, there are reasons to suggest that there may indeed be national cultural differences that are relevant to an understanding of leadership.

Global leadership and organisational behaviour effectiveness (GLOBE)

Project GLOBE was a large-scale research project which sought to identify those leader behaviours and attributes which would be accepted and therefore effective in all societies and, contrastingly, those which would only be accepted and effective in some cultural contexts. This study was conducted by an international team of researchers led by *Robert House* and encompassed 62 countries across the world, including some which had not always featured in cross-cultural study – for example newly capitalist states in Eastern Europe. The GLOBE study commenced in 1991 and led to a series of publications in the early twenty-first century.[48]

The results are some significant variations in leadership style, attributes and behaviour. Charismatic and team-oriented leaders were shown to be globally endorsed – and hence universally effective. Leaders who displayed high levels of trust, integrity and vision were supported by subordinates in all societies. It was also found that there were so-called universal impediments to success; for example, *self-protective* leaders characterised by malevolence and 'face-saving' were viewed negatively by subordinates in all cultures.

Some aspects of leadership varied between societies. In common with Hofstede **(see Chapter 1)** the GLOBE study identifies clusters of societies with important points of commonality. To take one example, in a situation which might imply a directive style of leadership, subordinates in the 'Anglo' cluster of societies (in effect the main

English-speaking countries) would prefer some degree of informality on the part of the leader and as much of a participative style as the situation allowed. The GLOBE study recognises that strategic organisational contingencies such as the sector an organisation operates in will affect leadership style and behaviour. However, researchers concluded that such factors would be moderated by the national cultural context. Leader effectiveness will be influenced by interaction between leaders and subordinates, which is dependent on the nature of power relations within the particular culture, and organisational contingencies applying in all societies.[49]

According to *Walker* too much focus in recent decades has been in Western approaches to leadership and that a study of alternative methods can help inspire leaders – wherever they are. In the Far East, for example, face-to-face contact and relationship-building is prized more highly than here. Walker suggests that new thinking sees Asian business culture not as a challenge to be overcome but as a source of leadership inspiration.[50]

 What situations can YOU relate of national culture influencing the behaviour of leaders and followers?

Leadership effectiveness

Attention to style of leadership has come about through better understanding of the needs and expectations of people at work. It has also been influenced by such factors as: broader standards of education and training; advances in scientific and technical knowledge; pressure for a greater social responsibility towards employees, for example through schemes of participation in decision-making and work/life balance; and legislation, for example in the areas of employment protection. These factors have combined to create resistance against purely autocratic styles of leadership. There is an assumption that subordinates are more likely to work effectively for managers who adopt a certain style of leadership than for managers who adopt alternative styles.

Goleman reports the most effective executives use a collection of distinct leadership styles, each in the right measure, at just the right time. Although the authoritative style of leadership can be occasionally overbearing, it was found to be most effective and can motivate and inspire commitment to the goals of the organisation. The affiliative style has potential to create harmony within teams and can be used in conjunction with the authoritative style. The democratic approach was seen as positive, and encourages input from staff and helps build consensus through participation. The coaching style, although the least frequently used, can help staff identify their strengths and encourage long-term development goals. The study concludes that the most effective leaders rely on more than one leadership style, and were able to master a mixture of authoritative, democratic, affiliative and coaching styles. Leaders with the best results use most of the styles in a given week – seamlessly and in different measure – depending on the business situation.[51]

The shadow of leadership

Leadership is clearly a major feature of effective teamwork. Good leaders surround themselves with talented and capable members of staff, and their behaviour and actions serve as a role model. *McCabe* suggests that leaders who want to transform their performance and the effectiveness of the team should look at how their own shadow could be getting in the way. Leaders focus on what they see as important and they are typically quite unconscious of the unintended but massive impact they are having on their colleagues, teams and clients. All leaders cast a shadow and whatever a particular leadership style, the shadow will affect others and can compromise people's engagement at work and business effectiveness. Leaders need to be fully aware of the shadow they cast and the impact they have on others.[52]

Authority without arrogance

Reeves and Knell suggest being a successful leader is less about who you are or what you do than about what you know. This includes four pieces of knowledge: where the organisation is heading; what is going on; who they are; and how to build a strong team. Leaders in the most successful organisations are authoritative but their secret is that they use their authority without arrogance. Successful leaders:

- build a 'culture of discipline' and are about getting things done, controlling costs and marshalling resources;
- keep in touch with how people are feeling. They don't waste time worrying if everyone is happy but understand the emotional temperament of the organisation and emotional responses from people;
- know where they are strong but also know their weaknesses and display a fierce humility;
- are motivated by what they build, such as great teams and talent people, rather than what they get;
- have a clear sense of where the organisation is going, but very often this is the result of collective decision-making in a talent team.[53]

Variables affecting leadership effectiveness

Clearly, there is no one 'best' form of leadership that will result in the maintenance of morale among group members and high work performance. We have seen that there are many alternative forms and styles of leadership and within an organisation different individuals may fulfil the functions of leadership. An effective manager will clearly recognise that different styles of leadership are called for in different situations. As an extreme example, emergency situations demand an assertive, directive style of action. **(Recall the actual example of the Mumbai hotel attack given earlier in this chapter.)** Different types of leadership may also be most appropriate at different stages in the development of a business organisation. Leadership can also vary between public and private sectors and depend upon the size of the organisation.

Three main aspects to be considered in determining the most appropriate style are the leader, the group and the work environment. However, there are many variables that underlie the effectiveness of leadership in work organisations. More specifically, these include the following:

- characteristics of the leader; personality, attitudes, abilities, value-system, and personal credibility;
- type of power and basis of the leadership relationship;

- characteristics of the followers; diversity, needs and expectations, attitudes, knowledge, confidence and experience, and motivation and commitment;
- type and nature of the organisation, organisation culture and structure;
- nature of the tasks to be achieved and time scales;
- technology, systems of communication and methods of work organisation;
- informal organisation, and the psychological contract;
- nature and influence of the external environment and national culture.

In addition there is an argument that physical attributes, such as height, can be associated with good leadership **(discussed in Chapter 6).**

Overuse of the term 'leader'

Owen argues that the increasing use of the leadership title for people who are not leading serves only to devalue both leadership and management. Once we start calling everyone a leader, we no longer know what real leadership is. There are people such as CEOs who are not leading and equally people lower in the organisation who may not have the title but are making change and leading people. This means leadership is about what you do not about your position. Owen suggests the skillset for leaders and managers is very similar but becoming more demanding as we move from a relatively simple world of command and control to one of influence and commitment.[54]

To what extent do YOU believe the leadership title is misused and the only real indicator of who is a leader is about what a person actually does?

Acas 'framework for effective leadership'

This framework is intended to help both junior and senior managers identify the qualities in themselves, and those around them, that can build workplace relationships that are productive, trusting and mutually rewarding. The leadership triangle **(Figure 9.8)** is based upon four levels of understanding and action. It is not intended to be prescriptive, but sets out the skills, legal requirements and values that can help any leader be effective in their role. It also points to further advice that can be found in other Acas guidance. The triangle is informed by the millions of customer interactions Acas advisors have every year. The four levels are:

1 **Know your stuff.** This refers to all the nuts and bolts of working life, everything from employment law to disciplinary policies and procedures.
2 **Refine your skills.** Here the focus is on communicating, listening, telling, motivating and liaising – in essence, the ability to engage well with people.
3 **Be aware of organisational responsibilities.** The hardest part of leadership is often balancing individual and group concerns, and encouraging the right behavioural norms.
4 **Strive for those essential characteristics.** The best leaders have a personal style that is reflexive, emotionally intelligent and openly accommodates both strength and vulnerability.[55]

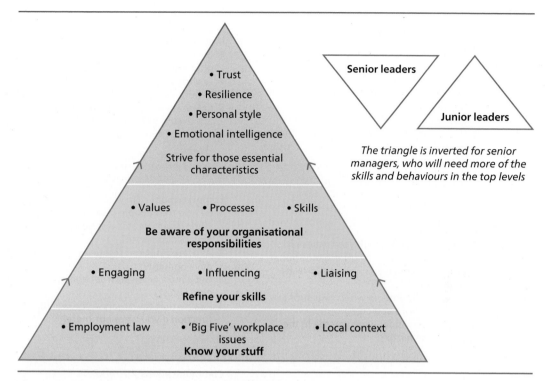

Figure 9.8 Acas framework for leadership effectiveness
Source: Acas Strategy Unit, 'The Acas framework for effective leadership', Employment Relations Comment, ACAS, September 2016. Used with permission from Acas National.

Leadership development

The most effective form of leadership behaviour is a product of the total leadership situation and demands not only interpersonal skills but a flexibility of approach and diagnostic ability. *Melville-Ross* refers to the importance of developing leadership skills in everyone, not just those at the top. Even people in the most junior positions can play a leadership role. It is about the dissemination of ideas, taking the initiative and encouraging others to see it that way. For this to happen, you need an open leadership culture that runs right through the organisation. People are encouraged to take personal responsibility and are not afraid to speak up with ideas or take risks.[56]

The leadership jigsaw

Cutler has designed a 'jigsaw' of best practice. There are six interlinking pieces: vision, example, relationships, motivation, empowerment and communications as a guide to the measurement and development of leadership skills. Cutler believes that leadership is not such a difficult role if condensed to these essential elements and has devised a set of questions to help aspiring leaders to find out if they have all the necessary pieces of the jigsaw **(*see* Figure 9.9)**.[57]

Intuitive intelligence in leadership

According to *Bacon*, a critical factor in leadership development is the intuitive intelligence of leaders, especially when it comes to decision-making. We use our instinct and intuition in many facets of our personal lives but Bacon questions if we

Vision – Do you:
1 Work hard at communicating your vision for the organisation to all staff at all levels?
2 Understand that your vision must appeal to your staff at both an emotional and practical level if they are to join you on your journey?
3 Understand the culture and values of your organisation and their impact on its future development?
4 Recognise blind alleys?

Example – Do you:
1 Match your words with your actions?
2 Take full responsibility for organisational problems, even if you were not directly responsible?
3 Occasionally muck in when your staff are under pressure at work?
4 Regularly consider what you see in the bathroom mirror?

Relationships – Do you:
1 Work hard at countering a 'them and us' culture within your organisation?
2 Set clear codes of acceptable conduct and take action against breaches of them?
3 Stress that everyone contributes to the success of the team(s) they belong to?
4 Admit when you make a mistake?

Motivation – Do you:
1 Understand that every member has a different set of motivational stimuli?
2 Explain your decisions in terms of their benefit to the organisation and its members?
3 Celebrate and reward individual and team achievements?
4 Prefer to offer carrots, rather than wield sticks?

Empowerment – Do you:
1 Believe that people generally respond well when given greater responsibility for their own performance?
2 Allocate sufficient resources to training and development?
3 Get a buzz when staff set and achieve their own goals?
4 Realise that the organisation would still function if you were not there?

Communications – Do you:
1 Use your influence to encourage two-way communications at all levels in your organisation?
2 Encourage personal contact rather than written, mechanical or technological alternatives?
3 Encourage a diversity of opinion and constructive criticism?
4 Walk the talk?

Figure 9.9 The leadership 'jigsaw'
Source: Cutler, A. 'A Good Fit Is Essential', *Professional Manager*, vol. 14, no. 3, May 2005, p. 38. Reproduced with permission from Chartered Management Institute and Alan Cutler.

underutilise one of the most powerful leadership tool at work. Many people feel that intuition has little or no place in business, that decisions should be based on empirical evidence rather than on trusting your gut feeling. Much credence is given to emotional intelligence **(discussed in Chapter 4)** but perhaps the greatest weapon for business decision-making is intuitive intelligence.

Bacon maintains that intuitive intelligence can be trained and best leaders have learned not only to just trust their instincts, but to obey them by listening to their own internal voice. Situations in which leaders rely most consistently on their intuitive intelligence include:

- **in a crisis** when rapid response is required;
- **high-speed change** when situations are changing rapidly without warning;
- **in messy situations** when a problem or challenge is poorly constructed;
- **in ambiguous situations** when there are contradictory factors to consider.[58]

Importance of self-awareness

Blanchard believes that all good leadership starts with a shared vision. The best and most respected leaders share not just their visions for the future of their organisations with their people, but also their personal beliefs about how and why they lead as they do. Blanchard suggests clarifying and sharing your leadership point of view means answering seven questions.

1 Who are the people who have influenced you in your life?
2 What is your life purpose?
3 What core values will guide your behaviour as you live your life 'on purpose'?
4 What are your beliefs about leading and motivating people?
5 What can people expect of you?
6 What do you expect from your people?
7 How will you set an example?[59]

An underlying feature of effective leadership is self-awareness: understanding who you are, and what you are thinking and feeling. *Benjamin* sees a leader simply as someone who takes the lead and whom other people are inclined to follow willingly. The sense of who you are is so important because leadership is at heart about leading people.

Approaching leadership with a clear sense of self will give you the strength to work with others respectfully but also the confidence to challenge another's opinion or authority because you know what you stand for, and what your principles and beliefs are.[60]

How good do YOU think you are or will become as a leader? What do you believe are your best leadership skills and what areas are in need of most development?

Critical Thinking Zone
Reflections on Leadership and Management

In this zone, we critically discuss the concepts of leadership and management and evaluate whether there is a clear dichotomy between them or whether definitional and practical overlaps exist.

For decades, it has been mooted that leadership and management are two separate and distinct functions, dichotomised by, among other things, their principal philosophies, key objectives and outcomes.[61,62] The concepts have been subject to definitional complexity, a menagerie of metaphorical conceptualisations and academic and practitioner debate and discourse that shows no sign of abating. A recurring theme in the debate is the interchangeability of leadership and management and the inference and prevalent confusion that they are one and the same.[61,63] However, according to Clemmer[64] 'management is as distinct from leadership as day is from night.' Kotter[65] (p. 3) concurs and professes that 'leadership and management are two distinctive. . . systems of action.' Rather than competing against each other, Kotter, Bedian and Hunt[66] and Gosling[67] advocate that they are complementary, work in tandem and both are needed to help organisations survive and succeed in volatile and complex business environments. Before we discuss these concepts further, it is necessary to explore contrasting definitions and conceptualisations.

The Theoretical Roots and Definitional Challenges of Leadership and Management

The literature surrounding the concepts of leadership and management has been described as a 'longstanding enigma'[66] (p. 198) and is beset with definitional challenges.[61] In terms of leadership, Toor and Ofori[61] note that its theoretical roots can be traced back several centuries, where writers and philosophers such as Confucius, Plato (The Republic), Niccolo Machiavelli (The Prince) and Sun Tzu (The Art of War) made major contributions to developing its theoretical base. Grace[68] records that the origins of leadership can be traced back to pre-Anglo Saxon culture. From a definitional perspective, leadership is defined by the Merriam-Webster Online Dictionary[69] as 'the office or position of a leader . . . capacity to lead . . . the act or an instance of leading.' It relates the concept to a leader, who has 'commanding authority or influence' and who 'tells people . . . especially workers what to do.' This is contrasted with Yukl[70] (p. 7), who defines leadership as 'the process of influencing others to understand and agree about what needs to be done and how to do it.' He also proffers that it is a 'process of facilitating individual and collective efforts to accomplish shared objectives.' Northouse[71] (p. 5) views it as 'a process whereby an individual influences a group of individuals to achieve a common goal.' The above definitions highlight the important role influence plays in engendering the achievement of collective and shared objectives. Northouse and Rowe and Guerrero[72] argue that defining leadership as a process means that it is not perceived as a characteristic or trait that exclusively resides in the leader. It thus makes the opportunity of becoming a leader available to everyone, not just to those who may be born to it (nature versus nurture) or formally designated or selected as a group leader. Rather than being a linear process, Northouse advocates that it involves two-way interaction with followers.

Although more formal management theorisation began and developed in the wake of the Industrial Revolution of the eighteenth and nineteenth centuries, Pindur et al.[73] contend that it can be traced all the way back to Biblical times and early Egyptian and ancient Chinese cultures, where the importance of organisation and administration were recorded and acknowledged. The Merriam-Webster Online Dictionary defines management as 'the act or art of managing...the conduct or supervising of something (such as a business)... the collective body of those who manage or direct an enterprise.' It likens the task of management to direction, administration, governance and *leadership*. This is compared with the theoretical definitions of the concept, which, first, describe it as the task of forecasting and planning, organising, coordinating, commanding (directing/*leading*) and controlling the organisation's activities.[74] Second, Hannagan[75] (p. 5) defines management in a similar vein. He suggests it is a 'process of achieving organisational goals and objectives effectively and efficiently through planning, organising, *leading* and controlling the human, material and financial resources available to it.' Fayol and Hannagan, along with Merriam-Webster, suggest that the management task involves an element of *leadership*, which infers that both concepts are an integral, and one could argue, symbiotic and interrelated part of the process and therefore cannot be separated. On this note, as with leadership, Hannagan and Kotter view management as a process, which is key to helping the organisation consistently produce quality, on-budget products and services daily. Kotter advises that although this is a complex task, which is largely underestimated, it is not leadership.

Key Differences between Leadership and Management

Literature is awash with a litany of views and perspectives on the key differences between the two concepts, four of which are presented here. First, Armandi et al.[76] espouse that managers are appointed by the organisation and are given formal authority to direct the activities of individuals to fulfil its goals. On the other hand, leaders can informally emerge as the 'people's choice' for leadership or can be formally appointed as such by the organisation. They emphasise that 'a leader can be a manager, but a manager is not necessarily a leader' (p. 107b). They add, 'employees willingly do what leaders ask or follow leaders, because they want to, not because they have to.' Second, Capowski[77] advocates that managers 'manage from the head', exercise positional or legitimate power, and, arguably are thus more psychologically distant from their direct reports. On the other hand, leaders 'lead from the head' using personal power or charisma and share a psychologically close relationship with their followers. Third, Bennis[78] (p. 108) states that 'management is getting people to do what needs to be done. Leadership is getting people to want to do what needs to be done.' He adds, 'Managers push. Leaders pull. Managers command. Leaders communicate.' Fourth, Kotter[65] (p. 4) proposes that 'management is about coping with complexity . . . by planning and budgeting – setting targets or goals for the future.' In contrast, he advises 'leadership is about coping with change . . . by setting a direction – developing a vision for the future.' Kotter does not suggest that one concept is better than the other but sees them as 'distinctive and complementary systems of action' (p. 3) that are necessary to achieve organisational success.

Implications for Organisational Behaviour in the Workplace

To conclude, the four views and perspectives outlined above, coupled with extant literature, make the case for viewing leadership and management as two separate and distinct concepts, each with their own unique part to play in ensuring the organisation's survival and longevity. It could be argued that the literature, along the views expressed here, privilege leadership over management and suggest that although both concepts are needed to make the organisation function, it is leadership that is the critical factor in making people *want* to subscribe to, and engage with, the organisation's mission, objectives and strategies and accept change. Peeling back the layers, it could be further argued that rather than there being a clear dichotomy, there is a degree of theoretical and

practical overlap and shades of grey between them, as the dictionary, Fayol and Hannagan definitions suggest. Instead of viewing them as opposite ends of a spectrum, which, arguably, so much of the literature encourages us to do, we should consider and apply both concepts as vital components in the organisation's metaphorical engine. Clemmer concurs and concludes 'both management and leadership are needed to make teams and organisations successful. Trying to decide which is more important is like trying to decide whether the right or left wing is more important to an airplane's flight. I'll take both, please!'

Questions

In view of the above, answer the following questions.

1. Fayol's 1916 definition of management includes 'to command,' which literature espouses can translate to 'directing/leading.' This, arguably, suggests that he felt leadership was a key part of the management task. Having conducted appropriate research, *build a case for* the interchangeability, rather than dichotomy, of leadership and management.

2. Capowski suggests that leaders are more emotionally in tune with their followers than a manager is with direct reports. *What* are the implications of this for organisational behaviour in the workplace?

3. It could be argued that the literature privileges leadership over management. With reference to theory and practice, *to what extent* do you agree?

Summary – Chapter 9 'Leadership in work organisations'

There are many ways of looking at leadership but essentially it is a relationship through which one person influences the behaviour or actions of other people. There is a close relationship between leadership and management but it does not follow that every leader is a manager. The leadership role is not clearly defined and there are many approaches to study of the subject area. A simple threefold heading of leadership behaviour is authoritarian, democratic or laissez-faire. Four main styles of leadership are tells, sells, consults and joins. Contingency theories draw attention to major variables and forces in the situation influencing effective leadership. Increasing business competitiveness has focused attention on transformational, inspirational or visionary leadership and renewed attention to servant leadership. Leadership is a dynamic form of behaviour. The leadership relationship is a social process dependent upon the type of power and influence exercised over other people. Culture is also a contingent factor. There is no one 'best' form of leadership and there are many variables that underlie effectiveness. Attention needs to be given to sets of skills to work within less hierarchical-based systems of command and control. Leadership development needs to emphasise interpersonal skills and recognise that successful leadership behaviour is a product of the total leadership situation.

Group discussion activities

Undertake each of these activities in small groups as indicated by your tutor. Before you start your discussion establish a non-threatening environment within the group and confirm confidentiality will be honoured.

First, form your own views and then share and compare in open critical discussion with colleagues. Reflect honestly on the extent to which: (i) you influenced the thinking and ideas of your colleagues; and (ii) you were influenced by your colleagues.

To what extent was your group able to reach consensus?

Agree one of your members to produce a brief written summary of the discussion and prepared to present in a plenary session.

Activity 1

(a) Explain fully a situation from university and/or any work experience where you have been inspired by a person through their charisma and natural leadership influence.

(b) Identify clearly the specific personal qualities exhibited by the person.

(c) Describe how the experience has influenced your views on the nature of leadership.

(d) Debate the extent to which it is possible to learn charisma.

(e) To what extent do you have charisma and the ability to inspire other people?

(f) How great is the danger of infatuation or hubris from 'great' or charismatic leaders?

Activity 2

List, *in rank order,* all the different approaches to leadership mentioned in this chapter on the basis of what you believe their practical relevance for today's workplace. Where possible provide supporting details for your ranking.

How much agreement is there amongst your colleagues?

What have you learnt from undertaking this activity?

Activity 3

(a) To what extent do you believe the term 'leadership' is misused and/or overused?

(b) Provide specific examples from the work situation of: (i) people with a leadership title but who have little if any real managerial influence over other people; and (ii) people who clearly behave as a leader but without the title in their job description.

(c) Do you regard your university lecturers as true leaders?

(d) How much would you learn from an in-depth study of sportspeople who are generally regarded as inspirational leaders?

Organisational behaviour in action case study

Portsmouth Hospitals NHS Trust Leadership Development Programme 2018

High quality leadership is now widely accepted as critical to the success of an organisation. The context in which 'leadership' takes place is important because the culture of individual teams and the challenges they face, vary greatly. This may explain why a seemingly successful leadership strategy in one care setting translates poorly to another. Understanding the context in which leadership takes place is therefore central to success.

Whilst there are a plethora of leadership courses available, they do not address the specific challenges faced by doctors, nurses and managers in our organisations. Furthermore, the unique leadership challenges within specific teams are often poorly appreciated ahead of taking on a leadership role.

We suggest that a fully developed sense of organisational culture, memory and politics are required to lead successfully in our health community. In the modern and more collaborative NHS, we believe that some leadership styles are better suited than others.

What is different about this leadership programme?

Integration through education

One of the biggest challenges facing modern health services is integrating care between acute and community providers. This programme will seek to develop leaders from both the hospital and community trust in the same classroom. By educating leaders together we will break down the artificial divides that can naturally build up between organisations. The mission for both organisations is the same; to deliver high quality patient care. It therefore makes sense to develop our leaders together.

Delivery by local leaders

The programme is delivered by Medical and Nursing facilitators who have extensive experience of leadership within Portsmouth Hospitals NHS Trust and more recently Southern Health Foundation Trust. They have been recently awarded Masters Degrees in leadership and will bring an understanding of what 'real life' leadership challenges exist in this organisation.

Learning from patients

We will be using patient pathways that are shared between both organisations to illustrate how leadership skills can empower front line staff to drive change to improve clinical effectiveness, for example the discharge pathway from Portsmouth Hospitals to Gosport War Memorial Hospital or admission avoidance pathway to ambulatory or step up to step down.

Leading together

A completely fresh approach to leadership training, delivered by staff that have not only studied the latest theory but have lived the practical experiences.

Development sets

Delegates will spend some time in small groups discussing the 'real-life' leadership challenges they face. This environment offers leaders support and encouragement in a highly confidential environment. Development sets are highly valued and often thought to be the most memorable and practical part of any development course.

Learning outcomes

By the end of this course, students should be able to:

* Demonstrate a broad understanding of the variety of approaches to leadership and how the NHS leadership applies locally
* Understand your own leadership style and how you can develop it
* Understand the causes of leadership success and failure
* Understand and lead change
* Have the practical knowledge and skills to be able to analyse widely different contexts and situations
* Develop leadership potential in others

Key benefits

* Taught by frontline leaders
* Innovative approach
* Integration of healthcare through shared learning
* Opportunity to network and share the burdens of difficult decision making – 'the loneliness of command'

What do you need to commit?

We require energy, enthusiasm and an on-going desire for self-development. The number of places is limited and so you must be committed to complete course work, an end of course assessment as well as undertake coaching/mentorship meetings. You will be on an overarching Leadership and Management Development Programme or nominated by your line manager who in turn will give you time to attend the teaching sessions.

Source for case: Extract from Portsmouth Hospitals NHS Trust 'LEADING TOGETHER: Leadership Development Programme 2018' with kind permission from Abigail Wilson, Organisational Development Manager.

Tasks

1. Explain your immediate impression of this leadership development programme.

2. What is your view of delivery from staff who have both studied the latest theory and also lived the practical experience? Do you think this is necessarily the best or most realistic approach?

3. To what extent do you believe leadership development courses should take account of the culture and challenges of a specific organisation?

Chapter 9 – Personal skills and employability exercise

Objectives

Completing this exercise should help you to enhance the following skills:

* Recognise your self-awareness and understanding of who you are
* Explore attributes associated with leadership
* Evaluate your readiness for a leadership role

Exercise

Self-knowledge about who you are, and what you are thinking and feeling is crucial if you are to become an effective and inspiring leader. Work together in small groups.

To gain maximum benefit from this exercise it is important to be completely honest with yourself.

First, for each of the following twenty-five items, consider honestly and fully the extent to which you:

1. Have a strong work ethic;
2. Are adaptable to changes in the work situation;
3. Place emphasis on service to others over self-interest;
4. Stretch yourself to meet objectives;
5. Take time in connecting with group members;
6. Set yourself clear goals and criteria for success;
7. Believe in doing things right the first time;
8. Have strong moral values;
9. Think leadership is simple if you have the right personality;
10. Find it easy to compliment fellow colleagues;
11. Are competitive and take pride in winning;
12. Communicate easily your ideas, thoughts or concerns to others;
13. Tolerate genuine mistakes by others that affect your work
14. Believe respect for superiors is more important than popularity
15. Enjoy others relying on you or coming to you for help;
16. Respect hierarchical authority and chain of command;
17. Believe leadership depends on confidence and courage;
18. Are prepared to place trust in your fellow colleagues;
19. Believe everyone is responsible for their actions and behaviour;
20. Get upset by disagreements or confrontation with your peers;
21. Simplify and explain complex situations to others;
22. Tend naturally to take the initiative in group situations;
23. Encourage challenging debate and dialogue;
24. Do not put off for tomorrow what can be done now;
25. Believe you would make an effective leader.

There are no right or wrong answers but score and record each item from 1–10 with 10 as the highest.

Second, share and discuss fully and openly your scoring amongst other members of the group.

Discussion

* How difficult was it for you to complete this exercise? How well do you think you know yourself?

* To what extent do colleagues agree with your own scoring including an honest evaluation of your perceived readiness for a leadership role?

* What benefits have you gained from this exercise and what have you learned about yourself as a potential leader?

Notes and references

1. See, for example, Adair, J. *Leadership and Motivation,* Kogan Page (2006).
2. CBI 'The Path to Leadership: Developing a Sustainable Model within Organisations', Caspian Publishing (2005), p. 4.
3. Zaleznik, A. 'Managers and Leaders: Are They Different?', *Harvard Business Review,* May–June 1977, pp. 67–78.
4. Kent, T. W. 'Leading and Managing: It Takes Two to Tango', *Management Decision,* vol. 43, no. 7/8, 2005, pp. 1010-17.
5. Radcliffe, S. *Leadership: Plain and Simple,* Financial Times Prentice Hall (2010).
6. Mintzberg, H. *Managing,* Financial Times Prentice Hall (2009), p. 8.
7. Moorcroft, R. 'To Lead or to Manage? That Is the Question', *Manager, The British Journal of Administrative Management,* November 2005, p. 4.
8. Drucker, P. F. *The Practice of Management,* Heinemann Professional (1989), p. 156.
9. See, for example, Bryman, A. 'Leadership in Organisations', in Clegg, S., Hardy, C. and Nord, W. (eds) *Managing Organisations: Current Issues,* Sage (1999), pp. 26–62.
10. Kotter, J. P. 'What Leaders Really Do', *Harvard Business Review,* May–June 1990, p. 103.
11. Adair, J. *Action-Centred Leadership,* Gower Press (1979). See also Adair, J. *The Skills of Leadership,* Gower Press (1984).
12. Tannenbaum, R. and Schmidt, W. H. 'How to Choose a Leadership Pattern', *Harvard Business Review,* May–June 1973, pp. 162–75, 178–80.
13. Fiedler, F. E. *A Theory of Leadership Effectiveness,* McGraw-Hill (1967).
14. See, for example, Yukl, G. *Leadership in Organizations,* seventh edition, Prentice Hall (2010).
15. Vroom, V. H. and Yetton, P. W. *Leadership and Decision-Making,* University of Pittsburgh Press (1973).
16. Vroom, V. H. and Jago, A. G. *The New Leadership: Managing Participation in Organizations,* Prentice Hall (1988).
17. House, R. J. 'A Path–Goal Theory of Leadership Effectiveness', *Administrative Science Quarterly,* vol. 16, September 1971, pp. 321–38.
18. House, R. J. and Dessler, G. 'The Path–Goal Theory of Leadership', in Hunt, J. G. and Larson, L. L. (eds) *Contingency Approaches to Leadership,* Southern Illinois University Press (1974).
19. Nadler, D. A. and Tushman, M. L. *Competing by Design: The Power of Organizational Architecture,* Oxford University Press (1997).
20. Hersey, P. and Blanchard, K. H. *Management of Organizational Behavior: Utilizing Human Resources,* sixth edition, Prentice-Hall (1993).
21. Burns, J. M. *Leadership,* Harper & Row (1978).
22. Bass, B. M. *Leadership and Performance Beyond Expectations,* Free Press (1985).
23. Bass, B. M. and Avolio, B. J. *Improving Organizational Performance Through Transformational Leadership,* Sage Publications (1994).
24. Yukl, G. *Leadership in Organizations,* seventh edition, Pearson (2010).
25. Goffee, R. and Jones, G. *Why Should Anyone Be Led By You?,* Harvard Business School Press (2006).
26. Weber, M. *The Theory of Social and Economic Organization,* Oxford University Press (1947).
27. Conger, J. 'Charisma and How to Grow It', *Management Today,* December 1999, pp. 78–81.
28. Conger, J. 'The Danger of Delusion', *Financial Times,* 29 November 2002.
29. Adair, J. *The Inspirational Leader: How to Motivate, Encourage and Achieve Success,* Kogan Page (2003).
30. Kingsmill, D. 'Leaders who can Recruit and Reward Teams for their Unique Skills Will Always Achieve the Best Results', *Management Today,* September 2014, p. 20.
31. Tourish, D. 'Poisonous power: The infatuation with the myth of the great leader is damaging to business' *Governance + Compliance,* August 2017, pp. 32–3.
32. Lord Owen, 'The danger of runaway leadership', *Governance + Compliance,* May 2017, pp. 32–4.
33. Greenleaf, R. K., *Servant Leadership: A Journey into the Nature of Legitimate Power and Greatness,* Paulist Press (1977). See also, for example: Spears, L. C. and Lawrence, M. (eds.), *Practicing servant leadership: Succeeding through trust, bravery and forgiveness,* Jossey-Bass (2004).
34. See also, for example: Smith, B. N., Montagno, R. V. and Kuzmenko, T. N. 'Transformational and Servant Leadership: Content and Contextual Comparisons', *Journal of Leadership & Organizational Studies,* vol. 10, no. 4, 2004, pp. 80–91.
35. See, for example: Brownell, J. 'Leadership in the Service of Hospitality', *Cornell Hospitality Quarterly,* vol. 51, no. 3, 2010, pp. 363–78.
36. Wong, P. T. P. 'Best Practices in Servant Leadership', *School of Global Leadership & Entrepreneurship,* Regent University, July 2007, pp. 1–15.
37. Yukl, G. *Leadership in Organizations,* seventh edition, Pearson (2010).
38. Metcalfe, H. and Urwick, L. (eds) *Dynamic Administration – The collected papers of Mary Parker Follett,* Harper (1941).
39. See also: Semler, R. 'Managing without Managers', *Harvard Business Review,* September–October 1989, pp. 76–84.
40. Day, D. V., Gronn, P. and Salas, E., 'Leadership Capacity in Teams', *Leadership Quarterly,* vol. 15, 2004, pp. 857–80.

41. Hewlett, S. A., Luce, C. B. and West, C. 'Leadership in your Midst: Tapping the Hidden Strengths of Minority Executives', *Harvard Business Review,* vol. 83, 2005, pp. 74–82.
42. 'Responsible leadership', Business in The Community. www.bitc.org.uk/issues/responsibleleadership (accessed 3 October 2014).
43. 'Responsible leadership', Financial Times. http://lexicon.ft.com/term=responsible-leadership (accessed 4 October 2014).
44. Jones, P. 'Masterclass on Correlative Leadership', *Professional Manager,* Winter 2017, pp. 67–8.
45. Bass, B. M. *Handbook of Leadership: Theory, Research and Managerial Applications,* third edition, The Free Press (1990), p. 11.
46. McGregor, D. *The Human Side of Enterprise,* Penguin (1987), p. 182.
47. Kouzes, J. M. and Posner, B. Z. 'The Janusian Leader', in Chowdhury, S. (ed.) *Management 21C,* Financial Times Prentice Hall (2000), p. 18.
48. House, R. J., Hanges, P. J., Javidan, M., Dorfman, P. J. and Gupta, V. (eds) *Culture, Leadership and Organisations: The GLOBE Study of 62 Societies,* Sage (2004).
49. For a fuller account of Project GLOBE see French, R. *Cross-Cultural Management,* second edition, Chartered Institute of Personnel and Development (2010).
50. Walker, B. 'Feast on The East', *Professional Manager,* Spring 2014, pp. 46–9.
51. Goleman, D. 'Leadership That Gets Results', *Harvard Business Review,* vol. 78, no. 2, March–April 2000, pp. 78–90.
52. McCabe, B. 'The Disabling Shadow of Leadership', *Manager, British Journal of Administrative Management,* April/May 2005, pp. 16–17.
53. Reeves, R. and Knell, J. 'Your Mini MBA', *Management Today,* March 2009, pp. 60–4.
54. 'Owen, J. 'Leader v manager: who's the boss?' *Professional Manager,* Spring 2016, p. 70.
55. Acas Strategy Unit, 'The Acas framework for effective leadership', Employment Relations Comment, ACAS, September 2016. Used with permission from Acas National.
56. Melville-Ross, T. 'A Leadership Culture has to Run Right Through an Organisation', *Professional Manager,* vol. 16, no. 1, 2007, pp. 18–21.
57. Cutler, A. 'A Good Fit Is Essential', *Professional Manager,* vol. 14, no. 3, May 2005, p. 38.
58. Bacon, B. 'Intuitive intelligence in leadership', *Governance + Compliance,* September 2013, pp. 24–5.
59. Blanchard, K 'Developing your Leadership Point of View', *Manager, The British Journal of Administrative Management,* Spring 2010, p. 15.
60. Benjamin, D. 'In my opinion', *Management Today,* May 2011, p. 58.
61. Toor, S. R. and Ofori, G. 'Leadership versus Management: How They Are Different and Why', *Leadership and Management in Engineering*', April, 2008, pp. 61–71.
62. Nienaber H. 'Conceptualisation of Management and Leadership', *Management Decision,* vol. 48, no. 5, 2010, pp. 661–75.
63. Edwards, G., Schedlitzki, D., Turnbull, S. and Gill, R. 'Exploring Power Assumptions in the Leadership and Management Debate', *Leadership and Organization Development Journal,* vol. 36, no. 3, 2015, pp. 328–43.
64. Clemmer, J. (2018). 'Management vs Leadership', https://www.clemmergroup.com/articles/management-vs-leadership/ (accessed 28 August 2018).
65. Kotter, J. 'What Leaders Really Do', *Harvard Business Review,* December, 2001, pp. 3–12.
66. Bedian, A. G. and Hunt, J. G. 'Academic Amnesia and Vestigial Assumptions of our Forefathers', *The Leadership Quarterly,* 17, 2010, pp. 190–205.
67. Gosling, J. 'What's the difference between leadership and management?', in Ratcliffe, R. (ed), *The Guardian,* 29 July 2013, http://www.theguardian.com/careers/difference-between-ledership-management (accessed 28 August 2018).
68. Grace, M. 'Origins of Leadership: The Etymology of Leadership', *Proceedings of International Leadership Association Conference,* 6–8 November 2003, Guadalajara, Mexico.
69. Merriam-Webster Dictionary Online, https://www.merriam-webster.com, accessed 12 April 2019. Used with permission.
70. Yukl, G. *Leadership in Organisations,* eighth edition, Pearson Education (2013).
71. Northouse, P. G. *Leadership Theory and Practice,* sixth edition, Sage Publications (2013).
72. Rowe, W. G. and Guerrero, L. *Cases in Leadership,* second edition, Sage Publications (2010).
73. Pindur, W., Rogers, S. E. and Kim, P. S. 'The History of Management: A Global Perspective', *Journal of Management History,* vol. 1, no. 1, 1995, pp. 59–77.
74. Fayol, H. In *General and Industrial Management,* Pitman and Sons, 1949.
75. Hannagan, T. *Management: Concepts & Practices,* fifth edition, Pearson Education, 2008.
76. Armandi, B., Oppedisano, J. and Sherman, H. 'Leadership Theory and Practice: A "Case" in Point', *Management Decision,* 41/10, 2003, pp. 1076–88.
77. Capowski, G. 'Anatomy of a Leader: Where Are the Leaders of Tomorrow?', *Management Review,* vol. 83, no. 3, 1994, pp. 10–18.
78. Bennis, W. 'Leading Change: The Leader as the Chief Information Officer', in Renesch, J. (ed.), *Leadership in a New Era: Visionary Approaches to the Biggest Crises of Our Time,* Paraview Special Editions (2002), pp. 103–10.

Chapter 10
Managing people at work

Management is an integrating activity permeating all operations of an organisation. Attention must be given to forms of managerial behaviour and the manner in which managing people at work is exercised.

Learning outcomes

After completing this chapter you should have enhanced your ability to:

- explain the essential nature of management;
- debate suggested philosophies for managing with and through people;
- contrast suppositions about human nature and behaviour at work;
- examine styles of managerial behaviour;
- review the role and organisation of the human resource function;
- explain the nature of performance management;
- assess main criteria for evaluating managerial effectiveness.

Outline chapter contents

Overview topic map: Chapter 10 – Managing people at work

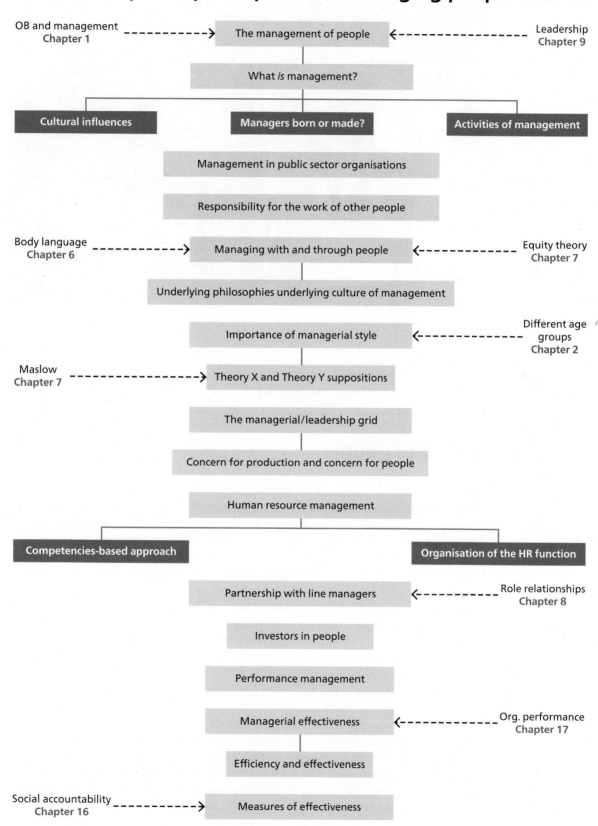

Cruise ship: compulsory crew drill

Before commencing to read this chapter, what do YOU immediately think of when you hear the term 'management'?

The management of people

The central underlying feature of organisational behaviour is concerned with the study of behaviour of people within an organisational setting. Although often studied as separate subject areas, there is a substantial interrelationship between organisational behaviour and management As discussed in **Chapter 1,** however much of a cliché, it is still an inescapable fact that people are the main resource of any organisation. Without its members, an organisation is nothing and only as good as the people who work within it.

Whatever the individual's orientations to work, the nature of the work organisation or cultural influences, efforts of members of the organisation need to be directed and guided towards the achievement of its goals. It is by the processes of management, execution of work and co-ordinated efforts of their members that activities of the organisation are carried out. The efficiency and performance of staff, and their commitment to the objectives of the organisation, are fostered by good human relationships at work.

In today's increasingly dynamic, global and competitive environment understanding human behaviour at work and effective management of the people resource is even more important for organisational survival and success. **Management** is fundamental to the effective operation of work organisations. It is essentially an integrating activity that should help reconcile needs of people at work with requirements of the organisation (*see* **Figure 10.1**).

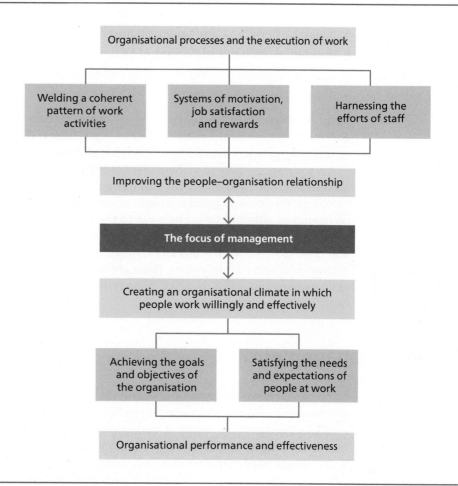

Figure 10.1 The central focus of management

Who is a manager?

In certain respects everyone could be regarded as a manager. We all manage our own time and everyone has some choice whether or not to do something, and some control, however slight, over the planning and organisation of their work. However, we are concerned with management as involving people looking beyond themselves and exercising formal authority and/or influence over the activities and performance of other people. Even within a work organisation you cannot necessarily identify a manager by what a person is called or their job title.

In some organisations there is a liberal use of the title 'manager' in an apparent attempt to enhance the status and morale of staff. As a result, there are a number of people whose job title includes the term manager but who, in reality, are not performing the full activities of a manager. Yet there are many people whose job title does not include the term manager but who, in terms of the activities they undertake and the responsibility and influence they exercise, may be very much a manager.

For our purposes, therefore, we can regard management as:

- taking place within a structured organisational setting with prescribed roles;
- directed towards the attainment of aims and objectives;
- achieved through the efforts of other people; and
- using systems and procedures.

At its most basic, management may be viewed as 'making things happen'. Recall also the discussion on the nature of leadership **(Chapter 9).** Whereas leaders are not necessarily managers it could be argued that all managers should be leaders.

It is the responsibility of management to manage. But organisations can achieve their aims and objectives only through the co-ordinated efforts of their members. This involves good people management. A heavy responsibility is placed on managers. Attention must be given to the work environment and appropriate systems of motivation, job satisfaction and rewards. The activity of management also takes place within the broader context of the organisational setting, external environment and cultural norms. There are also variations in systems and styles of management and in the choice of managerial behaviour. **Figure 10.2** shows a basic five-stage framework of study.

What *is* management?

Management is a generic term and subject to many interpretations. It is also a complex and discursive subject with contrasting ideas on the meaning of management and the work of a manager.[1] The nature of management is variable. It is not a separate, discrete function but relates to all activities of the organisation. It cannot be departmentalised or centralised. Management is seen best, therefore, as a process common to all other functions carried out within the organisation. However, 'management' is not homogeneous. It takes place in different ways and at different levels of the organisation.

Significance of cultural influences

Schneider and Barsoux contend that trying to define the meaning of management shows up differences in beliefs and values. Cultural influences are a significant feature of management. Managers in some countries might have more concern for the 'spiritual' aspects of management, while in others there would be greater

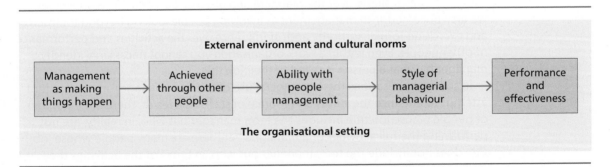

Figure 10.2 A basic framework of study

concern for the business sense. Developing people through work could be seen as an intrusion of privacy, and others may perceive empowerment as another name for manipulation.[2] According to *Francesco and Gold*, if international managers are to perform successfully in the global economy they need to understand the effects of different cultures on organisational behaviour. Reliance on theories developed in one culture is not sufficient.[3]

Managers born or made? Management an art or science?

There is frequent debate about whether managers are born or made or whether management is an art or a science. Briefly, the important point is neither are mutually exclusive alternatives. Even if there are certain innate qualities that make for a potentially good manager, these natural talents must be encouraged and developed through proper guidance, education and training, and planned experience. Clearly, management must always be something of an art, especially in so far as it involves practice, personal judgement and dealing with people. However, it still requires knowledge of the fundamentals of management, and competence in the application of specific skills and techniques – as illustrated, for example, with developments in information technology.

The discussion of management as an art or a science is developed by *Watson* who suggests that in order to make sense of the complex and highly ambiguous situations in which managers find themselves, management can be viewed not only as both art and science but also as magic and politics **(see Figure 10.3).**[4]

Dib provides an account of hearing contrasting views on management as a science. One view is YES – there is clearly science in management although a purely scientific approach omits human beings as the most important factor. Management is about the application of knowledge. 'The most successful managers are those who use scientific models, theories and concepts, and then apply them using their own style, experience and personality.' The other view is NO – both management and science apply and extend our knowledge but management needs more than just observations and experiments and needs to be based on practice, reflection and action. Management is too eclectic to be a science it itself. 'The very nature of management means that without applying and reflecting upon the practice of management we will be more inclined to measure than to take action'.[5]

Thinking about management at university level

Foppen questions the relationship between management practice and education, and whether management hasn't always been illusory. However, Foppen emphasises the importance of management performance.

> **Management is of pivotal importance for modern society. It is for this reason that, no matter what, thinking about management, certainly at university level, is of great relevance to management practice. So apart from the question of whether management's claim that it is indispensable is really valid or not, the fact that practically everyone believes it is, is what counts.**[6]

Activities of management

A common approach to viewing the nature of management, favoured by the classical writers such as *Henri Fayol* was the search for common activities

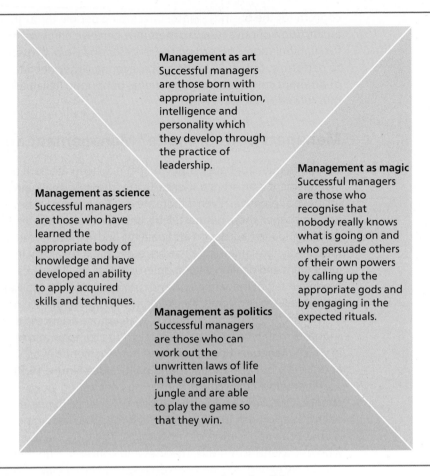

Figure 10.3 Management as art, science, magic and politics
Source: From Watson, T. J. *Management, Organisation and Employment Strategy,* Routledge & Kegan Paul (1986), p. 29. Reproduced by permission of the publishers, Routledge, a division of Taylor & Francis, Ltd.

applicable to managers in any organisation.[7] Inevitably there are doubts about the relevance of these activities and principles today but it is hard to argue against their continuing, underlying importance. What is perhaps debatable is the manner of their interpretation and implementation. *McLean* maintains that although proposed almost a hundred years ago, Fayol's definition of management remains one of the most cited of modern times. Fayol has left an indelible mark on management history, and forged an inextricable link between the manager and the organisation.[8]

Hamel suggests that there would be little argument from modern-day executives about Fayol's description of the work of a manager but puts forward his own synthesis of what the *practice* of management entails:

- Setting and programming *objective;*
- Motivating and aligning *effort;*
- Co-ordinating and controlling *activities;*
- Developing and assigning *talent;*
- Accumulating and applying *knowledge;*

- Amassing and allocating *resources;*
- Building and nurturing *relationships;*
- Balancing and meeting *stakeholder demands.*[9]

Rostrum from where John F. Kennedy announced the decision to land on the moon

To what extent do YOU believe thinking about management at your university level is likely to be relevant to your future managerial career?

Management in public sector organisations

The general movement of major organisations away from direct governmental control to greater responsibility for managing their own affairs has led to blurring of the traditional distinction between the private and public sectors. Basic principles of management apply in any series of activities in any organisation and both private enterprise and public sector organisations face the same common activities and general problems. However, actual methods and procedures will of necessity differ.

There are perceived differences between people management in the private and public sectors which arise from particular features of public sector organisations. For example:

- aims concerned with providing a service for, and for the well-being of, the community rather than just of a commercial nature;
- the scale, variety and complexity of their operations;

- the tendency for them to be subject more to press reports on their activities;
- the political environment in which they operate, and in the case of local government, for example, the relationship between elected members and permanent officers;
- high levels of statutory regulations, legislation and ministerial guidance;
- the generally high level of trade union involvement;
- difficulties in measuring standards of performance of services provided compared with profitability;
- demand for uniformity of treatment and public accountability for their operations;
- tendency towards more rigid HR policies, for example specific limitations on levels of authority and responsibility, fixed salary grades based on general pay scales, long-term career structures and set promotion procedures.

A number of these features frequently combine to result in increased bureaucracy within public sector organisations.

Importance of skills and behaviour

A report from CIPD points out that although public services are not homogeneous and specific issues facing managers will differ between sectors and localities, there is a shared agenda in improving people management in the public sector workplaces. It is important to recognise that without more effective people management there is no chance of introducing positive and lasting change. Management need to support and empower front line staff. The report makes clear that:

> **an improvement in the quality of people management, particularly among line managers and supervisors, is central to more effective delivery of public services and greater local accountability. Inadequate people management skills are also often at the heart of catastrophic service failure.**[10]

Sir Howard Bernstein refers to the challenging economic climate that has focused the public sector on the need for radical reform to tackle the cost pressures on it and the development of the skills to deliver public sector reform. Significant long-term culture change is required across a range of partners to overcome professional, organisational and technical barriers. All levels of managers and leaders have a vital role in delivering community services in a more integrated way. *This type of reform will require different skills and behaviours across all levels of management.*[11]

Walker points out that despite the talent in all sectors of the economy, cultural differences, alien working practices and even mutual suspicion mean moving between the private, public and voluntary sectors can be a bumpy ride. Beyond differences in management styles a key factor is that in the private sector there is more of a strategic focus; while in the public sector it is much more about here and now. Nine out of ten private sector employers would be unlikely to take employees offloaded from the public sector.[12]

Responsibility for the work of other people

One of the most popular ways of defining management today is that it involves getting work done second-hand, through the efforts of other people. Managers are judged, ultimately, not just on their own performance but on the results achieved by subordinate staff. If we look at how people at work actually spend their time, we should be able to distinguish between those whose main occupation is the carrying out of discrete tasks and the actual doing of work themselves, and those who spend proportionally more of their time in determining the nature of work to be undertaken by other people, the planning and organising of their work, providing directions and advice and guidance, and checking on their performance. Staff need **to perform well in the right areas,** and to be effective as well as efficient. Leadership is clearly important but the efforts of staff need to be **directed** towards the achievement of given objectives in accordance with stated policy.

The efforts of other people

Rosemary Stewart attempts to integrate the various definitions of management and summarises the manager's job, broadly defined as: *deciding what should be done and then getting other people to do it.*

> The first task comprises setting objectives, planning (including decision-making), and setting up formal organization. The second consists of motivation, communication, control (including measurement), and the development of people. The two tasks are separated for convenient analysis, but in practice they may often overlap.[13]

The middle managers

Middle managers have a particular part to play in managing people at work. A CMI report refers to the important role of middle managers as critical for creating 'civic' engagement across the workforce – through communications, integrity, visibility, interactions and connections. Middle managers are the lifeblood of an organisation and play a central role in managing and guiding its people. However they are not always treated in a way that reflects this. The report calls for improved trust and communication in recognising and supporting middle managers in their role at the heart of the organisation.[14]

Rock reminds us that the middle manager's goal is more about the accomplishment of the team than their own personal achievement and suggests eight reasons to love middle managers. They make organisations perform better; get stuff done; embody your culture; make sure information is trusted; cascade strategy; do detail; build relationships quickly; and soothe troubled waters.[15]

However, a BBC radio programme pointed out that the job of middle managers is inherently horrid. They are first to be fired when times get hard and in a study of 300,000 people those who liked their jobs least were middle managers who, despite privileges, felt unappreciated and all round miserable.[16]

Do YOU accept that 'getting work done second-hand, through the efforts of other people' is the best possible description of what management is basically all about?

Managing with and through people

One essential ingredient of any successful manager is the ability to handle people effectively. Genuine concern for their welfare goes a long way in encouraging them to perform well. A positive policy of investment in people and an interpersonal relationship approach to management is, in the longer term, worth the effort. For example, the UK government-sponsored initiative Investors in People **(discussed later in this chapter)** is based on a commitment to the benefits organisations can gain through their people and on the vital role of managers.

It is possible to put forward a number of underlying philosophies that underlie the culture of management and arguably likely to make for the successful management of people, and lead to both improved work performance and more contented staff **(see Figure 10.4). These philosophies are not intended to be prescriptive but to encourage discussion on the extent to which you agree with the points of view.**

Consideration, respect and trust

People generally respond according to the way they are treated. If you give a little, you will invariably get a lot back. Make people feel important and give them a sense of personal worth. The majority of staff will respond constructively if treated with consideration and respect, and as responsible individuals who wish to serve the organisation well. However, how can members of staff show that they can be trusted unless trust is first placed in them? **The initiative must come from management.**

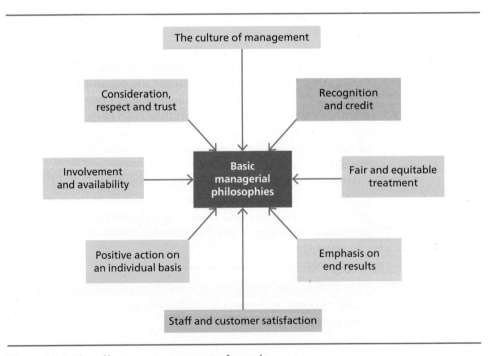

Figure 10.4 The effective management of people

Recognition and credit

People can be praised to success. Give genuine recognition and credit when it is due and let people know you appreciate them. Too often managers appear unresponsive to good performance, taking this for granted. But they are quick to criticise on the occasions when performance falls below expectations. **It should not be assumed staff would necessarily take a lack of response as a sign of positive recognition rather than just the absence of criticism.** So often you hear the comment: 'Well nobody has complained so I suppose everything is all right.' What a poor indictment of management style! Positive feedback on good performance is a strong motivator and staff are then more likely to accept and respond to constructive criticism.

Involvement and availability

Involve yourself with the work of the staff and make sure you fully understand the difficulties and distastes of their job. Ensure an open flow of communications and encourage participation and feedback. Take an active interest in the work of staff but without excessive supervision or inhibiting their freedom of action. Wherever possible be available to staff as a priority, rather than to administration. Remember the importance of giving time to listen genuinely to the feelings and problems of staff. This means giving staff your full attention including adopting appropriate body language **(recall the discussion in Chapter 6).**

Fair and equitable treatment

Treat people fairly but according to merit. Ensure justice in treatment, equitable systems of motivation and rewards, clear HR policies and procedures, avoidance of discrimination, and full observance of all laws and codes of conduct relating to employment. People expect certain outcomes in exchange for certain contributions or inputs. A feeling of inequality causes tension and motivates the person to indulge in certain forms of behaviour in order to remove or to reduce the perceived inequity. **(Recall the discussion on equity theory of motivation in Chapter 7.)**

Positive action on an individual basis

Deal with individual situations on an individual basis and avoid the 'blanket' approach. For example, it has come to the manager's attention that a couple of members of staff have failed to provide some urgently requested information on time. The manager's reaction is to send a circular email to *all* members of the department reminding them of the need for, and importance of, meeting deadlines. But what are the likely reactions of staff? The two members concerned might shield behind the generality of the e-mail and persuade themselves that it doesn't apply particularly to them. In contrast, the majority of staff in the department who do have a good record of providing requested information on time may well be annoyed or upset by the circular.

Emphasis on end-results

Place emphasis on end-results and levels of actual performance and achievement rather than on compliance with detailed instructions, rules or regulations. For example, where set attendance times are *clearly* seen as a necessary requirement of the job, it is right that managers should ensure that timekeeping is adhered to and enforced as appropriate. But in many cases rigid times of attendance are not an essential requirement for effective performance. The increasing movement to work/life balance, flexible working patterns and teleworking coupled with demands to boost productivity are placing growing emphasis on what staff actually achieve rather than the time spent at work. The important criteria are the level and quality of performance.

Staff and customer satisfaction

The starting point for customer, or consumer, satisfaction is good manager–subordinate relationships. Supportive and harmonious working relationships are more likely to create a working environment that results in high levels of both staff *and* consumer satisfaction. Managers need to adopt a positive attitude towards staff and to develop a spirit of mutual co-operation. Staff should feel that they are working *with* the manager rather than *for* the manager.

> How far do YOU support the idea of underlying philosophies for the effective management of other people; or are such philosophies naïve and unrealistic?

A looser approach to managing

It is not suggested managers should give up the right to manage: it is a question of *how* they manage and use their authority. *Thomas* suggests the need for a loose approach to business in which tight controls and specific rules are replaced with broad principles, a culture of trust and a more relaxed management style. As a result of employee and customer expectations, and social and technological change the modern workforce expects to play a greater role in service delivery and not be hampered by strict rules and inflexible regulations. However, Thomas believes the biggest obstacle is middle managers who fear they do not have authority to make big decisions and rely on management by the rule book, their process, templates and rigid structures.[17]

The importance of emotions and mood

We have mentioned previously that people are not homogeneous and human behaviour is capricious. People bring to work their own perceptions, feelings and attitudes. The importance of human foibles and emotions should not be forgotten. *Robbins,* for example points out that emotions are part of our lives: we not only think, we feel! Employees bring an emotional component with them to work every day.

> But the field of management has been guilty for a long time of treating employees as if they're non-emotional. All work behavior is assumed to be fully rational. While this makes for simpler analysis of workplace behavior, it also creates highly unrealistic and inaccurate assessments.[18]

Bolchover draws attention to the importance of mood as crucial to job performance in areas such as decision-making, creativity, teamwork, negotiation and leadership. Leaders' moods are highly contagious and what makes moods even more potentially beneficial or destructive is their infectiousness. Bolchover suggests that this 'emotional contagion' lies at the root of what we call corporate morale. Managers must appreciate that their own attitudes are contagious, profoundly affecting those who work for them. 'Pretty much everything that determines an employee's fundamental attitude at work is under the control of the manager.'[19]

Importance of managerial style

There appears to be a growing recognition that managers can no longer rely solely on their perceived formal authority as a result of a hierarchical position in the structure of the organisation. More than ever, an essential ingredient of any successful manager is the ability to handle people successfully. This changing relationship places a heavy responsibility on managers, and on the systems and styles of management adopted.

It is, however, interesting to note the views of *Watson* who, while acknowledging that to create the goods, services and quality of life that people look for in the modern world, rather complex patterns of co-operative behaviour have to be orchestrated and 'managed', identifies three major problems in thinking about organising and managing work in terms of 'managing people'.

First, in a modern democratic society, is it realistic even to contemplate the possibility of managing people and that there are people willing to be managed?

Second, can it be argued that a manager has no moral right to direct, manage or boss any individual?

Third, does the focus on people management tend to blur the part played by structures, systems, cultures, processes and the rest?[20]

Good people management

Whatever the veracity of these problems the organising and management of work depends ultimately on the people who make up the organisation. Without people, systems and procedures and indeed organisations themselves are meaningless. And people need to be managed. But, of course, of increasing importance are:

- how the process of management is actually carried out;
- the style of managerial behaviour; and
- its effectiveness for *both* organisational performance and the satisfaction of its members.

With the general movement towards flatter organisation structures, flexible working and greater employee empowerment, there is more emphasis on an integrating rather than a traditional controlling style of management. Management style and behaviour can be as important as management competence.

The style of managerial behaviour needs to take account of the likely orientations to work of different generations and wider range of age groups in the modern workplace **(discussed in Chapter 2).** For example compared with other age groups, Generation Y (born between 1980 and 1995) are less frightened by the future, will not stay long in a job they do not enjoy and are likely to be technologically sophisticated.

Theory X and Theory Y management

The way in which managers approach the performance of their jobs and the behaviour they display towards subordinate staff is likely to be conditioned by underlying predispositions about people, and human nature and work. Drawing on Maslow's hierarchy of needs model **(discussed in Chapter 7)**, *McGregor,* in 1960, put forward two suppositions about human nature and behaviour at work. He argued that the style of management adopted is a function of the manager's attitudes towards people and assumptions about human nature and behaviour. McGregor's work still proves debate today. The two suppositions are called Theory X and Theory Y and are based on polar assumptions about people and work.[21]

Theory X assumptions

Theory X represents the carrot-and-stick assumptions on which traditional organisations are based:

- the average person is lazy and has an inherent dislike of work;
- most people must be coerced, controlled, directed and threatened with punishment if the organisation is to achieve its objectives;
- the average person avoids responsibility, prefers to be directed, lacks ambition and values security most of all; and
- motivation occurs only at the physiological and security levels.

The central principle of Theory X is direction and control through a centralised system of organisation and the exercise of authority. Assumptions based on a Theory X approach, and the traditional use of rewards and sanctions exercised by the nature of the manager's position and authority, are likely to result in an exploitative or authoritarian style of management.

Theory Y assumptions

At the other extreme is Theory Y based on the **central principle of the integration of individual and organisational goals.** Theory Y assumptions are:

- for most people work is as natural as play or rest;
- people will exercise self-direction and self-control in the service of objectives to which they are committed;
- commitment to objectives is a function of rewards associated with their achievement;
- given the right conditions, the average worker can learn to accept and to seek responsibility;
- the capacity for creativity in solving organisational problems is distributed widely in the population;
- the intellectual potential of the average person is only partially utilised; and
- motivation occurs at the affiliation, esteem and self-actualisation levels as well as at the physiological and security levels.

Demands of the situation

The two views of Theory X and Theory Y tend to represent extremes of the natural inclination of managers towards a particular style of behaviour. In practice, however, the actual style of management behaviour adopted will be influenced by the demands of the situation.[22] Where the job offers a high degree of intrinsic satisfaction or involves a variety of tasks, an element of problem-solving and the exercise of initiative, or where output is difficult to measure in quantitative terms, an informal, participative approach would seem to be more effective. Where commitment to the goals of the organisation is almost a prerequisite of membership, such as in certain voluntary or charity organisations, for example, a Theory Y approach would clearly seem most appropriate.

However, even if a manager has a basic belief in Theory Y assumptions, there may be occasions when it is necessary, or more appropriate, to adopt a Theory X approach. This approach may be indicated in emergency situations, or where shortage of time or other overriding factors demand the use of authority in directing actions to the tasks in hand. For example, in the hustle, heat and noise of a busy hotel kitchen preparing fresh meals for a large banquet, with many tasks to be co-ordinated over very short time scales, it seems to be recognised that a Theory X style of management is most appropriate. In such circumstances this style of management appears often to be accepted by the kitchen staff.

Do YOU agree the underlying concept of Theory X and Theory Y is still one of the most meaningful insights into our understanding of managerial behaviour?

The Managerial/Leadership Grid®

One means of describing and evaluating different styles of management is the *Blake and Mouton* **Managerial Grid**®. First published as the Managerial Grid® in 1964, restated in 1978 and 1985[23] and republished in 1991 as the **Leadership Grid**®,[24] the Grid provides a basis for comparison of managerial styles in terms of two principal dimensions: concern for production and concern for people.

- **Concern for production** is the amount of emphasis that the manager places on accomplishing the tasks in hand, achieving a high level of production and getting results or profits. This is represented along the horizontal axis of the Grid.
- **Concern for people** is the amount of emphasis that the manager gives to subordinates and colleagues as individuals and to their needs and expectations. This is represented along the vertical axis of the Grid.

Five basic combinations

The four corners and the centre of the Grid provide five basic combinations of degree of concern for production coupled with degree of concern for people.

- **Managers with a 1,1 rating,** the impoverished manager, tend to be remote from their subordinates and believe in the minimum movement from their present position.
- **Managers with a 9,1 rating,** the authority-compliance manager, are autocratic. They tend to rely on a centralised system and the use of authority.
- **The 1,9 rating managers,** country club managers, believe that a contented staff will undertake what is required of them and achieve a reasonable level of output.
- **The 5,5 rating,** middle-of-the-road manager, with the approach of 'live and let live' and a tendency to avoid the real issues.
- **Managers with a 9,9 rating, the team manager,** believe in the integrating of the task needs and concern for people.

These five styles of management represent the extremes of the Grid. With a nine-point scale on each axis there is a total of 81 different 'mixtures' of concern for production and concern for people. Most people would come up with a score somewhere in an intermediary position on the Grid.

Two additional grid styles

The 1991 edition of the Grid covers two additional styles: opportunism and 9 + 9 paternalism/maternalism, which take account of the reaction of subordinates. In opportunistic management, organisational performance occurs according to a system of exchanges, whereby effort is given only for an equivalent measure of the same. People adapt to the situation to gain maximum advantage of it. In 9 + 9 paternalistic/maternalistic management, reward and approval are granted to people in return for loyalty and obedience; and punishment is threatened for failure to comply. A summary of the seven basic combinations of the Grid is given in **Table 10.1.**

Table 10.1 Leadership Grid® style definitions

9,1 Authority–compliance management	Managers in this position have great concern for production and little concern for people. People are seen as 'tools' for production. They demand tight, unilateral control in order to complete tasks efficiently. They consider creativity and human relations to be unnecessary.
1,9 Country club management	Managers in this position have great concern for people and little concern for production. They try to avoid conflicts and concentrate on being liked, even at the expense of production. To them the task is less important than good interpersonal relations. Their goal is to keep people happy. (This is a soft Theory X and not a sound human relations approach.)
1,1 Impoverished management	This style is often referred to as laissez-faire. Leaders in this position have little concern for people or productivity. They avoid taking sides and stay out of conflicts. They do just enough to maintain group membership.
5,5 Middle-of-the-road management	Leaders in this position have medium concern for both people and production. They rely on tried and true techniques and avoid taking untested risks. They attempt to balance their concern for both people and production, but are not committed strongly to either. Conflict is dealt with by avoiding extremes and seeking compromise rather than sound resolution.
9 + 9 Paternalistic 'father knows best' management	This leader takes the high 9 level of concern from 9,1 and 1,9 to create a combined style of controlling paternalism. The paternalist strives for high results (high 9 from 9,1) and uses reward and punishment to gain compliance (high 9 from 1,9). The paternalist uses a high level of concern for people to reward for compliance or punish for rejection.
Opportunistic 'what's in it for me' management	The opportunist uses whatever Grid style is needed to obtain selfish interest and self-promotion. They adapt to situations to gain the maximum advantage. They may use 9,1 to push their own goals with one person, and 1,9 to gain trust and confidence with another. Performance occurs according to a system of exchanges. Effort is given only for an equivalent measure of the same.
9,9 Team management	These managers demonstrate high concern for both people and production. They work to motivate employees to reach their highest levels of accomplishment. They explore alternatives openly and aggressively. They are flexible and responsive to change. This style is considered ideal.

Source: Blake, R. R. and McCanse, A. A. *Leadership Dilemmas – Grid Solutions*, Gulf Publishing Company (1991), p. 29.

Relevance today

The structure, plan and concept of an organisation are crucial to its effectiveness. However, beyond, this a single significant factor is the behaviour of the management team. Managers must act as leaders, they must guide, motivate and integrate the efforts of others. The ultimate purpose of studies of managerial style is to aid in the training and development of those who wish to become better leaders. Grid organisation development identifies and applies relevant aspects of behavioural science.

Newborough maintains that the Managerial/Leadership Grid is as relevant today as when it was first launched.[25] And according to *Crainer and Dearlove*: 'Crude at it is, the Grid helps people who are not conversant with psychology to see themselves and those they work with more clearly, to understand their interactions, and identify the sources of resistance and conflicts.'[26]

To what extent do YOU believe the Managerial/Leadership Grid helps to see yourself more clearly and influences your thinking about managing people?

Human resource management

The significance of human resources and recognition of people as the most important asset of any organisation is emphasised by *Gratton* who as the basis of her 'Living Strategy' puts forward four basic propositions:

1 there are fundamental differences between people as an asset and the traditional assets of finance or technology;

2 an understanding of these fundamental differences creates a whole new way of thinking and working in organisations, a shift in mindset;

3 business strategies can only be realised through people;

4 creating a strategic approach to people necessitates a strong dialogue across the organisation.[27]

In recent years there has been noticeable popularity in the use of the term 'human resource management' to replace the term 'personnel management'. Whatever the debate on comparative meanings, terms such as 'human resource management' or 'human capital' have overtones of a cold, impersonal approach. Referring to people as resources, assets or capital is an instrumental approach implying a means to an end. It is pleasing, therefore, to see what appears to be the increasing use of the terminology 'people management' or the 'management of people'.

Competencies-based approach

In most organisations, people are the largest asset. Without taking a strategic approach to the management of that asset, its skills and ability, knowledge development and deployment, even the best business strategy may not succeed. Developments in information and communications technology (ICT), new forms of work organisation and structure, and increasing attention to empowerment, flexible working arrangements and new psychological contracts provide a challenge to traditional HRM theories and practices. Only by having a truly strategic approach to managing people at work where all discussions regarding policies, activities, priorities and goals relate with wider organisational goals and with each other, is the organisation more likely to succeed in achieving optimum operational performance.

Implementation of practices and procedures should be based on underlying philosophies of managerial behaviour and employee relationships, embracing:

• recognition of people's needs and expectations at work;

• respect for the individual;

- attention to ethical responsibilities, diversity and inclusion;
- justice in treatment and equitable reward systems;
- stability of employment;
- good working environment and conditions of service;
- opportunities for personal development and career progression;
- democratic functioning of the organisation; and
- full observance of all laws and codes of conduct relating to employment.

Policies, activities and functions

Success in managing people at work is influenced by the philosophy of top management and the attitudes they bring to bear on relationships with staff, and problems which affect them. Recognition of the needs and wants of staff and the nature of their grievances is a positive step in motivating them to perform well and their commitment to the aims of the organisation. There should be open consultation with employee and union representatives, and clear lines of communication through managers and supervisors to staff at all levels. An example is the need for a clearly stated policy on the use of ICT resources (including email and the internet) that is clear about prohibited activities and consequences of failure to adhere to the policy such as disciplinary action and potential sanctions.

Organisation of the human resource (HR) function

Organisation of the HR function is determined primarily by the requirement the business places upon it. Is it a strategic partner or operational task master? To what extent are line management responsible for functional tasks within their own departments or reliant on a centralised specialised function? The size of the enterprise concerned also has a significant impact.

Smaller organisations may not justify a specialist human resource manager or a separate department. But it is still necessary to have an effective HR function, whether the responsibility of the owner, manager or administrative assistant. Even in the smallest organisations, or organisations where a specialist department has not been established, there will be a need to recruit staff, to train, motivate, reward them, and to comply with the law relating to employment. HR work must still be carried out even if an organisation is too small to justify a separate department or chooses not to establish one.

In the larger concerns, where more time is taken up with problems of organisation and the management of people, there is arguably greater need for a specialist member of staff to whom are delegated full-time responsibilities for advising top management on human resource matters and development and implementation of clearly defined policies which permit implementation of consistent HR practices. For example, high staffing costs together with increasing employment legislation and the changing nature of the work organisation (discussed in previous chapters) combine to suggest that personnel activities and employee relations are areas of increasing specialisation.

Even where HR work is established as a separate, specialist function the range of responsibilities varies from one organisation to another, as do the title and status of the head of department and position in the management structure. In larger organisations activities might be divided between two or more specialists, so that it would be possible to have, for example, a human resource manager, training officer and employee relations advisor. Whatever the range of responsibilities, the manager operates by consent, by delegated authority. How much consent is dependent upon attitudes of top management, the role they see the HR specialist(s) performing and formal organisational relationships with 'line' managers.

Would YOU accept the contention that too strong a separate HR department leads to the danger of line managers abdicating responsibility for managing their own staff?

Partnership with line managers

The HR function is part of the generality of management and responsibility of all managers and supervisors. The HR manager, as a separate entity, operates in terms of a 'functional' relationship: that is, as specialist advisor on matters of policy and implementation through all departments of the organisation. It is the job of the HR manager to provide specialist knowledge and services for line managers, and support them in the performance of their jobs. In other respects the HR manager's contacts with other managers, supervisors and staff is indirect: it is an advisory relationship.

Line managers are departmental or unit managers with responsibility for the 'production' process – for the operational functions directly related to the purpose and aims of the organisation. They form a hierarchical level in the chain of command throughout the organisation structure and are responsible for the management of their own staff. For example, according to the *Health and Safety Executive* stress management is part of the normal general management activities and about the way line managers behave on a day-to-day basis towards those they manage.[28] It is the line managers who have authority and control over staff in their departments and who have the immediate responsibility for day-to-day human resource activities, although there will be times when they need specialist help and advice.

However, although line managers are specialists in their own area of work, they are not necessarily specialists in human resource management. Just as line managers turn to specialists on legal and accounting matters and the use of technology, so they will need help, guidance and specialist advice on HR activities. CIPD, however, point out that although most organisations manage conflict through formal procedures, HR professionals and others are often guilty of 'hiding behind' procedures and failing to address the low-level conflict that rumbles on all the time.[29]

Success in managing people at work is dependent upon an effective working partnership between line managers and HR members of staff. There has to be clear lines of responsibility within the formal structure, good teamwork, and co-operation and open consultation. Top management should agree clear terms of references within a framework of sound human resource policies. Within this framework the HR function can be seen as operating at two levels: the organisational level and the departmental level **(*see* Figure 10.5).** This partnership is made easier when top management take an active part in fostering goodwill and harmonious working relationships among departments. It is important to have

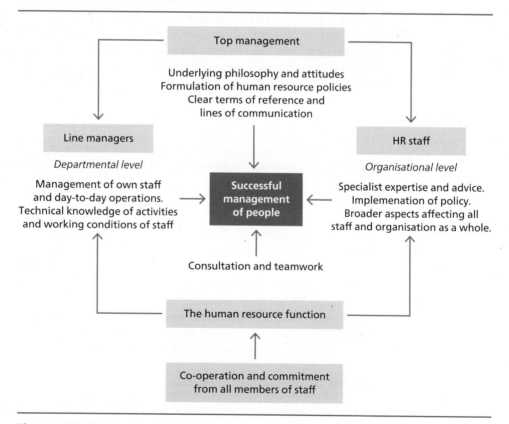

Figure 10.5 The human resources function – a shared responsibility

clear role relationships and avoid difficulties with role incongruence or role conflict **(discussed in Chapter 8).**

The organisational level

At the organisational level, detailed involvement of work activities of several departments, available time and the need for specialisation suggest HR has a prominent role to play and is the main executor of policies but acting in consultation with, and taking advice from, line managers. On this basis the HR would be concerned mainly with broader aspects of procedures that affect the organisation as a whole or staff generally. This could include such activities as human resource planning, procedures for recruitment and selection, induction and training, consultations with trade unions or staff representatives, employee development, compliance with the law relating to employment, maintaining records and statistics, and liaison with outside bodies such as Acas, employers' organisations, government agencies, the government Disclosure and Barring Service, training organisations and professional associations.

The departmental level

At the departmental or unit level line managers might assume a prominent role for day-to-day managing people at work with the HR as advisor and if necessary arbitrator. Line managers would be more concerned, at least in the first instance, with the operational aspects of HR activities within their own departments, for example the organisation of work and allocation of duties, minor disciplinary matters, standards of work performance, safety, on-the-job training, communication of information, and grievances from staff. In this respect it could be said that **all line managers are their own human resource managers.** Line managers are on hand to observe directly the performance of their staff. They will actually see, and be directly affected by, for example, lateness of staff, unsatisfactory work, insufficient training, low morale, staff unrest, or poor planning of work duties and responsibilities.

How far do YOU agree it is line managers who have the right and duty to manage their own staff and HR specialists should have only an advisory, supportive role?

Whatever the respective roles the effective management of people can only be achieved if based and implemented on sound policies and procedures. It also requires the co-operation and commitment of all members of staff, no matter their duties or positions within the organisation. Whatever the formal organisational structure, the HR function cannot be housed within one discrete department or as the sole responsibility of selected members of staff. It permeates all levels of the organisation and all phases of its operations. It is the concern of top management, all line managers and supervisors, and HR staff.

Nature of the organisation

The extent to which authority and responsibility for the HR function is devolved to line managers is a decision for top management and is likely to be influenced by the nature, culture, structure and characteristic features of the particular industry or organisation. For example, in the hospitality industry, *Rocco Forte* has emphasised the importance of a caring and efficient personnel function to assist line managers in what is one of their primary responsibilities. The nature of the hospitality business, with many separate units of differing size, location and mix of skills, means of necessity the personnel function is decentralised and prime responsibility has to be with line management.

Forte believed that the prime responsibility for personnel falls on line managers, not specialists. The nature of work means that active participation by management in every day operations and that workers need to know that their line managers have responsibility for and the authority to take action to affect their work. The link therefore is a direct one.[30]

This philosophy is still very much part of the structure of many hospitality organisations.

Relationship between organisational behaviour and HRM

Whatever the choice of terminology or decisions about its role and structure, effective human resource management is essential to maintaining and improving organisational performance. *Lynch* refers to the importance of people as a vital resource for sustainable competitive advantage. 'For most organisations, people are a vital resource. There are some industries where people are not just important but are the **key factor** for successful performance.'[31]

It is important to note that the theoretical frameworks for the study of organisational behaviour (psychology, sociology, anthropology, economics and politics) provide the conceptual basis for many specialist HRM activities. For example, perception affects the selection process; motivation theory informs the design of reward systems; learning theory supports the design of training and development activities; communication processes influence employment relations structures, and so on. The broader context of organisational behaviour provides an insight into the way HR professionals can help manage people more effectively.

Investors in People

Investors in People (IIP) is the Standard for people management. In 2017, IIP was established as a community interest company. IIP exists to shape a working world where employers, employees and the community succeed by understanding the value of investing in people.

The Investors in People framework describes what it takes to lead, support and develop people well for sustainable results. IIP specialises in highlighting and championing best practice in people management through a Framework for assessment and accreditation. It is a flexible framework that organisations of any size or sector can work with, putting their organisation's objectives at the heart of tangible improvement. IIP believe that people are an organisation's greatest asset, and their contribution is critical to continued business success.

'Put your people at the heart of your vision and they'll use their talents to achieve it' says Paul Devoy, Head of Investors in People.[32]

The Investors in People Standard was most recently updated in 2015, following a rigorous research and piloting programme involving industry experts and employees.

The IIP framework reflects the latest workplace trends and is constantly updated and reviewed by world leading academics, practitioners and industry experts. A unique performance model underpins the Investors in People framework, enabling organisations to measure and recognise their success, as well as highlighting areas for improvement and progression.

A key feature is the online employee survey, a powerful tool for giving employees a voice. The Investors in People survey measures an organisation's performance against the Framework. The survey offers detailed benchmarks at industry, sector and engagement driver level, providing insights to compare performance to the very best organisations.

The performance model

The performance model creates a roadmap for continuous improvement against the Standard's framework. This approach is based on extensive research into the concepts of performance and change management and sets out the criteria for different levels of accreditation: Accredited; Silver; Gold; and Platinum.

Simply put, the model describes the practices and outcomes required for better performance and higher accreditation. Progression through the model maps out how practices are embedded within an organisation, starting at the 'Developed' stage and progressing towards 'High Performing'. *See* **Figure 10.6.**

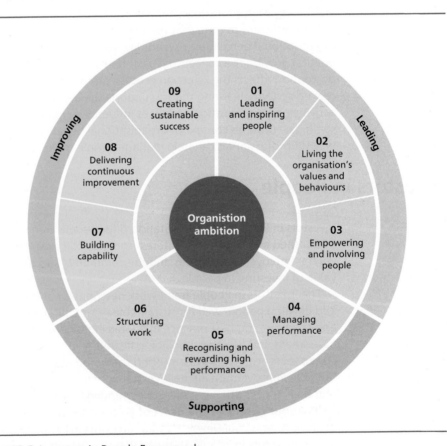

Figure 10.6 Investors in People Framework
Source: www.investorsinpeople.com (accessed 15 November 2017), reprinted with permission.

The Investors in People Silver, Gold and Platinum levels highlight an organisation's standard of people management quality and help create a competitive edge in their ability to deliver a service and also as an employer of choice.

The IIP framework is internationally recognised as a leading quality standard for people management and has proven to support businesses through times of change and economic uncertainty using recognised best practice.

> What do YOU see as the practical value of Investors in People framework for helping to champion best practice in people management?

Performance management (PM)

The process of management involves making a continuous judgement on the skills, behaviours, activities and contributions of staff. It is important that members of the organisation know exactly what is expected of them and how their performance will be measured. **Performance management** is a process which brings together many aspects of people management. It is about aligning the performance of individuals, teams, and departments with organisational aims, and uses tools such as training and reward to encourage and enhance productive activity. If there are good working relationships, individuals and teams are more likely to perform well together, and so it requires more than a simple focus on individual performance.

The performance review should ideally be a two-way conversation. PM should be about communicating organisational objectives, and providing information about individual performance and progress against targets. However, it should allow for open dialogue, and discussion would ideally come to some agreement about the nature of the individual's performance and any measures being put in place to address any concerns. Today, the majority of appraisal systems allow staff to view and agree their line manager's comments; indeed data protection legislation makes such personal assessments accessible to employees. It is also an opportunity for managers to collect information about the operational challenges or problems affecting their staff, any particular stress points or frustrations, and to ensure staff are fully supported to do their jobs.

Appraisal as a tool of PM

One of the most commonly used tools of PM is the performance appraisal or personal development review. This is usually a formal and regular review by a line manager of an individual's performance when past performance is assessed, new objectives are set and training and development needs are identified. Performance appraisals should review performance against agreed criteria and measures based on expectations and objectives which ultimately derive from the organisation's business plan. They should not be a one-way process but an opportunity for two-way discussion of performance in the past review period.

They should generally be both retrospective (reviewing actual performance in the past review period against any standards or targets) and also developmental, establishing future objectives, training needs and career development opportunities. They may also be corrective; identifying shortfalls and improvement plans. However, it is worth noting that no line manager should delay addressing performance problems until a formal review is due. In some organisations they form the basis for financial rewards (for instance performance-related pay) or career progression and promotion; they also offer the opportunity to highlight talent that the organisation is keen to retain and to offer opportunities to nurture and develop this talent.

Performance management and the HR specialist

Performance management is therefore a crucial part of managing people; but it is mostly conducted by line managers not HR specialists. So what, therefore, is the role of the HR professional in relation to performance management? As with talent management, the HR specialist is often charged with designing a suitable system, including the appraisal system; ensuring its operation throughout the organisation and providing the necessary training to support it, for example review training for both appraisers and appraisees. HR departments may also collate and act upon aggregate training needs identified across the organisation as the result of performance appraisals and reviews.

Integrating the system

In order to ensure the establishment of a successful performance review system, the system should not be viewed in isolation but in relation to the corporate objectives of the organisation. 'Vertical' integration means that the system is designed to suit the culture, strategy and particular requirements of the organisation. It also needs to be 'horizontally' integrated; in other words it matches reward, training and promotion systems. The purpose and nature of the system should be made clear and continually reinforced during appraisals. It is often the role of HR to ensure that there is all necessary consultation with trade unions, staff representatives and managers in the design and operation of the system.

Goddard calls for a fundamental shift in thinking on annual appraisal with conversations taking place with staff on the frontline and part of everyday life for employees. Feedback should be part of open, natural conversations and received when the relevant action is fresh in mind. A big problem with appraisals is nobody wants to take a risk and they incentivise a safe approach. Most performance appraisals standardise and erode confidence of the players. Unless feedback is given in the right way it demotivates staff and drags down overall performance.

Performance management is meant to improve your organisation's output, but, more often than not, an ill-conceived and ill-suited process is put in place that does little more than waste time and demotivate your staff.[33]

Do YOU agree that formal performance reviews are a complete waste of time? Monitoring performance should be an integral part of the line manager's day-to-day responsibility.

Managerial effectiveness

The overall responsibility of management can be seen as the successful attainment of the given objectives of the organisation, upon which rests the ultimate survival of the organisation. There is therefore a clear and important need for effective management. And this need is just as strong in public sector and voluntary organisations as in private enterprise organisations. Indeed, it could be argued that in local government, for example, the accountability of public servants to elected members for their actions means that professional standards of management of the highest order are even more essential.

According to *Berriman* everything is about people; whether you are leading, developing, supporting or designing services for them. Bringing people with you, leading and motivating them on the journey, is a vital ingredient of success.

The most effective managers and leaders understand their people and focus on how best to get them to collaborate for the common good, rather than compete internally. And they guide and advise their teams by drawing out and applying practical lessons that enable their people to see what works best and what does not. This is a subtle skill, often learned rather than taught and applied instinctively.[34]

Efficiency and effectiveness

Managerial efficiency can be distinguished from managerial effectiveness. **Efficiency** is concerned with 'doing things right' and relates to inputs and what the manager does. **Effectiveness** is concerned with 'doing the right things' and relates to outputs of the job and what the manager actually achieves. To be efficient the manager must attend therefore to the **input requirements of the job** – to clarification of objectives, planning, organisation, direction and control. But in order to be effective, the manager must give attention to **outputs of the job** – to performance in terms of such factors as obtaining best possible results in the important areas of the organisation, optimising use of resources, increasing profitability, and attainment of the aims and objectives of the organisation.

Effectiveness must be related to the achievement of some purpose, objective or task – to the performance of the process of management and the execution of work. Criteria for assessing the effectiveness of a manager should be considered in terms of measuring the results that the manager is intended to achieve. But **what is also important is the manner in which the manager achieves results and the effects on other people.** This may well influence effectiveness in the longer term. Managerial effectiveness results from a combination of success in managing people, personal attributes and dimensions of the manager's job in meeting the demands of the situation, and satisfying the requirements of the organisation.

What makes a good manager?

According to GOV.UK managers play a central role in any organisation. They connect people to the purpose of their work and help them understand why their work is important. They set tasks and track performance, and they recognise the contribution of each individual in achieving the organisation's goals. They also play a leading role in helping their team to identify the areas they need to develop.

What all inspirational managers have in common is they have taken the time to demonstrate one or more of the following positive behaviours that people look for in a good manager:

- they understand how to model leadership behaviours, inspire a shared vision and enable and support others to act;
- they champion learning and development for themselves and their teams and create an environment where the giving and receiving of feedback is the norm;
- they know and listen to their team and encourage open discussion and constructive challenge.[35]

Measures of effectiveness

Management involves getting work done through the co-ordinated efforts of other people. As a result **managers are most likely to be judged not just on their own performance but also on the results achieved by other staff.** The manager's effectiveness may be assessed in part, therefore, by such factors as:

- the strength of motivation and morale of staff;
- the success of their training and development;
- levels of staff retention;
- creation of an organisational environment in which staff work willingly and effectively.

The difficulty is in determining objective measurement of such factors. Some possible indication might be given by, for example:

- the incidence of sickness, conflict or stress;
- absenteeism;
- accidents at work ;and
- poor timekeeping.

However, such figures are likely to be influenced by broader organisational or environmental considerations, for example poor job security due to the economic climate, which are outside the direct control of the individual manager. In any case, there is the general question of the extent to which such figures bear a direct relationship to the actual performance of subordinate staff.

Other criteria of effectiveness

Other criteria that may give some indication of managerial effectiveness include the efficiency of systems and procedures, and standard of services afforded to other departments. Again, however, there is the question of how to determine objective measurement. For some management jobs it might be possible to identify more quantitative factors which *may* give an indication of managerial effectiveness, including:

- meeting important deadlines;
- accuracy of work carried out by the department, perhaps measured by the number of recorded errors;

- level of complaints received from superiors, other departments, customers or clients, suppliers, the public;
- adherence to quality standards, for example, the amount of scrap or waste material;
- keeping within agreed cost or budgetary control limits.

Another broad, qualitative criterion of increasing significance today is in terms of perceived social accountability, and the ethical behaviour of individual managers and the organisation as a whole **(discussed in Chapter 16)** (*see* Figure 10.7). **The qualities of a manager and organisational performance are discussed in Chapter 17.**

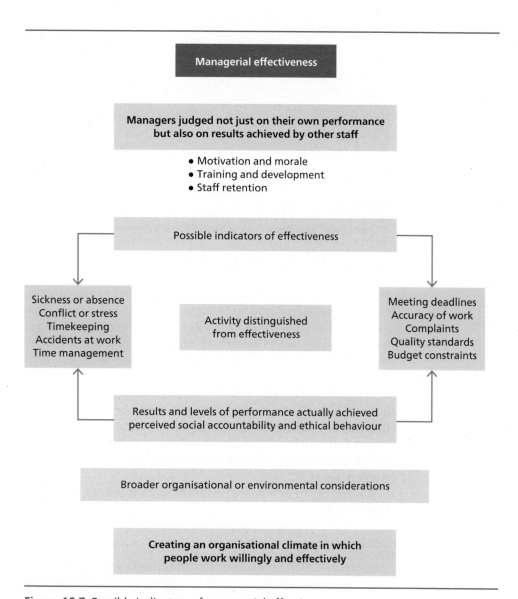

Figure 10.7 Possible indicators of managerial effectiveness

courageous	charismatic
committed	passionate
curious	*inspiring*
confident	
	visionary
candid	energetic/enthusiastic
reflective	upbeat/optimistic
insightful	ambitious
open-minded/tolerant (of people, ambiguities, and ideas)	tenacious/persistent/zealous
innovative	collaborative/participative/cooperative
communicative (including being a good listener)	*engaging*
connected/informed	supportive/sympathetic/empathetic
perceptive	stable
thoughtful/intelligent/*wise*	dependable
analytic/objective	fair
pragmatic	accountable
decisive (action-oriented)	ethical/honest
proactive	consistent
	flexible
	balanced
	integrative
	tall

Figure 10.8 Composite list of basic managerial qualities
Source: Henry Mintzberg, *Managing,* Financial Times Prentice Hall (2009), p. 197. Compiled from various sources; my own favourites in italics. Reproduced with permission from Pearson Education Ltd.

Composite list of basic qualities

Mintzberg refers to the many lists of the qualities of effective managers. These lists are usually short and incomplete as they do not include important aspects such as native intelligence, being a good listener or just having energy. For the 'sake of a better world' Mintzberg provides a composite list of fifty-two qualities **(Figure 10.8)**. 'Be all fifty-two and you are bound to be an effective manager, if not a human one.'

Mintzberg refers also to the romance of leadership that on one hand puts ordinary mortals on managerial pedestals and on the other hand allows us to vilify them as they come crashing down. 'Yet some managers do stay up, if not on that silly pedestal. How so? The answer is simple: **successful managers are flawed – we are all flawed – but their particular flaws are not fatal, at least under the circumstances.**'[36]

A summary of managing people at work is set out in the concept map Figure 10.9.

How would YOU list in rank order the criteria you believe most appropriate for evaluating the effectiveness of managing other people at work?

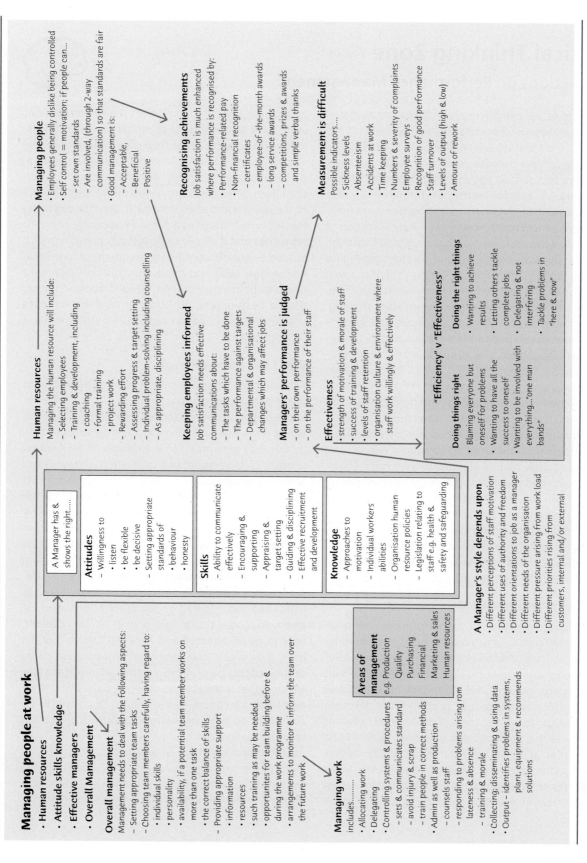

Figure 10.9 Managing people at work
Source: Copyright ©2018 The Virtual Learning Materials Workshop. Reproduced with permission.

Critical Thinking Zone
Reflections on Performance Management

In this zone, we critically examine the concept of performance management and evaluate whether it still has a role in the changing twenty-first century workplace.

For over three decades, researchers and practitioners have focused on engendering a greater understanding of, and facilitating an influence on, the development and improvement of performance management systems in organisations.[37] A proliferation of research in the past few years has sought to challenge existing thinking and determine whether managing performance in an individual context still has a role in the changing twenty-first century workplace.[38] The findings of such researches have been rather startling. Even though tools, methods, processes and systems have been developed to aid the execution of performance management, overall operational implementation has been disappointing.[37] The CIPD[38] report that traditional performance management practices, specifically performance appraisal, are outdated and do not work. They advise that more and more employers have begun to question the actual relevance and value of traditional performance management systems and processes. They add, 'if employers were once enamoured with performance appraisals, they clearly aren't now' (p. 8). So, why, arguably, do employers appear to have fallen out of love with performance management? Before attempting to answer this question, it is necessary to define the concept (in the absence of a definitive definition) and identify its key activities and objectives.

Defining Performance Management

According to Aguinis[39] (p. 2), performance management is defined as 'a continuous process of identifying, measuring and developing the performance of individuals and teams and aligning performance with the strategic goals of the organisation.' This differs from performance appraisal, which Aguinis describes as the 'depiction of the strengths and weaknesses of employees in a non-continuous manner, typically just once a year' (p. 2). The CIPD define it as an activity that encompasses three key activities. First, it establishes objectives, through which individuals and teams identify their role in achieving the organisation's mission and strategy. Second, it improves the performance of individuals, teams and the organisation. Third, it holds individuals to account for their own performance and how it relates to other aspects of the people-organisation relationship, including reward and career progression. Both definitions emphasise the strategic nature of the process and alignment with what the organisation ultimately wants to achieve. Importantly, The CIPD advocates that it should not just focus on performance outcomes but also on the development of individual knowledge, skills and behaviour. Such development needs to be continuous and forward-thinking, rather than a perfunctory, ad hoc, transactional exercise that only focuses on an individual's strengths and weaknesses.[39,40]

What has Gone Wrong?

According to Cappelli and Tavis,[40] many organisations are rethinking performance management reviews/appraisals because it no longer fits with their business needs. It has been described as a 'last century practice' (p. 60) that generates large amounts of paperwork, restricts collaboration and innovation and does not serve a real purpose. In addition, the authors assert that some organisations are acknowledging the loathing that managers and their direct reports have for the performance review/appraisal process. Rather than being an opportunity for individuals to discuss their past and future performance and likely learning and development needs, Jones[41] laments that performance management is, instead, often manifested as a dreaded and resented paper-based, annual exercise that is relegated to the desk drawer or filing cabinet, only to be resurrected and revisited twelve months later. She caveats that the review process is, for many organisations, painfully ineffective, inconsistent and all too often unrelated to business objectives, strategies and outcomes. In this respect, it does little to contribute to building a strong people-organisation relationship and, one could argue, a positive relational psychological contract. In a rather damning indictment of performance management, Culbert[42] (p. 46) contends that the review is a 'broken system' that is 'fatally flawed.' Commenting in the *Wall Street Journal,*

Culbert[43] proffered that it has a negative impact on corporate performance, is obstructive to 'straight-talk relationships' and a major cause of low morale in the workplace. He notes 'even the mere *knowledge* that such an event will take place damages daily communication and teamwork.'

Finding a Way Forward

To conclude, one could argue that the negative viewpoints of performance management presented here make a compelling case for it to be supplanted with a system that will engender more engagement from, and commitment to, the process by all parties concerned in the people-employment relationship. Cappelli and Tavis concur and report that some organisations have replaced annual performance reviews with feedback and coaching, particularly after the completion of key projects or milestones have been achieved. Removing the emphasis from performance to the identification of strengths and goals means that individuals and their organisations can be more strategic, collaborative, holistic rather than fragmented and focus on skill development for the future. Performance management still has a role in the changing twenty-first century workplace – but not in its traditional form. As we have seen, it will need to metamorphose into a process that is welcomed, not dreaded, future-oriented rather than retrospective and concentrates on developing knowledge and creativity that serves a real purpose. As Jones[41] (p. 102) concludes 'performance management is not dead, but the old way of doing it certainly is.'

Questions

Based on the above, answer the following questions.

1. Pulakos and O'Leary and Cappelli and Tavis report that many organisations have begun to think differently about performance management and how it is used. With reference to theory and practice, *discuss* the reasons why this is the case.

2. *What* strategies can organisations adopt to engender a greater level of engagement with, and commitment to, reviewing individual performance?

3. *Evaluate* the benefits and drawbacks of adopting feedback and coaching as alternative tools to review/monitor performance.

Summary – Chapter 10 'Managing people at work'

There is a substantial interrelationship between organisational behaviour and management. People are the main resource of any organisation. A popular way of describing the essential nature of management is getting work done second-hand, through the efforts of other people. An essential ingredient of any successful manager is the ability to handle people effectively. A number of underlying philosophies arguably make for success in managing with and through people. Growing importance is attached to managerial style. Behaviour displayed by managers is likely to be influenced by suppositions about people, human nature and behaviour at work – called Theory X and Theory Y. One means of evaluating styles of management is the Managerial/Leadership Grid, and concern for production and concern for people. The human resource function is part of the generality of management and responsibility of all managers and supervisors. Success in managing people at work calls for an effective partnership between line managers and HR staff. Investors in People specialises in highlighting and championing best practice in people management. Performance management should be a two-way review and part of everyday life of employees. There is a clear and important need for effective management. Managers are most likely to be judged not just on their own performance but also on results achieved by other members of staff.

Group discussion activities

Undertake each of these activities in small groups as indicated by your tutor. Before you start your discussion establish a non-threatening environment within the group and confirm confidentiality will be honoured.

First, form your own views and then share and compare in open critical discussion with colleagues. Reflect honestly on the extent to which: (i) you influenced the thinking and ideas of your colleagues; and (ii) you were influenced by your colleagues.

To what extent was your group able to reach consensus?

Agree one of your members to produce a brief written summary of the discussion and prepared to present in a plenary session.

Activity 1

Drawing on your own beliefs, observations and experience debate the extent to which you would challenge the following cynical view of management. Where possible give support examples.

Managers do not really have much influence. They follow where the organisation appears to be going and avoid upsetting other people or making serious errors. People regarded as good managers are usually those who are remembered as not being bad managers.

Activity 2

(a) Describe what you see as the most appropriate style of management for each of the different generations and age groups discussed in **Chapter 2**.

(b) What other factors are likely to play a significant influence in choice of managerial style? Where possible provide examples.

(c) What style of managerial behaviour is most likely to influence you to work willingly and effectively?

Activity 3

Recall Foppen's emphasis on the importance of management performance but questioning the relationship between management practice and education.

(a) Debate critically the extent to which you agree:

* management is of pivotal importance for modern society; and
* thinking about management, certainly at university level, is of great relevance to management practice.

(b) Explain fully what you expect to gain from your studies and how this will help benefit your future managerial career.

Organisational behaviour in action case study

Happy and productive workplace

Henry Stewart of the training company Happy draws attention to the positive correlation between staff engagement and profitability. Employee contentment is an underlying key to maximising growth and performance. Key factors to a happy workplace include a no-blame culture, a good work/life balance, transparency and a genuine commitment to the wider community. Applying the ten guiding principles of the Happy Manifesto across many organisations has created happier and more productive workplaces.[15]

Ten steps to a happy workplace

1. Trust your team. Step out of approval. Instead, pre-approve and focus on supporting your people.

2. Make your people feel good. Make this the focus of management.

3. Give freedom within clear guidelines. People want to know what is expected of them. But they want freedom to find the best way to achieve their goals.

4. Be open and transparent. More information means more people can take responsibility.

5. Recruit for attitude, train for skill. Instead of qualifications and experience, recruit on attitude and potential ability.

6. Celebrate mistakes. Create a truly no-blame culture.

7. Community: create mutual benefit. Have a positive impact on the world and build your organisation too.

8. Love work, get a life. The world, and your job, needs you well-rested, well-nourished and well-supported.

9. Select managers who are good at managing. Make sure your people are supported by somebody who is good at doing that, and find other routes for those whose strengths lie elsewhere. Even better, allow people to choose their own managers.

10. Play to your strengths – make sure your people spend most of their time doing what they are best at.

Source: Stewart, H., *The Happy Manifesto: Make Your Organisation a Great Workplace – Now!* Happy (2012), p. 121. Reproduced with permission.

Tasks

1. Explain fully how you relate the Happy Manifesto to the contents of this chapter. How *you* would place in order of importance the ten steps to a happy workplace?

2. Discuss how you view the relationship between a genuine commitment to the wider community and a happy workplace.

3. To what extent and under what circumstances do you believe people should be allowed to choose their own managers?

Chapter 10 – Personal skills and employability exercise

Objectives

Completing this exercise should help you to enhance the following skills:

∗ Act in the role of the manager to handle a number of real-life situations.

∗ Conduct management–staff interviews and discussions.

∗ Review critically your ability to deal with emotionally difficult situations.

Exercise

Given below are a number of real-life situations. You are required to:

(a) Think through each one and explain how you as the manager might best handle the discussion with your member of staff.

(b) Record how you would approach each discussion/interview.

(c) What specific questions might you be likely to ask – and why?

(d) Share and compare your responses with colleagues in a small group situation.

Situation 1

One of your employees who is hard-working and conscientious with tasks continually arrives late for work. This is the sixth time this has happened. Their excuse is that they have to take their child to nursery because they are getting divorced and their spouse refuses to do this task.

Situation 2

You receive a complaint from one of your female employees who claims to have accidently found a pornographic image on the PC of another employee and finds this offensive.

Situation 3

One of your permanent employees has been accused of assaulting another member of staff who works in the same organisation but as an independent contractor.

Situation 4

You overhear a member of your department commenting that 'you have no idea about the technical complexity of their work, and don't know how you are able to manage a department like this!'

Situation 5

A key client calls you to complain about sarcastic and impatient comments made by one of your more experienced technicians. Comments like 'Your people must be really thick if they think that's how it works . . .' have proved less than helpful. You know this person has been working long hours, achieving excellent results and is clearly committed to their job and the department. In fact, you have recently promoted the technician for these very reasons.

Situation 6

In a recent management meeting, a relatively new colleague repeatedly contradicted you and appeared to be 'scoring points' at your expense. Although the colleague had made some valid, even perceptive comments, it isn't exactly helping your relationship get off to an encouraging start. Furthermore, this has happened on a previous occasion.

Discussion

* How would you summarise the essential nature of the manager–subordinate relationship?

* Using your own examples, explain the importance of using appropriate approaches when dealing with potentially difficult situations.

* What have you learned about your potential skills of effective management of people?

Notes and references

1. See, for example, Margretta, J. *What Management Is: How it Works and Why it's Everyone's Business,* HarperCollins (2002).
2. Schneider, S. C. and Barsoux, J. *Managing Across Cultures,* second edition, Financial Times Prentice Hall (2003).
3. Francesco, A. M. and Gold, B. A. *International Organizational Behavior,* second edition, Prentice Hall (2005).
4. Watson, T. J. *Management, Organisation and Employment Strategy,* Routledge and Kegan Paul (1986).
5. Dib, F. 'Is management a science?', *Professional Manager*, Autumn 2014, pp. 38–9.
6. Foppen, J. W. 'Knowledge Leadership' in Chowdbury, S (ed) *Management 21C,* Financial Times Prentice Hall (2000) pp. 160–1.
7. Fayol, H. *General and Industrial Management,* Pitman (1949).
8. McLean, J. 'Fayol – standing the test of time', *Manager, The British Institute of Administrative Management,* Spring 2011, pp. 32–3.
9. Hamel, G. with Breen, B. *The Future of Management,* Harvard Business School Press (2007), p. 20.
10. 'Building productive public sector workplaces: Part One, Improving People Management', CIPD January 2010.
11. Bernstein, Sir Howard, 'In My Opinion', *Management Today,* February 2012, p. 62.
12. Walker, B. 'How to switch sides', *Professional Manager,* Spring 2013, pp. 40–7.
13. Stewart, R. *The Reality of Management,* third edition, Butterworth Heinemann (1999), p. 6.
14. 'The Middle Manager Lifeline', Charter Management Institute, September 2016.
15. Rock, S. 'Strengthen Your Core', *Professional Manager,* Winter 2017, pp. 37–41.
16. 'The Joy of 9 to 5: Do we need managers?' BBC Radio 4, 13 April 2016.
17. Thomas, M. cited in Smith, P. 'Why it's time to break the rules', *Professional Manager,* vol. 20, no. 2, March/April 2011, pp. 33–5. See also: Thomas, M. *Loose: The Future of Business is Letting Go,* Headline Publishing Group (2011).
18. Robbins, S. P. *The Truth About Managing People,* second edition, Pearson Education, 2008, p. 202.
19. Bolchover, D. 'Why Mood Matters', *Management Today,* November 2008, pp. 46–50.
20. Watson, T. *Organising and Managing Work,* second edition, Financial Times Prentice Hall (2006).
21. McGregor, D. *The Human Side of Enterprise,* Penguin (1987).
22. See, for example, Mullins, L. J. 'Management and Managerial Behaviour', *International Journal of Hospitality Management,* vol. 4, no. 1, 1985, pp. 39–41.
23. Blake, R. R. and Mouton, J. S. *The Managerial Grid III,* Gulf Publishing Company (1985).
24. Blake, R. R. and McCanse, A. A. *Leadership Dilemmas – Grid Solutions,* Gulf Publishing Company (1991).
25. Newborough, G. 'People vs Production', *The British Journal of Administrative Management,* May/June 1999, pp. 13–14.
26. Crainer, S. and Dearlove, D. (eds) *Financial Times Handbook of Management,* second edition, Financial Times Prentice Hall (2001), p. 364.
27. Gratton, L. *Living Strategy: Putting people at the Heart of Corporate Purpose,* Financial Times Prentice Hall (2002). Reprinted and electronically reproduced by permission of Pearson Education, Inc.
28. 'Management competencies for preventing and reducing stress at work', Health and Safety Executive, 2007, p. 73.
29. Simms, J 'There's more than one way to solve a dispute', CIPD, 25 July 2017 www.cipd.co.uk.
30. Forte, R. 'How I See the Personnel Function', *Personnel Management,* vol. 14, no. 8, August 1982, p. 32.
31. Lynch, R. *Corporate Strategy,* fourth edition, Financial Times Prentice Hall (2006), Chapter 7.
32. www.investorsinpeople.com (accessed 15 November 2017).
33. Berriman, J. 'The most effective managers focus on how best to get their people to collaborate', *Management Today,* December 2011, p. 86.
34. Scott, M. in conversation with Goddard, J 'Performance management after the annual appraisal', *Professional Manager,* Summer 2016, pp. 37–9. Copyright © 2016 Chartered Management Institute.
35. 'Guidance to Good management' GOV.UK, 27 October 2014.
36. Mintzberg, H. *Managing,* Financial Times Prentice Hall (2009), pp. 196–7.
37. Pulakos, E. D. and O'Leary, R. S. 'Why is Performance Management Broken?', *Industrial and Organizational Psychology,* 2011, pp. 146–64.
38. CIPD 'Could do better? Assessing what works in performance management', Research Report, Chartered Institute of Personnel and Development, December 2016, pp. 1–47.
39. Aguinis, H. *Performance Management,* second edition, Pearson Prentice Hall (2009b).
40. Capelli, P. and Travis, A. 'The Performance Management Revolution', *Harvard Business Review,* October 2016, pp. 58–67.
41. Jones, D. 'The Future of Performance Management Beyond Appraisals', *Strategic HR Review,* vol. 15, no. 2, 2016, pp 100–2.
42. Culbert, S. 'Interview with Samuel Culbert, author of "Get Rid of the Performance Review"', Bell, G. (ed.), *Human Resource Management International Digest,* vol. 20, no. 4, 2012, pp. 45–8.
43. Culbert, S. 'Get Rid of the Performance Review', *The Wall Street Journal,* 20 October 2008, http://online.wsj.com/article/SB1224263187484933.html (accessed 2 September 2018).

Part 4
Focus on the workplace

Chapter 11
Organisational theory and structure

Major trends in organisational theory, work of leading writers and approaches to structure and management provide a perspective for the study of organisational behaviour.

Learning outcomes

After completing this chapter you should have enhanced your ability to:

- provide a framework in which to study organisational theory and structure;
- detail the work and views of leading writers;
- identify major trends in the development of organisational behaviour;
- outline alternative approaches to the study of organisations;

- assess contrasting views of organisations, their structure and management;
- evaluate benefits and criticisms of the different approaches;
- debate applications of organisational theory to the present-day work situation.

Outline chapter contents

Overview topic map: Chapter 11 – Organisation theory and structure

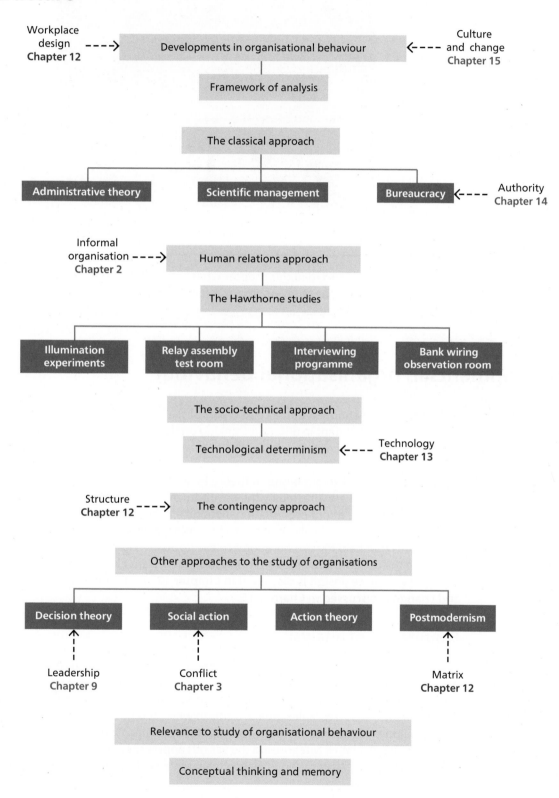

Before commencing to read this chapter what value do YOU place on the work of leading writers to the study of organisation theory and structure?

Developments in organisational behaviour

In Chapter 1 we mentioned that a central part of the study of organisational behaviour is development in different thinking on the structure and management of organisations and their relationship with the external environment, which is usually termed organisational theory.

Gareth Jones refers to organisation theory as how organisations function and how they affect and are affected by the environment in which they operate. Jones suggests knowledge about organisational design and change enables people to analyse the structure and culture of the organisation, diagnose problems and make adjustments that help the organisation achieve its goals.[1] **Figure 11.1** provides an outline of the relationships among organisation theory, structure, culture, design and change. **Workplace design is discussed in Chapter 12 and Organisational culture and change is discussed in Chapter 15.**

Framework of analysis

In order to help identify main trends in the development of organisational behaviour theory, it is helpful to categorise the ideas and work of writers into various 'approaches', based on their views of organisations, their structure and management. This is a complex area of study in which it is possible to identify a large number of writers and range of comparative points of view. There are, therefore, many ways of categorising the various approaches. For example, *Skipton* attempts a classification of eleven main schools.[2] The choice of a particular

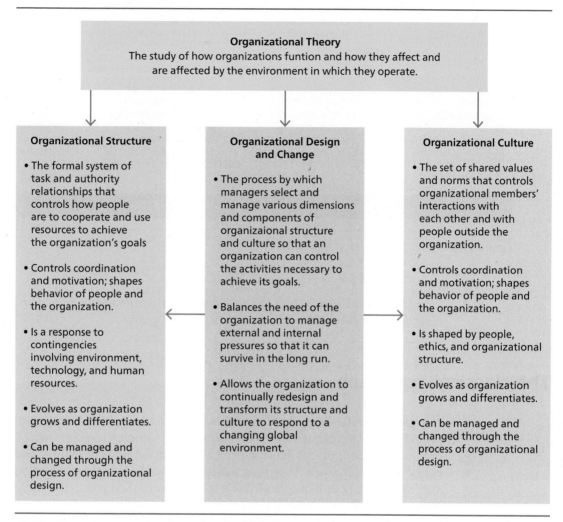

Organizational Theory
The study of how organizations funtion and how they affect and are affected by the environment in which they operate.

Organizational Structure

- The formal system of task and authority relationships that controls how people are to cooperate and use resources to achieve the organization's goals

- Controls coordination and motivation; shapes behavior of people and the organization.

- Is a response to contingencies involving environment, technology, and human resources.

- Evolves as organization grows and differentiates.

- Can be managed and changed through the process of organizational design.

Organizational Design and Change

- The process by which managers select and manage various dimensions and components of organizaional structure and culture so that an organization can control the activities necessary to achieve its goals.

- Balances the need of the organization to manage external and internal pressures so that it can survive in the long run.

- Allows the organization to continually redesign and transform its structure and culture to respond to a changing global environment.

Organizational Culture

- The set of shared values and norms that controls organizational members' interactions with each other and with people outside the organization.

- Controls coordination and motivation; shapes behavior of people and the organization.

- Is shaped by people, ethics, and organizational structure.

- Evolves as organization grows and differentiates.

- Can be managed and changed through the process of organizational design.

Figure 11.1 Relationship between organizational theory and organizational structure, culture, design, and change

Source: Jones, G. R. *Organizational Theory, Design and Change,* seventh edition, Pearson Education (2013), p. 30. Reprinted and electronically reproduced by permission of Pearson Education, Inc.

categorisation is therefore largely at the discretion of the observer and makes demands of the reader.

For convenience, the following analysis revolves around a framework based on four main approaches **(*see* Figure 11.2)**:

- classical – including scientific management and bureaucracy;

- human relations – including neo-human relations;

- socio-technical;

- contingency.

Although a simplistic process, it provides a useful framework in which to direct study and focus attention on the progression of ideas concerned with improving organisational performance.

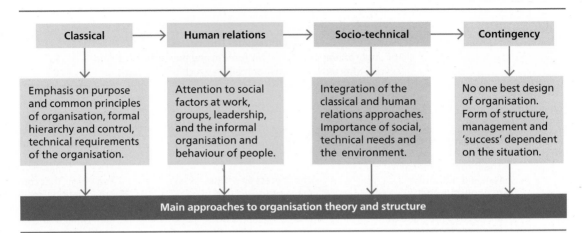

Figure 11.2 A basic framework of analysis

 To what extent do YOU believe the analysis of structure and culture helps the organisation diagnose problems and achieve its goals?

The classical approach

The **classical** writers thought of the organisation in terms of its purpose and formal structure. Emphasis is on planning of work, technical requirements of the organisation, principles of management, and the assumption of rational and logical behaviour. Identification of general objectives would lead to the clarification of purpose and responsibilities at all levels of the organisation and to the most effective structure. Attention is given to division of work, clear definition of duties and responsibilities, and maintaining specialisation and co-ordination. Emphasis is on a hierarchy of management and formal organisational relationships.

The analysis of organisation in this manner is associated with work carried out initially in the early part of the last century by such writers as Fayol, Urwick, Brech and Taylor. Such writers were laying the foundation for a comprehensive theory of organisation.

The classical approach and can be view under three broad headings: administrative theory, scientific management, bureaucracy. *See* **Figure 11.3.**

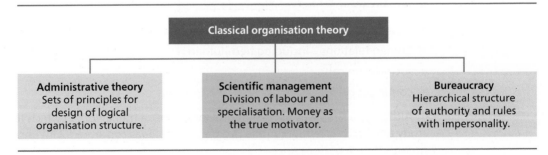

Figure 11.3 Main headings of classical organisation theory

Administrative theory

The classical writers were concerned with improving the organisation structure as a means of increasing efficiency. They emphasised the importance of principles for the design of a logical structure of organisation. Their writings were in a normative style and they saw these principles as a set of 'rules' offering general solutions to common problems of organisation. Most classical writers had their own set of principles but among the most publicised are those of Fayol, Urwick and Brech.

One of the first, and most widely quoted, analyses is that given by *Henri Fayol* (1841–1925) who divided the managerial activity into five elements of management and structure.[3]

- **Forecasting and planning** – examining the future, deciding what needs to be achieved and developing a plan of action.
- **Organising** – providing the material and human resources and building the structure to carry out the activities of the organisation.
- **Command** – maintaining activity among personnel, getting the optimum return from all employees in the interests of the whole organisation.
- **Co-ordination** – unifying and harmonising all activities and efforts of the organisation to facilitate its working and success.
- **Control** – verifying that everything occurs in accordance with plans, instructions, established principles and expressed command.

Fayol's theory of organisation is a set of fourteen well-established principles that relate directly to, or are influenced by, the organisation structure in which the process of management takes place. He emphasises, however, that these principles must be flexible and adaptable to changing circumstances. Fayol's set of principles can be compared, therefore, with those given by *Urwick* who originally specified eight principles of the requirements of the formal organisation, but these were revised to ten in his later writing.[4]

Brech attempts to provide a practical approach to organisation structure based on tried general principles as opposed to concentration on specific cases or complex generalisations of little value to the practising manager. He sets out the various functions in the organisation and the definition of formal organisational relationships.[5] Although clearly a strong supporter of the formal approach in some of his views such as, for example, on the principle of span of control, Brech is less definite than other classical writers and recognises a degree of flexibility according to the particular situation.

Brech does place great emphasis, however, on the need for written definition of responsibilities and the value of job descriptions as an aid to effective organisation and delegation. This work builds on the ideas of earlier writers, such as Urwick, and therefore provides a comprehensive view of the classical approach to organisation.

Evaluation of the classical approach

The classical writers have been criticised generally for not taking sufficient account of social factors and creating an organisation structure in which people can exercise only limited control over their work environment. The idea of sets of principles to guide managerial action has also been subject to much criticism. For example, *Simon* writes:

> **Organisational design is not unlike architectural design. It involves creating large, complex systems having multiple goals. It is illusory to suppose that good designs can be created by using the so-called principles of classical organisation theory.[6]**

Research studies have also expressed doubt about the effectiveness of these principles when applied in practice.[7]

However, the classical approach prompted the start of a more systematic view of management and attempted to provide some common principles applicable to all organisations. These principles are still of relevance in that they offer a useful starting point in attempting to analyse the effectiveness of the design of organisation structure. However, the application of these principles must take full account of the particular situational variables of each individual organisation and the psychological and social factors relating to members of the organisation.

Do YOU agree that criticism against general principles of organisation should be directed not against the need for such principles but the manner in which they are implemented?

Scientific management

Many of the classical writers were concerned with the means of increasing productivity from individual workers through technical structuring of the work organisation and monetary incentives as the motivator for higher levels of output. A major contributor to this approach was *F. W. Taylor* (1856–1917), the 'father' of **scientific management**.[8] Taylor believed in the same way there is a best machine for each job, so there is a best working method by which people should undertake their jobs. All work processes could be analysed into discrete tasks and that by scientific method it was possible to find the 'one best way' to perform each task. Each job was broken down into component parts, each part timed and the parts rearranged into the most efficient method of working.

Principles to guide management

Taylor was concerned with finding more efficient methods and procedures for co-ordination and control of work, and a believer in the rational-economic needs concept of motivation. If management acted on his ideas, work would become more satisfying and profitable for workers motivated by obtaining the highest possible wages through the most efficient and productive way. He set out a number of principles to guide management usually summarised as:

- development of a true science for each person's work;
- scientific selection, training and development of workers;
- co-operation with workers to ensure work is carried out in the prescribed way;

- hierarchical structures of authority and close supervision;
- clear division of tasks and responsibility between management and workers.

In the famous studies at the Bethlehem Steel Corporation, Taylor applied his ideas on scientific management to a group of 75 men loading pig iron. Taylor selected a Dutch labourer, Schmidt, whom he reported as a 'high-priced' man with a reputation for placing a high value on money, and of limited mental ability. By following detailed instructions on when to pick up the pig iron and walk, and when to sit and rest, and with no back talk, Schmidt increased his output from $12\frac{1}{2}$ tons to $47\frac{1}{2}$ tons per day. He maintained this level of output throughout the three years of the study.

In return, Schmidt received a 60 per cent increase in wages compared with what was paid to the other men. One by one other workers were selected and trained to handle pig iron at the rate of $47\frac{1}{2}$ tons per day and in return they received 60 per cent more wages. Taylor drew attention to the need for the scientific selection of the workers. When the other labourers in the group were trained in the same method, only one in eight was physically capable of the effort of loading $47\frac{1}{2}$ tons per day, although there was a noticeable increase in their level of output.

Reactions against scientific management

There were strong criticisms of, and reaction against, scientific management methods from workers who found work boring and requiring little skill. Despite these criticisms Taylor attempted to expand the implementation of his ideas in the Bethlehem Steel Corporation. However, fears of mass redundancies persuaded the management to request Taylor to moderate his activities. Yet Taylor's belief in his methods was so strong that he would not accept management's interference and eventually they dispensed with his services. Continued resentment and hostility against scientific management led to an investigation of Taylor's methods by a House of Representatives Committee which reported in 1912. The conclusion of the committee was that scientific management did provide some useful techniques and offered valuable organisational suggestions, but gave production managers a dangerously high level of uncontrolled power.

Taylorism as management control

Taylor placed emphasis on the content of a 'fair day's work' and optimising the level of workers' productivity. A major obstacle to this objective was 'systematic soldiering' and what Taylor saw as the deliberate attempt by workers to promote their best interests and to keep employers ignorant of how fast work, especially piece-rate work, could be carried out.

According to *Braverman,* scientific management starts from the capitalist point of view. Taylor's work was more concerned with the organisation of labour than development of technology. A distinctive feature of Taylor's thought was the concept of management control.[9] Braverman suggests Taylor's conclusion was that workers should be controlled not only by the giving of orders and maintenance of discipline but also by removing from them any decisions about the manner in which their work was to be carried out. By division of labour, and by dictating precise stages and methods for every aspect of work performance, management could gain control of the actual process of work. The rationalisation of production processes and division of labour tends to result in the de-skilling of work and this may be a main strategy of the employer.[10]

Cloke and Goldsmith also suggest that Taylor was the leading promoter of the idea that managers should design and control the work process scientifically in order to guarantee maximum efficiency. Taylor believed in multiple layers of management to supervise the work process and in rigid, detailed control of the workforce. Managers saw this as an opportunity to solidify their power. His theories justified managerial control over the production process and removed decision-making from employees and from owners as well.[11]

> How far do YOU believe a scientific management approach is more about control over workers rather than the search for improved organisational efficiency?

Relevance today

Taylor's work is often criticised today[12] but it should be remembered that he was writing at a time of industrial reorganisation and the emergence of large, complex organisations with new forms of technology. Whatever the opinions on scientific management, Taylor and his disciples left to modern management the legacy of such practices as work study, organisation and methods, payment by results, management by exception and production control.

Taylor did give a major impetus to the development of management thinking and the later development of organisational behaviour. For example, *Crainer and Dearlove* suggest that although Taylor's theories are now largely outdated, they still had a profound impact throughout the world and his mark can be seen on much of the subsequent literature.[13] And *Stern* goes a stage further:

> **The 'scientific management' of Frederick Taylor . . . shaped the first coherent school of thought with application to the industrialised world. He was our first professional guru and Taylorism – with its twin goals of productivity and efficiency – still influences management thinking 100 years on.[14]**

Principles of Taylor's scientific approach appear still to have relevance today. We can see examples of Taylorism alive and well, and management practices based on the philosophy of his ideas. As an example, large hotel organisations often make use of standard recipes and standard performance manuals. It is common for housekeeping staff to have a prescribed layout and daily schedule for each room. Training is based on detailed procedures and the one best way. Staff may be expected to clean a given number of rooms per shift with financial incentives for additional rooms.[15] Modern customer call centres can also be seen to exhibit many features of Taylorism.[16] The strict routine, uniformity, clearly specified tasks, detailed checklists and close control in fast-food restaurants such as McDonald's also suggest close links with scientific management. **McDonaldisation is discussed later in this chapter.**

It is difficult to argue against the general line of Taylor's principles but they are subject to misuse. It seems that Taylor did not so much ignore (as is often suggested)

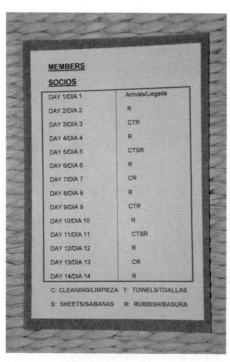

| MEMBERS | |
SOCIOS	
DAY 1/DIA 1	Arrivals/Liegada
DAY 2/DIA 2	R
DAY 3/DIA 3	CTR
DAY 4/DIA 4	R
DAY 5/DIA 5	CTSR
DAY 6/DIA 6	R
DAY 7/DIA 7	CR
DAY 8/DIA 8	R
DAY 9/DIA 9	CTR
DAY 10/DIA 10	R
DAY 11/DIA 11	CTSR
DAY 12/DIA 12	R
DAY 13/DIA 13	CR
DAY 14/DIA 14	R

C: CLEANING/LIMPIEZA   T: TOWELS/TOALLAS

S: SHEETS/SABANAS   R: RUBBISH/BASURA

Room attendant's checklist: thoughts of scientific management?

but was more *unaware* of the complexity of human behaviour in organisations and the importance of the individual's feelings and sentiments, group working, managerial behaviour and the work environment. However, we now have greater knowledge about social effects within the work organisation and about the value of money, incentives, motivation, and job satisfaction and performance.

Bureaucracy

A form of structure to be found in many large-scale organisations is **bureaucracy**. The term has common connotations with criticism of red tape and rigidity, but in the study of organisations it is important that bureaucracy is seen not necessarily in a depreciative sense but applying to certain structural features of formal organisations. *Weber,* a German sociologist, showed particular concern for what he called 'bureaucratic structures', although his work in this area came almost as a side issue to his main study on power and authority.[17]

Weber saw the development of bureaucracies as a means of introducing order and rationality into social life. He suggested that 'the decisive reason for the advance of bureaucratic organization has always been its purely technical superiority over any other form of organization'. Weber pointed out that the definition of tasks and responsibilities within the structure of management gave rise to permanent administration and standardisation of work procedures notwithstanding changes in the actual holders of office. Underlying Weber's work is the idea that there are three different sources of authority: traditional, charismatic and legal, **discussed in Chapter 14.**

Main characteristics of bureaucracies

Weber did not actually define bureaucracy but identified main characteristics of this type of organisation. He emphasised the importance of administration based on expertise (rules of experts) and administration based on discipline (rules of officials).

- Tasks of the organisation are allocated as official duties among the various positions.
- An implied clear-cut division of labour and a high level of specialisation.
- A hierarchical authority applies to the organisation of offices and positions.
- Uniformity of decisions and actions is achieved through formally established systems of rules and regulations. Together with a structure of authority, this enables the co-ordination of various activities within the organisation.
- An impersonal orientation is expected from officials in their dealings with clients and other officials. This is designed to result in rational judgements by officials in the performance of their duties.
- Employment by the organisation is based on technical qualifications and constitutes a lifelong career for the officials.[18]

Criticisms of bureaucracy

Weber's concept of bureaucracy has a number of potential disadvantages and has been subject to severe criticism.

- The over-emphasis on rules and procedures, record keeping and paperwork may become more important in its own right than as a means to an end.
- Officials may develop a dependence upon bureaucratic status, symbols and rules.
- Initiative may be stifled and when a situation is not covered by a complete set of rules or procedures there may be a lack of flexibility or adaptation to changing circumstances.

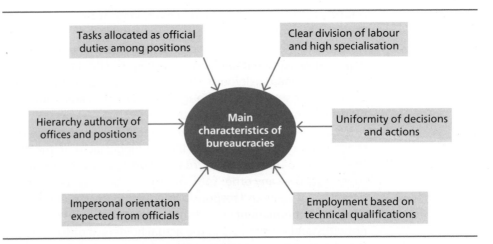

Figure 11.4 Main characteristics of bureaucracies
Source: Based on Blau, P. M. and Scott, W. R. *Formal Organizations,* Routledge & Kegan Paul (1966).

- Position and responsibilities in the organisation can lead to officious bureaucratic behaviour. There may also be a tendency to conceal administrative procedures from outsiders.

- Impersonal relations can lead to stereotyped behaviour and a lack of responsiveness to individual incidents or problems.

Restriction of psychological growth

One of the strongest critics of bureaucratic organisation, and the demands it makes on the worker, is *Argyris*.[19] He claims that bureaucracies restrict the psychological growth of the individual and cause feelings of failure, frustration and conflict. Argyris suggests that the organisational environment should provide a significant degree of individual responsibility and self-control; commitment to the goals of the organisation; productiveness and work; and an opportunity for individuals to apply their full abilities.

A similar criticism is made by *Caulkin* who refers to the impersonal structure of bureaucracy as constructed a round the post rather than the person and the ease with which it can be swung behind unsocial or even pathological ends.

> **The overemphasis on process rather than purpose, fragmented responsibilities and hierarchical control means that it's all too easy for individuals to neglect the larger purposes to which their small effort is being put.[20]**

Adhocracy

A number of writers refer to 'adhocracy' as the opposite of bureaucracy. **Adhocracy** is a flexible, loosely structured, adaptable, organic and informal form of organisation. According to *Morgan* adhocracy is an organic form of organisation, highly suited for the performance of complex and uncertain tasks. It is frequently used for research and development.[21] *Waterman* sees adhocracy as any form of organisation that cuts across normal bureaucratic lines to capture opportunities, solve problems and get results.[22] *Miner* views adhocracy as the project organisation built around project teams of experts with senior managers linking and dealing to secure the projects.[23]

To what extent do YOU believe large-scale organisations can ever work effectively without displaying at least some characteristics of bureaucracy?

Evaluation of bureaucracy

Growth of bureaucracy has come through the increasing size and complexity of organisations and associated demand for effective administration. Bureaucracy is founded on a formal, clearly defined and hierarchical structure. However, with rapid changes in the external environment, de-layering of organisations, empowerment and greater attention to meeting the needs of customers, there is an increasing need to organise for flexibility. For example, the crisis IBM experienced in the 1980s/1990s over the market for personal computers is explained at least in part by its top-heavy corporate structure, cumbersome organisation and dinosaur-like bureaucracy.[24]

By their very nature, bureaucracies have always tended to attract criticism. Much of this criticism is valid, but much also appears unfair. For example, according to *Drucker*:

> **Whenever a big organization gets into trouble – and especially if it has been successful for many years – people blame sluggishness, complacency, arrogance, mammoth bureaucracies. A plausible explanation? Yes. But rarely the relevant or correct one.[25]**

As organisations face increasing global competitiveness and complex demands in the information and technological age, the need arises for alternative forms of corporate structure and systems. For example, there appears to be a particular dilemma for management in personal service industries. The underlying characteristics of bureaucracy would seem to restrict personal service delivery which requires a flexible approach, responsiveness to individual requirements and the need for initiative and inventiveness.[26]

Public sector organisations

However, despite new forms of organisation which have emerged, many writers suggest that bureaucracy is still relevant today as a major form of organisation structure. In the case of public sector organisations, in particular, there is a demand for uniformity of treatment, regularity of procedures and public accountability for their operations. This leads to adherence to specified rules and procedures and to the keeping of detailed records. In their actual dealings with public sector organisations people often call for what amounts to increased bureaucracy, even though they may not use that term. The demands for equal treatment, for a standard set of regulations that apply to everyone, and that decisions should not be left to the discretion of individual managers are in effect demands for bureaucracy.

Green argues that, although bureaucracies are becoming less and less the first-choice format for organisational shape, there is still a place for bureaucracy in parts of most organisations and especially public sector organisations such as local authorities and universities. The use and implementation of tried and tested rules and procedures help to ensure essential values and ethics, and that necessary functions are run on a consistent and fair basis.[27] New forms of information technology such as electronic transactions processed from home or public access terminals are likely to change processes of government service delivery, administrative workloads and the nature of bureaucracy.[28]

McDonaldisation

McDonald's, the world's largest restaurant chain, is often quoted as exemplifying rational organisational behaviour and implementing underlying features of both scientific management and bureaucracy. Work is broken down into clear distinct tasks with detailed specifications, automated procedures, predictability and uniformity, centralised planning and training, strong managerial supervision and control.[29]

Ritzer refers to the principles of the fast-food restaurant:

- efficiency
- calculability

- predictability and
- control.

as exemplified by the process of **McDonaldisation** as an increasingly dominant part of our social and organisational fabric.[30] There is even a film *The Founder* with Michael Keaton released in the United States, January 2017.

However, *Gwyther* points out that it hasn't all been plain sailing and questions the future of McDonald's with the notorious McLibel case, worries over the obesity epidemic, the McJob debate and the growth of fast-food rivals. Although McDonald's is regarded highly in HR circles for their training and education, Gwyther suggests the McJob tag – unstimulating, low pay, with few prospects – hurt more than almost anything.[31]

In what ways do YOU identify features of both scientific management and bureaucracy with McDonald's? How do feel about a future career working in the fast-food industry?

Human relations approach

The main emphasis of the classical writers was on structure and the formal organisation, but during the 1920s greater attention began to be paid to the social factors at work and to the behaviour of employees within an organisation – that is, to **human relations** (the social organisation is an alternative heading).

The Hawthorne studies

The turning point in the development of the human relations movement came with the famous studies at the Hawthorne plant of the Western Electric Company near Chicago, America (1924–32) and subsequent publication of the research findings.[32] Among people who wrote about the Hawthorne studies was Elton Mayo (1880–1949), who is often quoted as having been a leader of the researchers. However, there appears to some doubt as to the extent of Mayo's actual involvement.[33]

There were four main phases to the Hawthorne studies:

- the illumination experiments;
- the relay assembly test room;
- the interviewing programme;
- the bank wiring observation room. **(*See* Figure 11.5)**.

Illumination experiments

The original investigation was conducted on the lines of the classical approach and was concerned, in typical scientific management style, with the effects of the intensity of lighting upon the workers' productivity. Workers were divided into two groups, an experimental group and a control group. Results of these tests were inconclusive as production in the experimental group varied with no apparent relationship to the level of lighting, but actually increased when conditions were

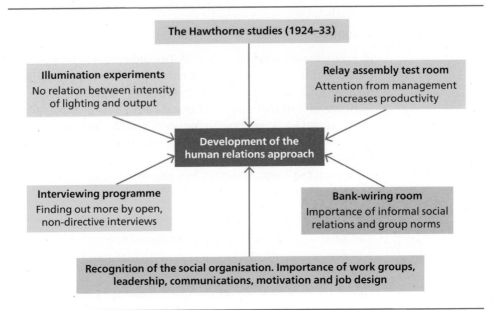

Figure 11.5 The Hawthorne studies

made much worse. Production also increased in the control group although the lighting remained unchanged. The level of production was influenced, clearly, by factors other than changes in physical conditions of work. This prompted a series of other experiments investigating factors of worker productivity.

Relay assembly test room

In the relay assembly test room work was boring and repetitive. It involved assembling telephone relays by putting together a number of small parts. Six women workers were transferred from their normal departments to a separate area. Researchers selected two assemblers who were friends, then chose three other assemblers and a layout operator. The experiment was divided into thirteen periods during which the workers were subjected to a series of planned and controlled changes to their conditions of work, such as hours of work, rest pauses and provision of refreshments. The general environmental conditions of the test room were similar to those of the normal assembly line.

During the experiment the observer adopted a friendly manner, consulting the workers, listening to their complaints and keeping them informed. Following all but one of the changes (when operators complained too many breaks made them lose their work rhythm) there was a continuous increase in the level of production. This has become famous as the '**Hawthorne Effect**' – the conclusion was the extra attention given to the workers and apparent interest in them shown by management, and that people behave differently when being observed.

Interviewing programme

Another significant phase of the experiments was the interviewing programme. The lighting experiment and the relay assembly test room drew attention to the form of supervision as a contributory factor to the workers' level of production. In an attempt to find out more about the workers' feelings towards their supervisors and their general conditions of work, a large interviewing programme was introduced. More than 20,000 interviews were conducted before the work was ended because of the Depression.

Initially, interviewers approached their task with a set of prepared questions, relating mainly to how the workers felt about their jobs. However, this produced only limited information. As a result, the style of interviewing was changed to become more non-directive and open-ended. There was no set list of questions and the workers were free to talk about any aspect of their work. The interviewers set out to be friendly and sympathetic. They adopted an impartial, non-judgemental approach and concentrated on listening.

Using this approach, interviewers found out far more about workers' true feelings and attitudes. They gained information not just about supervision and working conditions but also about the company itself, management, work group relations and matters outside of work such as family life and views on society in general. Many workers appeared to welcome the opportunity to have someone to talk to about their feelings and problems and to be able to 'let off steam' in a friendly atmosphere. The interviewing programme was significant in giving an impetus to present-day human resource management and the use of counselling interviews, and highlighting the need for management to listen to workers' feelings and problems. Being a good listener is arguably even more important for managers in today's work organisations and it is a skill which needs to be encouraged and developed.[34]

Bank wiring observation room

Another experiment involved the observation of a group of fourteen men working in the bank wiring room. It was noted that the men formed their own informal organisation with sub-groups or cliques, and natural leaders emerging with the consent of the members. The group developed its own pattern of informal social relations and 'norms' of what constituted 'proper' behaviour. Despite a financial incentive scheme where the workers could receive more money the more work produced, the group decided on a level of output well below the level they were capable of producing. Group pressures on individual workers were stronger than financial incentives offered by management. The group believed that if they increased their output, management would raise the standard level of piece rates. The importance of group 'norms' and informal social relations is **discussed in Chapter 8.**

How far would YOU support the contention that the human relations approach pays insufficient attention to the realities of the actual working environment?

Evaluation

The Hawthorne studies have received much criticism, for example, on methodology and on failure of the investigators to take sufficient account of environmental factors – although much of this criticism is with the value of hindsight. The human relations writers have been criticised generally for the adoption of a management perspective, their 'unitary frame of reference' and their over-simplified theories.[35] Other criticisms of the human relations approach are that it is insufficiently scientific and that it takes too narrow a view. It ignores the role of the organisation itself in how society operates.

Sex power differential

There are a number of interpretations of the results of the Hawthorne studies, including the possible implications of the 'sex power differential' between the two groups. In the bank wiring room where output was restricted, the group was all male. In the relay assembly room where output increased all members were young unmarried women. All except one were living at home with traditional families of immigrant background. In the work environment of the factory women had been subjected to frequent contact with male supervisors and therefore 'the sex power hierarchies in the home and in the factory were congruent'. It is suggested, therefore, that it was only to be expected that the women agreed readily to participate with management in the relay assembly test room experiment.[36]

Recognition of the social organisation

Whatever the interpretation of the Hawthorne studies, they generated significant new ideas concerning the importance of work groups and leadership, communications, output restrictions, motivation and job design. The studies undoubtedly marked a significant step forward in providing further insight into human behaviour at work and recognition of the social organisation. The human relations approach also recognised the importance of the informal organisation which will always be present within the formal structure. This informal organisation will influence the motivation of employees who will view the organisation for which they work through the values and attitudes of their colleagues. **The informal organisation is discussed in Chapter 2.**

Supporters of the classical approach adopted a more managerial perspective and sought to increase production by rationalisation of the work organisation. By contrast, the human relations movement led to ideas on increasing production by humanising the work organisation and strove for a greater understanding of people's psychological and social needs at work. Human relations writers demonstrated that people go to work to satisfy a complexity of needs and not simply for monetary reward. It has been commented that the classical school was concerned about 'organisations without people' and the human relations school about 'people without organisations'.

Neo-human relations

Certainly there were shortcomings in the human relations approach and assumptions which evolved from studies such as the Hawthorne studies were not necessarily supported by empirical evidence. For example, the contention that a satisfied worker is a productive worker was not always found to be valid. However, subsequent attention given to the social organisation and to theories of individual motivation gave rise to the work of a group of writers under the heading of neo-human relations in the 1950s and 1960s who adopted a more psychological orientation.

New ideas on management theory arose and a major focus of concern was the personal adjustment of the individual within the work organisation and the effects of group relationships and leadership styles.

Socio-technical approach

Criticisms of earlier approaches to organisation are based in part on the attempt to study the activities and problems of the organisation solely in terms of the internal environment. The classical approach emphasised technical requirements of the organisation and its needs – 'organisations without people'; the human relations approaches emphasised psychological and social aspects, and consideration of human needs – 'people without organisations'. The socio-technical approach attempts to reconcile these two earlier approaches. The idea of socio-technical systems arose from the work of *Trist* and others, of the Tavistock Institute of Human Relations, in their study of the effects of changing technology in the coal-mining industry in the 1940s.[37]

The traditional method of working was small, self-selecting groups of miners working together, as an independent team, on one part of the coalface – the 'single place' or 'shortwall' method. Increasing use of mechanisation enabled coal to be extracted on a 'longwall' method. Shift working was introduced, with each shift specialising in one stage of the operation – preparation, cutting or loading. Technological change had disrupted psychological and sociological properties of the old method of working. There was a lack of co-operation between different shifts and within each shift, an increase in absenteeism, scapegoating and signs of greater social stress. The new method did not prove as economically efficient as it could have been with the new technology.

Researchers saw the need for a socio-technical approach in which an appropriate social system could be developed in keeping with the new technical system. The result was the 'composite longwall' method with more responsibility to the team as a whole and shifts carrying out composite tasks, reintroduction of multiskilled roles and a reduction in specialisation. The composite method was psychologically and socially more rewarding and economically more efficient than the 'longwall' method.

The **socio-technical system** is concerned with interactions between psychological and social factors and structural and technological requirements. The 'socio-technical' system directs attention to the transformation or conversion process itself, to the series of activities through which the organisation attempts to achieve its objectives. Recognition of the socio-technical approach is of particular importance today. People must be considered as at least an equal priority along with investment in technology. For example, *Lane et al.* point out that major technological change has brought about dramatic changes in worker behaviour and requirements. It is people who unlock the benefits and opportunities of information communication technology.[38]

Technological determinism

The socio-technical system provides a link with writers under the technology heading. This approach attempts to restrict generalisations about organisations and emphasise the effects of varying technologies on organisation structure, work groups and individual performance and job satisfaction. This is in contrast with the socio-technical approach which did not regard technology, *per se,* as a determinant of behaviour. Under the heading of the technology approach could be included the work of such writers as *Walker and Guest* (effects of the assembly line production method on employee behaviour);[39] *Sayles* (relationship between technology and the nature of work groups);[40] *Blauner* (problems of 'alienation' in relation to different work technologies);[41] and *Turner and Lawrence* (technology and socioculture).[42] **Technology and organisations is examined in Chapter 13.**

Socio-technical approaches

With increasing automated innovations what do YOU see as the likely developments with the socio-technical approach to organisational theory?

Contingency approach

The classical approach suggested one best form of structure and placed emphasis on general sets of principles while the human relations approach gave little attention at all to structure. In contrast the **contingency approach** showed renewed concern with the importance of structure as a significant influence on organisational performance. The contingency approach highlights possible means of differentiating among alternative forms of organisation structures and systems of management. There is no one optimum state. For example, the structure of the organisation and its 'success' are dependent, that is contingent upon, the nature of tasks with which it is designed to deal and the nature of environmental influences.

The most appropriate structure and system of management is therefore dependent upon the contingencies of the situation for each particular organisation. The contingency approach implies that organisation theory should not seek to suggest one best way to structure or manage organisations but should provide insights into the situational and contextual factors which influence management decisions. Situational variables may be identified in a number of ways and include type of organisation and its purpose, culture, size, technology and environment. **Contingency models of organisation structure are discussed in Chapter 12.**

A summary of management theory is set out in the concept map in Figure 11.6.

Analysing some organisational approaches

Organisation theory	Approach		Outcomes
Classical Emphasis on purpose & common principles of organisation, formal hierarchy & control, technical requirements of the organisation.	• Classical organization theories- the formal organization & concepts to increase management efficiency • Taylor- scientific management concepts Weber- the bureaucratic approach • Fayol- administrative theory of the organization.	• Insufficient account of social factors • Creating an organisation structure in which people can exercise only limited control over their work environment • Doubts about the effectiveness set of principles to guide managerial action in practice • Principles must take full account of the particular situational variables of each individual organisation & the psychological & social factors relating to members of the organisation	• Prompted a more systematic view of management • Attempted to provide some common principles applicable to all organisations • Principles a useful starting point in attempting to analyse the effectiveness of the design of organisation structure
Human relations Attention to social factors at work, groups, leadership, the informal organisation & behaviour of people	• Increasing production by humanising the work organisation & • Understanding of people's psychological & social needs at work. • People work to satisfy a complexity of needs & not simply for monetary reward • The classical school-'organisations without people' & the human relations school 'people without organisations'	• Ignores role of the organisation in how society operates • New ideas - importance of work groups & leadership • The importance of the informal organisation will always be present within the formal structure • Employees view their organisation through the values & attitudes of their colleagues - can influence their own motivation	• Provided further insight into human behaviour at work & recognition of the social organisation, increasing production by humanising the work organisation Leading to....... • Neo-human relations the contention that a satisfied worker is a productive worker, not always found to be valid. • Move to adopting psychological orientation in 1950s & 1960s
Socio-technical Integration of the classical & human relations approaches Importance of social, technical needs & the environment	• Interactions between psychological & social factors & structural & technological requirements • All organizations consists of the people (the social system) use tools, the technical system (techniques & knowledge) & the environment	• Reconciles classical & human relation approaches • Directs attention to the transformation or conversion process itself to the series of activities through which the organisation attempts to achieve its objectives	• People must be considered as at least as an equal priority along with investment in technology • Major technological change has brought about dramatic changes in worker behaviour & requirements
Contingency No one best design of organisation. Form of structure, management & 'success' dependent on the situation	• Structure & system of management depends upon the contingencies of the situation • Organisation theory should not seek to suggest one best way to structure or manage organisations • Providing insights into the situational & contextual factors which influence management decisions	• There are common elements in the hierarchies of different organisations but very many differences peculiar to the local situation • Possible to find bureaucracies, project teams, matrix structures, loose ad hoc structures within the same organisations in both commercial & public sector	• Should not necessarily treat every situation as being unique • Striking a balance between universal prescriptions & stating that all situations are different
The systems approach The organization is viewed as multidisciplinary, emphasizing the dynamic nature of communication & importance of integration of individual & organizational interests	• The organization, defined as a designed & structured process • Individuals interacting for objectives is defined as a system • Managers encouraged to view the organisation as a whole & part of a larger environment • Adapts to changes in its environment • Any part can affect other parts	Separate organisational sub-systems (illustrative activities) **Task** - the goals & objectives **Technology** - how the tasks are carried out **Structure** - patterns of organisation **People** - attitudes, skills, knowledge, needs expectations leadership styles **Management** - coordination of tasks technology structure & people, focus on total work organisation & interaction between variables	• Attempts to reconcile the classical & human relations approaches • Businesses are analysed as systems with interrelated sub-systems • Focus on total work organisation & the interrelationship of structure & behaviour & within a range of variables within the organisation • Systems control gave insight into application of cybernetics

©2018 The Virtual Learning Materials Workshop

Figure 11.6 Concept map of management theory
Source: Copyright © 2018 The Virtual Learning Materials Workshop. Reproduced with permission.

Other approaches to the study of organisations

The fourfold framework of classical, human relations, social-technical and contingency approaches provides a helpful if rather simplistic categorisation. The study of organisations, their structure and management is a broad field of inquiry. Depending on preferences of the writer, other possible main approaches include decision theory, social action and postmodernism. **(*See* Figure 11.7.)**

Decision theory

Successful management lies in responding to internal and external change. This involves the clarification of objectives, the specification of problems and the search for and implementation of solutions. Viewing the organisation as a system emphasises the need for good information and channels of communication in order to assist effective decision-making in the organisation. This draws attention to **decision theory**. Here the focus of attention is on managerial decision-making and how organisations process and use information in making decisions. The organisation is seen as an information-processing network with numerous decision points. An understanding of how decisions are made helps in understanding behaviour in the organisation. Decision-making writers seek to explain the mechanisms by which conflict is resolved and choices are made.

Some leading writers

Leading writers on the decision-making approach include Barnard, Simon and Cyert and March. The scope of the decision-making approach, however, is wide and it is

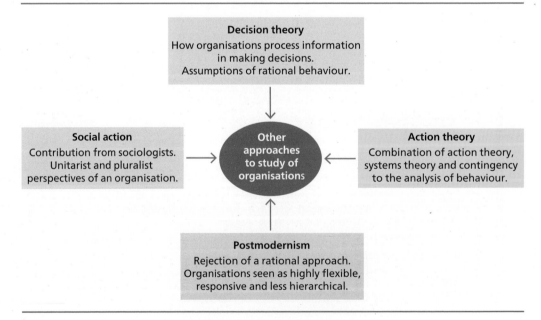

Figure 11.7 Other approaches to the study of organisations

possible to identify contributions from engineers, mathematicians and operational research specialists in addition to the work of economists, psychologists and writers on management and organisation.

Barnard stressed the need for co-operative action in organisations. He believed people's ability to communicate, and commitment and contribution to the achievement of a common purpose, were necessary for the existence of a co-operative system.[43] These ideas were developed further by *Simon*. He sees management as meaning decision-making and his concern is with how decisions are made and decision-making improved. Simon is critical of the implication of man as completely rational and proposes a model of 'administrative man' who, unlike 'economic man', 'satisfices' rather than maximises. Administrative decision-making is the achievement of satisfactory rather than optimal results in solving problems.[44]

Cyert and March contrast economic models of decision-making, based on the assumption of rational behaviour in choosing from known alternatives in order to maximise objectives, with behavioural models based not so much on maximisation of objectives as on short-term expediency where a choice is made to avoid conflict and to stay within limiting constraints. Managers are more concerned with avoiding uncertainties than with the prediction of uncertainties.[45] **(See also decision models of leadership in Chapter 9.)**

Social action

Social action represents a contribution from sociologists to the study of organisations. Social action writers attempt to view the organisation from the standpoint of individual members (actors) who will each have their own goals and interpretation of the work situation in terms of the satisfaction sought and the meaning that work has for them. The goals of the individual, and the means selected and actions taken to achieve these goals, are affected by the individual's perception of the situation. Social action looks to the individual's own definition of the situation as a basis for explaining behaviour. Conflict of interests is seen as normal behaviour and part of organisational life. According to *Silverman,* 'The action approach . . . does not, in itself, provide a theory of organisations. It is instead best understood as a method of analysing social relations within organisations.'[46]

A main thrust of social action is criticism of earlier approaches to organisation and what is claimed failure to provide a satisfactory basis for the explanation or prediction of individual behaviour. The human relations approaches have been criticised because of their focus on generalised theories of good management, group psychology and the suggestion of needs common to all individuals at work. The socio-technical approach has been criticised for attributing feelings of alienation to the nature of technology and the status of work groups rather than an analysis which focused on concern for the individual's expectations of, and reactions to, work.

Unitarist or pluralist perspectives

Important contributors to a social action approach include *Goldthorpe* (industrial attitudes and behaviour patterns of manual workers)[47] and *Fox*. In a research paper written for the Royal Commission on Trade Unions and Employers' Associations (the Donovan Report), Fox suggests two major ways of perceiving an industrial organisation – a 'unitarist' approach and a 'pluralist' approach.[48] In the search for effective employee relations and common commitment to the goals of the organisation, consideration should be given to both unitarist and pluralist perspectives. While neither of the approaches can be seen as 'right' or 'wrong', these contrasting views will influence the nature of employment relations and the management of human resources. **(See discussion in Chapter 3 on contrasting views of conflict.)**

The **unitarist perspective** views the organisation as an integrated and harmonious whole with managers and other staff sharing common interests and objectives. There is an image of the organisation as a team with a common source of loyalty, one focus of effort and one accepted leader. Conflict is perceived as disruptive and unnatural and can be explained by, for example, poor communications, personality clashes or the work of agitators. Trade unions are seen as an unnecessary evil and restrictive practices as outmoded or caused by trouble-makers. HR policies and managerial development can be seen as reflecting a unitary ideology. *Horwitz* suggests that the unitary perspective views company and trade union loyalty as mutually exclusive. Developments in HRM, in seeking to optimise co-operation and organisational loyalty, can be seen as imposing new forms of control. A managerial approach to facilitating organisational goals and the direct involvement of employees furthers a unitary perspective and can mask an underlying distaste for unionism.[49]

The **pluralist perspective** suggested by *Fox* views the organisation as made up of powerful and competing sub-groups with their own legitimate loyalties, objectives and leaders.[50] These competing sub-groups are almost certain to come into conflict as inevitable and induced in part by the very structure of the organisation. Conflict is not necessarily a bad thing but can be an agent for evolution, and internal and external change. Restrictive practices may be seen as a rational response from a group that regards itself threatened. The role of the manager would be less commanding and enforcing, and more persuading and co-ordinating. Fox suggests that the pluralist perspective is a more realistic frame of reference. He argues the importance of viewing work situations through the different groups involved rather than attempting a wished-for unitarist approach.

To what extent do YOU agree that social action theory may seem interesting in the classroom but offers little constructive application in the actual work situation?

Action theory

A theory of human behaviour from an 'action approach' is presented by *Bowey* who suggests action theory, systems theory and contingency theory are not necessarily incompatible approaches to the understanding of behaviour in organisations. It would be possible to take the best parts of the different approaches and combine them into a theory that would model empirical behaviour and also facilitate the analysis of large numbers of people in organisations.[51] The three essential principles of action theory can be summarised as:

- Sociology is concerned not just with behaviour but with 'meaningful action'.
- Particular meanings persist through reaffirmation in actions.
- Actions can also lead to changes in meanings.

These three principles apply mainly to explanations of individual, or small-scale, behaviour. Bowey gives four additional concepts on which analysis of large-scale behaviour can be based. These concepts are redefined in accordance with an action approach.

- **Role.** This is needed for the analysis of behaviour in organisations. It explains the similar action of different people in similar situations within the organisation and the expectations held by other people.
- **Relationships.** This is needed to explain the patterns of interaction among people and the behaviours displayed towards one another.
- **Structure.** The relationships among members of an organisation give rise to patterns of action which can be identified as a 'transitory social structure'. The social factors, and non-social factors such as payment systems, methods of production and physical layout, together form the behavioural structure.
- **Process.** Human behaviour can be analysed in terms of processes, defined as 'continuous interdependent sequences of actions'. The concept of process is necessary to account for the manner in which organisations exhibit changes in structure.

The three principles of action theory, together with the four additional concepts from systems theory, provide an action approach to the analysis of behaviour in organisations. Bowey goes on to illustrate her theory with case studies of five different types of organisations, all in the restaurant industry.

Postmodernism (Post bureaucratic)

With the development of the information and technological age a more recent view of organisations and management is the idea of **postmodernism or post-bureaucratic.** *Cooper and Burrell* refer to the contrasting postmodern view of 'organisation less the expression of planned thought and calculative action and a more defensive reaction to forces intrinsic to the social body which constantly threaten the stability of organised life'.[52]

In the 1990s, writers such as *Clegg* described the postmodern organisation in terms of the influence of technological determinism, structural flexibility, premised on niches, multiskilled jobs marked by a lack of demarcation, and more complex employment relationships including subcontracting and networking.[53] Postmodernism rejects a rational systems approach to our understanding of organisations and accepted explanations of society and behaviour. Postmodern organisations are perceived as highly flexible and responsive, with decentralised decision-making, fluid, less hierarchical structures and with the ability to change quickly to meet present demands. **Matrix structures, discussed in Chapter 12,** can be seen as a form of post-bureaucratic organisation.

Generalised sociological concept

The idea of postmodernism is, however, not easy to explain. Arguably it is more of a generalised sociological concept rather than a specific approach to organisations. There is even some discussion of two connotations, and theories or philosophies of the concept depending on whether the term is hyphenated or not.[54] Perhaps understandably, therefore, the concept of postmodernism appears to have little interest or appeal to the practical manager. *Watson,* for example, questions the value of labelling more flexible forms of bureaucratic structure and culture as postmodern or post-bureaucratic and differentiating these from the modernist bureaucratic organisation.

> The labelling of more flexible forms of bureaucratic structure and culture as 'postmodern' or 'post-bureaucratic' is unhelpful. It is unrealistic to suggest that there is something new occurring to work organisations at the level of the basic organising principle. There is no postmodern or post-bureaucratic organisational form available to us that is **essentially** different from the modernist bureaucratic organisation.[55]

Nevertheless, postmodernist organisation can arguably be seen as a healthy challenge to more traditional approaches. It puts forward alternative interpretations of rationality, credibility and ambiguity, and a thoughtful critical perspective on disorders in work organisations, and reminds us of the complexities in our understanding of organisational behaviour.

An outline summary of main approaches to organisational theory is set out in Figure 11.8.

What examples can YOU provide of the adaptive value of postmodernism to the study of organisation theory and structure?

Relevance to study of organisational behaviour

Different perspectives on organisation theory are not necessarily a bad thing; they illustrate the discursive and complex nature of organisational behaviour. Discussion on various categorisations of approaches and identification of individual writers within a particular approach can provide a useful insight into the subject. Division of writers on organisation into various approaches offers a number of positive advantages. It is helpful in the arrangement and study of material and provides a setting in which to view the field of organisational behaviour. Review of the different approaches helps in organisational analysis and in the identification of problem areas. For example, is the problem one of structure, of human relations or of the socio-technical process?

The various approaches represent a progression of ideas, each building on from the other and adding to it. They are not in competition and no one approach should be viewed as replacing or superseding earlier contributions. Many ideas of earlier writers are still of relevance today and of continuing importance in modern management practice. *McLean* acknowledges that some critics see organisational

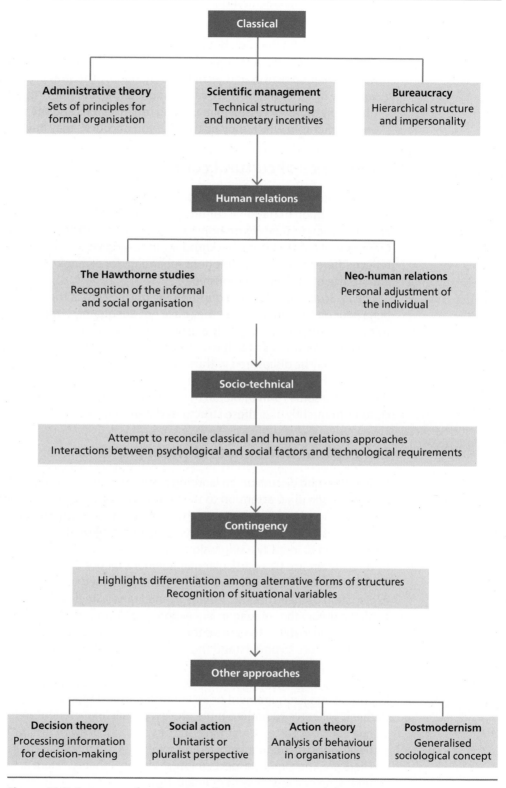

Figure 11.8 Summary of main approaches to organisational theory

philosophies as management fads that will be replaced by new ones as other theories are proposed.

> **That may well be the case, but it is good for management theories to evolve, because organisations change, the environment changes, and as a result, management practices and techniques change . . . Theories provide us with valuable insights into how we can be more understanding, influential and ultimately more successful in managing organisations and the turbulent dynamic environments in which they operate . . . you of course, may have a different view![56]**

Importance of cultural contexts

A major criticism of the attempt to define generalised models of organisation theory is the assumption of national culture. *Schneider and Barsoux* draw attention to how the different theories on how to organise all reflect societal concerns of the times as well as the cultural backgrounds of the individuals. Different approaches reflect different cultural assumptions regarding, for example, human nature and the importance of task and relationships.[57]

Cheng, Sculli and Chan also question the universality of theories of organisational behaviour on the grounds that they have not adequately addressed the factor of culture. 'Traditionally, the greatest aspiration of researchers is to discover objective, universalistic principles of behaviour. The tacit assumption behind this is that these principles may be discovered without reference to cultural contexts.' They conclude that while there may be some universality to organisation structures, for example the need for some form of hierarchy whatever its shape may be, different national cultures frequently give those structures different meanings.[58]

Conceptual thinking and theory

In an interesting discussion on learning classic management theories *Robinson and Francis-Smythe* draw attention to the importance of conceptual thinking and how far knowledge of formal academic theory helps in the discharge of managerial responsibilities. The overwhelming majority of established senior managers will be hard-pressed to identify a single significant occasion of decision-making guided by direct reference to a particular management theory. Even if names of respected theorists can be recalled managers will be hard-pressed to provide a succinct explanation of their theories. Robinson and Francis-Smythe question what happens to all the theory that managers are exposed to during their training and education. However, 'the inability to name either a theory or a theoretician should not be taken to imply a failure to understand the theory in a more generalised, more abstract, more conceptual way'.

Robinson and Francis-Smythe suggest that academic knowledge is not, *per se,* a key professional requirement or an important aspect of managerial competence. Rather it will serve to underpin the process of building a repertoire of concepts that will be held in long-term memories in the way most likely to facilitate subsequent retrieval, good managerial moves and solutions to managerial challenges.[59]

There are, then, many aspects to organisational theory. There are no simple solutions, no one best way to manage. However, study of different approaches to organisations, their structure and management is still important and remains an indispensable part of the job.

Egyptian pyramids: impressive structures served as burial sites for pharaohs and kings

How would YOU best explain to a sceptical audience the practical benefits from the classroom study of organisational theory?

Critical Thinking Zone

Reflections on Fayol's Five Elements of Management

In this zone, we critically examine Fayol's Five Elements of Management and consider whether they are still pertinent to organisations over a century after they were first proposed.

Jules Henri Fayol has been described as 'the most distinguished figure which Europe contributed to the management movement'[61] (p. 21). The French industrialist was widely acknowledged as the founding father of the administrative school of management, for catalysing the professionalisation of management and for providing a theoretical foundation upon which subsequent management theory and practice have been built.[62–64] Fayol's contribution to classical organisation theory, and, arguably, continued influence on contemporary management theory and practice, was espoused during the Industrial Revolution, an era of factorisation and unprecedented societal, economic and environmental change that promulgated a steep rise in theorisation of how organisations should be managed.[65] Fayol's theories were developed through his extensive experience (his entire career[66]) in a French mining company, including tenure as Chief Executive Officer, and undertaking roles such as Mining Engineer

and Researcher.[62] His empirical investigations also engaged him in the extensive analysis of management tasks through observation, experiential learning on the job and personal insights,[67] many of which were compared to the work of Frederick Winslow Taylor, a fellow classical management theorist.[62]

Key Managerial Activities

According to Holmblad Brunsson,[68] Fayol viewed the organisation from a top down perspective, as opposed to Taylor who took a bottom up approach[69] and believed that senior managers and boards were responsible for administering its entire business affairs.[62, 70] He saw organisations as homogeneous entities and thus proffered that managerial work displays common traits or characteristics. Based on his notion of general management principles, Fayol proposed that an organisation's business operations comprised an amalgam of six major activities[67, 62] (Pugh and Hickson[67], p. 97; Parker and Ritson[62]). First, technical activities, incorporating manufacture, production and adaptation. Second, commercial activities, including buying, selling and exchange. Third, financial activities, encompassing the search for, and optimal use of, capital. Fourth, security activities, such as the protection of people and property. Fifth, accounting activities, which includes stocktaking, costs, balance sheet and statistics. Finally, and importantly, managerial activities, namely planning, organising, commanding, coordinating and controlling. Based on his experience, Fayol espoused that most jobs, in varying degrees, contain all six managerial activities, but a shift in emphasis and significance occurs as managers climb the hierarchical ladder. He also noted that managerial activities increase while technical ones decrease. Fayol therefore concluded that the development and utilisation of managerial knowledge was an important prerequisite and criterion for administering the organisation's business affairs and thus advocated an on-going programme of management education to facilitate this.[62]

History in the Making

Smith and Boynes[63] profess that Fayol's ideas, the foundation of which were his own extensive experiences, were developed for senior management, based on his top down approach. The espousal of his fourteen general principles of management birthed 'the first real definition of management as a distinct and important contribution to organisation effectiveness' (p. 1322). Thus, in 1916, Fayol concluded[71] 'to manage is to forecast and plan, to organise, to command, to coordinate and to control'[67] (p. 96). George[69] (p. 114) argues that Fayol's definition, which is also known as the five elements of management, provided a 'complete and comprehensive theory of management which could be applied to all endeavours' and generalised to a wide variety of organisational and managerial contexts.[72]

Is Fayol's Theory Applicable to Twenty-First Century Organisations?

Despite its espousal over a century ago, it could be argued that Fayol's five elements of management are still pertinent to twenty-first century organisations. A discussion of this argument now follows (Pugh and Hickson,[67] (p. 98); McLean[73] (p. 33); Rausch[74]).

To Forecast and Plan (Prévoyance in French)

Fayol professed that forecasting involved analysing the future and formulating an appropriate plan of action.[67] Arguably, the global knowledge economy, along with ubiquitous change and hypercompetition, engages managers in activities such as forecasting, appraising the micro environment and analysing the macro environment to aid strategic planning. Indeed, Mintzberg[75] acknowledged Fayol as one of the earliest proponents of planning.

To Organise

Fayol espoused that the organisation's structure was important to its survival, as it facilitated the optimal conduct of its business affairs.[67] Organising, in contemporary terms, requires managers to design and implement an appropriate infrastructure, which optimises the organisation's systems, services, processes, resources (human, material, financial) and procedures and enables the dissemination of knowledge and information in a timely manner.[73,76]

To Command

Fayol, in his original writing, used 'command' to describe a manager's responsibility to lead individuals towards organisational goal and strategy achievement.[67] In contemporary parlance, 'command' may sound rather harsh and control-orientated, but Fayol's theory was espoused during the era of the classical school of management, where, it could be argued, top-down, directive management styles prevailed over more participative ones. Using a twenty-first century lens, Hill and McShane[77] supplant 'command' with 'leadership' to highlight the importance of directing, influencing and engaging individuals to buy into the achievement of the organisation's goals and objectives.[78] Furthermore, Fayol proffered that managers should develop an in-depth knowledge of their staff.[67] This could, arguably, be promoted through the development of a positive people-organisation relationship and relational psychological contract.[79,80]

To Coordinate

Fayol advocated that managers should bind together, unify and harmonise all the organisation's activities.[67] This is relevant to contemporary management, especially since managers have a responsibility to ensure there is coordination, synergy and symbiosis between organisational processes and functions, including the input-conversion-output process.[73] Hill and McShane proffer that coordination works in synergy with organising.

To Control

Fayol acknowledged the importance of control in an organisational setting and posited that it makes sure 'everything occurs in conformity with established rules and expressed command'[67] (p. 100). Using less formal, contemporary parlance, as one of the most important managerial responsibilities, control involves deploying contextual leadership (e.g. transformational or transactional) to ensure plans, strategies, etc are achieved within allocated budgets, resources and timescales.[77] As metaphorical controllers, managers should ensure that contingency plans are in place to deal with system anomalies and deviations and avoid infrastructural and organisational disruption. It could be argued that Fayol placed 'control' as the fifth element of management to emphasise the underpinning and overarching support it gives to the previous four.

The discussion of the five elements, arguably, highlight their relevance to twenty-first century organisations. Fells[81] (p. 347) concurs and attests that Fayol's model is 'relevant and appropriate to contemporary management. . . Fayol's five elements. . . are quite general and therefore may pass the test of time.' However relevant Fayol's work may be to contemporary management practice, it is not without its critics. Hatchuel and Segrestin[66] (p. 2) highlight criticisms that have been levelled towards the translation from French into English. They report 'Urwick (1949) . . . complained about the translation of administration as 'management', which would narrow the scope of Fayol's theory to the realm of industrial management.' Parker and Ritson[62] (p. 178–179) state that Fayol is often portrayed as 'an inflexible and authoritarian generalist. . . ' who was described as a 'fellow traveller of the scientific management movement.' They claim that the only distinguishing feature between the two theorists is Fayol's extensive senior management experience, which 'led him to adapt a perspective that focused on managing the total organisation.'

An Indelible Impact on History

To conclude, it could be argued that Fayol's five elements of management are still pertinent to organisations, over a century after they were first proposed. Of course, based on your own experiences, you may have a different view. Fells[81] (p. 354) contends that 'Fayol's work is still very much alive and still relevant today.' Smith and Boyns[63] (p. 1320) also highlight the impact that Fayol's work has had on the management role 'not just for their originality but for their continuing influence on management thinking in the West to this day.' Mintzberg[82] (p. 49) noted the influence of Fayol and stated, 'if you ask a manager what he does, he will tell you that he plans, organises, coordinates and controls.' It is evident that Fayol's five elements of management have made an indelible impact on history and the theorisation of management, from an empirical, conceptual and practical perspective. In recognition of Fayol's influence, Hales[83] (p. 3) concludes 'if all philosophy is a set of footnotes to Plato, management theory is, in large measure, a reply to Fayol's original memo.'

Questions

Based on the above, answer the following questions.

1. Fayol viewed organisations as homogeneous entities and thus espoused that managerial work displays common traits. Using reference to theory and practice, *to what extent* do you agree?

2. Fayol's theory has been described as generalisable across other contexts. Using an organisation of your choice, *apply* the five elements of management and *identify* the implications for organisational behaviour in the workplace.

3. It has been mooted that the only distinguishing feature between administrative theory and scientific management is Fayol's extensive senior management experience. *Discuss* this assertion, referring to appropriate theories.

Summary – Chapter 11 'Organisational theory and structure'

A central part of the study of organisational behaviour is the development of different thinking on structure and management, and what might be termed organisation theory. The work of leading writers can be categorised into various 'approaches' based on their views of organisations, their structure and management. The classical writers placed emphasis on purpose and structure, technical requirements of the organisation, and assumption of rational and logical behaviour. Human relations writers emphasised the informal organisation, group relationships, and the psychological and social needs of people at work. The socio-technical approach focuses attention on the interactions between technical and social variables and influences of the external environment. Contingency theory highlights possible means of differentiating between alternative forms of structures and systems of management. It is possible to identify a number of other approaches including decision-making, social action and postmodernism. The various approaches are not in competition but represent a progression of ideas. There are many aspects to organisational theory and no simple solutions. Division into various approaches and identification of leading writers offers a number of positive advantages but there are criticisms including the significance of cultural contexts. Formal academic theory may help in the discharge of managerial responsibilities.

Group discussion activities

Undertake each of these activities in small groups as indicated by your tutor. Before you start your discussion establish a non-threatening environment within the group and confirm confidentiality will be honoured.

First, form your own views and then share and compare in open critical discussion with colleagues. Reflect honestly on the extent to which: (i) you influenced the thinking and ideas of your colleagues; and (ii) you were influenced by your colleagues.

To what extent was your group able to reach consensus?

Agree one of your members to produce a brief written summary of the discussion and prepared to present in a plenary session.

Activity 1

(a) For the following types of organisation suggest what features of each of the different approaches to organisational theory discussed in this chapter are most likely to predominate.

Explain your reasoning and support with examples.

* six-star luxury international hotel
* major civil service department
* medical research university
* maternity hospital
* motor car manufacturer
* large comprehensive school
* maximum security prison
* leisure centre

(b) How much agreement was there among members of your group?

(c) What conclusions do you draw?

(d) How does the activity relate to your knowledge of different approaches to organisation theory and structure?

Activity 2

Place in *rank order* the four main experiments of the Hawthorne studies in terms of:

(i)   their relevance to the study of organisational theory; and

(ii) practical applications today for the structuring and management of work organisations.

Attempt to achieve consensus among your colleagues.

Activity 3

(a) Which *one* approach to approach to organisations, their structure and management and/or *one* writer on the subject has the greatest influence on you?

(b) How would you defend criticisms of the study of social action theory and post-modernism as too 'academic' and abstract to have any real meaning outside of the classroom?

Organisational behaviour in action case study

Vanguard Method' for systems thinking – beyond command and control

A different, more recent approach to thinking about organisation and structure applied to the service industry is that of the 'Vanguard Method' which is based on the pioneering work of among others, W. Edwards Deming, Chris Argyris and Taiichi Ohno. Ohno, the father of the Toyota Production System, drew attention to managers' lack of control on the shop floor and to the importance of continuous revisions, and his ideas gave rise to concepts such as Total Quality Management and Just In Time. Ohno viewed the work organisation as an integrated system with the focus on flow throughout the system rather than on individual functions. As *Seddon* notes: 'In Ohno's philosophy each person's work is connected to the needs of customers, as opposed to arbitrary and counterproductive measures of activity'.[60]

Vanguard helps organisations change from command and control thinking to a systems thinking on the structure and design of work.

Command and control thinking		Systems thinking
Top-down, hierarchy	**Perspective**	Outside-in system
Functional specialisation and procedures	**Design of work**	Demand, value and flow
Contractual	**Attitude to customers**	What matters?
Separated from work	**Decision-making**	Integrated with work
Output, targets, activity, standards, related to budget	**Measurement**	Capability, variation: related to purpose
Contractual	**Attitude to suppliers**	Co-operative
Control budgets, manage people	**Management ethos**	Learn through action on the system
Extrinsic	**Assumptions about motivation**	Intrinsic

Emphasis is placed on the customer and measurement of success as opposed to targets of expected performance. The consequences are improved service to customers, at lower costs and improved morale. Service is different to manufacturing. In simple terms there is inherently greater variety in customer demand, hence the need to design to absorb that variety. We recommend that service organisations avoid the 'tools' developed for 'lean manufacturing' as they don't apply well in service organisations.

Intrinsic to The Vanguard Method is the transfer of expertise to people (managers and staff) in the organisation. Vanguard uses 'sensei', people who are experts in both intervention theory (how you make a change) and systems theory (how to analyse and design work). Vanguard senseis are experts in the 'what': how a systems design improves performance and the 'how': how to make this change.

Steps in the Vanguard Methods

Understanding the distinctions – Top management must understand what it means to change from command and control to systems thinking.

Scoping – Assessing the scope for improvement; knowledge about customer demand, revenue and service flows, waste and the causes of waste; the potential scope and value of making this change in practical terms.

Check – People who do the work given technical support and check their understanding of the what and why of performance as a system.

Measures and method – In parallel with 'check', managers work on the relationship between measures and method, understanding the need to change and use of measures for managing and improving performance.

Prototyping – The 'check' team and managers work on measures and establish a prototype of the re-design. The purpose is to develop the re-design and determine anticipated economies.

Leader's review – In order to make informed choices about benefits from adopting the new systems design and authorises preparation for implementation.

Proof of concept – Prototype is extended and developed to handle all customer demands; the consequential improvements are tracked with new (system) measures while management develop a new budgeting and management information system.

Constancy of purpose – Leadership of the change with the top management team including in particular roles and measures. Clarity about future state and means of implementation.

Implementation – Here a choice can be made: establishing a working pilot (a complete re-design but limited in volume or scope); or making a complete change to the organisation.

Changes to policy and practice – Review matters of policy and practice. Typically they will include budgeting, HR policy and practice, interpretation of regulations and IT.

Finding out what matters to your customers – Having re-designed and improved your service, it is a natural extension to step over the boundary and learn about what matters to your customers. The work leads to new services, designed with customers.

Source: Thanks to David Puttick, Vanguard. Reproduced with permission.

Tasks

1. What is your view of systems thinking as a further approach to organisation theory and structure?

2. To what extent do you agree with emphasis on the customer and measurement of success as opposed to targets of expected performance?

3. How far do you believe the *idea* of systems thinking could apply to both service and manufacturing organisations?

Chapter 11 – Personal skills and employability exercise

Objectives

Completing this exercise should help you to enhance the following skills:

* Awareness of the type of organisation structure in which you would feel comfortable working.
* Greater recognition about the type of job and work you would enjoy.
* Improved knowledge about the likely direction of your work career.

Exercise

Answer each question 'mostly agree' or 'mostly disagree'. Assume that you are trying to learn something about yourself.

	Mostly agree	Mostly disagree
1 I value stability in my job.	❑	❑
2 I like a predictable organisation.	❑	❑
3 The best job for me would be one in which the future is uncertain.	❑	❑
4 The army would be a nice place to work.	❑	❑
5 Rules, policies and procedures tend to frustrate me.	❑	❑
6 I would enjoy working for a company that employed 85,000 people worldwide.	❑	❑
7 Being self-employed would involve more risk than I'm willing to take.	❑	❑
8 Before accepting a job, I would like to see an exact job description.	❑	❑
9 I would prefer a job as a freelance house painter to one as a clerk for the Department of Motor Vehicles.	❑	❑
10 Seniority should be as important as performance in determining pay increases and promotion.	❑	❑
11 It would give me a feeling of pride to work for the largest and most successful company in its field.	❑	❑
12 Given a choice, I would prefer to make £40,000 per year as a vice-president in a small company to £50,000 as a staff specialist in a large company.	❑	❑
13 I would regard wearing an employee badge with a number on it as a degrading experience.	❑	❑

	Mostly agree	Mostly disagree
14 Parking spaces in a company lot should be assigned on the basis of job level.	❑	❑
15 If an accountant works for a large organisation, he or she cannot be a true professional.	❑	❑
16 Before accepting a job (given a choice), I would want to make sure that the company had a very fine programme of employee benefits.	❑	❑
17 A company will probably not be successful unless it establishes a clear set of rules and procedures.	❑	❑
18 Regular working hours and holidays are more important to me than finding thrills on the job.	❑	❑
19 You should respect people according to their rank.	❑	❑
20 Rules are meant to be broken.	❑	❑

Source: Adapted from DuBrin, A. J. *Human Relations: A Job-Oriented Approach,* Reston Publishing/Prentice Hall (1978), pp. 296–7. Copyright © 1978. Reproduced with permission from Pearson Education Inc.

You should then consider the further information supplied to you by your tutor.

Discussion

✳ How easy was it for you to agree or disagree with each question?

✳ How far did members relate the questions to different ideas or studies on the structure and management of work organisations?

✳ To what extent do you think personal skills and employability are influenced by the type of organisation structure?

Notes and references

1. Jones, G. R. *Organizational Theory, Design and Change,* seventh edition, Pearson (2013).
2. Skipton, M. D. 'Management and the Organisation', *Management Research News,* vol. 5, no. 3, 1983, pp. 9–15.
3. Fayol, H. *General and Industrial Management,* Pitman (1949). See also Gray, I. *Henri Fayol's General and Industrial Management,* Pitman (1988).
4. Urwick, L. *Notes on the Theory of Organization,* American Management Association (1952).
5. Brech, E. F. L. *Organisation: The Framework of Management,* second edition, Longman (1965).
6. Simon, H. A. *Administrative Behaviour,* third edition, Free Press (1976), p. xxii.
7. Woodward, J. *Industrial Organization: Theory and Practice,* second edition, Oxford University Press (1980).
8. Taylor, F. W. *Scientific Management,* Harper & Row (1947). Comprises 'Shop Management' (1903), 'Principles of Scientific Management' (1911) and Taylor's testimony to the House of Representatives' Special Committee (1912).
9. Braverman, H. *Labor and Monopoly Capital,* Monthly Review Press (1974).
10. For a study of employers' labour relations policies, including comments on the work of Braverman, see Gospel, H. F. and Littler, C. R. (eds) *Managerial Strategies and Industrial Relations,* Heinemann Educational Books (1983).

11. Cloke, K. and Goldsmith, J. *The End of Management and the Rise of Organizational Democracy,* Jossey-Bass (2002), p. 27.

12. See, for example: Rose, M. *Industrial Behaviour,* Penguin (1978), p. 31. See also Rose, M. *Industrial Behaviour,* second edition, Penguin (1988), ch. 2.

13. Crainer, S. and Dearlove, D. *Financial Times Handbook of Management,* second edition, Financial Times Prentice Hall (2001).

14. Stern, S. 'Guru Guide', *Management Today,* October 2001, pp. 83–4.

15. See also: Mullins, L. J. and Dossor, O. P. *Hospitality Management and Organisational Behaviour,* fifth edition, Pearson Education (2013).

16. See for example: Beirne, M., Riach, K. and Wilson, F. 'Controlling business? Agency and constraint in call centre working', *New Technology, Work and Employment,* vol. 19, no. 2, 2004, pp. 96–109.

17. Weber, M. *The Theory of Social and Economic Organization,* Collier Macmillan (1964).

18. Blau, P. M. and Scott, W. R. *Formal Organizations,* Routledge and Kegan Paul (1966). Reproduced with permission.

19. Argyris, C. *Integrating the Individual and the Organization,* John Wiley & Sons (1964).

20. Caulkin, S. 'Faceless Corridors of Power', *Management Today,* January 1988, p. 65.

21. Morgan, G. *Images of Organization,* second edition, Sage Publications (1997).

22. Waterman, R. *Adhocracy: The Power to Change,* Norton & Company (1994).

23. Mintzberg, H. *Managing,* Financial Times Prentice Hall (2009).

24. Tibballs, G. *Business Blunders,* Robinson Publishing (1999).

25. Drucker, P. F. *Classic Drucker,* Harvard Business School Press (2006), p. 22.

26. See Mullins, L. J. and Dossor, P. *Hospitality Management and Organisational Behaviour,* fifth edition, Pearson Education (2013).

27. Green, J. 'Is Bureaucracy Dead? Don't Be So Sure', *Chartered Secretary,* January 1997, pp. 18–19.

28. See, for example, Waller, P. 'Bureaucracy Takes New Form', *Professional Manager,* May 1998, p. 6.

29. For a fuller account see, Wilson, F. M. *Organizational Behaviour and Work,* fourth edition, Oxford University Press (2014).

30. Ritzer, G. *The McDonaldization of Society,* Sage (2015).

31. Gwyther, M. 'Can McDonald's Stand The Heat?', *Management Today,* Issue 2, 2017, pp. 36–8.

32. There are many versions of the Hawthorne experiments. Among the most thorough accounts is Roethlisberger, F. J. and Dickson, W. J. *Management and the Worker,* Harvard University Press (1939). See also Landsberger, H. A. *Hawthorne Revisited,* Cornell University Press, Ithaca (1958).

33. See, for example, Rose, M. *Industrial Behaviour,* second edition, Penguin (1988).

34. See, for example, Buggy, C. 'Are You Really Listening?', *Professional Manager,* July 2000, pp. 20–2.

35. Silverman, D. *The Theory of Organisations,* Heinemann (1970).

36. Stead, B. A. *Women in Management,* Prentice Hall (1978), p. 190.

37. Trist, E. L., Higgin, G. W., Murray, H. and Pollock, A. B. *Organizational Choice,* Tavistock Publications (1963).

38. Lane, T., Snow, D. and Labrow, P. 'Learning to Succeed with ICT', *The British Journal of Administrative Management,* May/June 2000, pp. 14–15.

39. Walker, C. R. and Guest, R. H. *The Man on the Assembly Line,* Harvard University Press (1952). See also Walker, C. R., Guest, R. H. and Turner, A. N. *The Foreman on the Assembly Line,* Harvard University Press (1956).

40. Sayles, L. R. *Behaviour of Industrial Work Groups,* Wiley (1958).

41. Blauner, R. *Alienation and Freedom,* University of Chicago Press (1964).

42. Deutsch, S. E. 'Industrial Jobs and the Worker: An Investigation of Response to Task Attributes by Arthur Turner and Paul Lawrence', *Technology and Culture,* vol. 7, no. 3, Summer 1966, pp. 436–38.

43. Barnard, C. *The Functions of the Executive,* Oxford University Press (1938).

44. Simon, H. A. *The New Science of Management Decision,* revised edition, Prentice Hall (1977).

45. Cyert, R. M. and March, J. G. *A Behavioural Theory of the Firm,* second edition, Blackwell (1992).

46. Silverman, D. *The Theory of Organisations,* Heinemann (1970), p. 147.

47. Goldthorpe, J. H., Lockwood, D., Bechhofer, F. and Platt, J. *The Affluent Worker,* Cambridge University Press (1968).

48. Fox, A. *Industrial Sociology and Industrial Relations,* HMSO (1966).

49. Horwitz, F. M. 'HRM: An Ideological Perspective', *International Journal of Manpower,* vol. 12, no. 6, 1991, pp. 4–9.

50. Fox, A. *Industrial Society and Industrial Relations,* HMSO (1966).

51. Bowey, A. M. *The Sociology of Organisations,* Hodder & Stoughton (1976).

52. Cooper, R. and Burrell, G. 'Modernism, Postmodernism and Organizational Analysis: An Introduction', *Organization Studies,* vol. 9, no. 1, January 1988, pp. 91–112.

53. Clegg, S. R. *Modern Organizations: Organization Studies in the Postmodern World,* Sage (1990).

54. See, for example, Legge, K. *Human Resource Management: Rhetorics and Realities,* Macmillan Business (1995).

55. Watson, T. J. *Organising and Managing Work,* second edition, Financial Times Prentice Hall (2006), p. 271.

56. McLean, J. 'Management Techniques and Theories', *Manager, The British Journal of Administrative Management,* August/September 2005, p. 17. Reproduced with permission.

57. Schneider, S. C. and Barsoux, J. *Managing Across Cultures,* second edition, Financial Times Prentice Hall (2003).

58. Cheng, T., Sculli, D. and Chan, F. 'Relationship Dominance – Rethinking Management Theories from the Perspective of Methodological Relationalism', *Journal of Managerial Psychology,* vol. 16, no. 2, 2001, pp. 97–105.

59. Robinson, L and Francis-Smythe, J. 'Managing to abstraction', *Professional Manager,* vol. 19, no.5, September 2010, pp. 36–8.

60. Seddon, J. *Freedom from Command & Control: A better way to make the work work,* Vanguard Consulting Ltd. (2005).

61. Urwick, L. *A Short Survey of Industrial Management,* British Institute of Management, London (1950).

62. Parker, L. D. and Ritson, P. 'Fads, Stereotypes and Management Gurus: Fayol and Follett today', *Management Decision,* vol. 43, no. 10, 2005, pp. 1335–57.

63. Smith, I. and Boyns, T. 'British Management Theory and Practice: The Impact of Fayol', *Management Decision,* vol. 43, no. 10, 2005, pp 1317–34.

64. Dale, E. *Management: Theory and Practice,* fourth edition, McGraw-Hill (1978).

65. Burnes, B. *Managing Change: A Strategic Approach to Organisational Dynamics,* second edition, Financial Times/Prentice Hall (1996).

66. Hatchuel, A. and Segrestin, B. 'A century old and still visionary: Fayol's innovative theory of management', *European Academy of Management*', June 2018, pp. 1–14.

67. Pugh, D. S. and Hickson, D. J. *Writers on Organisations,* sixth edition, Penguin Books (2007).

68. Holmblad Brunsson, K. 'Some Effects of Fayolism', *International Studies of Management and Organization,* vol. 38, no. 1, 2008, pp. 30–47.

69. George, C.S. Jr. *The History of Management Thought,* second edition, Prentice Hall (1972).

70. Davidson, P. and Griffin, R. W. *Australia in a Global Context,* John Wiley and Sons (2000).

71. Fayol, H. (1916). In Pugh, D. S. and Hickson, D. J. (2007).

72. Rees, W. D. and Porter, C. *The Skills of Management,* fifth edition, Thomson Learning (1996).

73. McLean, J. 'Fayol – standing the test of time', *British Journal of Administrative Management,* Spring, 2011, pp. 32–3.

74. Rausch, E. 'A practical focus on leadership and management – for research, education and management development', *Management Decision,* vol. 43, no. 7/8, 2005, pp. 988–1000.

75. Mintzberg, H. *The Rise and Fall of Strategic Planning,* Prentice Hall (1994).

76. Stonehouse, G. H. and Pemberton, J. D. 'Learning and knowledge management in the intelligent organisation', *Participation and Empowerment: An International Journal,* vol. 7, no. 5, 1999, pp. 131–44.

77. Hill, C. W. L. and McShane, S. *Principles of Management,* McGraw-Hill (2008).

78. Yukl, G. and Lespringer, R. 'Why Integrating the Leading and Managing Role is Essential for Organizational Effectiveness', *Organizational Dynamics,* 34, No. 4, 2005, pp. 361–75.

79. Dabos, G. E. and Rousseau, D. M. 'Mutuality and Reciprocity in the Psychological Contracts of Employees and Employers', *Journal of Applied Psychology,* 89, 2004, pp. 52–72.

80. Hui, C., Lee. C. and Rousseau, D. 'Psychological contract and organizational citizenship behaviour in China: Investigating generalizability and instrumentality', *Journal of Applied Psychology,* 89, 2004, pp. 311–21.

81. Fells, M. J. 'Fayol stands the test of time', *Journal of Management History,* vol. 6, no. 8, 2000, pp. 345–60.

82. Mintzberg, H. 'The Manager's Job: Folklore and Fact', *Harvard Business Review,* vol. 53, no. 4, 1975, pp. 49–61.

83. Hales, C. *Managing Through Organization: The Management Process, Forms of Organization and the Work of Managers*, Routledge (1993).

Chapter 12
Patterns of structure and workplace design

Structure provides the framework of an organisation to make possible effective performance of key activities and support the efforts of staff.

Learning outcomes

After completing this chapter you should have enhanced your ability to:

- detail the purpose and importance of organisation structure;
- review underlying principles and dimensions of structure;
- explain formal organisational relationships between individuals;
- relate the nature of role structure of the organisation and role conflict;

- review the nature of the contingency approach and main contingency models;
- assess the changing nature of the workplace;
- debate realities of structure and organisational behaviour.

Outline chapter contents

Overview topic map: Chapter 12 – Patterns of structure and workplace design

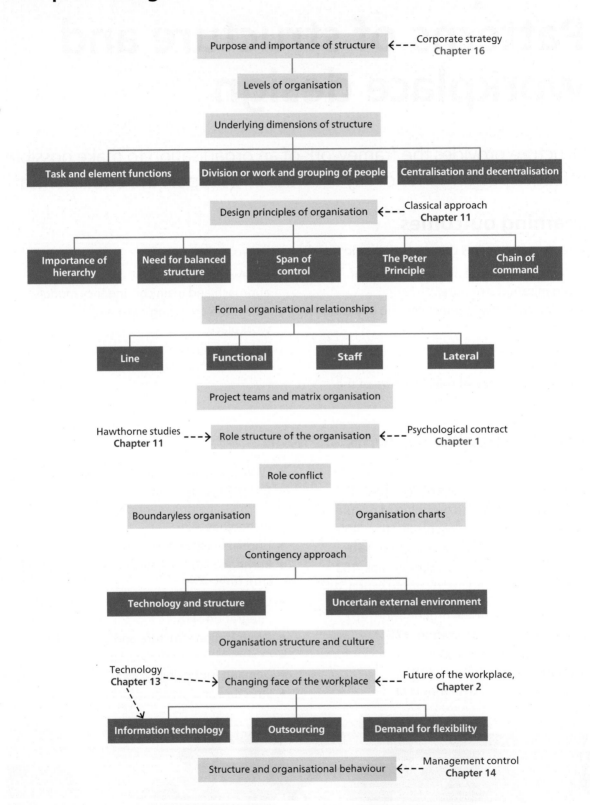

Workplace design is highly important

Before commencing to read this chapter how much emphasis would YOU place on the importance of effective structure to organisational performance?

Purpose and importance of structure

Structure is the defining feature of a work organisation. Whatever the goals and objectives, systems of management or quality of its members, an organisation will not achieve optimum performance without a sound and appropriate structure. The purpose of structure is the division of work among members of the organisation, and the co-ordination of their activities so they are directed towards the goals and objectives of the organisation. It is by means of structure that the work of the organisation is carried out. Structure defines tasks and responsibilities, work roles and relationships, and channels of communication.

Structure provides the framework for the activities of the organisation and must harmonise with its goals and objectives, and environmental influences, the continued development of the business, and the management of opportunities and risks. There is a close relationship between organisation structure and corporate strategy, **discussed in Chapter 16.** It is by means of the organisation's structure that its goals and objectives are attained.

The purpose of structure may be summarised as to provide for:

- economic and efficient performance of the organisation and level of resource utilisation;

- monitoring activities of the organisation;

- accountability for areas of work undertaken by groups and individual members of the organisation;

- co-ordination of different parts of the organisation and different areas of work;
- flexibility in order to respond to future demands and developments, and to adapt to changing environmental influences; and
- social satisfaction of members working in the organisation.[1]

It is not easy to describe, in a positive manner, what constitutes a 'good' or effective organisation **structure** although the negative effects of a poorly designed structure can be identified more easily. In his discussion on the principles of organisation and co-ordination, *Urwick* (writing in 1947) suggests a large proportion of friction and confusion may be traced back directly to faulty organisation in the structural sense. 'Lack of design is Illogical, Cruel, Wasteful and Inefficient'.[2]

More recent writers have drawn similar conclusions as to the consequences of badly designed structure. The importance of good structure is also emphasised by *Child* who maintains the form of organisation employed is not just a means to achieving better economic performance but also carries a message about how to treat other people. Child points out the consequences of structure deficiencies as exacerbating problems of (1) low motivation and morale, (2) late and inappropriate decisions, (3) conflict and lack of co-ordination, (4) a generally poor response to new opportunities and external change and (5) rising costs.[3]

The functions of the formal structure, and the activities and defined relationships within it, exist independently of the members of the organisation who carry out the work. Structure should be designed, therefore, so as to encourage both the willing participation of members of the organisation and effective organisational performance. *Lord Forte,* for example, has drawn attention to the importance of the human element in organisation structure and lines and squares and the diagrams mean nothing unless within these squares you have people deeply involved with the business.[4]

Structure, though, is not an end in itself but a means of improving organisational performance. According to *Drucker,* it is the correct design of structure that is of most significance in determining organisational performance.

> **Good organisation structure does not by itself produce good performance. But a poor organisation structure makes good performance impossible, no matter how good the individual managers may be. To improve organisation structure . . . will therefore always improve performance.**[5]

 To what extent do YOU agree with Drucker that correct design of structure is of most significance in determining organisational performance?

Levels of organisation

Determination of policy, decision-making, execution of work, and exercise of authority and responsibility are carried out by different people at varying levels of seniority throughout the structure. In small organisations, these activities tend to be less distinct, but in the larger organisations it is possible to view organisations in terms of three broad interrelated levels in the hierarchical structure: the **technical level**, the **managerial level** and the **community level**.[5]

The **technical level** is concerned with specific operations and discrete tasks and actual job or tasks to be done. Examples are the physical production of goods, administrative processes giving direct service to the public in government departments, and actual process of teaching in an educational establishment. The technical level interrelates with the **managerial** (or organisational) **level** concerned with the co-ordination and integration of work at the technical level. This level is sometimes further viewed in terms of junior, middle or senior management. In turn, the managerial level interrelates with the **community** (or institutional) **level,** concerned with broad objectives and the operations of the organisation as a whole including the wider environment. Examples of the community level are the board of directors of joint stock companies, governing bodies of educational establishments, and trustees of non-profit organisations.

Blurring of differentiation

Effective co-ordination and communication among the three levels is essential for successful performance. Decisions taken at the institutional level determine objectives for the managerial level, and decisions at the managerial level set objectives for the technical level *(see Figure 12.1)*. In practice however there is not always a clear division. Empowerment, an increase in knowledge workers and technological advances have contributed to lack of clear distinction between policy, management and the execution of work. Flatter structures, the dismantling of hierarchies and virtual teams all contribute to a further blurring of differentiation.

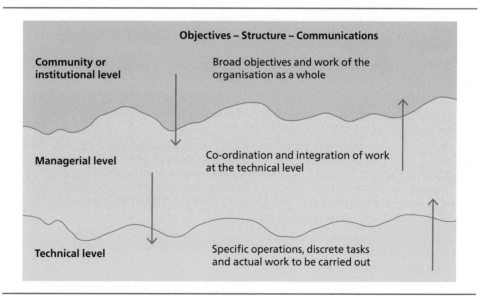

Figure 12.1 Interrelated levels of organisation

The three broad levels do, however, provide a basis for a critical analysis of the interrelated activities of the organisation.

Underlying dimensions of structure

There are many variables that influence the most appropriate pattern of organisation structure. There is nevertheless an underlying need to establish a framework of order by which the work to be undertaken is accomplished successfully. **Note** that these principles and considerations are not prescriptive but present a series of important decision points for design of organisation structure, or in reviewing the effectiveness of an existing structure **(see Figure 12.2).**

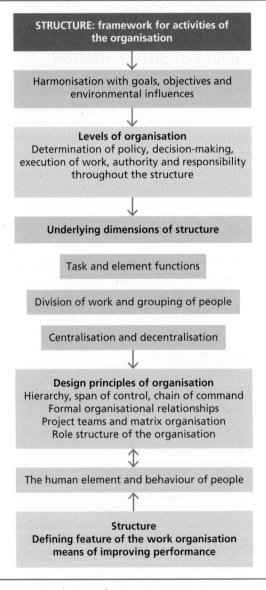

Figure 12.2 Considerations in design of organisation structure

Task and element functions

In order to produce some good, or provide some service, there are four essential functions that the organisation must perform.

1. The good or service must be developed.
2. Something of value must be created: the production or manufacture of a product or provision of a service.
3. The products or services must be marketed and distributed or made available to those who are to use them.
4. Finance is needed in order to make available resources for the development, creation and distribution of the products or services provided.

These essential functions, what *Woodward* refers to as the **'task' functions**, are the basic activities of the organisation related to the actual completion of the productive process and directed towards specific and definable end results.[6] Other activities of the organisation not directed towards specific and definable ends are supportive of the task functions and an intrinsic part of the management process. These are referred to as **'element' functions** and include, for example, human resources, public relations, quality control and maintenance. In certain organisations, however, noticeably in service industries involving direct customer contact, human resource management can arguably be seen as closely associated with a task function.[7]

Failure to distinguish between the two types of functions can lead to confusion in the planning of structure and in the relationship between members of the organisation. For example, in her study of the management organisation of firms in this country, Woodward comments on the bad relationships between accountants and other managers referred to during the study. One reason for this hostility was the bringing together of two quite separate financial functions essential to the efficient operation of a business.

> **People concerned with works accounting tended to assume responsibility for end results that was not properly theirs; they saw their role as a controlling and sanctioning one rather than as a servicing and supportive one. Line managers resented this attitude and retaliated by becoming aggressive and obstructive.**[8]

How far do YOU identify with the importance of differentiating task and element functions? How does this difference manifest itself in your university?

Division of work and grouping of people

Within the formal structure work has to be divided among its members and different jobs related to each other. The division of work and the grouping together of people should, wherever possible, be organised by reference to some common characteristic

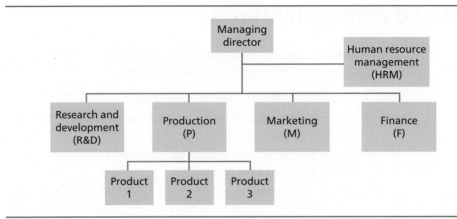

Figure 12.3 Division of work by major purpose or function

which forms a logical link between the activities involved. Work can be divided, and activities linked together, in a variety of ways.

- **Major purpose or function** – The most common basis for grouping activities is according to specialisation, the use of the same set of resources, or the shared expertise of members of staff. It is a matter for decision in each organisation as to which activities are important enough to be organised into separate functions, departments or sections. Work may be departmentalised and based, for example, on differentiation between task and element functions, discussed above, *see* **Figure 12.3.**

- **Product or service** – Contributions of different specialists are integrated into separate, semi-autonomous units with collective responsibility for a major part of the business process or for a complete cycle of work. An example is the bringing together of all activities concerned with a particular production line, product or service. Another example is a hospital where staff are grouped together in different units dealing with particular treatments such as accidents and emergency, medical or surgery, *see* **Figure 12.4.**

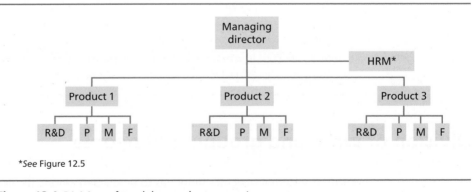

*See Figure 12.5

Figure 12.4 Division of work by product or service

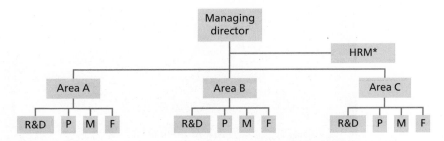

*In the case of division of work by product or service, or by geographical location, it is possible that certain aspects of support services, such as human resource management, may also be assigned to individual units of the organisation. However, the main responsibility of the HRM manager, as a separate entity, is to provide a specialist advisory service to all unit managers and to ensure implementation of HRM policy throughout the organisation as a whole. Responsibility for the main aspects of the HRM function is likely to remain, therefore, in a direct line of authority from top management.

Figure 12.5 Division of work by location

- **Location** – Different services are provided by area or geographical boundaries according to particular needs or demands, the convenience of consumers, or for ease of administration. Examples are the provision of local authority services for people living in a particular locality, sales territories for business firms or the grouping of a number of retail shops under an area manager, *see* **Figure 12.5.**

- **Nature of work performed** – Where there is some special common feature of the work such as the need for speedy decisions, accuracy, confidentiality/security, or where local conditions require first-hand knowledge not immediately available elsewhere. Another example may be the grouping of equipment or machinery which is noisy or which produces dust, fumes or unpleasant odours.

- **Common time scales** – Division according to time scales, for example shift working. In a further education college there may be separate departments or groupings to deal with the different needs of full-time day and part-time evening students. In a hotel, activities in the kitchen tend to be short-term with a range of different tasks to be co-ordinated very quickly. Other activities, for example forecasting future room occupancy, are longer-term decisions and subject to different organisational requirements.

- **Nature of staff employed** – Division based on a particular skill, special qualification or responsibility – for example, the division of work between surgeons, doctors and nurses, or between barristers, solicitors and legal executives. Work may also be planned deliberately to give a variety of tasks and responsibilities to provide improved job satisfaction or to assist in the training of staff.

- **Customers of clients served** – Separate groups may be established to deal with different consumer requirements – for example, division between trade or retail customers or between home or export sales. In hospitals there are different groupings dealing with, for example, patients in the gynaecology, geriatric and children's wards. Government departments are often grouped according to whom services are provided for example the unemployed, low-pay families, students, or senior citizens.

Structure of work to suit the organisation

Centralisation and decentralisation

The balance between centralisation and decentralisation is one of the major debates in organisation structure. Advantages often claimed for centralisation tend to relate to economic and administrative considerations. However, such advantages frequently are not realised fully, and do not lead to an actual improvement in service. There are a number of contrary arguments against centralisation, including the criticism that it creates a more mechanistic structure and may result in lengthening the chain of command. There are also positive arguments, which tend to relate more to behavioural considerations, in favour of decentralisation (*see* **Figure 12.6**).

Advantages of centralisation

- the easier implementation of a common policy for the organisation as a whole;
- provides a consistent strategy across the organisation;
- prevents sub-units from becoming too independent;
- makes for easier co-ordination and management control;
- improved economies of scale and a reduction in overhead costs;
- greater use of specialisation, including better facilities and equipment:
- improved decision-making, which might otherwise be slower and a result of compromise because of diffused authority.

Advantages of decentralisation

- enables decisions to be made closer to the operational level of work:
- increased responsiveness to local circumstances;
- improved level of personal customer service;
- more in keeping with developments in flatter and more flexible structures;
- support services, such as adminstration, are more likely to be effective if provided as close as possible to the activities they are intended to serve;
- provides opportunities for training and development in management;
- usually, it has an encouraging effect on the motivation and morale of staff.

Figure 12.6 Advantages of centralisation or decentralisation

Extent of decentralisation

Most organisations necessarily involve a degree of **decentralisation** arising from such features as increase in size, geographical separation of different parts of the organisation, or need to extend activities or services to remote areas. Growing emphasis on participation and empowerment also suggest focus attention on decentralisation, but there is still a need to maintain effective co-ordination and control of the activities of the organisation as a whole. Balance between centralisation and decentralisation will be affected by such factors as importance of decision-making, urgency of the situation and time scales, technological developments, changes in structure, the prevailing organisational climate and the nature of staff employed. Decentralisation generally tends to be easier to implement in private sector organisations than in the public sector organisations where there is a greater demand for the accountability of their operations, regularity of procedures and uniformity of treatment.

Would YOU agree that the extent of decentralisation is often under recognised by organisations as a major factor influencing customer service and staff satisfaction?

Design principles of organisation

As mentioned in **Chapter 11,** the classical writers placed emphasis on the requirements of the formal organisation and the search for a common set of principles applicable to all circumstances. The idea of common sets of principles on organisation and management has been subject to much criticism but it is difficult to argue against providing general guidance on the structuring of organisations. The basic concepts can be of value to the practical manager, **if modified to suit the demands of the particular situation.** Three of the more specific principles of general interest in the structuring of organisations are: (i) the hierarchy; (ii) the span of control; and (iii) the chain of command.

Importance of the hierarchy

Early writers on management drew attention to the importance of the **hierarchy** – clearly delineated levels of authority throughout the organisation as a means of co-ordination and control. However, the changing nature of work has led to discussion on the continuing role and importance role of the hierarchy and reliance on their perceived formal authority within the structure of the organisation.

Importance of the hierarchy is emphasised strongly by *Drucker,* who asserts that 'One hears a great deal today about "the end of the hierarchy". This is blatant nonsense. In any institution there has to be a final authority, that is, a "boss" – someone who can make the final decisions and who can expect them to be obeyed.'[9] However, contrary to the view of Drucker, *Cloke and Goldsmith* question whether we are accustomed to and have accepted that hierarchy, rules and managers are an essential part of organisational life. Have managers been seduced by the apparent power over others that a hierarchical organisation offers and by the disproportionate rewards it can provide to those at the top? If so, this is depriving individuals of the chance to develop themselves to their full potential and cluttering organisations with wasteful and counter-productive processes.[10]

Holocracy

Attention on decentralisation has given rise to the idea of 'holocracy', organisational governance in a structure without any hierarchy. Authority and decision-making is invested to self-managing teams and wider roles throughout the organisation. Robertson suggests holocracy replaces conventional hierarchy with a radical change in the nature of work. Holocracy is about processes not people. Attention is not on personal positional power and authority is distributed to roles not to people. The whole process is intended to be highly impersonal. For example, meetings are supposed to be factual and based on qualifying questions rather than personal opinions.[11]

Span of control

Span of control refers to the number of subordinates who report **directly** to a given manager or supervisor. It does not refer to the total of subordinate operating staff, those who report first to another person. Hence the term 'span of responsibility' is sometimes considered to be more appropriate. *V. A. Graicunas* developed a mathematical formula for the span of control.

$$R = n\left\{\frac{2^n}{2} + n - 1\right\}$$

The limitation of the number of subordinates who can effectively be supervised is based on the total of direct and cross relationships, where n is the number of subordinates, and R is the number of interrelationships. For example, with five subordinates the total number of interrelationships requiring the attention of the manager is 100; with six subordinates the number of interrelationships is 222.[12]

If span of control is **too wide,** it becomes difficult to supervise subordinates effectively. With larger groupings, informal leaders and sub-groups or cliques are more likely to develop. If the span of control is **too narrow,** this may present a problem of co-ordination and consistency in decision-making and hinder effective communications. Morale and initiative of subordinates may suffer as a result of too close a level of supervision. Narrow spans of control can lead to additional levels of authority in the organisation creating an unnecessarily long chain of command.

Chain of command

This refers to the number of different levels in the structure of the organisation. The **chain of command** establishes the vertical graduation of authority and responsibility, and framework of relationships in an unbroken line down from the top of the organisation. Every person should know their position within the structure of the organisation. Most organisation charts demonstrate that this principle is used widely as a basis for organisational design. It seems generally accepted that for reasons of morale and to help decision-making and communications there should be as few levels as possible in the chain of command. There is danger in adding to the structure in such a way that it results in increased hierarchical authority and control, and leads to the risk of empire building and the creation of unnecessary work in justification of the new position. However, if efforts are made to reduce the number of levels this may bring about an increase in the span of control.

Need for a balanced structure

The balance of span of control and chain of command determines the overall pyramid shape of the organisation and whether the hierarchical structure is 'flat' or 'tall' **(see Figure 12.7**). Broader spans of control and fewer levels of authority result in a **flat hierarchical structure** as tends to be found, for example, in universities. Narrower spans of control and more levels of authority result in a **tall hierarchical structure** as tends to be found, for example, in the civil service or the armed forces. There is no one, ideal combination of span of control and scalar chain. This depends upon the particular situation for each organisation, but it is important to provide an appropriate, balanced structure.

The Peter Principle

An interesting situation which can arise from the hierarchical structure is that of occupational incompetence. The analysis of hundreds of cases led to the formulation of the '**Peter Principle**', which is:

In a hierarchy every employee tends to rise to their level of incompetence.[13]

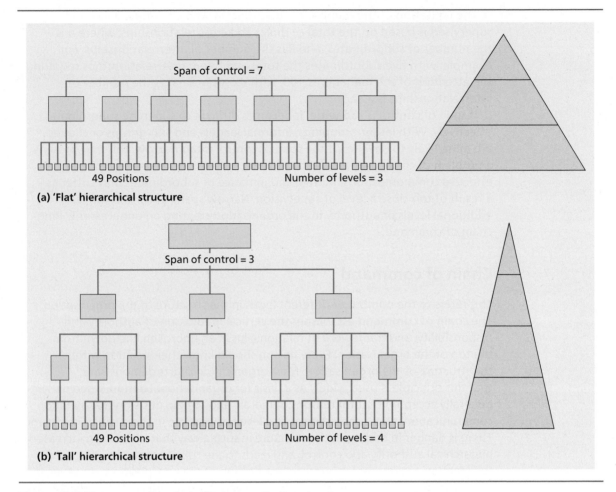

Figure 12.7 How span of control affects organisation structure

Employees competent in their position are promoted and competence in each new position qualifies for promotion to the next highest position until a position of incompetence is reached. The principle is based on perceived incompetence at all levels of every hierarchy – political, legal, educational and industrial – and ways in which employees move upwards through a hierarchy and what happens to them after promotion.

Ann Franke (Chief Executive CMI) refers to the dangers of 'accidental managers'. Someone well trained in their core function and excels so is promoted but they fail to grasp how managerial responsibility has changed their role and carry on as usual.[14]

To what extent do YOU believe medium- or large-scale organisations can ever function effectively without a defined hierarchical structure?

Formal organisational relationships

In any organisation structure certain formal relationships between individuals will arise from the defined pattern of responsibilities. There is often confusion over the meaning of different terms and their implications for organisational structure, but these **individual relationships** may be identified as:

- line;
- functional;
- staff or;
- lateral **(see Figure 12.8).**

In **line relationships**, authority flows vertically down through the structure – the chain of command. There is a direct relationship between superior and subordinate, with each subordinate responsible to only one person. Line relationships are associated with departmental division of work and organisational control. Line managers have authority and responsibility for matters and activities within their own department.

Functional relationships apply to people in specialist or advisory positions. They offer a common service throughout all departments of the organisation but

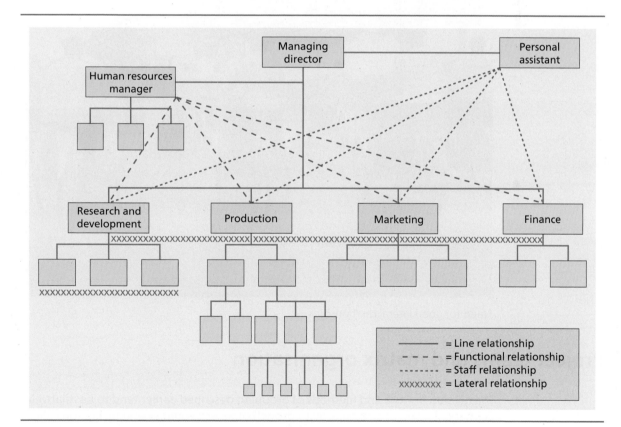

Figure 12.8 Illustration of formal organisational relationships

have no direct authority over those who make use of the service. For example, the HR manager has no direct authority over staff in other departments – this is the responsibility of the line manager. However, as the position and role of the HR manager would have been sanctioned by top management, other staff might be expected to accept the advice which is given.

Staff relationships arise from the appointment of personal assistants, advisers or aides to senior members of staff. They exercise only 'representative' authority and often act in a 'gatekeeper' role. There is no formal relationship with other staff except where delegated authority and responsibility have been given for some specific activity. In practice however personal assistants often have influence over other staff. This may be because of the close relationship between the personal assistant and the superior, their knowledge and experience or strength of personality.

Lateral relationships exist between individuals in different departments or sections, especially individuals on the same level. These lateral relationships are based on contact and consultation and are necessary to maintain co-ordination and effective organisational performance. Lateral relationships may be specified formally but in practice they depend upon the co-operation of staff and in effect are a type of informal relationship.

Need for good lateral relationships

Project teams and matrix organisation

The division of work and methods of grouping described earlier tend to be relatively permanent forms of structure. With growth of newer, complex and technologically advanced systems it has become necessary for organisations to provide greater integration of a wide range of functional activities. People with specialist knowledge have to be integrated into the managerial structure. Bureaucratic structures and hierarchies still exist in many organisations but increasing attention is given to the creation of groupings based on project teams and matrix organisation.

A **project team** may be set up as a separate unit on a temporary basis for the attainment of a particular task. Members of staff from different departments or sections are assigned to the team for the duration of a particular project. When this task is completed the project team is disbanded or members of the unit are reassigned to a new task. Project teams may be used for people working together on a common task or to co-ordinate work on a specific project such as the design and development, production and testing of a new product; or the design and implementation of a new system or procedure. For example, project teams have been used in many military systems, aeronautics and space programmes.

The matrix structure

The matrix structure is a combination of:

- departments which provide a stable base for specialised activities and a permanent location for members of staff; and

- units that integrate various activities of different functions on a project team, product, programme, geographical or systems basis.

A **matrix structure** might be adopted in a university or college, for example, with grouping both by common subject specialism, and association with particular courses or programmes of study. The matrix organisation therefore establishes a grid, or matrix, with a two-way flow of authority and responsibility **(see Figure 12.9).** Within

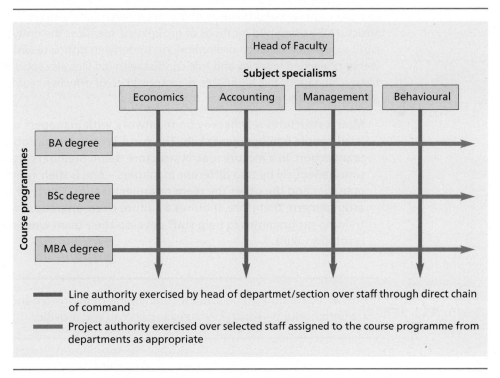

Figure 12.9 Outline of a matrix structure in a university

the functional departments authority and responsibility flow vertically down the line, but the authority and responsibility of the 'project' manager (or course programme manager) flow horizontally across the organisation structure.

A matrix design might be adopted in the following circumstances:

1. **More than one critical orientation to the operations of the organisation.** For example, an insurance company has to respond simultaneously to both functional differentiation (such as life, fire, marine, motor) and to different geographical areas.

2. **A need to process simultaneously large amounts of information.** For example, a local authority social services department seeking help for an individual will need to know where to contact outside agencies (such as police, priest, community relations officer) and at the same time contact internal resources within the organisation (such as the appropriate social worker, health visitor or housing officer).

3. **The need for sharing of resources.** This could be justified only on a total organisational basis such as the occasional or part-time use by individual departments of specialist staff or services.

Developing an effective matrix organisation, however, takes time and a willingness to learn new roles and behaviour; this means that matrix structures are often difficult for management to implement effectively.[15]

Difficulties with matrix structures

Matrix structure offers advantages of flexibility, greater security and control of project information, and opportunities for staff development. There are, however, a number of potential difficulties and problem areas, and can result in a more complex structure. By using two methods of grouping it sacrifices the unity of command and can cause problems of co-ordination. An underlying difficulty with matrix structures is that of divided loyalties and role conflict with individuals reporting simultaneously to two managers; this highlights the importance of effective teamwork. *Senior and Swailes* make the point that:

> Matrix structures rely heavily on teamwork with managers needing high-level people management skills. The focus is on solving problems through team action. In a mature matrix structure, team members are managed simultaneously by two different managers – one is their functional line manager and the other the team or project leader. This type of organizational arrangement, therefore, requires a culture of co-operation, with supportive training programmes to help staff develop their team working and conflict-resolution skills.[16]

How effective do YOU believe the functioning of matrix organisation structures are within your university? What examples can you provide?

Role structure of the organisation

In order for the organisation to achieve its goals and objectives, the work of individual members must be linked into coherent patterns of activities and relationships. This is achieved through the 'role structure' of the organisation. A '**role**' is the expected pattern of behaviours associated with members occupying a particular position within the structure of the organisation. The concept of role differentiation helps to clarify structure and define the pattern of complex relationships within the group. The role, or roles, that the individual plays within the group is influenced by a combination of:

- **situational factors,** such as requirements of the task, nature of technology employed, time scales, style of leadership, position in the communication network; and

- **personal factors** such as values, culture, attitudes, motivation, ability and personality.

However, everyone within a group is expected to behave in a particular manner and to fulfil certain role expectations. The formal organisational relationships (line, functional, staff or lateral) **discussed above** can be seen as forms of role relationships that determine the pattern of interaction with other roles.

A person's role set

In addition to role relationships with members of their own group – peers, superiors, subordinates – the individual will have a number of role-related relationships with outsiders – for example, members of other work groups, trade union officials, suppliers, consumers. This is a person's '**role set**'. The role set comprises the range of associations or contacts with whom the individual has meaningful interactions in connection with the performance of their role (*see* **Figure 12.10**).

Role incongruence

This arises when a member of staff is perceived as having a high and responsible position in one respect but a low standing in another respect. Difficulties with role incongruence can arise from the nature of groupings and formal relationships within the structure of the organisation. There are a number of work-related relationships such as doctor and nurse, chef and waiter, senior manager and personal assistant which can give rise to a potential imbalance of authority and responsibility.

Difficulties with role incongruence can also arise within functional relationships: for instance, a relatively junior member of the HR department informing a senior departmental manager that a certain proposed action is contrary to the policies of the organisation. Another example with staff relationships is where a person establishes themselves in the role of 'gatekeeper' to the boss[17] – for instance, where a comparatively junior personal assistant passes on the manager's instructions to one of the manager's more senior subordinates.

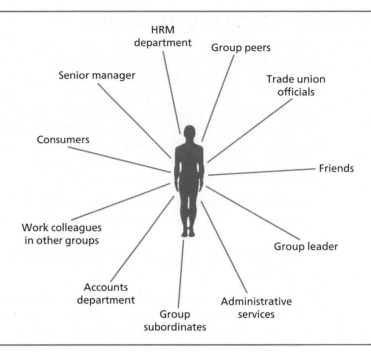

Figure 12.10 Representation of a possible role set in the work situation

Role expectations

Many **role expectations** are prescribed formally and indicate duties and obligations and provide guidelines for expected behaviours. Examples are written contracts of employment, rules and regulations, standing orders, policy decisions, job descriptions, or directives from superiors. Formal role expectations may also be derived clearly from the nature of the task. They may, in part at least, be defined legally: for example under Health and Safety at Work legislation; obligations of a company secretary under the Companies Acts; or responsibilities of a district auditor under the Local Government Acts.

Not all role expectations are prescribed formally, however. There will be certain patterns of behaviour which, although not specified formally, will be expected of members. These informal role expectations may be imposed by the group itself or at least communicated to a person by other members of the group. **Recall the Hawthorne studies discussed in Chapter 11.** Examples include general conduct, mutual support to co-members, attitudes towards superiors, means of communicating, dress and appearance. Members may not always be consciously aware of these informal expectations yet they still serve as important determinants of behaviour. Under this heading could be included the concept of a psychological contract **(discussed in Chapter 1).**

Self-established roles

Some members may have the opportunity to determine largely their own role expectations, where, for example, formal expectations are specified loosely or only in very general terms. Opportunities for **self-established roles** are more likely in senior positions, but also occur within certain professional, technical or scientific groups, for example senior research staff, or where there is a demand for creativity or artistic flair, for example head chefs. Such opportunities may be greater within an 'organic' organisation and will also be influenced by the style of leadership adopted – for example, where a laissez-faire approach is adopted.

How much would YOU prefer a job with opportunities for self-established roles? To what extent is this likely to influence your choice of career?

Role conflict

Patterns of behaviour result from both the person's role and personality. The concept of role focuses attention on aspects of behaviour existing independently of an individual's personality. **Role conflict** arises from inadequate or inappropriate role definition and needs to be distinguished from personality clashes. These arise from incompatibility between two or more people as individuals even though their roles may be defined clearly and understood fully. In practice, the manner in which a person behaves may not be consistent with their expected pattern of behaviours. This inconsistency may be a result of role conflict. Role conflict as a generic term can include:

- role incompatibility;
- role ambiguity;
- role overload;
- role underload.

These are all problem areas associated with the creation of role expectations (*see* Figure 12.11).

- **Role incompatibility** arises when a person faces a situation in which simultaneous different or contradictory expectations create conflict or inconsistency. Compliance with one set of expectations makes it difficult or impossible to comply with other expectations. A typical example concerns the person 'in the middle', such as the supervisor or section head, who faces opposing expectations from workers and from senior management.

- **Role ambiguity** occurs when there is lack of sufficient information or clarity as to the precise requirements of the role and the person is unsure what to do. The person's perception of their role may differ from the expectations of others. It is likely to arise in large, diverse groups or at times of constant change. Uncertainty often relates to such matters as extent of the person's authority and responsibility, standards of work, time for completion, and evaluation and appraisal of performance.

- **Role overload** is when a person faces too many separate roles or too great a variety of expectations. This leads to a conflict of priority and potential stress. Some writers distinguish between role overload and work overload. Role overload is seen as the total role set and implies that the person has too many separate roles to handle. Work overload is a problem of quantity with too many expectations of a single role.

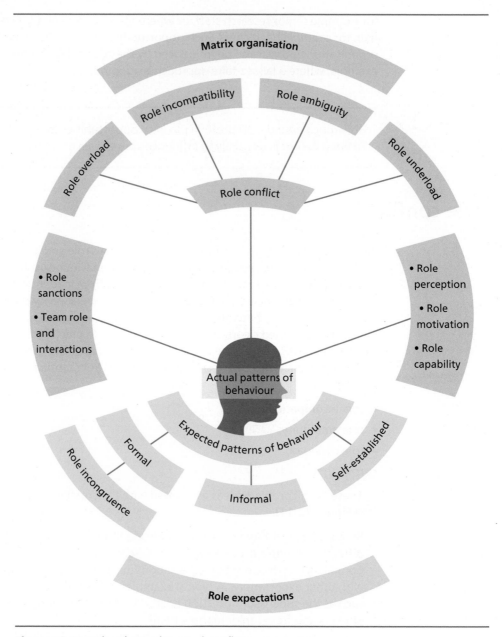

Figure 12.11 Role relationships and conflicts
Source: based on Miner, J. B. *Management Theory*, Macmillan (1971), p. 47.

- **Role underload** can arise when the prescribed role expectations fall short of the person's perception of their role. The person may feel their role is not demanding enough and that they have the capacity to undertake a larger or more varied role, or an increased number of roles. Role underload may arise, for example, when a new member of staff is first appointed or from the initial effects of empowerment.

Role conflict and matrix organisation

Problems of role conflict can often arise from the matrix form of organisation **(discussed above)** and, for example, from the use of flexible project teams. Where staff are assigned temporarily, and perhaps on a part-time basis, from other groups this creates a two-way flow of authority and responsibility. Unless role differentiations are defined clearly this can result in conflicting expectations from the manager of the person's own functional grouping and from the manager of the project team (role incompatibility). It can also lead to uncertainty about the exact requirements of the part the person is expected to play as a member of the project team (role ambiguity). The combinations of expectations from both managers may also result in role overload.

Application of sanctions

Organisations apply a number of sanctions as inducements for members to contribute and behave in accordance with their prescribed roles. Typical examples are: an increase in salary or wages; promotion; upgrading to the latest equipment or technology; a sideways or downwards move in the organisation structure; the threat of dismissal. A number of less direct sanctions may also be adopted; for example size of office or work area, allocation of unpopular tasks, opportunities for paid overtime, priority for holiday rotas. Role sanctions may also be applied through operation of the informal organisation. Members of the group may impose their own sanctions and discipline individuals who contravene the norms of the group or expected standards of behaviour.

Boundaryless organisation

The idea of boundaryless organisation originated with Jack Welch, former chairman of General Electric, in the 1990s. Despite the enormous size of the organisation, the idea was to eliminate internal barriers: both vertical boundaries between different levels of the management hierarchy and horizontal boundaries between different departments; and external barriers between the company, suppliers and customers. The concept has been popularised by *Ashkenas* and colleagues.[18] A number of organisations have since attempted to follow this idea.

Francesco and Gold refer to the globalisation of the economy that has created new types of structures such as the 'boundaryless organization' which breaks the traditional demarcations of authority and task specialisation associated with bureaucracies and other structures. 'Features of a boundaryless organization include a widespread use of project teams, interfunctional teams, networks, and similar structural mechanisms, thus reducing boundaries that typically separate organizational functions and hierarchical levels.' A key management challenge is the socialisation and training of members of the organisation away from the effects of the bureaucratic mentality. Although there is still some form of authority structure, and task and political boundaries, such boundaries are flexible and unlike the rigid horizontal and vertical dimensions of traditional organisations.[19]

Advances in information communications technology and the growth of social networking together with the general movement towards less rigid chains of command and empowered teamwork has given impetus to the boundaryless organisation.

How practical do YOU think the idea of boundaryless organisations? Do you think you would enjoy working in such an organisation?

Organisation charts

The organisation may be depicted in the form of a chart that provides a pictorial representation of the overall shape and structural framework. Some charts are very sketchy and give only a minimum amount of information. Other charts give varying amounts of additional detail such as an indication of the broad nature of duties and responsibilities of the various units.

Charts are usually displayed in a traditional, vertical form such as those already depicted in Figures 12.7 and 12.8. They can, however, be displayed either horizontally with the information reading from left to right, or concentrically with top management at the centre. There are, however, a number of limitations with traditional organisation charts. They depict only a static view of the organisation, and show how it looks and what the structure should be. Neither do charts show the extent of personal delegation from superior to subordinates, or the precise relationships between line and staff positions. Organisation charts can become out of date quickly and are often slow to be amended to reflect changes in the actual structure.

Despite the limitations organisation charts are useful in explaining the outline structure of an organisation. They may be used as a basis for the analysis and review of structure, indicating apparent weaknesses in structure and formulating changes. As *Rosenfeld and Rosen* point out:

> **Probably the most immediate and accessible way to describe any formal organisation is to outline its structure. For the student of organisations, knowledge of its structure is indispensable as a first step to understanding the processes which occur within it. When asked to describe their organisation, managers will frequently sketch an organisation chart to show how their organisation 'works'.[20]**

> **A summary of formal organisations and organisation charts is set out in the concept map in Figure 12.12.**

Contingency approach

Earlier approaches to organisation believed in one best form of structure and tended to study the organisation in isolation from its environment. According to *Bouchikhi and Kimberly,* a feature that differentiates the nineteenth-, twentieth- and twenty-first-century management paradigms is that as customers and shareholders have been more proactive, market-driven strategies and flexible organisations have developed as a consequence. The changing nature of the work environment, the increasing demands for flexibility and concerns with the contextual factors influencing structure have drawn attention to the contingency approach to organisational design.[21]

The contingency approach takes the view that there is no one best, universal structure. There are a large number of variables, or situational factors, which influence organisational design and performance. The contingency approach emphasises the need for flexibility. *Lynch* points out: 'Every organisation is unique

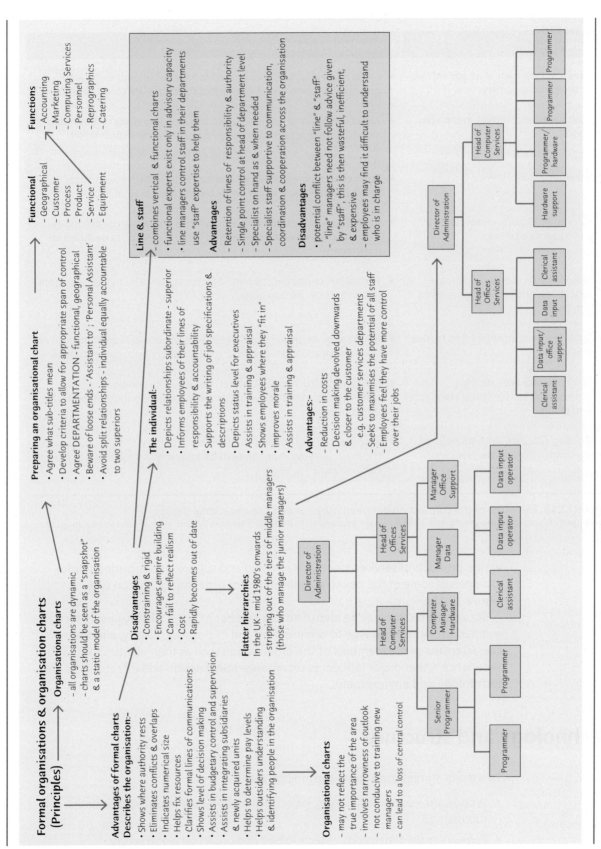

Figure 12.12 Formal organisations and organisation charts

Source: Copyright ©2018 The Virtual Learning Materials Workshop. Reproduced with permission.

Purpose	Implications for organisation design
• 'Ideas factory' such as an advertising or promotions agency	• Loose, fluid structure with limited formalised relationships. As it grows in size, however, more formal structures are usually inevitable
• Multinational company in branded goods	• Major linkage and resource issues that need carefully co-ordinated structures, e.g. on common suppliers or common supermarket customers for separate product ranges
• Government civil service	• Strict controls on procedures and authorisations. Strong formal structures to handle major policy directions and legal issues
• Non-profit-making charity with a strong sense of mission	• Reliance on voluntary members and their voluntary contributions may require a flexible organisation with responsibility devolved to individuals
• Major service company such as a retail bank or electricity generating company	• Formal structures but supported by some flexibility so that variations in demand can be met quickly
• Small business attempting to survive and grow	• Informal, willingness to undertake several business functions such as selling or production, depending on the short-term circumstances
• Health service with strong professional service ethics, standards and quality	• Formalised structure that reflects the seniority and professional status of those involved while delivering the crucial complex service provisions
• Holding company with subsidiaries involved in diverse markets	• Small centralised headquarters acting largely as a banker, with the main strategic management being undertaken in individual companies

Figure 12.13 Examples of the connection between purpose and organisational design
Source: Lynch, R. *Strategic Management,* sixth edition, Pearson Education (2012), p. 464. Reprinted by permission of Pearson Education Ltd.

in size, products or services, people, leadership and culture' and provides helpful examples of some of the possible implications for organisation design **(*see* Figure 12.13).**[22]

Situational factors may be identified in a number of ways. Obvious bases for comparison include the type of organisation and its purpose, history, and the characteristics of the members of the organisation such as their abilities, skills and experience. Other major influences on organisational design and effectiveness are **technology and environment.**

Technology and structure

Two major studies concerning technology are:

- Woodward – patterns of organisation, production technology and business success; and
- Perrow – main dimensions of technology and organisation structure.

Technology and structure

Woodward – structure and production technology

A major study of the effects of technology on organisation structure was carried out by *Joan Woodward* in the 1950s.[23] Her pioneering work presents the results of empirical study of 100 manufacturing firms in south-east Essex and the relationships between the application of principles of organisation and business success. The main thesis was:

> **that industrial organisations which design their formal organisational structures to fit the type of production technology they employ are likely to be commercially successful.[24]**

Firms were divided into nine different types of production systems, from least to most technological complexity, with three main groupings of:

- unit and small batch production;
- large batch and mass production;
- process production.

The Woodward study emphasised importance of the relationship between production technology and organisation structure. Another important finding was the nature of the actual cycle of manufacturing and the relationship between three key 'task' functions of development, production and marketing. The most critical of these functions varied according to the type of production system **(see Figure 12.14).** Woodward acknowledges technology is not the only variable that affects an organisation but is one that could be isolated more easily for study. She does, however, draw attention to the importance of technology, organisation and business success.

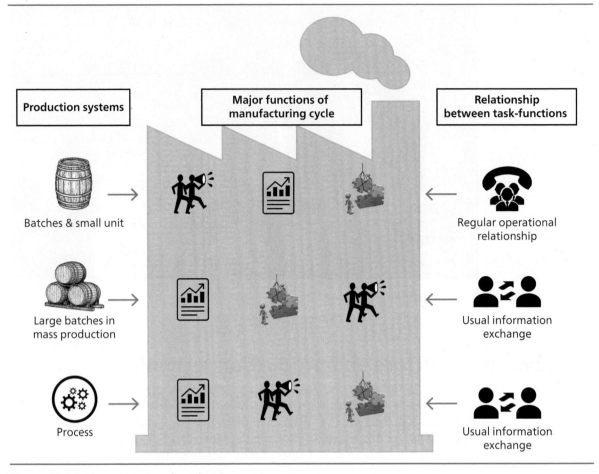

Figure 12.14 Characteristics of production systems
Source: Woodward, J. *Industrial Organization: Theory and Practice,* second edition, Oxford University Press (1980), p. 128.

Perrow – major dimensions of technology

The work by Woodward was extended by *Perrow,* who drew attention to two major dimensions of technology:

- the extent to which the work task is predictable or variable; and
- the extent to which technology can be analysed.[25]

Variability refers to the number of exceptional or unpredictable cases and the extent to which problems are familiar. For example, a mass production factory is likely to have only a few exceptions but the manufacture of a designer range of clothing would have many exceptional and unpredictable cases. The **analysis of technology** refers to the extent to which task functions are broken down and highly specified, and extent to which problems can be solved in recognised ways or by the use of routine procedures. Combining the two dimensions provides a continuum of technology from routine to non-routine. With non-routine technology there are a large number of exceptional cases involving difficult and varied problem-solving. The two dimensions of variability and the analysis of problems can also be represented as a matrix **(*see* Figure 12.15**).

		Task predictability or variability	
		Few exceptions	Many exceptions
Analysis of technology	Problems cannot be analysed	*Craft technology* Making a whole product probably in the same way e.g. fine glassware	*Non-routine technology* e.g. psychiatric care in a mental hospital, manufacture of nuclear fuel systems
	Problems can be analysed	*Routine technology* Manufacture of standard products; highly mechanised mass production	*Engineering technology* e.g. made-to-order machines such as electric components; research consultancy

Figure 12.15 Matrix of technology variables
Source: Adapted from Perrow, C. *Organizational Analysis: A Sociological View*, Tavistock Publications (1970), p. 78.

Predictability of work tasks

The classification of each type of technology relates to a particular organisation structure. Perrow suggests that by classifying organisations according to their technology and predictability of work tasks, we should be able to predict the most effective form of structure. Variables such as the discretion and power of sub-groups, the basis of co-ordination and the interdependence of groups result from the use of different technologies.

In the **routine type of organisation** there is minimum discretion at both the technical and supervisory levels, but the power of the middle management level is high, co-ordination is based on planning and there is likely to be low interdependence between the two groups. This arrangement approaches a bureaucratic structure. In the **non-routine type of organisation** there is a high level of discretion and power at both the technical and supervisory levels, co-ordination is through feedback and there is high group interdependence. This model resembles an organic structure.

How far do YOU accept the suggestion that the nature of technology is *the* most important determinant of organisation structure?

Uncertain external environment

Two important studies that focused not just on technology but also on the effects of uncertainty and a changing external environment on the organisation, and its management and structure, are those by:

- Burns and Stalker – divergent systems of management practice, 'mechanistic' and 'organic'; and
- Lawrence and Lorsch – the organisation of specific departments, and the extent of 'differentiation' and 'integration'.

Burns and Stalker – mechanistic and organic structures

The study by *Burns and Stalker* was an analysis of twenty industrial firms in the UK and effects of the external environment on their pattern of management and economic performance. The firms were drawn from a number of industries: a rayon manufacturer, a large engineering company, Scottish firms attempting to enter the electronics field and English firms operating in varying sectors of the electronics industry. From an examination of settings in which the firms operated, Burns and Stalker distinguished five different kinds of environments ranging from 'stable' to 'least predictable'. They also identified two divergent systems of management practice and structure – the 'mechanistic' system and the 'organic' system.[26]

The **mechanistic system** is a more rigid structure unable to deal adequately with rapid change; it is therefore more appropriate for stable environmental conditions. The characteristics of a mechanistic management system are similar to those of bureaucracy. An example might be a traditional high-class and expensive hotel operating along classical lines with an established reputation and type of customer. Major fast-food chains that tend to operate along the lines of scientific management may also require a mechanistic structure.

The **organic system** is a more fluid structure appropriate to changing conditions. It appears to be required when new problems and unforeseen circumstances arise constantly and require actions outside defined roles in the hierarchical structure. A holiday or tourist hotel with an unpredictable demand, offering a range of functions and with many different types of customers, requires an organic structure.

A summary of the characteristics of mechanistic and organic organisations is provided by *Litterer* **(see Table 12.1).**[27]

Burns and Stalker point out that there are intermediate stages between the two extreme systems that represent not a dichotomy but a polarity. The relationship between the mechanistic and organic systems is not rigid. An organisation moving between a relatively stable and a relatively changing environment may also move between the two systems.

'Mixed' forms of organisation structure

Organisations *tend* towards mechanistic or organic, and many will be hybrid – that is, a mix of both mechanistic and organic structures – and often this is an uneasy mix that can lead to tension and conflict. A typical example of a hybrid organisation could be a university with differences in perception between academic staff and non-teaching staff. Academic staff may feel they can work effectively only within an organic structure, and tend to see non-teaching staff as bureaucratic and resistant to novel or different ideas.

Non-teaching staff have an important function in helping to keep the organisation operational and working effectively, and may fail to understand why academics appear to find it difficult, or resent, working within prescribed administrative systems and procedures. Universities may also tend to be more mechanistic at top management level, with an apparent proliferation of committees and sub-committees, because of their dealings with, for example, government bodies and other external agencies.

Lawrence and Lorsch – differentiation and integration

Lawrence and Lorsch undertook a study of six firms in the plastics industry followed by a further study of two firms in the container industry and two firms in the consumer

Table 12.1 Characteristics of mechanistic and organic organisations

Mechanistic		Organic
High, many and sharp differentiations	SPECIALISATION	Low, no hard boundaries, relatively few different jobs
High, methods spelled out	STANDARDISATION	Low, individuals decide own methods
Means	ORIENTATION OF MEMBERS	Goals
By superior	CONFLICT RESOLUTION	Interaction
Hierarchical, based on implied contractual relation	PATTERN OF AUTHORITY CONTROL AND COMMUNICATION	Wide net based upon common commitment
At top of organisation	LOCUS OF SUPERIOR COMPETENCE	Wherever there is skill and competence
Vertical	INTERACTION	Lateral
Directions, orders	COMMUNICATION CONTENT	Advice, information
To organisation	LOYALTY	To project and group
From organisational position	PRESTIGE	From personal contribution

Source: Litterer, J. A. *The Analysis of Organizations,* second edition, John Wiley & Sons (1973), p. 339. Reproduced with permission from the estate of Joseph A. Litterer.

food industry. They extended the work of Burns and Stalker and examined not only the overall structure but also the way in which specific departments were organised to meet different aspects of the firm's external environment. The internal structures of the firms were analysed in terms of 'differentiation' and 'integration'.[28]

- **Differentiation** describes 'the difference in cognitive and emotional orientation among managers in different functional departments' with respect to goal orientation, time orientation, interpersonal relations, and formality of structure.

- **Integration** describes 'the quality of the state of collaboration that exists among departments required to achieve unity of effort by the demands of the environment'. It is the degree of co-ordination and co-operation between different departments with interdependent tasks. Lawrence and Lorsch's view of integration was not minimising differences between departments and provision of a common outlook: it was the recognition that different departments could have their own distinctive form of structure according to the nature of their task, and the use of mediating devices to co-ordinate the different outlooks of departments.

This view of differentiation and integration was confirmed in the subsequent study of firms in the container and consumer food industries. It was concluded that the extent of differentiation and integration in effective organisations will vary according to the demands of the particular environment.

- The more diverse and dynamic the environment, the more the effective organisation will be differentiated and highly integrated.

- In more stable environments, less differentiation will be required but a high degree of integration is still required. Differences in the environment will require different methods of achieving integration.

Given the possibility that different demands of the environment are characterised by different levels of uncertainty, it follows that individual departments may develop different structures.

Integrating mechanisms

Mechanisms used to achieve integration depend on the amount of integration required and difficulty in achieving it. In mechanistic structures, integration may be attempted through use of policies, rules and procedures. In organic structures, integration may be attempted through teamwork and mutual co-operation. As the requirements for the amount of integration increase, additional means may be adopted, such as formal lateral relations, committees and project teams. It is important, however, to achieve the right balance of integration. Too high a level of integration may involve costs that are likely to exceed possible benefits. Too low a level of integration is likely to result in departments 'doing their own thing', poorer quality decisions and failure to make the best use of resources.[29]

Evaluation of contingency approach

The contingency approach draws attention to situational factors that influence variations in the structure of organisations. It is more concerned with differences among organisations than with similarities and rejects assumptions of the classical and human relations approaches, and the idea of one best form of structure. For its part, however, the contingency approach tends to assume that organisational performance is dependent upon the degree to which the structure of the organisation matches the prevailing contingencies.

According to *Robey,* modern contingency theory defines variables ignored in earlier work, and directs attention of the manager to contingencies to be considered in the design of organisation structure. However, the contingency approach runs the risk of concluding that 'it all depends on everything', and the greatest danger is the over-emphasis on differences between organisations and the exclusion of similarities. If the contingency approach is to be useful in guiding organisational design it should not treat every situation as being unique. 'Rather it must strike a balance between universal prescriptions and the statement that all situations are different (which is really no theory at all). Thus, modern theory uses a limited number of contingencies to help explain structural differences between organizations.'[30]

What practical benefits do YOU see from an organisation adopting a contingency approach to structure and what do you think the potential greatest dangers?

Organisation structure and culture

The pervasive nature of culture in terms of both external influences and 'how things are done around here', common values, beliefs and attitudes will have a significant effect on organisational processes including the design of structure. *Schneider and Barsoux* suggest that while managers are ready to accept national culture as an influence on the way people relate to each other, they are less convinced of its real effect on the structure, systems and process of the organisation. However emerging approaches to organisation reflect different cultural assumptions and models of management have diffused across countries at different rates in different ways Schneider and Barsoux discuss the multidimensional impact of culture on organisations and management and maintain that it would be a mistake to base a prediction regarding structure or process on a single cultural dimension.

> **Managers need to recognise that the relationship between cultural dimensions and structure (or processes) are not simple cause–effect links, but instead, are multidetermined. Similar approaches may exist for the same reason. Thus formalized rules and procedures or participative management approaches may have a different raison d'être on different sides of the national border.[31]**

Watson suggests that we must be careful not to treat structures or cultures as if they were solid 'things' that exist separately from the processes and relationships that the two concepts are intended to help us make sense of. The structure of work organisations also involves the wider context of societal structures and cultures. 'Societal structures both contribute to and result from organisational structures.' Watson also refers to the closeness and overlap of structure and culture. 'Many of the processes and practices we observe in an organisation could as readily be said to be part of the structure of the organisation as part of its culture.'[32]

An interesting set of caricatures for organisation charts of different countries is given in **Figure 12.16.**

Changing face of the workplace

Birchall refers to the changing world of organisations and its impact on management. Much of the work undertaken by middle management no longer requires the considerable layers of management. Tasks that used to take up a great deal of management time in hierarchical structures are now possible with minimal supervision or intervention. Much of the organisation's work is carried out in projects. Many managers will find themselves managing people who spend much of their time outside the office. There is a strong move towards the use of consultants. Managers will need to be familiar with electronic networks, the operation of dispersed teams and virtual organisations.[33] **(See also discussion on the future of the workplace in Chapter 2.)**

A similar point is made by *Cloke and Goldsmith* who maintain that management is an idea whose time is up and the days of military command structures are over.

> **Rather than building fixed structures with layers of middle management, many innovative organizations function as matrixed webs of association, networks, and fast-forming high-performance teams . . . The most significant trends we see in the theory and history of management are the decline of the hierarchical, bureaucratic, autocratic management and the expansion of collaborative self-management and organizational democracy.[34]**

Information technology

The impact of **information technology** has significant effects on the structure, management and functioning of most organisations. Information technology

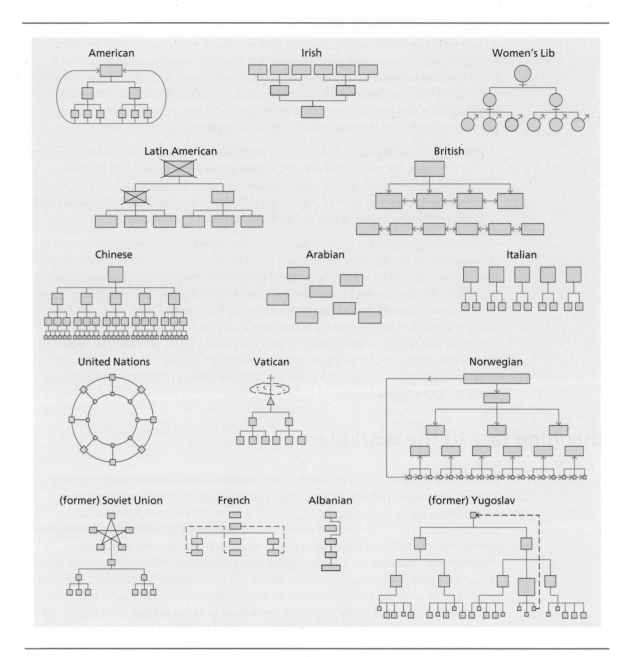

Figure 12.16 Caricatures of organisation charts for different countries
Source: Copyright © Reed Business Information, reprinted with permission.

influences the need for restructuring the organisation and changes to lines of command and authority. Computer-based information and decision-support systems influence choices in design of production or service activities, hierarchical levels and organisation of support staffs. Information technology may influence the centralisation/decentralisation of decision-making and control systems. New technology has typically resulted in a 'flatter' organisational pyramid with fewer levels of management. In the case of new office technology it allows the potential for staff at clerical/operator level to carry out a wider range of functions and to check their own work. The result is a change in the traditional supervisory function and a demand for fewer supervisors. **See also Chapter 13 on Technology and organisations.**

Most manufacturing and industrial organisations still require the physical presence of staff at the place of work. However, for many service or creative organisations such physical presence is not always necessary. For knowledge workers their work can be undertaken from home or where there is access to a computer. Nine-to-five working is no longer enough. With the growth in workspace hosting, businesses will have less need for fixed premises.

Outsourcing

In order to free concentration on core activities, businesses are making increasing use of outsourcing and a wider range of non-core services provided by specialist service providers. A Management Consultancies Association and *Management Today* survey drew attention to changing relationship between organisations and individuals. The survey refers to the significant increase in outsourcing with some of the highest growth in business process outsourcing (BPO) where entire functions are moved outside the organisation. However, one of the consequences of increased outsourcing is that the boundaries of the organisation are becoming blurred.[35]

Thomas reports on the increase in outsourcing legal and company secretarial activities. Outsourcing can address cost reduction, lack of expertise or work that does not make a full-time role but it is a very radical answer to cost cutting. It may cause more difficulties than it solves. When a company outsources an activity, it cannot just forget about it. The company and its directors are still accountable for the activity, and needs to review and monitor the outsourced work.[36] *Overell* suggests that although there is lack of hard evidence of consequences of outsourcing, there are grounds for prospective concern. With outsourcing, power seems to be no longer about direct control but about the ability to coordinate an intricate web of organisations, contractors, sub-contractors, bit-part-players and middlemen known as a supply chain.[37]

According to *The Chartered Management Institute* outsourcing has evolved into a strategic option for businesses of all sizes. Often seen as a threat by employees and an opportunity by organisations, outsourcing has nonetheless become standard practice in many businesses. 'If you focus on identifying the core competencies of your organisation and on what differentiates the company and makes it unique, then those areas which make up the support, administration, routine and internal serving of the organisation will become potential areas for outsourcing.'[38]

Demand for flexibility

The nature of work is being redefined and this has created strong pressures for greater flexibility in patterns of work organisation and in the workforce. Recent advances in computerisation and telecommunications have had a further significant effect on opportunities for flexible working. People can work from almost any geographic location: from head office, a satellite office, a shared access telecentre; or from their home, hotel room or car. An increasingly popular means of teleworking is **telecommuting** where staff work from home with a computer network, telephone and fax.

A recent report from *Acas* comments on an increase in flexibility in the workplace. Employees allowed to work flexibly tend to demonstrate greater commitment and a willingness to give back to the organisation. The report concludes flexible working acts as a motivator for employees but whilst this has positive benefits for teams and organisations in terms of increased productivity there are potential negative effects for the individual such as leading to work intensification.[39]

One-sided flexibility

The Government review of modern working practices (*The Taylor Review*) found the UK labour market characterised by flexibility which is both a strength as well as an obvious risk. Concern was expressed about the way some employers use this flexibility to transfer risk to, and exert control over workers. The review expresses concern over 'one-sided flexibility' and employers must not use flexible working simply to reduce costs. Further consideration should be given to incentivise employers who take a one-sided view of flexibility encouraging them to use fairer and more responsible models.[40]

> What do YOU believe is *the* most significant feature of the changing nature of the workplace, and why? What future changes do you envisage?

Structure and organisational behaviour

There is a clear need to give full attention to the structure of an organisation. However, this is not always an easy task and involves balancing a series of trade-offs. In analysing the effectiveness of structure, consideration should be given to both:

* a definable structure of management, system of order and control, technological requirements, principles of design; and
* social factors, and the needs and demands of the human part of the organisation.

Trends towards flatter hierarchies, teamwork, empowerment, and flexible working has reduced significantly the importance of formal structures. What really matters is that individuals know what is expected of them, work well with other people and perform their tasks successfully. Structure should be designed so as to maintain the balance of the socio-technical system of the organisation and encourage the willing participation of its members.

Whatever its structure, the various operations of the organisation have to be distributed among its members. It is necessary to plan, organise, direct and control their activities. The demand for flexibility and greater freedom and autonomy for individuals raises questions about the extent and nature of delegation and empowerment, the manager–subordinate relationship, and the maintenance of management control within the formal structure of the organisation. **(This is discussed more fully in Chapter 14.)**

Reality of organisational behaviour

Structure or charts do not describe what really happens in work organisations. Individuals differ and people bring their own perceptions, feelings and attitudes towards the organisation, styles of management and their duties and responsibilities. The behaviour of people cannot be studied in isolation and we need to understand interrelationships with other variables that comprise the total organisation, including the social context of the work organisation and the importance of the informal organisation.

How we look

How we work

Figure 12.17 How the organisation should be, compared with how it actually works
Source: Gray, J. L. and Starke, F. A. *Organizational Behavior: Concepts and Applications,* fourth edition, © 1988. Reprinted and electronically reproduced by permission of Pearson Education, Inc., New York.

Gray and Starke provide a humorous but perhaps realistic illustration of how an organisation actually works *(see* **Figure 12.17).**[41] *Heller* also refers to 'the gap between the aims of big company organisations and what actually happens. Organisational form and organisational behaviour are not one and the same thing.'[42]

Critical Thinking Zone
Reflections on the Peter Principle

In this zone, we critically discuss the concept of the Peter Principle and determine whether factors, other than espoused incompetence, are the root cause of poor performance and organisational ineffectiveness.

The concept of the Peter Principle has been caricatured, satirised, refuted and ignored by organisational theorists.[43,44] Five decades after the theory was first proposed, opinion appears to be divided as to whether it is a myth, parody or organisational reality, with which managers in bureaucracies still wrestle. According to Madden,[45] the theory has 'become a hotly debated human resource phenomenon,' despite its original

presentation as a 'sort of absurd-yet-true comic relief to the overworked.' Regardless of the apparent ridicule surrounding the concept, Romaine[44] highlights that theorists have sought to investigate, empiricise and validate the Peter Principle and thus demystify the promotion process and the current and future performance expectations required of promotees, who have been elevated to positions at higher levels in the organisation.

The Peter Principle Debunked

The concept of the Peter Principle was developed by Canadian academic, Dr Laurence J. Peter and co-author

Raymond Hull. Described as the 'Dilbert of its times,' the book, 'The Peter Principle: Why Things Always Go Wrong,' posited that in hierarchies, 'incompetence' is an inevitable by-product of promotion. Individuals are appointed to positions for which they are qualified or have the potential to develop and grow in the role. As they achieve success in that role, they are promoted to higher level positions, each of which presents them with a new set of challenges. In due course, they are promoted to roles in which their previous 'competence' or ability is no longer sufficient to sustain them. While their performance continues to decline, any future promotions cease from that point onwards.[43,46] Peter and Hull[47] (p. 27) thus concluded 'given enough time - and enough ranks in the hierarchy - each employee rises to, and remains at, his level of incompetence.' Their theory infers that all managerial positions in organisations are tenured by individuals who are already incompetent or are approaching their level of incompetence to deal with the increased demands of the job. Beeman[46] describes this reasoning as 'spurious. . . logic' and proffers that other factors contribute to organisational ineffectiveness following promotions are discussed below.

Contributory Factors to Organisational Ineffectiveness

According to Kane,[48] time is an essential prerequisite for new promotees to develop and optimise their performance. He suggests that if incumbent individuals have been in post for several years, they may have strengthened their capability to perform the job through experiential learning and qualifications. They may thus feel more confident, comfortable and settled in that role. In contrast, those who gain promotion face fresh challenges in, and must learn new things for, their elevated role, which may, arguably, be outside their existing knowledge base, skills set and comfort zone. They might also feel somewhat unprepared and inefficient, but one could argue, not necessarily incompetent. In his 1976 article 'The Real Peter Principle: Promotion to Pain,' Hess,[49] an occupational psychologist, contended that incompetence was not the root cause of poor performance. He noted that people are 'often promoted, not to their level of incompetence, but to their level of anxiety and depression. . . it is anxiety and depression, not incompetence, that causes inability to do the job' (p. 12). He suggests that new promotees are often left on their own to cope with the job and its increased demands, without appropriate support from their line managers. This leads to further non-performance, which may eventually end their careers or lead to demotion. However, in many large organisations or bureaucracies, Hess outlines that underperforming individuals may continue in post in a 'semi-functioning capacity' and 'wring little fulfilment from their jobs' (p. 12).

Chan[50] advocates that the promotion system, which is managed by the HRM function, is a key contributor to sub-optimal promotee performance. He proposes that many organisations make promotional decisions based on *current* performance rather than *expected* performance in the higher role. In this instance, the 'best' performer may not necessarily be the ideal candidate for the promotion. Chan therefore caveats that promoting someone based on their current job performance may run the risk of the promotee being unsuitable for the new role; thus, one could argue, catalysing poor performance. In a similar vein, using microdata from research undertaken with a sample of the salesforce in 214 firms, Benson et al.[51] found that promotion decisions privilege current performance over best potential performance to undertake a higher role. They state, 'the most productive worker is not always the best candidate for manager and yet some firms are significantly more likely to promote top frontline sales workers into managerial positions' (p. 30). Not only does the new promotee's performance deteriorate but so does their staff. Thus, Benson et al. caveat 'promoting based on lower-level job skills, rather than managerial skills, can be extremely costly.' Finally, Beeman argues that the notion of 'incompetence' is created and perpetuated by organisational culture and political interplay. He counsels 'incompetent persons are often promoted (or not demoted) for political reasons. . . for fitting in and not making waves.' He also contends that it is the so-called 'old boy network' or the 'politics of the 'ole buddy' system of family connection' that is the 'root of the incompetency problem' in organisations (p. 49).

The Peter Principle: Incompetence or Poor Performance?

To conclude, the arguments presented suggest that the Peter Principle has less to do with 'incompetence' and more to do with poor performance that has been catalysed and exacerbated by a litany of factors, many of which, it could be argued, are outside the promotee's control. Beeman and Hess feel strongly about the original premise of the Peter Principle, which evidence suggests is still being disputed fifty years after its first espousal. Beeman caveats that it has 'nothing to do with reality' (p. 48), while Hess suggests that 'it must be seen for what it is – a gag' (p. 10). Other views advocate that it is the organisation's culture, political objectives and behaviour, along with HR systems and policies that are perpetuating the situation and letting many promotees down by not providing them with the support they need to develop, perform and succeed in their elevated role. Such support may include preparing potential junior, middle and senior managers to step into higher positions through succession planning[52] and providing mentoring and appropriate learning and development programmes for aspiring managers, especially if their current performance, as Chan and Benson et al. espouse, does not make them the best candidate to take on the higher role and they suffer anxiety and depression as a result. With that in mind, Hess concludes that the *real* Peter Principle should state 'a person can be promoted to the point where his psychological problems cause him enough pain to neutralise or exceed his ambition and desire for mastery' (p. 158).

Questions

Based on the above, answer the following questions.

1. The Peter Principle was espoused in 1969, amid controversy that it parodied, among other things, the promotion process in bureaucracies. Using reference to theory and practice, *critically examine* the relevance of the concept to contemporary organisational practice.

2. Theorists suggest that there is a plausible explanation for individuals who experience a reduction in performance following their promotion to a higher level. *Identify* these issues and *explain* the implications for organisational behaviour in the workplace.

3. *What* strategies can the HR function implement to a) counter the potential negative effects of selection decisions that are made during the promotion process, and b) support new promotees to higher positions?

Summary – Chapter 12 'Patterns of structure and workplace design'

Structure is the defining feature of a work organisation and makes possible application of the process of management. Organisations can be viewed in three broad interrelated levels – technical, managerial and community. Attention is focused on certain underlying dimensions of organisation that provide important decision points. Critical decisions arise from distinguishing task and element functions, division of work and grouping of activities, and extent of decentralisation. Design principles include role of the hierarchy, formal organisational relationships, project teams and matrix organisation, and role structure of the organisation. The contingency approach suggests there is no one best structure but a number of situational variables including size, technology, external environment, and the influence of culture. The changing nature of the workplace has drawn attention to influences such as information technology, outsourcing, and demands for flexibility on organisation structure. It is essential to give full attention to structuring an organisation but this is not an easy task. There is no perfect structure. Organisational design involves balancing a series of trade-offs and attention to both the needs of staff and effective performance. Consideration should be given to the realities of structure and organisational behaviour.

Group discussion activities

Undertake each of these activities in small groups as indicated by your tutor. Before you start your discussion establish a non-threatening environment within the group and confirm confidentiality will be honoured.

First, form your own views and then share and compare in open critical discussion with colleagues. Reflect honestly on the extent to which: (i) you influenced the thinking and ideas of your colleagues; and (ii) you were influenced by your colleagues.

To what extent was your group able to reach consensus?

Agree one of your members to produce a brief written summary of the discussion and prepared to present in a plenary session.

Activity 1

(a) Create a visual representation of a role set for university students in general.

(b) How might this role set vary for students on different course or at different levels of their study?

(c) Now look more closely at how the role set represents a map of *yourself*. You could use different sizes and coloured pens to enhance the degree and/or importance of various relationships.

(d) To what extent would family, friends or colleagues outside the university identify with your visualisation?

What conclusions do you reach?

Activity 2

'We trained very hard, but it seemed every time we were beginning to form into teams we would be reorganised. I was to learn later in life that we tend to meet any new situation by reorganising and a wonderful method it can be for creating the illusion of progress while producing confusion, inefficiency and demoralisation' (Gaius Petronius, AD 66).

To what extent do you think this is still true for the modern work organisation? Can you relate an example of reorganisation in your university that has been clearly beneficial?

Activity 3

To cope with the changing nature of the workplace many writers are calling for more creative forms of organisation structure.

(a) Explain how you believe the structure of your university, or other organisation with which you are familiar, affects your level of motivation and performance.

(b) Detail fully, with supporting reasons, how you would design a more creative form of organisation structure.

(c) Where appropriate prepare a revised organisation chart.

Organisational behaviour in action case study

Working structure: Geoplan Spatial Intelligence Limited

Geoplan, a consultancy organisation in Yorkshire and Humberside was in meltdown. As well as a growing number of market and technological challenges, the company was grappling with a structure that didn't work and in which all roads led back to managing director John Taylor. Finance Director Sara McCartney explains: 'John would go out and win new business, which created a buzz of excitement. But this was quickly overtaken by a feeling of dread about how we were going to deliver on that promise.'

John and Sara realised that they had to find a better way of working. This meant finding a way of decentralising the business to get away from a line management structure that put John – and everyone else – under huge pressure. They also recognised that they needed to invest in developing their people if they were going to succeed.

Initially Geoplan used a facilitator to help John share his vision and mission for the company, something he found difficult: 'It felt like being in a padded cell, kicking it around until it all came out.' But ultimately Investors in People gave the team a 'Geoplan way of working'. Next, Geoplan used Investors in People to help them develop a new 'matrix' structure for the company. This meant that the business became increasingly self-managed and anyone – rather than just John – could lead a project. John credits the leadership and management criteria in the Investors in People framework with helping him to realise that everyone could be a leader at some point in their role. But now Geoplan's staff had to step up to that challenge. Sara: 'We've worked very hard to develop an Investors in People framework that helps people to understand their own competences. That knowledge has given them confidence that they know their stuff and can deliver to global businesses.'

Now people focus on outputs and the value they add to the business. Effective planning and organisation, team work and prioritisation has delivered a significant increase in performance.

In 2003, Geoplan was making a loss of nearly half a million pounds a year. In 2011, it made a profit of £400,000. The value of the average contract has risen from £20,000 to £150,000–£200,000, and productivity has gone up from £56k per head in 2002 to £93k per head in 2011. Geoplan puts its improved results down to the increased confidence and ability of their people, who now form project teams to win new business and work much more closely with clients. They win and retain more customers, and their improved performance has enabled them to move from 'data assembly' work to large, bespoke jobs where Geoplan can add value. This consultancy approach is also more profitable, and the average value of a contract has risen from 'about £20k' to £150–200k.

Involving all staff in management and strategy has also enabled Geoplan to cope with rapid technological change in their sector. This meant Geoplan had to change from being a desktop-based business used by specialists, to online systems used by a wide range of business customers and sectors. This change has also enabled them to expand from being a UK business to working with global clients such as TNT and KFC owners Yum! Brands. John says that Investors in People also helps Geoplan 'to explain to a billion-pound business why they should work with you rather than a big company.'

Source: for case study: Investors in People content provided by the UK Commission for Employment and Skills. www.investorsinpeople.co.uk. Reprinted with permission.

Tasks

1. Discuss potential problem areas in decentralising a business away from a line management structure.

2. What do you see as the advantages of a matrix structure with a business becoming more self-managed?

3. Discuss the implications for organisation structure with a change from desktop-based business to online systems.

Chapter 12 – Personal skills and employability exercise

Objectives

Completing this exercise should help you to enhance the following skills:

* Diagnose specific features of structure within your university.
* Evaluate the significance and effects of structure on people within the university.
* Provide meaningful advice to senior management.

Exercise

Remind yourself of key features in the text of this chapter relating to:

* Technical, managerial and community levels
* Task and element functions
* Centralisation and decentralisation;
* Project teams and matrix structures; and
* Mechanistic and organic structures of organisation.

Now observe your own university and any other organisation with which you are familiar.

1. Prepare a detailed report with specific examples on the manner in which these features are manifested in your university (and/or some other organisation well known to you).
2. Comment on how these features impact upon the apparent effectiveness of structure and influence various activities of the university, styles of management, the people employed, and you as students.
3. Give examples of tensions and conflicts which arise from the implementation of these features, *for example* between task and element functions or from a mix of mechanistic and organic structures.
4. Explain fully what changes you would recommend to organisation structure and actions to help overcome these tensions and conflicts.

Discussion

* To what extent does organisational structure influence the actions, behaviour and effectiveness of: (i) lecturing staff (ii) non-teaching staff and (iii) students?
* Who should realistically be involved in decision-making relating to structure?
* Explain what specific changes you expect to see in the organisation structure of universities in the next five to ten years.

Notes and references

1. Adapted from Knight, K. (ed.) *Matrix Management: A Cross-Functional Approach to Organization,* Gower (1977), pp. 114–15.
2. Child, J. *Organization: Contemporary Principles and Practice,* second edition, Wiley (2015), p. 17.
3. Forte, C. (Lord Forte) *Forte: The Autobiography of Charles Forte,* Sidgwick and Jackson (1986), p. 122.
4. Drucker, P. F. *The Practice of Management*, Heinemann Professional (1989), p. 223.
5. Parsons, T. 'Some Ingredients of a General Theory of Formal Organization', in Litterer, J. A. *Organizations: Structure and Behaviour,* third edition, Wiley (1980).
6. Woodward, J. *Industrial Organization: Theory and Practice,* second edition, Oxford University Press (1980).
7. See, for example, Mullins, L. J. and Dossor, P. *Hospitality Management and Organisational Behaviour,* fifth edition, Pearson Education (2013).
8. Woodward, J. *Industrial Organization: Theory and Practice,* second edition, Oxford University Press (1980), p. 113.
9. Drucker, P. F. *Management Challenges for the 21st Century,* Butterworth-Heinemann (1999), p. 11.
10. Cloke, K. and Goldsmith, J. *The End of Management and the Rise of Organizational Democracy,* Jossey-Bass (2002).

11. Robertson, B. J. *Holacracy: The New Management System for a Rapidly Changing World,* Penguin (2015) and Stern, S. 'Creating a World Without Managers', *Management Today,* July/August 2015, p. 23. For further information see www.holocracy.org.

12. Graicunas, V. A. 'Relationship in Organization', in *Papers on the Science of Administration,* University of Columbia (1937).

13. Peter L. J. and Hull, R. *The Peter Principle,* Pan Books (1970), p. 22.

14. Franke, A. 'Accidental Managers Wreck Business', *Professional Manager,* Summer 2015, p. 5.

15. Adapted from Kolondy, H. F. 'Managing in a Matrix', *Business Horizons,* March/April 1981, pp. 17–24.

16. Senior, B. and Swailes, S. *Organizational Change,* fourth edition, Financial Times Prentice Hall (2010), p. 84.

17. Learner, P. M. 'Beware the Gatekeeper', *Amtrak Express,* July/August 1994, pp. 14–17.

18. Ashkenas, R., Ulrich, D., Jick, T. and Kerr, S. *The Boundaryless Organization: Breaking the Chains of Organizational Structure,* second edition, Jossey-Bass (2002).

19. Francesco, A. M. and Gold, B. A. *International Organizational Behavior,* second edition, Pearson Prentice Hall (2005), p. 246.

20. Rosenfeld, R. H. and Wilson, D. C. *Managing Organizations: Text, Readings and Cases,* second edition, McGraw-Hill (1999), p. 255.

21. Bouchikhi, H. and Kimberly, J. R. 'The Customised Workplace' in Chowdhury, S. (ed.) *Management 21C,* Financial Times Prentice Hall (2000), pp. 207–19.

22. Lynch, R. *Corporate Strategy,* fourth edition, Financial Times Prentice Hall (2006), p. 582.

23. Woodward, J. *Industrial Organization: Theory and Practice,* second edition, Oxford University Press (1980).

24. Dawson, S. and Wedderburn, D. 'Introduction' to Woodward, J. *Industrial Organization: Theory and Practice,* second edition, Oxford University Press (1980), p. xiii.

25. Perrow, C. *Organisational Analysis: A Sociological View,* Tavistock Publications (1970).

26. Burns, T. and Stalker, G. M. *The Management of Innovation,* Tavistock Publications (1966).

27. Litterer, J. A. *The Analysis of Organizations,* second edition, Wiley (1973).

28. Lawrence, P. R. and Lorsch, J. W. *Organisation and Environment,* Irwin (1969).

29. Boschken, H. L. 'Strategy and Structure: Reconceiving the Relationship', *Journal of Management,* vol. 16, no. 1, March 1990, pp. 135–50.

30. Robey, D. *Designing Organizations,* Irwin (1982), p. 59. See, for example, Fincham, R. and Rhodes, P. S. *The Individual, Work and Organization,* second edition, Weidenfeld and Nicolson (1992).

31. Schneider, S. C. and Barsoux, J. *Managing Across Cultures,* second edition, Financial Times Prentice Hall (2003), p. 101.

32. Watson, T. *Organising and Managing Work,* second edition, Financial Times Prentice Hall (2006), pp. 254–62.

33. Birchall, D. W. 'What Managers Do', in Crainer, S. and Dearlove, D. (eds) *Financial Times Handbook of Management,* second edition, Financial Times Prentice Hall (2001), pp. 110–31.

34. Cloke, K. and Goldsmith, J. *The End of Management and the Rise of Organizational Democracy,* Jossey-Bass (2002), p. 41.

35. Czerniawska, F. 'From Bottlenecks to Blackberries: How the Relationship between Organisations and Individuals is Changing', Management Consultancies Association (September 2005).

36. Thomas, A, 'At Arm's Length', *Chartered Secretary,* June 2010, pp. 28–9.

37. Overell, S. 'The Blurring of Control and Responsibility', ACAS, December 2012.

38. 'Deciding Whether to Outsource', Checklist 079, *Chartered Management Institute,* September 2014.

39. Clarke, S. and Holdsworth L. 'Flexibility in the Workplace' Research Paper, ACAS, March 2017.

40. 'Good Work: The Taylor Review of Modern Working Practices' GOV.UK. July 2017.

41. Gray, J. L. and Starke, F. A. *Organizational Behavior: Concepts and Applications,* fourth edition, Merrill Publishing Company, an imprint of Macmillan Publishing (1988).

42. Heller, R. *In Search of European Excellence,* HarperCollins Business (1997), p. 4.

43. Romaine, J. 'The Peter Principle Resuscitated: Are Promotion Systems Useless?', *Human Resource Management Journal,* vol. 24, no. 4, 2014, pp. 410–23.

44. Bailey, A. M. 'The Peter Principle: A Literature Review', Research Paper, School of Global Leadership and Entrepreneurship, Regent University, 2011, pp. 1–22.

45. Madden, K. 'Have an incompetent boss? You're not alone', CNN, 3 November 2010, http://edition.cnn.com/2010/LIVING/11/02/cb.peter.principle/index.html (accessed 17 September 2018).

46. Beeman, D. R. 'A Public Execution of the Peter Principle', *Business Horizons,* vol. 24, no. 6, 1981, pp. 48–50.

47. Peter, L. J. and Hull, R. *The Peter Principle: Why Things Always Go Wrong,* HarperCollins Publishers (1998).

48. Kane, J. 'Dynamics of the Peter Principle', *Management Science,* 16, 1970, B800-B810.

49. Hess, H. 'The Real Peter Principle: Promotion to Pain', *Harvard Business Review,* July–August, 1976, pp. 10–12, 158–9.

50. Chan, E. W. 'Promotion, Relative Performance Information, and the Peter Principle', *The Accounting Review,* vol. 93, no. 3, 2018, pp. 83–103.

51. Benson, A., Li, D. and Shue, K. (2018). 'Promotions and the Peter Principle' Research Paper, 12 February, pp. 1–34, https://dx.doi.org/10.2139/ssrn.3047193 (accessed 17 September 2018).

52. CIPD 'Succession Planning. Factsheet, Chartered Institute of Personnel and Development, 2017, https://www.cipd.co.uk/knowledge/strategy/resourcing/succession-planning-factsheet (accessed 17 September 2018).

Chapter 13
Technology in the workplace

Peter Scott

Technology and technological change are increasing influences on the way in which organisations deliver their products and services and how people experience the nature of work.

Learning outcomes

After completing this chapter you should have enhanced your ability to:

- explain the role and increasing relevance of technology within organisations;
- assess applications, problems and risks of technology;
- review technology, work and organisational behaviour;
- debate the potential impacts of technology on the nature and experience of work;
- explain the impact of technology on relationships with customers and users;
- evaluate different schools of thought on how technology interacts with the experience of work in organisations.

Outline chapter contents

Overview topic map: Chapter 13 – Technology in the workplace

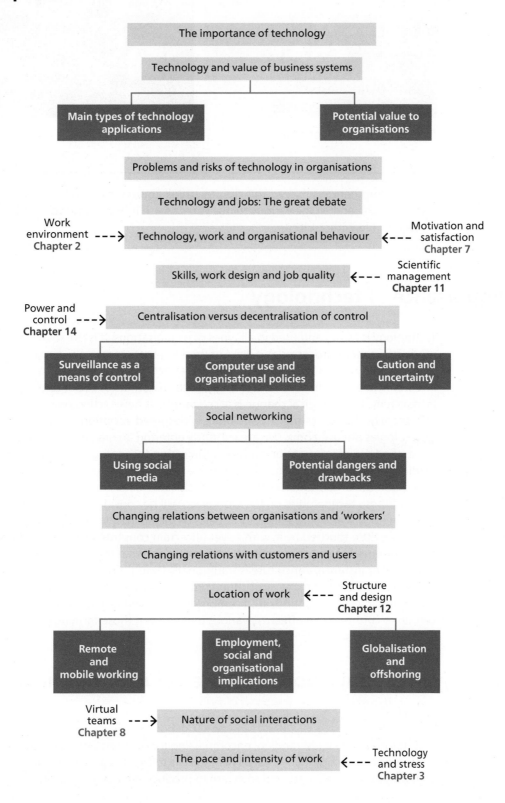

Technology and the workplace

Before commencing to read this chapter, think about how YOU use your smartphone and all the various things you do with it. How easy would it be to live your life without it?

The importance of technology

Technology is found and used in all types of organisations. It is the source of new products, services, processes and ways of working that create new demands and improve productivity. Technical innovation is affecting the way in which workers interact with each other and, increasingly, with customers of the organisation. Increasingly, technological change is accelerating, as new technologies come on stream or the cost barriers to the more widespread adoption of particular technologies are overcome. We are currently entering an era where the evolving design and use of information and communication technology (ICT), such as social media and social networking, are likely to be associated with further rapid major changes in the organisation of work and businesses alike. The potential impacts of some of these technologies on the workplace will be considered further below.

Technology is also spreading out to parts of the economy and organisations previously little touched by it, with as yet uncertain consequences for the shape of the labour market and the numbers and types of job that may be available in years to come. For instance, agriculture is traditionally thought of as a low-skilled, labour-intensive industry, but many agricultural processes and parts of the sector are now dominated by highly sophisticated computer-controlled technology. This process is certain to continue and affect, by various means, even those farming processes that still require considerable manual input.[1]

Technology in organisations and the value of business systems

Technology is very wide-ranging, encompassing innovations from ultra-small-scale nanotechnology incorporated in materials to the merger of computing and communications hardware and software to produce what are generally known as information and communications technologies (ICTs). The latest developments in ICTs emphasise a number of additional capabilities that are likely to significantly enhance the potential applications of technology and hence the value of organisational systems. These include, **first**, considerably larger data storage capacity, which enables the development of so-called immersive technologies, such as augmented reality and virtual reality. These impinge on – indeed, go some way to recreating – the user's conscious experience of an environment, and may be useful in creating more cost-effective applications like training simulations.

Second, recent advances in artificial intelligence have brought nearer the elusive goal of enabling machines to 'think' and act in a way more akin to the conscious human. This is evident in various applications such as voice and object recognition that potentially challenge areas in which human perception has hitherto reigned largely supreme. Commercial devices such as voice-activated 'personal assistants', into the development of which the tech giants have sunk considerable resources, may seem something of a novelty, but presently only scratch the possibilities of such developments. The implications of artificial intelligence will be discussed further below.

Third, the so-called 'internet of things' involves the integration of hitherto stand-alone devices, including mundane ones such as refrigerators or utility supply meters, into enabled communications systems where the data generated is used to monitor and pre-empt logistical and operational problems (in these examples, being aware of one's food or energy consumption). This is linked to a **fourth** area of development: what is known as big data. 'Big data' is underpinned by the data capture and storage potential of current generations of ICTs, but takes this a step further by breaking down the barriers to *analysis* of these vast quantities of data in order to establish connections and behaviour patterns that may further improve business efficiency and new opportunities. The ethical and political dilemmas that are raised for organisations by many of these new possibilities will be considered later in this chapter.

What do YOU see as the additional capabilities and potential applications of technology that can enhance the value of organisational systems of your university?

Main types of technology applications

Technology's main forms or applications may be summarised as follows:

- Manufacturing, engineering and design technology, for the provision of goods. Nowadays, this is usually interlinked and draws on common databases.

- Technology used for information capture, storage, transmission, analysis and retrieval. This covers many forms of computing and telecommunications equipment.

- Technology employed in the provision of services to for example customers, clients, patients in service sector applications, such as in internet banking or shopping.

- Technology as the product itself, or as a significant addition to the product, such as devices incorporating microprocessors, forms of artificial intelligence such as speech recognition, or the addition of nano-materials to existing products (enabling, for example, self-cleaning clothes or glass). Rapid technological development of new products incorporating information technology, such as new generations of smartphones, are a prime source of competitive advantage to many firms in current markets.

- Data generated by the above technological innovations can itself be classified as a product. The rise of social media, and the proliferation of information posted on it, has turned personal data itself into a valuable commodity for firms. Data are capable of gaining competitive advantage, for example through improved targeting of products and services.

Potential value to organisations

Taken together, these various types of application are capable of generating considerable value to organisations especially if separate applications can be combined successfully into systems and networks. Business benefits can be divided into two main types.

- **Quantitative value, or economies of scale.** This is where technology can be used to achieve greater efficiency in the use of resources, such as lower costs, reductions in the time taken to deliver a product or service, or a need for fewer staff.
- **Qualitative value, or economies of scope.** The real benefits of the use of technology in business systems, however, come when firms use it to exploit new opportunities that were often not originally envisaged. Because this type of benefit cannot easily be quantified under conventional business accounting rules, it is sometimes overlooked, but the long-run opportunities may be greater. Examples might include the generation of new business because technology has been able to improve service quality, the ability to manufacture entirely new types of product.

Tokyo train station

Problems and risks of technology in organisations

Despite the undoubted benefits, organisations' increasing dependence on technology carries with it a considerable number of potential reputational and operational risks. The dangers of some of these factors are only recently starting to become fully apparent. This is as a result of the unintended consequences of some technological developments, and how they have been introduced and used in practice.

- **Risks of overdependence on technology** without adequate back-up, contingency plans, or in-house knowledge of how complex systems operate. At the time of writing, the crash of TSB's online banking services for several days in April 2018 when it tried to move to a new system after its demerger with Lloyds Bank provides a high-profile example. Most UK banks' systems still bear strong hallmarks of when banks first automated in the 1960s. However, most of the personnel who understood these systems had exited over time, TSB's new owners had no previous experience of attempting a switchover on the required scale, and there appeared to be no effective 'shadow' system in the background in case of the kind of problems that did occur.[2] At the extreme, lack of human understanding and oversight of incredibly complex ICT systems may lead to catastrophic failures, such as 'flash crashes' in the case of high-speed automated trading in the financial services sector.[3]

- **Vulnerability to reputational damage** through the increasing transparency of information and the rapid spread of adverse publicity through social media. Protest campaigns can be organised rapidly through social media, and it may be difficult for organisations to weather the storm created by large campaigns.

- **Data breaches and hacking of organisational systems,** by state-sponsored or criminal actors. This appears to be a growing problem for organisational security and the privacy of the individual. In some cases, problems have been compounded where the organisations hacked have only belatedly discovered a breach or have not been perceived as proactive in dealing with the breach when it comes to light. A related issue is the misuse of data. This issue has become much more significant with the rise of giant internet and social media monopolies such as Google and Facebook, whose primary 'product' to sell is the personal data that is gathered from the millions of individuals who use their services. The case of the now defunct Cambridge Analytica, which used personal data gathered from millions of individuals via what purported to be a 'personality quiz' Facebook app to target voters in elections, is a cautionary tale for a number of reasons.

How realistic do YOU think it for organisations to be able to guard against the risk of data breaches? What sort of measures do you think should be taken to avoid data breaches?

- **Neglect of the human factor.** Sadly, there is a long history in the UK of designers, engineers and managers failing to consult with end users to optimise technical designs to fulfil their intended purposes.[4] Employee resistance to technology is also becoming an increasing issue in some environments, because of its potential to displace jobs and downgrade the ability to achieve business benefits other than those of efficiency and cost savings. For example, there have been a number of long-running disputes on the UK railway network in recent years over the attempted introduction of driver-only operated trains. While trade unions representing train conductors have been concerned to protect their members' jobs, they and some passengers' groups have attempted to highlight the role of conductors on trains in protecting passenger safety and assisting disabled passengers to access public transport.

- **Opportunity cost.** New opportunities for employees to engage in social activities in work time due to the difficulty in separating 'work' and 'personal' communications devices and software.

- **Conflict between the goal of using technology** to improve business efficiency and other organisational and social goals. This may be particularly acute where government organisations use technology to try to cut costs. For instance, the UK Government has increasingly been using ICTs and online methods to restructure access to the justice system in an attempt to make it more efficient. This includes techniques such as making more court hearings 'virtual' rather than face to face and also the automation of the conviction process. While this may make justice more 'efficient' and cheaper to administer, some have questioned whether such developments undermine the need for fairness to be seen in the administration of justice.[5]

Do YOU think it is acceptable for automation of the conviction process and a machine to decide a criminal sentence or should such decisions be better made by a judge?

Finally, we need to remember that technology cannot solve all problems in either the workplace or society more generally. It is not a panacea, especially in cases where extremely complex systems would be required! A good example of this is the public debate, at the time of writing, over whether technology can be used to solve the problem of monitoring movements of goods and people between the borders of Northern Ireland and the Irish Republic after the UK leaves the European Union. Strong differences of opinion have been expressed over whether the technology exists, or can be developed, to effectively undertake this task.[6]

Crossed wires in India

Technology and jobs: the great debate

Perhaps the main current debate about technology and the workplace is the impact of new technologies on jobs. This is the latest instalment of an old controversy. Since the dawn of the Industrial Revolution, there have been repeated predictions of advances in technology leading to the end of work and to new opportunities for leisure (by optimists) or to mass poverty and job losses (by pessimists). In practice, technological unemployment has tended to be absorbed by the rise of new types of jobs. The new jobs have arisen because of new products enabled by new technologies, or they have come in growth sectors that have been labour-intensive, like the service sector.

Why the controversy again now? A number of writers, in recent years, have looked at developments in computerisation and artificial intelligence (AI) and drawn projections about how many jobs might potentially be displaced and how job content might change. A large literature has developed on this topic in the last few years, so here we will concentrate on just giving a flavour of some of the main issues in the debate.

Writers such as *Brynjolfsson and McAfee* and *Frey and Osborne* have analysed the US labour market and forecast the possibility of large-scale job losses. In 2013, Frey and Osborne hit the headlines by arguing that 47 per cent of US jobs are at high risk from computerisation, 19 per cent at medium risk, and the remaining third at low risk, in current conditions of low growth and high levels of inequality. As before, low skilled jobs are at the greatest risk, but they suggest that the next generation of technologies, such as robotics, driverless vehicles, artificial intelligence, drones, etc., will also threaten more highly skilled and professional jobs.[7]

A more recent report by some of the same team reduced the 'high risk' prediction to 18.7 per cent of US jobs and 21.2 per cent of the UK workforce.[8] These lower predictions are typical of other recent studies, which emphasise change in the nature of remaining jobs as well as job losses. However, such studies still point out that this leaves large numbers of jobs potentially at risk, and there is doubt about whether automation will not affect hitherto 'safe' jobs in the service sector this time.[9]

Where jobs remain, some fear an increasing digital divide, with its divergent implications for skills, wages and job security, and 'jobs' consisting solely of residual, lowly skilled and paid tasks that are not worth automating, such as hand car washing services.[10]

If jobs, in the traditional sense, are to become much rarer, there is a question about how those displaced should be supported, and whether this is the responsibility of organisations or of society as a whole. In countries such as Finland and Switzerland, there have been discussions about introducing a system of universal basic income, paid to citizens of working age by the government, as a way of resolving what could be a potential crisis of employment and incomes. **Recall discussion in Chapter 7.**

Whose responsibility do YOU think it is to support the potential large numbers of people becoming jobless because of technological change: organisations or society as a whole?

Technology, work and organisational behaviour

The rest of this chapter reviews seven main ways in which technology and technological change has an impact on those in the workplace. Some of these subjects have engendered lengthy academic debates and controversy, while others are emerging areas, particularly where they concern the implications of the most recent technological innovations.

1. It influences the specific design of each member's pattern of work, affecting the skills exercisable and the overall quality of jobs.
2. Technologies affect the degree of control that workers can exercise within their jobs. There is a fertile, unresolved debate over whether centralisation and closer control of workers or decentralisation and democratisation of technology in the workplace is the dominant trend.
3. It changes the relationship between organisations and those who perform the work of the organisation.
4. It also changes the relationship between organisations and external customers or users in further ways that have implications for the structure and reputation of organisations.
5. It affects where the 'workplace' is located.
6. It affects the nature of social interactions between workers, particularly in cases where those working on a project are doing so from different places.
7. It can influence the pace and intensity of work.

These factors are likely to affect the experience of work, and therefore ultimately the levels of job satisfaction that individuals are able to attain. We should also recognise that many of the seven factors are inter-linked. For example, the setting-up of offshore telephone call centres represents a change in the location of work, but such moves are often also accompanied by the routinisation of the tasks in these establishments (a reduction in skill levels) and an expectation of faster throughput of calls (a change in the pace and intensity of work). **Recall the discussion in Chapter 2.**

Skill, work design and job quality

The impact of technological change on the nature and variety of job activities performed, the skills that workers can exercise and the amount of autonomy and control they have over their jobs have been among the most hotly contested areas in social science.[11] In this section we concentrate particularly on skills and work organisation. There are basically three schools of thought that have developed on this issue, which can still be found reflected in current debates about automation **(discussed above)**: an association between introduction of new technologies and a general reduction in skill requirements; an overall increase because automation is said to need additional skills; or a more mixed overall picture.

*Braverman***'s** influential work viewed automation, in the hands of managers, as the next logical step in a strategy to de-skill and eliminate jobs that had started with Taylor's techniques of scientific management. Subsequent contributors to the so-called 'labour process' debate that followed the publication of Braverman's work[13] argued that the exact effects of technical change on skill levels depend on how managers organise job design and the patterns of work organisation more broadly. This varies considerably between different workplaces and across different countries.[14] **(See the discussion on scientific management in Chapter 11.)**

Other writers took the view that microprocessor-based automation required additional programming skills, and therefore led to a general rise in skill requirements. *Zuboff* was one of the first to argue that ICTs were different, because they generate new streams of previously unavailable information about processes that require interpretation by human operators. To use her term, it 'informates' processes in ways that require new human skills to exploit successfully.[15] Nevertheless, some have cast doubt on the idea that ICTs require a new generation of 'knowledge workers'.[16] *Fleming, Harley and Sewell* argue, on the basis of a study of jobs in Australia that might be classified as 'knowledge work', that many such occupations involve merely relatively low-level information-processing skills, and thus it could be mistaken to anoint them as 'knowledge work'.[17]

Other studies of the use of computing applications in different forms of clerical and professional work, such as the work of *Huws,* suggest that many of the 'skills' simply involve navigating standardised software interfaces, producing increasingly uniform work experiences.[18]

The third perspective seems more reasonable. Rather than talking about general trends of deskilling or upskilling, it seems more likely that skill trends and trajectories may be moving in different directions, and this will vary across occupations, the workforce as a whole, and even across countries.

Centralisation versus decentralisation of control

The debate about the effect of technology upon skills and work organisation necessarily raises the question of the consequences of technology for workers' autonomy and discretion. In other words, to what extent can it be an instrument of tighter monitoring and control or of greater liberation in the workplace? **(Organisational power and control are discussed in Chapter 14.)**

Surveillance as a means of control

Recently *Foster and McChesney* have talked of the emergence of a form of **'surveillance capitalism'**, enabled by the information-gathering potential of ICTs and the growing monopoly power of data-driven companies such as Google, Facebook, Microsoft and Apple.[19] In the workplace, the ICT revolution has reinvigorated concern with the use of technology as a means of workplace control, through technically monitoring or conducting surveillance on workers' performance and activity. Contributory factors include the sheer growth in the numbers and usage of technologies available to capture and store data generated within organisations,[20] coupled with higher pressures on staff to perform because of increased competition, financial constraints, or large firms' domination of integrated ICT networks in some sectors, such as retail.[21] The potential for surveillance encompasses technologies as established as closed circuit television[22] through to newer methods such as voice and image recognition software and RFID tags, which can be placed in goods and even people so as to enable tracking of their location and movement.[23] It is commonplace for RFID devices to be installed in delivery vans.

The origins of such concerns can be traced back to the writings about 'disciplinary power' of the French postmodernist *Foucault,* and particularly to his popularisation of Jeremy Bentham's proposed design for a prison that perfected the capability for surveillance of the prisoners' activities in their cells: a 'panopticon', the literal meaning of which is 'all-seeing eye'.[24] Some writers liken the information-gathering potential of ICTs to an '**electronic panopticon**'.

This literature draws attention to insidious and not-so-insidious ways in which IT has been used by managers to monitor and record the work of employees, in some cases in such a way they do not know exactly when they are being watched, but are aware this could be at any time. For instance, the systems in telephone call centres typically permit managers to listen in randomly to the calls of selected operatives (a practice usually justified on the grounds of quality control). However, operatives have no way of being aware when managers may be monitoring their conversations with customers. Hence, it is argued, employees amend their behaviour to act as if they are under unseen surveillance all the time, just like the prisoners in Bentham's panopticon.[25]

To what extent do YOU believe the sentiment 'invent a system and workers will always find a way to subvert it' is true of the way technology is used in the workplace?

Caution and uncertainty

Mason et al. strike a note of caution, echoing previous debates on labour control: there is disagreement over whether the ability to collect such performance data necessarily means that managers always refer to, or act on it; whether technologies are actually capable of living up to their claimed surveillance potential; and to what extent employees can resist such techniques, rationalise their existence, or even turn them to their own advantage.[26]

The conditional and partial nature of the potential for control within ICT is illustrated in a number of workplace studies, such as *Eriksson-Zetterquist, Lindberg and Styhre*'s work on the introduction of new technology into professional jobs and *Fisher*'s research into the introduction of ICTs and the restructuring of work within an agency of the UK Civil Service. Fisher, for example, shows how the complexity of the case work undertaken by the civil servants largely thwarted management attempts to de-skill the work technically and to exert more control over it, although managers were nevertheless able to use the new ICT systems to generate previously unavailable information about the work process that might assist future attempts to exert greater control.[27]

Further, in particular organisational contexts, some workers may also view surveillance as legitimate in proving their own levels of performance against allegedly less productive colleagues, as *Sewell, Barker and Nyberg* find in a call centre.[28] Similarly, some workers support technology as protecting their safety, as *Grampp, Houlihan and McGrath* find with the introduction of global positioning systems (GPS) for dispatch of taxi drivers in Dublin. GPS facilitated closer management control over the movements of drivers and limited their autonomy. Drivers were resigned to this rather than resistant: inasmuch as the system reduced the time that taxis were unoccupied it also maximised driver income and, in many respects, the interests of company and drivers coincided. However, what really sold the GPS system to the drivers, and was emphasised by employer and equipment suppliers alike, was its potential to improve driver safety.[29] This study, and others like it, shows that we cannot conceive of organisational control as simple or unproblematic, and it is clearly mediated by other salient issues within the workplace.

Computer use and organisational policies

The generic nature of software included on organisational networks and computing devices creates novel problems and dilemmas for managers about the control of employees' computer use in working hours. Access to the internet, social networking sites and email is increasingly available within the workplace, and further applications similar to those already likely to be on employees' home computers and smartphones. This raises real problems about the boundaries between 'work' and 'personal' use of computers, what usage workers may legitimately make of the computing facilities available to them, and how any restrictions should be devised, monitored and enforced. The extended hours that some employees spend at, or doing, work clearly exacerbate the likelihood that the employer's computing facilities may be the vehicle used for personal or social internet traffic.[30]

A growing number of disciplinary, dismissal and Employment Tribunal (ET) cases have centred on the abuse of email, distribution of inappropriate images, and negative posts by employees on social media.[31] ETs have ruled employees were fairly dismissed even if the posts were not primarily work-related, distribution was only to a small group of 'Facebook friends' or 'Twitter followers', or the employer was not mentioned by name. In cases where the employee won, ETs sometimes reduced compensation on the grounds that, by posting in a public forum, the employee contributed to the problem.[32] Even if used for work purposes, email can be used excessively or distributed to mailing lists beyond those who need to – or, in some cases, should – see the message concerned, thus contributing to information overload.

As both a legal defence and good HR policy, organisations should therefore put in place clear and transparent guidelines to minimise the likelihood of abuse or misunderstandings about the nature and extent of computer use for reasons that may be considered unrelated to work. A number of such guidelines exist, including those produced by organisations like the Advisory, Conciliation and Arbitration Service.[33] These cover issues of access to computer systems, monitoring of employee usage, the degree to which personal use of computing facilities may be permissible in work time, data protection, use of disclaimers in emails to safeguard against legal action, the relative responsibilities of employers and employees, and so on. New technological developments, such as social networking, carry with them the need for organisational policies to be regularly updated if they are to remain relevant.

How far do YOU think employees should have any right to use organisational IT systems for personal use in the workplace and what limits should be placed on any such right?

Social networking

We have discussed the vertical control that employers can exercise over workers' tasks through ICT, and their ability to monitor the use employees are making of the technologies made available to them. Social networking and other interactive technologies, such as Facebook, Twitter, virtual worlds (such as Second Life), weblogs (blogs), permit the more lateral use of technologies to share information and digital content. Such developments create new problems for traditional authority relations and communications within organisations as these interactive technologies short-circuit existing organisational hierarchies.[34]

Online social networking has increased rapidly, and at least some of this must be taking place in work time. One response is to clamp down on use of social media, internet or personal phones in the workplace. Apart from social media's potential for new work-related misbehaviours, employers are also concerned about reputational damage. For example, cases exist of blogging employees being dismissed when the offending employer about whom they were blogging could be identified from details included in the posts.[35]

Using social media

Others argue that organisations should come to terms with the new participatory opportunities offered by social media and should not 'kill the conversation'.[36] Social networking can be a positive phenomenon for recruitment, publicity, to build necessary business contacts and to expand sales and goodwill beyond organisational boundaries. *Acas* argues it can be used to strengthen employee voice.[37] In relation to blogging, for example, *Ellis and Richards* dispute the common perception that it is solely a manifestation of covert resistance to the employer. Their research with bloggers finds other motivations for blogging include using it as an outlet for workers' underemployed creativity, to build a virtual network of the like-minded, and as a form of public relations for the job. This raises the worrying possibility that such employees are finding a form of autonomy and control in their blogs that they do not feel in their everyday jobs.[38]

Using networking sites such as Facebook and LinkedIn for business communications and marketing purposes appears to be considered important in some organisations, particularly those in creative industries and those whose business methods have traditionally relied heavily on more established forms of social networking. As with most electronic technologies, networking appears equally capable of being used for work and social purposes, thus one cannot draw blanket conclusions that such developments bode well or ill from a work perspective. *Bradwell and Reeves* argue that any distinction between 'social' and 'professional' networking is becoming increasingly artificial, especially in relation to younger employees, and that the latter type of network is spreading its boundaries horizontally across organisations. Although they argue that such developments have considerable promise, dangers can be identified too.[39]

Potential dangers and drawbacks

The development of individual workers' networks with those outside the organisation raises questions about the nature of commercial confidentiality, of loyalty, and also conceal dangers of iniquitous practices in hiring staff, awarding contracts, and suchlike. Others have indicated further drawbacks with networks, although some of these disadvantages accrue to different parties in the employment relationship. First, one needs to question whether the forms of social interaction enabled by such sites are as rich in quality as traditional face-to-face networking,[40] considered further in the section on social interactions below. Second, employees may easily forget that the electronic traces they leave on the web and networking sites can be accessed by anyone who is able to track them down, including curious prospective future employers!

> Do YOU think social networking is a friend or foe for employers? Would you be happy for a potential employer to have access to your social media profile?

Computer work stations

Changing relations between organisations and their 'workers'

There has been considerable debate in recent years about the implications of changing organisational forms for the employment status of those who do the work for such new bodies. This is connected to the development of the so-called '**gig economy**' and a class of organisations that use the internet as a giant free market to bring together those who want certain tasks done and those who are prepared to provide them. This is basically the concept attributed to the Microsoft founder, Bill Gates, of 'friction-free capitalism', where the internet breaks down the barriers that separate buyers and sellers of services from easily contracting with each other.

Think of this as a large, glorified noticeboard to bring the two groups into contact with each other. A number of firms, such as Uber and Deliveroo, have grown rapidly through a business model of – as they see it – offering a platform to bring self-employed contractors into contact with those who wish to be supplied with taxi rides or deliveries respectively. However, are such firms simply platforms or are they employers? This question has now been debated frequently in the UK court system, deciding more often than not in favour that they are actually employers. A number of employment tribunal cases has found that those supplying the services should be considered as workers rather than self-employed, because they do not, in reality, have the freedoms to pick and choose how they work in the way the genuinely self-employed do.

Moreover, what is the nature of this work? While certain studies find that some appreciate the relative freedom and opportunity for earnings, particularly if those doing this work are combining it with other jobs, others are more pessimistic. [41] For instance, a study of those undertaking tasks for Amazon's 'Mechanical Turk' system interprets the experience as a further step on the road to casualised, insecure and poorly paid self-employment.[42]

Changing relations with customers and users

As the previous sections suggest, current internet developments blur the boundaries between the organisation and its external context in ways previously not experienced. This section considers three aspects of how such technologies impact on organisations' relations with their customers or service users. These are the implications for organisational structure and work of user-generated content and 'crowd-sourcing'; the use of technology to enable customer self-service; and organisations' increasing transparency and vulnerability to the views and opinions of external customers and service users.

Interactive technologies have increased the power of the user of products and services. One sees this, first, in user-generated content on internet sites, such as in amateur reviews of products and services purchased. Organisations have little or no control over such content, but poor reviews may cause considerable reputational damage. When reviews are located on social media sites, a similar problem crops up to that discussed in the previous section: are social media sites such as Facebook or YouTube merely platforms enabling individuals to express their opinions publicly, or are they publishers, in which case surely they have a responsibility to ensure that the content appearing on their sites is not potentially defamatory or otherwise unlawful?

A more far-reaching development is the 'open source' or '**crowd-sourcing**' movement, where enthusiastic amateurs, often working unpaid, engage in dispersed 'mass collaboration' to author, develop and improve artefacts.[43] Computer operating systems such as Linux, software ('freeware') such as Audacity and the on-line encyclopaedia Wikipedia are among the better-known products of this movement. Torch-bearers for this movement, such as *Shirky,* consider it as 'organising without organisations'.[44] Such developments in mass co-operation have implications for traditional organisational structures, the distribution of power, the nature and value of professional expertise, and even the nature and value of paid work itself that are as yet in their infancy. The likely implications are as yet imperfectly understood and require further research.

Free labour

A second trend enabled by increasingly interactive technologies is the transfer of what used to be paid work to the free labour of the customer or service user. Although a move from paid service to self-service has been visible for some time – think of the use of ATMs by banks over several decades – the internet and user-friendly software has taken this to a new level. Self-service supermarket checkouts, on-line-only ordering (for example, flight booking for certain budget airlines) and the development of so-called e-government services[45] provide examples of this. Such innovations change the relationship between the organisation and the customer/user. This has potential equality implications for organisations. For instance, a report by Age UK points to potential problems for older consumers in accessing services that may increasingly be moving to being provided online only.[46]

Power and performance

Third, interactive technologies have changed the dynamics of organisational power, not only internally within the organisation (as suggested in the previous section), but also in relation to interactions with customers, users and the wider public. This can happen in several ways. The perceived performance of workers in organisations can become more transparent to current and prospective customers. For instance, crowdsourced taxi drivers for the smartphone-powered UberTAXI service are rated by customers according to the service they give. The visibility of drivers' ratings to potential customers acts as a powerful disciplinary force on the drivers concerned if they wish to continue receiving jobs.

Even if one accepts that one can readily quantify the quality of a taxi riding experience, it is reasonable to ask whether a one-to-five-star rating can adequately encapsulate the quality of a complex service received from a professional. Similarly, *Williams and Beck* show how organisations are using performance management software that assigns numerical rankings, which are essentially based on *subjective* criteria, to continuously measure employees' job performance. These rankings are then presented as *objective* indicators that can be used to identify and take action against those deemed to be 'underperforming'.[47]

To what extent do YOU think performance rating systems or satisfaction surveys based on a 1–5 scale are an adequate and fair way of judging the performance of employees?

Location of work

New technologies have facilitated the redistribution of where work is carried out in a number of ways, the full implications of which are not yet clear. Here we focus on two main developments. First, the availability of ICTs has made the displacement of workers from the traditional individual location (desk or office) considerably easier. Thus workers may be working from home, on the move, or in some form of collective office space part or all of the time. Second, technology has made easier the move nationally or even internationally of certain forms of service sector activity that can be carried out over the telephone or via an internet connection. This is one part of the phenomenon known as offshoring. In each of these cases, technology is certainly not the only factor in play, but it is an important one.

Remote and mobile working

The fragmentation of the 'workplace' is a multi-faceted phenomenon, and some aspects are discussed elsewhere in this text **(see, for example telecommuting in Chapter 12).** Here we concentrate more specifically on the trends towards working while on the move. Sociologists such as *Urry* have noted the simultaneous expansion in recent years of human travel and of the desire to maintain contact with other people at a distance through various communication technologies.[48] Such developments have expanded into the world of work in a variety of forms. Sixty-four per cent of the firms responding to a 2011 survey by Virgin Media Business claim to be equipping workers to work out of the office, a rapid growth that suggests that the relative positions of mobile and fixed desktop computing are gradually being reversed.[49]

Felstead, Jewson and Walters conducted perhaps the most comprehensive study to date of workers whose jobs are located wholly or partly away from a conventional workplace. Felstead *et al.* detail the many ways in which traditional conceptions and routines of work are fragmented and displaced in such settings, but the most instructive lesson is that workers actively attempt to reconstruct for themselves some of the certainties of the traditional workplace, although sometimes in new ways. These include attempts to reconstruct 'personal' work space and a division between 'working' and 'non-working' time. Workers also invent new ways to circumvent the electronic supervision of their activities **(as discussed above)** and to alert their superiors to their 'presence' and productivity, by sending emails very early or late in the day, for example.[50]

Globalisation and offshoring

The emergence as economic powers of new nations with skilled but relatively inexpensive workforces has combined with the availability of ICTs to produce the phenomenon of offshoring. This has created new options for organisations about where to locate the functions that need to be performed, and contributed to the fragmentation of organisational forms and structures.

The development of Information and Communication Technology (ICT) is, along with deregulation, the other key enabling factor for the changed nature of globalisation. It enables both a closer coordination of supply chain activities and more cost-efficient delivery across national borders. The other important implication of technological advances in ICT is that it has eroded some of the geographical limitations to the provision of services and opened up a wide range of service activities to international competition that were previously confined to national markets.[51]

Employment, social and organisational implications

Much of the debate about **offshoring** has been concerned with the employment, social and organisational implications of what the new technological possibilities unleash. The initial impetus of offshoring was to reorganise service sector work in such a way that it did not need to be performed face-to-face, especially in finance, insurance and other customer service operations. Early public debate focused on the export from Western countries of such work and its concentration into telephone call centres in countries like India, which have a highly qualified and plentiful supply of English-speaking labour and a developing technical infrastructure.

Nevertheless, such workers are paid a fraction of the wages that comparable work in the UK would attract, although the wages in the recipient country may still seem high by its average standards and the relative 'wage gap' between the 'sender' and 'receiver' countries has declined over time. Research suggests that firms involved in offshored work tend to reorganise it along Taylorised lines, giving the workers limited discretion and subjecting them to a high degree of monitoring.[52] Similarly, internet-based commercial activities can be based where the labour needed to run and maintain them is relatively cheap.

More recently, higher value and professional activities have been considered candidates for offshoring, and a number of offshore service providers offer, for example, staff planning and other HR services, programming and software development, and so on. *Garner* classifies the types of service jobs that are economically attractive to move abroad as those that do not require the provider to be in physical contact with the recipient and are labour-intensive, information-based, codifiable (i.e. routinised) and highly transparent (involve dealing with easily measurable and verifiable information, such as the analysis of financial ratios).[53]

The future of offshoring

At the time of writing, the future for offshoring looks rather mixed. While some firms are continuing to diversify the locations of their suppliers globally, there has also been something of a reaction against offshoring in several of the Western countries where the trend originated. This is sometimes occurring for commercial reasons. Think, for example, of the advertising hoardings seen on British streets where major UK organisations try to attract customers by trumpeting the fact that they only use UK-based call centres. In the wake of political changes in some Western countries, such as the Brexit referendum vote, for example, some firms and governments now say they support the 'reshoring' of business functions.[54] In other words, they wish to bring back 'home', in order to create domestic jobs, tasks that had previously been offshored abroad. **See the discussion in Chapter 12.**

What do YOU think about offshoring? Make a list comparing what you believe are its main advantages and disadvantages for organisations.

Nature of social interactions

Technology is likely to change the extent and manner in which managers and workers interact and workers interact with each other. It may affect the size and nature of work groups and the extent of physical mobility and of contacts with other people. These factors will certainly be magnified with ICTs, where people working on linked tasks may be at a variety of locations, including at home, and individuals may work more on their own, from personal work stations, or work more with machines than with other people. There are clear dangers for organisations here that workers may become isolated from the workplace and that it becomes harder for the informal channels of information exchange on which organisations depend to flow freely.

Worse, information about developing problems can be more easily hidden when workers are not interacting face-to-face. A comment from a knowledge management worker participating in a research study of virtual working sums up the difficulty of creating high-quality social interactions when workers are communicating from different locations: 'We try to have what we call virtual coffee sessions, which were dreadful . . . all around the world we tried to get together and have a cup of coffee and sit down and look at each other, and you can't be spontaneous now, you can't do it, you can't force it.'[55]

Remote versus office-based workers

It is well established that remote workers face particular problems in being able to interact successfully with the organisation, and particular care is needed to integrate them and to assure that they face no detriment to their career development. Equally important, but subject to considerably less attention, is the quality and nature of interaction between staff who remain office-based and their remote co-workers. The limited research that does exist suggests that office workers can resent their remote colleagues, both for the perceived advantages of the remote lifestyle and for the fact that their own presence in the office means they pick up tasks that the remote workers can avoid. **See the discussion on virtual teams in Chapter 8.**

Golden studied the job satisfaction and turnover intentions of office-based workers who have colleagues who telework.[56] He found that 'the prevalence of teleworkers in a work unit alters the flexibility and workload of non-teleworking colleagues, thereby impacting their satisfaction with co-workers and turnover intentions'.[57] Such negative findings for co-workers of teleworking are moderated the fewer the hours teleworked, the greater the opportunity for face-to-face interactions with teleworkers, and the greater the degree of job autonomy experienced.

Fogarty, Scott and Williams studied predominantly office-based workers in a publishing firm where some staff work remotely on an informal basis, alongside the existence of other employees on a formal teleworking scheme and yet others who always work in the office. Their findings question the practicalities of the 'virtual organisation'. They found communications and social interactions between office-based and remote workers, as well as continuity of operations, can all be adversely affected by the uncertainties generated, especially by the practice of ad hoc informal off-site working.[58]

Working from home – just like at the office?

The pace and intensity of work

A number of academic studies point out that technology contributes to a quickening pace and intensification of work.[59] Technology can dictate the speed at which workers react, such as mechanical pacing of work on a mass-production assembly line or the manner in which electronic control devices can be programmed to demand a human response within a given time frame. If such demands are perceived as excessively frequent, persistent or intrusive, then this may result in the development of stress. For instance, press reports of working conditions in warehouses like Amazon's point to health problems among workers, some of whom are required to wear devices that monitor the speed at which they work.[60]

The instantaneous connectivity of new technologies, notably easily accessible email and social media, has created a working climate in which there is a greater expectation of the immediacy of receipt and response, regardless of location or time, and this has added to the dangers of information overload. The ease of use only exacerbates the frequency of use.

iDisorder

Views on ICT's contribution to workers' stress and impact on work–life balance split into three broad categories. The more negative research finds that the ever-increasing use of ICT, and workers' propensity to check for messages repeatedly (with or without managerial expectations they will do so), are causes of rising stress levels in the workplace.[61] This is part of a wider social issue: the potentially addictive qualities of new technologies are increasingly being recognised by bodies as diverse as the World Health Organization and the big social media firms themselves.

Rosen has related the phenomenon of obsessive use of, and near-permanent connectedness to technology to various recognised psychological disorders and mental health problems. He terms this syndrome 'iDisorder'. Although different generations in the workplace may experience this to different extents, depending on what technologies they have grown up with, he cautions against the ways in which intrusive technologies are changing our perceptions of what constitutes normality.[62] ***See also Chapter 3.***

Conversely, others argue fears of increasing user stress are exaggerated and users – especially those who have grown up with ICT – can develop coping mechanisms to process and retrieve information without experiencing overload.[63] *Symon* points out that the volume of information leads workers to develop strategies to ignore much of it, although this may itself be problematic if significant information is thus screened out.[64] A third view, typified by *Madden and Jones'* PEW/Internet and American Life Project, suggests a more mixed, nuanced picture, where ICT's contribution to workers' productivity and flexibility is offset by difficulties in disengaging from an intensified work experience.[65]

A number of major European employers have started to introduce organisational solutions to reduce the impact of ICT overload on staff. These include preventing the firm's servers from sending out email after the end of shifts, banning managers from contacting employees outside working hours and allowing staff to delete emails sent to them while they were on leave.[66]

How do YOU believe problems of information and work overload because of technology should best be solved?

A summary of impacts of new technology is set out in the concept map, Figure 13.1.

To what extent do YOU think that all managers in their everyday jobs should have knowledge of available technologies and how they work? Or do you think that only engineers, designers and technical specialists need this kind of knowledge?

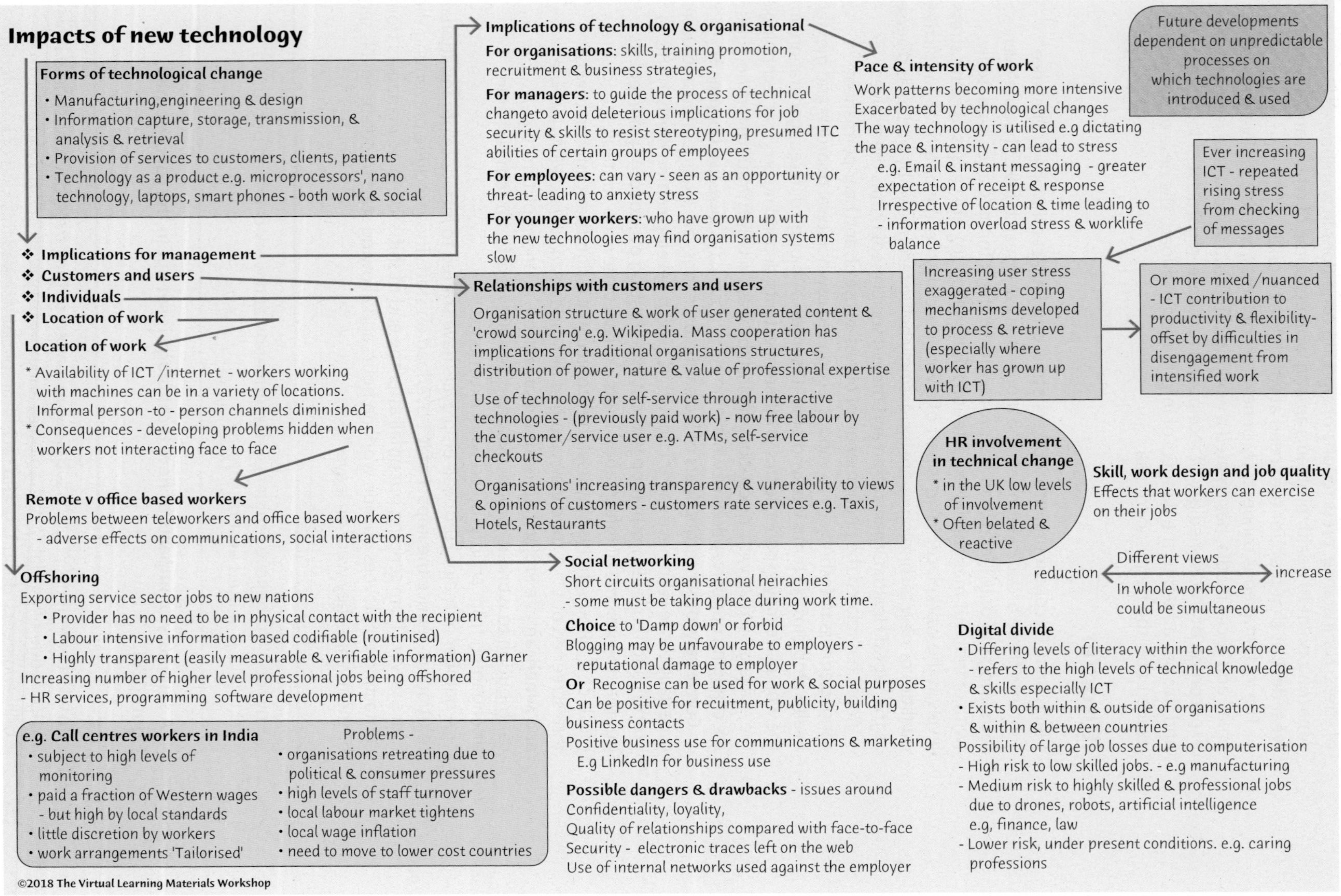

Impacts of new technology

Forms of technological change
- Manufacturing, engineering & design
- Information capture, storage, transmission, & analysis & retrieval
- Provision of services to customers, clients, patients
- Technology as a product e.g. microprocessors', nano technology, laptops, smart phones - both work & social

❖ Implications for management
❖ Customers and users
❖ Individuals
❖ Location of work

Location of work
* Availability of ICT /internet - workers working with machines can be in a variety of locations. Informal person -to - person channels diminished
* Consequences - developing problems hidden when workers not interacting face to face

Remote v office based workers
Problems between teleworkers and office based workers - adverse effects on communications, social interactions

Offshoring
Exporting service sector jobs to new nations
- Provider has no need to be in physical contact with the recipient
- Labour intensive information based codifiable (routinised)
- Highly transparent (easily measurable & verifiable information) Garner
Increasing number of higher level professional jobs being offshored
- HR services, programming software development

e.g. Call centres workers in India
- subject to high levels of monitoring
- paid a fraction of Western wages - but high by local standards
- little discretion by workers
- work arrangements 'Tailorised'

Problems -
- organisations retreating due to political & consumer pressures
- high levels of staff turnover
- local labour market tightens
- local wage inflation
- need to move to lower cost countries

©2018 The Virtual Learning Materials Workshop

Implications of technology & organisational
For organisations: skills, training promotion, recruitment & business strategies,
For managers: to guide the process of technical change to avoid deleterious implications for job security & skills to resist stereotyping, presumed ITC abilities of certain groups of employees
For employees: can vary - seen as an opportunity or threat- leading to anxiety stress
For younger workers: who have grown up with the new technologies may find organisation systems slow

Relationships with customers and users
Organisation structure & work of user generated content & 'crowd sourcing' e.g. Wikipedia. Mass cooperation has implications for traditional organisations structures, distribution of power, nature & value of professional expertise
Use of technology for self-service through interactive technologies - (previously paid work) - now free labour by the customer/service user e.g. ATMs, self-service checkouts
Organisations' increasing transparency & vunerability to views & opinions of customers - customers rate services e.g. Taxis, Hotels, Restaurants

Social networking
Short circuits organisational heirachies
- some must be taking place during work time.
Choice to 'Damp down' or forbid
Blogging may be unfavourable to employers - reputational damage to employer
Or Recognise can be used for work & social purposes
Can be positive for recruitment, publicity, building business contacts
Positive business use for communications & marketing E.g LinkedIn for business use
Possible dangers & drawbacks - issues around
Confidentiality, loyality,
Quality of relationships compared with face-to-face
Security - electronic traces left on the web
Use of internal networks used against the employer

Pace & intensity of work
Work patterns becoming more intensive
Exacerbated by technological changes
The way technology is utilised e.g dictating the pace & intensity - can lead to stress
e.g. Email & instant messaging - greater expectation of receipt & response
Irrespective of location & time leading to
- information overload stress & worklife balance

Increasing user stress exaggerated - coping mechanisms developed to process & retrieve (especially where worker has grown up with ICT)

Future developments dependent on unpredictable processes on which technologies are introduced & used

Ever increasing ICT - repeated rising stress from checking of messages

Or more mixed /nuanced - ICT contribution to productivity & flexibility- offset by difficulties in disengagement from intensified work

HR involvement in technical change
* in the UK low levels of involvement
* Often belated & reactive

Skill, work design and job quality
Effects that workers can exercise on their jobs

Different views

↓ reduction   ↑ increase

In whole workforce could be simultaneous

Digital divide
- Differing levels of literacy within the workforce - refers to the high levels of technical knowledge & skills especially ICT
- Exists both within & outside of organisations & within & between countries
Possibility of large job losses due to computerisation
- High risk to low skilled jobs.- e.g manufacturing
- Medium risk to highly skilled & professional jobs due to drones, robots, artificial intelligence
e.g, finance, law
- Lower risk, under present conditions. e.g. caring professions

Figure 13.1 Impacts of new technology
Source: Copyright © 2011 The Virtual Learning Materials Workshop.

Critical Thinking Zone

Reflections on Remote and Office-Based Working

In this zone, we critically examine remote and office-based working and explore whether the social aspects of working with technology have been overlooked, ignored or appropriately addressed by organisations.

The twenty first century, always-on, hyperconnected workplace has heralded a raft of challenges for the organisation and its members. The drive for flexibility and paradigm shift to non-traditional modes of working have impacted on those who choose to work remotely, others who prefer to retain their status as an office-based worker and managers, who must balance the needs of both parties with maintaining organisational efficiency and optimising productivity. Theorists such as Tietze and Nadin[67] have voiced their concerns regarding the shift in paradigm and the inevitable impact on workplace dynamics, which it could be argued, has disturbed the status quo. Their first concern centres on the social and organisational relationships that have either been severed, disrupted or destabilised and the ensuing tensions between colleagues and managers that the organisation has had to address. Their second concern is the 'relational impoverishment' (p. 1525) that remote and office-based workers, along with their managers, have suffered, which has been catalysed by the increased physical and psychological distance and reduced interpersonal interaction between them. Although remote workers are supported by computer-mediated technologies, Bélanger et al.[68] and Bentley et al.[69] proffer that restricted communication is a major issue for organisations, which can significantly impact on levels of job satisfaction and productivity. With all the hype surrounding virtual working, Gajendran and Harrison[70] caveat that it is unclear whether extant research can say, with any authority, if remote working is a positive or negative technological and workplace innovation for individuals concerned.

Remote vs Office-Based Working

Despite the tranche of well-publicised benefits that can be derived from remote working, theorists acknowledge some of the negatives that may be experienced. First, as individuals are working away from the main office location, they could encounter reduced face-to-face interaction with their colleagues, line managers, clients and customers.[71] Of course, the acuteness of the situation depends on the level of virtuality adopted by the organisation, the local, national and international geographical location at which the work is undertaken and the amount of computer-mediated communication technologies with which individuals work[72] (see Chapter 8: Critical Thinking Zone: Reflections on Managing Virtual Teams). The reduced physical interaction might lower the social and relational capital that is generated between stakeholders[73,74] and, arguably, lead to significant knowledge gaps in various parts of the organisation. Second, Bélanger et al. and Bentley et al. contend that remote workers face social isolation and workplace exclusion in the absence of co-location, which impedes their innate need for affiliation with others. It might, therefore, result in reduced organisational commitment, higher turnover, lower job satisfaction, burnout and disinterest in, and rejection by, office-based workers. Hence, Morganson et al.[71] advocate the importance of workplace inclusion in designing virtual working arrangements and, where possible, ensuring that remote workers have an appropriate amount of social contact with their office-based colleagues.

To counter the negativity and promote more synergy and co-ordination between remote and office-based workers, Bentley et al. and Bélanger et al. profess the adoption of a socio-technical systems approach, to achieve some equilibrium between individuals' need for affiliation and their interaction with, and utilisation of, technology. This would promote the psychosocial aspects of organisational behaviour in the workplace, such as personality, motivation and attitudes to work, colleagues and the organisation at large.[68,75]

Transitioning from Office-Based to Remote Working

The transition from office-based to remote working is a major strategic change for the organisation and its stakeholders. Research conducted by Tietze and Nadin with a sample of homeworkers in the benefits and taxation units of a local authority, found that it yielded a range of positive and negative issues. First, although participants reported feelings of social isolation, it did not adversely affect productivity, which consequently increased. Many participants overcame the isolation by building networks with other homeworkers, which satiated their need for affiliation and belongingness. Participants felt they had a greater level of control over their work, which meant they were able dichotomise their work and home lives more effectively and achieve a better work–life balance in the process (see Chapter 2: Critical Thinking Zone: Reflections on Work–Life Balance). The introduction of homeworking by the local authority created tensions, negativity and resentment among office-based colleagues, who were not given the option to work from home. Tietze and Nadin concluded that although remote working can be a win-win for all parties concerned, caution should be exercised by organisations, particularly in terms of ensuring that relational aspects of the transition are not ignored but appropriately addressed.

Transitioning from Remote to Office-Based Working

Despite the espoused and evidence-based benefits of flexibility, not all organisations are in favour of remote working.[76] The former President and Chief Executive Officer of Yahoo, Marissa Mayer, reportedly banned home working on the basis that it harmed the tech giant's speed of delivery and innovation, which she believed were the bedrock of its success. Google and Hewlett Packard are further examples of organisations that have curtailed, though not discontinued, their working from home policies and programmes, preferring instead to exploit the benefits of co-location, which include increased collegiality and collaboration, enhanced tacit communication and improved understanding and appreciation of task interdependence within projects.[76] Although office-based working is a favourable choice for individuals who prefer the affiliation and sense of belonging that is related to being in one place, Pathak et al.[76] caveat that it may not be the best strategy for every organisation – or indeed, every information technology one.

Implications for Organisational Behaviour in the Workforce

To conclude, in the scrum to embrace the always-on, hyperconnectedness of the twenty-first-century business environment, and exploit consumer and business demand for 24/7 flexibility, McDowall and Kinman[75] profess that many organisations have overlooked, underestimated, ignored and thus not appropriately addressed the human, psycho-social aspects of working with technology and the requirement to preserve team cohesion and engender support from colleagues and managers, who may or may not have taken up the option to work remotely. As 'human capital remains organisations' greatest asset' (p. 264), McDowall and Kinman advocate that organisations, along with researchers and practitioners, have a common interest in, and joint responsibility to, generate a better understanding of people–technology interaction, identify how ICTs are influencing major changes in the nature of work and highlight how effective, conducive, healthy and sustainable working can be engendered for all parties in the people–employment relationship. As technology is here to stay, they conclude 'we cannot put the genie back in the bottle. . . so we need to take an evidence-based approach to how we can work most-effectively with it' (p. 264).

Questions

Based on the above, answer the following questions.

1. The viewpoints presented suggest there are pros and cons of remote and office-based working. *Identify* and *critique* the implications of each for organisational behaviour in the workplace.

2. It could be argued that a major issue with remote working is the lack of tacit knowledge creation and transfer between all parties concerned. Considering the different levels of virtuality an organisation can adopt, *what* steps would you *recommend* to managers to engender more tacit contact?

3. Having reversed their decision to allow homeworking, *consider* the strategies organisations such as Yahoo can deploy to promote the socio-technical and psychosocial aspects of working with technology.

Summary – Chapter 13 'Technology in the workplace'

Technology is found and used in all types of organisations and has an important influence on the nature of structure and work. It has an increasing impact on how and where products and services are delivered. We are currently on the verge of what may be a new revolution in 'intelligent' technologies, which has uncertain, but potentially far-reaching consequences for the numbers and types of job available. Technology has many forms of applications and the potential to improve the experience of work in many ways. However increasing dependence on technology carries potential reputational and operational risks and malign consequences, particularly when it comes to how much autonomy individuals have at work, and how it can drive an increasing pace and intensity of work in an information-hungry society. Current internet developments have implications for relations between organisations and their workers and also with customers and users. The experience of work is not a result just of the technology itself, but of decisions that are made within organisations by managers about how technologies will be applied. Managers therefore need an understanding of the practical, organisational and ethical dimensions of how technology is put to work.

Group discussion activities

Undertake each of these activities in small groups as indicated by your tutor. Before you start your discussion establish a non-threatening environment within the group and confirm confidentiality will be honoured.

First, form your own views and then share and compare in open critical discussion with colleagues. Reflect honestly on the extent to which: (i) you influenced the thinking and ideas of your colleagues; and (ii) you were influenced by your colleagues.

To what extent was your group able to reach consensus?

Agree one of your members to produce a brief written summary of the discussion and prepared to present in a plenary session.

Activity 1

Divide into two groups: one representing managers and the others representing employees. Separately, each group should come up with a number of arguments about the degree to which employees have a reasonable expectation of privacy and freedom from surveillance of their activities in the workplace. Each group can also consider to what extent employers have any right to exert control over what workers do outside the workplace too.

The two groups should then present their respective cases to the other. Can the two groups reach any consensus about the extent to which employers should be able to exercise surveillance and control over workers?

Activity 2

(a) To what extent do organisations have any responsibility to manage technical change in a way that preserves numbers of jobs?

(b) Whatever your answer to the above question, to what extent do firms have any responsibility to manage the introduction of technical change in a way that maximises the chances of producing high quality jobs?

Activity 3

Think of the innovation of the driverless vehicle, which is currently being pioneered by a number of major companies.

(a) What does the group think are the economic and social implications of this? You may want to consider the impact on jobs, skills, the economy, legal implications in the event of an accident, implications for personal freedom, and so on.

(b) On balance, do you think the driverless vehicle is a development to be welcomed or feared?

Organisational behaviour in action case study
Negotiating the use of vehicle tracking technology

The use of vehicle tracking technology by managers of those who drive company vehicles as part of their job is controversial. For instance, parcel delivery firms routinely use such technology so that managers, and sometimes even customers, can check drivers' progress on their routes. It has also resulted in a number of disputes between firms and trade unions about the monitoring of drivers. Among other things, drivers and their unions have been concerned about privacy and the possible use of such systems to monitor driver location and performance. For management's part, such workers have traditionally been very difficult to control, as they often work alone and cannot be readily supervised when off the company premises.

In 2009 British Telecom (BT) engineers in Southampton belonging to the Communication Workers' Union (CWU) organised a demonstration about the proposed installation of GPS vehicle tracking systems in their vehicle cabs. In response to this disquiet, BT managers entered discussions with CWU representatives and the outcome was a jointly negotiated Memorandum of Understanding that stipulated how GPS equipment was to be used in the future. The agreement stated that the system would not be used as a means of engaging in surveillance of employees, nor would it be used as the sole basis for opening disciplinary proceedings against, or questioning the performance of individuals. The agreement reached also gave guarantees about employees' reasonable expectations of privacy

while out on the road and committed BT management and the CWU to consulting jointly in order to engage trust. As a result of the agreement, BT line managers were forbidden from accessing the GPS system to view data in real time on tracked vehicle movements. This does not imply that they cannot access historical data.

As a result of this agreement, a potentially serious dispute was averted and relations between the company and the CWU appear to have been strengthened.

Source: The main source for this case study is Labour Research Department 'The Enemy Within: Negotiating on Monitoring and Surveillance', *Workplace Report,* no. 97, December, 2011, pp. 15–16.

Tasks

1. Explain fully ways in which you think it was possible to avoid this dispute.

2. How does this case illustrate the management dilemma of the extent to which employees should be *controlled* or *trusted*? What factors complicate this dilemma in the case of employees who mainly work off-site?

3. To what extent do you think the case demonstrates the value of reaching joint agreement on technological change? What other possible approaches do you think could have been adopted and would have been the likely outcome in each scenario you can identify?

Chapter 13 – Personal skills and employability exercise

Objectives

Completing this exercise should help you to enhance the following skills:

* Understand better the impact of technology on an organisation and its members.
* Apply your theoretical knowledge to the analysis of organisational processes.
* Evaluate benefits and drawbacks resulting from technological change.

Exercise

Select and examine examples of two different jobs in your university, if possible, or in some other organisation with which you are familiar. Detail the main duties of the chosen jobs and both the technical skill and equipment necessary in undertaking each job.

Taking each job in turn, detail:

* Those aspects of job that you think could, or should, be further automated, and why?
* Those aspects of the job that cannot, or should not, be further automated, and why?
* How the nature of the job would change if your suggestions were followed? What do you think would be the reaction of the occupant? Would the job become more or less fulfilling?
* To what extent do you think senior managers would come to the same conclusions as yourself, taking into account factors such as costs, product and service quality?

Discussion

* On the basis of the jobs you have studied, does it suggest that further automation results in more positive or more negative implications for individuals in an organisation? Would you come to the same conclusion about further automation in general?
* Think back to the present occupants of each job. In what ways do you think there might be a different response depending upon the generation and age group of the occupants **(discussed in Chapter 2),** for example Generation Y, and the technological sophistication of the occupants?

Notes and references

1. King, A. 'Technology: The Future of Agriculture', *Nature,* vol. 544, 2017, pp. S21–S23.
2. See, for example, Flinders, M. 'TSB IT Meltdown has the Makings of an Epic', *Computer Weekly,* 25 April 2018, https://www.computerweekly.com/news/252439859/ TSB-IT-meltdown-has-the-makings-of-an-epic (accessed 19 June 2018).
3. See, for example, Tarafdar, M., Gupta, A. and Turel, O. 'Special issue on "Dark Side of Information Technology Use": An Introduction and a Framework for Research', *Information Systems Journal,* vol. 25, 2015, pp. 161–70.
4. See notably Advisory Council on Science and Technology, *People, Technology and Organisations: The Application of Human Factors and Organisational Design,* HMSO (1993).
5. Easton, J. 'Where to Draw the Line? Is Efficiency Encroaching on a Fair Justice System?', *Political Quarterly,* vol. 89, no. 2, 2018, pp. 246–53.
6. Hayward, K. 'Can Technology and "Max Fac" Solve the Irish Border Question? Expert Explains', *The Conversation,* 23 May 2018, http://theconversation.com/ can-technology-and-max-fac-solve-the-irish-border- question-expert-explains-96735 (accessed 19 June 2018).

7. Brynjolfsson, E. and McAfee, A. *The Second Machine Age: Work, Progress and Prosperity in a Time of Brilliant Technologies,* Norton (2014); Frey, C. and Osborne, M. 'The Future of Employment: How Susceptible are Jobs to Computerisation?', Oxford University Working Paper (2013). See also Frey, C. and Osborne, M. *Technology at Work: The Future of Innovation and Employment,* Citi GPS (2015). Their analysis has been applied to the UK in Frey, C. and Osborne, M. *London Futures – Agiletown: The Relentless March of Technology and London's Response,* Deloitte LLP (2014).

8. Bakhshi, H., Downing, J., Osborne, M. and Schneider, P. *The Future of Skills: Employment in 2030,* Pearson (2017).

9. See, for example, de Cameron, N. *Will Robots Take your Job?* Polity (2017); Eurofound *Automation, Digitalisation and Platforms: Implications for Work and Employment,* (2018); OECD, *Automation, Skill Use and Training,* OECD (2018).

10. Clark, I. and Colling, T. 'Work in Britain's Informal Economy: Learning from Road-side Hand Car Washes,' *British Journal of Industrial Relations,* vol. 56, no. 2, 2018, pp. 320–341.

11. See Peng, G., Wang, Y. and Han, G. 'Information Technology and Employment: The Impact of Job Tasks and Worker Skills', *Journal of Industrial Relations,* vol. 60, no. 2, 2018, pp. 201–23, for a recent review.

12. Braverman, H. *Labor and Monopoly Capital: The Degradation of Work in the Twentieth Century,* Monthly Review Press (1974).

13. See Thompson, P. *The Nature of Work,* Macmillan (1989) for an overview of the main positions in the labour process debate.

14. Jones, B. *Forcing the Factory of the Future,* Cambridge University Press (1997).

15. Zuboff, S. *In the Age of the Smart Machine,* Harvard Business School Press (1988).

16. Darr, A. and Warhurst, C. 'Assumptions, Assertions and the Need for Evidence: Debugging Debates about Knowledge Workers', *Current Sociology,* vol. 56, no. 1, 2008, pp. 25–45; Thompson, P., Warhurst, C. and Callaghan, G. 'Ignorant Theory and Knowledgeable Workers: Interrogating the Connections between Knowledge, Skills and Services', *Journal of Management Studies,* vol. 38, no. 7, 2001, pp. 923–42.

17. Fleming, P., Harley, B. and Sewell, G. 'A Little Knowledge Is a Dangerous Thing: Getting Below the Surface of the Growth of "Knowledge Work" in Australia', *Work, Employment and Society,* vol. 18, no. 4, 2004, pp. 725–47.

18. Huws, U. 'The Making of a Cybertariat? Virtual Work in a Real World', in U. Huws (ed.) *The Making of a Cybertariat? Virtual Work in a Real World,* Merlin Press (2003), p. 166.

19. Foster, J. B. and McChesney, R. 'Surveillance Capitalism', *Monthly Review,* vol. 66, no. 1, https://monthlyreview. org/2014/07/01/surveillance-capitalism/ (accessed 19 June 2018).

20. Blakemore, M. *From Workplace Watch to Social Spy: Surveillance in (and by) the Workplace – Updated Briefing Paper for GMB,* GMB Union (2011); Labour Research Department, *Social Media, Monitoring and Surveillance at Work,* Labour Research Department (2012).

21. See for example Newsome, K., Thompson, P. and Commander, J. '"You Manage Performance at every Hour": Labour and the Management of Performance in the Supermarket Supply Chain', *New Technology, Work and Employment,* vol. 28, no. 1, 2013, pp. 1–15; De Vita, G. and Case, P. '"The Smell of the Place": Managerialist Culture in Contemporary UK Business Schools', *Culture and Organization,* vol. 22, no. 4, 2016, pp. 348–64.

22. A 2015 survey of members by UK teachers' union NASUWT reports more extensive problems with the use of CCTV in schools to monitor teachers' performance than found in a parallel survey in 2014. See NASUWT 'Teachers subjected to professionally demeaning practices', NASUWT press release, April 2015, http:// www.nasuwt.org.uk/Whatsnew/NASUWTNews/ PressReleases/NASUWT_013937 (accessed 6 May 2015).

23. See House of Lords Select Committee on the Constitution, *Surveillance: Citizens and the State: Report,* HL18-I, Second Report of Session 2008/9, Stationery Office (2009), p. 17.

24. Foucault, M. *Discipline and Punish – The Birth of the Prison,* Penguin (1977).

25. See, for example, Lyon, D. *The Electronic Eye: The Rise of the Surveillance Society,* Polity Press (1994); Sewell, G. 'The Discipline of Teams: The Control of Team-Based Industrial Work through Electronic and Peer Surveillance', *Administrative Science Quarterly,* vol. 43, no. 2, 1998, pp. 397–428.

26. Mason, D., Button, G., Lankshear, G. and Coates, S. 'Getting Real about Surveillance and Privacy at Work', in Woolgar, S. (ed.) *Virtual Society? Technology, Cyperbole, Reality,* Oxford University Press (2002), pp. 137–52.

27. Eriksson-Zetterquist, U., Lindberg, K. and Styhre, A. 'When the Good Times are Over: Professionals encountering New Technology', *Human Relations,* vol. 62, no. 8, 2009, pp. 1145–70; Fisher, M. 'The New Politics of Technology in the British Civil Service', *Economic and Industrial Democracy,* vol. 28, no. 4, 2007, pp. 523–51.

28. Sewell, G., Barker, J. and Nyberg, D. 'Working under Intense Surveillance: When does "Measuring Everything that Moves" Become Intolerable?', *Human Relations,* vol. 65, no. 2, February 2012, pp. 189–215.

29. Grampp, C., Houlihan, M. and McGrath, P. 'Who's Driving Now? GPS and the Restructuring of Taxi Work', in Bolton, S. and Houlihan, M. (eds) *Work Matters: Critical Reflections on Contemporary Work,* Palgrave (2009), pp. 232–49.

30. HR Grapevine 'Shopping, Gaming and Gambling – How are your Staff using Company Devices?', HR Grapevine, 21 November 2014, http://www.hrgrapevine.com/

markets/hr/article/2014-11-21-shopping-gaming-and-gambling-how-are-your-staff-using-company-devices?utm_source=eshot&utm_medium=email&utm_campaign=RR%20-%2021/11/2014 (accessed 19 June 2018).

31. See, for example, the case of three judges sacked for viewing internet pornography through their work IT accounts: BBC News 'Judges sacked for watching porn', www.bbc.co.uk, 17 March 2015, http://www.bbc.co.uk/news/uk-31920906 (accessed 6 May 2015). Also see the first 'Twitter unfair dismissal' case: Laws v. Game Retail Ltd.: [2014] UKEAT_0188_14_0311.

32. See, for example: Labour Research Department, *Social Media, Monitoring and Surveillance at Work,* Labour Research Department, 2012.

33. Advisory, Conciliation and Arbitration Service, *Social Media in the Workplace,* ACAS (n.d.), http://www.acas.org.uk/index.aspx?articleid=3375 (accessed 18 June 2018).

34. Broughton, A., Higgins, T., Hicks, B. and Cox, A. *Workplaces and Social Networking: The Implications for Employment Relations,* ACAS Research Paper 11/11 (2011); Jennings, S., Blount, J. and Wetherly, M. 'Social Media – A Virtual Pandora's Box: Prevalence, Possible Legal Liabilities and Policies', *Business and Professional Communication Quarterly,* vol. 77, no. 1, 2014, pp. 96–113.

35. Ellis, V. and Richards, J. 'Creating, Connecting and Correcting: Motivations and Meanings of Work-Blogging among Public Service Workers', in Bolton, S. and Houlihan, M. (eds) *Work Matters: Critical Reflections on Contemporary Work,* Palgrave (2009), pp. 253–4.

36. Stevens, M. 'Employers are Urged not to "Kill the Conversation" on Social Media', *People Management,* 29 February 2012, http://www.peoplemanagement.co.uk/pm/articles/2012/02/employers-urged-not-to-kill-the-conversation-on-social-media.htm (accessed 23 July 2012).

37. ACAS 'Does Social Media Strengthen or Dilute Employee Voice?', *ACAS Employment Relations* Comment, August 2014.

38. Ellis, V. and Richards, J., op. cit., pp. 250–68.

39. Bradwell, P. and Reeves, R. *Network Citizens: Power and Responsibility at Work,* Demos (2008).

40. Ibid.

41. Broughton, A. et al. *The Experiences of Individuals in the Gig Economy,* Department of Business, Energy and Industrial Strategy (2018).

42. Bergvall-Kåreborn, B. and Howcroft, D. 'Amazon Mechanical Turk and the Commodification of Labour', *New Technology, Work and Employment,* vol. 29, no. 3, 2014, pp. 213–23.

43. See, for example: Surowiecki, C. *The Wisdom of Crowds,* Abacus (2005); Tapscott, D. and Williams, A. *Wikinomics,* Penguin (2007).

44. Shirky, C. *Here Comes Everybody: The Power of Organizing without Organizations,* Penguin (2009).

45. Pollitt, C. 'Mainstreaming Technological Change in the Study of Public Management', *Public Policy and Administration,* vol. 26, no. 4, 2011, pp. 377–97.

46. Age UK *Everything is Online Nowadays,* Age UK (2018).

47. Williams, G. and Beck, V. 'From Annual Ritual to Daily Routine: Continuous Performance and its Consequences for Employment Security', *New Technology, Work and Employment,* vol. 33, no. 1, 2018, pp. 30–43.

48. Urry, J. *Mobilities,* Polity (2007).

49. Anon 'Mobile Working – Massive Growth Seen', at http://www.newbusiness.co.uk/news/mobile-working-massive-growth-seen, Newbusiness.co.uk, 2011 (accessed 20 July 2012).

50. Felstead, A., Jewson, N. and Walters, S. *Changing Places of Work,* Palgrave (2005).

51. European Foundation for the Improvement of Living and Working Conditions, *Global Competition and European Companies' Location Decisions, Background Paper,* European Foundation (2008), p. 2.

52. For research on the labour process and employment systems in Indian call centres see Taylor, P. and Bain, P. '"India Calling to the Far Away Towns": The Call Centre Labour Process and Globalization', *Work, Employment and Society,* vol. 19, no. 2, 2005, pp. 261–82.

53. Garner, C. 'Offshoring in the Service Sector: Economic Impact and Policy Issues', *Federal Reserve Bank of Kansas City Economic Review,* Autumn 2004, pp. 12–15.

54. The Economist 'Brexit triggers a round of reshoring', *The Economist,* 19 October 2017, https://www.economist.com/britain/2017/10/19/brexit-triggers-a-round-of-reshoring (accessed 18 June 2018).

55. Cited in Jackson, P. (ed.) *Virtual Working: Social and Organisational Dynamics,* Routledge (1999), p. 53.

56. Golden, T. 'Co-workers Who Telework and the Impact on Those in the Office: Understanding the Implications of Virtual Work for Co-worker Satisfaction and Turnover Intentions', *Human Relations,* vol. 60, no. 11, 2007, pp. 1641–67.

57. Ibid., p. 1643.

58. Fogarty, H., Scott, P. and Williams, S. 'The Half-Empty Office: Dilemmas in Managing Locational Flexibility', *New Technology, Work and Employment,* vol. 26, no. 3, 2011, pp. 183–95.

59. On work intensification, and the contribution of technology, see the following *inter alia*: Beynon, H. *et al. Managing Employment Change: The New Realities of Work,* Oxford University Press (2002); Burchell, B. *et al.* (eds) *Job Insecurity and Work Intensification,* Routledge (2002); Green, F. 'It's Been a Hard Day's Night: The Concentration and Intensification of Work in Late Twentieth Century Britain', *British Journal of Industrial Relations,* vol. 39, no. 1, 2001, pp. 53–80; White, M., Hill, S., McGovern, P., Mills, C. and Smeaton, D. 'High Performance Management Practices, Working Hours and Work–Life Balance', *British Journal of Industrial Relations,* vol. 41, no. 2, 2003, pp. 197–214.

60. Butler, S. 'Amazon Accused of Treating UK Warehouse Staff like Robots', *The Guardian,* 31 May 2018, https://www.theguardian.com/business/2018/may/31/amazon-accused-of-treating-uk-warehouse-staff-like-robots?CMP=share_btn_tw (accessed 18 June 2018).

61. Berkowsky, R. 'When you just Cannot get Away', *Information, Communication and Society,* vol. 16, no. 4, 2013, pp. 519–41. See also NASUWT's survey of the impact of email on teachers' work–life balance: NASUWT 'Home invasion on a grand and unacceptable scale', press release, 6 April 2015, http://www.nasuwt.org.uk/Whatsnew/NASUWTNews/PressReleases/NASUWT_013939 (accessed 6 April 2015).

62. Rosen, L. *iDisorder: Understanding our Obsession with Technology and Overcoming its Hold on Us,* Palgrave Macmillan (2012).

63. For example, Bittman, M., Brown, J. and Wajcmann, J. 'The Mobile Phone, Perpetual Contact and Time Pressure', *Work, Employment and Society,* vol. 23, no. 4, 2007, pp. 673–91; Bucher, E., Fieseler, C. and Suphan, A. 'The Stress Potential of Social Media in the Workplace', *Information, Communication and Society,* vol. 16, no. 10, 2013, pp. 1639–67.

64. Symon, G. (2000) 'Information and Communication Technologies and the Network Organization: A Critical Analysis', *Journal of Occupational and Organizational Psychology,* vol. 73, p. 395.

65. Madden, M. and Jones, S. *Networked Workers,* PEW Research Center (2008), p. iii.

66. De Castella, T. 'The Big Ideas of 2014', *BBC News Magazine,* 1 January 2015 http://www.bbc.co.uk/news/magazine-30576672 (accessed 6 May 2015).

67. Tietze, S. and Nadin, S. 'The Psychological Contract and the Transition from Office-based to Home-based Work', *Human Resource Management Journal,* vol. 21, no. 3, 2011, pp. 318–32.

68. Bélanger, F., Watson-Manheim, M. B. and Swan, B. R. (2013). 'A Multi-level Socio-technical Systems Telecommuting Framework', *Behaviour and Information Technology,* vol. 32, no. 12, 2013, pp. 1257–79.

69. Bentley, T. A., Teo, S. T. T., McLeod, L., Tan, F., Bosua, R. and Gloet, M. (2016). 'The Role of Organisational Support in Teleworker Well-being: A Socio-technical Systems Approach', *Applied Ergonomics,* vol. 52, pp. 207–15.

70. Gajendran, R. S. and Harrison, D. A. 'The Good, the Bad and the Unknown about Telecommuting: Meta-Analysis of Psychological Mediators and Individual Consequences', *Journal of Applied Psychology,* vol. 92, no. 6, 2007, pp. 1524–41.

71. Morganson, V. J., Major, D. A., Oborn, K. L., Verive, J. M. and Heelan, M.P. 'Comparing Telework Locations and Traditional Work Arrangements: Differences in Work–Life Balance Support, Job Satisfaction, and Inclusion', *Journal of Management Psychology,* vol. 25, no. 6, 2010, pp. 578–95.

72. Gibson, S. G. and Gohan, S. G. *Virtual Teams That Work: Creating Conditions for Virtual Team Effectiveness,* Jossey-Bass (2003).

73. Pfaff, C. C. and Hasan, H. 'Wiki-based Knowledge Management Systems for more Democratic Organizations', *Journal of Computer Information Systems,* vol. 52, no. 2, 2011, pp. 73–82.

74. Bontis, N. 'Intellectual Capital: An Exploratory Study that Develops Measures and Models', *Management Decision,* vol. 36, no. 2, 1998, pp. 63–76.

75. McDowall, A. and Kinman, G. 'The New Nowhere Land? A Research and Practice Agenda for the "Always on" Culture', *Journal of Organizational Effectiveness: People and Performance,* vol. 4, no. 3, 2017, pp. 256–66.

76. Pathak, A. A., Bathini, D. R. and Kandathil, G. M. 'The ban on working from home makes sense for Yahoo', *Human Resource Management International Digest,* vol. 23, no. 3, 2015, pp. 12–14.

Chapter 14
Organisational control and power

Work organisations are complex systems of formal and social relationships. An underlying feature of organisational behaviour is the nature of control and power.

Learning outcomes

After completing this chapter you should have enhanced your ability to:

- explain the nature and importance of control in work organisations;
- detail functions and essential elements of organisational control;
- review different forms, strategies and characteristics of control;
- assess management control, leadership influence and pluralistic approaches to power;

- debate the nature and importance of behavioural factors of organisational control;
- explore the concept of empowerment and the manager–subordinate relationship;
- examine the process, benefits of and concerns about delegation.

Outline chapter contents

Overview topic map: Chapter 14 – Organisational control and power

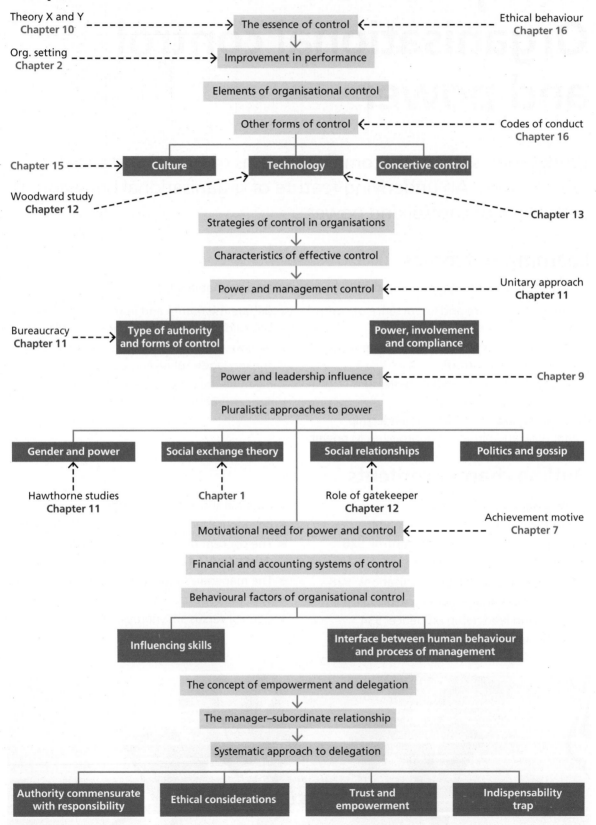

Exercising control and power

Before commencing to read this chapter think honestly about how YOU react when you hear the words 'control' and 'power'.

The essence of control

As discussed in **Chapter 10** control is generally acknowledged as part of the essential function of management. Control systems exist in all spheres of the operations of the organisation and are a necessary part of the process of management. What is important is the manner in which control is exercised and nature of the manager–subordinate relationships as the basis of improved work behaviour and organisational performance.

Feature of organisational behaviour

By their very nature, control systems are concerned with the regulation of behaviour. Unfortunately 'control' often has an emotive connotation and interpreted in a negative manner to suggest an indication of authoritarian management, the giving of orders, and a means of exerting pressure and maintaining discipline.

Child suggests that although control is an essential process of management, it is strangely neglected by many writers on organisation. Among possible reasons for this is that 'control has a sinister ring to it, associated in people's minds with power and manipulation. As a result, there may be some reluctance among many business school writers to discuss control, in order to avoid embarrassment'.[1]

Traditional views of control

Traditional views of control placed emphasis on the need for conformity of activities with the organisation and a prerogative of management. Tannenbaum, for example, sees control as an inherent characteristic of the nature of organisations. The process of control is at the centre of the exchange between the benefits that the individual derives from membership of an organisation and the costs of such benefits.[2]

Individual responses and behaviour

According to *Cloke and Goldsmith,* many employees have grown up in hierarchical organisations and become accustomed to external authority and the dead weight of organisational history.

> **Many employees actually prefer being told what to do by autocratic managers and are willing to accept being treated like children in exchange for irresponsibility and reduced stress. They are willing to blindly obey hierarchical authority and keep silent before their superiors in exchange for job security. It is easier by far to be an unthinking drone who obeys orders from above than a self-managing team member who is responsible for results.[3]**

(You may wish to remind yourself of the discussion on Theory X and Theory Y management in Chapter 10.)

There is however far more to control than simply a means of restricting behaviour or the exercise of authority over others. Control is not only a function of the formal organisation and a hierarchical structure of authority: it is also a feature of organisational behaviour and a function of interpersonal influence. With both control and power, **discussed later**, it is important to remember they are the *perceived* influences over other people. It is the way in which people are seen rather than the actual control or power they are in a position to exercise.[4]

Concern for the regulation of behaviour and improvement in performance raises questions as to the ethical nature of control. (Ethical behaviour in business is discussed in Chapter 16.)

As *Wilson* reminds us, individuals are not just passive objects of control: 'They may accept, deny, react, reshape, rethink, acquiesce, rebel, or conform and create themselves within constraints imposed on them.'[5]

Watson points out that although process-rational thinking recognises the aspiration of those 'in charge' of work organisations to achieve control over work behaviours, it also recognises two other things.

- Only partial control can ever be achieved. This is because organisations only exist through human relationships, and human relationships never allow the total control of some people over others. Power is rarely uncontested and, to a greater or less extent, attempts at control are typically resisted.

- Whatever control is achieved over work behaviour is brought about as much through processes of negotiation, persuasion, manipulation and so on, as through system 'devices' like rules and official procedures.[6]

Behaviour factors of organisational control are discussed later in this chapter.

Improvement in performance

From an organisational perspective, control completes the cycle of managerial activities. It involves the planning of work functions, and guiding and regulating the activities of staff. The whole underlying purpose of management control is improvement in performance at both the individual and organisational level **(see Figure 14.1).** According to *Zimmermann* an organisation without control is

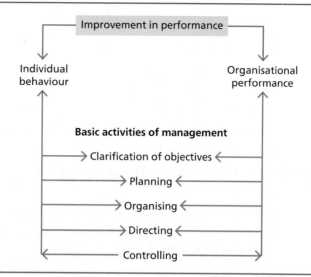

Figure 14.1 The nature of management control

impossible. Control systems are about influencing the behaviour of individuals in the interest of the corporation. Control systems measure the effective translation of decisions into results and goal achievement of the organisation.[7]

Features of poor organisational performance can even lead to the collapse of a company.[8] A major international report undertaken by Proudfoot Consulting found that poor management in terms of inadequate planning and control and insufficient day-to-day supervision of work is still the largest single reason for lost productivity.[9]

Expression of managerial behaviour

The nature of management control is an organisational variable. Recall the discussion on the organisational setting in **Chapter 2** and consider likely variations in the extent and form of control among a range of diverse organisations. While the need for some form of control is constant, the extent and manner of control is variable. The exercise of control is an expression of management systems and styles of behaviour. What is really important is what control is intended to achieve and the manner in which it is exercised.

To what extent do YOU accept the need for some form of control as a prerequisite for improved individual and organisational performance?

Function of control systems

Control is far-reaching; it can serve a number of functions concerned with general results or specific actions and can be manifested in a number of forms. For example, controls can be concerned with:

- observance of legislation, standing orders and policies and procedures;
- day-to-day operational activities that call for more specific standards of performance and speedy corrective action;

- health and safety of all members of the organisation or people in contact with the organisation;
- the structure of the organisation and role relationships;
- type of production system and use of technology;
- measurement of inputs, outputs, processes or the behaviour of people;
- recruitment and selection, socialisation, training and development;
- performance of the organisation as a whole or with major parts of it.

Elements of organisational control

Whatever the nature of control, whatever form it takes or whoever is responsible for its implementation there are five essential elements in an organisational control system (*see* **Figure 14.2):**

- planning what is desired;
- establishing standards of performance;
- monitoring actual performance;
- comparing actual achievement against the planned target; and
- rectifying and taking corrective action.

1. **Planning what is desired** – clarification of aims to be achieved. It is important people understand exactly what is required of them, and objectives and targets are specified clearly, particularly key activities. Planning provides the framework against which the process of control takes place.

2. Related to planning is the **establishment of defined standards of performance** This requires realistic measurements by which achievement can be determined. Whenever possible measurements given some measurable attribute and stated in quantitative terms. Reasonable time scales should also be specified. Planning and measurement are prerequisites of control.

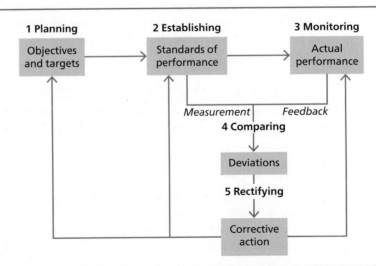

Figure 14.2 The five essential stages of organisational control

3. **Monitoring actual performance** – requires clear channels of communication and feedback, a system of reporting information that is accurate, relevant and timely. Feedback also provides the basis for decisions to adjust the control system, for example the need to revise the original plan.

4. **Compare actual performance against planned targets** – requires a means of interpreting and evaluating information to give details of progress, reveal deviations and identify probable causes.

5. **Taking corrective action to rectify** the situation that has led to any failure to achieve objectives or targets, or other forms of deviations identified. This requires authority to take appropriate action to correct the situation, review the operation of the control system and make any necessary adjustments to objectives and targets or to the standards of performance.

Other forms of control

More recent approaches question the extent to which **culture is a means of organisation control.** For example, *Ray* suggests that managers view organisational culture as an effective control tool[10] and *Egan* refers to culture as the largest organisational control system.[11] **(See the discussion on organisational culture in Chapter 15.)**

According to *McKenna,* organisational codes of conduct **(discussed in Chapter 16)** can constitute another form of control:

> Developing and distributing a code of conduct is a form of control that sets out the rules of behaviour and values with which an organisation's senior managers expect their subordinates will conform. Such a code will only be accepted if subordinates observe that managers at all levels live this code in their actions, beliefs and involvement in collective learning.[12]

Technology and control systems

From a further analysis of the data collected from Woodward's South Essex study of 100 manufacturing firms **(discussed in Chapter 12),** clear links emerged between the original classification of technology and managerial control systems. From the analysis, Reeves and Woodward suggest that control systems may be the underlying variable that links organisational behaviour and technology. The classification of control systems they propose might provide a better means of predicting certain facets of organisational behaviour than the classification of technology.[13]

Wilson points out that technology is not just about devices and machines but also about social relations that encourage some form of interaction. Technology is a human, political and social activity. 'The locus of control cannot always be moved from workers to managers during technical change nor from managers to workers. Control does therefore ultimately lie with management – although workers may resist it.'[14]

Information communications technology

Previous chapters have referred to the impact of developments in information communications technology and these developments will also have a significant impact on organisational control systems. Processes of communication are increasingly linked to computer systems with the rapid transmission of more information to more people including immediate access to other national or international offices. Information technology and office automation are changing the nature of the workplace and the way in which people work. For example, advances in telecommunications have resulted in a significant growth in telecommuting, with staff working from home with a computer network, telephone and fax. This has many potential advantages but also raises questions of self-motivation, security and systems of management control. Another interesting situation arising from the increasing use of information technology is the legal position on organisations monitoring staff emails and internet usage. **(A more detailed discussion on technology, work and organisational behaviour is included in Chapter 13.)**

Concertive control

Barker refers to a change from hierarchical, bureaucratic control to concertive control through the interaction of members in self-managing teams. **Concertive control** is not exerted by managers but by the value consensus of the team to a system of normative rules. Workers form their own cultural norms rather than bureaucratic rules and develop means for their own control.

> I don't have to sit here and look for the boss to be around; and if the boss is not around, I can sit there and talk to me neighbor or do what I want. Now the whole team is around me and the whole team is observing what I'm doing.[15]

However, *Wright and Barker* refer to the need for some form of functional self-control as an element of teamwork but research has identified concertive control as a factor constraining teamwork. Teams can struggle with the collective manner in which teams control their own behaviours. Concertive peer enforced control can create powerful constraining or oppressive systems. Negative implications can arise within a team when a concertive control system is either too constraining or too loose and which parallel disadvantages of external control systems.[16]

 Do YOU believe concertive control is a realistic way in which to monitor the behaviour and performance of self-managing teams?

Strategies of control in organisations

Six significant strategies of control in organisations are explained by *Child* (*see* **Figure 14.3**):

1. personal centralised control;
2. bureaucratic control;
3. output control;
4. control through electronic surveillance;
5. HRM control; and
6. cultural control.[17]

1. Personal centralised control

   1.1 direct supervision of people's activities

   1.2 centralised decision-taking

   1.3 personal leadership: founded upon ownership rights, charisma, and/or technical expertise

   1.4 reward and punishments reinforcing conformity to personal authority

2. Bureaucratic control

   2.1 breaking down of task into easily definable elements

   2.2 formally specified methods, procedures and rules applied to the conduct of tasks

   2.3 budgetary and standard cost-variance accounting controls

   2.4 technology designed to limit variation in conduct of tasks, with respect to pace, sequence and possibly physical methods*

   2.5 routine decision-taking delegated within prescribed limits

   2.6 reward and punishment systems reinforcing conformity to procedures and rules

3. Output control

   3.1 jobs and units designed with responsibility for complete outputs

   3.2 specification of output standards and targets

   3.3 use of 'responsibility accounting' systems

   3.4 delegation of decisions on operational matters: semi-autonomy

   3.5 reward and punishment linked to attainment of output targets

4. Control through electronic surveillance

   4.1 speed and quality of work recorded and assessed remotely via information and communication technology (ICT)

   4.2 employee's performance assessed against that of other employees and trends

   4.3 such monitoring of performance used to reward and discipline employees

5. HRM control

   5.1 use of selection methods to ensure that new recruits 'fit' the profile of attitude, behaviour, and capabilities desired by management

   5.2 training and development designed to reinforce this desired profile

   5.3 assessment procedures and reward systems used to encourage conformity

6. Cultural control

   6.1 development of employees' personal identification with management goals

   6.2 strong emphasis on the collective and mutually supportive character of the organisation - e.g. analogy with the 'family'

   6.3 employment characterised by security of tenure and progression within the organisation

   6.4 semi-autonomous working: few formal controls

*Some authorities distinguish this as a separate control strategy. For example, Richard Edwards (1979), *Contested Terrain: The Transformation of the Workplace in the Twentieth Century,* New York, Basic Books.

Figure 14.3 Strategies of organisational control
Source: Child, J. *Organization: Contemporary Principles and Practice,* Blackwell Publishing (2015), second edition, p. 154. Reproduced with permission from Wiley-Blackwell.

- **Personal centralised controls** – Often found in small owner-managed organisations and characterised by centralisation of decision-making and initiative around a leadership figure. Control consists largely of personal supervision and inspection. The authority of the leader will usually rest upon the rights of ownership, special personal qualities (charisma) or technical expertise.

- **Bureaucratic control** – Familiar in public sector organisations and many other types of large organisations. It is based on the specification of how members should behave and carry out their work. There is an attempt to ensure predictability through formal job descriptions and procedures, and the specification of standard methods for the performance of tasks. The bureaucratic strategy also permits delegation without loss of control. Compliance can be rewarded by upgrading, improved status, favourable employment benefits and job security.

- **Output control** – Relies upon the ability to identify specific tasks having a measurable output or criterion of overall achievement – for example, an end-product, a part manufactured to agreed standards, batch production or a sub-assembly. Rewards and sanctions can be related to performance levels expressed in output terms.

- **Control through electronic surveillance** – The essence of control is that the speed and quality of work is recorded and assessed remotely through the use of ICT without reliance on personal supervision. Monitoring of performance can be used readily as the basis for reward and discipline. Control through electronic surveillance is applied to many types and levels of activity. A common example is call centres.

- **HRM control** – HRM procedures can be used both to develop people at work and to control their behaviour and performance. Systematic selection techniques are designed to ensure new recruits fit the profile and technical competencies required by management. Performance evaluation and appraisal provide feedback to both management and employees. Appraisals should provide the basis for reward and for an assessment of the need for further training or development.

- **Cultural control** – Moves away from conventional forms of organisation and is based on maintaining control through internalised compliance rather than external constraint. The basis of cultural control is the acceptance and willing compliance with the requirements of management and belief of the organisation. Despite criticisms of cultural control, it is in tune with the increasing number of professional and knowledge workers and is consistent with self-managing units or teams working with only limited formal controls.

Nelson Mandela's cell at Robben Island – a form of cultural control?

Characteristics of effective control

Whatever the nature or form of control there are a number of characteristic features of an effective control system. Control systems can have positive as well as negative effects. It is important therefore that they are designed and implemented in a constructive and rewarding way. An effective control system should:

- **Be understood by those involved in its operation.** The purpose of the control system and the information it provides must be fully comprehensible to those who have to act on the results.

- **Draw attention to the critical activities important to the success of the organisation.** Careful control must be maintained in key result areas and in those activities that are crucial to the success of the organisation.

- **Conform with the structure of the organisation and be related to decision centres responsible for performance.** Information should be supplied to those managers who have the responsibility for specified areas of activity and presented in a form that shows clearly when corrective action is necessary.

- **Be consistent with the objective of the activity to which it relates.** The control system should be sophisticated enough to indicate ways in which performance can be improved. For example it may not be sufficient just to know that expenditure has been kept within the budget. It would be more helpful to know in what areas expenditure has been incurred.

- **Report deviations from the desired standard of performance as quickly as possible.** Ideally, indications of likely deviations should be discovered before they actually occur. For example, information that the budget is likely to be overspent should arrive in sufficient time to enable those responsible to avoid drastic last-minute action.

- **Be flexible** and yield information that is not influenced by other factors unconnected to the purpose of the control system. For example, a control system which specifies that reports to top management should be made whenever expenditure exceeds the same set amount means high-spending departments may be subject to excessive control and low-spending departments not monitored closely enough.

- **Subject to continual review** to ensure they are effective and appropriate in terms of the results they produce. They should not be too costly or elaborate, but should satisfy the characteristic features suggested above.

How far can YOU identify the effectiveness of these characteristics with control systems in your university?

Power and management control

Work organisations are not only systems of hierarchical structure, they are also systems of intricate social relationships, status and power. **Power** is a complex and dynamic concept and difficult to define easily. **At a broad level, power can be interpreted in terms of control or influence over the behaviour of other people with or without their consent.** Sometimes power is interpreted in terms of the *extent* of the influence which can actually be exercised over other people, and sometimes it is taken to include influence over objects or things as well as people. Like the meaning of control, power can have an emotive connotation.

However, power is an inherent feature of work organisations and is often the underlying reality behind the decision-making process. It is central to the framework of order and system of command through which the work and activities of the organisation are carried out, and the implementation of policies, and procedures. Lack of power and influence, and office politics, are among the main sources of managerial stress within organisations.

Caulkin points out that visible or not, power shapes everything. Hierarchy occurs everywhere in the natural order.

> **Yet for all the words devoted to 'official' topics such as strategy, leadership, shareholder value and customer focus, the truth is that the drive to win and keep power is the 'invisible hand' that yanks the strings which determine much of what happens in business.[18]**

The view of power as of functional importance is in keeping with a unitary approach to organisation, **discussed in Chapter 11.** Management control is the predominant means by which the activities of staff are guided towards the achievement of organisational goals. The exercise of power is that which comes from a position of formal authority within the management structure of the organisation and which legitimises control over subordinate staff.

Types of authority and forms of control

In one of the earliest studies of formal organisations, *Weber* distinguished three types of authority: **traditional, charismatic** and **legal–rational.**[19] These types of authority are based on the form of control regarded as legitimate by subordinates and their acceptance of the power of superiors. The three types of authority relate to different types of organisations.

- In **traditional organisations,** authority is legitimised by custom and a longstanding belief in the natural right to rule, or is possessed by traditional ('proper') procedure. Examples would be the authority of the pope, kings or queens or a paternalistic employer.

- In **charismatic organisations,** authority is legitimised by belief in the personal qualities of the leader; authority is based on the leader's strength of personality and inspiration. Winston Churchill might be quoted as an example. On the impending demise of the charismatic leader the movement might collapse unless a 'legitimate' heir is found. This process tends to transform a charismatic organisation into either a traditional organisation or a bureaucratic organisation.

- In **legal–rational (legitimate) organisations,** authority is based on the acceptance of the law of formal rules and procedures, and on impersonal principles. Bureaucratic organisations are associated with legal–rational authority which stems from a legitimate hierarchical position in the organisation and not from personality. Examples are the armed forces, authority of government ministers or a university chancellor.

The concept of legal–rational authority is of most interest to us because most business organisations, particularly large-scale ones, tend to be of the bureaucratic type of structure, although there are variations in degree. Bureaucracy, as applying to certain structural features of organisation, is the most dominant type of formal organisation. **(Bureaucracy as a form of structure is discussed in Chapter 11.)**

To what extent do YOU accept the idea of legal-rational authority and the exercise of legitimate power from the position in the formal organisation structure?

Power, involvement and compliance

From a comparative analysis of complex organisations, *Etzioni* provides a classification of organisational relationships based on structures of control and the use of power resources as a means of ensuring compliance among members.[20]

Power differs according to the means by which members of the organisation comply.

- **Coercive power** relies on the use of threats, or physical sanctions or force, for example, controlling the need for food or comfort.
- **Remunerative power** involves the manipulation of material resources and rewards, for example, through salaries and wages.
- **Normative power** relies on the allocation and the manipulation of symbolic rewards, for example, esteem and prestige.

Involvement is the degree of commitment by members to the organisation.

- **Alienative involvement** occurs where members are involved against their wishes. There is a strong negative orientation towards the organisation.
- **Calculative involvement** occurs where attachment to the organisation is motivated by extrinsic rewards. There is either a negative orientation or a low positive orientation towards the organisation.
- **Moral involvement** is based on the individual's belief in, and value placed on, the goals of the organisation. There is high positive orientation towards the organisation.

When considered together Etzioni suggests that a particular kind of power usually goes with a particular kind of involvement *See* **Figure 14.4**:

- coercive power with alienative involvement – typified, for example, by prisons;
- remunerative power with calculative involvement – typified, for example, by business firms;
- normative power with moral involvement – typified, for example, by churches.

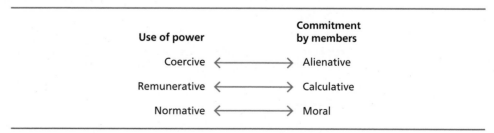

Figure 14.4 Etzioni's considered best fit between use of power and kind of involvement

The matching of these kinds of power and involvement is congruent with each other and represents the most common form of compliance in organisations. Etzioni suggests that organisations with congruent compliance structures will be more effective than organisations with incongruent structures.

Power and leadership influence

Leadership influence is a social process and may be seen in terms of the type of power that the leader can exercise over the behaviour and actions of others. **(Leadership is discussed in Chapter 9.)** An early view of social power upon which the influence of the leader is based have been identified by *French and Raven* who identify five main sources: reward power, coercive power, legitimate power, referent power and expert power.[21] We shall consider these in terms of the manager (as a leader) and subordinate relationship. It is important to note that these sources of power are based on the subordinate's perception of the influence of the leader, whether it is real or not.

- **Reward power** is based on the subordinate's *perception* that the leader has the ability and resources to obtain rewards for those who comply with directives; for example, pay, promotion, praise, recognition, increased responsibilities, allocation and arrangement of work, granting of privileges.

- **Coercive power** is based on fear and the subordinate's *perception* that the leader has the ability to punish or to bring about undesirable outcomes for those who do not comply with directives; for example, withholding pay rises, promotion or privileges; allocation of undesirable duties or responsibilities; withdrawal of friendship or support; formal reprimands or possibly dismissal. This is in effect the opposite of reward power.

- **Legitimate power** is based on the subordinate's *perception* that the leader has a right to exercise influence because of the leader's role or position in the organisation. Legitimate power is based on authority, for example that of managers and supervisors within the hierarchical structure of an organisation. Legitimate power is therefore 'position' power because it is based on the role of the leader in the organisation, and not on the nature of the personal relationship with others.

- **Referent power** is based on the subordinate's *identification* with the leader. The leader exercises influence because of perceived attractiveness, personal characteristics, reputation or what is called 'charisma'. For example, a particular manager may not be in a position to reward or punish certain subordinates, but may still exercise power over the subordinates because the manager commands their respect or esteem.

- **Expert power** is based on the subordinate's *perception* of the leader as someone who is competent and who has some special knowledge or expertise in a given area. Expert power is based on credibility and clear evidence of knowledge or expertise including 'functional' specialists such as the management accountant or systems analyst.

French and Raven point out that the five sources of power are interrelated and the use of one type of power (for example, coercive) may affect the ability to use another type of power (for example, referent). Furthermore, the same person may exercise different types of power, in particular circumstances and at different times.

Yukl suggests that a further relevant source of power is **control over information.**[22]

We can distinguish between **legitimate (organisational) power,** which derives from a person's position within the formal structure of the organisation and **personal (informal) power,** which derives from the individual and is in the eye of the beholders who believe that person has the ability to influence other people or events and to make things happen. For example, charisma or personal power as a feature of transformational leadership.

What form(s) of control and power are featured here?

Pluralistic approaches to power

Power arises not only from sources of structure or formal position within the organisation but from interpersonal sources such as the personality, experience, characteristics and talents of individual members of the organisation. *See* **Figure 14.5.**

We can distinguish between **legitimate (organisational) power**, which derives from a person's position within the formal structure of the organisation and

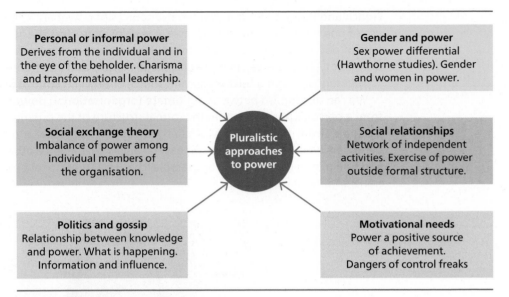

Figure 14.5 Pluralistic approaches to power

personal (informal) power, which derives from the individual and is in the eye of the beholders who believe that person has the ability to influence other people or events and to make things happen. For example, charisma or personal power as a feature of transformational leadership.

The exercise of power is, then, a social process that derives from a multiplicity of sources and situations.[23] This suggests a more pluralistic approach and recognises power as a major organisational variable. Many different groups and individuals have the ability to influence the behaviour and actions of other people, and in a number of different ways. This is not a new concept, however. In the 1920s the renowned management writer Mary Parker Follett focused on a human behaviour aspect, rejected the notion of domination and the exercise of power over other people, and argued for developing power with others in the organisation to make things happen. Effective control over work processes and social relationships would be achieved through group power and co-operative management. Follett advocated the replacement of personal power with the authority of task or function, and successful management based on the 'law of the situation'.[24]

Gender and power

You may recall the suggestion of the sex power differential between the all male group and all female group as part of the evaluation of the Hawthorne experiments **(discussed in Chapter 11)**. An example of gender and power is given by the Equality and Human Rights Commission who report on a survey on women in positions of power and influence. The survey found noticeable examples of the lack of women in senior positions of power, including those in the senior civil service, top management, judiciary, health service, directors of FTSE companies, Members of Parliament, and senior appointments in the armed forces and the police force. Where women do find positions of power and influence it is more likely to be in the public and voluntary sectors.[25]

Social exchange theory

Social exchange theory, **discussed in Chapter 1**, can give rise to an imbalance of power among individual members of the organisation. Social exchanges are influenced by a web of power relationships and are not always equal. Individuals will seek to achieve a positive balance for themselves by maximising benefits and minimising costs of exchanges. Those with more power are likely to fare better in their dealings with others. As an example, part-time or casual staff often feel they have less power than their full-time colleagues. *Bloisi* suggests that one negative outcome is when ethnic minorities or women are confined to the low end of the power spectrum, caused in part by their fewer numbers and by token dynamics. Bloisi also suggests that in some cases, language is used as a power tactic to put down a minority or to be condescending.[26]

Network of social relationships

Organisations function on the basis of networks of interdependent activities. Certain jobs or work relationships enable people to exercise a level of power in excess of their formal position within the structure of the organisation. A classic example is someone, perhaps a personal assistant or office manager, who fulfils the role of gatekeeper to the boss **(discussed in Chapter 12)**. Another example is with information technology problems where comparatively junior members of staff with particular technical expertise may have a way of ignoring the normal chain of command.

Many people within organisations also have the ability to grant or withhold 'favours' within the formal or the informal interpretation of their job role – for example, caretakers, security staff and telephonists. Staff may exercise negative power – that is, 'the capacity to stop things happening, to delay them, to distort or disrupt them'.[27] Negative power is not necessarily related proportionately to position and may often be exercised easily by people at lower levels of the hierarchical structure.

> What examples can YOU give of people outside the formal hierarchical structure who have been in a position to exercise power over other people?

Politics and gossip

A reality of organisational life is the vagaries of social relationships including power, office politics, and also the grapevine and gossip. *Misselhorn*, for example suggests that:

> Power is often seen as a dirty word. Yet it is a reality of human experience. We all use power in one way or another. We are also strongly influenced by our values. Then we draw on both our values and our power in what we believe to be our rational thinking about a problem situation. The difficulty we have is that 'power' and 'values' are mostly hidden forces which are at work from international politics to shop floor problem solving.[28]

Although a difficult topic to pin down, *Mann* refers to the key role that gossip plays in power relationships and knowledge production in organisations and maintains that 'There is an undeniable relationship between knowledge and power which lies at the root of gossiping.'[29]

Hazlehurst refers to the hoary old question of office politics. Although supposed to abhor it, power games are instinctive and most people enjoy at least a modest level of politicking – either as players or amused spectators. Hazlehurst also refers to *Sheryl* Sandberg, COO of Facebook who 'retains that most traditional symbol of corporate power, a corner office'.[30]

Alexander suggests that although office politics has a bad press you cannot sit it out and suggests it is reframed as 'office dynamics' or 'office relationships'. The author quotes a framework which distinguishes politics aligned with game-playing; and political awareness with integrity. There are also the non-political, principled and hard-working employees; or the game-playing employees who see themselves as power players but are usually outmanoeuvred.[31]

Yew and Gregory maintain that although rumour and gossip are often viewed as misbehaviour they are important in the workplace as they involve detailed knowledge of not just what is happening but who is doing what, with whom, how and why.[32]

Motivational need for power and control

Power can be a positive source of motivation for some people **(see the discussion on achievement motivation in Chapter 7)**. There is often a fine line between the motivation to achieve personal dominance and the use of social power. It has to be acknowledged, however, that there are some people who positively strive for and enjoy the exercise of power over other people. Some managers seek to maintain absolute control over subordinates and the activities of their department/section, and welcome the feeling of being indispensable. The possession of power is an ultimate ego satisfaction and such managers do not seem unduly concerned if as a result they are unpopular with, or lack the respect of, their colleagues or subordinate staff.

Kirwan-Taylor discusses control freaks who exist in every office and are capable of making everyone's life a misery. Control freaks try to dominate the environment by establishing order on what they perceive as chaos and attempting to control how other people think and behave. At one end of the spectrum are motivated and organised employees and at the other end obsessional, temperamental bullies. Sometimes, however, being a control freak is considered a positive attribute and key to success. Although control freaks function to a high standard, few people can bear to work with them.[33]

Be honest – do YOU see yourself as a control freak? If so, does it concern you? How do you feel about working closely with others you believe are control freaks?

Financial and accounting systems of control

Management control systems are frequently thought of in terms of financial and accounting systems. The reasons for this are easy to understand. The stewardship of financial resources is of vital concern to the majority of organisations. In both private enterprise and public sector organisations there is an increasing need to demonstrate value for money expended. Results are measured and reported in financial terms. Money is quantifiable, a precise unit of measurement and often used as a common denominator and as a basis for comparison. Financial limits are easy to apply as a measure of control and easy to relate to. For example, as part of the process of delegation, **discussed later in this chapter**, a measure of control might permit the subordinate to incur expenditure on certain items up to a given financial cost limit.

Accounting systems and human behaviour

However, accounting statements focus on only a limited area of activity. Management control embraces far more than just financial or accounting considerations. It is concerned with the whole process of management: with the extent to which organisational aims are achieved and with improvement in performance. Accounting control systems such as internal audit, management by exception and budgetary control tend to operate in a negative way and to report only on the unfavourable, or on favourable variances which may have adverse consequences, for example less spent than budgeted. 'Success' for the accounting staff may be equated with the 'failure' of other staff. As a result there is no specific recognition from management and little if any positive motivation.

There is, of course, nothing wrong with the use of accounting systems of control that have positive as well as negative effects. But, as with other forms of control, accounting systems should be designed and implemented in a constructive and rewarding way. To do this, they must take account of individual, social and organisational factors that determine people's patterns of behaviour.

Hilton suggests that the modern manager often lacks any feel for the unique culture of a business and therefore has an insufficient understanding or appreciation of the true drivers of its success. Unlike most developed countries UK boardrooms are dominated by people with a financial background. The problem is that financial control is not enough. Conventional risk control systems can cover hard data, technical know-how, systems and strategies. What they don't do is handle softer issues such as management style, employee motivation, shared values and corporate culture.[34]

Behavioural factors of organisational control

Most people show ambivalence towards control. While they may not wish to have them applied by other people to their own performance they recognise (even if reluctantly) the need for, and usefulness of, control systems. Individuals may feel a sense of unease with what they perceive as lack of control over disruptive or anti-social actions or behaviour of work colleagues.

Control systems can help fulfil people's needs at work and their presence may be welcomed by some members of staff. Under certain conditions, individuals may actually desire greater control over their work performance. Whenever a person inquires 'I would like to know how well I am doing', this can *arguably* be seen as asking for control in the form of improved feedback. Members of staff want to know what is expected of them and how well they are progressing towards their objectives. Control can stand for reliability, order and stability. It is a basis for training needs, for the motivation to achieve standards and for the development of individuals.

Often, however, control systems are perceived as a threat to the need satisfaction of the individual. Even when control systems are well designed and operated they may be viewed with a certain amount of suspicion and possible resentment by members of staff. Control over behaviour may be resented and provoke an emotional response from those affected including a dislike of those responsible for its operation.

Influencing skills

Clearly some degree of power, in whatever form, is needed to get work done. As *Owen* points out power skills are becoming more important because the nature of the manager's job is changing.

> It is now normal for managers to find that their responsibilities exceed their authority. In the past, the art of management was getting things done through other people, whom the manager controlled. Now managers have to get things done through other people whom they do not control. The lack of control changes everything. New skills are required to make things happen when you lack formal authority.

These skills include:

- building networks of trust and influence;
- creating alliances to make things happen;
- dealing with conflict;
- shaping the organisation's agenda to meet your needs;
- dealing with organisational conflict and resistance;
- managing ambiguity and uncertainty;
- finding the right assignments and projects to work on;
- discovering the real rules of survival and success in your firm.[35]

Yukl suggests that rather than focusing exclusively on power as a source of potential influence more attention is being given to specific types of behaviour used to exercise influence.

Rational persuasion – the use of logical arguments and factual persuasion

Apprising – explaining the personal benefits or career advancement

Inspiration appeals – to values and ideas or attempt to gain commitment

Consultation – seeking support and assistance by asking for assistance

Exchange – incentives or willingness to reciprocate

Collaboration – providing relevant resources and assistance in exchange for proposed change

Personal appeals – based on friendship or personal favour

Ingratiation – use of praise or flattery

Legitimating tactics – establish legitimacy or verify authority

Pressure – use of demands, threats, frequent checking

Coalition tactics – seeking the aid or support of others[36]

Jimmy Wales, founder of Wikipedia, suggests a redefinition of management and a change to the usually quoted functions of command and control to 'inspiring and coaching'. Management is inspiring people to do what needs to be done. Managers need new skills including delegation and allowing more autonomy for teams to be

> How good are YOU in influencing other people? What parts of your influencing behaviour are in need of further development?

more agile. There is no longer the luxury of communicating up the old command and control hierarchy: organisations need to be nimble at the end points.[37]

Interface between human behaviour and process of management

The manner in which control is exercised and the perception of staff will have a significant effect on the level of organisational performance. Control systems provide an interface between human behaviour and the process of management. There are a number of factors, **discussed in other chapters**, that can affect the successful implementation of management control systems, including the following.

- **Attitudes and response of staff.** Perception of reasons for, and methods of control. Consideration by management to the influences of diversity and inclusion. Extent to which control may help as a learning and development experience.

- **Motivation.** Motivation is a function of the relationship between effort expended and perceived level of performance. Recognition for a satisfactory level of attainment coupled with a suitable reward system, as integral parts of control, can do much to motivate staff and encourage improved performance.

- **Groups and the informal organisation.** Membership of a harmonious and effective work group can be a source of motivation and job satisfaction. Socialisation can help create a feeling of commitment to the group and reduce the need for formal management control. With the development of autonomous work groups, members have greater freedom and wider discretion over the planning, execution and control of their own work. Informal group 'norms' and peer pressure can be one of the most powerful forms of control.

- **Leadership and managerial style.** The style of managerial leadership is a function of the manager's attitudes towards people, and assumptions about human nature and behaviour – for example McGregor's Theory X and Theory Y. The balance between concern for production and for people.

- **Consultation and participation.** If staff are committed personally to particular objectives they are more likely to direct themselves and exercise self-control over their level of performance.

- **Organisation structure.** Organisations with a mechanistic structure are more readily suited to the operation and implementation of traditional systems of control. In organic structures the effectiveness of control is more dependent upon individual involvement and commitment to the aims of the organisation. Increased flexible working arrangements and homeworking call for greater trust from managers.

The concept of empowerment and delegation

Discussion on the balance between control versus autonomy, draws attention to the importance of empowerment. Despite general movement towards less mechanistic structures and the role of managers as facilitators, there appears to be some reluctance especially among top managers to dilute or weaken hierarchical control.

Empowerment is generally explained in terms of allowing employees greater freedom, autonomy and self-control over their work, and responsibility for decision-making. However, there are differences in the meaning and interpretation of the term. For example, how does it differ in any meaningful way from other earlier forms of employee involvement? Is the primary concern of empowerment getting the most out of the workforce? Is empowerment just another somewhat more fanciful term for delegation? Some writers see the two as quite separate concepts while other writers suggest empowerment is a more proactive form of delegation.

Attempting to distinguish clearly between empowerment and delegation is not always clear. However, empowerment is viewed generally as the more embracing term that describes a management style and granting of genuine additional power to other members of staff. Empowerment is viewed as the more embracing process. **It is the process of empowerment that gives rise to the act of delegation.**

At the individual (or personal) level, **delegation** is the process of entrusting authority and responsibility to others throughout the various levels of the organisation. It is the authorisation to undertake activities that would otherwise be carried out by someone in a more senior position.

According to *Mills and Friesen,* 'Empowerment can be succinctly defined as the authority of subordinates to decide and act.'

> It describes a management style. The term is often confused with delegation but, if strictly defined, empowerment goes much further in granting subordinates authority to decide and act. Indeed, within a context of broad limits defined by executives, empowered individuals may even become self-managing.[38]

Skill of empowerment and delegation

Empowering other people is a matter of judgement and delegation is not an easy task. It involves behavioural as well as organisational and economic considerations. Effective delegation is a social skill and requires reliance on other people, confidence and trust, and courage. It is important that the manager knows what to delegate, when and to whom. Matters of policy and disciplinary power, for example, usually cannot legitimately be delegated.

Extreme forms of behaviour

The nature of delegation can have a significant effect on the morale, motivation and work performance of staff. In all but the smallest organisation the only way to get work done effectively is through delegation, but even such an important practice can be misused or over-applied. There are two extreme forms of behaviour that can result.

- At one extreme is the almost total lack of meaningful delegation. Subordinate staff are only permitted to operate within closely defined and often routine areas of work, with detailed supervision. Staff are treated as if they are incapable of thinking for themselves and given little or no opportunity to exercise initiative or responsibility. This can be exemplified by the expression 'If you want something done properly, do it yourself'.

- At the other extreme there can be an excessive zeal for so-called delegation when a manager leaves subordinates to their own resources, often with only minimal guidance or training, and expects them to take the consequences for their own actions or decisions. The expression 'slopping shoulders' is often used to explain this form of behaviour. These 'super-delegators' misuse the practice of delegation and are often like the Artful Dodger, and somehow contrive not to be around when difficult situations arise. Such a form of behaviour is not delegation; it is an abdication of the manager's responsibility.

Either of these two extreme forms of behaviour can be frustrating and potentially stressful for subordinate staff, and unlikely to lead to improved organisational effectiveness.

How far do YOU honestly believe you would be capable of avoiding either of these two extreme forms of behaviour?

The manager–subordinate relationship

Delegation is not just the arbitrary shedding of work. It is not just the issuing and following of orders or carrying out of specified tasks in accordance with detailed instructions. Within the formal structure of the organisation, delegation creates a special manager–subordinate relationship. It is founded on the concept of:

- authority;
- responsibility; and
- accountability (ultimate responsibility).

Authority is the right to take action or make decisions that the manager would otherwise have done. Authority legitimises the exercise of empowerment within the structure and rules of the organisation. It enables the subordinate to issue valid instructions for others to follow.

Responsibility involves an obligation by the subordinate to perform certain duties or make certain decisions and having to accept possible reprimand from the manager for unsatisfactory performance. The meaning of the term 'responsibility' is, however, subject to possible confusion: although delegation embraces both authority and responsibility, effective delegation is not abdication of responsibility.

Accountability is interpreted as meaning ultimate responsibility and cannot be delegated. Managers have to accept 'responsibility' for the control of their staff, for the performance of all duties allocated to their department/section within the structure of the organisation, and for the standard of results achieved. That is, 'the buck stops here'.

The subordinate is responsible to the manager for doing the job, while the manager is responsible for seeing that the job gets done. The manager is accountable to a superior for the actions of subordinates.

Authority commensurate with responsibility

Delegation, therefore, embraces both authority and responsibility. It is not practical to delegate one without the other **(see Figure 14.6)**. Responsibility must be supported by authority and by power to influence areas of performance for which the subordinate is held responsible. Authority can be delegated readily, but many problems of delegation stem from failure to delegate sufficient authority to enable subordinates to fulfil their responsibilities. For example, if a section head is held responsible to a departmental manager for the performance of junior staff but is not empowered (given authority) to influence their selection and appointment, their motivation, the allocation of their duties, their training and development, or their sanctions and rewards, then the section leader can hardly be held responsible

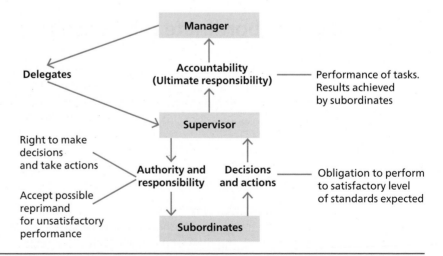

Empowerment

Broader term for a management style that grants genuine additional power and responsibility to other members of staff.

Gives rise at the individual (or personal) level to the act of **Delegation**.

Figure 14.6 The basis of empowerment and delegation

for unsatisfactory performance of the junior staff. To hold subordinates responsible for certain areas of performance without also conferring on them the necessary authority within the limits of that responsibility is an abuse of delegation.

The manager should accept the blame as the person **accountable** for the performance of the department/section, and obligated to see that the task was completed satisfactorily. It is necessary to maintain the organisational hierarchy and structure of command. Managers should protect and support subordinate staff and accept, personally, any reprimand for unsatisfactory performance. It is then up to managers to sort out things in their own department/section, to counsel members of staff concerned and to review their system of delegation.

Bushe emphasises the continuing importance of authority.

> Contrary to popular images and poorly thought through books on the subject, collaborative work systems do not decrease or eliminate authority even if they do flatten hierarchies and reduce command and control – quite the contrary. Authority and hierarchy are two separate things. Authority is the power to make and enforce decisions. Collaborative organizations create much more authority than command and control systems do because in collaborative organizations, authority is dispersed widely . . . But collaborative organizations still require hierarchy for focus and direction.[39]

Ethical considerations

Properly handled, delegation offers many potential benefits to both managers and staff. Delegation should help make the best use of time, provide a means of training and development, and lead to improved morale by increasing motivation and job satisfaction. Effective delegation results in optimum use of human resources and improved organisational performance.

Moorcroft suggests that although delegation is a useful business tool it needs only occasional use and is one that demands strong ethical issues, for example:

- managers may be overwhelmed with work but it is what they get paid to do;
- some larger consultancy companies 'selling' the consultancy through senior staff but then sending junior staff;
- using the argument of 'development of staff' to delegate tasks beyond the level of the subordinate with an unrealistic timescale hoping that the subordinate will fail and reinforcing the status of the manager.

When delegation does occur, it is important to establish ethical rules relating to agreement on responsibility for outcomes, effective training and recognising credit for success.[40] Mistakes will inevitably happen and the subordinate will need to be supported by the manager, and protected against unwarranted criticism. The acceptance of ultimate responsibility highlights the educational aspect of the manager's job. The manager should view mistakes as part of the subordinate's training and learning experience, and an opportunity for further development. 'Even if mistakes occur, good managers are judged as much by their ability to manage them as by their successes.'[41]

Trust and empowerment

Empowerment is also a matter of confidence and trust – both in subordinates and the manager's own performance and system of delegation. In allowing freedom of action to subordinates within agreed terms of reference and the limits of authority, managers must accept that subordinates may undertake delegated activities in a different manner from themselves. This is at the basis of the true nature of trust. However, learning to put trust in other people is one of the most difficult aspects of successful delegation for many managers, and some never learn it.

As *Stewart* points out, managers who think about what can be done only in terms of what they can do, cannot be effective. Managing is not a solo activity.

> **Managers must learn to accept their dependence upon people. A key part of being a good manager is managing that dependence. Managers who say that they cannot delegate because they have poor staff may genuinely be unfortunate in the calibre of the staff that they have inherited or been given. More often this view is a criticism of themselves: a criticism either of their unwillingness to delegate when they could and should do so, or a criticism of their selection, training and development of their staff.**[42]

To what extent would YOU welcome having delegated authority and responsibility or would you be concerned about the ethical considerations?

The indispensability trap

Jolly comments on the 'curse of knowledge' – those individuals who have demonstrated technical expertise, worked hard, and developed skills and competence. Your skill has become automatic and when moving into management you are faced with supervising people who not know how to do what for you is obvious. If you have then managed to demonstrate your expertise and ability to supervise others, you're too good at your current job and risk getting stuck in it. You have become indispensable and too important to promote. To be an effective executive you need a strong desire and ability to control and this focus on control leads to 'I don't have time to delegate'. Delegation feels like losing control and takes valuable time. Hence the instinct to control can increasingly become a liability rather than an asset.[43]

Systematic approach to delegation

In order to realise the full benefits of empowerment without loss of control, it is necessary to adopt a planned and systematic approach. Setting up a successful system of delegation involves examining five basic questions.

- How can I make better use of my time and expertise?
- What tasks could be performed better by other staff?
- What opportunities are there for staff to learn and develop by undertaking delegated tasks and responsibilities?
- How should increased responsibilities be implemented and to whom should they be given?
- What forms of monitoring control system would be most appropriate?

Delegation is not an irrevocable act and can always be withdrawn. In order to set up an effective system of delegation, subordinates should know exactly what is expected of them, what has to be achieved, the boundaries within which they have freedom of action, and how far they can exercise independent decision-making. It is possible to identify six main stages in a planned and systematic approach to delegation (*see* Figure 14.7).

- **Clarification of objectives and suitable patterns of organisation** in order to provide a framework for authority and responsibility.
- **Agreement on terms of reference and acceptance of authority and responsibility** with emphasis placed on end results rather than set of detailed instructions.
- **Guidance, support and training, and patterns of communication** including where they can go for further help or advice.
- **Effective monitoring and review procedures** including time limits and system to monitor progress and provide feedback.
- **Freedom of action within agreed terms of reference** and leaving the subordinate alone to get on with the job within the boundaries established.
- **Related reward system** including opportunities for promotion, personal development or further empowerment.

A summary of delegation, authority, power and responsibility is given in the concept map set out in Figure 14.8.

Figure 14.7 Main stages in the process of delegation

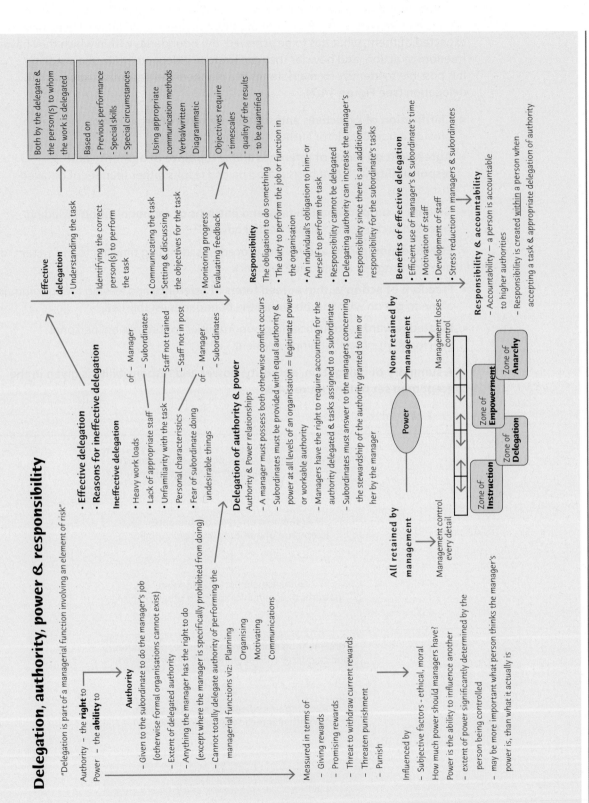

Figure 14.8 Delegation, authority, power and responsibility
Source: Copyright © 2012 The Virtual Learning Materials Workshop. Reproduced with permission.

Control versus autonomy

Whatever the extent of employee empowerment, there is still a requirement for some form of management control and this gives rise to a number of important behavioural considerations. From their study of top-performing companies in the 1990s, *Goldsmith and Clutterbuck* refer to the sharing of power, and to the balance between control and autonomy. They question how companies manage to balance giving people maximum freedom against exerting controls to ensure the benefits of size and a common sense of direction. To exert the most effective control, Goldsmith and Clutterbuck suggest it is limited to the few simple, readily understandable processes. Autonomy is, in essence, an absence of formal control: once clear goals are set, there is greater or lesser freedom to determine how they will be met. There are still controls in place, but they are much less obvious or intrusive. Control and autonomy are therefore two sides of the same coin.[44]

How do YOU view the importance of empowerment and delegation, and maintaining the balance between controls versus autonomy?

Critical Thinking Zone

Reflections on Employee Empowerment

In this zone, we critically discuss the construct of employee empowerment and evaluate whether it is managerial rhetoric or organisational reality.

According to Cunningham et al.,[45] the 1980s and 90s witnessed a rise in the implementation of employee involvement schemes, such as employee participation, participative management and participative decision-making,[46] with the intent of increasing individuals' commitment to their jobs and employer while engendering a culture of inclusion and flexibility. They argue that employee empowerment is a contemporary manifestation of involvement and typifies a conscious move away from the philosophy of Taylorist scientific management control to augmenting commitment as a strategy to enhance organisational performance. Appelbaum et al.[47] and Honold[48] profess that employee empowerment is a constantly evolving, multidimensional concept, which is subject to multiple interpretation and application, depending on the context, corporate culture and organisational actors involved. They thus attest that these factors conflate to make defining empowerment inherently problematic.

Defining Employee Empowerment

Although theorists have made progress in developing the employee empowerment construct, Fernandez and Moldogaziev[49] profess that disagreement is still rife among the research community about what it means and how it translates, in practical terms, in organisations. With its intellectual roots planted firmly in the human relations movement, employee empowerment is defined by Ghosh[50] (p. 95) as 'the process of shifting authority and responsibility to employees at a lower level in the organisational hierarchy. It is a transfer of power from the managers to their subordinates.' In a similar vein, Conger and Kanungo[51] (p. 473) suggest it is 'the process by which a leader or manager shares his or her power with subordinates.' In this context, power is 'interpreted as the possession of formal authority or control over organisational resources' which, they argue, emphasises the notion of both parties sharing authority between them. The Oxford Living Dictionary Online[52] also likens empowerment with the assignment of authority and power, but also relates the concept to delegation, authorisation and entitlement. However, its definition of delegation does not suggest the relinquishing of power from one person to another. Although empowerment is often used interchangeably with delegation, one could argue that empowerment can be delegated, but delegation is not empowerment. *Power* is a key theme running throughout the vein of these definitions and importantly, Greasley et al.[53] advocate that assignment of this power is intended to ascribe individuals with a greater level of responsibility, flexibility and freedom to make work-related decisions and implement them, without the shackles of Taylorist control. Such em*power*ment, according to Greasley et al., encourages autonomy and heightens job satisfaction. Lee and Koh[54] view empowerment as a paradigm shift from, but not a substitute for, motivation schemes, such as job enrichment[55] (see Chapter 7: Work Motivation and Satisfaction).

Perspectives of Employee Empowerment

Extant literature proffers that there are two distinct, and one could argue, competing perspectives of employee empowerment: structural and psychological, which Greasley et al. attest appears to have been researched as separate rather than complimentary concepts. First, structural empowerment encompasses a redistribution of power from managers to individuals via enabling organisational structures, policies and practices that are intended to engender collaboration and trust between parties in the people–organisation relationship through power sharing. While it may be a positive move by the organisation to be more inclusive and give individuals the opportunity to be involved in managing its business operations, Greasley et al. and Mills and Ungson[56] suggest that structural empowerment poses a quandary for managers. Its successfulness is dependent on their ability to alleviate the tension between relinquished control, and a certain amount of power, with the important task of achieving congruence between individual and organisational goals.

Second, psychological empowerment centres on an individual's emotional state and their cognition of, and the meaning they assign to, the completion of work tasks.[57] The perspective encompasses four aspects. First, the fit between their work roles and personal values. Second, their competence in, and belief in their ability to, perform the job. Third, self-determination or perception of autonomy on the job, and fourth, impact or the sense of influence they may have over job outcomes. Peccei and Rosenthal[57] point out that overarching this is the individual's belief that they have the requisite skills and abilities to complete the tasks for which they have been empowered. On this point, Dainty et al.[46] caveat that an individual can only feel empowered if they *believe* they have been empowered. Therefore, perceptions that are subjective and socially constructed, play a major role in the empowerment experience. Managers need to bear this in mind when implementing structural empowerment programmes and ensure that the rhetoric of empowerment is translated to reality and psychological issues are not overlooked.[53]

The Espoused Benefits of Empowerment

Greasley et al. posit that the espoused benefits that can be derived from employee empowerment appear to be heavily skewed towards the organisation, which may, arguably, suggest that managers have implemented such initiatives for the organisation's benefit, not the individual.[45] Employee empowerment benefits individuals by increasing their motivation, skill utilisation, job satisfaction levels, capacity to innovate and loyalty to the organisation.[58]

Critical Perspectives of Employee Empowerment

Foster-Fishman and Keys[59] espouse that management efforts to implement employee empowerment is doomed to fail unless the organisation's culture engenders inclusion and trust, encourages and tolerates risk taking and supports its staff to 'take delegated power' and exercise control over the work to be undertaken. This includes giving them discretionary choice in how the work is done and appropriate access to information, knowledge and resources. Honold[48] (p. 210) contends that 'employee empowerment will not happen naturally in organisations' as too many disabling and 'disempowering structures have been built into them over the years.' Arguably, this suggests that a culture of disempowerment is institutionalised and inherent within the organisation's culture.

Mills and Ungson profess that the organisation's need to foster greater commitment among the workforce through empowerment is juxtaposed with the necessity to coordinate and control. The authors suggest that this juxtaposition can be overcome via two mechanisms: organisational constitution and trust. First, organisational constitution is a 'set of agreements and understandings that define the limits and goals of the group. . . as well as the responsibilities and rights of participants'[60] (p. 225). These are the tacit, implied, unwritten work rules that operate through the organisation's culture. Rather than stifling empowered individuals, it moderates the relationship between the expectations of the empowered and organisational requirements of empowerment itself.[56] Second, trust, which the Merriam-Webster Dictionary Online[61] defines as 'assured reliance on the character, ability, strength or truth of someone or something . . . to place confidence in. . .' It relates trust to faith, acceptance and integrity. Mills and Ungson profess that trust, in its various interpretations, is imperative within empowerment as it enables those empowered to enact their imbued authority and, ostensibly, power, with ability, discretion and confidence and without the need for contracts and formal control mechanisms.

One could argue that parallels can be drawn between organisational constitution and trust with aspects of the relational psychological contract, which is also based on trust, mutual obligations and attitudinal and emotional commitment[62,63] that are unwritten and inherently perceptual and subjective. As such, both parties in the 'empowerer–empoweree' relationship face risks. Managers place trust in individuals to act with discretion when making decisions and take risks that will not be injurious to the organisation. Equally, individuals face comparable risks in accepting imbued empowerment because, as Mills and Ungson[56] (p. 148) caveat, 'he or she may fail.'

Implications for Organisational Behaviour in the Workplace

To conclude, Honold contends that employee empowerment goes far beyond managers delegating power to their direct reports. That, she claims, is a rather outdated, one-dimensional perspective. She advocates viewing the construct through a multiplicity of lenses and suggests it therefore involves the ways in which leaders lead, how individuals react to their leadership and how peers interact with each other and their leaders. Ultimately, it involves the structuration of the organisation's work-related processes, culture and management philosophy that enable empowerment to become an organisational reality rather than managerial rhetoric. Holt et al.[64] concur and conclude that turning rhetoric into reality involves cultural change and a holistic rationalisation of the organisation's business operations, rather than a token gesture of managers relinquishing control and calling it 'empowerment.'

Questions

Based on the above, answer the following questions:

1. Theorists suggest that employee empowerment is a regurgitation of previous employee involvement initiatives. With reference to theory and practice, *to what extent* do you agree?

2. *Critically analyse* the differences between empowerment and delegation.

3. It could be argued that parallels can be drawn between structural and psychological empowerment and the relational psychological contract. *How* can organisations marry these concepts closer together, as part of implementing their employee empowerment initiatives?

Summary – Chapter 14 'Organisational control and power'

Control systems exist in spheres of all organisations as part of the process of management with the purpose of improvement in performance. By its very nature, control is concerned with the regulation of behaviour. Often it has an emotive connotation and interpreted in a negative manner. There are important elements, characteristics and strategies of effective control systems. Work organisations are not only systems of hierarchical structure: they are complex systems of social relationships, status and power. Leadership influence may be seen as a type of power over the actions of other people. Control systems are frequently thought of in terms of accounting or financial systems, but consideration must also be given to social considerations. Pluralistic approaches recognise power as a social process that derives from a multiplicity of interpersonal sources, social relationships and realities of organisational life. Most people show ambivalence towards control and under certain conditions their presence may be welcomed. Control is the interface between human behaviour and process of management. Discussion on the balance between order and flexibility draws attention to the nature of empowerment and delegation and greater freedom for staff.

Delegation creates a special manager–subordinate relationship based on the concept of authority, responsibility and accountability.

Group discussion activities

Undertake each of these activities in small groups as indicated by your tutor. Before you start your discussion establish a non-threatening environment within the group and confirm confidentiality will be honoured.

First, form your own views and then share and compare in open critical discussion with colleagues. Reflect honestly on the extent to which: (i) you influenced the thinking and ideas of your colleagues; and (ii) you were influenced by your colleagues.

To what extent was your group able to reach consensus?

Agree one of your members to produce a brief written summary of the discussion and prepared to present in a plenary session.

Activity 1

To what extent do you agree:

(a) The changing nature of the workplace with flatter structures, a diminishing hierarchy, empowerment, remote working, demands for flexibility and working from home have all contributed to the loss of effective organisational control over the actions and behaviour of people at work.

(b) It is a poor manager who relies on the exercise of formal power and position within the hierarchy for the maintenance of order and control. Personal influence is the only truly effective way to ensure members of staff act and behave in the manner expected of them.

Activity 2

On a scale from 1 (least) to 5 (highest) rate yourself in terms of the degree of influence you believe you exercise other your colleagues for each of the following three headings:

* **Expertise power:** Will others see you as someone who can exercise influence because of your expertise, skill or knowledge?

* **Charismatic power**: Will others see you as someone who can exercise influence because of your personality and extent to which are liked, admired or respected?

* **Administrative power:** Will others see you as someone who can exercise influence because of your ability to change the way things appear or are done to advantage?

Activity 3

(a) Stewart points out managers who think about what can be done only in terms of what they can do cannot be effective.

(b) Managers are encouraged to empower staff with greater authority and responsibility but still held accountable for their actions and performance. It is only right they should continue to exercise close supervision and control.

(c) Reasons for lack of effective delegation are easy to understand. It is faster and easier to do the work yourself. The main problem is that few people ever learn how to put trust in other people or are coached in the skills of empowerment.

Organisational behaviour in action case study
The police custody officer and empowerment

The Police Service has statutory responsibility for the treatment of persons detained by them (and other agencies such as HMRC which brings people into a police station). These people must be treated in accordance with the Police & Criminal Evidence Act 1984 (PACE) that was enacted in January 1986 and any code of practice issued under the Act.

Section 39 of PACE specifies that these duties should be the duty of the custody officer at a police station. The same section goes on to declare:

> where an officer of **higher** rank than the custody officer gives directions . . . which are at variance with any **decision** or **action** taken by the custody officer in the performance of a duty imposed on him under this Act the matter **shall** be referred at once to an officer of the rank of Superintendent or above who is responsible for that police station.

There is statutory backing for the decisions and actions taken by custody officers in the performance of their duties.

PACE sets out the provisions regarding the appointment of custody officers (Section 36). Custody officers are appointed to designated police stations, which are effectively police stations equipped to receive and house detained persons in the conditions that PACE requires. Subject to limited exceptions all detained persons must go to a designated police station. Custody officers are appointed by the Chief Officer of Police for that area or by an officer directed by that Chief Officer

of Police to do so. Importantly no police officer may be appointed a custody officer unless at least the rank of sergeant, and significantly none of the functions of a custody officer shall be performed by an officer who is involved in the investigation of an offence for which the person is in detention (and there is case law that identifies what being involved in an investigation entails).

Most forces have adopted the sergeant rank as the best suited to the custody officer role (custody officers no longer have to be a police officer). On appointment training is given in the role of sergeant and specifically custody officer duties. Custody officers, though they work for the same organisation, have an element of impartiality through the statement that they must not be involved in the investigation of an offence for which that person is detained. This allows for their decision-making to be non-partisan. There is an argument perhaps that for the decision-making to be completely impartial custody provisions should be independent of the police service but in practice it is argued that custody officers value their impartiality and their decision-making is reflected in this.

The Act clearly defines the process for any challenge to custody officers' decision-making and that is by appeal to the station commander, a Superintendent. As well as providing support for custody officers in their decision-making it also affords protection for them from **rank pulling** in a hierarchically structured organisation such as the police.

Custody officers deal with people's liberty and determine whether they enter the prosecution process. The decision to detain is a serious business and in practical terms it is taken very seriously. In the case of a person detained on the suspicion of committing a criminal offence, their decision-making in this process is subject to periodic review. In the first 24 hours of a person's detention that review is undertaken at the 6-, 15- and 24-hour stages. Any detention beyond 24 hours requires the authority of a Superintendent and any detention beyond 36 hours requires a warrant from a court. The custody officer's decision-making is subject to close scrutiny through the training process, accreditation process and local inspection processes. Most importantly, it is a legal requirement now that all designated custody centres are subject to visual and audio recording, which is perhaps the ultimate scrutiny. The arrival of visual and audio recording in custody centres was welcomed by custody officers as it saw a corresponding fall in the number of complaints against them in the charge room process.

In practical terms it is rare that decisions of a custody officer are challenged by a more senior officer (a Detective Chief Inspector). The fact that these occasions are so rarely reported is evidence of the seriousness and professionalism adopted by custody sergeants in their decision-making process. **A process that would only work with empowerment.**

(With thanks to Sergeant Keith Poultney, Hampshire Constabulary for providing this information.)

Tasks

1. Discuss critically the extent to which you believe this case illustrates the importance and potential benefits of empowerment.
2. How would you relate this case to the concept of authority commensurate with responsibility?
3. Explain the importance of protection from rank pulling in any other hierarchically structured organisations.

Chapter 14 – Personal skills and employability exercise

Objectives

Completing this exercise should help you to enhance the following skills:

* Review honestly and reflect upon features of your own personality.
* Assess the extent to which you are in danger of becoming a control freak.
* Sensitivity to your reaction towards control and power.

Control in its many forms is an inherent and essential feature of organisational behaviour. However the manner in which control is exercised is a variable dependent upon the extent to which an individual either prefers or believes it necessary to use positional power to maintain control. For some people power can be a positive source of motivation.

Exercise

Working in small self-selected groups, individually record honestly the extent to which you agree with the following ten questions. If necessary think how you would be likely to behave in a given situation. Then compare and discuss responses with your colleagues.

1. I enjoy and strive for power over other people. It is a natural human characteristic.
2. I am generally happy to put my trust in others to get work done on time and to a good standard.

3. Charisma and personal power is the most effective source of control.

4. I am happy to accept that other people often have better ideas than me.

5. If you are put in charge of a group project or assignment it is only natural to expect obedience based on your formal authority.

6. Office politics, manipulation and the grapevine should be accepted as realities of organisational life.

7. I believe that I am right most of the time.

8. Control over employees through electronic surveillance is nothing more than an unwelcomed invasion of privacy.

9. Financial and accounting systems are the most reliable and fairest forms of control.

10. If you want a job done properly then do it yourself.

Discussion

∗ Do you think you have controlling issues or can you exercise flexibility?

∗ How can you attempt to develop charisma and the use of personal power?

∗ To what extent has this exercise provoked further thoughts on your attitude towards organisational control and power?

Notes and references

1. Child, J. *Organization: Contemporary Principles and Practice,* second edition, Wiley (2015), p. 144.
2. Tannenbaum, A. S. *Control in Organizations,* McGraw-Hill (1968), p. 3.
3. Cloke, K. and Goldsmith, J. *The End of Management and the Rise of Organizational Democracy,* Jossey-Bass (2002), p. 5.
4. Misselhorn, H. *Values, Power and Problem Solving,* MOD Associates, South Africa, 10 March 2014.
5. Wilson, F. M. *Organizational Behaviour and Work: A Critical Introduction,* third edition, Oxford University Press (2010), p. 222.
6. Watson, T. J. *Organising and Managing Work,* second edition, Financial Times Prentice Hall (2006), pp. 55–6.
7. Zimmermann, J. 'The Different Centres of Control', *Mastering Management,* Financial Times/Pitman Publishing (1997), p. 21.
8. For examples, see Tibballs, G. *Business Blunders,* Robinson Publishing (1999).
9. 'Untapped Potential: The Barriers to Optimum Corporate Performance', Proudfoot Consulting, October 2002.
10. Ray, C. A. 'Corporate culture: the last frontier of control?' *Journal of Management Studies,* vol. 23, no. 3, 1986, pp. 287–97.
11. Egan, G. 'The Shadow Side', *Management Today,* September 1993, p. 37.
12. McKenna, R. *New Management,* Irwin/McGraw-Hill (1999), pp. 430–1.
13. Reeves, T. K. and Woodward, J. 'The Study of Managerial Control', in Woodward, J. (ed.) *Industrial Organization: Behaviour and Control,* Oxford University Press (1970).
14. Wilson, F. M. *Organizational Behaviour and Work: A Critical Introduction,* third edition, Oxford University Press (2010), p. 313.
15. Barker, J. R. 'Tightening the Iron Cage: Concertive Control in Self-Managing Teams', *Administrative Science Quarterly,* vol. 38, 1993, pp. 408–37.
16. Wright, B. M. and Barker, J. R. 'Assessing concertive control in the term environment', *Journal of Occupational and Organizational Psychology,* vol. 73, 2000, pp. 345–61.
17. Child, J. *Organization: Contemporary Principles and Practice,* second edition, Wiley (2015).
18. Caulkin, S. 'The Real Invisible Hand', *Management Today,* November 2011, pp. 40–4.
19. Weber, M. *The Theory of Social and Economic Organization,* Collier Macmillan (1964).
20. Etzioni, A. *A Comparative Analysis of Complex Organizations: On Power, Involvement and Their Correlates,* revised edition, Free Press (1975).
21. French, J. P. and Raven, B. 'The Bases of Social Power', in Cartwright, D. and Zander, A. F. (eds) *Group Dynamics: Research and Theory,* third edition, Harper and Row (1968).

22. Yukl, G. *Leadership in Organizations,* sixth edition, Pearson Prentice Hall (2006).

23. For an account of the use of power, see, for example, Guirdham, M. *Interactive Behaviour at Work,* third edition, Financial Times Prentice Hall (2002), Chapter 9.

24. Parker, L. D. 'Shock of the New a Century On', *Professional Manager,* November 2005, pp. 34–5; and 'Mary Parker Follett,"Prophet of Management"' Thinkers Checklist No. 24, Chartered Management Institute, March 2002.

25. 'Sex and Power 2011', *Equality and Human Rights Commission,* August 2011.

26. Bloisi, W., Cook, C. W. and Hunsaker, P. L. *Management and Organisation Behaviour,* McGraw-Hill (2003).

27. Handy, C. B. *Understanding Organizations,* fourth edition, Penguin (1993), p. 131.

28. Misselhorn, H. *Values, Power and Problem Solving*, MOD Associates, South Africa, 10 March 2014. Reproduced with permission.

29. Mann, S. 'Oh I Heard It On the Grapevine', *Professional Manager,* July 1997, p. 33.

30. Hazelhurst, J. 'The Way We Work Now', *Management Today,* June 2013, pp. 47–9.

31. Alexander, R. 'Don't be a donkey', *Management Today*, May 2016, p. 52.

32. Yew, L. T. and Gregory, G. 'Organisational misbehaviour: Should management intervene?' Borneo Post online, 26 July 2011, www.theborneopost.com (accessed 30 April 2017).

33. Kirwan-Taylor, H. *'People Who Can't Let Go',* *Management Today,* March 2007, pp. 45–7.

34. Hilton, A. 'People power', *Chartered Secretary*, September 2011, p. 14.

35. Owen, J. *The Death of Modern Management*, Wiley (2009), p. 230.

36. Yukl, G. *Leadership in Organizations,* seventh edition, Pearson (2010), p. 219.

37. Scott, M in conversation with Jimmy Wales, 'The end of control', *Professional Manager,* Winter 2016, p. 35.

38. Mills, D. Q. and Friesen, G. B. 'Empowerment', in Crainer, S. and Dearlove, D. (eds) *Financial Times Handbook of Management,* second edition, Financial Times Prentice Hall (2001), p. 323.

39. Bushe, G. R. 'The Skills of Clear Leadership', *Manager, The British Journal of Administrative Management*, Summer 2009, p. 26. See also: Bushe, G. R. *Clear Leadership: sustaining real collaboration and partnership at work,* revised edition, Davies-Black (2010).

40. Moorcroft, R. 'Delegation, not relegation', *Manager, The British Journal of Administrative Management,* Autumn 2009, pp. 4–6.

41. Gracie, S. 'Delegate Don't Abdicate', *Management Today,* March 1999, p. 94.

42. Stewart, R. *The Reality of Management,* third edition, Butterworth Heinemann (1999), p. 180.

43. Jolly, R. 'The Indispensability Trap', *Management Today,* November 2012, pp. 48–52.

44. Goldsmith, W. and Clutterbuck, D. *The Winning Streak Mark II,* Orion Business Books (1998), pp 12–13.

45. Cunningham, I., Hyman, J. and Baldry, C. 'Empowerment: The Power to do what?', *Industrial Relations Journal,* vol. 27, no. 2, 1996, pp. 143–54.

46. Dainty, A. R. J., Bryman, A. and Price, A. D. F. 'Empowerment Within the UK Construction Sector', *Leadership and Organization Development Journal,* vol. 23, no. 6, 2002, pp. 333–42.

47. Appelbaum, S. H., Karasek, R., Lapointe, F. and Quelch, K. 'Employee Empowerment: Factors Affecting the Consequent Success or Failure – Part 1', *Industrial and Commercial Training,* vol. 46, no. 7, 2014, pp. 379–86.

48. Honold, L. 'A Review of the Literature on Employee Empowerment', *Empowerment in Organizations,* vol. 5, no. 4, 1997, pp. 202–12.

49. Fernandez, S. and Moldogaziev, T. 'Employee Empowerment, Employee Attitudes, and Performance: Testing a Causal Model', *Public Administration Review,* vol. 73, no. 3, 2013, pp. 490–506.

50. Ghosh, A. K. 'Employee Empowerment: A Strategic Tool to Obtain Sustainable Competitive Advantage', *International Journal of Management,* vol. 30, no. 3, part 1, 2013, pp. 95–107.

51. Conger, J. A. and Kanungo, R. N. 'The Empowerment Process: Integrating Theory and Practice', *Academy of Management Review,* vol. 13, no. 3, 1988, pp. 471–82.

52. Oxford Living Dictionary Online: https://www.oxforddictionaries.com, 2018 (accessed 28 August 2018).

53. Greasley, K., Bryman, A., Dainty, A., Price, A., Naismith, N. and Soetanto, R. 'Understanding Empowerment from an Employee Perspective: What Does it Mean and Do They Want It?' *Team Performance Management,* vol. 14, no. 1/2, 2008, pp. 39–55.

54. Lee, M. and Koh, J. 'Is empowerment really a new concept?', *International Journal of Human Resource Management,* vol. 12, no. 4, June, 2001, pp. 684–95.

55. Hackman, J. R. and Oldham, G. R. *Work Redesign,* Addison-Wesley (1980).

56. Mills, P. K. and Ungson, G. R. 'Reassessing the Limits of Structural Empowerment: Organizational Constitution and Trust as Controls', *Academy of Management Review'*, vol. 28, no. 1, 2003, pp. 143–53.

57. Peccei, R. and Rosenthal, P. 'Delivering Customer-Oriented Behaviour through Empowerment: An Empirical Test of HRM Assumptions', *Journal of Management Studies,* vol. 38, no. 6, 2001, pp. 831–57.

58. Mullins, L. J. and Peacock, A. 'Managing Through People: Regulating the Employment Relationship', *Administrator,* December 1991, pp. 32–33.

59. Foster-Fishman, P. G. and Keys, C. B. 'The Inserted Pyramid: How A Well Meaning Attempt to Initiate Employee Empowerment Ran Afoul of the Culture of a

Public Bureaucracy', *Academy of Management Journal Best Papers Proceedings,* 1995, pp. 364–72.

60. Zald, M. 'Political Economy: A Framework for Comparative Analysis', in Zald, M. (ed.) *Power in Organizations,* Vanderbilt University Press (1970), pp. 221–61.

61. Merriam-Webster Dictionary Online, https://www.merriam-webster.com, accessed 12 April 2019. Used with permission.

62. Dabos, G. E. and Rousseau, D. M. 'Mutuality and Reciprocity in the Psychological Contracts of Employees and Employers', *Journal of Applied Psychology,* 89, 2004, pp. 52–72.

63. Hui, C., Lee, C. and Rousseau, D. 'Psychological Contract and Organizational Citizenship Behaviour in China: Investigating Generalizability and Instrumentality', *Journal of Applied Psychology,* vol. 89, 2004, pp. 311–21.

64. Holt, G. D., Love, P. E. D. and Nesan, L. J. 'Employee Empowerment in Construction: An Implementation Model for Process Improvement', *Team Performance Management: An International Journal,* vol. 6, no. 3/4, 2001, pp. 47–51.

Part 5
Focus on organisational environment

Chapter 15
Organisational culture and change

A central feature of the successful organisation is the diagnosis of its culture and ability to adapt to change. This involves applications of organisational behaviour.

Learning outcomes

After completing this chapter you should have enhanced your ability to:

- detail the nature, types and main features of organisational culture;
- evaluate influences on the development and importance of culture;
- debate the importance and characteristic features of a healthy organisational climate;
- explain the nature and forces of organisational change;
- explore the nature of, and reasons for, resistance to change;
- examine the management of change, and human and social factors of change.
- review relationships between organisational culture and control.

Outline chapter contents

Overview topic map: Chapter 15 – Organisational culture and change

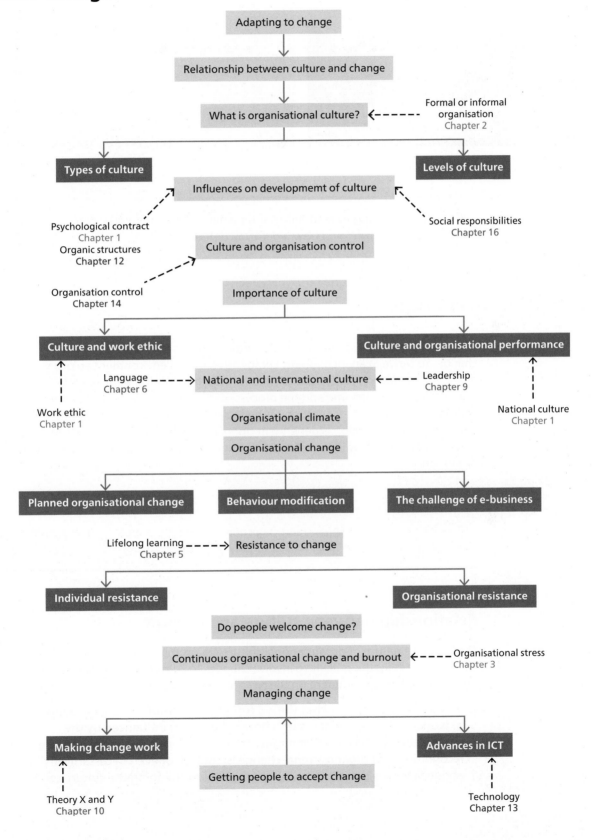

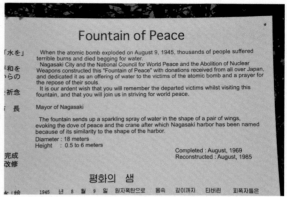

 Before commencing to read this chapter what do YOU understand by 'organisation culture' and how would you define the term?

Adapting to change

An underlying feature of the successful organisation is the ability to adapt to change. To thrive in an increasingly competitive, global environment an organisation must pay attention to its continual effectiveness and development. No two organisations are the same and the process of change must be in harmony with its overriding culture and recognition of the social processes of the organisation. To perform well and develop is dependent upon a culture of openness, participation and acceptance of new ideas achieved through involvement of people who are the organisation.

'Rapid technological changes create huge opportunities for companies bold enough to seize them.' (Attributed to Jeff Bezos, founder and CEO, Amazon)

Relationship between culture and change

The pervasive nature of organisational culture means that if change is to be brought about successfully, this is likely to involve changes to culture. For example, *Stewart* makes the following comment on the relationship between culture and change:

> In recent years attention has shifted from the effects of the organization of work on people's behaviour to how behaviour is influenced by the organizational culture. What is much more common today is the widespread recognition that organizational change is not just, or even necessarily mainly, about changing the structure but often requires changing the culture too.[1]

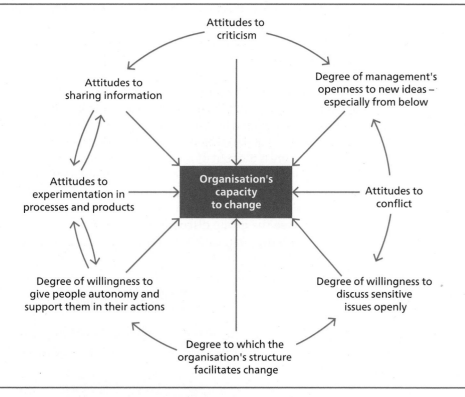

Figure 15.1 Organisational culture and change
Source: Senior, B. and Swailes, S. *Organizational Change,* fourth edition, Financial Times Prentice Hall (2010), p. 161, Reprinted and Electronically reproduced by permission from Pearson Education, Inc., New York.

A similar view is held by *Naylor,* who points out that 'In the holistic system, any change will affect the culture and the culture will affect or constrain the change . . . Cultural change is intimately bound up with the process of organisational change.'[2]

However, in practice, organisations usually appear to alter their underlying ethos only on a gradual basis and the complexity of environmental pressures may itself hinder rapid change. Culture is often deep-rooted and commitment to the objectives and policies of the organisation, people's cognitive limitations and their uncertainties and fears, may mean a reluctance to accept a change in behaviour. Culture is reinforced through the system of rites and rituals, patterns of communication, the informal organisation, expected patterns of behaviour and perceptions of the psychological contract. **(Organisational change is discussed later in this chapter.)**

A depiction of the way elements of culture can support and/or defend against change is given in **Figure 15.1.**

What is organisational culture?

Although people may not be aware consciously of culture, it still has a pervasive influence over their behaviour and actions. There is, however, no consensus on its meaning or applications to the analysis of work organisations. There is also sometimes confusion over the difference between the interpretation of organisational culture and organisational climate **(discussed later in this chapter).**

Organisational culture is a general concept with different meanings and difficult to explain precisely. A popular and simple way of defining culture is 'how things are done around here'. For example, *Atkinson* explains organisational culture as reflecting the underlying assumptions about the way work is performed; what is 'acceptable and not acceptable'; and what behaviour and actions are encouraged and discouraged.[3] *Rachel Johnson,* the Editor of *Governance & Compliance* magazine suggests that our understanding of culture in the workplace is that it is the embodiment of the ethos of a whole organisation which finds expression through the operation and practices that the organisation undertakes. If the ethos of an organisation is deemed to be incorrect, then the culture is the root of the problem and needs to be addressed for these issues to be resolved. Changing the ethos without changing the culture would be purely superficial and not have any long term impact.

The culture of an organisation is also often likened to the personality of an individual[4] **(see the group discussion activity at the end of this chapter).**

A summary of organisational culture is set out in Figure 15.2.

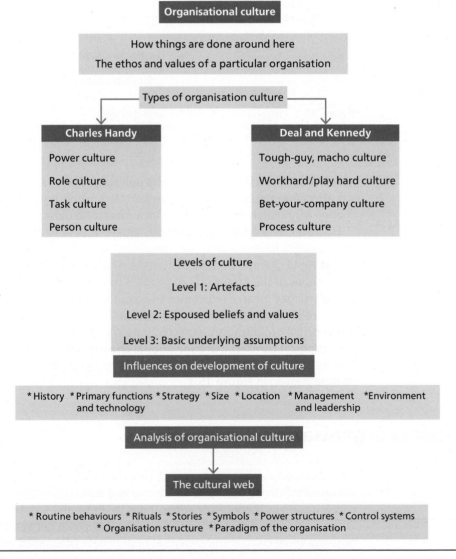

Figure 15.2 Summary of organisational culture

How would YOU describe the culture of your university in terms of how things are done around here and in what ways does it impact upon your life as a student?

Types of organisation culture

There are a number of ways to classify different types of organisational culture. Two common classifications are those by Handy and by Deal and Kennedy.

Developing the ideas of *Harrison,*[5] *Charles Handy* describes four main types of organisational cultures: power culture; role culture; task culture; and person culture.[6]

- **Power culture** depends on a central power source with influence throughout the organisation. A power culture is frequently found in small entrepreneurial organisations and relies on trust, empathy and personal communications. There are few rules and procedures, and little bureaucracy. It is a political organisation with decisions taken largely on the balance of influence.

- **Role culture** is often stereotyped as a bureaucracy and works by logic and rationality. Role culture rests on the strength of strong organisational 'pillars' – the functions of specialists in, for example, finance, purchasing and production. Role or job description is often more important than the individual, and position is the main source of power.

- **Task culture** is job-oriented or project-oriented. Task culture can be likened to a net, some strands are stronger than others and with much of the power and influence. An example is the matrix organisation. Task culture seeks to bring together the right resources and people, and utilises the unifying power of the group. Influence is widely spread and based more on expert power than on position or personal power.

- **Person culture** is where the individual is the central focus and structure exists to serve the individuals within it. When a group of people decide to band together to do their own thing and share office space, equipment or clerical assistance, then the resulting organisation would have a person culture. Examples are groups of barristers, architects, doctors or consultants. Many individuals have a preference for person culture, for example university professors and research specialists. Management hierarchies and control mechanisms are possible only by mutual consent.

Every organisation will have its own unique culture and most large businesses are likely to be something of a mix of cultures with examples for each of the four types in varying areas of the organisation. Different people enjoy working in different types of organisation culture and they are more likely to be happy and satisfied at work if their attributes and personalities are consistent with the culture of that part of the organisation in which they are employed.

Four generic types of culture

From an examination of hundreds of business organisations and their environments, *Deal and Kennedy* categorise corporate cultures according to two determining factors in the marketplace:

- the degree of risk associated with the organisation's activities; and
- the speed at which organisations and their employees receive feedback on the success of decisions or strategies.

These factors give rise to four generic types of culture: the tough-guy, macho culture; the work-hard/play-hard culture; the bet-your-company culture; and the process culture.[7]

- **Tough-guy, macho culture** – an organisation of individualists who frequently take high risks and receive quick feedback on the right or wrong of their actions. Examples include police departments, surgeons, construction, cosmetics, management consulting and the entertainment industry. Financial stakes are high and there is a focus on speed.
- **Work-hard/play-hard culture** – characterised by fun and action where employees take few risks, all with quick feedback. Organisations tend to be highly dynamic and the primary value centres on customers and their needs. There is a high level of relatively low-risk activity. Examples include sales organisations such as estate agents and computer companies, mass consumer companies such as McDonald's, office equipment manufacturers and retail stores.
- **Bet-your-company culture** – where there are large-stake decisions with a high risk but slow feedback so that it may be years before employees know if decisions were successful. Examples include oil companies, investment banks, architectural firms and the military. The focus is on the future and the importance of investing in it. There is a sense of deliberateness throughout the organisation typified by the ritual of the business meeting.
- **Process culture** – a low-risk, slow-feedback culture where employees find difficulty in measuring what they do. Typical examples include insurance companies, financial services and the civil service. The individual financial stakes are low and employees get very little feedback on their effectiveness. Their memos and reports seem to disappear into a void. Lack of feedback forces employees to focus on how they do something, not what they do.

Criticisms of cultural typologies

Some writers are critical of the generic typologies of culture that suggests organisations have a single overriding cultural environment representative of management ideology and all stakeholders. The complex nature of organisations may give rise to many different cultures and overlapping and/or conflicting sub-cultures including ways in which members of staff distinguish themselves within the organisation.

A notable critic of a unitary approach to a dominate culture imposed by senior management is *Smircich* who uses the metaphor of a plant root. Culture is something that 'is' and has developed and spread (like plant roots) together with an organisation's history, structure and staff. It is culture that drives organisations and shapes their structure and interactions. Smircich views culture as usually defined hierarchically and is elevated as a critical variable that controls the nature of organisational life, and determines its performance and effectiveness.[8]

Martin contrasts an integrationist perspective of a single unified culture as a basis for organisational effectiveness with a differentiation or pluralistic perspective which views organisation culture in terms of diverse interest groups within their own objectives.[9] *Parker* also suggests that rather than a strong single culture, organisations possess multiple sub-cultures that may overlap or contradict each other. An organisation's culture may also be perceived differently in terms of either the formal or informal structure (*see* **Chapter 2**).[10]

In what type of organisation culture are YOU more likely to be happy and satisfied at work, and is most consistent with your personality and attributes?

Levels of culture

Schein suggests a view of organisational culture based on distinguishing three levels of culture, from the shallowest to the deepest: artefacts and creations; values; and basic assumptions.[11]

- **Level 1: Artefacts.** The most visible level of the culture is artefacts and creations – the constructed physical and social environment. This includes physical space and layout, the technological output, written and spoken language and the overt behaviour of group members.

- **Level 2: Espoused beliefs and values.** Cultural learning reflects someone's original values. Solutions about how to deal with a new task, issue or problem are based on convictions of reality. If the solution works, the value can transform into a belief. Values and beliefs become part of the conceptual process by which group members justify actions and behaviour.

- **Level 3: Basic underlying assumptions.** When a solution to a problem works repeatedly it comes to be taken for granted. Basic assumptions are unconsciously held learned responses. They are implicit assumptions that actually guide behaviour and determine how group members perceive, think and feel about things.

Culture – how things are done around here

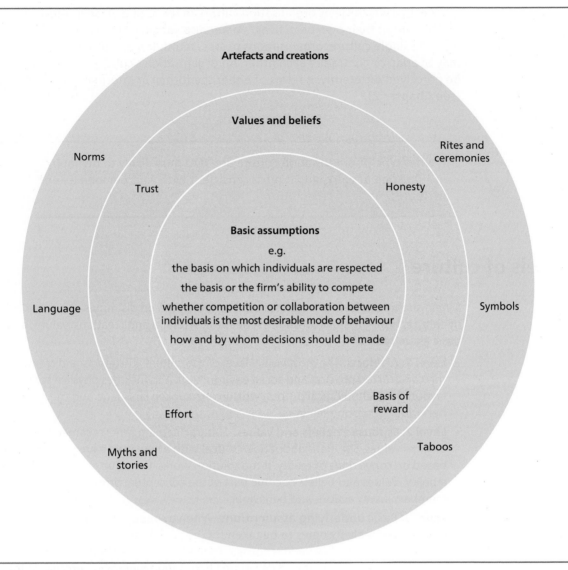

Figure 15.3 Schein's levels of culture

Source: Rollinson, D. *Organisational Behaviour and Analysis: An Integrated Approach*, fourth edition, Financial Times Prentice Hall (2008), p. 592, Reprinted and Electronically reproduced by permission from Pearson Education, Inc., New York.

Schein suggests that the basic assumptions are treated as the essence – what culture really is – and values and behaviours are treated as observed manifestations of the culture essence. *See* **Figure 15.3.**

Influences on the development of culture

The culture and structure of an organisation develop over time and in response to a complex set of factors. We can, however, identify a number of key influences that are likely to play an important role in the development of any corporate culture.

These include history, primary function and technology, strategy, size, location, management and leadership, and the environment.[12]

- **History.** The reason, and manner in which, the organisation was originally formed, its age, and the philosophy and values of its owners and first senior managers will affect culture. Corporate history can be an effective induction tool to assist a growth programme, and help integrate new employees by infusion with the organisation's culture and identity.[13] Failure in mergers and acquisitions can arise from cultural clashes and failure to integrate different cultures.[14]

- **Primary function and technology.** The nature of the organisation's 'business' and its primary function have an important influence on its culture. This includes the range and quality of products and services provided, the importance of reputation and the type of customers. The primary function of the organisation will determine the nature of the technological processes and methods of undertaking work, which in turn also affect structure and culture.

- **Strategy.** Although a business organisation may pursue profitability, this is not by itself very clear or a sufficient criterion for its effective management. The organisation must give attention to objectives in all key areas of its operations. For example, the emphasis placed on long-term survival or growth, avoiding risks and uncertainties, or concern for broader social responsibilities. The combination of objectives and resultant strategies will influence culture, and may itself be influenced by changes in culture. **(See also Chapter 16.)**

- **Size.** Usually larger organisations have more formalised structures and cultures. Increased size is likely to result in separate departments and possibly split-site operations. This may cause difficulties in communication and inter-departmental rivalries with the need for effective co-ordination. A rapid expansion, or decline, in size and rate of growth, and resultant changes in staffing will influence structure and culture.

- **Location.** Geographical location and physical characteristics can have a major influence on culture – for example, whether an organisation is located in a quiet rural location or a busy city centre can influence the types of customers and the staff employed. An example could be a hotel or restaurant. Location can also affect the nature of services provided, the sense of 'boundary' and distinctive identity, and opportunities for development.

- **Management and leadership.** Top executives can have considerable influence on the nature of corporate culture. Examples could include the key roles played by Sir Richard Branson, Anita Roddick, founder of The Body Shop.

  Another example is *Louis Gerstner,* who remade the ossified culture of computing giant IBM bred by the company's success, rebuilt the leadership team and gave the workforce a renewed sense of purpose.[15] A further example is Harriet Green who between 2012 and 2014 completely transformed the financial fortunes of travel operator Thomas Cook. Before her appointment as CEO, Thomas Cook was described by the *Financial Times* as 'a near-death experience'. Such was the impact of Harriet Green that after her sudden departure £360 million was wiped off the share price of the company. However, all members of staff help to shape the dominant culture of an organisation, irrespective of what senior management feel it should be. Another important influence is the match between corporate culture and employees' perception of the psychological contract **(discussed in Chapter 1)**.

- **The environment.** In order to be effective, the organisation must be responsive to external environmental influences. For example, if the organisation operates within a dynamic environment it requires a structure and culture that are sensitive and readily adaptable to change. An organic structure is more likely to respond effectively to new opportunities and challenges, and risks and limitations presented by the external environment. **Recall the discussion on mechanistic and organic systems in Chapter 12**.

What examples can YOU provide of people who have exercised considerable influence over corporate culture? What about the vice-chancellor of your university?

The cultural web

In order to help describe and understand the culture of an organisation, *Johnson et. al.* present a cultural web, which brings together different aspects for the analysis of organisational culture **(see Figure 15.4).**

- **Routine behaviours** – ways in which members of the organisation behave towards each other and towards those outside the organisation and which make up how things are done or how things should happen.
- **Rituals** – particular activities or special events through which the organisation emphasises what is particularly important; can include formal organisational processes and informal processes.

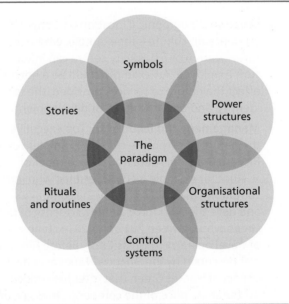

Figure 15.4 The cultural web

Source: Johnson, G., Whittington, R., Scholes, K., Angwin, D. and Regnér, P. *Exploring Strategy,* tenth edition, Pearson Education Ltd (2014), p. 156. Reprinted and Electronically reproduced by permission from Pearson Education, Inc., New York.

- **Stories** told by members of the organisation that embed the present and flag up important events and personalities, and typically have to do with successes, failures, heroes, villains and mavericks.
- **Symbols** – such as logos, offices, cars, titles, type of language or terminology commonly used – which become a shorthand representation of the nature of the organisation.
- **Power structures** – power of the most powerful individuals or groups in the organisation may be based on management position and seniority, but in some organisations power can be lodged with other levels or functions.
- **Control systems** – measurement and reward systems that emphasise what it is important to monitor, and to focus attention and activity upon – for example, stewardship of funds or quality of service.
- **Organisation structure** – which reflects power structures and delineates important relationships and activities within the organisation, and involves both formal structure and control and less formal systems.
- **The paradigm of the organisation,** which encapsulates and reinforces the behaviours observed in other elements of the cultural web.[16]

Culture and organisation control

A number of writers have referred to an alternative view of culture as a means of organisational control. For example, *Cartwright* sees culture as a system of management authority. When accepted by employees, cultural values increase the power and authority of management in three ways. Employees:

- identify themselves with their organisation and accept its rules when 'it is the right thing to do';
- internalise the organisation's values when they believe they are right; and
- are motivated to achieve the organisation's objectives.[17]

Egan refers to culture as the largest organisational control system that dictates how crazy or idiosyncratic people can be. Companies and institutions have both an overt and covert culture that influences both business and organisational behaviour.

> **The covert set can be quite dysfunctional and costly, and the largest and most controlling. It affects not only overt organisational behaviour but also the shadow-side behaviour. There may be no published rule, but culture still lays down norms for the social system. Culture tells the kind of politics allowed and how employees are allowed to play the political game.**[18]

Watson refers to the cultural design of an organisation and the link between direct and indirect controls. In a highly centralised organisation with a tight bureaucratic structure and culture there would be an emphasis on direct controls with prescribed rules and procedures, and a low level of psychological commitment from employees. In a less centralised organisation with a loosely bureaucratic structure and culture there would be more attention to indirect controls with relatively loose rules and procedures, greater flexibility and discretion, and a culture of high level commitment.[19] **See also organisation control in Chapter 14.**

Two different forms of culture

Acas distinguishes two different organisation cultures and different ways of doing things:

* control culture with the emphasis on rules and procedures, control and compliance with precedent providing guidelines; and
* quality of working life culture with the emphasis on core values, with mission statements providing guidance and commitment via shared goals, values and traditions.[20]

Kershaw contrasts rules-based or values-based culture.

> In rules-based cultures, people follow the rules and procedures assuming they are in place for good reasons, as a result of the regulatory nature of the work they undertake, or because of a particular management style. In value-driven organisations, there is an expected code of conduct. People should understand the values of the organisation and know how to behave and perform. Diverse organisations need a mix of 'command and control' and 'culture and values' to be successful.[21]

Importance of culture

Applications of organisational behaviour and effective management of people are dependent not only upon the nature of the industry or business, but also upon the characteristic features of the individual organisation – and its culture. The pervasive nature of culture in terms of 'how things are done around here' and common values, beliefs and attitudes will therefore have a significant effect on organisational processes such as decision-making, design of structure, group behaviour, work organisation, motivation and job satisfaction, and management control. With increasing globalisation, work organisations are becoming even more complex and internationally based. There is greater emphasis on the understanding and management of a diverse group of people from different nationalities into a coherent culture.

Reigle refers to culture as an important factor in successful technology implementation, innovation, mergers, acquisitions, job satisfaction, organisational success and team effectiveness, and to the importance of determining whether organisations exhibit organic or mechanistic cultures.[22]

> A director of Glassdoor Europe, *Joe Wiggins,* suggests that apart from money and compensation, company culture is the most important influence on the decision of candidates to join an organisation, followed by company reputation/employer brand.[23]

Culture and work ethic

Culture can influence people's attitudes and behaviour at work. *Bunting* draws attention to the link between work ethic **(discussed in Chapter 1)** and culture, and the extent to which people have a choice over how hard they work. Although some people have no choice, for the vast majority of people there is a degree of choice but the choices are not made in isolation:

> they are the product of the particular organisational culture of our workplaces, which promote concepts of success, of team spirit so that we don't let colleagues down, and a powerful work ethic. We are also influenced by a culture that reinforces that work ethic and its cycle of continual achievement and consumption as measures of self-worth.

Bunting maintains it is through work that we seek to satisfy our craving for a sense of control, mastery and security and clever organisations exploit this cultural context by designing corporate cultures that meet the emotional needs of their employees.[24]

The competitive environment and concerns about job security have contributed to a prevailing work culture of 'presenteeism'. In many organisations working long hours is seen as a necessary feature of acceptable behaviour and career progression. Presenteeism does not necessarily imply physical presence at your place of work but ready availability at most hours, including weekends and evenings, by email and mobile.

National cultural environment **(discussed in Chapter 1)** can have a noticeable effect on presenteeism. As the author experienced for himself in Australia work - related activities are often undertaken comfortably away from the workplace, in local coffee houses for example, without concern about not being seen by management. This is in contrast to the typical work ethic throughout much of the USA where again the author experienced the almost obsessive concern for always being seen about the place.

How has YOUR work ethic been influenced by the cultural environment of your university? To what extent is there an expectation of presenteeism for staff and for students?

Culture and organisational performance

Culture is clearly an important ingredient of effective organisational performance. *Stanford* suggests that although people have difficulty in explaining why, intuitively they know that 'yes, of course' culture matters. It is an intangible asset that is both distinctive to that organisation and adds value to it (or diminishes value). Ten typical characteristics that form the typical organisation culture are:

- a story or stories
- a purpose
- set of values
- an attitude to people
- a global mindset
- a relationship network
- a digital presence
- a reputation

- a customer proposition, and
- horizon scanning ability.

Although links between culture and business success are difficult to prove, Stanford maintains that even when there is a strong and healthy culture, a business cannot be successful if there is a flawed business model. However, with a strong and healthy culture there is less likelihood of a flawed business model.[25]

Hilton believes the key to understanding any business is to understand its culture, yet often it is the most neglected and taken for granted part. There is a strong link and companies both succeed and decline because of their culture. Most management systems such as risk management neglect the importance of culture and treat business as a mechanical operation when its outcomes depend fundamentally on the way people behave and interact. The biggest reason for the failure of two thirds of mergers and acquisitions would probably be the incompatibility in culture of the businesses.[26]

As *Clifton* points out, an organisation's culture whether official defined and promoted or just established organically will determine a whole range of performance indicators. A happy and engaged workforce is widely acknowledged to outperform one where negativity and office politics thrive. 'Business leaders should re-evaluate the importance of culture when embarking on any change management programme focused on performance improvement.'[27]

Klugerman maintains that culture will happen whether you like it or not. It is all - embracing touching every interaction or decision in an organisation. For many it is difficult to know how to get a grip on their culture. The power of culture can be illustrated by the expression 'That's just how we did things' as a familiar sentiment in the wake of an organisational scandal. Although changing culture is never easy the rewards can be substantial.[28]

National and international culture

With greater global competition, an understanding of national culture has become of increasing importance for managers. *Schneider and Barsoux* suggest that cultural beliefs and values influence the meaning of management and also show up differences in conceptions of organisations. National differences and cultural reasons raise concerns about the transferability of organisational structures, systems and processes and question the logic of universal 'best practice'.[29] *Cheng, Sculli and Chan* also question the universality of theories of management and organisational behaviour on the grounds that they have not adequately addressed the factor of culture.[30]

According to *Francesco and Gold,* culture has recently been accepted as an explanation of organisational behaviour. One reason is the increase in competitiveness of nations and a second reason is that managers encounter different cultures in their contacts with people from other nations. However, there are limits to the use of culture to explain organisational behaviour, and the relationship between national cultural values and actual behaviour in organisations is complex.[31]

Menzies points out that understanding the culture of doing business in a particular country can give you the upper hand. While the cultural differences in doing business abroad represent one of the biggest barriers to efficient working, these barriers can be easily overcome by taking the time to understand the nuances of business culture including different legal frameworks, and local business culture and language.[32]

See also discussion on language as part of culture in Chapter 6, and culture as a contingent factor of leadership in Chapter 9.

 What examples of different cultural behaviours or etiquettes have YOU observed? Have these differences resulted in misunderstandings or conflict situations?

Case study
Brazil

Full of colour and rhythm, Brazil has become the new land of opportunity in South America. Currently the seventh largest economy in the world, Brazil is wrought by its diverse culture and geography. Its growing economy is a thriving fusion of Portuguese, African and indigenous Indian influences, all of which have left their mark on Brazilian society. When in Brazil to do business, having an understanding of the diversity of its society and the unique values and attitudes of its citizens will help you to develop better relationships and do business more successfully with your Brazilian colleagues.

Under its motto: 'Ordem e Progresso', Brazilian culture is known for its hospitality, openness and traditional events, such as the carnival. The climate of Brazil comprises a wide range of weather conditions across a large area and a varied topography, but most of the country is tropical. It is important to appreciate that the Brazilian football team is a key component of national pride. As such you shouldn't schedule a business meeting during a soccer match and you should always comment about the game when on a conference call.

In Brazil family is at the centre of the social structure. Families in Brazil tend to be large and close-knit, providing members with security and connections. The importance of family is also evident in Brazilian business culture, where family members will often be found working for the same company, whether or not it is family-owned.

Relationships are one of the most important elements of Brazilian business culture. It is essential therefore to spend time getting to know your Brazilian counterparts, both personally and professionally. By cultivating close personal relationships and building trust, you will have a greater chance of successfully doing business in Brazil.

When you meet someone for the first time, it is polite to say 'muito prazer' (my pleasure). Expressions such as 'como vai' and 'tudo bem' are common forms of saying hello once you know someone and can demonstrate that you are making an effort to develop a relationship with a person. The use of titles and first names varies across Brazilian society. It is polite to address your Brazilian counterpart with their title and surname at the first meeting or when writing to them. Once you know them, it is common to use just first names, or else their title followed by their first name.

Advancing your company's relationship with a Brazilian company may rest upon your ability to gain trust. So, on your next meeting, remember to make eye contact, as this shows you are paying attention and are interested and honest. Make sure to accept any food or coffee that is offered to you, saying no can be seen as insulting. Do not show feelings of frustration or impatience as this will reflect poorly on you as an individual. Brazilians pride themselves on their ability to be in control, so acting in a similar fashion will improve your relationship with your Brazilian counterparts.

You should bear in mind that Brazilian companies tend to have vertical hierarchies, where managers at the top make most of the decisions. These positions tend to be dominated by men, but women are slowly gaining employment in executive roles. Time in Brazil is approached in a flexible manner; punctuality and defined plans are not common. This carries over into business, which can result in negotiations taking much longer than scheduled. Meetings are also often delayed or cancelled without any prior warning.

Finally, Fique tranquilo, if Brazilians value any single trait, it's optimism and being able to solve problems. If the problem can't be fixed, you should just relax and forget about it. At the first signs of someone becoming stressed, a Brazilian will often say: Fique tranquilo (fee-kee kdang-kwee-loh), which means don't worry; it has a very calming effect.

Paola Fonseca is a Manager at TMF Costa Rica.

Source: This case was published originally in ICSA Global Outlook, a supplement to the May 2011 issue of *Chartered Secretary* magazine.

A generic model of cultural categorisation

With the wide range of national cultures and regional variations, and a world of rapidly globalising business, *Lewis* draws attention to the importance of cross-cultural training and a generic model of cultural categorisation. The model classifies cultures under three main headings: linear-actives; multi-actives; and reactives (*see* **Figure 15.5**).

- **Linear-active people** tend to be task-oriented, highly organised planners who complete action chains doing one thing at a time. They prefer straightforward and direct discussion, adhere to logic rather than emotion, have faith in rules and regulations, honour written contracts and are process oriented.

- **Multi-active people** are emotional, loquacious and impulsive and attach great importance to family, feelings and relationships. They like to do many things at the same time. Relationships and connections are more important than products. They have limited respect for authority, often procrastinate, flexible and often change their plans.

- **Reactive people** are listeners who rarely initiate action or discussion. They concentrate on what is being said, listen before they leap and show respect. Reactives are introverts and adept at non-verbal communications. Silence is regarded as a meaningful part of discourse. Smalltalk is not easy and lack of eye contact is typical.[33]

Do YOU believe cross-cultural training and understanding of cultural categorisation should be included in classroom courses on Organisational Behaviour?

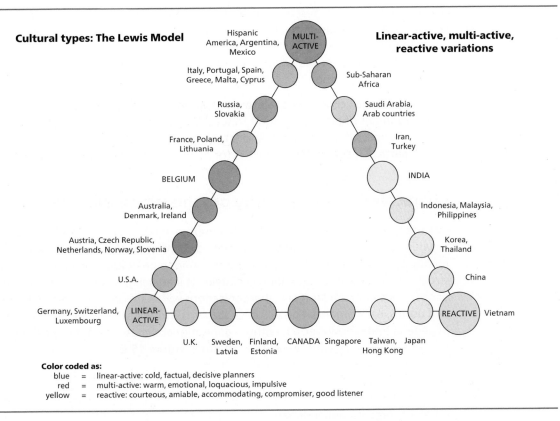

Figure 15.5 Cultural categorisation
Source: from *The Cultural Imperative: Global Trends in the 21st Century,* Nicholas Brealey (Lewis, R.D. 2007) © 2003 Richard Lewis. Reproduced by permission of Nicholas Brealey Publishing.

Organisational climate

Organisational climate is another general concept and difficult to define precisely. It is more something that is felt. **Organisational climate** can be said to relate to the prevailing atmosphere surrounding the organisation, to the level of morale, and to the strength of feelings of belonging, care and goodwill among members. The climate of an organisation is often likened to our description of the weather and the way in which the climate of a geographical region results from the combination of environmental forces. Some of these forces are better understood than others. In a similar way that culture was defined simply as 'how things are done around here', climate can be defined as 'how it feels to work around here'.

Both culture and climate relate to the value system of the organisation and both have an influence on the behaviour of their members. Climate will influence the attitudes that members of the organisation bring to bear on their work performance and personal relationships. The extent to which employees accept the culture of the organisation will have a significant effect on climate. Whereas organisational culture describes what the organisation is about, organisational climate is an indication of the employees' feelings and beliefs of what the organisation is about.

According to *Tagiuri and Litwin,* climate is based on the perceptions of members towards the organisation.

> **Organisational climate is a relatively enduring quality of the internal environment of an organisation that (a) is experienced by its members, (b) influences their behavior, and (c) can be described in terms of the values of a particular set of characteristics (or attributes) of the organisation.**[34]

Characteristics of a healthy organisational climate

Organisational climate is characterised, therefore, by the nature of the people – organisation relationship and the superior – subordinate relationship. These relationships are determined by interactions among goals and objectives, formal structure, the process of management, styles of leadership and the behaviour of people. Although similar types of organisations will share certain common features and norms, each organisation will have its own different and distinctive features. In general terms, however, a healthy organisational climate might be expected to exhibit such characteristic features as set out in **Figure 15.6.**

A healthy organisational climate
The extent to which members of staff believe there is:

- acceptance of the psychological contract between the organisation and its members
- managerial and leadership behaviour appropriate to the particular work situation
- mutual trust, consideration and support among different levels of the organisation
- easy access to senior staff with open channels of communication
- respect for individual differences, diversity, equality and inclusion
- attention to work environment and reduction of alienation or frustration at work
- genuine concern for flexibility and work/life balance
- opportunities for personal development and career progression
- democratic functioning of the organisation and opportunities for participation
- recognition of trade unions or staff representatives
- open discussion of conflict with attempt to avoid confrontation
- sense of identity with the organisation
- feeling of being a valued and appreciated member of the organisation

---

Figure 15.6 Characteristic features of a healthy organisational climate

A healthy climate will not by itself guarantee improved organisational effectiveness. However, an organisation is most unlikely to attain optimum operational performance unless the climate evokes a spirit of support and co-operation throughout the organisation, and is conducive to motivating members to work willingly and effectively. *Gray* maintains from his research to have found a clear correlation between successful workplace outcomes and a range of climate characteristics and that a climate conducive to successful outcomes also tends to be conducive to individual happiness. The climate of an organisation has a significant impact on the quality and quantity of work that gets done and on the well-being of employees.[35]

Six dimensions of climate

Atkinson and Frechette of Forum Corporation maintain there is a direct correlation between organisational climate and financial results. A healthy climate increases employee motivation, catalysing more effective performance. Research by Forum identifies six dimensions that influence the work environment and employee motivation.

- **Clarity** – people's degree of understanding of the organisation's goals and policies, as well as the requirement of their job.
- **Commitment** – the expression of continuing dedication to a common purpose and to achieving goals.
- **Standards** – the emphasis management places on high performance standards and the amount of pressure it exerts on teams to improve performance.
- **Responsibility** – the degree to which people feel personally responsible for their work.
- **Recognition** – the feeling that people are recognized and rewarded for doing good work, and that they receive accurate performance feedback.
- **Teamwork** – the feeling of belonging to an organisation characterised by cohesion, mutual support, trust and pride.

A corporate imperative now is to cultivate a positive organisational climate in a negative economic one. Successful leaders take pains to ignite a chain reaction that improves climate, increases motivation, and enhances performance. Strong leaders have the motivation and influence skills to develop the workforce in these six measurable dimensions.[36]

How would YOU explain the organisational climate of (i) your university; and (ii) your faculty or department? What specific examples can you provide?

How important is organisational climate to your university life?

Organisational change

Change is an inevitable part of both social and organisational life and we are all subject to continual change of one form or another. Change is also a pervasive influence and change at any one level is interrelated with changes at other levels. It is difficult to study one area of change in isolation and much of the following discussion provides links with topics referred to in other chapters. The effects of change can be studied over different time scales and studied at different levels. Change can be studied in terms of its effects at the individual, group, organisation, society, national or international level.

At the individual level there could for example, be a **personal transformational change** where external circumstances have not changed but because of some emotional or spiritual happening the individual was transformed or changed. This transformation may have some effect on their behaviour and actions at work and relationships with colleagues. But our main focus of attention is on the management of organisational change which can be initiated deliberately by managers, evolve slowly within a department, imposed by specific policies or procedures or arise through external pressures. Change can affect all aspects of the operation and functioning of the organisation.[37]

Planned organisational change

Change also originates within the organisation itself. Much of this change is part of a natural process of ageing – for example, as material resources such as buildings, equipment or machinery deteriorate or lose efficiency, human resources get older, the demand for new skills and abilities. Some of this change can be managed through careful planning – for example, regular repairs and maintenance, introduction of new technology or methods of work, effective human resource planning, training and staff development. However, the main pressure of change is usually from external forces and the organisation must be properly prepared to face the demands of a changing environment.

A summary of planned organisational change is set out in Figure 15.7.

Most planned organisational change is triggered by the need to respond to new challenges or opportunities presented by the external environment, or in anticipation of the need to cope with potential future problems, for example, uncertain economic conditions, intended government legislation, new product development by a major competitor or further technological advances. Planned change represents an intentional attempt to improve, in some important way, the operational effectiveness of the organisation.

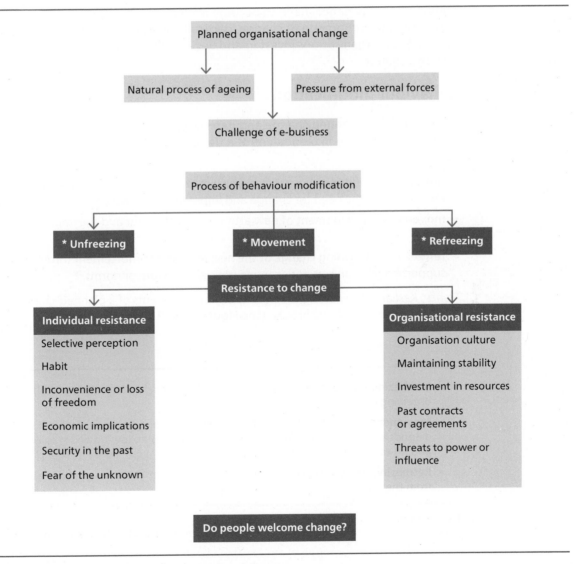

Figure 15.7 Summary of planned organisational change

The underlying objectives can be seen as:

- modifying the behavioural patterns of members of the organisation; and
- improving the ability of the organisation to cope with changes in its environment.

The challenge of e-business

Whatever the future of e-business it will continue to bring tremendous change. One of the biggest changes for managers, especially within large organisations, is learning how to get to grips with an increasingly flexible workforce. As a result of the e-business environment many people can work at anytime, anywhere and at any place. Many employees work at home but although the virtual office may help organisations to cut costs, it also poses many management challenges including the challenge to put structures in place to ensure regular meetings take place. Flexible working calls for flexible managers. This means that the traditional line managers need to become leaders, coaches and facilitators. Given the accelerating rate of change, particularly with the internet, it is essential that organisations invest in and develop their managers to succeed with this change.

Behaviour modification

A programme of planned change and improved performance developed by *Lewin* involves the management of a three-phase process of behaviour modification:

- **unfreezing** – reducing those forces which maintain behaviour in its present form, recognition of the need for change and improvement to occur;
- **movement** – development of new attitudes or behaviour and the implementation of the change;
- **refreezing** – stabilising change at the new level and reinforcement through supporting mechanisms, for example policies, structure or norms.[38]

French, Kast and Rosenzweig list eight specific components of a planned-change effort related to the above process **(see Figure 15.8).**[39]

- **Unfreezing** relates to the stages of (1) initial problem identifi cation and (2) obtaining data.
- **Movement** relates also to stage (2) obtaining data; and stages (3) problem diagnosis, (4) action planning, (5) implementation, (6) follow-up and stabilisation, and (7) assessment of consequences.
- **Refreezing** relates also to stage (7) assessment of consequences; and (8) learning from the process.

Figure 15.8 Stages in a planned-change effort
Source: based on French, W. L., Kast, F. E. and Rosenzweig, J. E. *Understanding Human Behavior in Organizations*, Harper and Row (1985), p. 9.

Transformational change

Organisations may be faced with the need for large-scale **transformational change** involving a fundamental shift in the culture, conduct of business and working practices of the organisation. Transformational change is often enacted over a period of time. CIPD report on the increasing demand for transformational change programmes as organisations emerge from the recession and once more seek more growth and development-oriented opportunities. Investment in change capability and capacity is essential for organisations wishing to have an ability to affect transformational change.[40] **See the Organisational Behaviour in Action Case Study at the end of this chapter.**

   A concept map of sources of organisational change is presented in Figure 15.9.

How successfully are YOU able to apply Lewin's three-phase process of behaviour modification at a personal level in order to accommodate change?

Changing nature of the workplace

Resistance to change

Despite the potential positive outcomes, change is often resisted at both the individual and the organisational level. Resistance to change – or the thought of the implications of the change – appears to be a common phenomenon. As long ago as 1970, *Toffler* wrote about the psychological dimension of 'future shock', and that people are naturally wary of change. 'Among many there is an uneasy mood – a suspicion that change is out of control.'[41]

   Resistance to change can take many forms and it is often difficult to pinpoint the exact reasons. Forces against change in work organisations include: ignoring the needs and expectations of members; lack of sufficient information about the nature of the change or perceived need for change. Fears may be expressed over such matters as employment levels and job security, de-skilling of work, increased workloads, loss of job satisfaction, wage rate differentials, changes to social structures and working conditions, loss of individual control over work. The impact of change on work organisations and their management draws attention to the importance of lifelong learning and self-development **(discussed in Chapter 5).**

Sources of change

Change may originate from
- outside the organisation
- inside the organisation

In order to
- promote change
- adapt to change

It is essential to define
- the Origin of the Need to change
- the Nature of any Proposed change

The need for reorganisation
within an organisation can arise from several sources:

ORGANISATION IS GROWING
& requires more staff & requires tighter control of
- administrative procedures
- employment conditions
- wages structure e.g.
In small company salaries / wages agreed on a personal basis
In large companies – a hierarchical structure of salaries
                wage levels & bargaining conditions

ORGANISATION IN DECLINE
- staff reduction
- frozen or reduced wages
- lack of motivation

Organisation takes new direction/additional direction
- changes in staff roles

Reorganisation is accompanied by changes in culture
- less social contact between staff at all levels
- less opportunity for cooperation between management & staff
- decrease in motivation by staff

External forces for change
Include
- Market forces
- Legislation
- Tax structures
- New technologies
- Political

Internal forces for change
Include:
- profitability
- reorganisation
- conflict between organisational components
        – departments
        – people
        – changes in culture/social environment

Conflict can be a source of change
Between
- senior management on strategy
- departments on respective roles/areas of responsibility
- all staff on levels/areas of responsibility
    e.g. in a company
    • production manager/service manager has tie up
      with clients on technical matters
    • accounts manager has tie up with clients
      on payment of bills
    • one manager commandeers the dual role

Market forces frequently dictate need for change
- Financial pressures – e.g. increased cost of imports, effect of VAT on fuel
- Competition – need to develop new/improved products
        e.g. supermarket price wars, travel agent price wars
        – need to provide new & improved services & quality of services

New technologies
- these may be
    • New process equipment
    • New computer technology
    • New information/data
      processing systems

Tax structures
- Value Added Tax changes
- National Insurance contributions
- Windfall taxes
- Local taxes e.g. community charge,
  business rates

Legislation
- in particular environmental
  & employment legislation
- Quota controls
- Equal opportunities
- Discrimination
- Workers charter
- Data protection

Political reasons for change
A source of change which encompasses
many of the above –
    • world politics/transnational policies
    • national politics
    • organisational politics

Profitability is a major thrust for change
Sources of change to improve profitability
- attitudes & skills of senior management
- products of research
- improved production facilities
- reductions in staff
- take-overs/mergers
    • of other organisations
    • by other organisations

Take-overs/mergers
This source (origin) of change:
- to improve efficiency/efficient use of assets
    e.g. economics of scale
        reduce duplication
        increased market pull
        more dynamic management

Example
A travel company is losing money/making lower profits
Causes may be – inefficient management
        – more efficient management of competitors
        – more attractive holidays from competitors
        – less competitive in price
        – poor exchange rates
        – improved weather conditions in the UK
Having identified causes, solutions can be planned at
        • company level
        • branch level

Figure 15.9 Sources of change

Source: Copyright © 2011 The Virtual Learning Materials Workshop. Reproduced with permission.

Individual resistance

Some common reasons for individual resistance to change within organisations include the following:

- **Selective perception.** People's interpretation of stimuli presents a unique picture or image of the 'real' world. This can result in selective perception and to a biased view of a particular situation. For example, trade unionists may have a stereotyped view of management as untrustworthy and therefore unduly suspicious of any management change, however well founded might have been the intention.

- **Habit.** People tend to respond to situations in an established and accustomed manner. Habits may serve as a means of comfort and security and proposed changes may well be resisted. However, if there is a clearly perceived advantage, for example a reduction in working hours without loss of pay, there is likely to be less, if any, resistance to the change, although some people may, because of habit, still find it difficult to adjust to the new times.

- **Inconvenience or loss of freedom.** If the change is seen as likely to prove inconvenient, make life more difficult, reduce freedom of action or result in increased control, there will be resistance.

- **Economic implications.** People are likely to resist change that is perceived as reducing either directly or indirectly their pay or other rewards, requiring an increase in work for the same level of pay or acting as a threat to their job security. People tend to have established patterns of working and a vested interest in maintaining the status quo.

- **Security in the past.** There is a tendency for some people to find a sense of security in the past. In times of frustration or difficulty, or when faced with new or unfamiliar ideas or methods, people may reflect on the past. There is a wish to retain old and comfortable ways. For example, in bureaucratic organisations, officials often tend to place faith in well-established ('tried and trusted') procedures and cling to these as giving a feeling of security.

- **Fear of the unknown.** Changes which confront people with the unknown tend to cause anxiety or fear. Many major changes in a work organisation present a degree of uncertainty, for example the introduction of new technology or methods of working. A person may resist promotion because of uncertainty over changes in responsibilities, longer working hours or increased social demands of the higher position.

Organisational resistance

Although organisations have to adapt to their environment, they tend to feel comfortable operating within the structure, policies and procedures which have been formulated to deal with a range of present situations. To ensure operational effectiveness, organisations often set up defences against change and prefer to concentrate on the routine things they perform well. Some of the main reasons for organisational resistance against change are as follows.

- **Organisation culture.** Recall that the culture of an organisation develops over time and may not be easy to change. The pervasive nature of culture in terms of 'how things are done around here' also has a significant effect on organisational processes and the behaviour of staff. An out-dated culture may result in a lack of flexibility for, or acceptance of, change.

- **Maintaining stability.** Organisations, especially large-scale ones, pay much attention to maintaining stability and predictability. The need for formal structure and the division of work, narrow definitions of assigned duties and responsibilities, established rules, procedures and methods of work, can result in resistance to change. The more mechanistic or bureaucratic the structure, the less likely it is that the organisation will be responsive to change.

- **Investment in resources.** Change often requires large resources that may already be committed to investments in other areas or strategies. Assets such as buildings, technology, equipment and people cannot easily be altered. For example, a manufacturer may not find it easy to change to a socio-technical approach and the use of autonomous work groups because it cannot afford the cost of a new purpose-built plant and specialised equipment.

- **Past contracts or agreements.** Organisations enter into contracts or agreements with other parties, such as the government, other organisations, trade unions, suppliers and customers. These contracts and agreements can limit changes in behaviour – for example, organisations operating under a special licence or permit, or a fixed-price contract to supply goods/services to a government agency. Another example might be an agreement with unions that limits the opportunity to introduce redundancies, or the introduction new technology or working practices.

- **Threats to power or influence.** Change may be seen as a threat to the power or influence of certain groups within the organisation, such as their control over decisions, resources or information. For example, managers may resist the introduction of worker-directors because they see this as increasing the role and influence of nonmanagerial staff, and a threat to the power in their own positions. Where a group of people have, over a period of time, established what they perceive as their 'territorial rights', they are likely to resist change.

Cultural and change

Katzenbach, Steffen and Kronley suggest that when a major change runs aground, leaders often blame their company's culture for pushing it off course. Too often culture becomes an excuse and diversion rather than an accelerator and energiser. Leaders see cultural initiatives as a last resort, except for top-down exhortations to change.

Must cultures are too well entrenched to be jettisoned. The secret is to stop fighting your culture – and to work with and within it, until it evolves in the right direction.[42]

 What do YOU see as the most likely reasons for resistance to change at (i) the individual; and (ii) the organisational level? Can you give specific examples?

Do people welcome change?

In order to help ensure its survival and future success the organisation must be responsive to change and adaptable readily to the external demands placed upon it from an increasingly volatile environment. According to *Dan Wagner,* change is good.

> **It is the whole dynamic that creates successful companies in the first place, whether you are trying to do something differently or more efficiently, or something that leverages the technology that has become prevalent to do something better.**[43]

Although change is often resisted, *Lockhead* maintains that 'most successful organisations develop a culture that welcomes change and the opportunities it brings'.[44] *Cunningham* maintains that one of the greatest myths in management is the generalisation that people resist change. In fact people love change. The commonest reason for resistance is where people perceive a potential loss. For example, because of negative rumour-mongering, people may perceive that they will be worse off from a proposed change even if the opposite is in fact true. In a different context, changes that result, for example, in the loss of one's job, can create real, fact-based resistance. While people welcome change that they want, they have to be careful about the pace of change. In a more general context people may be enthusiastic for change, for example in large organisations where some people want to see changes and improvements in communication.[45]

Continuous organisational change and burnout

Rees and Rumbles point out that the pace and scope of change has been unprecedented and they examine the extent to which continuous organisational change leads to organisational burnout. Organisational causes of burnout include excessive workload, lack of autonomy and authority, insufficient reward and disparity between personal and organisational values. Burnout may also have a 'spill over' effect on people's home lives. Rees and Rumbles question the extent to which organisations 'care' about the amount of stress that occurs during change and whether organisations can assess whether their human capital is close to burnout. Organisations need to determine how to get out of the burnout rut by becoming more resilient to change and engaging employees in a positive and productive manner in order to ensure long term success.[46] **(Organisational Stress is discussed in Chapter 3.)**

Managing change

Whatever the extent to which people resist or welcome change it is an inevitable feature of work organisations. The successful management of change is clearly essential for continued economic performance and competitiveness and is the life-blood of business success. New ideas and innovations should not be perceived as threats by members of the organisation. Efforts to maintain the balance of the socio-technical system will influence people's attitudes, the behaviour of individuals and groups, and thereby the level of organisational performance and effectiveness.

Many books and articles refer to the steps or actions to be taken to secure successful and sustainable change.[47] *Arnold* refers to the influential work of *John Kotter*[48] who following research into 100 American companies in 1996 set out an 8-step process for leading transformational change. In view of the volatile world, Arnold suggests a revised five-step process of Kotter's work.

- **It's all about agility** – to adapt rapidly to a changing market agile thinking must be applied to the digital world and to fundamental corporate behaviour.

- **Change has many leaders** – with thousands of incremental changes involved in a change programme responsibility and ownership of results rests with a larger number of leaders.

- **There's no end to change** – rather than a linear change process, people must be open and receptive to change which can emerge both bottom-up as well as top-down.

- **Change cannot be standardised** – today's change programmes are not just about people but about technical solutions and genuine change across the whole organisation.

- **Millennials change everything** – millennials are flexible and innovative, and the new generation may be able to make constant change a reality.

Arnold points out that successful management of change is now a source of competitive advantage and companies that do not change, suffer. It is only a matter of time before all organisations embrace the idea of constant change.[49]

Making change work

If change is to work, it must alter the perceptions, attitudes and behaviour of people.

Despite the views of Lockhead and Cunningham **(discussed above)**, it is important to remember that change is a complex and powerful psychological experience. Most people are not detached from their work but experience a range of emotional involvements through their membership of the organisation, and they feel threatened and disoriented by the challenge of change. Emotions such as uncertainty, frustration or fear are common reactions. It is understandable therefore that people often adopt a defensive and negative attitude, and demonstrate resistance to change.

According to *Atkinson,* a major problem in driving change in organisations is dealing with and managing the resistance that will be encountered – but that resistance should be welcomed as a healthy response. Resistance is natural and should not be viewed only as a negative response to change. In the absence of really positive benefits from the proposed change, the 'default' response of resistance is acceptable.[50]

Taylor points out that one of the most stressful aspects of change is often the sense of loss of control that accompanies it. The individual can feel powerless and helpless. Many organisations spend a great deal of attention and energy focusing on the operational outcomes of proposed changes but often pay scant attention to enabling employees to adapt psychologically to the new situation.[51] *Reeves and Knell* suggest that 'knowledge leaders understand that change provokes an emotional response, that successful change involves allowing people to feel angry, resentful and afraid as well as excited, hopeful and energised'.[52]

One of the most important factors in the successful implementation of organisational change is the style of managerial behaviour. Some members may actually prefer, and respond better, to a directed and controlled style of management. **(Recall, for example, the discussion on Theory X and Theory Y styles of managerial behaviour in Chapter 10.)** In most cases, however, the introduction of change is more likely to be effective with a participative style of managerial behaviour. If staff are kept fully informed of proposals, are encouraged to adopt a positive attitude and have personal involvement in the implementation of the change, there is a greater likelihood of their acceptance of the change.

Advances in ICT

A report published jointly by the Chartered Management Institute, the British Computer Society and the Change Leadership Network refers to challenges facing senior executives to ensure they are better prepared to lead technological change. Change always involves risk and on the basis of examination of ten detailed organisational case studies the report identifies five key challenges in obtaining best value from IT-enabled change:

- Creating transformational value rather than just implementing IT projects.
- Building capability for ongoing change. Being able to predict future business needs and how IT can help shape new business models and deliver the desired benefits.
- Creating a climate of open communication.
- Managing confidence and trust – understanding the impact of external changes.
- Building personal capability, learning and confidence.[53]

Considerations of the need to change arising from advances in information technology simply cannot be ignored. An important priority is to create an environment of trust and shared commitment, and involve staff in decisions and actions that affect them. There should be full and genuine participation of all staff concerned as early as possible, preferably well before the actual introduction of new equipment or systems. Information about proposed change, its implications and potential benefits should be communicated clearly to all interested parties. Staff should be actively encouraged to contribute their own ideas, suggestions and experiences, and to voice openly their worries or concerns.

As part of the pre-planning for new technology there should be a carefully designed 'human resource management action programme' and close involvement of HR. **See also the discussion in Chapter 13.**

Getting people to accept change

Anne Riches, an internationally recognised leader in neuroscientific research, questions why some organisations struggle to change and applies an interesting approach to resistance to change based on a neuroscientific understanding. Resistance to change is one of the most powerful drivers of human behaviour, and the key to dealing with it effectively is to understand both its physical and emotional components. Most organisations make two fatal errors when dealing with resistance. First, they underestimate the strength of current patterns that employees are comfortable and familiar with. Second, they underestimate what will be required to change those patterns and deal with the automatic, though sometimes subtle, fight or flight responses that occur when employees interpret changes as threats.

The amygdala and The Almond Effect®

According to Riches, our brains are hard-wired to do three things: match patterns, resist or fight any threats to survival, and respond first with emotion over logic. Our neural pathways and amygdalae are the key players in these reactions. The **amygdala** is an almond-shaped piece of the brain that triggers the 'fight or flight' reaction. Sometimes, though, the amygdalae set off a false alarm. This is what Riches calls The Almond Effect®. Put simply, you act without thinking and get it wrong. You can probably think of many times when this has happened, times when you said or did something in the heat of the moment, and almost immediately afterwards regretted it.

At work, the Almond Effect often gets in the way. It is the reason why all too often, human beings automatically react to change with resistance, even before they fully understand the nature of the change. The amygdala has activated the fear response based on previous memories of change (old neural pathways) associated with, for example, job losses, more work, new skills required, change of roster, cost cutting and so on. Stress hormones are released as part of the inbuilt flight/fight mechanism and show up at work as anger, anxiety, lethargy, poor performance and reluctance to change.

Mechanisms of change

Riches points out that people don't change behaviours easily. This is especially true in workplaces with cultures and histories that are slow and resistant to change. The nature and intensity of our motivation to change will differ in various circumstances but regardless of our reasons for wanting to change behaviours or thought patterns, we will have to create new neural pathways and then to use them in preference to the old ones.

It is worth remembering that:

- Humans are hard wired for survival above all else.
- Our default thinking is habitual and self-perpetuating.
- Everyone is the product of their own experiences with different motivations and unique memories.
- Change can be frustratingly slow because it's hard brain work to rewire – even if it is logical and in the person's best interests.[54]

How far do YOU accept the idea of the 'Almond Effect' which has caused you a false alarm and when you acted without thinking and got it wrong?

Critical Thinking Zone

Reflections on Resistance to Change

In this zone, we critically evaluate resistance to change and examine whether it positively or negatively influences the implementation and outcomes of organisational change programmes.

Resistance to change has been described as 'one of the most widely accepted mental models that drives organisational behaviour'[55] (p. 25). It has a long history of academic and practitioner recognition as a vitally important factor that can either positively or negatively influence the outcome of organisational change programmes.[56] As 'over half of all organisational changes fail'[57] (p. 24), managers and the organisation at large need to see beyond their perception of resistance as a foe, the enemy of change that must be defeated,[58] and appreciate the potentially devastating effect that it can have on the success and longevity of the business if it not appropriately addressed.

Defining Resistance to Change

Amarantou et al.[59] and Sharma[60] concur that a commonly accepted definition of resistance to change is difficult to find in the literature. It has been described as a ubiquitous, multidimensional organisational phenomenon that introduces unexpected delays, uncertainties and costs into the strategic change process.[58,61] Zaltman and Duncan[62] view it as any behaviour or way of behaving that seeks to perpetuate the status quo against the pressure to change it. Continuing the organisational behaviour theme, Waddell and Sohal[56] espouse that resistance is often associated with negative individual attitudes or counterproductive overt and covert behaviours, such as making dissenting or critical comments, not doing something when an agreement has been made to do it and tardiness in responding to requests.[57]

Deconstructing Resistance to Change

Resistance to change has been traditionally understood as an underlying cause of conflict that is unwelcome and injurious to the organisation. According to Waddell and Sohal, in classical management theory, unitarism espoused everyone working towards a single, unitary sense of purpose and direction, which was driven and perpetuated by top management. This

was a vehicle to promote organisational efficiency and effectiveness through the introduction of change that managers deemed necessary for organisational success and survival. Pluralism generated individual multiple viewpoints and attitudes to change that managers perceived as incongruous to their own and the organisation at large. Any form of resistance was seen by management as subversion and an attempt by individuals to derail the introduction of change through their own self-interest and catalyse a reduction of organisational effectiveness and performance. Resistance rapidly gained a reputation as a foe, an enemy of change that protracted transformation programmes by in-fighting and factional dissent. Management's response was to eradicate resistance by quashing it as soon as it erupted, to make way for the change to be implemented. This negative view of change was, according to Waddell and Sohal, also considered by early human resource theorists as conflict. Rather than being addressed by managers and tackled head on, it was largely avoided to keep the peace and promote workplace harmony.

Waddell and Sohal report that initial perceptions of resistance as being rooted in parochial self-interest and conflict have been somewhat softened by anthropological, psychological and social research, which identified that the phenomenon was far more complex and multidimensional than originally thought. Studies highlighted that resistance to change is a by-product of four key social factors. First, incongruences between individual and management perceptions of change objectives and outcomes (rational). Second, the impact the change will have on the individual's context and the extent to which they will be displaced by it, such as a change of location (non-rational). Third, management exercising favouritism or point scoring (political) and fourth, poor or inappropriate management styles (management). Following on from this, developments in organisational theory has, according to Waddell and Sohal, identified that resistance is also embedded in institutional systems and processes, which, it could be argued, are perpetuated through, and fuelled by, corporate culture. Additionally, the classical view of resistance as an arch nemesis of change, has, over the years, been recognised as a friend rather than foe that could potentially play a major role in an organisation's change endeavours.

Resistance: Help or Hindrance?

Extant literature suggests there is a tussle between theorists who label resistance as something negative to be eradicated or minimised as quickly as it emerges and others who contend that it is to be welcomed as an aide to change implementation.[63] According to Dent and Galloway Goldberg[55] (p. 26), both the literature and organisational practice have perpetuated the 'people resist change' mental model that has, they argue, proven to be problematic for individuals and the organisation at large. They assert that the 'best way to challenge the conventional wisdom is to suggest that people do *not* resist change per se' (p. 26), a view that is shared by Waddell and Sohal. People may resist a loss of pay, comfort, status, the unknown, management ideas that are incongruent with their own or even being dictated to by managers. However, Dent and Galloway Goldberg argue that the above issues are not the same as resisting or refusing to accept change and make an impassioned plea for theorists and practitioners to 'dispense with the phrase *resistance to change*' and identify more constructive and pertinent models for 'describing what the phrase has come to mean - employees are not wholeheartedly embracing a change that management wants to implement' (p. 26). In view of this, Ford and Ford[57] (p. 25) attest that 'resistance is more in the eye of the beholder than an objective report by an unbiased and disinterested observer.' Arguably, it is also perceptual and socially constructed, driven by multiple perspectives of reality and prior experiences. As such, the authors suggest that one manager's perception of resistance is not resistance at all through someone else's eyes. Critically, Ford and Ford contend that managers use resistance as a conception against which to label communications and behaviours they dislike or don't think should occur and for which they attribute will increase their workload and the time they need to contribute to making the change successful.

Like Dent and Galloway Goldberg, Ford and Ford and Waddell and Sohal profess that resistance might not be resistance at all, but a bona fide, perfectly natural reaction to something within the planned change that individuals may not understand. This, they assert, is a valuable opportunity for managers to listen to what stakeholders have to say and use the intel as a potentially positive force for good, to enhance and improve the change process. Waddell and Sohal add that feedback might highlight aspects of the proposed change that are inappropriate, wrong or poorly thought through and therefore need amending. Rather than being a hindrance, they advise that resistance might also inject a modicum of energy into an apathetic situation and when questioning the status quo should be privileged over silent acquiescence. It is thus an opportunity for managers to evaluate whether the change implementation is on trajectory or whether catharsis is needed to examine, evaluate and put right any problems that individuals can see, to which they may be blinded. In doing so, Waddell and Sohal advocate that resistance and its resisters may become a vital source of innovation and, it could be argued, metamorphose into change champions rather than perceived antagonists.

Implications for Organisational Behaviour in the Workplace

To conclude, resistance to change is a multidimensional, complex phenomenon that both positively and negatively influences the implementation and outcomes of change. Waddell and Sohal advocate that classical, adversarial perceptions of, and approaches to, resistance have been superseded with softer, more psychosocial attitudes that are intended to aide, rather than hinder, change. Furthermore, Ford and Ford contend that if the organisation blames resistance for the demise of change programmes, it runs the risk of failing to notice a raft of opportunities to strengthen its operational outcomes and modify subjective biases that could otherwise derail implementation. They add that the organisation may also lose a certain amount of credibility in the eyes of the recipients of change, who may consequently refuse to share their specialist knowledge and thus obstruct planned changes. They conclude 'resistance, properly understood as feedback, can be an important resource in improving the quality and clarity of the objectives and strategies at the heart of a change proposal.' They advise that if the feedback gained through the process is strategically used, it can 'enhance the prospects for successful implementation' (p. 103).

Questions

Based on the above, answer the following questions:

1. Theorists suggest that a definition of resistance to change is difficult to find in the literature. *Why* do you think this is the case? *How* would you define the concept?

2. Resistance to change has classically become known as an enemy or foe of change. In your role as a Consultant, *what* strategies would you suggest to the Senior Management Team to alter negative perceptions and attitudes to change?

3. With reference to theory and practice, *argue* the case *for* individuals challenging the status quo. *Critically evaluate* the implications for organisational behaviour in the workplace.

Summary – Chapter 15 'Organisational culture and change'

A central feature of the successful organisation is the diagnosis of its culture, health and performance, and the ability to adapt to change. Culture is a general concept that helps to explain what the organisation is all about and how things are done in different organisations. There are a number of ways to classify different types and levels of organisation culture. The culture of an organisation develops over time and in response to a complex set of factors. Culture has an important effect on the behaviour and actions of individuals, on the process of management and on organisational performance. Organisational climate is based on the perception of members towards the organisation, and is the state of mutual trust and understanding among its members. Organisations operate within an increasingly volatile environment. Change is a pervasive influence and an inescapable part of social and organisational life.

Planned organisation change involves a process of behaviour modification. Change may be welcomed by some people but is often resisted at both the individual and organisational level. Resistance to change can take many forms and it is not always easy to pinpoint exact reasons. The successful initiation and management of change must be based on a clear understanding of social factors and human behaviour at work.

Group discussion activities

Undertake each of these activities in small groups as indicated by your tutor. Before you start your discussion establish a non-threatening environment within the group and confirm confidentiality will be honoured.

First, form your own views and then share and compare in open critical discussion with colleagues. Reflect honestly on the extent to which: (i) you influenced the thinking and ideas of your colleagues; and (ii) you were influenced by your colleagues.

To what extent was your group able to reach consensus?

Agree one of your members to produce a brief written summary of the discussion and prepared to present in a plenary session.

Activity 1

Understanding your organisation's personality

The culture of an organisation is often likened to the personality of an individual. One of the most effective ways to explore the personality of your organisation is by describing it as if it were a person. **Ask yourself the following questions about your organisation.**

* What gender would it be?
* How old would it be?
* Where would it live?
* Where would it prefer to holiday?
* What car would it drive?
* What interests or hobbies would it have?
* If it were to win the lottery, what would it do?

Source: Adapted with permission from David Hill, Director, Echelon Learning Ltd.

Activity 2

(a) How important was perception of the organisational culture in the decision of your chosen university?

(b) Referring back to **Figure 15.5** discuss with specific examples the extent to which your university displays characteristic features of a healthy organisational climate.

(c) Explain fully any areas in which you believe the organisational climate of your university could be enhanced.

Activity 3

(a) To what extent do you believe in the suggestion of the psychological dimension of future shock and that people are naturally wary of change?

(b) How would YOU explain your emotional response to change? Detail fully your experiences of:

    (i) anger, resentment or fear; and

    (ii) excitement, hopefulness and feeling energised.

(c) What did you learn from this activity and in what ways were your surprised by the responses of your colleagues?

Organisational behaviour in action case study

Transformational change

Harriet green, Chief Executive, Thomas Cook

Harriet Green told the Commission about her personal 'transformation toolkit', which she has used to overhaul a number of organisations on different continents, including Thomas Cook.

'Driving transformation is a 24/7 job,' she said. 'Organisations are like living organisms and, when looking to transform them, you need to consider all elements, whilst addressing the most urgent priorities.' The critical three elements are:

The psychology: how people think, feel and act – in other words, the organisation's culture, values, ways of working and 'the way we get things done round here'.

The physiology: the systems and processes that underpin and connect the business, like nerve endings and blood flows.

And, finally, *its anatomy*: the organisational structure. Businesses need to create a lean, agile structure as befits a digitally enabled business, supporting fast decision-making, and reducing the layers of management between the CEO and customers.

Harriet believes a CEO must lead change in all three areas to truly transform the organisation. An effective CEO today needs to operate at the centre of the vortex – not from the top of the pyramid in a historical, hierarchical construct – and has to gather information from all the organisation's communities, both internal and external.

> *Organisations are like living organisms and, when looking to transform them, you need to consider all elements, whilst addressing the most urgent priorities.*

Harriet described some of the key 'tools' in her personal leadership toolkit that are helping her to drive the ongoing turnaround at Thomas Cook.

Investigate the problem

On her first day as CEO, Harriet sent a survey to everyone in the business asking what was wrong with it. In under a month, over 8,000 people had replied. Those at the frontline usually know what's not working and have a passion for fixing it.

Be visible

Communicate often, update the organisation regularly, and use different media, like video. Be available and reply quickly. Be visible, share honestly and celebrate success.

Be open

Ensure you are open to feedback from employees. At Thomas Cook, Harriet developed an 'Ask Harriet' email address, so employees could email in confidence on any issue. At its peak, Harriet received 200 emails a day and prides herself on replying to everyone.

Identify talent

Leaders need to identify their talented performers quickly. Engage with people across the organisation – meet the key players in every area, know their direct reports, and meet with up and coming talent. Identify quickly those who are not 'on the bus' – make decisions quickly. When transforming an organisation, moving at pace is essential – don't waste time trying to convert those managers and leaders who don't want to change and who make it clear that they will never support the new ways. give everyone a fair chance to change but then take the tough decisions. Middle- management is often a big part of the problem – and also the solution. By engaging and fostering belief at the top and the bottom of the organisation, those in the middle who might be slower to change begin to feel the squeeze and move forward positively.

Build a winning team

Bringing in fresh talent, different industry experience and a different perspective is vitally important, as is identifying the skills and knowledge gaps early on. At Thomas Cook, Harriet personally recruited close to 80 people, believing that, when transforming the leadership of an organisation, the principle of 'a third, a third and a third' is usually the right balance: keep one-third of the original leadership team, promote one-third from within and bring in one-third to give fresh perspective and learnings from other industries, and then involve and engage them to work together as one aligned team.

Develop the culture

From the very start, focus on the culture. Develop and agree together the values and the ways of working. Create a strong code of conduct and involve the whole organisation. Everyone needs to clearly know what the organisation believes in, how it works and 'how we do things round here'. Together, these will create a culture and build trust. Every employee needs to see themselves and their beliefs reflected in the culture to succeed – like a flamingo looking into a pool. Develop clear leadership competencies to measure the performance of your leaders and enforce the code of conduct fairly and clearly for everyone without exception. Lead with integrity and by example every day. Be a role model.

Break down barriers

Silos and organisational politics have no place in transformations – build new teams, share best practice and encourage openness.

Celebrate success

Remember to take time to celebrate success – it's an important part of rebuilding belief, particularly in an organisation that's been through a tough time. Pride in the company, its performance, its products and its services is important for everyone.

Listen to stakeholders

Never stop listening to your customers. Never be so remote or so arrogant to think you can stop listening to any of your key stakeholders.

Source: 'MANAGEMENT 2020', Commission on The Future of Management and Leadership, *Chartered Management Institute,* July 2014, p. 33. www.managers.org.uk/management2020. Reproduced with permission.

Tasks

1. Explain fully what you understand by transformational change. Give your own views on Harriet Green's 'transformation toolkit'.

2. To what extent do you believe sending a survey to everyone in the business is *ordinarily* likely to produce constructive and meaningful feedback? How well do you think this would work in your own university?

3. What particular problems do you foresee in attempting to 'create a strong code of conduct and involve the whole organisation'?

Chapter 15 – Personal skills and employability exercise

Objectives

Completing this exercise should help you to enhance the following skills:

* Work together effectively in a small group.
* Evaluate organisation culture and cultural norms and applications to organisational behaviour.
* Undertake a critical review of the socialisation process.

Exercise

Through the process of socialisation new people into an organisation tend to inculcate themselves and adopt cultural norms. Socialisation into the culture of the organisation is an important aspect of organisational behaviour.

Working in small groups, you are required to undertake a detailed review of the socialisation of new members into the culture of your own university.

Comment critically, with supporting examples where possible, on the extent to which the socialisation process successfully addresses such topics as, for example:

* Design and nature of the induction programme
* Introduction to top management and key members of staff
* Expected patterns of behaviour
* Unwritten codes of behaviour, including dress codes
* Attempts to build cohesiveness among close working colleagues
* Mentoring relationships
* Responsibilities for human resource management
* Nature of discipline and grievance procedures
* Social facilities and activities
* Housekeeping arrangements such as canteen and refreshment facilities, car parking
* Opportunities for further studies, training and development, career progression

Discussion

* How successfully did the socialisation process indoctrinate new members into the ways of the university and its cultural norms? What changes would you recommend?
* How much did you learn about the informal organisation or how things really work?
* To what extent did the socialisation process help generate an initial feeling of engagement with the university or did you detect an element of management control and manipulation?

Notes and references

1. Stewart, R. *The Reality of Management,* third edition, Butterworth Heinemann (1999), p. 123.
2. Naylor, J. *Management,* second edition, Financial Times Prentice Hall (2004), p. 79.
3. Atkinson, P. E. 'Creating Cultural Change', *Management Services,* vol. 34, no. 7, 1990, pp. 6–10.
4. See, for example, Oswick, C., Lowe, S. and Jones, P. 'Organisational Culture as Personality: Lessons from Psychology?', in Oswick, C. and Grant, D. (eds) *Organisation Development: Metaphorical Explorations,* Pitman Publishing (1996), pp. 106–20.
5. Harrison, R. 'Understanding Your Organization's Character', *Harvard Business Review,* vol. 50, May/June 1972, pp. 119–28.
6. Handy, C. B. *Understanding Organizations,* fourth edition, Penguin (1993).
7. Deal, T. E. and Kennedy, A. A. *Corporate Cultures: The Rites and Rituals of Corporate Life,* Penguin (1982).
8. Smircich, L. 'Concepts of Culture and Organizational Analysis', *Administrative Science Quarterly,* vol. 28, no. 3, September 1983, pp. 339–58.
9. Martin, J. *Cultures and Organizations: Three Perspectives,* Oxford University Press (1992).
10. See, for example: Parker, M. *Organizational Culture and Identity: Unity and Division at Work,* Sage (2000).
11. Schein, E. H. *Organizational Culture and Leadership,* fourth edition, Jossey-Bass (2010).
12. See, for example, Handy, C. B. *Understanding Organizations,* fourth edition, Penguin (1993); and McLean, A. and Marshall, J. *Cultures at Work,* Local Government Training Board (1988).
13. Kransdorff, A. 'History – A Powerful Management Tool', *Administrator,* October 1991, p. 23.
14. See, for example, Beckett-Hughes, M. 'How to Integrate Two Cultures', *People Management,* vol. 11, no. 5, 10 March 2005, pp. 50–1.
15. Gerstner, L. V. Jr. *Who Says Elephants Can't Dance?: Inside IBM's Historic Turnabout,* HarperBusiness (2002).
16. Johnson, G. *et. al. Exploring Strategy,* tenth edition, Pearson Education (2014). Reprinted and electronically reproduced by permission of Pearson Education, Inc.

17. Cartwright, J. *Cultural Transformation,* Financial Times Prentice Hall (1999), p. 34.

18. Egan, G. 'The Shadow Side', *Management Today,* September 1993, p. 37.

19. Watson, T. J. *Organising and Managing Work,* second edition, FT Prentice Hall (2006).

20. 'Effective Organisations: The People Factor', Advisory Booklet, ACAS, November 2001.

21. Kershaw, P. 'Culture and Control', *Governance + Compliance*, July 2014, p. 4.

22. Reigle, R. F. 'Measuring Organic and Mechanistic Cultures', *Engineering Management Journal,* vol. 13, no. 4, December 2001, pp. 3–8.

23. Wiggins, J. 'The Rise of the "Informed Hire"', *Professional Manager,* Winter 2018, p. 22.

24. Bunting, M. *Willing Slaves,* HarperCollins (2004), p. xxiii.

25. Stanford, N. *Organisation Culture: Getting it right,* The Economist/Profile Books (2010).

26. Hilton, A. 'Hearts and Minds', *Chartered Secretary,* April 2011, p. 14.

27. Clifton, K. 'Values Added', *Manager,* Autumn 2012, p. 14.

28. Klugerman, M. 'Aspire higher: Changing organisational culture is never easy, but the rewards can be substantial', *Governance + Compliance*, November 2017, pp. 30–2.

29. Schneider, S. C. and Barsoux, J. *Managing Across Cultures,* second edition, Financial Times Prentice Hall (2003).

30. Cheng, T., Sculli, D. and Chan, F. 'Relationship Dominance – Rethinking Management Theories from the Perspective of Methodological Relationalism', *Journal of Managerial Psychology,* vol. 16, no. 2, 2001, pp. 97–105.

31. Francesco, A. M. and Gold, B. A. *International Organizational Behavior,* second edition, Pearson Prentice Hall (2005).

32. Menzies, J. 'Cultural Advantage', *Global Outlook, Chartered Secretary,* May 2011, pp. 10–12.

33. Lewis, R. D. *The Cultural Imperative: Global Trends in the 21st Century,* Nicholas Brealey (2007).

34. Tagiuri, R. and Litwin, G. H. (eds) *Organizational Climate,* Graduate School of Business Administration, Harvard University (1968), p. 27.

35. Gray, R. *A Climate of Success,* Butterworth-Heinemann (2007).

36. Atkinson, T and Frechette, H. 'Creating a Positive Organizational Climate in a Negative Economic One' *Forum Corporation*, www.trainingindustry.com.media (accessed 8 October 2011).

37. For a discussion of change in relation to the complexities of organisational life, see Senior, B. and Swailes, S. *Organizational Change,* fourth edition, Financial Times Prentice Hall (2010).

38. Lewin, K. *Field Theory in Social Science,* Harper and Row (1951).

39. French, W. L., Kast, F. E. and Rosenzweig, J. E. *Understanding Human Behavior in Organizations,* Harper and Row (1985).

40. 'Leading transformational change', Research report, CIPD, September 2014.

41. Toffler, A. *Future Shock,* Pan Books (1970), p. 27.

42. Katzenbach, J. R., Steffen, I. and Kronley, C. 'Cultural Change That Sticks', *Harvard Business Review,* vol. 90, July/August 2012, pp. 110–17.

43. In conversation with Saunders, A. 'How to Cope with a Changing World', *Management Today,* October 2012, pp. 52–5.

44. Lockhead, Sir M. 'In My Opinion', *Management Today,* September 2008, p. 12.

45. Cunningham, I. 'Influencing People's Attitudes to Change', *Professional Manager,* vol. 14, no. 3, May 2005, p. 37.

46. Rees, G and Rumbles, S. 'Continuous Organizational Change and Burnout', *The International Journal of Knowledge, Culture & Change Management,* vol. 11, 2012.

47. See, for example, Yukl, G. *Leadership in Organizations,* seventh edition, Pearson Education (2012).

48. Kotter, J. P. *Leading Change,* Harvard Business School Press (1996).

49. Arnold, P. 'The Evolution of Change', *Professional Manager,* Winter 2016, pp. 50–3.

50. Atkinson, P. 'Managing Resistance to Change', *Management Services,* Spring 2005, p. 15.

51. Taylor, G. 'Managing the Situational and Psychological Pressures Brought About by Change', *Professional Manager,* vol. 16, no. 4, July 2007, p. 14.

52. Reeves, R. and Knell, J. 'Your Mini MBA', *Management Today,* March 2009, pp. 60–4.

53. Tranfield, D. and Braganza, A. *Business Leadership of Technological Change: Five Key Challenges Facing CEOs,* Chartered Management Institute (2007).

54. Material in this section reproduced with kind permission of Anne Riches, creator of The Almond Effect® and author of CLUES: tips, strategies and examples for change leaders. For further information see www.AnneRiches.com.

55. Dent, E. B. and Galloway Goldberg, S. 'Challenging "Resistance to Change"', *The Journal of Applied Behavioural Science,* vol. 35, no. 1, 1999, pp. 25–41.

56. Waddell, D. and Sohal, A. S. 'Resistance: A Constructive Tool for Change Management', *Management Decision,* vol. 36, no. 8, 1998, pp. 543–8.

57. Ford, J. D. and Ford, L. W. 'Stop Blaming Resistance to Change and Start Using It', *Organization Dynamics,* vol. 39, no. 1, 2010, pp. 24–36.

58. Schein, E. (1988). *Organizational Psychology,* third edition, Prentice Hall.

59. Amarantou, V., Kazakopoulou, S., Chatzoudes, D. and Chatzoglou, P. 'Resistance to Change: An Empirical Investigation of its Antecedents', *Journal of Organizational Change Management,* vol. 31, no. 2, 2018, pp. 426–50.

60. Sharma, R. R. *Change Management: Concepts and Applications,* Tata McGraw-Hill (2008).

61. Ansoff, I. *The New Corporate Strategy,* Wiley & Sons (1998).

62. Zaltman, C. and Duncan, R. *Strategies for Planned Change,* Wiley (1977).

63. Thomas, R. and Hardy, C. 'Reframing Resistance to Organizational Change', *Scandinavian Journal of Management,* vol. 27, pp. 322–31.

Chapter 16
Strategy, corporate responsibility and ethics

Strategy, the process of management and applications of organisational behaviour must be tempered by decisions relating to broader social obligations and ethical responsibilities.

Learning outcomes

After completing this chapter you should have enhanced your ability to:

- explain the nature and importance of organisation strategy;
- debate the significance of organisational ideologies, principles and values;
- assess the significance of organisational goals, objectives and policy;
- review the concept, nature and scope of corporate social responsibilities;
- detail approaches to the consideration of organisational values and business ethics;
- review the nature and impact of codes of conduct or ethics;
- assess the nature and importance of human rights in business.

Outline chapter contents

Overview topic map: Chapter 16 – Strategy, social responsibility and ethics

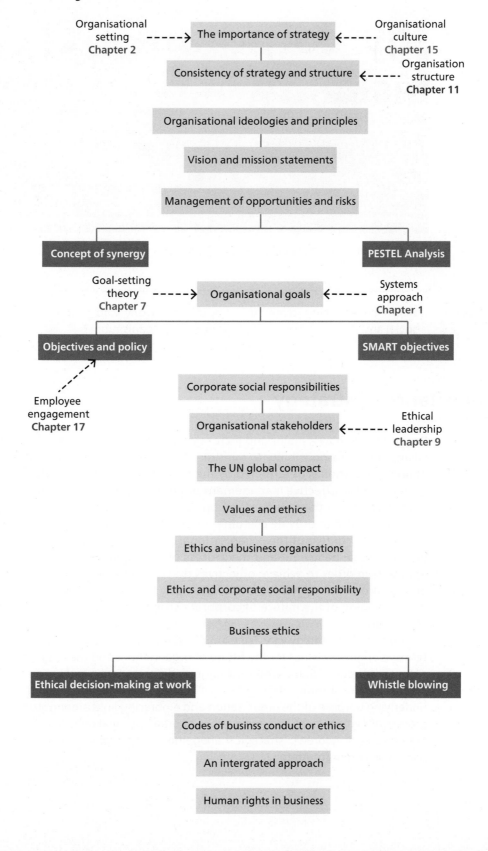

Success depends upon overall strategic purpose and vision

Before commencing to read this chapter how strongly do YOU feel about the social and ethical responsibilities of business organisations?

The importance of strategy

Organisations play a major and increasingly important role in the lives of us all and have a responsibility to multiple stakeholders. The overall direction of an organisation is determined by the nature of its corporate strategy. Underlying the effective management of people is the requirement for a clear understanding of the nature of the business that the organisation is engaged in and how best to provide customer or consumer satisfaction. In **Chapter 2** we saw that the context of the organisational setting is central to the application of organisational behaviour and the process of management. It is the interaction of people in order to achieve objectives that form the basis of the particular organisation. An integral feature of the study of organisational behaviour is an understanding of the nature of corporate strategy for the formal organisation as a whole.

Definitions of strategy vary. For example, *Johnson et al.* view strategy in simple terms as about key issues for the future of organisations and the long-term direction of an organisation.[1] Some writers distinguish different terms and various levels of 'strategy', but **corporate strategy** is seen here as a generic term relating to the underlying purpose of the organisation and embracing links among structure, the process of management and applications of organisational behaviour. For some writers, such as *Andrews,* 'strategic management' is emerging as a more popular term than corporate strategy.[2]

Consistency of strategy and structure

There is obviously a close relationship between strategy and organisation structure, **discussed in Chapter 11.** It is by means of the organisation's structure that its goals and objectives are attained. *Chandler* suggests a clear distinction between devising a strategy and implementing it. Drawing on major empirical evidence *Chandler* concluded that the organisation first needed to develop strategy and after this devise the organisation structure to deliver that strategy.[3]

However, *Lynch* points out that a major debate has been taking place over recent years regarding the relationship between the strategy and structure of the organisation. The nature of this relationship, and whether structure follows strategy or strategy follows structure, is not clear. The concept of strategy first and then structure may oversimplify the situation. Although it may not be possible to define which comes first, there is a need to ensure that strategy and structure are consistent with each other. To be economically efficient the organisation must undertake a process of strategic fit matching strategy and structure. In order to undertake the proposed strategy effectively, the organisation needs to adopt an internally consistent set of practices. Lynch maintains that for most organisations it is essential to have some structure and there is a connection between an organisation's strategy and most appropriate organisation structure, *see* **Figure 16.1.**[4]

Nature of business strategy	Likely organisational structure
Single business – one major set of strategies for the business	Functional
Range of products extending across a single business – several strategies for each product area but business still run as one entity, perhaps with some common functions	Functional but monitor each range of products using separate profit and loss accounts
Separate businesses within group with limited links – assuming that each business is not related and operates in a separate market	Divisional
Separate businesses within group with strong links needed across parts of the group	Matrix (or divisional with co-ordination if matrix is difficult to manage)
Ideas factory – strategy needs to be strongly experimental and emerge	Innovative structure
Unrelated businesses – series of businesses each with its own strategic issues	Holding company
Related businesses owned jointly or by minority shareholdings – series of businesses where each needs to have its own strategies and be managed separately	Holding company

Figure 16.1 Nature of business strategy and organisation structure
Source: Richard Lynch, *Strategic Management*, sixth edition, Pearson Education (2012), p. 481. Reprinted and electronically reproduced by permission of Pearson Education, Inc.

Strategy and people

Allen and Helms suggest that different types of reward practices may more closely complement different generic strategies and are significantly related to higher levels of perceived organisational performance.[5] According to *Stern* it seems acceptable again to acknowledge the human factor in business. 'Niceness is back in vogue, at least for some of the time. People are talking about strategy not just in visionary terms but also in emotional ones.'[6] *Gratton* draws attention to people at the centre of business success and the importance of people-centred strategies as one of the means by which the organisation balances the needs of the short term with those of the long term, as well as balancing financial capital with human potential.

> **Creative and engaging people strategies have, at their core, an understanding of how the vision and business goals can be delivered through people, and of the specific actions which need to be taken in the short and longer term to bridge from reality to aspirations.[7]**

Strategy and culture

Schneider and Barsoux discuss the close link between culture and strategy and address such questions as: how does national culture affect strategy; how do different approaches to strategy reflect different underlying cultural assumptions; how do managers from different cultures respond to similar business environments; and in what ways does culture affect the content and process of decision-making**? See also organisational culture in Chapter 15.** Among the examples quoted by Schneider and Barsoux are Japanese companies that challenge the Western view of strategic management and adopt a broader notion of strategy; managers from Nordic and Anglo countries who are less likely to see environments as uncertain; whereas managers from countries within Latin Europe or Asia are likely to perceive greater uncertainty when faced with similar environments and perceive less control over what will happen.[8]

Sir Win Bischoff, Chair of the Financial Reporting Council reports on the importance of a strong culture for generating value to a business. Strategy and culture are equally important and inextricably linked. You cannot have a business model and strategy change without impeding the long-term cultural aspects of a company.[9]

> How would YOU explain the relationship between: (i) strategy and structure; and (ii) strategy and culture?

A summary of strategy, social responsibilities and ethics is set out in Figure 16.2.

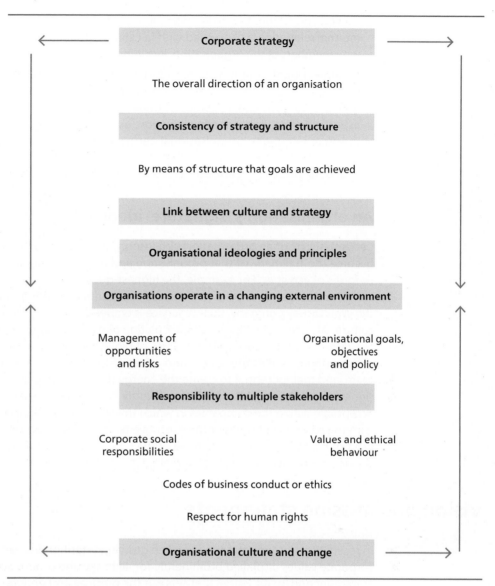

Figure 16.2 Summary of strategy, social responsibilities and ethics

Organisational ideologies and principles

The strategy of an organisation may be pursued in accordance with an underlying ideology, or philosophy, based on beliefs, values and attitudes. This **organisational ideology** determines the 'culture' of the organisation and provides a set of principles that govern the overall conduct of the organisation's operations, codes of behaviour, the management of people and its dealings with other organisations.[10] These sets of principles may be recognised and implemented informally as 'accepted conventions' of the organisation or they may be stated formally in writing.

Over forty years ago, *Brech* wrote about the ideology of an organisation related to the idea of both an ethical foundation and an organisational or operational foundation.

- **Ethical foundation** embodies the basic principles which govern the external and internal relations of the organisation. External relations concern standards of fair trading and relations with, for example, customers, suppliers and the general public. Internal relations are concerned with fair standards of employment and relations with members of the organisation, including authorised union representatives.

- **Organisational or operational foundation** is concerned with the structure, operation, and conduct of the activities of the organisation. External aspects relate to, for example, methods of trading and channels of distribution. Internal aspects include methods of production, use of equipment and managerial practices relating to organisational performance, productivity and profitability.[11]

Ethical behaviour of organisations is discussed later in this chapter.

An organisation's 'signature' ideology

Certain aspects of an organisation's philosophy may be so dominant that they become the 'hallmark' of that organisation and place constraints on other areas or forms of activities. For example, the highest-quality hallmark of Rolls-Royce cars would presumably prevent entry into the cheaper mass-production market. With the Walt Disney Company, quality service is embedded deeply within its corporate culture. Also, the John Lewis hallmark pledge of never knowingly undersold.

Gratton refers to 'signature' processes of highly successful companies that are a direct embodiment of the history and values of the company and its top executive team, and their potential to create the energy to drive high performance. These signature processes, which differ significantly from general views of best practice, are acceptable within the companies in which they develop because of their association with the passion and value of the executive team, and are part of the fabric and ways of behaving.[12] A clear example of the point made by Gratton, is Apple with a signature that has survived the ultimate demise of its founder.

Vision and mission statements

In recent years organisations have given growing attention to a set of stated corporate values displayed prominently for all to see and production of a **mission statement** and/or its 'vision' that sets out the purpose and general direction for the organisation. There is sometimes an apparent uncertainty over the distinction between the terms 'mission' and 'vision' that tend to be used interchangeably. It seems to be generally accepted that the vision provides the overall frame of reference of what the organisation would like to reach and how it will look. Within this vision the mission statement defines what the organisation aims to achieve, and its core business and activities.

Value of mission statements

The desire to identify with as many stakeholders as possible means that many mission statements are all-embracing with bland and abstract wording. The value of a mission statement is dependent, however, upon the extent to which it is understood and accepted throughout the organisation, and translated in meaningful terms to all members of staff including those at the operational level. A mission statement is only likely to be of any value if the organisation actually practises what it preaches. The purpose (strategy) and guiding principles of the John Lewis Partnership is set out in **Figure 16.3.**[13]

The John Lewis Partnership – defining principles

The John Lewis Partnership's principles define how we run our business. They are as relevant today as they were when they were set out by our founder, John Spedan Lewis, in our constitution.

Purpose The Partnership's ultimate purpose is the happiness of all its members, through their worthwhile and satisfying employment in a successful business. Because the Partnership is owned in trust for its members, they share the responsibilities of ownership as well as its rewards profit, knowledge and power. The video 'Employee Ownership, A Shared Passion', explains how our employee owned business model operates in practice, and offers insight and advice to anyone wanting to learn more about this sort of model and its benefits.

Power Power in the Partnership is shared between three governing authorities: the **Partnership Council**, the **Partnership Board** and the **Chairman**.

Profit The Partnership aims to make sufficient profit from its trading operations to sustain its commercial vitality and finance its continued development, to distribute a share of those profits each year to its members and to enable it to undertake other activities consistent with its ultimate purpose.

Members The Partnership aims to employ and retain as its members people of ability and integrity who are committed to working together and to supporting its Principles. Relationships are based on mutual respect and courtesy, with as much equality between its members as differences of responsibility permit. The Partnership aims to recognise their individual contributions and reward them fairly.

Customers The Partnership aims to deal honestly with its customers and secure their loyalty and trust by providing outstanding choice, value and service.

Business relationships The Partnership aims to conduct all its business relationships with integrity and courtesy and to honour scrupulously every business agreement.

The community The Partnership aims to obey the spirit as well as the letter of the law and to contribute to the wellbeing of the communities where it operates.

Figure 16.3 John Lewis Partnership – defining principles
Source: http://www.johnlewispartnership.co.uk/about-our-principles.html. Used with Permission from John Lewis partnership.

How far are YOU able to identify clearly with the shared values or mission statement of your university? Do you believe mission statements serve any useful purpose?

Management of opportunities and risks

To survive and maintain growth and expansion every business needs a strategy related to changing environmental conditions, to protect the business from potentially harmful influences and ready to take maximum advantage of the challenges and opportunities presented. An effective business strategy depends upon the successful management of opportunities and risks. *Drucker* suggests that strategy should be based on the priority of maximising opportunities, and that risks should be viewed not as grounds of action but as limitations on action. The right opportunities will not be selected unless:

- focus is on maximising opportunities rather than on minimising risks;
- major opportunities are scrutinised collectively and in respect of their characteristics rather than singly and in isolation;

- opportunities and risks are understood in terms of the appropriateness of their fit to a particular business; and

- balance is struck between immediate and easy opportunities for improvement, and more difficult, long-range opportunities for innovation and changing the character of the business.[14]

SWOT analysis

In order to analysis its opportunities and risks an organisation may undertake a broader evaluation of the business environment and strategic capability by undertaking a **SWOT analysis** (sometimes also known as 'WOTS up'), which focuses on the Strengths, Weaknesses, Opportunities and Threats facing the organisation. **Strengths** are positive aspects or distinctive attributes or competencies which provide a significant market advantage or upon which the organisation can build. **Weaknesses** are negative aspects or deficiencies in the present competencies or resources of the organisation, or its image or reputation, which limit its effectiveness and which need to be corrected or need action taken to minimise their effect. **Opportunities** are favourable conditions and usually arise from the nature of changes in the external environment. **Threats** are the converse of opportunities and refer to unfavourable situations that arise from external developments likely to endanger the operations and effectiveness of the organisation. Although now less popular a SWOT analysis may still provide a framework for strategic management and used in conjunction with a PESTEL analysis, **discussed below.**

The concept of synergy

An important feature of corporate strategy and growth and development of organisations is the concept of synergy, developed in management applications by *Ansoff.*[15] **Synergy** results when the whole is greater than the sum of its component parts. It can be expressed simply in terms of the 2 + 2 = 5 effect. An example could be an organisation integrating its retail and on-line operations. Synergy is often experienced in situations of expansion or where one organisation merges with another. An example could be the merger of a computer firm with expertise in design and marketing of hardware with a firm expert in software systems design and manufacturing.

In the search for synergy and increased productivity, a number of organisations are creating more streamlined structures and concentrating on key activities with the outsourcing of non-core activities. It is possible, however, to experience **negative synergy** or the 2 + 2 = 3 situation. Such a position might arise when a merger occurs between organisations operating in different fields, with different markets or methods or where the new organisation becomes unwieldy or less cost-effective. Another situation could be customer, staff or union resistance to the outsourcing of call centres particularly to other countries.

PESTEL analysis

Strategic decision-making must be related to the external environment in which an organisation is operating. Organisational performance and effectiveness will be dependent upon the successful management of the opportunities, challenges and risks presented by changes identified in scanning this global external environment. One popular technique for analysing the general environment is a **PESTEL analysis** – that is, Political, Economic, Socio-cultural, Technological, Environmental and Legal influences. As an example, *Lynch* presents the main issues that might be considered when undertaking a PESTEL analysis **(*see* Figure 16.4).**[16]

Worthington and Britton refer to the complexity of the number and variety of influences from the external environment and no study could hope to consider them all. For students of business and managers alike, the requirement is to pay greater attention to those influences which appear the most pertinent and pressing for the organisation in question, rather than to attempt to consider all possible contingencies.[17]

Political future

- Political parties and alignments at local, national and European or regional trading-bloc level
- Legislation, e.g. on taxation and employment law
- Relations between government and the organisation (possibly influencing the preceding items in a major way and forming a part of future strategic management)
- Government ownership of industry and attitude to monopolies and competition

Socio-cultural future

- Shifts in values and culture
- Change in lifestyle
- Attitudes to work and leisure
- 'Green' environmental issues
- Education and health
- Demographic changes
- Distribution of income

Economic future

- Total GDP and GDP per head
- Inflation
- Consumer expenditure and disposable income
- Interest rates

- Currency fluctuations and exchange rates
- Investment–by the state, private enterprise and foreign companies
- Cyclicality
- Unemployment
- Energy costs, transport costs, communications costs, raw materials costs

Technological future

- Government and EU investment policy
- Identified new research initiatives
- New patents and products
- Speed of change and adoption of new technology
- Level of expenditure on R&D by organisation's rivals
- Developments in nominally unrelated industries that might be applicable

Environmental future

- 'Green' issues that affect the environment and impact on the company
- Level and type of energy consumed– renewable energy?
- Rubbish, waste and its disposal

Legal future

- Competition law and government policy
- Employment and safety law
- Product safety issues

Figure 16.4 Organisational sub-systems

What do YOU believe are the greatest opportunities and risks from changing environmental influences that face business organisations today?

You need clear goals to aim for

Organisational goals

Activities of an organisation are directed to the attainment of its goals. **Organisational goals** are future expectations; some desired future state, something the organisation is striving to accomplish. Goals will determine the nature of its inputs and outputs, the series of activities through which the outputs are achieved, and interactions with its external environment. The extent to which an organisation is successful in attaining its goals is a basis for the evaluation of organisational performance and effectiveness.

Goals are therefore an important feature of work organisations. To be effective, goals should be emphasised, stated clearly and communicated to all members of the organisation. At the individual level, the attainment of goals is the underlying influence on motivation. Movement towards greater delegation and empowerment through the hierarchy means that staff at all levels must be aware of their key tasks and actions, and exactly what is expected of them and their department/section. For example, goal-setting theory **(discussed in Chapter 7)** is widely recognised as a successful means of increasing work motivation and performance.[18]

In addition to performing some function, all organisations have some incentive for their existence and for their operations. The goals of the organisation provide

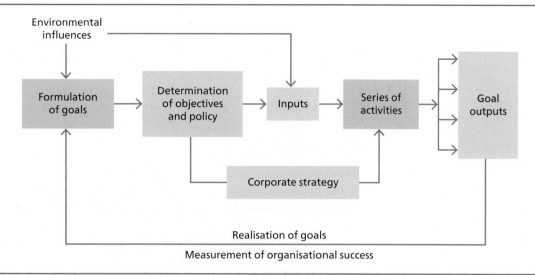

Figure 16.5 A systems view of organisational goals and objectives

corporate guidelines that are translated into objectives and policy. In terms of a systems approach **(discussed in Chapter 1)** the objectives of an organisation are related to the input–conversion–output cycle. In order to achieve its objectives and satisfy its goals the organisation takes inputs from the environment, and through a series of activities transforms or converts these inputs into outputs and returns them to the environment as inputs to other systems. The organisation operates within a dynamic setting and success in achieving its goals will be influenced by a multiplicity of interactions with the environment **(*see* Figure 16.5).**

Objectives and policy

Whatever the type of organisation formulation of objectives and policy is an essential part of corporate strategy and the process of management. Use of the two terms varies but objectives are seen here as the 'what' and policy as the 'how', 'where' and 'when' – the means that follow the objectives.

- **Objectives** set out more specifically the goals of the organisation, the aims to be achieved and the desired end results.
- **Policy** is developed within the framework of objectives. It provides the basis for decision-making and the course of action to follow in order to achieve objectives.

Objectives may be just implicit but formal, explicit definition will assist communications and reduce misunderstandings, and provide more meaningful criteria for evaluating organisational performance. Policy is a guideline for organisational action and translated into rules, plans and procedures; it relates to all activities of the organisation and all levels of the organisation. Some policy decisions are directly influenced by external factors – for example government legislation on equal opportunities and diversity. Together, objectives and policy provide corporate guidelines for the operations and management of the organisation.

Guidelines for individual behaviour

To be effective, goals should be emphasised, stated clearly and communicated to all members of the organisation. At the individual level, the attainment of goals is an underlying influence on motivation. Clearly stated, good objectives can help provide unity of direction and aid employee engagement and commitment. However, objectives should not be stated in such a way that they detract from the recognition of possible new opportunities, potential danger areas, the initiative of staff or the need for innovation or change.

According to *Reeves* a few well-chosen aims in goal-setting can sharpen focus and boost productivity but too many can lead to stress and even disaster. Clear objectives expressed as specific goals should improve performance, but measurement should not be confused with target-setting. Employee engagement **(discussed in Chapter 17)** is much more likely to follow from autonomy than from a battery of management-dictated targets. Problems occur when there are too many targets and they are closely attached to individual performance.[19]

'SMART' objectives

Clearly defined and agreed objectives are the first stage in the design of organisation structure and help facilitate systems of interaction and communication between different parts of the organisation. A commonly used mnemonic to summarise the characteristics of good objectives is 'SMART', usually interpreted as:

- **S**pecific – clear, detailed and understandable as to what is required
- **M**easurable – to monitor and measure progress towards achievement of the objective
- **A**chievable – challenging but obtainable by a competent person
- **R**ealistic – relevant to the goals of the organisation with a focus on outcomes of achievement
- **T**imebound – outcomes to be achieved within an agreed timescale

But note the observations from *Dryburgh*.

Why SMART objectives are really DUMB

Alastair Dryburgh

We have all read about how objectives should be SMART – Specific, Measurable, Achievable, Realistic and Timed. This is well meaning but profoundly limiting. Let's take the points one by one and see where they lead us.

- **Specific.** Why is this a good thing, when it excludes objectives like 'insanely great technology' (Apple), 'a totally new way of seeing' (Picasso) or 'customer service that gets customers raving about how good it is' (anyone? I wish someone would)?
- **Measurable.** Same problem as specific. Mediocrity is easy to measure, but greatness is harder – you know it when you see it.
- **Achievable and realistic.** This is where the real problem occurs. I don't know, cannot know, how much I can achieve. If I want to set myself a goal that I know I can achieve,

I have to set something which is much less than I could achieve. That's a recipe for mediocrity, at best. The worst thing that can happen with such a goal is that we do meet it, and we stop short of what we could have achieved. Consider instead the value of an impossible goal like 'be the world's greatest X.' It helps and inspires us. It sets a direction. We may never get there, but every day we know what to do to move closer.

- **Timed.** This creates the dangerous illusion that we make changes in order to arrive at a steady state at some defined point in the future. That's not how the world works – it keeps changing, and we need to keep changing with it.

SMART objectives are part of an obsolete management paradigm which assumes that we know what the future will look like (much like the present) and know how we will survive and thrive in that future. If Mother Nature had used SMART objectives instead of natural selection, we would still be no more than slightly improved monkeys.[20]

A 'SMARTER' option

A development of the SMART framework is proposed by *Taylor* who suggests that in today's demanding and fast-paced business environment a smarter option is to add the 'E' and 'R' to your smart goals.

- **E is for exciting** – unless you have the excitement and motivation to achieve your goal, it will remain just that, a written goal. There is more likelihood of achieving your goal if it's something you really want.

- **R is for recorded** – now take recording and writing down your goal one step further. Share your goal with someone else and say it out loud. By sharing your goal with others you're putting yourself on the line and more likely to be committed to achieving it.[21]

To what extent do YOU identify with the idea of SMART goals? Do you believe your goals should be exciting and shared with other people?

Corporate social responsibilities (CSR)

Organisations play a major and increasingly important role in the lives of us all, especially with the growth of large-scale business and expanding globalisation. The decisions and actions of management in organisations have an increasing impact on individuals, other organisations and the community. Organisations make a contribution to the quality of life and to the well-being of the community. The power and influence that many business organisations now exercise should be tempered, therefore, by an attitude of responsibility by management.

At the time of writing two examples of current issues of serious public and media concern are: (i) environmental effects from the continuing use of plastics and excessive packaging; and (ii) increasing number of gambling websites and association of betting companies with sporting organisations and activities.

Organisational survival is dependent upon a series of continual interactions and exchanges between the organisation and its environment which give rise to a number of broader responsibilities to society in general. These broader responsibilities, which are both internal and external to the organisation, are usually referred to as **corporate social responsibilities (CSR)**. For example, the core values of Red Carnation Hotels include care to the local communities.[22] *See Figure 16.6.*

Red Carnation Hotels – Core Values

Our core values reflect what is really important and matters to us as a company and group of individuals who make up the Red Carnation family. They are the solid foundation and main principles of our company culture. By consistently working hard to maintain our values, we endeavour to preserve what makes Red Carnation Hotels so special – a sincere and deep commitment to each other, our guests whom we serve every day and the communities within which we work and live.

To give personalised, warm and consistently exceptional service

We appreciate the myriad of options and alternatives our guests have to choose from, and therefore we set the bar high for ourselves to provide the highest quality services and products we possibly can.

We constantly challenge ourselves to update and enhance the guest experience. Innovation, constant training and refurbishment help create an environment which our guests and our employees regard as their home from home.

To value, respect and support each other

We believe that care comes from caring and so we provide a level of care for our team members that inspires by example, generates trust, respect, open and honest communication and appreciation. Staff feel valued and are offered opportunities to develop and progress, and as a result our staff loyalty far exceeds the industry average.

To create positive, memorable experiences for every guest

We work hard to meet and exceed our customers' expectations on every visit or touch point they have with us. By delighting and satisfying our guests, we ensure the longevity of our business and employment for our team.

By serving our customers with very personable, proficient, friendly, competent service, and listening to their needs we create memorable and distinctive experiences as well as loyal guests who return regularly.

To care about and give back to our local communities

We recognise and appreciate our responsibility to be active participants in our local communities. We believe in giving time to community and service organisations with the belief that it is important to give back and make a difference wherever possible. In a world of shrinking natural resources, we must endeavour to conserve, reuse and care about those around us.

All of our hotels make it an on-going priority to support and contribute positively to a variety of charitable organisations within their respective communities. The charities we support in England include The Starlight Foundation, Great Ormond Street Children's Hospital, Action Against Hunger, the National Autistic Society and the Cystic Fibrosis Trust. In Geneva we have provided help for The Red Cross and in South Africa we support the Nelson Mandela Children's Fund, and our bath amenities are purchased from Charlotte Rhys, a Founding Member of the Proudly South African Organisation, dedicated to the support of disadvantaged women and men in South Africa. Recycling efforts continue to be reviewed and improved upon wherever possible.

Our guests, staff, and suppliers have been wonderfully sympathetic to our aims, assisting us with their wholehearted support, and we would like to send a sincere 'thank you' to every one of them. While we believe our collective contributions do make a difference we are not content to sit back, and constantly challenge ourselves to increase our involvement with the global community. We welcome ideas and input from our customers, staff and suppliers.

Jonathan Raggett

Managing Director, The Red Carnation Hotel Collection

Figure 16.6 Core values of Red Carnation Hotels

Source: https://www.redcarnationhotels.com/about/core-values. Used by permission from Red Carnation Hotels.

Growing attention to social responsibilities

There has been growing attention given to the subject of CSR and an increasing amount of literature on the subject and on a new work ethic. According to The Chartered Management Institute, CSR is now an important and increasingly specialised aspect of strategy and management. Over recent decade, it has become a necessity rather than a choice, due to:

- legal changes that have made some aspects of CSR compulsory;
- increased public interest in environmental and ethical issues from consumers and potential employees;
- a convincing business case linking CSR to better performance;
- shareholder pressure on businesses to show they operate ethically and sustainably.

CSR demands a different way of working at strategic levels with basic changes to ensure CSR priorities are set, trust in the organisation builds, and stated values enacted. Codes of conduct reinforced by training, strong leadership and performance measures can establish responsible standards of corporate behaviour.[23]

To what extent do YOU believe concern for broader social responsibilities should be *the* overriding consideration in the strategy of all business organisations?

Organisational stakeholders

Social responsibilities are often viewed in terms of **organisational stakeholders** – that is, those individuals or groups who have an interest in and/or are affected by the goals, operations or activities of the organisation or the behaviour of its members. Stakeholders include a wide variety of potential interests and may be considered under a number of headings. For example, drawing on the work of *Donaldson and Preston*,[24] *Rollinson* suggests a comprehensive view of stakeholders in terms of the potential harm and benefits approach.[25] ***See Figure 16.7***.

According to *Willis* British companies' record on CSR is mixed at best. While for some companies CSR is deeply embedded in their institutional DNA and an intrinsic part of their identity for many others it can appear to be a bewildering prospect. Getting it wrong can lead to perceptions of tokenism and loss of faith from staff and customers. West, an advisor at BITC points out companies should undertake a gap analysis of how a business is performing in four key areas of environment, community, workplace and marketplace. CSR needs more than a list of values on the wall. Every part of the business needs to understand exactly what it actually means. Leadership can make a real difference in ensuring CSR filters down into core decisions and actions.[26]

A blurred distinction

Arguably, there is still something of blurred distinction between the exercise of a genuine social responsibility, on the one hand, and actions taken in pursuit of good business practice and the search for organisational efficiency on the other.

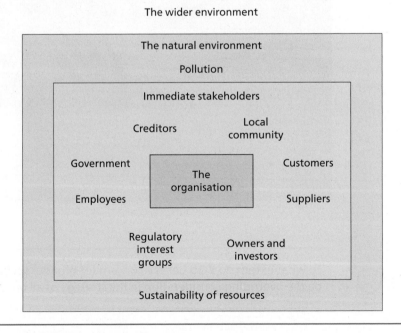

Figure 16.7 Areas of organisational social responsibilities
Source: Rollinson, D. *Organisational Behaviour and Analysis,* fourth edition, Financial Times Prentice Hall (2008), p. 592, Reprinted and Electronically reproduced by permission from Pearson Education, Inc., New York.

One approach is that attention to social responsibilities arises out of a moral or ethical motivation and the dictates of conscience – that is, out of genuine philanthropic objectives. An alternative approach is that the motivation is through no more than enlightened self-interest and the belief that, in the long term, attention to social responsibilities is simply good business sense. In practice, it is a matter of degree and balance, of combining sound economic management with an appropriate concern for broader responsibilities to society.

Ethical leadership

The importance of ethical behaviour, integrity and trust calls into question the extent to which managers should attempt to change the underlying values and beliefs of individual followers. **(See discussion on transformational leadership in Chapter 9.)** For example, *Yukl* discusses the controversy whereby some writers contend that this type of leader influence is clearly unethical even when intended to benefit followers as well as the organisation. A contrary view is that leaders have an important responsibility to implement major changes when necessary to ensure survival and effectiveness. Large-scale change would not be successful without some changes in member beliefs and perceptions.[27]

According to a report from the *Institute of Leadership and Management,* despite the high level of public focus on ethics managers are still placed under increased pressure from facing frequent ethical dilemmas at work. Although the majority of managers say their organisations have a statement of values, it is clear that they are not effective enough at influencing behaviour. Building a set of values that do not link with targets is an ineffective way to influence behaviour. Values need to be linked with strategy. When values tie into the strategic objectives of an organisation, the way people are expected to behave and the goals they are required to achieve work in tandem.[28]

The UN Global Compact

Corporate sustainability starts with a company's value system and a principled approach to doing business. This means operating in ways that, at a minimum, meet fundamental responsibilities in the areas of human rights, labour, environment and anti-corruption. Responsible businesses enact the same values and principles wherever they have a presence, and know that good practices in one area do not offset harm in another. By incorporating the Ten Principles of the UN Global Compact into strategies, policies and procedures, and establishing a culture of integrity, companies are not only upholding their basic responsibilities to people and planet, but also setting the stage for long-term success.[29]

The Ten Principles of the UN Global Compact

The UN Global Compact asks companies to embrace, support and enact, within their sphere of influence, a set of core values in the areas of human rights, labour standards, the environment and anti-corruption. The UN Global Compact's ten principles in the areas of human rights, labour, the environment and anti-corruption enjoy universal consensus and are derived from:

Human rights

Principle 1: businesses should support and respect the protection of internationally proclaimed human rights; and
Principle 2: make sure that they are not complicit in human rights abuses.

Labour

Principle 3: businesses should uphold the freedom of association and the effective recognition of the right to collective bargaining;
Principle 4: the elimination of all forms of forced and compulsory labour;
Principle 5: the effective abolition of child labour; and
Principle 6: the elimination of discrimination in respect of employment and occupation.

Environment

Principle 7: businesses should support a precautionary approach to environmental challenges;
Principle 8: undertake initiatives to promote greater environmental responsibility; and
Principle 9: encourage the development and diffusion of environmentally friendly technologies.

Anti-corruption

Principle 10: businesses should work against corruption in all its forms, including extortion and bribery.

Source: https://www.unglobalcompact.org/what-is-gc/mission/principles.

To what extent do YOU agree the principles of the UN Global Compact are to be applauded but in reality have little real influences on organisational behaviour?

Values and ethics

The question of values and ethics in business has been thrown into sharp focus in the years following the financial crisis of 2007/8. Since the dramatic events of Autumn 2008 that followed the collapse of prominent US investment bank Lehman Brothers, many of the major economies in the world have faced an extended period of low or negative growth, with rising unemployment and very low levels of business and consumer confidence, all of which made an early resumption of growth less likely. Some economists have published books suggesting that we must learn to accept, or even embrace a future with much lower economic growth.[30]

Many governments have had to attempt to rein in public spending, with growing levels of resentment and disillusionment in some countries. In a number of parts of Europe, this has been linked with increased support for new political parties with populist agendas, whose manifestos often reflect a sense of unease the effects of globalisation, together with a view that governments should intervene more, rather than less to protect the interests of ordinary people. Unsurprisingly, given the origins of the 2008 crisis, bankers – or at least highly paid senior managers in global banks – were the initial focus of public opprobrium, but dissatisfaction with business and with capitalism has spread more broadly.

A further trend in recent years has been the increasingly insistent demands that businesses – and particularly multinational businesses with global operations – should pay 'fair' levels of tax to the countries in which they sell products and services, rather than actively seeking to minimise the amounts due. Opinions as to exactly *what* went wrong in 2008 varied widely, however, commentators across the political spectrum have sometimes also alluded to a lack of moral awareness in business and public affairs – the absence of an intuitive sense of right and wrong (sometimes referred to as a '**moral compass**').

Ethics and business organisations

Ethics is concerned with the study of morality: practices and activities that are considered to be importantly right or wrong, together with the rules that govern those activities and the values to which those activities relate.[31] It seeks to understand what makes good things good, for example, in ways that can be generalised to other similar cases. Business ethics can be seen as an example of applied ethics – just as medical ethics is about the application of general ethics to the human activity called medicine, business ethics seeks to explore the implications of general ethics for the conduct of business. This apparently obvious point is important: by taking this stance, one rejects the view that moral principles have no bearing on business, or that 'the business of business is business', as the common saying has it.

A discussion of ethics in business organisations has to take account of the purpose of the organisation, as well as its strategy: what it is trying to achieve, usually in competition with other similar businesses. These two factors are important because of their influence on what the organisation chooses to do and thus on the consequences for people inside and outside the organisation. A decision by an airline, for example, to pursue a low-cost strategy will have significant impacts on what is required of its staff and how well that business fares in the market. A successful implementation of such a strategy may mean fast growth, with attractive career development opportunities for some staff, but also more negative consequences for others. On the other hand, the failure of a strategy can lead to the end of the organisation as an independent entity, with more widespread adverse consequences for the organisation's people.

Ethics and corporate social responsibility

One illustration of the complexity of issues in business ethics is the diversity of opinion on the issue of corporate social responsibility. On one side of the debate are those who would share *Milton Friedman's* view that the social responsibility of business is to make as much money as possible for the shareholders, within the law and the rules of the game (fair competition, no deception or fraud, and so on).[32] This **shareholder-centred view** sees the directors of a company as agents of the owners, who are duty bound to act so as to maximise the interests of those owners, this being taken as the reason for owners having made the investment in the first place.

A more recent development of this general approach is that of *Sternberg* who proposes a teleological view of business ethics, based upon the pursuit of the business purpose – that of maximising long-term owner wealth by selling products and services.[33] Actions by a firm that are consistent with this aim and which satisfy the additional tests of common decency (for example, refraining from stealing, cheating, coercion, and so on) and distributive justice (that is, ensuring that rewards are proportional to contributions made) are ethical. Actions that fail any one of these three tests are, in this model, unethical.

At the other end of the spectrum are some forms of **stakeholder theory**, which emphasise a much broader set of social responsibilities for business. *Charles Handy* maintains that the proper responsibility of a business community is to create wealth for the whole society. Handy questions whether we can safely trust big, bloated and selfish organisations with our future and is it not time to return to the idea of a business as a responsible community paying heed to all its constituents?

> **The proper responsibility of a business community surely is to create wealth for society as a whole, to produce the goods and services that their customers need and want, to provide employment and a way of life for those who work in them, all at fair prices, and to do no harm to the environment around them – in other words to do their job in the best possible way for the benefit not of themselves alone but of all their stakeholders, and to continue to do so for as long as possible.[34]**

Intelligent self-interest

It is also worth emphasising that a company seeking to maximise its owners' long-term wealth may well do very good things for its 'stakeholders', not necessarily through any direct intent but in pursuit of its main duty. Providing customers with excellent products and services is the central example, of course, but this form of intelligent self-interest may also – for example – drive a firm to build strong, trusting relationships with its suppliers and distributors (because it will be better off as a result), or an attractive working environment for its employees (because it wishes to recruit and keep the best, in order to be able to compete more effectively).

Even beyond its immediate commercial relationships, an intelligently self-interested company may deliberately set out to build strong relationships with other stakeholders, or to take a principled stance on an issue such as the use of child labour, because to do so is to maximise owner value. The 'value' in question is not just next year's dividends, but refers to the value of the investment as a whole and thus obliges the management to think long term as well as short term and to consider the impact of company actions as broadly as possible.

Offshoring example

By way of an illustration of the two approaches, we could imagine how a UK-based company might think about an opportunity to 'offshore' part of its operation to a lower-cost Anglophone country. The shareholder-centred view would place emphasis on the unit cost savings to be achieved by moving the operation to a lower-cost area, provided that the required quality of service can be maintained. However, the assessment would also take into account the possibility of additional risks to be managed, such as security and quality control issues. Furthermore, this view would also consider the competitive implications of the decision.

A stakeholder-centred company would place more emphasis on the impacts of the decision on the various stakeholder groups, notably including UK employees. Although the decision to offshore might still be seen as competitively necessary by such a company, it might feel impelled to make more generous arrangements for those whose jobs are to be replaced, both out of a sense of long-term obligation and also to preserve its image in the UK labour market.

How far can YOU explain your support for the shareholder-centred view OR the stakeholder theory on the issue of corporate social responsibility?

Business ethics

The large-scale issues of corporate social responsibility are to do with how a company should conduct itself within society: these questions certainly have an ethical aspect, as has been discussed, but they are not the whole of business ethics. Day-to-day decisions made by individual managers are not usually made on the basis of some detailed calculation of the consequences for shareholder value (however theoretically desirable that might be) and more general ethical considerations must play a part in resolving the dilemmas that sometimes arise in practice.

Hilton queries the meaning of ethics and how you define ethical behaviour. Individuals make personal value judgements, think in terms of doing the right thing and behaving with integrity but this does not deliver a universal ethical standard. Hilton questions if it is possible to be ethical and unethical at the same time.

> **It cannot be ethical to dump toxic waste in some remote corner of Africa because that is cheaper than disposing of it properly. Yet if management's duty is to shareholders, can it be considered ethical to create the best possible returns for them by putting the squeeze on suppliers, employers or customers and making extreme use of tax havens?**[35]

These questions can be complex, since there is no single view in general ethics of what makes something right or wrong. One school of thought emphasises **duties,** things that must be done (or refrained from) irrespective of the consequences. This deontological point of view holds that goodness or badness is evident only in the action itself: that, for example, lying is bad because it is bad in itself. By contrast, a **consequentialist** view of ethics holds that the goodness or badness of a proposed action is evident only in the consequences of that action: whether a lie is good or bad depends upon the consequences of that particular lie at the time. Utilitarianism, for example, is a consequentialist theory, in that it seeks to maximise the net happiness for everyone affected by a particular action ('the greatest good for the greatest number', as it is sometimes expressed).

Both of the perspectives on corporate social responsibility discussed above are also to some extent consequentialist, in that they are mainly concerned with an assessment of the effects of a firm's actions. We can also note that the idea of a moral compass typical of a duties-based approach to ethics – the sense that we just shouldn't do this – is one that is not reliant on any calculation of the consequences.

Work for those in need or breach of business ethics?

Ethical decision-making at work

Nonetheless, duties and principles clearly do inform our views of how people should treat each other at work. An exclusively consequentialist view of ethics is likely to entail methodological problems of forecasting reliably what the consequences of an action may be and of deciding how to measure those consequences. Some forms of utilitarianism can be very unjust to small minorities, by allowing their unhappiness (i.e. as a result of some proposed action) to be offset by the increased happiness of a much larger number. Again, however, we can hardly deny that our assessment of the likely consequences of different actions plays a part in our view of acceptable and unacceptable behaviour in an organisation.

How, then, are ethical choices to be made by people working for organisations? No simple and universal answer is available – ethical awareness is something that can be cultivated and the different perspectives will often help to shed light on a particular dilemma. Some perspectives may appear to be better suited to particular situations: whereas, for example, it is difficult to avoid some sort of consequentialist component in thinking about how a company should act, it is also clear that duty-based (or 'moral compass') arguments must also weigh heavily in thinking about the ethical treatment of people such as employees.

Personal integrity and individual values are important elements in ethical decision-making at work, but the increasingly common company, professional or industry codes of conduct may also provide support and guidance. This is not to say that these ethical 'resources' will always provide clear and comfortable guidance – sometimes, people in organisations will experience tension between the conflicting demands of, say, their own personal values and the demands placed on them by their organisation.

Whistleblowing

If these conflicts become intolerable and cannot be resolved through normal means, then an individual may decide to become a 'whistleblower' in the public interest,

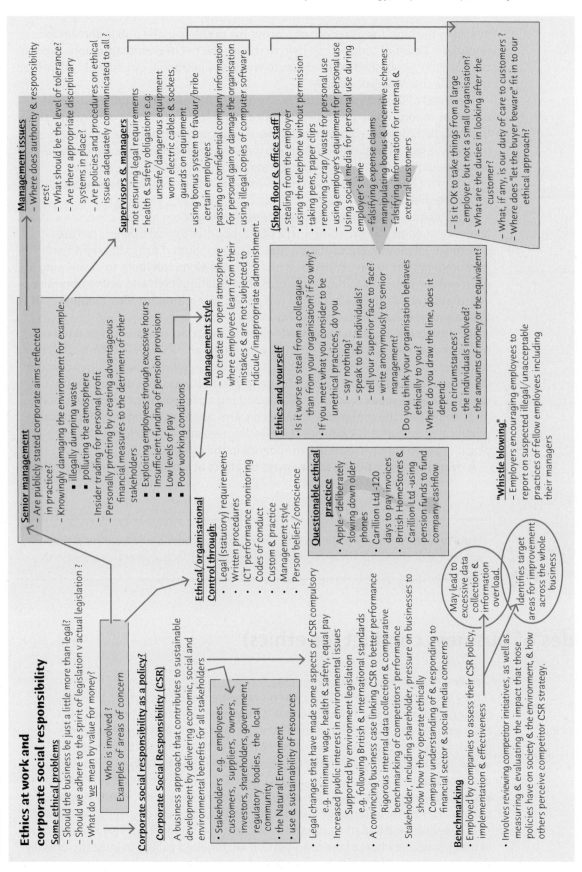

Figure 16.8 Concept map of ethics at work

Source: **Copyright © 2018 The Virtual Learning Materials Workshop. Reproduced with permission.**

by taking the high-risk approach of placing the problem in the public domain for resolution. Codes of conduct can help to reduce the risk of painful situations like this by providing a published set of values to which the individual can appeal, rather than taking the risk wholly personally.

The Head of Communication at *The Institute of Business Ethics* (IBE), *Katherine Bradshaw* reports on negative views of those who speak out about wrongdoing and that only half of those who witnessed misconduct raised their concerns. The main reason was fear of jeopardising their job with a quarter believing no appropriate action would be taken. It takes courage to raise concerns in an unsupportive environment and society needs to move away from the story that those who speak up are troublemakers.[36]

According to *The Institute of Business Ethics* the freedom to raise concerns without fear of retaliation is a core component of a supportive ethical business culture – one where employees are confident they will be supported to 'do the right thing'. Encouraging staff to raise concerns is just one step along the route to developing an open culture. Listening to those concerns, investigating them and acting upon the information received are essential. If companies do not support their employees in this way, they risk a concern becoming a crisis.

IBE distinguish 'Blowing the whistle' externally as a last resort and 'Speaking up' which implies raising a concern internally so that it can be remedied. Protecting those who raise concerns is a challenge when it comes to an effective speak up procedure. IBE have published a Good Practice Guide to practical ways that organisations can encourage a speak up culture by establishing a procedure for employees that gives employees the confidence to raise concerns about anything they find unsafe, unethical or unlawful. It examines the investigation process and looks at some ways which organisations can increase confidence in the process.[37]

A concept map outlining some issues of ethics at work is given in Figure 16.8.

How would YOU answer the question whether it is possible to be ethical and unethical at the same time? How difficult is it for you to answer this question?

Codes of business conduct (or ethics)

Detailed regulations, laws or codes may not by themselves guarantee ethical conduct if they are not accompanied by a clear moral sense on the part of the businesses making decisions about how to behave. Codes of Conduct may, however, play an important role in fostering ethical conduct in organisations, by sending clear guidance to employees about what is expected of them and to the outside world about the standards by which the organisation wishes to be judged. In some cases, concise and clear codes of conduct may also arise from a distillation of the knowledge and experience of the organisation over many years, which may be particularly helpful to junior or less experienced staff in their day-to-day work.

In American and Canadian organisations, codes of conduct are very common and in many cases members of the organisation are required to sign to indicate formally their acceptance. Codes may be updated on a regular basis.

Codes of conduct or ethics

In the UK an increasing number of organisations, of all types, also now publish a code of conduct or code of ethics. For example:

The Chartered Management Institute (CMI) has a Code of Conduct and Practice which is binding on all members.

It sets CMI and its members apart. It is what we stand for, as professional managers buying into and personifying the CMI vision. The Code is a real differentiator and refers to competence, professionalism, honesty and integrity and the duty to keep up-to-date with current good practice. The Code is binding on all members. As such, it forms a critical ingredient of our value proposition. It also sends a clear message to organisations that, by employing CMI members or, in fact, applying the Code within the organisation itself, they gain immediate added value.

The Code encapsulates, with supporting examples, six key principles:

* Behaving in an open, honest and trustworthy manner
* Acting in the best interest of your organisation, customers, clients and/or partners
* Continually developing and maintaining professional knowledge and competence
* Creating a positive impact on society
* Respecting the people with whom you work
* Upholding the reputation of the profession and the institute[38]

The University of Portsmouth has a detailed Ethics Policy. The document provides a general framework for professional practice and decision-making on ethical issues as they arise in the work of the University. The Policy is an integral part of the governance framework of the University of Portsmouth and under 'Ethical Values' includes:

Values are the shared, fundamental beliefs held by the University as a community of learning; they should be seen as a reflection of the culture of the institution. . . The University's Strategy 2015/16–2020/21 includes a commitment to 'act with integrity for the greater good' and to 'insist on upholding the highest academic and professional standards'. As a matter of social responsibility the University reserves the right to refuse funding from organisations that do not share its values, and requires members of its community to exercise due diligence when entering into agreements with such organisations. These commitments are also reflected in our Research and Innovation Strategy.[39]

An integrated approach

The late *Anita Roddick* (founder of The Body Shop) urged the need to develop a corporate code of conduct, a formal, articulated and well-defined set of principles which all global businesses agree to live up to. Roddick suggested that business leaders should make ethics part of their heritage and agree to embrace principles of socially responsible business and not to compete in ways that destroy communities or the environment.[40]

According to *Philippa Foster Back,* OBE (Director, Institute of Business Ethics), the globalisation of business has raised questions of applying ethical values to the different cultures and societies in which organisations operate. The challenge for everyone concerned with ethics now is to ensure that values are embedded throughout an organisation. A code of ethics needs to be translated into reality through training and enforcement and driven from the top.[41]

McEwan summarises the separate histories of corporate social responsibility, business ethics and corporate governance, and suggests a method of inquiry that attempts to integrate these different perspectives on business through three broad levels of inquiry:

- a **descriptive** approach that draws attention to the values and beliefs of people from different cultures and societies that influence their attitudes towards the various activities of business in their home countries and abroad;

- a **normative** approach that identifies sets of values and beliefs as a basis for making ethical decisions at the individual, group, or senior management level in an organisation;

- an **analytical** approach that attempts to explore the relationship between these normative values and beliefs and other value-systems or ideologies such as political or religious beliefs and culture or other social customs.[42]

A culture of ethics, integrity and compliance

Bennett points out that a culture of integrity focused on outstanding quality and business outcomes must be intentionally shaped and build on the values and principles of the organisation. This involves seven steps of:

1. Designate a compliance owner;
2. Implement written standards and procedures;
3. Conduct appropriate training;
4. Develop open lines of communication;
5. Centrally manage all reports and allegations;
6. Respond consistently and appropriately to alleged offences;
7. Audit, monitor and adapt as needed. Bennett also points out the need for an integrated effort.

> **Achieving an effective ethics and compliance programme requires more than simply adding rules and additional layers of controls. There must be an integrated effort that aligns financial and compliance requirements with the organisations mission and values.**[43]

What examples can YOU give of organisations that have achieved an effective integrated approach to ethics, integrity and compliance?

Human rights in business

Human rights in business is receiving increasing attention. The *United Nations* publish a set of guiding principles on implementing a 'Protect, Respect and Remedy' framework for business. The framework includes a number of foundation principles including to avoid infringing on the human rights of others; and operational principles including policy commitment and human rights due diligence for the corporate responsibility to respect human rights.[44]

The Equality and Human Rights Commission sets out six steps to respecting human rights in business. The six steps shown in the diagram will help you to identify and deal with your human rights impacts, *see* **Figure 16.9**.[45]

- **Step 1: Make a public commitment to respect human rights**

  A clear commitment from the top of your business to respect human rights backed by expectations about the behaviour of employees and subcontractors in your supply chain. Think about how you communicate your commitment publicly.

- **Step 2: Check for human rights risks**

  Looks at risks to the rights of people affected by your business and not simply the risks to the business. Begin by assessing human rights impacts that are particularly relevant for your sector. For example, an internet business might think about the right to privacy and the confidential information it holds about its customers.

- **Step 3: Take action to deal with the risks you identify**

  Take action to deal with the most important risks that may be within your own business that you can manage through training or improving your management systems. If these risks relate to your supply chain or partners you need to consider how to use your influence, for example through your contracting arrangements, to prevent or reduce the adverse human rights impact.

- **Step 4: Monitor your progress**

  Regular monitoring and managing risks helps to assess their human rights impacts and action to prevent harm and provide solutions when things go wrong. An open and responsive attitude to complaints enables people affected by your operations to report instances when they feel their human rights may have been harmed. Complaints may give you early warnings of human rights risks.

- **Step 5: Provide a solution if things go wrong**

  Take steps to improve performance where you identify risks at the heart of showing respect for human rights. Review your policies and procedures to reduce

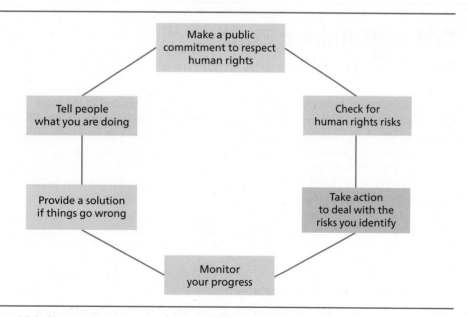

Figure 16.9 Six steps to respecting human rights in business

Source: A Guide to Business and Human Rights: How Human Rights Can Add Value to Your Business. *Equality and Human Rights Commission,* June 2014. The copyright in the document this publication has been adapted from and all other intellectual property rights in that material are owned by, or licensed to, the Commission for Equality and Human Rights, known as the Equality and Human Rights Commission ("the EHRC").

the risk of it happening again. Think about further training for staff or reminding suppliers of their obligations.

- **Step 6: Tell people what you are doing**
  If you identify adverse impacts and risks, you need to think about how you inform your customers, your suppliers or your contractors about the steps you have taken to put things right. When people complain it is important that they hear what has been done to address their complaint. You can enhance your credibility by being open about the human rights challenges that you are trying to address.

The Commission has also drawn attention to the importance of respect for human rights as an integral part of business and the need to be aware of the harms their activities could create and take steps to deal with them.[46] The Commission has produced a five-step guide to help board directors and ensure the company:

- embeds the responsibility to respect human rights into its culture, knowledge and practices;
- identifies and understands its salient or most severe risks to human rights;
- systematically addresses its salient or most severe risks to human rights and provides remedy when needed;
- engages with stakeholders to inform its approach to addressing human rights risks; and
- reports on its salient or most severe human rights risks and meets regulatory reporting requirements.

What do YOU regard as the most potential risks to the respect for, and safeguarding of, human rights by business organisations?

Critical Thinking Zone

Reflections on The Mission Statement

In this zone, we critically discuss the concept of the mission statement and examine whether it is espoused rhetoric or reflects organisational practice.

As a management concept, the mission statement has fuelled an interest in, and debate and discourse among, the academic, practitioner and business communities.[47,48] Although it has attracted a considerable amount of scepticism from numerous circles, it is often portrayed as a precursor to, and bedrock of, strategic planning and is thus utilised as an important tool to aid organisational effectiveness.[49,50]

Deconstructing the Mission Statement

According to Braun et al.,[49] the utilisation of the mission statement as a multipurpose organisational tool is

attributed to the work of Drucker[50] and his early writings on management. Thereafter, research in, and application of, the concept increased significantly. Based on this, Braun et al. profess that there is a widespread assumption that a mission statement a) facilitates consistency of purpose and direction within the organisation; b) functions as a control mechanism; c) guides organisational decision-making, and d) conveys a meaning to work that motivates and inspires organisational members. Deconstructing the concept further, Bart[51] (p. 9) defines it as 'a formal written document designed to capture and convey a firm's unique and enduring purpose.' He adds 'it should answer some fairly basic yet critical questions, such as: what is our purpose? and, why does our organisation exist?' Bart suggests that a mission statement's power lies in its ability to accomplish two results. First, to influence behaviour and thus encourage and enthuse the organisation's members to achieve outstanding performance. Second, to consistently and fairly steer the resource allocation process.

Three Key Meta-Components of the Mission Statement

Braun et al proffer that a mission statement contains three key meta-components: vision, mission and philosophy. First, the vision chronicles the comprehensive, long-term, future-oriented perspective of the organisation's development and predominantly focuses on presenting an emotionally-appealing portrait of its future. The vision also encompasses specific organisational goals, to which members can aspire. Second, the mission refers to the organisation's raison d'être or reason for being in business. Within this, it defines its core tasks and duties as related to a) its customers, such as offering high quality services; b) its members by, for example, making sure they have job security, and c) society at large by promoting education. Third, the philosophy affirms the organisation's values through, for instance, its intention to offer fair, honest and sustainable products and services, the objective being to guide and shape organisational behaviour, attitudes and decision-making. This aspect of the document also outlines the organisation's internal and external ethical commitments and corporate social responsibility to customers and society. Braun *et al.* caveat that although the three components are defined and espoused within the literature, they are not always differentiated and applied in practice. Arguably, the reality is incongruity between espoused theory (what should happen) and theory-in-use (what actually happens[52]).

Underpinning the mission statement is the organisation's culture, which drives the philosophy, values, identity and meaning that are embedded within the document. Babnik *et al.*[53] attest that an effective mission statement is characterised by the extent to which there is congruence between the espoused values defined within the statement and individuals' values that shape their emotional commitment towards both it and the organisation. One could argue that this commitment is mediated within the psychological contract and whether individuals perceive that the espoused values have been translated into practice or have been breached.[54,55]

Mission Impossible!

Evidence suggests that researchers are dissatisfied with the current field of research[56] and concerns have been expressed about the lack of quality in, and insufficient content and development of, the mission statement. Khalifa[56] highlights that such critique ranges from the document being a fabrication, irrelevant and superfluous; other unflattering descriptions include they are dull, vague and shallow. Importantly, the incongruity between what the organisation espouses in its mission statement, and what it does in reality, is explicit in the literature. Research conducted by Bart[51] identified some startling and revealing findings. He noted 'so much mendacity and misrepresentation appears to exist in the published and very public mission statements in our sample of firms' (p. 12). The research also found that there was precious little quality control or inclination from senior managers to make certain that only correctly worded and formulated mission statements were produced and released. Bart[51] concluded 'in any sample of mission statements, the vast majority are not worth the paper they are written on and should not be taken with any degree of seriousness' (p. 12). Arguably, this further demonstrates the gap between what is espoused and actual practice.

Following on from Bart, Nash[57] (p. 155) also considers mission statements with a degree of disdain. She lamented 'at their worst, these statements are ponderous or pompous, static summaries of past exploits and future inadequacies.' She adds 'some are nothing more than a passing fancy or a piece of corporate window dressing.' On a more positive note, Khalifa[56] (p. 242) hints that it is possible to produce a good mission statement, but caveats that certain conditions must be met. He stated 'it is proper to assume that a good mission has to be lived and committed to, that a sense of mission is essential'. He counsels that the mission should be 'reflected in culture and translated into strategy.' Moreover, he advocates organisations taking mission statements seriously and generating a document that is genuine, effective and affective enough to generate a unified sense of direction and meaning among its members. He caveats 'a fabricated mission is probably worse than no mission at all' (p. 242).

Implications for Organisational Behaviour in the Workplace

To conclude, evidence suggests that the mission statement is shrouded in rhetoric. There appears to be a gap between what the document espouses and actual practice, which critics claim somewhat nullifies its existence. On this note, Bart[51] stated 'all too frequently, the mission statement is itself a promise that appears to have been broken, often before the ink is dried' (p. 12). Bart caveats that a reason for this might be the lack of stakeholder engagement in its conception, development and production, to which he attaches a large amount of disappointment. He professes that 'mission statements can be the *élan vital* of corporate life' (p. 17), a vital force from which the organisation can derive emotional and financial benefits. However, he claims that their abuse, misuse and tarnished reputation precludes their numerous benefits being yielded and enjoyed. Rather than producing a statement that is full of 'fantasy, fiction and lies', Bart concludes 'clear and tangible benefits await those firms that have both the fortitude and foresight to invest – vigorously in their mission' (p. 17).

Following her rather damning indictment of the mission statement, Nash[57] identifies a glimmer of hope for the document. She notes 'at best. . . mission statements serve important and lasting purposes' (p. 155). Managers can use it as a benchmark for success and individuals can collectively aspire to achieve its espoused goals. Arguably, it can also serve to shape aspects of the psychological contract within the people-organisation relationship. She concludes 'mission statements can help nurture loyalty, create a sense of corporate community. . . and provide a unique window through which to gain a clearer understanding of a company's values and directions' (p. 155).

Questions

Based on the above, answer the following questions.

1. Bart suggests that a key purpose of the mission statement is to influence behaviour and enthuse the workforce to achieve outstanding performance. *Evaluate* the implications of the mission statement for organisational behaviour in the workplace.

2. Evidence suggests there is incongruity between what the organisation espouses it is going to do and what it does. *How* can managers and the organisation at large close the gap between rhetoric and actual practice?

3. *Critically analyse* the relationship between the mission statement and aspects of the psychological contract.

Summary – Chapter 16 'Strategy, corporate responsibility and ethics'

The overall direction of an organisation is determined by the nature of its corporate strategy. There is obviously a close relationship between strategy and organisation structure and also between culture and strategy. Strategy needs to be related to changing external environment conditions and the management of opportunities and risks. Strategy highlights the overall direction of an organisation its goals, objectives and policy which may be pursued in accordance with an underlying ideology based on beliefs, values and attitudes. Growing attention is given to a set of stated corporate vales in the form of a vision or mission statement. The organisation operates within its external environment and this gives rise to broader corporate social responsibilities. Two differing perspectives on corporate social responsibility are a shareholder-centred view or a stakeholder theory view. Growing attention is given to the question of values and ethics in business. An increasing number of organisations of all types publish a code of business conduct (or ethics) which sets out its practices and values of ethical conduct.

The globalisation of business highlights calls for an integrated approach to the application of ethical values. The Equality and Human Rights Commission has drawn attention to the importance of respect for human rights as an integral part of business.

Group discussion activities

Undertake each of these activities in small groups as indicated by your tutor. Before you start your discussion establish a non-threatening environment within the group and confirm confidentiality will be honoured.

First, form your own views and then share and compare in open critical discussion with colleagues. Reflect honestly on the extent to which: (i) you influenced the thinking and ideas of your colleagues; and (ii) you were influenced by your colleagues.

To what extent was your group able to reach consensus?

Agree one of your members to produce a brief written summary of the discussion and prepared to present in a plenary session.

Activity 1

(a) To what extent do you have a strong moral compass with an intuitive sense of right and wrong?

(b) How far do you accept the idea of intelligent self-interest?

(c) How strong is your sense of personal integrity and would you be prepared to become a whistleblower?

Activity 2

(a) What do you believe is the extent of correlation between good corporate governance, concern for social responsibilities and ethical behaviour and successful and profitable business organisations?

(b) To what extent should social and ethical responsibilities include an obligation for the physical and mental health and well-being of employees?

(c) Highlight what you believe are the most serious and important concerns over CSR and ethical behaviour of business organisations.

Activity 3

What is your point of view?

(a) A National Health Service Trust chairperson was criticised heavily for maintaining that the primary loyalty of doctors was owed to their employers and that their duty to patients came third after themselves.

(b) Provide companies comply fully with the laws of the land it is unfair to criticise them for behaving in a manner which benefits them most, even if it might be regarded as a breach of their social responsibilities.

(c) The harsh truth is that without government legislation or threat of adverse media coverage the majority of organisations would give little regard to their social or ethical responsibilities.

(d) It is unfair to criticise companies in other countries who are involved in bribery or corruption when this is an accepted and integral part of their national culture.

Organisational behaviour in action case study

Corporate Social Responsibility – Graham McWilliam, BSkyB

CSR is good for brands

It always strikes me as surprising, when talking to my peers at other companies, how many of them talk about the substantial time they have to spend lobbying their colleagues to take CSR seriously. Maybe one of the problems is the phrase itself – corporate social responsibility – which implies a commitment without a return; something you have to do, but from which you can derive little value. And why, in tough economic times, would companies prioritise something that doesn't help the bottom line? Why indeed.

At Sky, we look at things a little differently. We don't talk about CSR. Instead, we concentrate on long-term value creation, grounded in a focus on what really counts for customers. Looking at things from this angle, it makes perfect commercial sense to act responsibly day to day and to contribute broadly to the communities around you. After all, like it or not, your brand isn't only created by what you say about yourself. It's built on what others say and think about you, which itself is built on their experience of what you do. For good or bad, that influences customer loyalty, employee engagement, investor sentiment and the regulatory and political climate.

This point is increasingly important in business. All those stakeholder groups now have fast and easy access to a wealth of information and commentary about your company, from news reports to social media conversations. Segmenting your audiences and controlling the message is becoming an impossible task. And, anyway, all the research shows people are more likely to trust what they hear through their informal networks than what they hear directly from you.

Don't Just say It, do It

So, focus first on doing, rather than saying, the right things. Set it all in the context of long-term value creation, and you'll find it's no longer an unwanted responsibility to be discharged, but a positive opportunity to build trust, encourage reappraisal and open up new commercial avenues. At Sky, we're proud of the positive contribution that our business makes to the communities around us, from bringing choice in TV to consumers, to the jobs that have been created for the 16,500 people who work at Sky.

But we want to do more, because we know it's what our customers and employees expect of us, and because we know that it drives positive reappraisal of our brand by those who haven't yet joined Sky. So we've chosen three areas which we know our customers care about and where we think we can make the biggest difference: using our relationships with 10 million families across the UK and Ireland to inspire action on climate change, encourage participation in sport and open up the arts to more people.

How CSR creates opportunity

Our work in sport, for example, builds on our strong history and credibility in sports broadcasting to get more people active. Within this, our partnership with British Cycling takes a three-pronged approach: support for the GB cycling team, enabling our elite cyclists to be the very best they can be; the creation of Team Sky, the UK's only professional road racing team, to inspire a whole new generation of cyclists to get on their bikes; and Sky Ride, a series of mass summer cycling events across the UK, free to all and free of traffic, which more than 200,000 people took part in last year.

The long-term commercial benefits of such activity are clear to us at Sky, but are equally easy to see at a large and growing number of other successful UK companies. For such brands, CSR isn't about responsibility. It's about opportunity, creating sustainable value over the long term. And, if you want to be around for years to come, that's hard to argue with.

Source: *Management Today* May 2011. p. 69. www.managementtoday.co.uk. Reproduced with permission.

Tasks

1. To what extent do you associate CSR as a commitment without a return?

2. Discuss Sky's approach of CSR as central to strategy and long-term value creation.

3. Give your own examples of how CSR can create opportunity and commercial benefits for an organisation.

Chapter 16 – Personal skills and employability exercise

Objectives

Completing this exercise should help you to enhance the following skills:

* Clarify the work values and beliefs that are important to you.

* Examine your sensitivity to, and dealings with, other people.

* Debate and justify with colleagues the nature of your values and beliefs.

Exercise

You are required to: rate the following items according to the scale

> 5 (extremely important for me);
>
> 4 (very important for me);
>
> 3 (average importance for me);
>
> 2 (not important for me);
>
> 1 (I would oppose this).

What is required is your genuine beliefs and feelings about each item, not what others think or believe, but what you personally and honestly believe and feel about each item.

1. There should be clear allocation of objectives and accountability for them   ___
2. We should be open and honest in all our dealings with each other   ___
3. People's talents should be recognised, developed and correctly utilised   ___
4. One should give acknowledgement and praise to those in authority   ___
5. There are clear rules about what we should and should not do in getting the job done   ___
6. Conflicts should be surfaced and resolved rather than allowed to simmer   ___
7. The causes of problems should be directed away from oneself   ___
8. Encouragement and support should be placed above criticism   ___
9. Problems should be tackled and resolved in co-operation with others   ___
10. What is right should be placed above who is right   ___
11. Clear standard procedures should be in place for all important jobs   ___
12. One should become visible and build up one's personal image   ___
13. Equity and fairness should be applied to all regardless of status or standing   ___
14. Excellence should be our aim in all that we do professionally and administratively   ___
15. We give close attention to codes of conduct since this is what builds character   ___
16. We should keep each other informed and practise open and friendly communication   ___
17. We know who should be making the decisions and refer decisions to the right person   ___
18. Everyone and their contribution should be treated with respect and dignity   ___
19. We should meet all our commitments to one another – we do what we say we will do   ___

20. One should form networks of support among those with influence   ___
21. There are clear reporting relationships – who reports to whom – and we stick to them   ___
22. People should take responsibility for their own decisions and actions   ___
23. Everyone should be committed to personal growth and lifelong learning   ___
24. Situations or events should be created so as to justify the advancement of one's goals   ___
25. Performance should be assessed against objectives and standards declared up-front   ___
26. Policies should be clear and not changed until there is proof that they need changing   ___
27. Everyone's needs should be given equal standing regardless of their position or status   ___
28. We should be committed to the service of others rather than ourselves   ___
29. Positive relationships should be established with those who have influence   ___
30. Warmth and affection should be demonstrated in our work relationships   ___
31. Individual productivity and performance should be encouraged and actively promoted   ___
32. We all know what our jobs are and we stick to our defined responsibilities   ___
33. Those from disadvantaged backgrounds should be helped to catch up with others   ___
34. One should expect to get support from those to whom we have given past support   ___
35. Goals should be challenging and stretch people to higher levels of achievement   ___

Source for the exercise: Misselhorn, A. *Head and Heart of Leadership* (Reach Publishers SA) (2012), p. 86. Reproduced with permission.

Discussion

1. How difficult was it for you to complete your ratings?

2. How much agreement was there among members of your group? Did this surprise you?

3. To what extent were you influenced to rethink your values or beliefs?

Notes and references

1. Johnson, G., Whittington, R., Scholes, K., Angwin, D. and Regnér, P. *Exploring Strategy,* tenth edition, Pearson Education (2014).
2. Andrews, K. 'The Concept of Corporate Strategy', Irwin (1971), in Lynch, R. *Strategic Management*, sixth edition, Pearson Education (2012), p. 7.
3. Chandler, A. *Strategy and Structure: Chapters in the History of the American Industrial Enterprise,* MIT Press (1987).
4. Lynch, R. *Strategic Management,* sixth edition, Pearson Education (2012), pp. 459, 462.
5. Allen, R. S. and Helms, M. M. 'Employee Perceptions of the Relationship between Strategy, Rewards and Organizational Performance', *Journal of Business Strategies,* vol. 19, no. 2, Fall 2002, pp. 115–39.
6. Stern, S. 'The Next Big Thing', *Management Today,* April 2007, p. 50.
7. Gratton, L. *Living Strategy: Putting People at the Heart of Corporate Purpose,* Financial Times Prentice Hall (2000), p. 18.
8. Schneider, S. C. and Barsoux, J. *Managing Across Cultures,* second edition, Financial Times Prentice Hall (2003), Chapter 5.

9. Jones, A. in conversation with Sir Win Bischoff, 'Culture by design', *Governance + Compliance*, September 2016, pp. 18–21.

10. See, for example, Brown, A. 'Organizational Culture: The Key to Effective Leadership and Organizational Development', *Leadership and Organization Development Journal,* vol. 13, no. 2, 1992, pp. 3–6.

11. Brech, E. F. L. (ed.) *The Principles and Practice of Management,* third edition, Longman (1975).

12. Gratton, L. *Hot Spots,* Financial Times Prentice Hall (2007).

13. https://www.johnlewispartnership.co.uk/about/our-principles.html (accessed 14 January 2018).

14. Drucker, P. *Managing for Results,* Heinemann Professional (1989).

15. Ansoff, H. I. (ed), *Business Strategy,* Penguin (1969).

16. Lynch, R. *Strategic Management,* sixth edition, Pearson Education (2012).

17. Worthington, I. and Britton, C. *The Business Environment,* fifth edition, Financial Times Prentice Hall (2006), p. 13.

18. See, for example, Hannagan, T. *Management: Concepts & Practices,* fifth edition, Financial Times Prentice Hall (2008), p. 396.

19. Reeves, R. 'The Trouble with Targets', *Management Today,* January 2008, p. 29.

20. Alistair Dryburgh, www.dontyoubelieveitblog.com (accessed 8 June 2012).

21. Taylor, L. 'Why SMART goals need to get SMARTER', Institute of Administrative Management Newsletter, April 2017.

22. https://www.redcarnationhotels.com/about/core-values (accessed 14 January 2018).

23. 'Corporate Social Responsibility: Checklist 242' Chartered Management Institute, August 2016.

24. Donaldson, T. and Preston, L. E. 'The stakeholder theory of the corporation: concepts, evidence and implications, *Academy of Management Review,* vol. 20. no. 1 (1995), pp. 65–91.

25. Rollinson, D. *Organisational Behaviour and Analysis*, fourth edition, Financial Times Prentice Hall (2008).

26. Willis, B. 'The ABC of CSR', *Professional Manager,* Spring 2015, pp. 62–3.

27. Yukl, G. *Leadership in Organizations,* seventh edition, Pearson Education (2010), p. 333.

28. 'Added values: The importance of ethical leadership', The Institute of Leadership and Management, June 2013.

29. https://www.unglobalcompact.org/news/381-09-05-2013.

30. See, for example: Coyle, D. *The Economics of Enough: How to Run the Economy as If the Future Matters,* Princeton University Press (2011); and Skidelsky, R. and Skidelsky, E. *How Much is Enough? The Love of Money and the Case for a Good Life,* Allen Lane (2012).

31. De George, R. T. *Business Ethics,* fifth edition, Prentice Hall (1999).

32. Friedman, M. 'The Social Responsibility of Business Is to Increase Its Profits', *New York Times Magazine,* 13 September 1970, pp. 32, 122–6.

33. Sternberg, E. *Just Business,* Little, Brown (1994).

34. Handy, C. 'The glass towers', *Governance + Compliance*, March 2016, pp. 22–5.

35. Hilton, A. 'Ethical irony', *Governance + Compliance*, August 2016, pp. 12–13.

36. Bradshaw, K. 'Heroes or Traitors?', *Governance + Compliance*, February 2018, pp. 26–8.

37. 'Encouraging a Speak Up Culture', IBE Good Practice Guide, 09 November 2017. www.ibe.org.uk.

38. Chartered Management Institute. For full details, see www.managers.org.uk/code. Reproduced with permission.

39. University of Portsmouth, Ethics Policy April 2017, www.port.ac.uk.

40. Roddick, A. *Business As Unusual,* Thorsons (2000), p. 269.

41. Back, P. F. 'Taking a Proactive Approach to Ethics', *Professional Manager,* vol. 15, no. 3, May 2006, p. 37.

42. McEwan, T. *Managing Values and Beliefs in Organisations,* Financial Times Prentice Hall (2001).

43. Bennett, M. 'Shaping the Future', *Governance & Compliance,* June 2014, pp. 32–3.

44. 'United Nations Guiding Principles on Business and Human Rights' (2011) www.business-humanrights.org/en/un-guiding-principles.

45. 'A Guide to Business and Human Rights' Equality and Human Rights Commission June 2014, www.equalityhumanrights.com

46. Equality and Human Rights Commission, June 2016 https://www.equalityhumanrights.com/en/advice-and-guidance/five-steps.

47. Khalifa, A. S. 'Three Fs for the Mission Statement: What's Next?', *Journal of Strategy and Management,* vol. 4, no. 1, 2011, pp. 25–43.

48. Alegre, I., Berbegal-Mirabent, J., Guerrero, A. and Mas-Machuca, M. 'The Real Mission of the Mission Statement: A Systematic Review of the Literature', *Journal of Management and Organisation,* vol. 24, no. 4, 2018, pp. 456–73.

49. Braun, S., Wesche, J. S., Frey, D., Weisweiler, S. and Peus, C. 'Effectiveness of Mission Statements in Organizations – A review', *Journal of Management and Organization Development,* vol. 18, no. 4, 2012, pp. 430–44.

50. Drucker, P. E. *Management: Tasks, Responsibilities and Practices,* Butterworth & Heinemann (1974).

51. Bart, C. K. 'Sex, Lies and Mission Statements', *Business Horizons,* Nov–Dec 1997, pp. 9–18.

52. Argyris, C. and Schön, D. *Theory in Practice: Increasing Professional Effectiveness,* Jossey-Bass (1974).

53. Babnik, K., Breznik, K., Dermol, V. and Trunk Širca, N. 'The Mission Statement: Organisational Culture Perspective', *Industrial Management and Data Systems,* vol. 114, no. 2, 2014, pp. 612–27.

54. Cullinane, N. and Dundon, T. 'The Psychological Contract: A Critical Review', *International Journal of Management Reviews,* vol. 8, no. 2, 2006, pp. 113–29.

55. Jensen, J. M., Opland, R. A. and Ryan, A. M. 'Psychological Contracts and Counterproductive Work Behaviours: Employee Responses to Transactional and Relational Breach', *Journal of Business Psychology,* 25, 2010, pp. 555–68.

56. Khalifa, A. S. 'Mission, purpose, and ambition: redefining the mission statement', *Journal of Strategy and Management,* vol. 5, no. 3, 2012, pp. 236–51.

57. Nash, L. 'Missions Statements: Mirrors and Windows', *Harvard Business Review,* March–April, 1988, pp. 155–6.

Chapter 17
Organisational performance and effectiveness

The people–organisation relationship, quality of management and commitment of staff to their work are central to organisational performance and effectiveness.

Learning outcomes

After completing this chapter you should have enhanced your ability to:

- explain the relationship between organisational performance and management;
- assess the nature and importance of employee engagement and commitment;
- explain concepts that bear upon organisational performance and effectiveness;
- outline the role, attributes and qualities of a successful manager;
- explore the nature and main features of management development;
- detail the importance of building productivity in the UK;
- review the nature of successful organisations and people.

Outline chapter contents

Overview topic map: Chapter 17 – Organisational performance and effectiveness

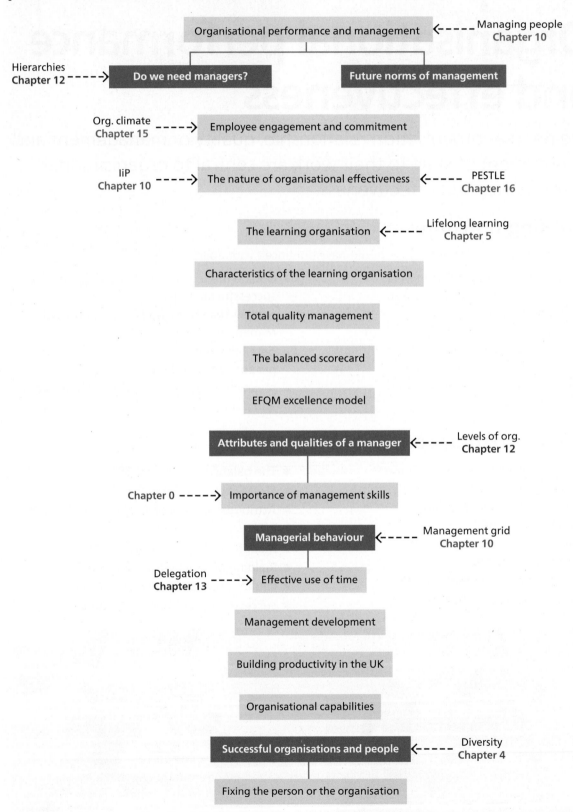

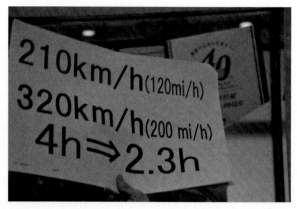

Japanese bullet train: not only very fast but extremely reliable

Before commencing to read this chapter, what do YOU believe is the most significant determinant of organisational performance and effectiveness?

Organisational performance and management

At the start of this book we referred to organisational behaviour in terms of individual and group behaviour, patterns of structure and management and organisational performance. Sooner or later every organisation has to perform successfully if it is to survive. An underlying basis for the study of organisational behaviour is the nature of the people–organisation relationship. A central feature of this relationship is the process of management as an integrating and co-ordinating activity. Whatever the type of the work organisation, it is through the process of management that the efforts of members of the organisation are co-ordinated, directed and guided towards the achievement of its goals. As can be seen from the discussion in **Chapter 10,** management is arguably the cornerstone of organisation effectiveness.

How important is the role of managers?

The 'Quality of Management' is one of nine measures of success by which *Management Today* rates performance in its annual survey of Britain's Most Admired Companies. A major survey undertaken by the Management Consultancies Association and *Management Today* drew attention to the changing relationship between organisations and individuals. More and more work is outsourced, teams are dispersed across multiple locations, an increasing number of people work away from the organisations and greater empowerment is shifting responsibility to individuals. This shift of responsibility from the organisation to the individual begs the question: are managers really necessary and what is the role of management?

> **Ironically, a time when people appear to require less management is also a time when they want it more than ever. Half of all respondents to the survey felt their bosses spent insufficient time actually managing their staff, a figure that was highest among employees of large organisations and in the manufacturing, financial services and the public sector.[1]**

Lucas reports on the crucial role of managers as the single most important factor in the success of innovation initiatives. Increasing global competition means companies can no longer compete simply on price and breaking the mould is more important than ever. 'Organisations need to be more creative in their approach to recognising, nurturing and turning innovative ideas into business reality – and managers are the key to that process.' This requires a leader and team with the ability and passion to turn ideas into business reality. Managers need to provide focus for their teams; generate the energy to make change happen; be good at coping with ambiguity and uncertainty; create a culture where people feel safe to experiment; and be willing to give agenda time to innovation.[2]

The democratic enterprise

According to *Gratton,* we have become accustomed to how contemporary organisations are structured, managed and run, but many more possibilities exist. Many people feel disconnected from their organisation and at times feel they have been treated unfairly and unjustly. Gratton believes we are witnessing the emergence of a new way of looking at people and their role in organisations and refers to the 'democratic enterprise': that is, organisations that are inspiring and meaningful, with the possibility for the individual and the organisation to create a win–win relationship and both benefiting but not at the expense of the other.

> **Over the last decade it has become increasingly clear that through the forces of globalization, competition and more demanding customers, the structure of many companies has become flatter, less hierarchical, more fluid and virtual. The breakdown of hierarchies provides us with fertile ground on which to create a more democratic way of working.[3]**

Do we need managers?

An interesting BBC radio programme discussed the nature and role of management as intrinsically controlling with always a likely element of resistance. Managers have a wretched time but what would happen if we got rid of them? It begged the questions: can organisations thrive without managers or without any hierarchy at all? The discussion suggested that hierarchies **(discussed in Chapter 12)** are a natural form of social organisation and the order and control suits us at least some of the time. In self-managed organisations everyone has to be responsible for everything and natural leaders will emerge. There are very few examples of companies that have worked effectively without managers. A conclusion was that managers are a necessary evil and often not really evil at all. Having a few people in charge is simply better than having everyone in charge.[4]

Future norms of management

Caulkin contrasts the traditional shareholder-driven, hierarchically managed and efficiency-obsessed Anglo-Saxon management with alternative models of management in other countries. For example:

- **India** – importance of employees and their development; putting employees first and customers second;

- **China** – entrepreneurial vigour at the heart of both corporate and individual performance; network family style relationships with incentives to work for the common good;
- **Gulf States** – engagement, loyal, reputation and stable relationships as the drivers in good time resulting in profits and success;
- **Japan** – an adaptive complex system of 'pull' and 'just in time' to make what is needed, when needed and amount needed;
- **Scandinavia** – high trust, high commitment workplace; stable ownership, egalitarian values, gender balance and an international outlook;
- **Germany** – high growth targets; focus on niches, innovation customer retention; high staff loyalty and minimal turnover; promotion of women to top jobs.[5]

Acceptance of failure

The founder of Wikipedia, *Jimmy Wales,* supports the belief of modern technology as an enabler rather than a redefiner of management. Technology may not have changed the fundamental role of management but is changing the way work is carried out. Managers can adapt to approaches to problems in real time and learn from experiments on the fly. To avoid the risk of falling behind competitors companies have to be innovating constantly and learning from their failures.

> **You never want an organisation to get into a position where no one is allowed to take a risk and fail, because what you are more likely to do is have the whole organisation fail as other people innovate and change faster than you do. It is important to have a culture that accepts reasonable failure.[6]**

Different types of organisations – and management

What do YOU see as the need for, importance and fundamental role of managers?

Employee engagement and commitment

A determining feature of the people–organisation relationship and role of management is the strength of employee engagement and commitment. It is often said that people join organisations but leave their bosses. Among the factors that contribute to a healthy organisational climate, **discussed in Chapter 15,** is the extent to which members of staff have a sense of engagement with, and commitment to, their work, their managers and to the organisation. Genuine commitment requires not just recognition or understanding of what the organisation expects but an emotional and behavioural response from staff. The extent of their commitment will have a major influence on staff retention and level of work performance. For example, *O'Reilly* refers to the term **'organisational commitment'** as 'typically conceived of as an individual's psychological bond to the organization, including a sense of job involvement, loyalty, and a belief in the values of the organization'.[7]

Underlying influences

There are a number of underlying influences on the extent of employees' engagement with and commitment to the organisation, discussed in previous chapters, including:

- People's behaviour and level of their commitment is also affected by the nature of the psychological contract and the degree to which it is perceived as fair by both the individual and the organisation.
- Individuals differ in their work ethic and the manner of their involvement with, and concern for, work and the extent to which they have an instrumental, bureaucratic or solidaristic orientation. Some people may well have a set attitude to work, whatever the nature of the work environment. It should also be accepted that a minority of people may not wish to be engaged.
- In terms of their relationship with the work organisation, employees may reasonably have the approach of 'what's in it for me?' An important influence on the strength of commitment is the nature of the reward system and the satisfaction of needs and expectations at work in terms of economic rewards, intrinsic satisfaction or social relationships.
- The broader organisational context including opportunities for learning and development, styles of leadership, management structures and systems, organisational culture and climate.

Circle of employee engagement

De Vita maintains employee engagement should not be written off as just another HR fad but neither should it be viewed as a quick fix. Engagement relates to the core of a business – its values, culture and way of managing and changing that is a tall order. But a truly engaged company is likely to be a 'great' one. As an example, De Vita quotes the success of the John Lewis Partnership as a result of its co-ownership by employees combined with a collective management approach and the full engagement of employees.[8] The positive behaviour of a deeply engaged employee will rub off on clients, customers and colleagues. A highly engaged company is

**The engaged
company**
- Better business
  performance
- High staff retention
- Sustained, long-term success
- Strong sense of purpose
  and identity
- Highly energised,
  productive and innovative
- Attractive reputation

**Its conditions
of engagement**
- Knows its values and
  communicates them
- Knows who fits the company
  and how to attract them
- Behaves as its employees
  would expect
- Engenders autonomy and trust
- Strong and authentic
  leadership and management
- Provides challenging work and
  personal development
- Values, respects and involves
  each employee
- Invokes a sense of community

**The
virtuous
circle of
employee
engagement**

The engaged employee
- Feels trusted, valued and empowered
- Gives their best; goes the extra mile
- Is loyal, motivated and enthusiastic
- Is an advocate for the company
- Understands the company's
  mission and their place in it; shares
  common values
- Is emotionally committed and
  personally involved

Figure 17.1 Virtuous circle of employee engagement
Source: De Vita, E. 'Get Engaged', *Management Today,* April 2007, p. 40. Reproduced from *Management Today*
magazine with the permission of the copyright owner, Haymarket Business Publications Limited.

known to perform better; enjoy high staff retention; sustain long-term success;
display energy, productivity and innovativeness; and win regard as an attractive place
to work. *See* **Figure 17.1.**

Employee engagement and performance

The importance of employee commitment and engagement for business success,
and the importance of people, have been highlighted in a 2009 report 'Engaging for
Success' to the Government by *David Macleod and Nita Clarke*.[9]

> Business organisations function best when they make their employees' commitment,
> potential, creativity and capability central to their operation. Clearly having enough
> cash, and a sensible strategy, are vital. But how people behave at work can make the
> crucial difference between business and operational success or failure.
>
> Employee engagement strategies enable people to be the best they can at work,
> recognising that this can only happen if they feel respected, involved, heard, well led
> and valued by those they work for and with.

> Engaged employees have a sense of personal attachment to their work and organisation; they are motivated and able to give of their best to help it succeed – and from that flows a series of tangible benefits for organisation and individual alike.
>
> Although improved performance and productivity is at the heart of engagement, it cannot be achieved by a mechanistic approach which tries to extract discretionary effort by manipulating employees' commitment and emotions. Employees see through such attempts very quickly; they lead instead to cynicism and disillusionment. By contrast, engaged employees freely and willingly give discretionary effort, not as an 'add on', but as an integral part of their daily activity at work.
>
> *Extracts from Macleod, D. and Clarke, N. Engaging for Success: Enhancing performance through employee engagement, A report to Government, Department for Business, Innovation and Skills (2009).*

Benefits of employee engagement

The *Chartered Management Institute* (CMI) point out that interest in the concept of employee engagement has been growing in recent years reinforced by pressures of economic recession. Engagement provides a range of benefits for both the employer including enhanced commitment, loyalty and performance and greater synergy and productivity: and for individuals including a sense of personal fulfilment and well-being; and increased morale and job satisfaction. Engagement is about developing productive working relationships and environment.[10]

The *CIPD,* who in January 2017 became Engage for Success prime sponsor, emphasise the relationship between how people are managed, their attitudes and behaviour, and business performance and point to the mutual benefits of employee engagement:

> **Employees who have good quality jobs and are managed well, will not only be happier, healthier and more fulfilled, but are also more likely to drive productivity, better products or services, and innovation. This mutual gains view of motivation and people management lies at the heart of employee engagement.[11]**

CIPD point out that successful employee engagement requires working with all areas of the organisation, HR but also action from leaders at all levels. Employers should pay attention to:

- employees empowered to make decisions and shape their jobs;
- effective channels for employee voice;
- fair treatment of employees and support for well-being;
- communications to keep employees informed and reinforce purpose and vision.

According to CIPD employee engagement is a broad concept and refer to a report 'Creating an engaged workforce' developed by Kingston Business School consortium which identifies three dimensions:

- **Intellectual engagement** – thinking hard about the job and how to do it.
- **Affective engagement** – feeling positively about doing a job.
- **Social engagement** – actively taking opportunities to discuss work-related improvements with others at work.

Fostering employee engagement

Stuart Rock points out that employee engagement can vary from poor to great. It can be measured and correlated with performance 'You cannot force people to engage but you create an environment that encourages people to engage.' Rock identifies twelve ways to foster amazing employee engagement.

1. **Do your homework** on the level of workers who feel engaged and to what extent.
2. **Healthy corporate culture and values** are the breeding ground for high engagement.
3. **Make the work matter** and instil a real sense of purpose and importance.
4. **Visible leadership,** stay close and articulate what the organisation is trying to achieve.
5. **Talk a lot,** open honest communication is the fuel of highly engaged companies.
6. **Honest conversation** listen and understand and do not get hung up by negative views.
7. **Tell good stories** articulate the purpose that binds employees and consumers to a successful brand.
8. **Know and trust your staff** engagement and empowerment are inextricably linked.
9. **Wage constant war against silos** find ways to keep high levels of internal engagement.
10. **Use technology imaginatively** consider if workplace and technology strategies are aligned.
11. **Don't let the system rule** enable individual employees to respond flexibly and imaginatively.
12. **Do have fun** help bring people together to build engagement and benefit the business.[12]

Some of the ways to foster employee engagement

> To what extent can YOU identify with Stuart Rock's twelve ways to foster amazing employee engagement?

A concept map of a summary of practical employee involvement is set out in Figure 17.2.

The nature of organisational effectiveness

An underlying theme of this book has been the need for organisational effectiveness based on an understanding of organisational behaviour, the people resource, and the role of management as an integrating activity. Organisational effectiveness, however, is affected by a multiplicity of variables. For example, *Handy* identifies over sixty factors that impinge on any one organisational situation and which illustrate the complicated nature of the study of organisational effectiveness.[13]

In addition to the factors identified by Handy there are a number of related concepts or approaches that have a bearing on organisational performance and effectiveness. These include the learning organisation, total quality management, and the balanced scorecard discussed below. Other related approaches discussed in previous chapters include Investors in People **(Chapter 10)** and PESTEL analysis **(Chapter 16).** Some main contributors to organisational effectiveness are set out in **Figure 17.3.**

The learning organisation

A key factor in organisational effectiveness is the successful management of change, innovation, and corporate renewal. Traditional views of managerial behaviour have placed emphasis on planning, organising, directing and controlling. However, increasing international competitiveness and the need for organisations to respond rapidly to constant change in their environment have drawn renewed attention in recent years to the concept of the **learning organisation**. It is associated with the concept of lifelong learning **(discussed in Chapter 5).** A central theme of the learning organisation is that **rapid learning is an essential ingredient of organisational performance and effectiveness.** It is therefore often associated with organisation development. The original idea has been around for many years, however, and was popularised in the 1960s–1980s by major writers such as Argyris.[14]

Characteristics of the learning organisation

Another significant contribution has been made by *Senge,* who defines the learning organisation as a place: 'Where people continually expand their capacity to create the results they truly desire, where new and expansive patterns of thinking are nurtured, where collective aspiration is set free, and where people are continually learning how to learn together'.[15]

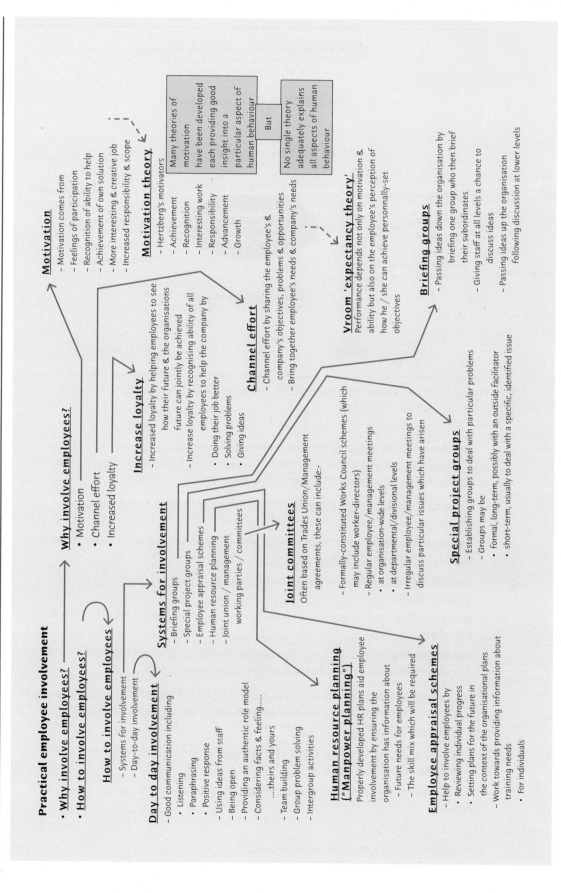

Figure 17.2 Concept map of practical employee involvement

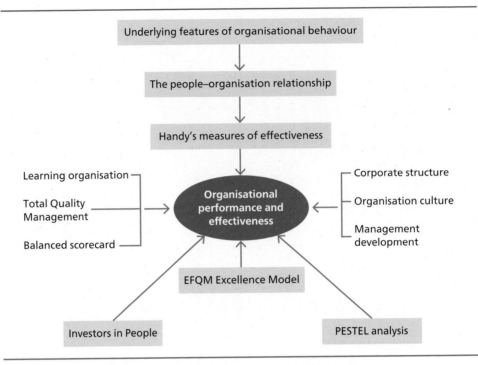

Figure 17.3 Some main contributions to organisational effectiveness

Senge maintains that organisations need to develop a culture of learning to instil people's commitment and capacity to learn at all levels in an organisation and suggests five basic features of a learning organisation:

- **systems thinking** – the recognition that things are interconnected and organisations are complex systems;
- **personal mastery** – the competencies and skills associated with management including spiritual growth;
- **mental models** – the driving and fundamental values and principles of the organisation;
- **shared vision** – the importance of co-operation and a shared vision by team members;
- **team learning** – the two mutually complementary practices of dialogue and discussion, first separating them and then combining them.

Garratt views learning organisations as essentially liberating and energising and as crucial for organisational survival and growth. He refers to four characteristics of the learning organisation:

- It encourages people at all levels of the organisation to learn regularly and rigorously from their work.
- It has systems for capturing and learning information and moving it where it is needed.
- It values its learning.
- It is able to transform itself continuously.[16]

Lane *et al.* suggest that there is no accepted definition of the term 'learning organisation' but list some key attributes of this type of organisation:

- Learning organisations understand that teams are the fundamental learning unit – not individuals.
- Learning organisations develop a shared vision through which a singular purpose is established and learning is based on this purpose.
- Learning organisations place learning in the mainstream of their operations. Learning, quality and customers are all so important that they are everyone's job.
- A learning organisation has a culture that embraces questioning and change.
- Learning takes place in anticipation of change rather than just responding tactically to problems.
- In a learning organisation technology serves the workforce, not vice versa.
- Learning is intentional and focused on the strategy of the organisation, not reactive.
- Learning organisations structure their processes and systems so that learning and teaching are included in the day-to-day work role; consequently, learning is pervasive and change created from it is permanent.[17]

Lane *et al.* emphasise that training in the organisation's ICT skills is essential for corporate survival and should be part of a continuous learning culture. The learning organisation model will create a solid foundation on which continually to build.

How would YOU assess the effectiveness of your university as a learning organisation for members of the non-teaching staff?

Total quality management (TQM)

One particular approach to improved organisational performance and effectiveness is the concept of the Japanese-inspired **total quality management (TQM)**. There are numerous definitions of TQM. These are generally expressed in terms of **a way of life for an organisation as a whole, committed to total customer satisfaction through a continuous process of improvement, and the contribution and involvement of people.**

A major influence on the establishment and development of TQM was the work of *Deming,* who emphasised the importance of visionary leadership and the responsibility of top management for initiating change. Deming drew attention to the importance of pride in work and process control, and made constant reference to the importance of 'good management' including the human side of quality improvement and how employees should be treated.[18]

The successful organisation should as a matter of policy be constantly seeking opportunities to improve the quality of its products and/or services and processes. The organisation must also couple quality with a required level of productivity. According to the *Chartered Management Institute,* TQM is not a single process but a philosophy and commitment to striving continuously for better quality. It is a style of management in which everyone in the organisation has responsibility for delivering quality to the end customer. TQM needs to be implemented across the whole organisation and evolve into an ongoing process of continuous improvement as a way of life. Successful implementation of TQM can lead to improvements in products and services, reductions in waste of resources and overall increases in efficiency and productivity.[19]

Implementation

If TQM is to be implemented successfully it must be seen as a total process involving all operations of the organisation and the active participation of top management. It demands a supportive organisational culture and a programme of planned management change. TQM places emphasis on the involvement of people as the key to improved quality. It involves changes to the traditional structure with greater emphasis on natural work groups, multi-disciplinary working and team-based management. Attention must be given to effective education and training, empowerment and the motivation to take ownership of quality, and systems of communications at all levels of the organisation. **A related successor to TQM is the balanced scorecard, discussed below**.

Kaizen

An integral part of a total quality approach is the Japanese concept of **Kaizen**, which means 'improvement', or is often interpreted as gradual progress of incremental change. Kai = change, Zen = for the better. In the work situation, Kaizen was introduced in several Japanese organisations after the Second World War and is particularly associated with Toyota. It is not a methodology for large-scale change or the introduction of new processes but focuses on the people aspect of improvement and the acceptance of change. The concept is based on a daily activity of continual evolutionary change, the elimination of waste, and the belief that the individual workers know more about their own jobs than anyone else. Kaizen is a culture of continuous improvement as a way of life involving the whole organisation and all its activities, and all members of staff from top managers to junior employees.

Cane suggests that the traditional Kaizen approach embeds it in a hierarchical structure, although it gives considerable responsibility to employees within certain fixed boundaries. The approach:

- analyses every part of a process down to the smallest detail;
- sees how every part of the process can be improved;
- looks at how employees' actions, equipment and materials can be improved; and
- looks at ways of saving time and reducing waste.[20]

Kaizen is a holistic approach touching everyone in the organisation working for the same goal. Kaizen is the practice of continuous improvement based on guiding principles of:

- good processes bring good results;
- go see for yourself to grasp the current situation;
- speak with data, manage by facts;
- take action to correct root causes of problems;

- work as a team;
- KAIZEN™ is everybody's business;
- and much more![21]

The balanced scorecard

The **balanced scorecard** is an attempt to combine a range of both qualitative and quantitative indicators of performance which recognise the expectations of various stakeholders and relates performance to a choice of strategy as a basis for evaluating organisational effectiveness. Citing the work of *Kaplan and Norton* in a year-long study of a dozen US companies,[22] *van de Vliet* suggests that in the information era, there is a growing consensus that financial indicators on their own are not an adequate measure of company competitiveness or performance and there is a need to promote a broader view.

> The balanced scorecard does still include the hard financial indicators, but it balances these with other, so-called soft measures, such as customer acquisition, retention, profitability and satisfaction; product development cycle times; employee satisfaction; intellectual assets and organisational learning.[23]

Bourne and Bourne suggest most people think about the balanced scorecard in terms of key performance indicators (KPIs) and target-setting, but it is about aligning actions to strategy and showing people what is important. A well-constructed scorecard tells everyone in the organisation where it is going and what they are trying to achieve. It clarifies objectives and communicates them widely.[24] According to 'Manager' magazine, the balanced scorecard has become well-established as a system that draws data across multiple functions to produce as full a picture of organisational performance as possible. Referring to Kaplan and Norton, in addition to, in order to reach a more balanced view of overall business performance attention must also be given not only to financial measures but also ongoing investments in areas such as organisational capacity, customer/stakeholder objectives, and internal processes.[25]

How do YOU view the practical value to organisational performance and effectiveness of (i) kaizen and (ii) the Balanced Scorecard?

The EFQM Excellence Model

Excellence is the goal for many organisations. EFQM is a global not-for-profit organisation, based in Brussels. The EFQM Excellence Model is a business model that builds on the experience of previous models and is now adopted by organisations across the globe to strive for sustainable excellence.

The **EFQM Excellence Model** is a management framework used by over 30,000 organisations in Europe and beyond. The Model takes a holistic view to enable organisations, regardless of size or sector, to assess where they are, help understand their key strengths and potential gaps in performance across the nine criteria. It is based on the concept that an organisation will achieve better results by involving all the people in the organisation in the continuous improvement of their processes. The 'Model' is designed to be non-prescriptive. It is not a standard; it does not tell you what to do but is there to provide guidelines.

Organisations are able to benchmark themselves against others both within and outside their sectors. The basic assumption is that excellent results in terms of Performance, Customers, People and Society (the Results) are achieved through Leadership driving Policy and Strategy, People, Partnerships and Resources, and Processes (the Enablers). Innovation and Learning are key to improving enablers that in turn improve results. *See* **Figure 17.4.**

Nine criteria of the 'Model'

Each of the nine criteria featured in the 'Model' are described as follows:

1. **Leadership.** How leaders develop and facilitate the achievement of the mission and vision, develop values for long-term success and implement these via appropriate actions and behaviours, and are personally involved in ensuring that the organisation's management system is developed and implemented.

2. **Strategy.** How the organisation implements its mission and vision via a clear stakeholder-focused strategy, supported by relevant policies, plans, objectives, targets and processes.

3. **People.** How the organisation manages, develops and releases the knowledge and full potential of its people at an individual, team-based and organisation-wide level, and plans these activities in order to support its policy and strategy and the effective operation of its processes.

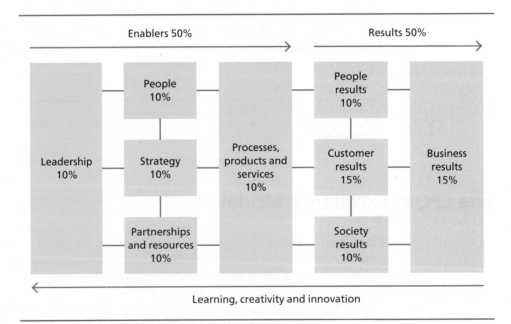

Figure 17.4 EFQM Excellence Model
Source: EFQM. Copyright © 2012 EFQM. The EFQM Excellence Model is a registered trademark of the EFQM. Reproduced with permission.

4. **Partnerships and resources.** How the organisation plans and manages its external partnerships and internal resources in order to support its policy and strategy and the effective operation of its processes.

5. **Processes, products and services.** How the organisation designs, manages and improves its processes in order to support its policy and strategy and fully satisfy, and generate increasing value for, its customers and other stakeholders.

6. **Customer results.** What the organisation is achieving in relation to its external customers.

7. **People results.** What the organisation is achieving in relation to its people.

8. **Society results.** What the organisation is achieving in relation to local, national and international society as appropriate.

9. **Business results.** What the organisation is achieving in relation to its planned performance.[26]

Do you believe external environment influences organisational performance?

Attributes and qualities of a manager

Whatever the role of the manager or whether in the private or public sector, in order to carry out the process of management and the execution of work, the manager requires a combination of technical competence, social and human skills, and conceptual ability.[27]

As the manager advances through the organisational hierarchy, greater emphasis is likely to be placed on conceptual ability, and proportionately less on technical competence, *see* **Figure 17.5. (See also the discussion on levels of organisation in Chapter 12.)**

- **Technical competence** relates to the application of specific knowledge, methods and skills to discrete tasks. Technical competence is likely to be required more at the supervisory level and for the training of subordinate staff, and with day-to-day operations concerned in the actual production of goods or services.

- **Social and human skills** refer to interpersonal relationships in working with and through other people, and the exercise of judgement. A distinctive feature of

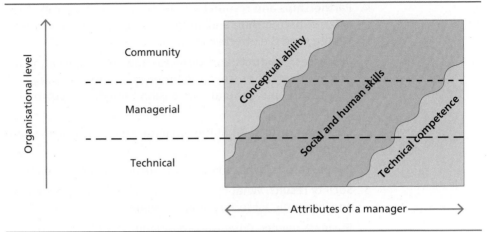

Figure 17.5 The combination of attributes of a manager

management is the ability to secure the effective use of the human resources of the organisation. This involves effective teamwork and the direction and leadership of staff to achieve co-ordinated effort. Under this heading can be included sensitivity to particular situations, and flexibility in adopting the most appropriate style of management.

- **Conceptual ability** is required in order to view the complexities of the operations of the organisation as a whole, including environmental influences. It also involves decision-making skills. The manager's personal contribution should be related to the overall objectives of the organisation and to its strategic planning.

Although a simplistic approach, this framework provides a useful basis from which to examine the combination and balance of the attributes of an effective manager. For example, the extent of technical competence or conceptual ability will vary according to the nature of the organisation and the level at which the manager is working. However, major technological change means that managers at all levels of the organisation increasingly require technical competence in the skills of information communications technology.

Importance of management skills

Chapter 0 drew attention to the importance of the development of personal skills. In recent years, increasing attention has been given by the government to the importance of the supply and application of skills attainment. *The UK Commission for Employment and Skills* (UKCES) aims to raise UK prosperity and opportunity by improving employment and skills levels across the UK, benefiting individuals, employers, government and society.

Developing influencing skills

According to *Sandi Mann* few would argue that an integral role of management involves influencing people especially in engaging and motivating employees without resorting to coercion, threats or manipulation. Influencing skills are wide-ranging and overlap more general spheres of interpersonal and communication skills, assertiveness and self-presentation. Some key strategies that can help one exert a positive influence include:

- **Empowerment** – don't tell staff what to do – empower them to develop their own strategies
- **Listen** – don't exert authority – listed to idea, thoughts and complaints of staff and you will win their support
- **Respect** – show respect to the viewpoints and wishes of your staff. Be sympathetic to their concerns and issues outside of work that may affect their work life
- **Nurture** – Nurture your team by being aware of their individual skills and abilities; encourage them to develop or build on their existing skill sets
- **Self-confidence** – Believing in your own abilities allows you to give people credit; accept your own mistakes and be decisive.
- **Engage** – Managers who use their spheres of influence to show appreciate of their team, listen to their opinions and support their team will be more successful.

Engaging managers use their spheres of influence to demonstrate appreciation of their team's efforts, listen to their opinions and ensure they feel supported.[28]

Growing emphasis on 'soft' skills

Management has become as much, if not more, about managing people than managing operations. Social and human skills which reflect the ability to get along with other people are increasingly important attributes at all levels of management. According to *Saunders,* the nature of management is changing and soft skills are on the rise. The stock of managers with the sharpest social and psychological skills is also on the rise because of today's lean, flat organisational structures. *Octavius Black,* CEO of MindGym, draws attention to the emotional side of work and claims that a degree in psychology would be a better training ground for managers.

> **We have done competitive advantage from strategy and from technology. What's left is competitive advantage from your people and the line manager is crucial to that. Get your people to flourish and your organisation will perform better.**[29]

 Do YOU believe a degree in psychology is good training for managers? How relevant do you think your present course of study for a future career is?

Managerial behaviour

However effectiveness is measured, managers are likely to be effective only if they adopt the most appropriate style of behaviour. A development of the Blake and Mouton Managerial Grid®, discussed earlier in **Chapter 10,** is the three-dimensional (3D) model of managerial behaviour suggested by *Reddin.* By adding

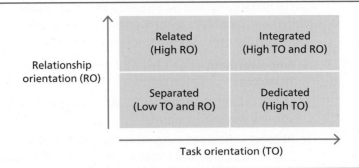

Figure 17.6 The four basic styles of managerial behaviour

a third dimension of managerial effectiveness to task orientation and relationship orientation, the 3D model identifies eight possible styles of managerial behaviour.[30]

- **Task orientation (TO)** is the extent to which the manager directs both personal and subordinates' efforts through planning, organisation and control.
- **Relationship orientation (RO)** is dependent upon the manager's personal job relationships. This is characterised by consideration for subordinates' feelings, mutual trust and encouragement.

The combination of TO and RO determines the manager's basic style of behaviour. The four possible basic styles **(see Figure 17.6)** are similar to those identified by Blake and Mouton in the Managerial Grid.

Apparent and personal effectiveness

Each of these four basic styles of management can be effective or ineffective depending on the situation in which they are applied. Effectiveness is defined by Reddin as output achieved by a manager. 'Managerial effectiveness has to be defined in terms of output rather than input, by what managers achieve rather than by what they do'.

Reddin distinguishes managerial effectiveness from (i) apparent effectiveness, and (ii) personal effectiveness.

- **Apparent effectiveness** is the extent to which the behaviour of the manager – for example punctuality, giving prompt answers, tidiness, making quick decisions and good public relations – gives the appearance of effectiveness. Such qualities may or may not be relevant to effectiveness.
- **Personal effectiveness** is the extent to which the manager achieves personal objectives – for example power and prestige – rather than the objectives of the organisation.

Applying the third dimension of managerial effectiveness provides eight styles of managerial behaviour – four effective styles, which achieve output requirements, and four ineffective styles. For each of the basic styles – separated, dedicated, related or integrated – there is a more effective or less effective version. Effectiveness results from the appropriateness of a particular style of management to the demands of the situation in which it is applied.

Birkinshaw questions how one can become a better boss. Employees are looking for challenging work, space, support, and recognition. But why do managers not do what they know they should? The busier you are, the more likely it is you'll get into bad management. 'Lack of time and resources are only part of the story. The underlying problem is that many aspects of good management involve going against our natural instincts.' The hallmarks of a good manager include:

- the capacity to let go and to give power and freedom to others and allow others to make mistakes;
- giving credit to others and downplaying your own achievements. Own your failures and share your successes;
- exercising self-control and the ability to regulate your own emotions and instincts. Be more attentive to your own shortcomings.[31]

Effective use of time

Whatever the attributes or qualities of a successful manager, one essential underlying criterion is the effective use of time. With many managers who complain that they do not have sufficient time it may be more that they have failed to organise themselves or their work properly. Although currently a popular topic of attention, the importance of time management has long been recognised as an inherent feature of management. *Drucker,* writing in 1988, refers to time as the limiting factor for effective executives. Time is a unique resource– you cannot rent, hire, buy or otherwise obtain more time. The supply of time is totally inelastic; time is totally irreplaceable and everything requires time.[32]

Effectiveness and activity

For many managers, appearing always to be busy, a cluttered desk and a continual flurry of activity are outward signs of their effectiveness. The trouble is that such managers may be too busy 'doing' rather than **thinking about what they, and their staff, should be doing and how they should be doing it.** Activity may be a substitute for actual achievement. It is important therefore to distinguish effectiveness from activity. *Rees and Porter* suggest that 'Activity-centred behaviour is in any case much more likely to spring from incompetence and/or insecurity rather than adroit political behaviour.'[33]

A similar point is made by *Hoyle and Newman* who refer to the many people who are satisfied being busy, but in their diligence and attention to detail mistake activity for achievement. Rather than the volume of work undertaken, it is what work creates that is important. Attention should be focused on what is achieved and the end result.[34]

Managers' checklist

There are numerous popular time management techniques, but still one of the most relevant approaches is that by *Rosemary Stewart* who suggests that it is often salutary for managers to compare what they think they do against what happens in practice. Answers to the following seven questions will help managers decide what, if anything, they should check, and to review their effective management of time, *see* Figure 17.7.[35] **(Delegation is discussed in Chapter 14.)**

The Seven Questions a Manager Should Ask Themselves

1. Am I giving attention to current activities, reviewing the past and planning for the future? Am I focussing enough on the future?
2. Am I dividing my time correctly? Is there a part of my work which I spend too much time doing?
3. Have I changed what I do and how I do it to allow for the effects of changes in my work?
4. Can I delegate some of my work?
5. Who should I be meeting? Am I spending too much or too little time with any of them?
6. Do I organise my working time according to priorities, or do I deal with each crisis as it happens without considering if it is the correct priorty?
7. Can I complete tasks? Am I constantly interrupted? If the latter, are these interruptions an essential?

There are three questions that managers should ask of each of their activities:

✱ Can it be done at all?

✱ If so, when?

✱ Can it be delegated?

Figure 17.7 Managers' checklist

To what extent are YOU able to apply Stewart's list of seven questions to the effective management of your own time and work as student?

Management development

The general movement towards greater employee involvement and managing the people resource has emphasised an integrating rather than a controlling style of management. Managers need a balance of technical, social and conceptual knowledge and skills, acquired through a blend of education and experience. There is, therefore, a continual need for organisations to ensure the development of both present and future managers. The 'Ability to Attract, Retain and Develop Top Talent' is another of the nine measures of success by which *Management Today* rates performance in its annual survey of Britain's Most Admired Companies.

From a national survey of 4,500 managers, together with focus groups, interviews and case studies, CMI report on the business benefits of management and leadership development (MLD). Findings highlight considerable scope for improving the effectiveness of UK management and by doing so, improving organisational performance. Higher performing organisations invest 36 per cent more on MLD than low-performing organisations. The research indicated that in addition to a financial commitment to MLD, a range of associated factors are associated clearly with higher performance. A combination of commitment to MLD, alignment to business strategy and supporting HR practices explains as much as 32 per cent of the increase in people performance and 23 per cent in overall organisational performance.[36]

The *CIPD* emphasise the crucial importance of effective management to organisational success in both the private and public sectors and, more broadly, to national economic well-being. Some critics, moreover, argue that the UK has certain deficiencies in respect of the qualities and skills of its management base when compared with managers at the global level. Management development is the structured process by which managers enhance their skills, competencies and/ or knowledge, via formal or informal learning methods, to the benefit of both individual and organisational performance. The development of managers to help sustain their performance at the highest levels possible is a particularly crucial element of wider organisational learning strategies.[37]

Succession planning

Management **succession planning** aims to ensure that a sufficient supply of appropriately qualified and capable people is available to meet the future needs of the organisation. Such people should be available readily to fill managerial or supervisory vacancies caused through retirement, death, resignation, promotion or transfer of staff, or through the establishment of new positions. Succession planning should be related to the overall corporate strategy.

McClements suggests smooth leadership succession can deliver significant returns including the transfer of organisational know-how and continuity in leadership culture. However, many companies have not made adequate succession plans resulting in lost productivity, negative culture and morale and leading to competitive decline. Succession planning should be aligned with the company culture, business objectives and long-term strategy.[38]

Allied to management development and succession planning should be a programme of planned career progression. This should provide potential managers with:

- training and experience to equip them to assume a level of responsibility compatible with their ability; and

- practical guidance, encouragement and support so that they may realise their potential, satisfy their career ambition and wish to remain with the organisation.

Career progression should involve individual appraisal and counselling. However, care should be taken to avoid giving staff too long or over-ambitious career expectations. If these expectations cannot be fulfilled, staff may become disillusioned and frustrated.

Continuing professional development (CPD)

In recent years, greater recognition has been given to the significance of lifelong learning and to **continuing professional development (CPD)**. Lifelong learning should, however, be the concern of all employees in the organisation and (despite the title) it is arguable that the concept of CPD should not be seen as applying only to professionals or managers as opposed to all employees. Clearly, however, CPD does have particular significance for management development. A number of professional bodies have developed a competence-based CPD scheme for their members. For example, the Chartered Management Institute regards CPD as vital to a successful career and requires all members to make a commitment to their own professional development. Submission of a detailed CPD record is an integral and compulsory part of gaining the status of 'Chartered Manager'.

Self-development

An important part of the process of improving personal performance is self-development. This demands the ability to identify clearly real development needs and goals, to take responsibility for actions to reach these goals and to recognise opportunities for learning. Self-development has to be self-initiated and continued throughout your working life. But if this is to be a realistic aim it requires an organisational climate that will encourage people to develop themselves and the active support of top management. People need sufficient authority and flexibility to take advantage of situations which are likely to extend their knowledge and skills. Superiors should be encouraged to empower staff and prepared to delegate new and challenging projects including problem-solving assignments.

What do YOU see as the main focus on management development? How well would you be capable of self-development for your chosen future career?

Building productivity in the UK

Based on discussions with a range of employers, employees, their representatives, and other thought leaders, *Acas* has produced a report aimed at stimulating debate amongst those with an interest in UK productivity. The UK workforce produces less per hour than our main economic competitors. Germany, France and the US produce much more than workers in the UK. A range of solutions have been offered by government, business and others, including training and investment in infrastructure. But these can only yield lasting improvements if workplaces are operating at their best. The way workplaces are organised, the part played by managers and leaders, and the role and involvement of employees can help deliver better outcomes for individuals, organisations and the economy.

As UK productivity levels continue to lag behind our competitors, we need to take a long hard look at all the factors that might have a part to play in addressing the problem. The UK's productivity challenge is an agenda shared by employers, trade unions, commentators, policy makers and government. Failure to take action poses considerable threats for growth, for jobs and for sustainable increases in real wages. Acas believes that there is real benefit to be gained from addressing this question through the prism of the workplace: to identify opportunities for workplaces to become more effective and, in turn, contribute to the bigger challenge.

Workplaces the key to productivity

Acas stress the importance of workplaces as the key to productivity. The long-term success of high-level solutions such as better physical infrastructure or capital investment and investment in skills depends on workplaces being efficient, responsive and innovative. This message applies across sectors and industries. The workplace is where the elements of productivity come together to deliver goods and services. How businesses manage and organise their workforce has a huge influence on delivering the improvements that the country needs. Acas has identified seven 'levers' for improving productivity through effective workplaces. *See* **Figure 17.8.**

- **Well-designed work**: jobs and work organised in a way that increases efficiency and makes the most of people's skills.
- **Skilled line managers**: managers with the confidence and training to manage and lead effectively.
- **Managing conflict effectively**: systems in place to reduce the likelihood of problems arising and to deal with problems at every stage.
- **Clarity about rights and responsibilities**: a working environment where everyone understands their rights and responsibilities.
- **Fairness**: employees who feel valued and treated fairly.
- **Strong employee voice**: informed employees who can contribute to decisions and are listened to.
- **High trust**: relationships based on trust, with employers sharing information at the earliest opportunity.

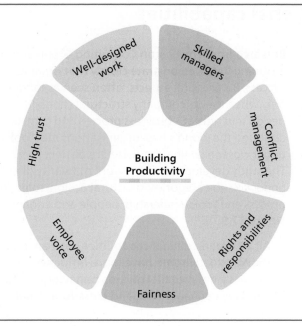

Figure 17.8 Seven levers for workplace productivity
Source: 'Building Productivity in the UK' Acas Strategy Unit, June 2015. Used with permission from Acas National.

These seven levers are not described in order of their importance. Many of them overlap and are interdependent. Nor do we assume that all employers will need to 'pull' all seven levers to improve their productivity. Building an effective and productive workplace that engages everyone takes time and priorities vary between organisations.[39]

To what extent can YOU apply the underlying principles of the seven levers for workplace productivity to your performance as a student?

Organisational capabilities

Research from The Boston Consulting Group and twelve partner organisations, including CMI, demonstrate clearly that organisational capabilities drive corporate success. Behavioural aspects, often seen as tangential, are vital differentiators – but only when they accompany structural capabilities such as superior organisational design and rigorous business process and controls. The study points out that although the world's best organisations may look like many of their competitors, under closer examination there are distinct combinations of winning attributes. The study developed a framework of twenty discrete organisational capabilities under six sub-categories: structural design, roles and collaboration mechanisms, process and tools, leadership, people and engagement, culture and change. **See Figure 17.9.**

> All 20 organizational capabilities have an impact on overall performance – though clearly some have more influence than others. Even more interesting: there is a definite tilt towards behavioral factors – in particular leadership, employee engagement, and cross-functional collaboration.[40]

Structural design	Description
1. Organization structure 2. Role of the center 3. Layers and spans of control 4. Organizational cost-efficiency 5. Shared services, offshoring, and outsourcing	• Reporting lines, including profit-and-loss accountabilities • The corporate center's role with regard to involvement and leadership • The number of reporting layers in the hierarchy; the number of people reporting directly to a manager • The level of cost-efficiency enabled by the organization • Internal service provider; cross-country relocation; subcontracting to other companies
Roles and collaboration mechanisms	
6. Role clarity 7. Cross-functional collaboration mechanisms 8. Informal/virtual networks	• Understanding of the role's responsibilities in the organization • Lateral coordination effort between functions or units • Important but informal channels for reinforcing culture and communicating key information
Processes and tools	
9. Process excellence/optimization 10. Project management 11. Business analytics and information management	• Processes optimized for high quality, short processing times, or low cost • For example, roles, processes, and tools • Skills, technologies, applications, and practices to drive business planning
Leadership	
12. Leadership performance 13. Leadership pipeline 14. Middle-management effectiveness	• Capable and effective individual leaders and leadership teams • Preparing for the next-generation leadership team • Middle managers empowered to carry strategy into the organization
People and engagement	
15. Recruitment and retention 16. Employee performance management 17. Employee motivation	• Providing the necessary talent to meet strategic and growth goals • Systems and processes aligned to ensure that goals are achieved • The willingness to exert discretionary effort
Culture and change	
18. Change management capabilities 19. Adaptability and flexibility 20. Culture	• The organization's ability to manage change efforts • A flexible structure that allows adapting to external challenges • The set of shared values in an organization

Figure 17.9 Twenty vital organisational topics
Source: Organizational Capabilities Matter © 2012, The Boston Consulting Group (BCG).

Successful organisations and people

The overall effectiveness of the organisation will be affected both by sound structural design and by individuals filling the various positions within the structure. Management will need to acknowledge the existence of the informal organisation that arises from the interactions of people working in the organisation. The operation of the organisation and actual working arrangements will be influenced by the style of management, the personalities of members and the informal organisation. These factors may lead to differences between the formal structure of the organisation and what happens in practice.

Stewart found the relationship between people and organisation to be reciprocal. Managers, therefore, need to be conscious of the ways in which methods of work organization may influence people's attitudes and actions. People modify the working of the formal organisation, but their behaviour is also influenced by it. 'Before behaviour is put down to individual or group cussedness, managers should look for its possible organizational causes'.[41]

Building an organisation involves more than concern for structure, methods of work and technical efficiency. The hallmark of many successful business organisations is the attention given to the human element; to the development of a culture which helps to create a feeling of belonging, commitment and satisfaction. Structure must be designed, therefore, so as to maintain the balance of the socio-technical system and the effectiveness of the organisation as a whole. Attention must be given to the interactions between both the structural and technological requirements of the organisation, and social factors and the needs and demands of the human part of the organisation.

The importance of people for organisational effectiveness is reinforced by a survey undertaken by the *MCA* and *Management Today.* The survey emphasises that the role of the organisation is social as well as economic and points to the desperate need for the basic, softer skills of managers in leadership, coaching and mentoring. Organisations need individuals they can trust, who are engaged in and committed to their work. If they want to survive, organisations need to recognise that they have to add value to their employees, that their social capital is just as important as their financial capital.[42]

People, diversity and organisational performance

An underlying consideration of the people element in work organisations of the future is attention to respect for individual differences and diversity, discussed in **Chapter 4,** and positive action on equality and inclusion. With increasing globalisation, it is of great importance to have a sound understanding of diverse countries and workforces. More than ever, effective organisational performance demands the successful management of diversity.

The *CMI* remind us that many work in diverse environments, and even in more homogeneous workplaces, employees could well be dealing with clients from a variety of backgrounds, particularly in global businesses. Unfortunately, there are still too many individuals and organisations that are 'diversity-sceptics' – those who can't or won't see the benefits that diversity can bring to an organisation. Greater diversity, and the benefits that diversity bring, will only occur if there is genuine enthusiasm for the concept throughout the organisation.[43]

Fixing the person or the organisation?

In terms of the people–organisation relationship it is arguably too easy and part of human nature to look to others as the source of problems. According to *Misselhorn* successful managers look beyond individual flaws in people and consider the broader context in which the people are working. The simple four-layer diagram **(Figure 17.10)** reminds us to view people not in isolation but with a more holistic approach to the people–organisation relationship.

Starter questions to open up all four layers

Effective organisational performance demands attention to all four layers: concerns for people doing their jobs (first two layers) in the context of the organisation and the socio-economic environment in which it operates (the outer two layers). Misselhorn suggests the following questions as thought-starters to open up thinking beyond the here-and-now practical issues under our noses. It is necessary to find time to think, reflect and consider the broader reality that (a) people don't do their jobs in a vacuum but in an easily-overlooked context that affects their motivation, their abilities, their skills and behaviour, and (b) the beginning of long-term significant changes and improvements starts with quality time spent on the first small steps taken now. These questions may open up the window on all four layers and the kind of issues raised for managers to consider:

Figure 17.10 Four layers of influence on performance
Source: Hugo Misselhorn, 'Do we fix the people or the organization?', 2 April 2016, www.jpsa.co.za. Reproduced with permission.

Person, including:

1. What is motivating the people to do their jobs?
2. How compatible are their goals and values with the goals and values of their organisation?
3. What do you know of their history of success/failure and the skills/knowledge they bring to the job?
4. What is the level of emotional and domestic stability?
5. What is the level of emotional intelligence and social skills?
6. What is the level of cognitive learning and problem solving (not the same as education)?

Job, including:

1. What are the specific requirements of the job?
2. What technology do they have to learn/use?
3. What are the most common technical problems encountered in doing their jobs?
4. What is the level of change and unpredictability?
5. How clear and meaningful are the goals of the jobs they do?
6. If standard procedures are required are these clear, relevant and useable?

Organisation context, including:

1. What is the culture of the organisation – political, bureaucratic, problem solving?
2. What kind of structures, reporting relationships and systems are in operation?
3. What is the dominant leadership style in the organisation?
4. How good are relationships and two-way communications – supportive, isolated, adversarial?
5. Do people work in teams and inter-teams or go solo?
6. What kind of material and financial resources are available to get the job done?

Socio-economic environment, including:

1. What external technological changes are taking place which affect the organisation – now and future?
2. What are the legal pressures on the organisation – tax, conformance, ecological, affirmative action etc?
3. How does the international market affect material supply and sales?
4. What are the effects of competitive products and services?
5. What is the impact of external financial and material resources on the organisation?[44]

How would YOU summarise essential criteria for successful organisational effectiveness and performance?

Critical Thinking Zone
Reflections on The Learning Organisation

In this zone, we critically evaluate the concept of the learning organisation and examine whether the phenomenon has been relegated to the vaults of history or whether it is alive and a vision to which organisations can still aspire.

During the 1980s and 90s, the concept of the learning organisation seized the imagination of global scholars, practitioners and business leaders. The seminal theories of US systems scientist, Peter Senge[46] and UK academics, Mike Pedler, John Burgoyne and Tom Boydell,[47] espoused how organisations could leverage its tenets to become more flexible, knowledgeable, adaptable and better prepared to survive and thrive in the turbulent and competitive business environment.[48]

Defining the Learning Organisation

Although the learning organisation concept is fully established in both the US and UK, by virtue of the work and advocacy of Senge,[46] Pedler *et al.*[47] and theorists such as Garavan,[49] Marquardt[50] and Marsick and Watkins,[51] consensus has yet to be reached as to what constitutes and defines a learning organisation. On this note, Örtenblad[52] (p. 150) acknowledges that 'many people still ask, "what is a learning organisation," "what does the concept mean?"' He accepts that this line of enquiry is 'entirely understandable. The LO . . . is a concept (or phenomenon) that is not easily defined.' As highlighted earlier in the chapter, Senge's rather abstract definition advocates the 'power' of the concept to expand people's capacity to create and achieve their desired results via freed collective aspiration, expansive thought patterns and continuous, collegial learning. In more concrete terms, Pedler *et al.*[47] (p. 3) define the concept as 'a company that facilitates the learning of all its members and continuously and consciously transforms itself and its context.' They contend that the practice of continuous and conscious transformation generates valuable individual and organisational learning opportunities that could be used to generate and sustain competitive advantage. Based on their empirical and practical research, the scholars charted their vision of an 'ideal' learning company and arrived at the eleven characteristics, which are outlined below.[53]

1. **A learning approach to strategy**. Everyone should be involved in strategy formation, implementation and monitoring, which is treated as a conscious learning process.

2. **Participative policy-making**. Individuals should be enabled or empowered to take part in policy making.

3. **Informating**. IT is used to facilitate the free flow of knowledge and information, to enable better decisions to be made.

4. **Formative accounting and control**. Working in collaboration with IT, discourse and feedback should be encouraged on how money is used in the business.

5. **Internal exchange**. Horizontal co-operation and dialogue are encouraged through inter-departmental customer/supplier exchange.

6. **Reward flexibility**. Designing a system that promotes monetary and non-monetary rewards, including supporting risk taking and experimentation.

7. **Enabling structures**. The structure is sufficiently adaptable and flexible to support learning through the implementation of more organic, decentralised structures.

8. **Boundary workers as environmental scanners**. Individuals, who are in contact with customers, suppliers and other stakeholders, are in a key position to bring knowledge and other intel back into the organisation.

9. **Inter-company learning**. Linked to Characteristic 8, enabling more conscious learning and knowledge acquisition from and with external organisations.

10. **Learning climate**. Fostering a climate through the organisation's overarching culture, which encourages learning from mistakes, experimentation and experience.

11. **Self-development opportunities for all**. Facilitating and empowering individuals to develop themselves, their careers and jobs.

Pedler *et al.* advocate that the eleven characteristics can be used by organisations as a blueprint to idiosyncratically interpret, tailor and implement them to their own contexts. Importantly, Thomsen and Hoest[53] view the work of Pedler *et al.* as less 'airy' and 'far more practice-oriented' than other theories of its ilk, providing managers with 'concrete tools to promote learning' (p. 471).

Emphasising the Importance of Knowledge in the Learning Organisation

With an emphasis firmly on knowledge rather than learning, Garvin *et al.*, (p. 110)[54] define the learning organisation as 'a place where employees excel at creating, acquiring and transferring knowledge.' For this to be enabled, they proffer that three essential building blocks must be present. First, an environment that supports learning. Second, learning processes and practices that are tangible, rather than abstract and third, behaviours from leaders that reinforces learning. Arguably, one can draw parallels between Garvin *et al.*'s building blocks and many of Pedler *et al.*'s characteristics. Both frameworks suggest the implementation of an infrastructure and culture that enables the creation, sharing and utilisation of knowledge for competitive advantage.

Critiquing the Learning Organisation

Although many of the theories espoused in the literature predominantly view the learning organisation as a 'thoroughly virtuous concept'[48] (p. 157), questions have been raised about the reasons why Senge's vision and widely-cited theory, which was proposed nearly three decades ago, has not been more fully realised. Daly and Overton[55] attest that a number of answers have been mooted. First, the model is overly theoretical and too disciplined to be implemented in practice. Second, leaders are not up to the job and are thus not capable of implementing the concept, and third, the myopia and short-term thinking of managers, who envision it purely as a one-off change programme. As a prescription for this, Senge counsels that a large dose of 'metanoia' or mind shift is needed to adopt the concept's premise and tenets. Arguably, it also requires a change in culture and climate[47] that encourages experimentation, experiential learning and continuous improvement through initiatives such as empowerment. Further critique is offered by Grieves[56] (p. 464), who refers to the concept as an 'impenetrable impossibility' and acknowledges the tendency of extant literature to express Senge's work as a string of

'clichéd aphorisms' (p. 467) that are difficult to apply in practice. One could argue that learning organisation models espouse unitarism and everyone collectively working towards a shared vision and mental models of learning and the optimisation of performance. With this in mind, Grieves contends that the concept is 'naively apolitical' because it 'assumes that people share the same interests, are not abused by exploitative managers' and 'are not driven by systems that seek to maximise effort at the expense of rewards' (p. 470).

Is the Learning Organisation Still Alive?

When Pedler and Burgoyne[57] (p. 125) posed the question 'is the learning organisation still alive in 2016?' based on research findings, they concluded 'no clear answer emerges . . . the yea-sayers will find plenty of evidence for the LO's continued existence and relevance . . . the nay-sayers will also feel at least partly vindicated.' Pedler and Burgoyne attest that the findings highlight the need for further research into the concept, the answers of which will determine 'whether the LO still has legs . . . we are left pondering: are all ideas fated to come and go, or are some more durable?' (p. 125).

Critics argue that becoming a learning organisation is not an easy feat. Garratt[58] contends that he has never come across a 'true' learning organisation and aspiring to become one is a journey towards a destination that is never reached. Garavan attests that the concept poses the important question whether learning can be managed and, ultimately, who is the benefactor and custodian of new knowledge and attitudes that the learning organisation is espoused to generate. Despite contention that the concept is alive and living on through its relationship with constructs such as knowledge management,[59] Garavan[49] proffers that its 'elusive and perhaps self-contradictory' nature 'raises the question of whether it is possible to create a learning organisation' (p. 25). Whilst he concludes that the concept is 'an idealised state that may never be attained' (p. 26), others may perceive it as a vision to which organisations can still aspire.

Questions

Based on the above, answer the following questions.

1. Pedler *et al.* advocate that boundary workers should be treated as environmental scanners, as they have direct interaction with a variety of stakeholders, each of which is a potential source of knowledge. With reference to knowledge management literature, a) *critically discuss* the types of capital that can be generated from such interface, and b) *how* can this intel be used to generate competitive advantage?

2. *Critically evaluate* the relationship between the learning organisation and knowledge management.

3. Since its first espousal, the learning organisation has been the subject of academic and practitioner praise as well as critique. Using relevant literature, *prepare* a compelling case *for* the concept being used as a tool to promote learning and knowledge.

Summary – Chapter 17 'Organisational performance and effectiveness'

Central to the success of the organisation is the process and quality of management. A determining feature of the people–organisation relationship is the strength of employee engagement and commitment. A key factor in organisational effectiveness is the successful management of change and attention to the learning organisation and the continuous learning for all staff. Other approaches to improved organisational performance are Total Quality Management, associated with the concepts of Kaizen, the Balanced Scorecard and EFQM excellence model. Other important contributions are the work of Investors in People and the PESTEL analysis. There is a clear and important need for managerial effectiveness. Attention must be given to the attributes and qualities of a manager, and development of social and human skills. In an increasingly competitive environment there is a continual need for organisations to ensure management development, succession planning and continuing professional development. Acas has identified seven 'levers' for improving UK productivity through effective workplaces. Boston Consulting Group has developed a framework of twenty organisational capabilities. Overall performance and effectiveness of an organisation is affected by sound structural design, the people within the structure and the broader socio-economic environment.

Group discussion activities

Undertake each of these activities in small groups as indicated by your tutor. Before you start your discussion establish a non-threatening environment within the group and confirm confidentiality will be honoured.

First, form your own views and then share and compare in open critical discussion with colleagues. Reflect honestly on the extent to which: (i) you influenced the thinking and ideas of your colleagues; and (ii) you were influenced by your colleagues.

To what extent was your group able to reach consensus?

Agree one of your members to produce a brief written summary of the discussion and prepared to present in a plenary session.

Activity 1

At Happy Training Company, people are asked who they would like as their manager.[45] 'Given how important a manager is to getting the most out of others, we let people choose theirs.'

* Detail fully what you see as the arguments for and against people choosing their own managers.
* To what extent does the type and nature of the organisation influence your views?
* Is choosing your own manager appropriate to a university?
* How would feel about choosing your own manager?
* If you were interested in a managerial career how would you feel about working in an organisation where people choose their own managers?

Activity 2

(a) Securing the engagement and commitment of staff is easy. Apply Herzberg's two factor theory of motivation **(Chapter 7)** with attention first to the hygiene factors and then the motivating factors.

(b) Given a *forced-choice situation* most people would prefer to work for an effective organisation that offers long-term security and consistently high wages rather than an organisation that is more about a pleasing and happy place to work.

(c) To what extent are you truly engaged with and committed to your course of study? What are the main determining factors?

Activity 3

(a) Many senior members of staff point out they have no formal management education or qualifications and emphasise the importance of experience on-the-job. Many organisations waste time and money on 'fancy' management development programmes.

(b) Technical competence can be learned easily and not everyone needs conceptual ability but someone lacking social and human skills will never succeed as an effective manager.

(c) The philosophy and actions of successful managers should include genuine acknowledgement of *mea culpa,* the open admission of responsibility for their failings and mistakes. This is a sign of strength not weakness.

Organisational behaviour in action case study

How to change a workplace culture: a case study in power of reflective learning

This case study looks at the experience of Wiltshire Fire & Rescue Service (WFRS), an organisation that faced a number of challenges in responding to considerable cultural and organisational changes. Having successfully worked with Acas before, WFRS decided to use training provided by Acas to enable the service to maintain and improve their productivity through this period of significant change.[1]

Where are they now? Wiltshire Fire & Rescue Service employs approximately 650 full-time and retained fire fighters and support staff in 24 local fire stations with its head office based in Devizes. Despite some restructures that have taken place over the years, staff turnover remains low, with a high proportion of employees having only worked at the Service. Most full-time firefighting staff in the organisation are represented by the Fire Brigades Union, with other staff represented by UNISON and the Retained Firefighters' Union.

In April 2016 the Service combined with Dorset Fire & Rescue Service. Over the last year or so the Service has reviewed and updated the way it carries out important personnel activities, such as managing performance and conflict, as well as addressing more underlying behavioural issues. The 'combination' project between Wiltshire and Dorset Fire Services provides a real opportunity to further reflect on how they can improve the way they work, but has also been the cause of uncertainty among staff about job security and terms and conditions of employment.

What challenges do Wiltshire Fire & Rescue Service face?

The culture of the Service is, in some ways, its greatest strength, but it can also raise challenges. Emotional and community bonds are often very strong and tight knit, but so are traditional views about obeying procedures to the letter. The day to day duties of the fire service have changed markedly over the last few years – with much more emphasis on prevention than responding to fires and other emergencies. The way the organisation sees itself, and the way it is perceived, has led to the need for some intense periods of reflective learning. The Service is having to adapt to the following challenges:

* **Public perception**: fire staff are stereotypically seen as jumping down poles and pouring water on fires. In reality, they are more likely to be seen in schools educating young people, advising builders on safety regulations or helping others, particularly the vulnerable in the community, to identify fire risks.

* **Different working patterns**: the decreasing need for 'firefighters' to put out fires has meant that fewer staff are needed at stations. Many fire fighters are 'retained' which means they can be on call and used only when needed. This has led to the adoption of different pay structures and working patterns.

* **Coming out of the shadow of the past**: the original 'Fire Services Disciplinary Regulation' that was in operation until the early 2000s, reflected a hierarchical organisation with very prescriptive procedures. For example, if someone appealed against a case of gross misconduct the appeal process could go all the way to the Home Secretary.

* **Facing up to behavioural issues**: the firefighter mindset is based upon the precept of 'you will' and many staff have difficulty dealing with grey areas where colleagues are not fully conforming to accepted standards of behaviour or conduct.

How did Wiltshire Fire Service respond to the need for cultural change?

Managers, employers and unions have worked hard to challenge cultural and behavioural norms by paying particular attention to the way in which they:

* **Communicate**: A culture based upon obeying orders has had to shift to allow staff to share experiences and exchange ideas more freely.

* **Balance the need for job autonomy:** With a deeper understanding of employee rights and line management responsibilities. In the past, some small fire stations were run like family businesses which led to a lack of consistency in how policies were applied.

* **Supported and trained line managers**: Encouraging line managers to take a more pro-active role in performance issues has revealed a lack of confidence that urgently needed to be addressed.

Where did Acas come in?

Acas has had a very productive working relationship with the Service over many years. This is partly based upon the recognised authority of the Acas brand, but also on the close personal rapport the Acas advisor developed with managers and union representatives. One union rep said he had a 'whole folder called Acas' and valued both the online and face-to-face services. Acas has previously delivered effective sessions to line managers on handling of TUPE[2] and redundancy processes and the Organisational Development (OD) Manager found that line managers were particularly receptive to Acas guidance.

This cultural shift is a work in progress, with much work still to be done around improving disciplinary and grievance procedures, but notable improvements so far include:

Much greater line manager confidence

An Acas programme of training sessions, specifically tailored to the needs of the Service, led 47 managers to undertake e-learning on handling disciplinary and grievance issues (78 per cent rated the 'overall usefulness' of the training as good or excellent). Managers were able to specify where they personally would benefit from further development and where they thought managers as a group required further training. This allowed the Service to target uncertainty around:

* **How to resolve problems early and take formal action.** Due to the close working ties within teams, managers were often inclined to delay taking action. Although they might say they were in the 'informal stage', they were rarely being pro-active about addressing issues and shied away from 'difficult conversations'.

* **Greater knowledge of the internal discipline and grievance procedures.** The Service acknowledges that there is still some room for improvement in its internal procedures, but Acas intervention has helped to simplify what were often lengthy and complex documents and improve consistency in the way they are applied.

* **Producing an investigation report.** Acas has experienced a great demand for training in this area from many of its customers. As well as how to conduct an investigation, support staff requested training in taking notes at meetings – a vital skill when accuracy is paramount.

More open and challenging communication forums

The training sessions also led to the creation of Communities of Practice in the Service. These are quarterly sessions held by each duty group in which experience, learning and good practice are discussed and shared over a range of issues, including discipline and grievance. The approach taken to improve the application of the discipline and grievance processes also reflects the wider 'Systems Thinking' initiative in the Service, which encourages all employees to question whether familiar and proposed ways of working are an efficient use of time. These forums also allowed managers to reflect more about the way jobs were designed. With a huge period of change underway, everyone has been encouraged to go back to basics and ask:

* Where should jobs be based?
* How can we use technology to improve the services we offer?
* What is the best way to combine the skills of both fire services?

Acas gave the Service the opportunity and the means to do some reflective learning about the kind of organisation it was – building on traditional strengths but letting go of unhelpful stereotypes and outdated procedures – and the kind of innovative and flexible organisation it wanted to become.

Conclusion: a work in progress but an appetite for continual learning

As the Acas advisor most involved with the Service said: 'in many ways, the journey that Wiltshire Fire & Rescue Service is embarking on reflects the journey that Acas has been on in the last few decades. They have had to change the public perception that firefighters purely fight fire. Acas largely focuses on preventing conflict in the same way that firefighters largely work on preventing fires. It's a shift in focus and how you see yourselves. The key is to be prepared to keep learning and be as innovative as you can.' A manager in the

Service also commented that Acas intervention did not always require a wholesale change of policies, but they were certainly simplified and made 'better versions of what they once were'. Skilled line managers, effective employee voice and well-designed work are three of Acas' 'seven levers of productivity'. Find out more here: http://www.acas.org.uk/media/pdf/7/9/Building-productivity-in-the-uk.pdf (accessed December 2015).

Endnotes

1. This case study is based on interviews conducted by the University of Plymouth with a human resources manager, a trade union representative and an organisation development manager at Wiltshire Fire Service, along with discussions with Acas staff.

2. TUPE refers to the 'Transfer of Undertakings (Protection of Employment) Regulations 2006'. The TUPE rules protect employees' rights when the organisation or service they work for transfers to a new employer. For more info see: www.acas.org.uk/tupe.

Source: Reproduced with permission of Acas. Crown Copyright. Open Government Licence, details of which can be found here: http://www.nationalarchives.gov.uk/doc/open-government-licence/version/3/

Tasks:

1. What do you see as the importance of reflective learning to improving organisational performance and effectiveness? How good is your skill of reflective learning?

2. How does this case study help to remind you of subjects you have read in previous chapters of the book?

3. Explain fully the overriding significance of workplace culture to organisational performance and effectiveness.

Chapter 17 – Personal skills and employability exercise

Objectives

Completing this exercise should help you to enhance the following skills:

* Participate meaningfully in a management development programme.
* Prepare for your future career progression.
* Take responsibility for your own self-development.

Exercise

You have recently been appointed to a trainee managerial position and selected for interview for an intensive management development training programme. You are pleased to have been invited for interview but unsure what to expect and nervous about your participation in the programme if selected.

* Explain fully how you can best prepare yourself for this development training programme.
* What questions might you expect to be asked?
* How would you explain benefits you have gained from your university course of study, including the balance between theory and practice?
* Detail the skills and abilities you would need to demonstrate at interview.
* What form of exercises, activities and assessments might you expect?
* How would you expect to benefit from the programme?
* How might you best attempt to apply what you have learned on the programme in your actual work situation?

> **Discussion**
> * Explain how you see the relationship between university education and employ-ability, and between off-the-job learning and on-the-job experience.
> * How would you attempt to evaluate the effectiveness of the programme?
> * To what extent should management development be suited to the individual or geared towards the needs of the particular organisation?

Notes and references

1. Czerniawska, F. 'From Bottlenecks to BlackBerries: How the Relationship between Organisations and Individuals Is Changing,' Management Consultancies Association (September 2005).
2. Lucas, E. 'Switched on to Innovation', *Professional Manager,* vol. 16, no. 3, May 2007, pp. 32–5 and Mahden, M. in conversation with De Vita, E. 'Best Fit', *Management Today,* September 2008, p. 54.
3. Gratton, L. *The Democratic Enterprise,* Financial Times Prentice Hall (2004), pp. xiii–xiv.
4. 'The Joy of 9 to 5: Do we need managers?' BBC Radio 4, 13 April 2016.
5. Caulkin, S. 'The New Geography of Management', *Professional Manager,* Autumn 2016, pp. 54–60.
6. Scott, M. in conversation with Jimmy Wales, 'The end of control', *Professional Manager,* Winter 2016, p. 39.
7. O'Reilly, C. 'Corporations, Culture and Commitment: Motivation and Social Control in Organizations', in Steers, R. M., Porter, L. W. and Bigley, G. A. (eds) *Motivation and Leadership at Work,* sixth edition, McGraw-Hill (1996), p. 374.
8. De Vita, E., 'Get Engaged', *Management Today,* April 2007, pp. 38–43.
9. Macleod, D. and Clarke, N. *Engaging for Success: Enhancing performance through employee engagement,* A report to Government, Department for Business, Innovation and Skills (2009).
10. 'Understanding employee engagement: Checklist 245', Chartered Management Institute, June 2015 and 'Engaging your team: Checklist 121', Chartered Management Institute, June 2015.
11. 'Employee engagement and motivation' Factsheet CIPD,14 September 2017.
12. Rock, S. '12 ways To Foster Amazing Employee Engagement' *Professional Manager,* Autumn 2016, pp. 50–3.
13. Handy, C. B. *Understanding Organizations,* fourth edition, Penguin (1993).
14. See, for example, Caulkin, S. 'Chris Argyris', *Management Today,* October 1997, pp. 58–9.
15. Senge, P. M. *The Fifth Discipline: The Art of Practice of the Learning Organization,* Doubleday (1990).
16. Garratt, B. *The Fish Rots From The Head,* HarperCollins (1996). See also Garratt, B. *The Learning Organization: Developing Democracy at Work,* HarperCollins Business (2000).
17. Lane, T., Snow, D. and Labrow, P. 'Learning to Succeed with ICT', *The British Journal of Administrative Management,* May/June 2000, pp. 14–15.
18. Deming, W. E. *Out of Crisis,* Cambridge University Press (1986) and *The New Economies for Industry,* Cambridge University Press (1993).
19. 'Total Quality: getting TQM to work', Checklist 030, Chartered Management Institute, July 2014.
20. Cane, S. *Kaizen Strategies for Winning Through People,* Pitman Publishing (1996), p. 8.
21. https://uk.kaizen.com/home (accessed 14 February 2018).
22. Kaplan, R. S. and Norton, D. P. *The Balanced Scorecard: Translating Strategy into Action,* Harvard Business School Press (1996).
23. Van de Vliet, A. 'The New Balancing Act', *Management Today,* July 1997, pp. 78–80.
24. Mann, S. in conversation with Bourne, M. and Bourne, P. 'Insights into Using Strategy Tool', *Professional Manager,* vol. 16, no. 6, November 2007, pp. 30–3.
25. 'On Balance', *Manager,* Autumn 2013, pp. 28–30.
26. Material on EFQM Excellence Model reproduced with permission of EFQM www.efqm.org.
27. Katz, R. L. 'Skills of an Effective Administrator', *Harvard Business Review,* September–October 1974, pp. 90–102.
28. Mann, S. 'Cultivating Influence', *Professional Manager,* January 2010, pp. 32–4.
29. Saunders, A. 'Rebuilding Management's Good Name', *Management Today,* May 2011, pp. 44–6.
30. Reddin, W. J. *Managerial Effectiveness,* McGraw-Hill (1970).
31. Birkinshaw, J. 'How to be a Better Boss', *Management Today,* September 2013, pp. 46–9.
32. Drucker, P. F. *The Effective Executive,* Heinemann Professional (1988).
33. Rees, W. D. and Porter, C. *Skills of Management,* fifth edition, Thomson Learning (2001), p. 22.

34. Hoyle, M. and Newman, P. *Simply a Great Manager,* Marshall Cavendish Business (2008).

35. Stewart, R. *Managers and Their Jobs,* second edition, Macmillan (1988), p. 123.

36. McBain, R., Ghobadian, A., Switzer, J., Wilton, P., Woodman, P and Pearson, G. 'The Business Benefits of Management and Leadership Development', Chartered Management Institute, February 2012.

37. 'Management Development' Factsheet, CIPD, 31 January 2018.

38. McClements, L. 'Building the Pipeline', *Governance + Compliance*, October 2017, pp. 38–9.

39. 'Building Productivity in the UK', Acas Strategy Unit, June 2015.

40. Roghē, F., Toma, A., Kilmann, J., Dicke, R. and Strack, R. 'Organizational Capabilities Matter', The Boston Consulting Group, January 2012.

41. Stewart, R. *The Reality of Management,* third edition, Butterworth-Heinemann (1999), p. 125.

42. Czerniawska, F. 'From Bottlenecks to BlackBerries: How the Relationship between Organisations and Individuals Is Changing', Management Consultancies Association, September 2005.

43. 'Managing for Diversity' Checklist 152, Chartered Management Institute, February 2015.

44. Source: Adapted with permission from Hugo Misselhorn, JPS Associates www.jbsa.co.za. Reproduced with permission.

45. Stewart, H. 'How to have a happy and productive office', *Management Today,* February 2012, pp. 38–42.

46. Senge, P. *The Fifth Discipline: The Art and Practice of the Learning Organization,* Doubleday Currency (1990).

47. Pedler, M., Burgoyne, J. G. and Boydell, T. *The Learning Company: A Strategy for Sustainable Development,* McGraw-Hill (1991).

48. Symon, G. 'The "Reality" of Rhetoric and the Learning Organization in the UK', *Human Resource Development International,* vol. 5, no. 2, 2002, pp. 155–74.

49. Garavan, T. 'The Learning Organization: a review and evaluation', *The Learning Organization,* vol. 4, no. 1, 1997, pp. 18–29.

50. Marquardt, M. J. *Building the Learning Organization,* McGraw-Hill (1996).

51. Marsick, V. J. and Watkins, K. E. *Facilitating Learning Organizations: Making Learning Count,* Gower (1999).

52. Örtenblad, A. 'What Does "Learning Organization" Mean?', *The Learning Organization,* vol. 25, no. 3, 2018, pp. 150–58.

53. Thomsen, H. K. and Hoest, V. 'Employees' Perception of the Learning Organization', *Management Learning,* vol. 32, no. 4, 2001, pp. 469–91.

54. Garvin, D. A., Edmondson, A. C. and Gino, F. 'Is Yours a Learning Organization?', *Harvard Business Review,* March, vol. 86, no. 3, 2008, pp. 109–16, 134.

55. Daly, J. and Overton, L. 'Driving the New Learning Organization: How to Unlock the Potential of L & D', In-Focus Report, Chartered Institute of Personnel and Development and Towards Maturity CIC, May 2017, pp. 1–47.

56. Grieves, J. 'Why We Should Abandon the Idea of the Learning Organization', *The Learning Organization,* vol. 15, no. 6, 2008, pp. 463–73.

57. Pedler, M. and Burgoyne, J. G. 'Is the Learning Organization Still Alive?', *The Learning Organization,* vol. 24, no. 2, 2017, pp. 119–26.

58. Garratt, B. 'An old idea that has come of age', *People Management*, vol. 1, no. 19, 1995, pp. 25–9.

59. Karkoulian, S., Messarra, L. C., and McCarthy, R. 'The Intriguing Art of Knowledge Management and its Relation to Learning Organizations', *The Journal of Knowledge Management,* 17, 2013, pp. 511–26.

APPENDIX Review of developing your personal skills and employability

This book has drawn attention to the importance of features that relate to the development of your personal skills and employability. Refer back to Chapter 0, look again at Figure 3 and consider carefully the following *examples*.

- **Self-awareness and confidence** – *for example*

  Be mindful of how your attitudes, beliefs and values impact on others; admit to your perceptual bias, distortions and errors; recognise the nature of your work orientation and work ethic; be able to exercise self-control; acknowledge your strengths and shortcomings.

- **Relationships with others** – *for example*

  demonstrate respect and empathy towards other people; display awareness of social interactions and influences; accept formal hierarchical and organisational relationships; acknowledge different personalities, and individual needs and expectations at work.

- **Communication and presentation skills** – *for example*

  be able to converse well with other people; sensitive to non-verbal communications and body language; contribute meaningful participation in group and seminar activities; present clear, coherent and persuasive verbal or written reports and other written documents.

- **Working in groups and teams** – *for example*

  work constructively and harmoniously with colleagues; accept group consensus and decision-making; recognise the roles you perform best and the contribution you make; accept the importance and impact of the informal organisation; work effectively in virtual teams.

- **Dealing with difficult situations** – *for example*

  be able to cope with conflict, personality clashes or misunderstandings as a reality of organisational behaviour; manage potentially stressful work situations; demonstrate calmness in difficult situations; display support and empathy in responding to practical or emotional needs of colleagues.

- **Influencing others and leadership** – *for example*

  interrelate well with colleagues; recognise how your own values and beliefs impact on others; awareness of how you are perceived by other people; understand leadership relationships and the attributes and qualities required of an effective leader; judge your readiness for a leadership role.

- **Coping with and managing change** – *for example*

  acknowledge the inevitable and continuous pace of change; recognise the forces and impact of change; be able to adapt effectively to change; understand resistance to change and how best to minimise problems of change; recognise the increasing importance of IT-enabled change.

- **Observing ethical behaviour** – *for example*

  adhere to social responsibilities to organisational stakeholders and codes of conduct; honour the ideologies, values and principles of the organisation; display ethical decision-making at work; respect the rights of whistleblowers; sustain a clear and strong moral compass.

- **Working in multicultural organisations** – *for example*

  embrace the impact and benefits of diversity and inclusion; avoid prejudice; understand the pervasive influence of organisation culture; demonstrate respect for and be able to work harmoniously with people of different ethnic origin, gender, age, sexual orientation, religious beliefs, or social class.

- **Displaying managerial potential** – *for example*

  be able to manage with and through people; relate meaningfully to the changing nature of the workplace; prioritise effectively your time; accept the need for lifelong learning and personal development; accept personal responsibility for your self-development and career progression.

Use these and other examples to reflect upon the extent to which you have enhanced your awareness and knowledge of such features, and are better prepared to demonstrate personal skills and employability, and aid your career progression.

Remember to update your personal profile.

Your concluding activity*

Definitions of organisational behaviour (OB) generally relate to improving organisational performance and effectiveness. Accordingly, underlying your study of OB has been the social and human skills which reflect the ability to work well with other people. The development of personal skills in management and leadership play a crucial role in terms of both your future career employability and continued contribution to organisational success.

How good are you at managing and leading at the same time?

In the table below there are two lists of different attributes. For each attribute in both columns rate yourself using the following scale. Where possible rate yourself in a particular situation or job context.

How well do the following describe your behaviour? Rate each item: always (5); mostly (4); sometimes (3); seldom (2); never (1)

(* Source for Activity: Adapted and reproduced with permission from Hugo Misselhorn, M.O.D. Consulting. August 2014. hugomodc@iafrica.com)

Column A	Column B
Quick to recognise problem situations that require attention and action	Willing to hear and consider alternatives from others, even if they are different to one's own
Know where one is headed and the results to be achieved	Good at listening to others and taking seriously what they have to say
Work to high standards of efficiency and effectiveness – get the job done well and on time	Take an interest in individuals and their abilities and what makes them tick
Focus on one issue at a time, giving full attention to reaching a conclusion	Favour listening and understanding to talking
Aware of what is and what is not important and focus on priorities	Handle conflict and disagreements with patience and try to find the answer to suit both parties
Think clearly and logically, working through problems in an orderly and logical manner	Aware of one's own strengths and weaknesses and how one comes across to others
Gather facts and information before drawing conclusions	Work well in a team and with others; can be described as co-operative and a team player
Work out, beforehand, the best way to tackle a problem or do the job	Know when to be tough and push hard and when to ease back when dealing with others
Fix problems and also prevent their recurrence by removing the cause	Consider who to involve and the best way to involve them before taking action
Follow up to check and rectify things if they have gone wrong	Explore what people feel and how they will react before taking action

Scoring

To score your own balance between 'managing' and 'leading', you can do so by adding up all the scores you gave yourself for those attributes in both Column A and Column B. Attributes listed in Column A are typically management orientation and the attributes listed in Column B are typically leadership orientation.

There is no one universal mixture of management + leadership behaviour. It will depend on the situation and the people involved. But we all have natural preferences which could lead us to a particular approach to a given situation regardless of the circumstances.

Key questions

What did you score?
Consider carefully how YOU might need to change your management + leadership mix to match a particular situation.

Comparison and discussion

Now attempt to compare and discuss your score with colleagues who have completed the same activity. You may also find it constructive to invite an observer from outside your immediate student group to undertake the activity. Discussion of the assessments supported with actual examples can provide a platform for gaining further insights into your self-development.

Virtues employers want in all employees

Finally, remind yourself from Chapter 0 of *Furnham*'s important issues considering a young person's employability and the five virtues employers want in all employees.**

- Hardworking and productive, a conscientious work ethic, and to pitch up and pitch in. Honest, reliable and dependable.
- Smart, bright, curious, fast-learners and not plodders. Inquisitive, widely-read, interesting in understanding.
- Concept of rewardingness, warm and trustworthy, sensitive and well-adjusted, sociable and sufficiently altruistic.
- Signs of being leader-like, able to make decisions for which accountable and with good judgement. Taking initiative and the strain when it counts.
- Have the big picture and globally minded and who look ahead. Anticipate and adapt to the future without being a victim.

** Furnham, A. 'How to make yourself more employable: the new employability skills of the 2016 worker' Insights, *Chartered Management Institute*, 06 May 2016.

Wishing you success and happiness in your future career.
Laurie J. Mullins

Glossary

Ability Generally defined as a stable characteristic of a person's capacity for physical or mental performance.

Accountability In delegation, the ultimate responsibility that managers cannot delegate. While managers may delegate authority, they remain accountable for the decisions and actions of their subordinates.

Action-centred leadership A theory of leadership that focuses on what leaders do. It states that the effectiveness of a leader is dependent upon meeting three areas of need within the work group: the need to achieve the common task, the need for team maintenance and the individual needs of group members.

Action learning An approach to management development that involves a small self-selecting team undertaking a practical, real-life and organisational-based project. The emphasis is on learning by doing with advice and support from tutors and other course members.

Adhocracy A flexible, loosely structured, adaptable, organic and informal form of organisation.

Adjourning The adjourning or disbanding of a group because of, for example, completion of a task, or members leaving the organisation or moving to other tasks.

Adoption phase A range of choices relating to the introduction of new technology into organisations consisting of initiation, progression/feasibility, investment decision, and planning and systems design.

Aggression A physical or verbal attack on some person or object.

Alienation Refers to the detachment of the person from their work.

Alienative involvement Where members are involved against their wishes. There is a strong negative orientation towards the organisation.

Anthropology The study of the cultural system, that is human behaviour as a whole and the science of humankind.

Attitudes Can be defined as providing a state of 'readiness' or tendency to respond in a particular way. They are learned through life and are embodied within our socialisation process.

Attribution theory The way in which individuals make sense of other people's behaviour through attributing characteristics to them by judging their behaviour and intentions on past knowledge and in comparison with other people they know.

Authoritarian (autocratic) style of leadership Where the focus of power is with the manager. The manager alone exercises decision-making and authority for determining policy, procedures and the allocation of work, and has control of rewards or punishments.

Authority The right of subordinates to take action or make decisions that the manager would otherwise have done.

Away days An approach to management development that uses activity-based exercises undertaken away from the workplace. The main objective is often building team spirit and working relationships.

Baby-boomers A generation and age group at work born between 1946 and 1963 and typified by a search for security.

Balanced scorecard An attempt to combine a range of both qualitative and quantitative measures of performance that recognise the expectations of various stakeholders.

Behaviourism A school of psychology developed out of research studies into learning that is interested in the study of behaviour and those actions that could be observed, measured and controlled.

Behaviourist theories of learning Based on the assumption our behaviour, actions and reactions to stimuli in our environment are a result of the learning process.

Brainstorming (thought showers) Where a group adopts a 'freewheeling' attitude aimed at generating as many ideas as possible. The focus is on freedom of expression and the quantity of ideas rather than quality.

Bureaucracy A form of structure found in many large-scale organisations. Bureaucracy is based on specialisation of tasks, hierarchy of authority and decision-making, systems of rules and regulations and an impersonal orientation from officials.

Bureaucratic organisations Authority is based on the acceptance of the law of formal rules and procedures, and on impersonal principles.

Bureaucratic orientation An individual's orientation to work in which he or she regards it as a central life issue. There is a sense of obligation to the work of the organisation.

Calculative involvement Where attachment to the organisation is motivated by extrinsic rewards.

Chain of command The number of different levels in the structure of the organisation; the chain of hierarchical command.

Charismatic organisation An organisation in which authority is legitimised by belief in the personal qualities of the leader and the leader's strength of personality and inspiration.

Classical approach The organisation is thought of in terms of its purpose and formal structure and this approach aims to identify how methods of working can improve productivity. Emphasis is placed on the planning of work, the technical requirements of the organisation, principles of management and the assumption of rational and logical behaviour.

Classical conditioning A theory on learning developed by Pavlov, using dogs. Pavlov found that instinctive reflexes could be 'conditioned' to respond to a new situation and new stimulus.

Coaching A supportive relationship aimed at creating understanding, direction and action. Coaching uses deductive techniques and the coach does not have to be an expert in the subject.

Coercive power Based on fear and the subordinate's perception that the leader has the ability to punish or bring about undesirable outcomes for those who do not comply with the directives (e.g. withholding promotion or privileges).

Cognitive theories of learning Underlined by a belief in our mental abilities and representations. Learning is based on our feelings and what takes place in our minds rather than our behaviour.

Community level The level within an organisation that is concerned with broad objectives and the work of the organisation as a whole.

Conceptual ability The ability to view the complexities of the operations of the organisation as a whole, including environmental influences, and the ability to make decisions.

Concertive control A system of control not exercised by managers but by the value consensus of the team to a system of normative rules.

Conflict Based on incompatibility of goals arising from opposing behaviours at the individual, group or organisational level. Particularly, conflict is behaviour intended to obstruct the achievement of some other person's goals.

Constructive behaviour A positive reaction to the blockage of a desired goal through problem-solving or restructuring.

Content theories of motivation These theories attempt to explain those specific things that actually motivate the individual at work and are concerned with identifying people's needs, the strength of those needs and the goals they pursue in order to satisfy those needs.

Contingency or situational approach to leadership Emphasises the situation as the dominant feature in considering characteristics of effective leadership in the work situation.

Contingency approach to structure Highlights possible means of differentiating alternative forms of organisation structure and systems of management. There is no one optimum state.

Continuing professional development (CPD) The process of planned, continuing development of individuals throughout their career.

Control By their very nature control systems are concerned with regulation of behaviour and improvement in performance. Control is not only a function of formal organisation but also organisational behaviour and interpersonal influence.

Corporate social responsibility This concept gives rise to how a company should conduct itself within society, and different views on what a business is for and how it should act. Social responsibilities arise from the interdependence of organisations, society and the environment.

Corporate strategy Relates to the underlying pupose of the organisation and embacing links among structure, process of management and applications of organisational behaviour.

Creative imagination Enables us to develop completely new and different ideas and concepts to solve problems and achieve goals.

Creativity The application of imaginative thought, which may lead to new ways of seeing things, and results in innovative solutions to a problem or the initiation of change.

Decentralisation Where specific delegation is given to sub-units or groups within an organisation such that they enjoy a measure of autonomy or independence.

Decision-making (decision theory) approach An approach to management that focuses on managerial decision-making and how organisations process and use information in making decisions.

Delegation The process of entrusting authority and responsibility to others throughout the various levels of the organisation, and the creation of a special manager–subordinate relationship.

Democratic style of leadership Where the focus of power is more with the group as a whole than with the manager. Leadership functions are shared with members of the group and the manager is more part of a team.

Differentiation Describes the difference in cognitive and emotional orientation among managers in different functional departments with respect to goal orientation, interpersonal relations and formal structure.

Displaced aggression When aggression is displaced towards some other person or object than that which is perceived as the source of frustration; A 'scapegoat' is found for the outlet of frustration.

Diversity The recognition of individual differences and that people are not homogeneous. Focuses on the multiplicity of visible and non-visible differences among people.

EFQM (European Foundation for Quality Management) Excellence Model A management model that enables organisations to assess their key strengths and potential gaps in performance across a set of nine criteria.

E-learning Learning via information and communications technology.

Electronic panopticon Use of information technology to monitor and record the work of employees.

Element functions Activities within an organisation that are not directed towards specific and definable ends but are supportive of the task functions and an intrinsic part of the management process.

Emotional intelligence The sum of a range of interpersonal skills that form the public persona, including the emotional qualities of individuals.

Emotional labour How employees are expected to manage and display their emotions and feelings.

Employee commitment (and engagement) Typically conceived as an individual's psychological bond to the organisation including a sense of job involvement, loyalty and a belief in the value of the organisation.

Empowerment Where employees are allowed greater freedom, autonomy and self-control over their work, and the responsibility for decision-making.

Equity theory A theory of motivation that focuses on people's feelings of how fairly they have been treated in comparison with the treatment received by others.

Ethics The study of morality – practices and activities that are considered to be importantly right and wrong, together with the rules that govern those activities and the values to which those activities relate.

Expectancy theory A theory of motivation based on the idea that people prefer certain outcomes from their behaviour over others. Motivation is a function of the relationship between effort, level of performance and rewards related to performance.

Experiential learning Emphasises the importance of synthesis between an individual's behaviour and evaluation of their actions. Reflecting on experiences as part of the learning process.

Expert power Based on the subordinate's perception of the leader as someone who is competent and who has some special knowledge or expertise in a given area. This power is based on credibility and clear evidence of knowledge or expertise.

External environment (and environmental factors) The external factors outside of the organisation that can influence and affect the performance of it, the major environmental factors being technical, economic, social and governmental.

Extrinsic motivation Related to tangible rewards such as salary, promotion, working conditions and fringe benefits. These tangible rewards are often determined at the organisational level and may be outside the control of individual managers.

Fixation When an individual is frustrated but persists in a form of behaviour that has no adaptive value and actions are continued that have no positive results.

Flat hierarchical structure An organisation that has broad spans of control and few levels of authority.

Flexible working arrangements A range of flexible working practices designed to help employees balance work and home life.

Formal groups Formal groups are created to achieve specific organisational objectives and are concerned with the co-ordination of work activities. Group members have defined roles and the nature of tasks to be undertaken is a predominant feature of the group.

Formal organisation A planned co-ordination of the activities of a number of people for the achievement of some common, explicit purpose or goal, through the division of labour and function, and through a hierarchy of authority and responsibility.

Forming The initial formation of a group and the first stage in group development.

Frustration A negative response to the blockage of a desired goal resulting in a defensive form of behaviour.

Functional relationships The formal relationships within an organisation between people in a specialist or advisory position and line managers and their subordinates. These occur when a person offers a common service throughout all departments of the organisation.

Functions of leadership Focuses attention on the functions of leadership, rather than the personality of the leader. This approach to leadership believes the skills of leadership can be learned, developed and perfected.

Generation X A generation and age group at work born between 1964 and 1980 and typified by, after the slog, the rewards.

Generation Y A generation and age group at work born between 1980 and 1995 and typified by travel first, then a career.

Globalisation In broad terms, organisations integrating, operating and competing in a worldwide economy.

Goal theory A theory of motivation based on the premise that people's goals or intentions play an important part in determining behaviour. Goals guide people's responses and actions and direct work behaviour and performance, leading to certain consequences or feedback.

Group Any number of people who interact with one another, are psychologically aware of one another and who perceive themselves as being in a group.

Group norm Codes and practices developed by a group that group members consider to constitute proper group behaviour.

Groupthink The tendency within a group to 'drift along' towards decisions that may be inappropriate or unquestioned due to various in-group pressures.

Halo effect When the perception of a person is formulated on the basis of a single favourable or unfavourable trait or characteristic and tends to shut out other relevant characteristics of that person.

Hawthorne effect The conclusion that people behave differently when observed for example when extra attention and interest shown by management.

Hierarchy Clearly delineated levels of management authority as a means of co-ordination and control.

Hierarchy of needs A theory of motivation developed by Maslow, which states that people's behaviour is determined by their desire to satisfy a progression of physiological, social and psychological needs.

Human capital A strategic approach to people management that focuses on issues critical to the success of an organisation. The people, their performance and their potential in the organisation.

Human relations approach A management approach based on the consideration of and attention to the social factors at work and the behaviour of employees within an organisation. Particular importance is paid to the informal organisation and the satisfaction of individuals' needs through groups at work.

Hygiene (maintenance) factors Factors within a job that serve to prevent dissatisfaction. They are related to the job environment, are extrinsic to the job itself and include job security, working conditions and salary.

Idiographic approaches Approaches to the study of personality that focus on understanding the uniqueness of individuals. These approaches regard personality as a process that is open to change.

Impression management (or self-presentation) The attempt to project our attitudes, personality and competence by particular attention to our appearance and impact on others.

Informal groups Serve to satisfy the psychological and social needs of the group members and are not necessarily related to tasks to be undertaken. Informal groups are based on personal relationships and membership can cut across the formal structure of an organisation.

Informal organisation An organisation arising from the interaction of people, their psychological and social needs, and the development of groups with their own relationships and norms of behaviour, irrespective of those defined within the formal structure.

Information technology A term used to cover the application of computers, computer networks and telecommunications to the retrieval, storage and transmission of information.

Inspirational (visionary) leadership Leadership associated with the concept of creating a vision with which others can identify, getting along with others and inspiring through personal qualities or charisma.

Instrumental orientation An individual's orientation to work in which he or she regards it as a means to an end and not as a central life issue.

Integration Describes the quality of the state of collaboration that exists among departments required to achieve unity of effort by the demands of the environment.

Intelligence The ability for constructive thinking, adaption, reasoning and problem-solving.

Interactionist perspective A view that believes conflict is a positive force and necessary for effective performance. This approach encourages a minimum level of conflict within a group in order to encourage self-criticism, change and innovation.

Internal environment Relates to the culture and climate of an organisation and to the prevailing atmosphere surrounding the organisation.

Intrinsic motivation Related to psychological rewards such as achieving appreciation, positive recognition and being given the opportunity to use one's ability. These psychological rewards can usually be determined by the actions and behaviour of individual managers.

Introduction phase The second main phase in the adoption and introduction of new technology into an organisation. This involves working on the technology and the associated organisational changes with a view to making them effective.

Investors in People (IIP) Owned by the UK government and specialises in highlighting and championing best practices through ten indicators for people management success.

Job satisfaction An attitude or internal state that is associated with, for example, a personal feeling of achievement either quantitative or qualitative.

Johari window A simple framework for looking at self-insight that classifies behaviour in matrix form between what is known–unknown to self and what is known–unknown to others. It is used frequently to help individuals in a T-group experience.

Kaizen A Japanese concept of a total quality approach based on continual evolutionary change with considerable responsibility to employees within certain fixed boundaries.

Knowledge management The promotion and formalisation of learning within the workplace with the aim of aligning training with the needs of the business.

Laissez-faire (genuine) style of leadership Where the manager consciously makes a decision to pass the focus of power to members of the group, allowing them freedom of action. The manager has observed that the members of the group work well on their own and does not interfere.

Lateral relationships Formal relationships within an organisation that exist between individuals in different departments or sections, especially between individuals on the same level.

Law of exercise and association Developed by Watson and refers to the process that occurs when two responses are connected and repeated such as fixed habits and routines.

Leadership A relationship through which one person influences the behaviour or actions of other people.

Leadership Grid® A grid that compares the varying styles of management based on the concern for production against the concern for people.

Learning Acquisition of knowledge that leads to change of a relatively permanent kind that may result in new behaviours and actions or new understanding.

Legal-rational (legitimate) organisations Authority is based on the acceptance of the law of formal rules and procedures, and on impersonal principles.

Learning organisation An organisation that encourages and facilitates the learning and development of people at all levels of the organisation, values the learning and simultaneously transforms itself.

Legitimate power Based on the subordinate's perception that the leader has a right to exercise influence because of the leader's role or position in the organisation. This power is based on authority and related to a person's position within an organisation.

Lifelong learning Changes and learning that continue throughout life, and take place in a variety of ways and range of situations.

Line and functional organisation A means of making full use of specialists while maintaining the concept of line authority. Creates an informal type of matrix structure.

Line relationships A formal relationship within an organisation between individual positions where authority flows vertically down through the structure.

Management An integration activity to help reconcile needs of people at work with requirements of the organisation. The process through which efforts of members of the organisation are co-ordinated, directed and guided towards the achievement of organisational goals.

Management development Concerned with improving both the effectiveness of individual managers and management performance as a whole. Managers need a balance of technical, social and conceptual knowledge acquired through a blend of education and experience.

Managerial effectiveness Concerned with 'doing the right things' and relates to the outputs of the job and what the manager actually achieves.

Managerial efficiency Concerned with 'doing things right' and relates to inputs and what the manager does.

Managerial Grid® A grid which compares the varying styles of management based on the concern for production against the concern for people.

Managerial level The level within an organisation that is concerned with the co-ordination and integration of work at the technical (organisational) level.

Managerial roles Organised sets of behaviour associated with a manager. Arise as a result of the formal authority, status and activities of a manager.

Matrix structure Where there is a two-way flow of authority and responsibility within an organisation due to the vertical flow of authority and responsibility from the functional departments and the horizontal flow of authority and responsibility from project teams.

McDonaldisation Quoted as an example of exemplifying rational organisational behaviour with features of both scientific management and bureaucracy. Seen as a dominant part of social and organisational fabric.

Mechanistic system A rigid system of management practice and structure that is characterised by a clear hierarchical structure, specialisation of task, defined duties and responsibilities, and knowledge centred at the top of the hierarchy.

Mentoring Aims to facilitate the individual's capability and potential, enhance performance and career progression. The mentor is typically not the line manager but an expert in an area or a leader within an organisation.

Mission statement Sets an organisation's purpose, guiding values and principles, and the way in which it intends to achieve its objectives, while recognising the interests of other stakeholders.

Moral compass Lack of moral awareness in business and public affairs – the absence of an intuitive sense of right and wrong.

Moral involvement Based on the individual's belief in, and value placed on, the goals of the organisation.

Motivation Concerned with why people behave in a certain way and do what they do. The direction and persistence of action.

Motivators (growth) factors Factors within a job that, if present, serve to motivate the individual to superior effort and performance. These factors are related to the job content of the work itself and include recognition, personal growth and sense of achievement.

Myers–Briggs Type Indicator (MBTI) A personality test that identifies sixteen types of personality based on individuals' extroversion or introversion and their cognitive functions of thinking, feeling, sensation and intuition.

Neo-human relations A management approach developed by such writers as Maslow, Herzberg and McGregor, which adopts a more psychological orientation than that of the human relations approach.

Nomothetic approaches Approaches to the study of personality that focus on people in general through the analysis of group data. These approaches claim that personality is largely inherited and resistant to change.

Normative power A form of power that relies on the allocation and manipulation of symbolic rewards (e.g. esteem and prestige).

Norming The third stage of group development during which members of the group establish guidelines and standards and develop their own norms of acceptable behaviour.

Objectives (organisational) Objectives set out the specific goals of the organisation, the aims to be achieved and the desired end results.

Open-systems model The organisation is viewed as an open system that takes inputs from the environment and through a series of activities transforms or converts these into outputs to achieve some objective.

Operant conditioning A theory of learning developed by Skinner showing the effects of reward and punishment and demonstrating that responses in behaviour are learned because of their outcomes.

Operationalisation A stage in technology introduction when the workforce can have direct impact on such aspects as working practices, tasks, decisions about methods, and tools and techniques.

Organic system A fluid and flexible system of management practice and structure that is characterised by the adjustment and continual redefinition of tasks, a network structure of control, authority and communication, and where superior knowledge does not necessarily coincide with positional authority.

Organisation structure The pattern of relationships among positions in the organisation and among members of the organisation. It defines tasks and responsibilities, work roles and relationships, and channels of communication.

Organisational behaviour The study and understanding of individual and group behaviour and patterns of structure in order to help improve organisational performance and effectiveness.

Organisational behaviour modification (OBMod) The application of learning principles to influence organisational behaviour. It can be seen as a form of operant conditioning or reinforcement theory.

Organisational climate Relating to the prevailing atmosphere surrounding the organisation, to the level of morale, and to the strength of feelings or belonging, care and goodwill among members. Organisational climate is based on the perceptions of members towards the organisation.

Organisational commitment (employee engagement and commitment) Typically conceived as an individual's psychological bond to the organisation including a sense of job involvement, loyalty and a belief in the value of the organisation.

Organisational culture The collection of traditional values, policies, beliefs and attitudes that constitute a pervasive context for everything we do and think in an organisation.

Organisational goals Something that the organisation is striving to achieve, a future expectation, a desired future state and something towards which the activities of the organisation are directed in an effort to attain this state.

Organisational ideology Based on the beliefs, values and attitudes of the individuals, this determines the culture of the organisation and provides a set of principles that govern the overall conduct of the organisation.

Organisational stakeholders Those individuals or groups who have an interest in and/or are affected by the goals, operations or activities of the organisation or the behaviour of its members.

Organisational sub-systems The interrelated sub-systems of an organisation: tasks, technology, structure, people and management. These sub-systems need to be co-ordinated to ensure that the activities of an organisation are directed towards the achievement of aims and objectives.

Organisations Structures of people that exist in order to achieve specific purposes, common aims and objectives by means of planned and co-ordinated activities.

Parkinson's Law The concept of the 'Rising Pyramid' and the idea that 'work expands so as to fill the time available for its completion'.

Path–goal theory A contingency model based on the belief that the individual's motivation is dependent upon expectations that increased effort to achieve an improved level of performance will be successful.

Perception The dynamic and complex way in which individuals select information (stimuli) from the environment, interpret and translate it so that a meaning is assigned that will result in a pattern of behaviour or thought.

Perceptual defence When people select information that is supportive of their own point of view and choose not to acknowledge contrary information. They avoid or screen out certain stimuli that are perceptually disturbing or threatening.

Performance management A process which brings together many aspects of people management. It is about aligning performance with organisational aims using tools such as training and reward.

Performing The fourth stage of group development during which the group concentrates on the performance of the common task.

Person culture Where the individual is the central focus and structure exists to serve the individuals within it.

Personal (informal) power Power that derives from the individual and is in the eye of the beholders who believe that person has the ability to influence other people or events to make things happen.

Personal transformational change Where circumstances have not changed but because of some emotional or spiritual happening the individual was transformed or changed.

Personality An individual's unique set of characteristics and tendencies that shape a sense of self, and what that person does and the behaviour they exhibit.

PESTEL analysis A technique for analysing the general external environment of an organisation in terms of the political, economic, socio-cultural, technological, environmental and legal aspects.

(The) Peter Principle Concerned with the study of occupational incompetence and hierarchies, and the idea that 'in a hierarchy every employee tends to rise to their level of incompetence'.

Pluralist perspective A work organisation is viewed as being made up of powerful and competing sub-groups with their own legitimate loyalties, objectives and leaders. These competing sub-groups are almost certain to come into conflict induced in part by the structure of the organisation.

Policy (organisational) Developed within the frame of the objectives and details the 'how', 'where' and 'when' in terms of the course of action that must be followed to achieve the objectives.

Positive organisational behaviour The study and application of positively oriented human resources and psychological capacities that can be measured, developed and effectively managed for performance improvement in today's workplace.

Positive psychology The scientific study of what makes life most worth living. Focuses on determining how things go right and how to enhance satis8ifaction and well-being.

Postmodernism (post-bureaucratic) A more recent view of organisations and management that rejects a rational, systems approach and accepted explanations of society and behaviour. Postmodernism places greater emphasis on the use of language and attempts to portray a particular set of assumptions or versions of the 'truth'.

Power The level of control or influence a person holds over the behaviour of others, with or without their consent.

Power culture Depends on a central power source which influences the whole organisation. Frequently found in small entrepreneurial organisations and relies on trust, empathy and personal communications.

Private-enterprise organisations Organisations owned and financed by individuals, partners or shareholders accountable to their owners or members. The main aim is of a commercial nature such as profit, return on capital employed, market standing or sales level.

Privatisation The transfer of business undertakings from state (government) control to the private sector. The extent of state ownership, and the balance between commercial and social interests.

Process theories of motivation Concerned with how behaviour is initiated, directed and sustained, that is the actual process of motivation.

Project team A team set up as a separate unit on a temporary basis for the attainment of a particular task. Members may be from different sections or departments. When the task is completed the team is disbanded or members reassigned to a new task.

Projection Attributing or projecting one's own feelings, motives or characteristics to other people. Projection is a distortion that can occur in the perception of other people.

Psychological contract An unwritten contract between employers and employees that covers a series of mutual expectations and satisfaction of needs arising from the people–organisation relationship.

Psychology The study of the personality system, that is human behaviour, traits of the individual and membership of small social groups.

Psychometric (psychological) tests Tests that assess an individual's typical responses to given situations based on his or her choices and strength of feeling; or that assess an individual's ability to perform effectively under standard conditions, including aptitude and ability.

Public-sector organisations Organisations created by the government and include, for example, municipal undertakings and central government departments that do not generally have profit as their goal but have political purposes.

Qualities (traits) approach to leadership This assumes that leaders are born and not made. Leadership consists of certain inherited characteristics, or personality traits, which distinguish leaders from their followers. Attention is focused on the person in the job and not the job itself.

Radical perspective A perspective on organisations that challenges the traditional view of conflict, and sees organisations in terms of disparity in power and control.

Rational–economic concept of motivation Based on the belief of earlier writers such as F. W. Taylor that employees want, more than anything else from their employer, the highest possible wages for their work and are motivated by their economic needs.

Referent power Based on the subordinate's identification with the leader. The leader exercises influence because of perceived attractiveness, personal characteristics, reputation or charisma.

Regression When an individual is frustrated and reverts to a childish or primitive form of behaviour, for example sulking, crying or tantrums.

Remunerative power A form of power that involves the manipulation of material resources and rewards (e.g. salaries and wages).

Responsibility Involves an obligation by a subordinate to perform certain duties or make certain decisions and having to accept possible reprimand for unsatisfactory performance.

Responsible leadership An organisation's approach to governance, social responsibilities and business ethics.

Reward power Based on the subordinate's perception that the leader has the ability and resources to obtain rewards for those who comply with directives (e.g. pay or promotion).

Risky-shift Where a group decides to take a riskier course of action rather than the more conservative or safer option.

Role The expected pattern of behaviours associated with members occupying a particular position within the structure of the organisation.

Role ambiguity This occurs when there is a lack of clarity as to the precise requirements of the role and the individual is unsure what to do.

Role conflict Arises from inadequate or inappropriate role definition and results in a person behaving in a way that may not be consistent with their expected pattern of behaviour.

Role culture Often stereotyped as a bureaucracy and works by logic and rationality. Rests on the strength of strong organisational 'pillars' and functions of specialists.

Role expectations Indicate what the person is expected to do and their duties and obligations.

Role incompatibility Arises when compliance with one set of expectations makes it difficult or impossible to comply with the other expectations. The two role expectations are in conflict.

Role incongruence This arises when a member of staff is perceived as having a high and responsible position in one respect but a low standing in another respect.

Role overload When an individual faces too many separate roles or too great a variety of expectations and is unable to meet all expectations satisfactorily.

Role set Comprises the range of associations or contacts with whom the individual has meaningful interactions in connection with the performance of their role.

Role underload When the prescribed role expectations fall short of the individual's own perception of his or her role.

Rusty halo effect Where general judgements about a person are formulated from the perception of a negative characteristic.

Scientific management Developed by F. W. Taylor, this classical approach to management advocates the breaking down of work processes into discrete tasks to find the 'one best way' of performing each task in terms of scientific procedures. Increased productivity is rewarded by financial rewards.

Self-established roles Where formal expectations are specified loosely or in very general terms, and members have the opportunity to determine their own role expectations.

Self-fulfilling prophecy The essence of the prophecy is that simply because it has been made, this will cause it to happen. People strive to validate their perceptions irrespective of the actual reality.

Servant leadership A philosophy based on ethical responsibility of leaders; a spiritual understanding of people and empowering people through honesty, respect, nurturing and trust.

Shared and distributed leadership As opposed to hierarchical leadership, this gives recognition to the sharing of leadership function, power and decision-making through all levels of the organisation.

Shareholder-centred view Sees the directors of the company as agents of its owners and duty-bound to act so as to maximise the interests of those owners.

Situational (or contingency) approach to leadership Where the person who is best suited to lead in a particular situation takes on the role of leader. The importance of the situation is the focus and the person who is seen as the most suitable leader is appointed by the group.

Social action A study of organisations in which the organisation is considered from the standpoint of the individual. Individual goals, interpretation of the work situation in terms of the satisfaction sought and the meaning that work has for them are used as a basis for explaining behaviour.

Social and human skills Abilities related to interpersonal relationships in working with and through other people, and the exercise of judgement.

Socialisation An aspect of social learning which reefers to the introduction of new members of staff into the culture of the organisation and expected standards of behavior and action.

Social-enterprise organisations Set up in response to community, social or environmental concerns and bring together aspects of both the private and public sectors.

Social exchange theory A fundamental feature of human interaction that gives rise to the exchange of social and material resources.

Social identity theory A means of understanding the psychological basis of intergroup discrimination. Individuals are perceived as having not just one 'personal self' but a number of 'selves' derived from different social contexts and membership of groups.

Social learning theory Based on the premise that people learn by observing and interacting with others, and through imitation.

Social loafing (Ringelmann effect) The tendency for individuals to expend less effort when working as a member of a group than as an individual.

Sociology The study of the social system, that is social behaviour, relationships among social groups and societies, and the maintenance of order.

Sociometry A method of indicating the feelings of acceptance or rejection among members of a group.

Socio-technical system A sub-division of the systems approach that is concerned with the interactions between the psychological and social factors and the needs and demands of the human part of the organisation and its structural and technological requirements.

Solidaristic orientation An individual's orientation to work in which group activities are most important. There is an ego involvement with work groups rather than with the organisation itself.

Span of control The number of subordinates who report directly to a given manager or supervisor.

Staff relationships These formal relationships within an organisation arise from the appointment of personal assistants to senior members of staff. Someone in a staff position usually has little or no direct authority in his or her own right but acts as an extension of his or her superior.

Stakeholder theory A business is for its stakeholders and the actions of management should be designed to balance stakeholder interests.

Stakeholders (organisational) *See* Organisational stakeholders.

Stereotyping The tendency to ascribe positive or negative characteristics to a person on the basis of a general categorisation and perceived similarities. It occurs when an individual is judged on the basis of the group to which it is perceived that person belongs.

Storming The second stage of group development, which involves members of the group getting to know each other and putting forward their views.

Strategic rewards Based on design and implementation of long-term policies and practices to support closely and advance both business and employee aspirations.

Stress A source of tension and frustration that tends to arise when an individual feels that a certain situation should not exist.

Succession planning Related to overall corporate strategy and aims to ensure a sufficient supply of appropriately qualified men and women to meet future needs of the organisation.

SWOT analysis An analysis of opportunities and risks an organisation may face through an evaluation of its Strengths, Weaknesses, Opportunities and Threats.

Synthetic imagination Enables the analysis of previous and imagined scenarios based on that experience and knowledge.

Systems approach (view) A management approach that attempts to reconcile the classical and human relations approaches. Attention is focused on the total work of the organisation and the interrelationships of structure and behaviour. The organisation is viewed within its total environment and emphasises the importance of multiple channels in interaction.

Tall hierarchical structure An organisation that has narrow spans of control and a relatively large number of levels of authority.

Task culture Job-oriented or project-orientated. Can be likened to a net with some strands stronger and more powerful than others. An example is a matrix organisation.

Task function (within organisations) The basic activities of the organisation that are related to the actual completion of the productive process and directed towards specific and definable end results.

Team role A pattern of behaviour, characteristic of the way in which one team member interacts with another, where performance facilitates the progress of the team as a whole.

Technical competence Relates to the application of specific knowledge, methods and skills to discrete tasks.

Technical level The level within an organisation that is concerned with specific operations and discrete tasks, with the actual job or tasks to be done and with the performance of the technical function.

Technology approach A sub-division of the systems approach that emphasises the effects of varying technologies on organisation structure, work groups and individual performance and job satisfaction.

Telecommuting Where staff work from home with a computer network and telephone.

Theory X A theory towards human nature and behaviour at work that assumes that most people are lazy, have an inherent dislike of work and must be coerced, controlled and directed through a central system of organisation and the exercise of authority, and that motivation occurs only at the lower levels of needs.

Theory Y A theory towards human nature and behaviour at work that assumes that most people enjoy work, are creative, can exercise self-direction and control and want to accept responsibility, and that motivation occurs at the higher as well as lower levels of needs.

Total quality management (TQM) An approach to quality within an organisation that is committed to total customer satisfaction through a continuous process of improvement, and the contribution and involvement of people.

Total rewards Encompasses all aspects of work valued by employees including learning and development opportunities and working environment in addition to pay and benefits.

Traditional organisations An organisation in which authority is legitimised through tradition, custom and a long-standing belief in the natural right to rule or is possessed through the 'traditional' procedure.

Transactional leadership Based on legitimate authority within the bureaucratic structure of the organisation. The emphasis is on the clarification of goals and objectives, work tasks and outcomes, and organisational rewards and punishment.

Transformational change Involves a fundamental shift in the culture, conduct of business and working practices of an organisation, and often enacted over a period of time.

Transformational (or creative) leadership Based on the objective of transforming the performance or fortunes of a business. The emphasis is on generating a vision for the organisation and the leader's ability to appeal to the values of followers in attempting to create a feeling of justice, loyalty and trust.

Type A personality Individuals who are excessively competitive, thrive on hard work and long hours, and have little interest outside of work. Type A personalities exhibit characteristics such as a high need for achievement, extreme competitiveness, impatience and aggressiveness.

Type B personality Individuals who exhibit the opposite characteristics from Type A and who are less preoccupied with achievement, not easily frustrated and enjoy leisure time.

Ultimatum game An economic behavioural game that can arguably be related to the concept of equity theory.

Unconscious bias Our preferred people preferences. The subtle, unconscious behaviours that are hard-wired into us and difficult to eliminate altogether.

Unitarist perspective A work organisation is viewed as an integrated and harmonious whole with managers and other staff sharing common interests and objectives. The image is the organisation with a common source of loyalty and conflict as disrupted.

Virtual teams Teams where instead of face to face proximity, the primary interaction among members is by some electronic information and communication process.

Withdrawal When an individual is frustrated and 'gives up' or resigns him- or herself to the situation.

Index